The Essential

GLUTEN-FREE
RESTAURANT GUIDE

5th Edition

Symbols Summary

 Gluten-free menu is available on site. See the Section 2 User's Guide for more information about what constitutes a gluten-free menu.

 Gluten-free specialty items, such as bread, beer, pasta, etc., are available. Always call ahead to confirm the availability of gluten-free specialty items. Restaurants may sell out and deliveries can arrive late.

100% **This is a 100% gluten-free establishment.** No gluten on site.

 This is a chain restaurant, and you can find its gluten-free menu or list in Section 3. More on this in the Section 3 User's Guide.

No Icon. None of the above apply. See the restaurant's description for information about its gluten-free accommodations.

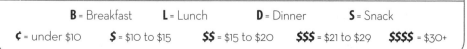

B = Breakfast   **L** = Lunch   **D** = Dinner   **S** = Snack

¢ = under $10   **$** = $10 to $15   **$$** = $15 to $20   **$$$** = $21 to $29   **$$$$** = $30+

THE ESSENTIAL GLUTEN-FREE RESTAURANT GUIDE, 5TH EDITION
Copyright © 2010 by Triumph Cookies, LLC

Published by Triumph Cookies, LLC
d/b/a Triumph Dining
124 E Broad Street
Suite B2
Falls Church, VA 22046

Find us on the web at: *www.triumphdining.com*
Find free gluten-free news and updates at: *www.triumphdining.com/blog*

ISBN 978-0-9776111-6-4

Printed in the United States of America.

CONTENTS

This book is about making dining out on a gluten-free diet safe, fun, and full of choices. It's packed with helpful tips and advice on getting gluten-free meals anywhere and contains thousands of restaurants (and many gluten-free menus) where other Celiacs have dined successfully. I hope you find this book as useful a tool as I have.

I've been gluten-free since 2001. For me, eating out on a gluten-free diet was a tough nut to crack. The thought of relinquishing control and not even being able to watch my food's preparation – especially when so many things could go wrong – made me very nervous. When I went gluten-free, I was a law student at Harvard in Cambridge, Massachusetts, later practicing law in nearby Boston. I was fortunate that I could draw on a set of resources created by a large, well-organized support group, The Healthy Villi. I followed the trails that other Celiacs had blazed, to places like the Elephant Walk, Tantawan, and Jake & Earl's – each with a gluten-free menu and/or extensive knowledge of our diet. But, even then, there wasn't a lot of variety in where or what I ate away from home. I was comfortable and safe, but I knew I was missing out on a world of interesting dining options.

Then, in 2004 I moved to Philadelphia to start an MBA program at The Wharton School. I searched in vain to find restaurants with gluten-free menus like the ones I was accustomed to in Boston. But, if Philadelphia had that level of resources, it was beyond my reach. I avoided eating out for as long as I could, but Kay, my fiancée (and now my wife), was persistent.

After some time, I reluctantly agreed to try a nearby Thai restaurant. I printed a free dining card from the Internet (it was in Thai, so I had no idea what it actually said) and brought it to the restaurant.

The dining card I found turned out to be overly restrictive. Among other things, it said that I categorically could not eat sauces and soups, which, of course, is untrue. Thai sauces and soups, in particular, are more often gluten-free than not. But, working with this information, and the many unnecessary restrictions it imposed, the owner of the restaurant made me a very plain, sauce-less version of Pad Thai. It was edible and safe, which was good enough for me. So, for the next few months, any time I needed to eat out, I went straight to that Thai restaurant and ordered the same dish.

I was well aware that I was foregoing one of Philadelphia's strongest assets – a diverse, vibrant restaurant scene. But, what I didn't realize was the enormous toll it was taking on my relationships.

I found myself making excuses to turn down dinner invitations and avoiding social opportunities that involved new restaurants. As a result, I was missing out on the friendships and camaraderie that my classmates were building. But, even more importantly, I was holding Kay back.

Kay is an enthusiastic traveler; she's been to over 25 countries and is a world-class cook. She's always had a strong interest in food, and there were a lot of restaurants in Philadelphia that she wanted to try. But, she wanted me to join her. Moreover, she was frustrated because she knew that I was missing out on many perfectly safe, delicious dining options – and missing out on a big part of life, which is trying new things.

Kay was intent on getting me to venture into new restaurants. She understood that my reluctance came in part from a fear of the unknown and the risk associated with trying to convey involved instructions in a restaurant setting. So, Kay came up with the idea to create a new kind of dining card that would contain detailed instructions on preparing food gluten-free and would be custom written for a particular cuisine. After all, Thai cuisine and American cuisine are very different in terms of ingredients and preparation – shouldn't the dining cards for both also be different? And so we started putting her vast knowledge of food and cooking to work. Together, we visited restaurant kitchens, interviewed chefs, read product labels, and studied dozens of cookbooks.

Over time, we built several lists of foods I could eat, foods to avoid, and the likely pitfalls we might encounter at the more common ethnic restaurants in Philadelphia. We turned these lists into very thorough, actionable kitchen instructions and found well-educated, native speakers to help us translate them, as appropriate.

I was the initial guinea pig for these dining cards and was amazed at their effectiveness. Within weeks they opened up a whole new world of dining for me. I ate in dozens of restaurants across Philadelphia, from the finest steak houses to little sushi shops. I had handmade corn tortillas at a Mexican greasy spoon and even had Indian food for the first time (it has since become one of my favorites)!

I'm not a chef or food expert. And before starting our research, I knew very little about food and its preparation. But, I saw that, without being an expert, I could use the instructions to quickly and concisely explain the gluten-free diet to chefs in such a way that they could easily prepare me a safe meal. And, surprisingly, these chefs were presenting me with a variety of options. In many types of restaurants, I could eat from a large portion of their menu with, at most, only slight modifications. And I wasn't just eating plain grilled chicken and steamed vegetables. For the first time, I was getting entrées with sauces, noodles, and even dessert. Eating out was no longer something to fear; it was becoming fun and exciting!

The success of our prototype dining cards and restaurant experiments confirmed that the idea had traction. If the cards worked so well for me, they could certainly help other people on the gluten-free diet, too. The prototypes formed the basis of our critically-acclaimed Triumph Dining Cards.

The response to our Dining Cards has been incredible, and it is the driving force behind the creation of this Restaurant Guide. We hear regularly from countless Celiacs who are using our cards to explore new restaurants and to successfully expand their dining options. They're educating restaurants across the country about how to prepare gluten-free meals and building great relationships in the process. This guide is a tool for taking those efforts one step further.

This guide is the start of a powerful network for all of us to share information about restaurants in our communities. It will provide you with immediate access to a list of restaurants that have handled the gluten-free diet well in the past. We hope that the list will give you some ideas for new restaurants to try and the inspiration to expand your dining options, both at home and when you travel.

And, this guide also provides you with an effective tool to help other Celiacs and reward restaurants that have gone the extra mile to help you. If a favorite restaurant of yours isn't already listed on these pages, let us know. A listing in this guide will help increase their gluten-free business – a "thank you" for taking care of you in the past and a strong incentive to provide great service and gluten-free options in the future. Let's work together to educate restaurants and build a network of Celiac-friendly restaurants across the country!

Please enjoy this edition of *The Essential Gluten-Free Restaurant Guide* and, as always, I would love to hear your questions and comments.

Ross Cohen
President, Triumph Dining
ross@triumphdining.com

Chapter 1 - Conveying Information Effectively

If you remember only two pieces of information from this guide, it should be these:

1. The first fundamental building block of successful gluten-free dining is the ability to share information in a clear, efficient manner.

2. The second is developing beneficial short and long-term relationships with restaurant staff.

Almost everything you will ever do to improve your gluten-free dining out experience will flow from these two skill sets. The next two chapters will start you on the path to building these essential skills.

Build the Right Knowledge Base

It seems obvious enough that in order to share knowledge, you must first possess it. And, when it comes to gluten-free dining, you are your own first line of defense. You should make educated decisions about what you are and are not willing to try, so that you can avoid inadvertently stepping into dangerous territory, or missing out on perfectly safe, enticing dining options.

That's why you should be vigilant about collecting information on different cuisines, restaurant dishes, ingredients, and common cooking techniques. It's important to think about each cuisine (e.g. Mexican, Chinese, American, etc.) separately because each one has different ingredients and cooking methods and, hence, different potential problems for Celiacs.

Read cookbooks, watch cooking shows, research common restaurant dishes, talk with knowledgeable people, and ask questions. Initially, this may require a big time commitment and a lot of work, but it becomes easier as you start to pick things up, and it's worth the investment. Knowing the details about a particular cuisine makes every other part of the dining out experience significantly easier.

Some of our customers use Triumph Dining Cards as reference materials for building knowledge about particular cuisines. They find that the cards help them understand what information to convey and the best way to organize it for a particular type of restaurant. Our Triumph Dining Cards offer a clean framework for thinking about a restaurant's kitchen – the cards present information in three broad sections, covering (a) foods we cannot ever eat, (b) foods that are possibilities but require additional research (such as reading a label), and (c) foods that are okay for us to eat. Each section goes into enough specific detail on individual items in the restaurant's kitchen that the cards are an effective learning tool to help you identify likely safe options and potential pitfalls of a particular cuisine.

The challenge then, of course, is effectively communicating this information in real time and in a restaurant setting. To accomplish this, it is necessary to focus on sharing the right information in a clear and concise manner. This involves boiling down the information you've been collecting into its most important components and presenting them in a way that a chef can understand and use.

Communicate Effectively

We all know that saying "no wheat, rye, barley, and oats" isn't enough to get a safe meal in a restaurant. It takes most Celiacs months to understand the nuances of what that really means; we can't expect a chef to make sense of it the first time he or she hears it. So, we need to give the chef enough information to really understand our needs. That means not leaving the chef to just guess where wheat, rye, barley, and oats might lurk. Give obvious examples like bread and pasta to start him or her on the right track, and then reinforce the nuances of the diet by explicitly mentioning hidden sources of gluten, like soy sauce.

Be careful, though, not to overwhelm the kitchen with irrelevant information that will impair the staff's ability to grasp the big picture and successfully accommodate you. For example, items you might want to bring up in an Indian restaurant are different from those you might mention in an Italian restaurant. Loading up an Indian kitchen with information about pasta or croutons (neither of which are typically found in Indian cuisine) or not cooking vegetables in pasta water, can lead to confusion. You might even distract the kitchen from the important task at hand – making you gluten-free Indian food. We need to strike a useful balance!

Strike a Useful Balance

The best way to do this is to pare your information down to only those instructions that are relevant to the restaurant you are currently visiting. Then, structure it in an order that's easy to follow and understand. For example, I prefer to start with a quick general statement (e.g. "I can't eat wheat…") and follow it up with a few obvious items that are prohibited (e.g. egg rolls and buns in a Chinese restaurant) to give a little context and help the kitchen staff comprehend the basic concepts of the gluten-free diet. Then, I lead into the potentially big problem areas that are less obvious (e.g. sticking with our Chinese restaurant example, I would now mention soy sauce and cross-contamination). Then, depending on the circumstances, I may provide some examples of foods I can eat to give the chef some starting points for preparing a safe dish.

At different restaurants, you should expect to provide different instructions, customized for the type and style of cuisine served. It's a good idea to practice your instructions and develop a personal style that feels comfortable for you.

Look for Evidence of Thorough Understanding

The gluten-free diet has received a lot of mainstream media attention in the last few years. As a result, we're seeing more and more restaurant employees who seem to "get it." Mention "no wheat, rye, barley or oats" to these staffers and you may immediately hear, "Oh, you're gluten-free" or "You have Celiac disease – I know how to handle that."

Staff awareness is the first step toward better restaurant accommodations and that initial sign of recognition can be very comforting. In fact, it might even make some diners comfortable enough just to hand over the reins and let the staffer take over. But, that willingness is likely a little premature, and here's why:

As you know, there's a huge difference between knowing generally what "gluten-free" means and understanding all the nuances of the diet. It took us months to learn all the details of eating safely, so we know that level of granularity can't be communicated in the mainstream newspapers and magazines from which most people learn about Celiac disease.

It's not reasonable to require that these well-intentioned servers should be familiar with all the ins and outs of the gluten-free diet, like hidden sources of gluten and the dangers of cross-contamination. Before allowing them to prepare your meal, it's essential that you make sure the restaurant staff is on the right page.

Don't Make Assumptions

There's a lot of conflicting information on the gluten-free diet out there, even among dieticians, support groups, and the many other experts in the field. Some people believe blue cheese is gluten-free; others believe it's a danger. Some say distilled vinegar is safe; others choose to steer clear. Don't expect a chef to guess what your definition of gluten-free is.

And don't expect the chef to be 100% up-to-date on the latest research (we've seen the old rumor that spelt is gluten-free circulating again. FYI, it is not). In an ideal world, the food service industry would be required to attend trainings on and stay informed about all food sensitivity issues. But, for now at least, keeping up-to-date is your job, not the chef's.

Now, it's impractical (and even a little rude) to lecture a server for half an hour on all the nuances of the gluten-free diet. But it is within bounds to go over a few key items just to make sure that they are fully on the same page with you. When I hear "oh you're gluten-free," I say something along the lines of "Great! I'm so glad you've heard about it. What a relief!" Then, I ask some basic cross-contamination questions, such as whether anything breaded is prepared on the same surface as what I want to order.

As I do this, I'm as concerned about the content of the actual answer as I am with the general tone and ease with which the staffer provides it. The important element of this communication is to get a feel for how educated this restaurant is. Does the server immediately grasp the underlying reasons for your concern? Does it sound like he's been trained on this, and/or that he knows the kitchen has safe, standard operating procedures in effect?

If this spot check produces good results, it gives me a strong level of comfort. If it doesn't, I fall back on some of the other communication techniques described in this Guide to make sure I convey the essentials of safe, gluten-free dining.

I advise doing this little verbal spot check at every restaurant you visit, no matter how highly recommended it comes.

Use a Dining Card

I don't want to present the illusion that communicating effectively to restaurant staff is easy. It can be a very challenging task. A lot of information needs to be conveyed effectively in very little time. For that and other reasons, I use a good dining card to supplement my verbal instructions.

A good dining card provides the kitchen with a written record of your conversation. They can reference it when preparing your meal, in case they forget or confuse any of the information you've provided them. It is also a good crutch for your verbal instructions – it serves as a visual cue to help you remember everything you want to share and gives you a safety net in case you forget to mention something.

Finally, when you're dealing with ethnic restaurants, a carefully translated dining card can help you bridge the language barrier. For example, in most Thai restaurants I can only get so far with an English explanation of our diet. But, with well-written Thai instructions, I can get most dishes on the menu prepared gluten-free!

It's important, however, not to choose just any dining card. Make sure the translation is one you can trust. And just as important, make sure you know what the card says.

Don't Say 'Gluten' ... at First

Some words are simple: They have only one meaning, and that meaning is clear. Unfortunately for us, gluten is not one of those words. Often, it means different things to different people.

Obviously, for Celiacs, "gluten" refers to the protein specifically found in wheat, rye, and barley. However, for chefs, "gluten" can be a much more expansive term that refers to plant proteins found in many cereal grains, even some that are safe for a gluten-free diet (including rice and corn). Common terms like "glutinous rice," which is also safe for a gluten-free diet, add further confusion. Without appropriate context, a chef may interpret a "gluten-free" meal to be free of flour, rice, corn, and other starches.

That's why we recommend spelling out "no wheat, rye, barley or oats" and avoiding the word "gluten" the first time you explain the diet to a new restaurant. It reduces the chance of a mix-up.

Now, that's not to say you'll never use the word "gluten" in a restaurant again. Providing information on the diet and appropriate terminology is an essential part of building long-term relationships and educating restaurants. The point here is simply that on your first visit to a new restaurant, the word "gluten" can do more harm than good.

Consider Using the Word 'Allergy'

We know and you know that Celiac disease is not an allergy. And it should never be a goal to spread misinformation. That said, some restaurants have reportedly approached "gluten-free" as if it were a version of Atkins or a voluntary, fad diet. In short, they didn't afford certain patrons the attention Celiac disease requires.

We've learned over the years that the word "allergy" means business in the restaurant world. It can often trigger special attention from the manager and special operating procedures in the kitchen. Depending on the circumstances, categorizing your gluten-free needs as an allergy may increase your chances of receiving a safe meal.

Now, we can't think of a good reason why the word "allergy" should carry more weight than "medically-restricted diet" or "food intolerance," but we're not interested in splitting semantic hairs. Our goal is simply to give you the tools necessary to get a gluten-free meal. It's ultimately your decision whether you're comfortable using the word "allergy," but we do at least want you to be aware of the option, should you have trouble getting the attention you deserve in a restaurant.

Talk to the Right Person

Finally, underlying this whole approach is one key assumption that I'd like to acknowledge: Your instructions, verbal or written, are only as good as the eyes or ears taking them in. Most Celiacs know that one of the easiest ways to get sick in any restaurant is to tell the wrong person about your special needs. Have you ever had a waiter who seemed too rushed to invest in understanding your instructions or just didn't seem to "get it"? Or, maybe you felt like he was playing a risky version of the old "telephone" game, selectively giving the kitchen only the bits and pieces he felt were important?

If you encounter situations like this, the most carefully prepared, expertly delivered instructions may not help you. It is absolutely essential to your success that you seek out and engage the right person early in your restaurant visit. Make sure your instructions are heard by someone who has the power, ability, and motivation to get you a gluten-free meal. Depending on the circumstances, this might be the manager, the maitre d', or the owner. We'll switch gears in the next chapter to develop a framework for identifying and reaching the right person, along with other techniques central to building successful relationships.

Chapter 2 - Building Short-Term Relationships

There are things you can do every time you're in a restaurant that will improve the service you receive right then and there, and these techniques build strong short-term relationships. There are other things you can do to build powerful long-term relationships. You might use these techniques now or in the near future, and they will pay dividends on every subsequent trip to a restaurant.

Consistently successful gluten-free dining requires the development of both short and long-term relationships. For example, I used the short-term techniques in this chapter to get a safe, delicious meal the first time I visited my favorite Thai restaurant in Philadelphia. In the next chapter, we'll cover the long-term relationship strategies that motivated the owner to invest the time and research to learn that he could prepare almost anything on his menu gluten-free.

Find the Right Restaurant

The first technique is deceptively simple: choose the right restaurant. There are a lot of factors to consider when picking a restaurant. First, some cuisines are better choices for Celiacs than others. For example, Indian and Thai cuisines often present dozens of options for the gluten-free diet, while the local pizzeria might not have any suitable options and could present a very high risk of cross-contamination.

Second, some restaurant business models create a better environment for Celiacs than others. For example, restaurants that focus on high-quality food, service, and providing fresh ingredients will be far more likely to offer you special treatment than restaurants geared toward high-speed table turning, low prices, and using pre-prepared items.

Finally, owner-operated restaurants are more likely to be Celiac-friendly than bigger chains and franchises (although there are some exceptions). At many large chains, dishes are prepared off-site with heavily-processed ingredients, making modifications very difficult. Furthermore, since the restaurant kitchen staff members receive dishes partially prepared, they are not always familiar with the composition of the dishes. On the other hand, owner-operated restaurants are far more likely to prepare dishes from scratch and therefore be more knowledgeable about the ingredients.

You should keep a close eye on these factors, along with other signals in the restaurant's environment. But the bottom line is that you should always trust your gut (no pun intended). If something about the restaurant feels off, or you aren't getting enough conscientious attention from the restaurant staff, choose another restaurant. I have walked out of restaurants when I've felt at risk, and you should feel empowered to do the same. There are plenty of other places that would be happy to have your business.

The timing of your restaurant visit is also very important. Restaurants have obvious peak hours (usually lunch and dinner rushes) during which they strain their resources just to accommodate all their customers. As a first-time customer, your objective is to convince the restaurant to invest in a short-term relationship with you, to find and prepare a gluten-free meal. This requires substantially more time and effort than accommodating a non-Celiac customer. If at all possible, your first visit to a new restaurant should be during non-peak hours (either well before or well after the peak rush), because the restaurant staff will be far better equipped and more likely to help you.

Notify the Restaurant Beforehand

It's usually best to make reservations, letting the restaurant know in advance about your special dietary needs. (But don't worry - not having a reservation isn't the end of the world.) And when making a reservation, be sure to speak with the right person.

Surprisingly, the person answering the phone sometimes has very limited knowledge of how the restaurant actually operates. The restaurant could have the best gluten-free service in the country, and the reservationist may never know! Don't get discouraged. If you sense confusion from the first person you're speaking with, ask for the manager or, even better, the chef, to make sure the restaurant can accommodate you and to find out what protocol they would like you to follow.

The Maitre D' = Your Best Friend

When you enter the restaurant, the first thing you should do (even before you sit down) is identify yourself as a special needs customer to the maitre d'. The last thing you want is to make a busy restaurant staff feel ambushed.

The maitre d' is a wonderful person to have on your side because he or she often serves as the restaurant's traffic cop. An experienced maitre d' knows every server and line cook, can speak to the kitchen on your behalf, and can determine which waiters are most capable of handling special needs. By talking with the maitre d' immediately upon arrival, you can substantially reduce the chances that you'll receive bad or disinterested service.

When I talk to the maitre d' on my first visit to a particular restaurant, I usually say something along the lines of the following: "Hi. My name is Ross. I've heard great things about your restaurant, and I'd really like to eat here tonight. I have a restricted diet and can't eat wheat and a few other things. This card has instructions on what I can and cannot eat." - I hand him or her my dining card - "Will you be able to help me tonight?"

Throughout hundreds of restaurant meals, I've only been turned away twice. But, I actually found that helpful. It's better to know you can't be accommodated as soon as you walk in the door, as opposed to after you've sat down and ordered drinks.

In addition to determining whether a restaurant can accommodate you, talking to the maitre d' immediately and honestly does one other extremely important thing: It humanizes you. The maitre d' may see hundreds of people a night, and it's very easy for him or her to start viewing everyone who comes in the door as just another customer, a source of revenue. When you ask for his or her help and he or she pledges it to you, you've formed a bond. Call it empathy, sympathy, or whatever – the chances are very good that your maitre d' will go that extra mile to make sure you eat safely.

If you're in a group and feel self-conscious about your diet, let the maitre d' seat you without mentioning your special needs. Then, excuse yourself from your group, return to the maitre d', and explain your situation privately. That should be enough to get you appropriate treatment, without drawing the group's attention to your special diet.

Make it Easy

Once you have a table, there are a few more things you can do to strengthen your immediate relationship with the restaurant staff. Keep in mind that the typical restaurant staff is usually busy, in a rush, and often stressed. Anything you can do to make their jobs easier will be greatly appreciated and result in better service.

For example, it's rarely enough to tell the waiter what you can't eat. Instead, be proactive. You know more about the gluten-free diet than he does, so don't make him guess the menu options that might be suitable for you. Scout the menu for choices that are likely to be gluten-free and present them to the waiter as items for further investigation. If you do this, you allow the waiter to use his valuable time to interface with the kitchen and to confirm that your choice is a safe one.

It's also important to be considerate and show appreciation when the restaurant staff goes the extra mile to accommodate you. Think back to the last time you went out of your way to help someone. Why did you do it? What made it worthwhile? For me, it's usually most rewarding when someone is really nice and genuinely appreciates my efforts. A restaurant's staff sees a lot of demanding and disgruntled customers in the course of an evening. Your smiling face and kind words will make you stand out from the crowd; you will be remembered and rewarded!

Double Check

Finally, when your meal is served, always confirm with the server that it was prepared gluten-free. Good restaurants will typically do this as a matter of course. If they don't, be proactive and ask. This simple step should provide confirmation that your special needs were not lost in the shuffle, and it will reduce the chances of an unpleasant surprise partway through your meal.

Chapter 3 - Building Long-Term Relationships

The real rewards in gluten-free dining come when you move beyond the transactional nature of a first-time restaurant visit and begin establishing substantial, long-term relationships with certain restaurants.

Over time, as you develop a relationship with a particular restaurant, you have the opportunity to open doors to even more specialized service. As I mentioned before, my favorite Thai restaurant learned to make me anything I want from scratch. Other Celiacs have inspired restaurants to stock gluten-free soy sauce or even create dedicated gluten-free menus! Every relationship with a restaurant will be different, but the sky is the limit when you start using the following tools to build mutually rewarding, long-term relationships.

Help Yourself by Helping Them

The key to building successful long-term relationships is to align the needs of the restaurant and its staff with your own. In other words, encourage an environment where helping you and providing for your needs meets their needs.

The first component of developing this environment is to understand the needs and interests of the restaurant and its staff. Every situation is different, but you can make some basic generalizations that will be more or less accurate the vast majority of the time.

For example, it's a safe bet that the restaurant's owner and manager are looking to build a strong business and satisfy customers. Likewise, the restaurant's employees are probably interested in generous tips and a pleasant work environment.

But also keep your eyes and ears open for less obvious information (and ways you can react to it). For example, maybe the restaurant is trying to increase traffic on slow evenings (offer to refer your friends) or build a business hosting events (arrange a support group dinner). Understanding the restaurant's interests will allow you to target your efforts and improve your effectiveness.

Reward Extra Service with an Extra Tip

The first and easiest strategy is to tip generously for good service. I generally tip 20-25% when someone handles my needs well, though I'll go higher if I receive exceptional service. I do this because waiting on Celiac patrons requires far more effort and involvement than serving typical diners. In giving you more thorough care, your server is spending less time attending to the needs of other tables. So if you tip like everyone else, the waiter could make less money for investing more time in you. That can actually create a disincentive for the waiter to spend extra time serving you well! If you reward his extra effort, however, you can actually incentivize him to go all out and be extra vigilant about your needs during future visits.

Make Yourself a Familiar Figure

The strategy of tipping generously can be complemented by returning to the restaurant often. Frequent visits have two impacts. First, working with you regularly helps the staff learn the specific needs of your diet. Second, regular visits increase your value as a customer. And the more valuable you are as a customer, the greater the restaurant's incentive to invest in providing a variety of suitable, delicious gluten-free options.

If you receive great service from a particular staff member, get that person's name. When you return to the restaurant, request to be seated in that server's section. You'll build loyalty and the server's gluten-free knowledge base. And if you follow the previous suggestion, the server will know she can earn a generous tip by taking care of your dietary needs. If she knows she's working toward a reward, she'll be attentive every time.

The Most Powerful Strategy: A Sincere Thank You

Believe it or not, the most effective tool for building long-term relationships is simply saying "thank you." Everyone likes to be appreciated and acknowledged for doing a good job.

Thanking the server directly is a great start. But, you can also take it to the next level by mentioning responsive staff to management.

Restaurant managers usually hear from customers when something goes wrong. Because they mostly hear complaints from customers, your compliments are a welcome breath of fresh air. They will make you stand out (in a good way) with management and help cement the long-term relationship you're building. And, you'll create positive karma that will benefit your responsive server, encouraging him to help you more in the future.

I'll give you an example of how effective this really is. Some time ago, I went to a Wendy's franchise during the lunch rush (not the ideal time, but I had little choice). With a line of people in back of me, I quickly ran through a set of instructions. When I was done, the cashier whirled around and spoke in rapid-fire Spanish to the cook behind him. I watched as my food was prepared exactly as I had asked. The cashier's name was Franco.

After finishing my meal, I filled out a comment card, letting the management know what a great job Franco had done. A few weeks later, I received a personal note and several vouchers for free meals from the franchise owner, thanking me for the positive feedback. And you can imagine the impact this had on the relationship between the owner and Franco! The next time I visited, with my free meal vouchers, Franco was thrilled, and he even remembered my instructions.

That's the wonderful thing about a sincere "thank you" – kindness finds its way back to you. Franco got the kudos he deserved, and I can now enjoy a safe meal at one of the busiest fast food restaurants in the nation.

Bring Your Friends

The next step in building a long-term relationship is to help grow the restaurant's business by referring your friends. Often, this goes hand-in-hand with a sincere "thank you."

For example, when I talk to the manager of a restaurant, I typically start by thanking him – both for the quality of his restaurant's food and the special care his staff showed in handling my dietary needs (assuming that's accurate). Then I ask him if they get many gluten-free customers and if he'd like to serve more in the future.

The managers I've spoken with are almost always happy to have more gluten-free business, so I tell the manager that I'll mention his restaurant to other Celiacs and in this Restaurant Guide. You should also feel free to use this Guide as a tool to reward Celiac-friendly restaurants. Just e-mail us if you'd like us to look into adding a restaurant to the next edition.

The key to this technique is recognizing that restaurants are businesses; restaurant owners worry about paying their bills and earning a profit. When you visit a restaurant regularly, you become a valuable customer. When you start sending your friends, you become an extremely valuable customer! The more you contribute to their bottom line, the more the restaurant will invest in catering to your special needs.

Remember that while referring additional Celiacs is great for our community, the friends you bring don't need to have Celiac disease to contribute to the restaurant's bottom line and make management happy. Just don't forget to mention your efforts to the manager, so that you get credit for any bump in business!

As you employ these strategies, you will notice that your relationships with restaurants will strengthen substantially over time. You may find that as you tip generously, visit frequently, thank the management, and send your friends, restaurants will become substantially more accommodating of your needs. And that's an amazing progress.

Just Ask

The most effective way to get something, whether you want to try a new dish or to get gluten-free soy sauce stocked, is to ask for it. It's really that simple! You'll be amazed at what you can get just by asking. Gluten-free restaurant dining is no exception. Use the techniques in this book to identify what makes you a valuable customer (the frequency of your visits, your plan to continue visiting regularly, your friend referrals, etc.) and ask if there's someone on staff who can work with you to find more menu options or even to create a dedicated gluten-free menu. Once you've established a good relationship, you'll most likely find that many of the restaurants you visit will be happy to go that extra mile to accommodate your needs.

Chapter 4 - A Few Final Words of Advice

We've covered a lot of ground in this section. We've discussed techniques to convey information on the gluten-free diet effectively, and strategies to develop productive short and long-term relationships. Now, we'll cover final, crucial concepts that will help you put these techniques to work.

Attitude is Everything

All of the strategies covered in this Guide work best when delivered, well, sweetly. Our attitudes are often reflected right back at us. Come in ready for battle, and you'll likely get one – your waiter, sensing your mood, will probably become defensive. Instead, come in smiling. It's hard for people, even overworked, stressed restaurant staff, to ignore genuine kindness. Be sure to ask for people's names, and use them often. Don't give orders, but ask for help.

Be careful that your instructions don't turn into a 10-minute lecture. People may zone out or, worse, become resentful. Instead, engage your server in a dialogue by involving her in your dining selections; make her your ally. The more involved she feels in the process, the more likely she is to go that extra mile for you.

Patience is a Virtue

The Celiac diet is complex, so don't expect the restaurant staff to catch on immediately. Don't be discouraged if your waiter asks you questions seemingly out of left field, like, "Is salt okay? How about vegetables?" Is the waiter displaying genuine curiosity? Does he seem to be catching on (even if slowly)? If so, be patient and hold your temper. If he's doing his best to learn how to serve you, try not to flare up at a few innocent, if misdirected, questions.

Give the Benefit of the Doubt

If someone who has been helpful so far makes a mistake – for example, if your salad comes with croutons – please give your server the benefit of the doubt. I've never been to a restaurant that intentionally tries to make its customers sick. Keep in mind the chaotic nature of restaurants, and please do not hurl accusations or insults.

The best way to handle this type of situation is to calmly point out the problem and reiterate that you can become ill without proper care. That is usually enough to correct any missteps. Making a scene, especially before trying to remedy the problem civilly, is a no-win situation all around. Remember that these restaurants are not obligated to serve gluten-free food. Please treat them with the respect and dignity they deserve, so that they will continue serving other Celiacs in the future.

Where to Start

We've now covered numerous strategies for successful gluten-free dining and how to apply them. I hope you've realized that gluten-free dining doesn't have to be scary or intimidating if you take the right approach and use the tools in this book.

The several thousand restaurants listed in this guide provide good, low-risk starting points for your gluten-free dining experiences. You can follow the paths of success enjoyed by other Celiacs by visiting restaurants with strong track records.

But, remember that before these restaurants were listed in this guide, a Celiac had to eat there for the first time, share information about our diet, and build that initial relationship. Now you too are equipped to do exactly that.

For every restaurant in this guide, there are hundreds more that may have no experience at all with gluten-free dining. This guide is designed to open doors for you, not shut them. So please visit the restaurants listed here, but don't necessarily rule out those that aren't in this guide. Some unlisted restaurants may present fantastic, unrealized opportunities. It's up to you to identify them. Use these tools to seek out more gluten-free opportunities to dine out, and make them successful.

Section 2: Restaurant Listings by State

User's Guide

In this section, there are over 6,500 restaurant locations listed alphabetically by state, with independent sub-categories for over forty of the nation's biggest and most Celiac-friendly cities. Each restaurant (or restaurant chain) was considered for inclusion in this guide based on recommendations from other Celiacs and thorough research by our editors. To determine its ability to accommodate gluten-free diners, we evaluated each restaurant for the availability of its gluten-free specialty items, the extensiveness of its gluten-free menu, and its staff's knowledge of the gluten-free diet. We used stories and suggestions from hundreds of Celiac diners, a variety of restaurant resources, and our own culinary savvy – in addition to information provided by the restaurants themselves – to come up with this broad listing of gluten-free aware restaurants.

Unfortunately, there's no such thing as worry-free gluten-free dining. By its nature, ordering a gluten-free meal will almost always take more time and effort than ordering a "regular" one. It requires constant vigilance, no matter how Celiac-friendly the restaurant may be. Our Guide is designed to help make this process as easy as possible for you.

The objective of this guide is to provide the tools you need to make safe dining choices. Not every Celiac will feel at ease frequenting every type of restaurant we've chosen to list (e.g., some people avoid pizza parlors because there is a stronger possibility of cross-contamination). Everyone has his/her own level of comfort, and we advise you to find your own and stick to it. We provide information about as wide a range of restaurants as possible, not to suggest that you could or should frequent these places, but to aid you in making that decision for yourself. This Guide is about enabling you to make safe, healthy choices. It is not about making them for you.

Please keep in mind that we are not recommending or endorsing any of the restaurants in this book. We have merely aggregated information for your convenience. Because the restaurant industry is constantly and rapidly changing, you should always independently verify the information presented in this Guide.

Overview of the Types of Restaurants Listed

The restaurants listed in this section of the guide can be broadly categorized into the following groups:

> Non-chain (independent) restaurants
>
> - Type 1: With gluten-free menus or specialty items
> - Type 2: Without gluten-free menus or specialty items
>
> Chain restaurants
>
> - Type 1: With gluten-free specialty items or gluten-free menus/lists
> - Type 2: Without gluten-free menus or lists

Non-Chain (Independent) Restaurants

By "non-chain" or "independent," we mean owner-operated restaurants. Generally speaking, these restaurants are more Celiac-friendly than large chain restaurants, where individualized service is harder to find. We've included two different types of non-chain restaurants in this guide:

Type 1: Non-Chain Restaurants with Gluten-Free Menus or Gluten-Free Specialty Items

In our book, a gluten-free menu has three qualities:

1. A gluten-free menu is printed. It's not in the chef's head or on the manager's computer.

2. A gluten-free menu is available to customers. This means that it is not an internal list hanging in the kitchen or in a service area; rather, it is something you can take to your table with you and choose a meal from.

3. A gluten-free menu, obviously, must list gluten-free items. It might be a separate menu or section on the menu listing only gluten-free items, or, alternatively, it can be a regular menu that clearly indicates gluten-free items (e.g. with an asterisk, a "GF," or another symbol).

A gluten-free specialty item is something that is not commonly gluten-free (like bread, pasta, pizza crust, or beer), but can be gluten-free if prepared specially.

Restaurants that have gluten-free menus or gluten-free specialty items are flagged with star-shaped icons. We've confirmed the availability of all gluten-free menus by phone, fax, or e-mail. We have not, however, independently verified the gluten-free status of the items on those menus.

In addition to flagging restaurants with gluten-free menus, we've tried to list some gluten-free menu items in the notes section, which is meant only to give you an idea of the type of cuisine served. **Never order directly from the notes section.** Many of the items listed can be prepared gluten-free only with the proper modifications, which the restaurant can make only if they know you are on a gluten-free diet!

Additionally, never assume that a gluten-free menu or gluten-free specialty items guarantee a gluten-free meal. Always show your dining card and carefully explain the gluten-free diet to your server. Please, don't make any assumptions when it comes to your health.

And don't forget: If you're going out for a gluten-free specialty item like pizza or pasta, be sure to call the restaurant ahead of time to make sure the item is in stock. Sometimes restaurants run out of these products.

Type 2: Non-Chain Restaurants without Gluten-Free Menus

In this section, we included some non-chain restaurants without gluten-free menus. These restaurants were selected based on recommendations from other Celiacs, as well as follow-up research that included conversations with restaurant management and staff. In the notes section, you will find important references to those conversations.

On occasion, the notes section also includes a few menu items that, according to the restaurant staff, are or can be modified to be gluten-free. These short lists are intended to give you an idea about what kind of food the restaurant serves. They are not designed to be comprehensive, and it is not appropriate or safe to order from these lists. When dining out at one of these establishments, please work with the restaurant staff to find a dish that's right for you. **Again, never order directly from the notes section of this guide.** Many of the items listed can be prepared gluten-free only with the proper modifications, which the restaurant can make only if they know you are on a gluten-free diet!

It's important to remember that these restaurants are listed because other Celiacs have safely enjoyed eating at them in the past, and they seemed aware during our conversations with management and staff. Many of them do not have any formally listed gluten-free offerings, and it's possible that certain employees at these restaurants have little to no experience with Celiac disease or the gluten-free diet.

As at any restaurant, even those with gluten-free menus, you should approach your dining experience with a certain amount of caution: Use your dining card, explain your diet carefully, and specify exactly how you'd like your food to be handled. Use your judgment, and if you're not entirely comfortable with the level of service being provided, leave the premises. Then, be sure to let us know, so we can revisit that restaurant's entry with extra caution when we prepare the next edition of this guide.

Chain Restaurants

In addition to owner-operated, "non-chain" restaurants, this section also contains two types of chain restaurants:

Type 1: Chain Restaurants with Gluten-Free Menus or Lists

In this section, we've included some or all locations of select chain restaurants that have gluten-free menus at each location, or gluten-free lists not present at each location but readily available from the corporate office or franchisor.

Next to Type 1 chain restaurants, you will see an icon of an open book. This means that you can find the corporate gluten-free list or menus in Section 3 of this guide. Please be sure to read the Section 3 User's Guide before consulting any of the gluten-free lists or menus included there. The lists typically indicate items available at all locations, but may, in certain circumstances, be unavailable. Call a specific restaurant location ahead of time to confirm the availability of items on the corporate gluten-free list or menu.

Note: Section 3 also contains many additional chain restaurants for which locations are not listed in Section 2. For more information about these restaurants and their gluten-free offerings, please see Section 3.

Type 2: Chain Restaurants without Gluten-Free Lists

Finally, this section includes listings for certain chain restaurants that do not have gluten-free lists, but do have on-site management that is generally regarded as very helpful, knowledgeable, and attentive. Each of these restaurants should be able to work with your dietary needs on an individual, local level.

Some Commonly Used Terms

GF Aware. The term "GF aware" appears occasionally in the restaurant notes section. That term simply means that our contact with the restaurant suggested that the managers and staff are familiar with the term "gluten-free" and the gluten-free diet. The term "GF aware" can indicate a range of knowledge, from "they have heard of the diet" to "they are formally trained on the requirements of the diet." You may still have to explain the details and nuances of the diet, but hopefully, you'll encounter staff members who have at least a baseline of knowledge on which to build.

Along the same lines, all the information presented here is "straight from the horse's mouth." We contacted every non-chain restaurant recommended for this guide and asked about gluten-free accommodations. In the following pages, we've reported their responses. We could not, however, quiz each restaurant to test the full extent and depth of the staff's knowledge. That's why it's important for you to remain vigilant and always ask questions.

Lunch vs. Dinner

The specific information provided in each restaurant's listing pertains to dinner, unless dinner is not served at that particular restaurant. Price categories apply to dinner entrées only; they do not include appetizers, drinks, etc. If dinner is not served at a particular restaurant, the price category refers to lunch or whatever meal is served.

Often, the dynamics of a restaurant change vastly between lunch and dinner. Lunch menus typically consist of lower-priced options like sandwiches, and many restaurants focus primarily on fast service. This makes it harder for restaurants to offer specialized attention.

Accordingly, the gluten-free options available at a restaurant may be very different for lunch and for dinner. For this reason, we recommend calling to get more information before visiting a restaurant for lunch.

A Few Final Notes

The restaurant business changes quickly and seems to be in a constant state of flux – even more so now, during an economic recession. New restaurants open while old ones close, owners sell businesses, chefs come and go, menus are updated, dish ingredients are modified, corporate policies change, managers leave, employees turn over or change shifts, etc. Any one of these (or other) factors could result in a one-time unpleasant dining experience at an otherwise reliable restaurant; they can also flat out ruin a formerly accommodating restaurant.

That's why it's important that you always individually verify the information presented in this Restaurant Guide (think of it as a starting point, not a definitive resource) and confirm that a restaurant can accommodate your needs before each visit. Remain vigilant, ask questions, make suggestions, and keep an eye on how the restaurant is handling your requests. If you're uncomfortable at any point, ask the manager to intervene. If that doesn't work, find another restaurant. It's not worth risking your health.

Finally, we would love to hear from you about your dining experiences – good or bad – at restaurants listed in this guide or new restaurants we haven't yet discovered. Future editions of this guide will be only as good as the feedback we receive from you, so if you'd like to see a restaurant added to these listings (or one removed), e-mail us or visit our website (www.TriumphDining.com) to let us know.

DINING OUT CHECKLIST

Before you visit a restaurant listed in this Guide, review this Summary Checklist and the User's Guides in Sections 2 and 3.

Before you Leave the House

☑ Research the restaurant. Is it a buffet, sandwich shop, or other type of cuisine that increases the risk of cross-contamination? If so, will you feel safe eating there?

☑ If dining at a chain restaurant, call the corporate office to request the most recent gluten-free menu or list. (See Section 3 for contact information.)

☑ Regardless of the type of restaurant, call the location you plan to visit in advance. Does the restaurant still have a gluten-free menu? (If not, can they accommodate you tonight?)

☑ Also, confirm that gluten-free specialty items are in stock. (E.g., if you're going for the gluten-free pasta, do they have it tonight?)

When You Get There

☑ Introduce yourself to the maitre d', and mention your dietary needs.

☑ Ask for the gluten-free menu, if applicable.

☑ Never make any assumptions. Present your dining card, even if they have a gluten-free menu. Ask a few questions. Confirm that they understand the diet, even if they have a gluten-free menu.

Also, review and use the tips and strategies on safe restaurant dining presented in the previous sections of this book.

And remember, there is no way any restaurant (or restaurant guide) can guarantee a gluten-free meal. Always independently verify information and be vigilant when eating out. A bit of caution goes a long way in getting a delicious, safe gluten-free meal.

ALABAMA

Amsterdam Café $$LD
Auburn ▪ *(334) 826-8181*
410 S Gay St ▪ *Seafood* ▪ Restaurant notes
that they are "comfortable" accommodating GF diners. In the kitchen, servers and
cooks have a list of which menu items can
be modified to be GF. Ask for a manager,
who will indicate GF menu options. ▪ *www.
theamsterdamcafe.com*

Berkeley Bob's Coffee   ¢$
Cullman ▪ *(256) 775-2944*
304 1st Ave NE ▪ *Coffee & Café* ▪ Owner
Bob reports that although he has stopped
regularly stocking GF bread, he can provide
it with advanced notice. They also serve GF
salads. Bob adds that GF diners need only
talk to him, and he will "work something
out." ▪ *www.berkeleybob.com*

Bonefish Grill   📖
Hoover ▪ *(205) 985-9545*
3430 Galleria Cir
Huntsville ▪ *(256) 883-0643*
4800 Whitesburg Dr S Ste 33
Mobile ▪ *(251) 633-7196*
6955 Airport Blvd
Montgomery ▪ *(334) 396-1770*
7020 Eastchase Pkwy

Cantina Laredo   📖
Huntsville ▪ *(256) 327-8580*
6782 Old Madison Pike

Carino's Italian   📖
Hoover ▪ *(205) 560-0505*
4330 Creekside Ave

Carrabba's Italian Grill   📖
Birmingham ▪ *(205) 980-1016*
4503 Riverview Pkwy
Huntsville ▪ *(256) 288-1333*
2801 Memorial Pkwy SW
Mobile ▪ *(251) 342-3662*
3917 Airport Blvd

Montgomery ▪ *(334) 271-7500*
1510 Eastern Blvd

Demo's Restaurant   ✪ $LD
Florence ▪ *(256) 246-1434*
339 Seville St ▪ *Italian* ▪ GF menu includes
shrimp cocktail, steak and feta salad,
stuffed potatoes, steaks, catfish, shrimp
scampi, mozzarella chicken, and more. ▪
www.demosrestaurants.com

Ellen's Creative Cakes   ★ $$$$$
Huntsville ▪ *(256) 217-1517*
603 Jordan Ln ▪ *Bakery* ▪ Non-dedicated
bakery offering a variety of GF cakes.
Flavors include carrot, hummingbird, and
chocolate, and each is available in a range
of sizes. Owner Ellen suggests placing an
order in advance, but she notes that she
usually has some GF cake stored in the
freezer for fast pickup. ▪ *www.ellenscre-
ativecakes.com*

Firebirds Wood Fired Grill   ✪ $$$LD
Hoover ▪ *(205) 733-2002*
191 Main St ▪ *American* ▪ GF menu includes a variety of salads and a selection
of entrées. Examples include sirloin, filet
mignon, ribs, and lobster tail. Restaurant
reports that servers are trained to alert the
chef when a customer orders from the GF
menu. ▪ *www.firebirdsrockymountaingrill.
com*

Hangout, The $$BLD
Gulf Shores ▪ *(251) 948-3030*
101 E Beach Blvd ▪ *American Regional* ▪
Restaurant reports that many menu items
can be modified to be GF, including sandwiches without buns and seafood dishes.
Confirm timeliness of this information before dining in. Alert a server upon arrival. ▪
www.thehangoutal.com

Jimmy's   ★ $$LD
Opelika ▪ *(334) 745-2155*
104 South 8th St ▪ *American Regional* ▪
Owner and Chef Jim reports that they will
prepare GF meals at "any time." He notes
that many dishes, including the fresh fish,
the beef tenderloin, and the lobster, are GF,

while other items can be modified to be GF. Confirm timeliness of this information before dining in. GF pasta is available. ▪ *www.jimmysopelika.com*

La Paz $**LD**

Birmingham ▪ *(205) 879-2225*
99 Euclid Ave ▪ *Mexican* ▪ Manager Ellen reports that GF diners can be easily accommodated. She recommends alerting a server, who will speak to the kitchen staff about preparing GF items in a separate frying pan. She notes that although the chips are not GF, customers are welcome to bring their own. Enchiladas, tacos, salads, and more can all be modified to be GF. Confirm timeliness of this information before dining in. ▪ *www.lapaz.com*

Lone Star Steakhouse & Saloon   📖

Birmingham ▪ *(205) 942-1902*
180 State Farm Pkwy
Huntsville ▪ *(256) 837-0010*
5901 University Dr NW
Montgomery ▪ *(334) 277-2455*
1060 Eastern Blvd
Oxford ▪ *(256) 831-7441*
171 Colonial Dr
Trussville ▪ *(205) 661-9339*
4720 Norrel Dr

Manna Grocery & Deli   ¢**L**

Tuscaloosa ▪ *(800) 752-9950*
2300 Mcfarland Blvd E Ste 12 ▪ *Deli* ▪ Manager Mike reports that the deli can accommodate GF diners and that the staff is "knowledgeable about the ingredients" in their food. He recommends asking for a manager upon arrival. ▪ *www.mannagrocery.com*

Melting Pot, The   📖

Birmingham ▪ *(205) 981-8001*
611 Doug Baker Blvd
Huntsville ▪ *(256) 327-8888*
340 Bridge St Town Centre

Oh! Bryan's Family Steak House $$**LD**

Madison ▪ *(256) 325-2792*
100 Plaza Blvd ▪ *Steakhouse* ▪ Manager Valerie reports that the kitchen can accom-

modate GF diners, but customers should be ready to explain GF requests. She notes that GF dining cards would be helpful. Alert a server, who will confer with the kitchen. ▪ *www.ohbryans.com*

Outback Steakhouse   📖

Birmingham ▪ *(205) 290-0099*
281 Lakeshore Pkwy
Birmingham ▪ *(205) 991-4418*
5231 Highway 280 S
Dothan ▪ *(334) 702-4939*
2925 Ross Clark Cir
Fultondale ▪ *(205) 849-0155*
1725 Fulton Rd
Hoover ▪ *(205) 979-7585*
1944 Hoover Ct
Huntsville ▪ *(256) 882-6283*
4777 Whitesburg Dr S
Madison ▪ *(256) 895-0257*
7640 Highway 72 W
Mobile ▪ *(251) 342-3276*
901 Montlimar Dr
Montgomery ▪ *(334) 270-9495*
1040 East Blvd
Opelika ▪ *(334) 741-4014*
2115 Pepperell Pkwy
Oxford ▪ *(256) 835-4644*
196 Spring Branch Rd
Prattville ▪ *(334) 285-6281*
1899 Sugar Exchange
Sheffield ▪ *(256) 383-0046*
4838 Hatch Blvd
Tuscaloosa ▪ *(205) 759-9000*
5001 Oscar Baxter Dr

P.F. Chang's China Bistro   📖

Huntsville ▪ *(256) 327-8320*
305 The Bridge St Ste 101
Vestavia ▪ *(205) 967-0040*
233 Summit Blvd

Papa Dubi's $**LD**

Guntersville ▪ *(256) 894-7878*
3931 Brashers Chapel Rd ▪ *Cajun & Creole* ▪ Owner Dan reports that the restaurant does not serve GF diners on a regular basis. He suggests alerting the server upon arrival, and asking the server to get him or his son, Patrick, who is the

kitchen manager. Dan notes that grilled chicken, fish, shrimp, and salads are among the items that can be modified to be GF. Confirm timeliness of this information before dining in.

Papageorge's Supper Club ★ $$LD
Mobile ▪ *(251) 478-9099*
2600 Government Blvd ▪ *American Regional* ▪ Owner Cindy reports that there are "a couple of items" that are naturally GF. She notes that most of the GF options are shrimp, oyster, or steak dishes. She recommends being very specific about GF requirements. GF beer is available.

Ruan Thai ★ $LD
Tuscaloosa ▪ *(205) 391-9973*
1407 University Blvd ▪ *Thai* ▪ Restaurant reports that they can modify anything to be GF, and that most items are naturally GF. GF items include rice noodles and salads, along wih shrimp and rice dishes. Alert a server upon arrival. ▪ *www.ruanthaituscaloosa.com*

Sunflower Café ✪★ $LD
Fairhope ▪ *(251) 929-0055*
320 Eastern Shore Shopping Ctr ▪ *Organic* ▪ GF menu includes hummus, sunflower salad, and an ahi sandwich. GF bread and pizza are available. ▪ *www.vafairhopehealthfoods.com*

Taylor's Bakery & Gourmet Coffee ★ ¢S
Auburn ▪ *(334) 502-1112*
132 N College St ▪ *Coffee & Café* ▪ Baker Eid notes that customers often call to order GF cakes, cookies, and bread. He requires advanced notice of three or four days. Eid also cautions that without calling ahead, there will most likely be no GF items available. ▪ *www.taylorsbakeryandcoffee.com*

Villaggio Grille $$$LD
Orange Beach ▪ *(251) 224-6510*
4790 Wharf Pkwy ▪ *Italian* ▪ Restaurant reports that it accommodates GF diners "at least once a day." They note that the staff is very GF aware. They also report that most

menu items, including seafood, steak, and chicken dishes, can be modified to be GF. Confirm timeliness of this information before dining in. Upon arrival, alert the server, who will notify the kitchen. ▪ *www.villaggiogrille.com*

ALASKA

Bear's Den $LD
Soldotna ▪ *(907) 262-6546*
45015 Kalifornsky Beach Rd ▪ *American Regional* ▪ Owner Laura reports that they are happy to accommodate GF diners. She notes that GF diners are "very common," and as long as they are "open" about their diet, the restaurant will be able to make a GF meal. She adds that most items are made from scratch, so they can control the ingredients. Alert a server, who will notify the chef. ▪ *www.bearsdenak.com*

City Diner $BLD
Anchorage ▪ *(907) 277-2489*
3000 Minnesota Dr ▪ *American* ▪ Manager Samantha reports that GF diners are welcome and notes that there are many GF options, like french fries made in a dedicated fryer, flat-iron steaks, and diner browns. Alert a server upon arrival. Servers have a "food allergy" button that tells the cooks to make careful preparations. ▪ *www.citydiner.org*

Ginger ✪ $$$LD
Anchorage ▪ *(907) 929-3680*
425 W 5th Ave ▪ *Pacific Rim* ▪ GF menu includes pomme frites and ahi tuna, among other things, as appetizers. It also lists the ribeye, Alaskan halibut, thai shrimp noodle soup, strawberry chili, and more as entrées. For dessert, there is crème brûlée. ▪ *www.gingeralaska.com*

Glacier Brewhouse $$$LD
Anchorage ▪ (907) 274-2739
737 W 5th Ave ▪ *American* ▪ Hostess Amy
reports that the "most important thing to
do" is alert the server upon arrival. Servers
are familiar with GF menu items. Amy
further notes that the baby back ribs and
the prime rib, among other things, are
naturally GF, but sauces are not. Confirm
timeliness of this information before dining in. ▪ *www.glacierbrewhouse.com*

Hangar on the Warf   ★ $$LD
Juneau ▪ (907) 586-5018
2 Marine Way ▪ *American* ▪ GF bread is
available. Bartender Michelle notes that
several vegetarian meals come with GF
bread, and other dishes can be modified
to be GF. She also notes that GF diners
"rarely" come in. Alert a server upon arrival. ▪ *www.hangaronthewharf.com*

Ivory Jacks Restaurant   ★ $BLD
Fairbanks ▪ (907) 455-6666
2581 Goldstream Rd ▪ *American* ▪ GF
pizza, bread, hamburger buns, and beer
are available, as are GF brownies and
cookies for dessert. Owner Joni reports
that she has GF family members, so she
is very GF aware. ▪ *www.mosquitonet.
com/~ivoryjacks/ij*

Johann's Restaurant $$BLD
Eagle River ▪ (907) 696-7222
11901 Old Glenn Hwy ▪ *American* ▪ Chef
Tony reports that there are three different
types of steaks, all of which are GF. The
grilled chicken breast with berry sauce is
also GF. Confirm timeliness of this information before dining in. Tony recommends
asking for himself or Josh upon arrival. ▪
www.johannsrestaurant.com

Kincaid Grill $$$D
Anchorage ▪ (907) 243-0507
6700 Jewel Lake Rd ▪ *Modern American*
▪ Kitchen Staffer Trerina reports that the
chefs are very good about accommodating GF diners "on the fly." Still, she recommends making reservations noting

GF and alerting the server upon arrival.
For dessert, they offer crème brûlée and
sometimes flourless chocolate cake. ▪ *www.
kincaidgrill.com*

Little Tokyo $$$LD
Sitka ▪ (907) 747-5699
315 Lincoln St ▪ *Japanese* ▪ Manager Sarah
reports that they can accommodate GF
diners as long as they are notified immediately of dietary needs. Alert a server upon
arrival. Sarah adds that there are many
menu items which can be prepared GF,
including the edamame, the vegetable roll,
the cucumber roll, and the tuna roll.

Lone Star Steakhouse & Saloon   📖
Anchorage ▪ (907) 562-7827
4810 C St

Ludvig's Bistro $$$D
Sitka ▪ (907) 966-3663
256 Katlian St ▪ *Mediterranean* ▪ Items
that are GF or can be modified to be GF
include king salmon with risotto, paella,
caesar salad with scallops, skewered lamb
kebabs, and lamb meatballs with pine nuts
and herbs. Alert a server upon arrival.
Reservations noting GF are recommended.
▪ *www.ludvigsbistro.com*

Marx Brothers Café $$$$LD
Anchorage ▪ (907) 278-2133
627 W 3rd Ave ▪ *Modern American* ▪
Owner Jack recommends reservations
noting GF. He explains that when a GF
reservation is made, the chef will "figure
something out" and advise the server on
how to accommodate the GF diner. ▪ *www.
marxcafe.com*

Middleway Café   ★ ¢S
Anchorage ▪ (907) 272-6433
1200 W Northern Lights Blvd ▪ *Bakery* ▪
Non-dedicated bakery offering GF banana
bread, chocolate bread, and blueberry muffins. Bakery adds that they are constantly
trying new GF recipes to add to their
selection.

Natural Pantry ${BLD}

Anchorage ■ *(907) 770-1444*
3801 Old Seward Hwy ■ *Café* ■ The menu changes day to day, but the café reports that there is usually one GF entrée or a GF soup available. Call ahead to find out the option for a given day. The café is located within the Natural Pantry Market. ■ *www.natural-pantry.com*

Orso ${LD}

Anchorage ■ *(907) 222-3232*
737 W 5th Ave ■ *Modern American* ■ Manager Josh reports that the restaurant can "absolutely" accommodate GF diners. He notes that while most servers are aware of GF menu modifications, less-experienced servers will ask the chef. Josh recommends reservations noting GF and alerting the server upon arrival. ■ *www.orsoalaska.com*

Outback Steakhouse 📖

Anchorage ■ *(907) 562-8787*
101 W 34th Ave

Red Beet Bistro & Beetniks Coffee

✪★ ${{LD}
Palmer ■ *(907) 745-4050*
320 E Dahlia Ave ■ *American Regional* ■ Owner and Chef Sally reports that "except on pasta or meat pie days," the restaurant is entirely GF. Confirm timeliness of this information before dining in. GF list is posted daily on the website, and usually includes a variety of breads and goodies like cookies, brownies, muffins, and more. ■ *www.redbeetcafe.com*

Sacks Café & Restaurant ${{LD}

Anchorage ■ *(907) 274-4022*
328 G St ■ *Modern American* ■ Owner Jo Ann reports that they serve GF diners often, and that all staff members are trained on the GF diet. The menus change seasonally, but the restaurant is always happy to prepare a GF meal. Jo Ann recommends making reservations noting GF and mentioning the word "allergy." ■ *www.sackscafe.com*

Simon and Seafort's Saloon & Grill

${{{LD}
Anchorage ■ *(907) 274-3502*
420 L St ■ *Seafood & Steakhouse* ■ Manager Angie reports that GF diners come in "every day." She adds that with one day's notice, she can prepare quinoa for a GF meal. She recommends calling ahead, but walk-in GF diners can also be accommodated. Alert a server upon arrival. ■ *www.simonandseaforts.com*

Snow City Café ★ ${BL}

Anchorage ■ *(907) 272-2489*
1034 W 4th Ave ■ *American* ■ General Manager Cynthia reports that several menu items, including five varieties of eggs benedict, tofu or chicken stir fry, and omelets, can be modified to be GF. The eggs benedict will come with brown rice or corn tortillas instead of the english muffin. Fruit smoothies and milkshakes are available, as are GF cookies and brownies. ■ *www.snowcitycafe.com*

Southside Bistro ${{{LD}

Anchorage ■ *(907) 348-0088*
1320 Huffman Park Dr ■ *American* ■ Manager Chance reports that GF diners are becoming "more and more common." He advises making reservations noting GF. Ask to speak with Chef Travis upon arrival. ■ *www.southsidebistro.com*

Spenard Roadhouse ✪★ ${BLD}

Anchorage ■ *(907) 770-7623*
1049 W Northern Lights Blvd ■ *American Regional* ■ GF menu includes blackened ahi tuna, jambalaya with salmon, tiger prawns and chorizo, autumn risotto, and more. Manager Sage reports that even other items listed on the regular menu can be prepared GF. GF beer is available. ■ *www.spenardroadhouse.com*

Starfire ${{LD}

Skagway ■ *(907) 983-3663*
4th Ave And Spring ■ *Fusion* ■ Owner Jeffrey reports that the restaurant serves many GF diners. He notes that all servers are

educated on the GF diet and can indicate GF items. Servers will flag all GF orders to help prevent cross-contamination. She also notes that there is an internal list of GF items, which includes lemongrass coconut soup, tom yum soup, curries, waterfall beef salad, spicy rockfish with vegetables, the big fat burrito, and more. Confirm timeliness of this information before dining in.

Terra Bella, Inc.   ★ ¢**BL**
Anchorage ▪ (907) 562-2259
601 E Dimond Blvd ▪ Café ▪ GF bread, cookies, cake, muffins, and brownies are available. Any sandwich can be prepared on GF bread, and soups are usually GF. President Linda reports that the bistro quiche from the regular menu is GF. Confirm timeliness of this information before dining in. ▪ www.terrabellacoffee.com

Thai Kitchen   ★ $**LD**
Anchorage ▪ (907) 561-0082
3405 E Tudor Rd ▪ Thai ▪ GF diners are welcome to bring their own pasta. Nearly all dishes in the restaurant are naturally GF, with the exception of fried spring rolls. Confirm timeliness of this information before dining in. GF soy sauce is available. Alert a server upon arrival. ▪ www.thaikitchenalaska.com

ARIZONA

PHOENIX

Basis New American $**LD**
Phoenix ▪ (602) 843-3689
410 E Thunderbird Rd ▪ American ▪ Staffer Jessica reports that both servers and chefs are GF aware, as the restaurant has regular GF customers. Alert the server upon arrival. ▪ www.atlastacatering.com

Bombay Spice Grill & Wine   ✪ $**LD**
Phoenix ▪ (602) 795-0020

10810 N Tatum Blvd ▪ Indian ▪ Extensive GF menu includes mango chicken salad, kebab skewers, tikka skewers, biryani, chicken keema, curries, and more. ▪ www.bombayspice.com

Capital Grille, The   📖
Phoenix ▪ (602) 952-8900
2502 E Camelback Rd

First Watch - The Daytime Café   📖
Phoenix ▪ (602) 340-9089
1 N 1st St
Phoenix ▪ (602) 265-2092
61 W Thomas Rd
Phoenix ▪ (602) 943-3232
9645 N Black Canyon Hwy

Giuseppe's on 28th   ★ $**LD**
Phoenix ▪ (602) 381-1237
2824 E Indian School Rd ▪ Italian ▪ Owner Richard reports that although very few menu items can be prepared GF, they can usually accommodate GF diners. He recommends reservations noting GF and mentioning the word "allergy" to the server. GF pasta may be available if requested in advance. ▪ www.giuseppeson28th.com

Gluten-Free Creations Bakery   100% ¢**S**
Phoenix ▪ (602) 522-0659
2940 E Thomas Rd ▪ Bakery ▪ Dedicated GF gourmet bakery offering a wide variety of products, all of which are made from scratch. GF bread, hamburger buns, pasta, and pizza crust are available. Breakfast and sandwiches can be prepared for take out. GF baked goods include cookies, pies, cakes, donuts, brownies, and more. Many items are offered in bulk, including bagels, donuts, and GF baking flours. They will soon be opening a second location, a cafette, which will serve sandwiches, bagels, tarts, pies, and cakes. ▪ www.glutenfreecreations.com

Havana Café   ✪ $$**LD**
Phoenix ▪ (602) 952-1991
4225 E Camelback Rd ▪ Cuban ▪ GF menu features entrées like ropa vieja, pollo Cubano, and paella de Havana. GF tapas, soups,

and salads are also available. For dessert, they offer coconut flan, rice pudding, and a Spanish custard with caramel sauce. ▪ *www.havanacafe-az.com*

Kincaid's Fish, Chop & Steak House
$$$LD

Phoenix ▪ (602) 340-0000
2 S 3rd St ▪ Seafood & Steakhouse ▪ The restaurant reports that they are "absolutely" able to accommodate GF diners. GF options include chicken, steaks, and fish with steamed vegetables. The restaurant advises making reservations noting GF. ▪ *www.kincaids.com*

Kona Grill
Phoenix ▪ (480) 289-5707
5310 E High St

La Fontanella
★ $$D
Phoenix ▪ (602) 955-1213
4231 E Indian School Rd ▪ Italian ▪ GF pasta is available. ▪ *www.lafontanellarestaurantphx.com*

Lone Star Steakhouse & Saloon
Phoenix ▪ (602) 371-8181
10004 N 26th Dr
Phoenix ▪ (602) 265-7827
1743 E Camelback Rd

Old Spaghetti Factory, The
Phoenix ▪ (602) 257-0380
1418 N Central Ave

Outback Steakhouse
Phoenix ▪ (602) 494-3902
4715 E Cactus Rd
Phoenix ▪ (480) 538-0122
7000 E Mayo Blvd Bldg 24
Phoenix ▪ (602) 943-2226
9801 N Black Canyon Hwy

P.F. Chang's China Bistro
Phoenix ▪ (623) 707-4495
2420 W Happy Valley Rd

Pei Wei Asian Diner
Phoenix ▪ (602) 707-2800
267 E Bell Rd Ste 1
Phoenix ▪ (602) 956-2300
4340 E Indian School Rd Ste 23 Bldg A

Phoenix ▪ (602) 308-0410
701 W Mcdowell Rd Ste 101
Phoenix ▪ (602) 707-0049
742 E Glendale Ave Ste 110

Picazzo's Organic Italian Kitchen
✪★ $$LD

Phoenix ▪ (602) 923-6001
4669 E Cactus Rd ▪ Pizza ▪ GF pizza and some GF baked goods like brownies and flatbreads are available at all locations. GF pasta and a full GF menu are available at all locations except Casa Grande and Goodyear, which were about to begin offering the GF menu when this guide was printed. GF menu at other locations includes caprese salad, organic roasted garlic and brie, pear gorgonzola salad, chicken and chorizo pasta, chipotle penne, pizzas, and more. Restaurant recommends specifying GF when ordering, as items may have GF and non-GF variations. ▪ *www.picazzos.com*

Pugzie's Restaurant
★ ¢L
Phoenix ▪ (602) 277-6017
4700 N 16th St ▪ Sandwich Shop ▪ GF bread is available. Manager Gina reports that they use only GF mayo and mustard, so all of the sandwiches can be made GF. Other GF items like soups are also available. GF cookies are available for dessert. ▪ *www.pugzies.com*

Roy's
✪★ $$$D
Phoenix ▪ (480) 419-7697
5350 E Marriott Dr ▪ Hawaiian Fusion ▪ GF menu includes blackened island ahi tuna and szechuan peppercorn crusted salmon, among other things. GF pasta is available with advanced notice. Administrator Heather reports that they see "more and more" GF diners, so they are able to accommodate GF requests well, but she still recommends making reservations noting GF so that the chefs can prepare. ▪ *www.roysrestaurant.com*

Ruffino Italian Cuisine
★ $$$LD
Phoenix ▪ (480) 893-8544
4902 E Warner Rd ▪ Italian ▪ Owner Steve

reports that all servers are "generally familiar" with the GF diet, and they serve GF diners frequently. They can modify many dishes, such as the chicken piccata, to be GF. Confirm timeliness of this information before dining in. Steve adds that with advanced notice of 48 hours, they can provide GF pasta. Alert a server upon arrival. ▪ *www.ruffinoaz.com*

Shane's Rib Shack   📖
Phoenix ▪ (623) 581-3704
2501 W Happy Valley Rd

Spinato's Pizzeria   ✪★ $**LD**
Phoenix ▪ (602) 277-0088
1219 E Glendale Ave
Phoenix ▪ (602) 867-1010
1614 E Bell Rd ▪ Pizza ▪ GF menu includes pizza with a variety of toppings, salads, and more. GF pizza is available. ▪ *www.spinatospizza.com*

True Food Kitchen   ✪★ $**BLD**
Phoenix ▪ (602) 774-3488
2502 E Camelback Rd ▪ Fusion ▪ GF items marked on the menu include local vegetable crudites with tzatziki dipping sauce, curry with rice noodles, and turkey bolognese, among other things. GF brown rice pasta is available. ▪ *www.foxrc.com*

Uno Chicago Grill   📖
Phoenix ▪ (602) 253-3355
455 N 3rd St

White Chocolate Grill, The   ✪ $$**LD**
Phoenix ▪ (480) 563-3377
7000 E Mayo Blvd ▪ Modern American ▪ GF menu includes grilled artichokes and tomato gin soup, among other things, as appetizers. As entrées, it lists a bunless cheeseburger, BBQ baby back ribs, center cut filet, and more. For dessert, it offers molten chocolate soufflé cake. ▪ *www.thewhitechocolategrill.wordpress.com*

Yard House   📖
Phoenix ▪ (480) 563-9273
21001 N Tatum Blvd

Z Pizza   ★ $**LD**
Phoenix ▪ (602) 254-4145
111 W Monroe St
Phoenix ▪ (602) 765-0511
13637 N Tatum Blvd
Phoenix ▪ (602) 997-4992
2815 W Peoria Ave
Phoenix ▪ (602) 234-3289
53 W Thomas Rd ▪ Pizza ▪ GF pizza is available. ▪ *www.zpizza.com*

Zinburger   ¢**LD**
Phoenix ▪ (602) 424-9500
2502 E Camelback Rd ▪ American ▪ Manager Doug of the Tucson location and Manager Mike of the Phoenix location report that they are very accustomed to serving GF diners. Alert a server upon arrival. All staff members are trained on the GF diet, and Doug reports that they accommodate GF diners "on a daily basis." There is a dedicated GF fryer, and all fries except for the zucchini fries are GF. Confirm timeliness of this information before dining in. ▪ *www.foxrc.com*

Z'Tejas Southwestern Grill   ✪★ $**LD**
Phoenix ▪ (480) 948-9010
10625 N Tatum Blvd ▪ Southwest ▪ One-page GF menu includes wild mushroom enchiladas and grilled salmon, along with smoked chicken and black bean salad. Frozen margaritas and GF beer are also available. ▪ *www.ztejas.com*

ARIZONA

SCOTTSDALE

Blanco Tacos & Tequila $**LD**
Scottsdale ▪ (480) 305-6692
6166 N Scottsdale Rd ▪ Mexican ▪ Manager Lindsey at the Scottsdale location and Manager Max at the Tucson location both report that they accommodate GF diners "very often." They note that with the excep-

tions of flour tortillas and enchilada sauce, most dishes are GF. Alert a server, who will indicate GF menu items. ▪ *www.foxrc.com*

Bloom　　　　　　　　　$$**LD**
Scottsdale ▪ *(480) 922-5666*
8877 N Scottsdale Rd ▪ *Modern American*
▪ Marketing Coordinator Julia reports that many menu items are naturally GF. She advises making reservations noting GF and calling ahead to speak with a manager or chef. She also notes that all chefs are trained on the GF diet. ▪ *www.foxrc.com*

Buca di Beppo　　　　　　　📖
Scottsdale ▪ *(480) 949-6622*
3828 N Scottsdale Rd

Capital Grille, The　　　　　📖
Scottsdale ▪ *(480) 348-1700*
16489 N Scottsdale Rd

Carrabba's Italian Grill　　　📖
Scottsdale ▪ *(480) 948-8881*
17007 N Scottsdale Rd

Culinary Dropout　　　　　$$**LD**
Scottsdale ▪ *(480) 970-1700*
7135 E Camelback Rd ▪ *Modern American*
▪ Executive Chef Clint reports that there is "plenty of stuff" on the menu that he can prepare GF. Examples include salmon, pork ribs, coq au vin, and bistro steak. Confirm timeliness of this information before dining in. Alert a server upon arrival. Clint notes that they serve GF diners "a couple times a week," and that the servers are trained to ask him if they have questions about GF items on the menu. ▪ *www.foxrc.com*

Don & Charlie's　　　✪ $$$**D**
Scottsdale ▪ *(480) 990-0900*
7501 E Camelback Rd ▪ *American* ▪ GF menu includes salads, BBQ ribs, chicken, and steaks. Manager Austin reports that the restaurant takes GF cooking "very seriously," and a manager supervises the entire GF preparation process, from the kitchen to table delivery. ▪ *www.donandcharlies.com*

du Jour Restaurant　　★ $$**L**
Scottsdale ▪ *(480) 603-1066*

10585 N 114th St ▪ *Modern American* ▪ GF bread and chocolate decadence cake are available with advanced notice. Manager Matthew reports that the GF diet "has been talked about to death" in class, so all servers and chefs are very familiar with it. He specifies that reservations noting GF are required, as is alerting the server upon arrival. Operated by the Arizona Culinary Institute, the restaurant offers a fine dining experience prepared by the student test kitchen. ▪ *www.arizonaculinary.com*

Earls　　　　　　　　✪ $**LD**
Scottsdale ▪ *(480) 607-1941*
15784 N Pima Rd ▪ *Global* ▪ GF menu includes edamame, chicken tacos, and a variety of salads. Most of the signature entrées are naturally GF. Manager Kim reports that all floor staff are trained to serve GF diners. She further notes that this is the only chain location with a GF menu, as one of the chefs has a GF family member. ▪ *www.earls.ca*

First Watch - The Daytime Café　📖
Scottsdale ▪ *(480) 248-9602*
16455 N Scottsdale Rd Ste 107

Fogo De Chao　　　　★ $$$$**LD**
Scottsdale ▪ *(480) 609-8866*
6300 N Scottsdale Rd ▪ *Brazilian* ▪ GF cheese bread made with yucca flour is available. ▪ *www.fogodechao.com*

Greene House, The　　　　$$$**LD**
Scottsdale ▪ *(480) 889-9494*
15024 N Scottsdale Rd ▪ *Modern American* ▪ Server Calen reports that one of the managers is GF, so they are "very" GF aware, and they accommodate "several" GF diners daily. Short ribs, scallops, and most of the salads are naturally GF. Calen recommends alerting the server upon arrival, and the server will forward requests on to the chef. ▪ *www.foxrc.com*

Havana Patio Café　　　　✪ $$**LD**
Scottsdale ▪ *(480) 991-1496*
6245 E Bell Rd ▪ *Cuban* ▪ GF menu features entrée items such as ropa vieja, pollo

Cubano, and paella de Havana. GF tapas, soups, and salads are also available. For dessert, they offer coconut flan, rice pudding, and a Spanish custard with caramel sauce. ▪ *www.havanacafe-az.com*

Kona Grill 📖
Scottsdale ▪ *(480) 429-1100*
7014 E Camelback Rd

Ling & Louie's Asian Bar & Grill ☺ *$LD*
Scottsdale ▪ *(480) 767-5464*
9397 E Shea Blvd ▪ *Asian* ▪ Extensive GF menu includes chicken and seafood, as well as not-so-sizzling platters. Examples include sweet and sour chicken, salmon, and edamame. For dessert, there is a chocolate volcano cake. ▪ *www.lingandlouies.com*

Los Sombreros Mexican Restaurant *$$D*
Scottsdale ▪ *(480) 994-1799*
2534 N Scottsdale Rd ▪ *Mexican* ▪ Owner Azucena reports that nearly the entire menu is GF, and servers are trained to indicate non-GF items. Alert a server upon arrival. Azucena adds that they serve GF diners "every day." ▪ *www.lossombreros.com*

Maggiano's Little Italy ★ *$$$LD*
Scottsdale ▪ *(480) 333-4100*
16405 N Scottsdale Rd ▪ *Italian* ▪ GF pasta is available. Call individual locations to inquire about additional GF options. ▪ *www.maggianos.com*

Marco's Italian Bistro ★ *$$BLD*
Scottsdale ▪ *(480) 767-3933*
10855 N Frank Lloyd Wright Blvd ▪ *Italian* ▪ GF rice pasta is available. Owner Marco reports that other dishes can also be made GF upon request. ▪ *www.marcosbistro.com*

Melting Pot, The 📖
Scottsdale ▪ *(480) 607-1799*
8260 N Hayden Rd

Modern Steak *$$$$LD*
Scottsdale ▪ *(480) 423-7000*
7014 E Camelback Rd ▪ *Steakhouse* ▪ Restaurant notes that GF diners are "reguarly" accommodated. They also note that several menu items are naturally GF. Upon

request, the chef is happy to come discuss GF options and modifications at the table. Reservations noting GF are highly recommended. ▪ *www.foxrc.com*

Olive & Ivy *$$$LD*
Scottsdale ▪ *(480) 751-2200*
7135 E Camelback Rd ▪ *Modern Mediterranean* ▪ Server Maddie reports that they have accommodated GF diners before. She notes that the hummus with vegetables, salads, several fish entrées, burgers without buns, and chicken dishes can be modified to be GF. Confirm timeliness of this information before dining in. Alert the server upon arrival. Reservations noting GF are recommended. ▪ *www.foxrc.com*

Outback Steakhouse 📖
Scottsdale ▪ *(480) 424-6810*
4180 N Drinkwater Blvd

P.F. Chang's China Bistro 📖
Scottsdale ▪ *(480) 367-2999*
7132 E Greenway Pkwy
Scottsdale ▪ *(480) 949-2610*
7135 E Camelback Rd Ste 101

Pei Wei Asian Diner 📖
Scottsdale ▪ *(480) 365-6002*
20851 N Scottsdale Rd Ste 105
Scottsdale ▪ *(480) 488-8630*
32607 N Scottsdale Rd Ste 107
Scottsdale ▪ *(480) 365-6000*
8787 N Scottsdale Rd Ste 214

Picazzo's Organic Italian Kitchen
✪★ *$$LD*
Scottsdale ▪ *(480) 990-2212*
7325 E Frank Lloyd Wright Blvd ▪ *Pizza* ▪ GF menu includes buffalo wings, avocado pasta, chicken fajita pizza, and pear gorgonzola salad. And if GF diners are not satisfied with the options on the GF menu, much of the regular menu can be modified to be GF. GF pizza and pasta are available. ▪ *www.picazzos.com*

Spinato's Pizzeria ✪★ *$LD*
Scottsdale ▪ *(480) 391-2347*
11108 N Frank Lloyd Wright Blvd ▪ *Pizza*

▪ GF menu includes pizza with a variety of toppings, salads, and more. GF pizza is available. ▪ *www.spinatospizza.com*

Sprinkles Cupcakes   ★ ¢S
Scottsdale ▪ *(480) 970-4321*
4501 N Scottsdale Rd ▪ *Bakery* ▪ GF red velvet cupcakes are available every day. They are not visible on display, as they are kept behind the counter to avoid cross-contamination. ▪ *www.sprinkles.com*

Yard House   📖
Scottsdale ▪ *(480) 675-9273*
7014 E Camelback Rd

Z Pizza   ★ $$LD
Scottsdale ▪ *(480) 515-9792*
20511 N Hayden Rd ▪ *Pizza* ▪ GF pizza is available. Manager Amy reports that the restaurant gets "a lot of requests" for GF pizza, so they are used to accommodating the GF diet. ▪ *www.zpizza.com*

Z'Tejas Southwestern Grill   ✪★ $LD
Scottsdale ▪ *(480) 946-4171*
7014 E Camelback Rd ▪ *Southwest* ▪ One-page GF menu includes wild mushroom enchiladas and grilled salmon, along with smoked chicken and black bean salad. Frozen margaritas and GF beer are also available. ▪ *www.ztejas.com*

ARIZONA

TUCSON

Blanco Tacos & Tequila $LD
Tucson ▪ *(520) 232-1007*
2905 E Skyline Dr ▪ *Mexican* ▪ Manager Lindsey at the Scottsdale location and Manager Max at the Tucson location both report that they accommodate GF diners "very often." They note that with the exceptions of flour tortillas and enchilada sauce, most dishes are GF. Alert a server, who will indicate GF menu items. ▪ *www.foxrc.com*

Bluefin Seafood Bistro $$$LD
Tucson ▪ *(520) 531-8500*
7053 N Oracle Rd ▪ *Seafood* ▪ Staffer Harrison reports that all servers are trained to accommodate GF diners, as they do so "more than you can imagine." He notes that GF diners have many menu choices, which can be explained by any server. ▪ *www.bluefintucson.com*

Bluepoint Kitchen   ★ $LD
Tucson ▪ *(520) 577-6000*
2905 E Skyline Dr ▪ *Seafood* ▪ Chef John reports that the kitchen staff is "very familiar" with GF and that servers are GF aware. He adds that all staff has access to an ingredients sheet, which indicates GF items. GF rice crackers are available for the hummus appetizer. ▪ *www.bluepointamerica.com*

Eclectic Pizza   ✪★ $$LD
Tucson ▪ *(520) 886-0484*
7065 E Tanque Verde Rd ▪ *Pizza* ▪ GF pizza and beer are available. GF menu also includes other items like spinach and artichoke dip, hummus tostada, and a variety of salads. For dessert, GF cakes and brownies are available. ▪ *www.eclecticpizza.com*

El Charro Café   ✪ $LD
Tucson ▪ *(520) 622-1922*
311 N Court Ave
Tucson ▪ *(520) 745-1922*
6310 E Broadway Blvd
Tucson ▪ *(520) 514-1922*
6910 East Sunrise
Tucson ▪ *(520) 229-1922*
7725 N Oracle Rd ▪ *Mexican* ▪ Extensive GF menu includes ceviche tostadas, corn quesadillas, tamales, soups, a shrimp platter, salmon, chicken adobo, and more. ▪ *www.elcharrocafe.com*

Elle $$LD
Tucson ▪ *(520) 327-0500*
3048 E Broadway Blvd ▪ *Modern American* ▪ Owner and Chef Jeff reports that they get "a number of" GF requests, and he notes that there are many naturally GF menu items. He advises alerting the server

upon arrival and seeking manager assistance when choosing an item from the menu. ▪ www.ellerestaurant.com

Firebirds Wood Fired Grill   ✪ $$$**LD**
Tucson ▪ **(520) 577-0747**
2985 E Skyline Dr ▪ *American* ▪ GF menu includes a variety of salads and a selection of entrées. Examples are the sirloin, filet mignon, ribs, and the lobster tail. Restaurant reports that servers are trained to alert the chef when a customer orders from the GF menu. ▪ *www.firebirdsrockymountaingrill.com*

Guadalajara Grill $**BLD**
Tucson ▪ **(520) 323-1022**
1220 E Prince Rd ▪ *Mexican* ▪ Hostess Maria reports that they accommodate GF diners "about once a week." She notes that most of the sauces and salsas are GF. Corn tortillas are available. Alert a server, who will ask the manager or kitchen staff if there are any questions. ▪ *www.ggrill.com*

Jonathan's Cork $$$**D**
Tucson ▪ **(520) 296-1631**
6320 E Tanque Verde Rd ▪ *American Regional* ▪ Owner Jonathan reports that they accommodate GF diners every day. He notes that reservations noting GF are "helpful," but alerting the server is sufficient. He hopes to provide a GF menu in the near future. ▪ *www.jonathanscork.com*

Kingfisher Grill $$$**LD**
Tucson ▪ **(520) 323-7739**
2564 E Grant Rd ▪ *Seafood* ▪ Chef Jim reports that the restaurant serves "quite a few people" who are GF. He notes that the kitchen frequently makes GF Hawaiian fish, scallops, salmon, and salads. He also notes that the kitchen can create GF items that are not on the menu. He recommends alerting the server, who will discuss GF options with the chef. ▪ *www.kingfishertucson.com*

Lovin' Spoonfuls   ✪★ ¢**BLD**
Tucson ▪ **(520) 325-7766**
2990 N. Campbell Ave ▪ *Vegetarian* ▪ GF

menu includes breakfast, lunch, dinner, and dessert items, and all sauces are made with GF thickeners. Confirm timeliness of this information before dining in. GF options include pancakes, waffles, sandwiches, and more. Also available are GF chocolate fudge cake and strawberry cake with lemon icing. ▪ *www.lovinspoonfuls.com*

Luna Bella Italian Cuisine & Catering   ★ $$$**LD**
Tucson ▪ **(520) 325-3895**
2990 N Swan Rd ▪ *Italian* ▪ GF pasta is sometimes available. Manager Elyse reports that the restaurant serves GF diners "at least two to three times per day." Alert a server upon arrival. The chefs will make GF sauces and sides from scratch to accommodate GF customers. ▪ *www.lunabellarestaurant.com*

Montana Avenue $$$**LD**
Tucson ▪ **(520) 298-2020**
6390 E Grant Rd ▪ *American* ▪ Restaurant reports that many GF diners come to eat, and the chef can modify any dish to be GF. They also note that all staff is trained on GF dining. Reservations noting GF are recommended but not required. ▪ *www.foxrc.com*

Outback Steakhouse   📖
Tucson ▪ **(520) 531-1231**
2240 W Ina Rd
Tucson ▪ **(520) 323-8892**
4871 E Grant Rd

P.F. Chang's China Bistro   📖
Tucson ▪ **(520) 615-8788**
1805 E River Rd Ste 100

Pei Wei Asian Diner   📖
Tucson ▪ **(520) 514-7004**
5285 E Broadway Blvd Ste 151
Tucson ▪ **(520) 297-3238**
633 W Ina Rd
Tucson ▪ **(520) 884-7413**
845 E University Blvd Ste 135

Roma Caffe   ★ $$**D**
Tucson ▪ **(520) 744-2929**

4140 W Ina Rd ▪ *Italian* ▪ GF pasta is available. It takes a bit longer to prepare than most other meals, so plan ahead. Manager Heidi reports that in addition, many menu items can be modified or grilled to be GF. ▪ *www.romacaffe.com*

Sir Veza's Taco Garage ✪ ¢LD
Tucson ▪ (520) 323-8226
4699 E Speedway Blvd ▪ *Tex-Mex* ▪
"Gluten Sensitive" menu includes guacamole, salads, wings, burgers without buns, chicken lettuce wraps, tacos, seafood, and more. ▪ *www.sirvezas.com*

Tasteful Takeout ✪ $LD
Tucson ▪ (520) 326-9363
4122 E Speedway Blvd ▪ *American* ▪ GF items marked on the menu include pork osso buco, grilled hanger steak, and saag paneer, among many other things. For dessert, they offer a flourless chocolate cake and homemade ice creams. ▪ *www.eatatfeast.com*

Wildflower $$$LD
Tucson ▪ (520) 219-4230
7037 N Oracle Rd ▪ *Modern American* ▪
Hostess Lauren reports that they accommodate GF diners "a lot." She notes that "everyone is aware" of the GF diet, so alert a server upon arrival. Servers are trained to know what modifications must be made to make meals GF. ▪ *www.foxrc.com*

Zinburger ¢LD
Tucson ▪ (520) 299-7799
1865 E River Rd ▪ *American* ▪ Manager Doug of the Tucson location and Manager Mike of the Phoenix location report that they are very accustomed to serving GF diners. Alert a server upon arrival. All staff members are trained on the GF diet, and Doug reports that they accommodate GF diners "on a daily basis." There is a dedicated GF fryer, and all fries except for the zucchini fries are GF. Confirm timeliness of this information before dining in. ▪ *www.foxrc.com*

ARIZONA
ALL OTHER CITIES

Alberto Italian Restaurant ★ $D
Cave Creek ▪ (480) 488-5800
7171 E Cave Creek Rd ▪ *Italian* ▪ GF pasta is available.

Beaver Street Brewery ✪ $$LD
Flagstaff ▪ (928) 779-0079
11 Beaver St ▪ *Fusion* ▪ GF menu includes steamed mussels in curry sauce and tortilla chips, caesar salad with no croutons, pesto cream cheese, hummus, and sandwiches or burgers without buns. Alert a server upon arrival. ▪ *www.beaverstreetbrewery.com*

Brandy's Bakery & Restaurant $$BLD
Flagstaff ▪ (928) 779-2187
1500 E Cedar Ave ▪ *American* ▪ Restaurant reports that after 5pm, anything on the dinner menu can be made GF. They also note that several lunch and breakfast items can be modified to be GF. The Celiac club in town frequently dines in, and since the chef is gluten-intolerant, he is very GF aware. ▪ *www.brandysrestaurant.com*

Buca di Beppo 📖
Chandler ▪ (480) 785-7272
7111 W Ray Rd
Mesa ▪ (480) 507-9463
1730 S Val Vista Dr
Peoria ▪ (623) 412-9463
16091 N Arrowhead Fountains Ctr Dr

Carrabba's Italian Grill 📖
Avondale ▪ (623) 936-0597
9920 W Mcdowell Rd
Chandler ▪ (480) 785-8586
1060 N 54th St
Gilbert ▪ (480) 726-7455
2709 S Market St
Glendale ▪ (602) 863-6444
5646 W Bell Rd
Mesa ▪ (480) 654-9099
1740 S Clearview Ave
Oro Valley ▪ (520) 742-7442

7635 N Oracle Rd
Surprise ▪ *(623) 214-3299*
14043 W Bell Rd

Cookies From Home   ★ ¢S
Tempe ▪ *(480) 894-1944*
1605 W University Dr ▪ *Bakery* ▪ Non-
dedicated bakery offering five flavors of GF
cookies. The GF cookie flavors are chocolate chewy chip, triple treat, fudgie, peanut
butter, and macademia. The bakery reports
that they started making GF cookies when
an employee was diagnosed with Celiac
Disease. ▪ *www.cookiesfromhome.com*

Cottage Place Restaurant, The $$$$D
Flagstaff ▪ *(928) 774-8431*
126 W Cottage Ave ▪ *Modern American*
▪ Owner and Chef Frank notes that the
restaurant accommodates GF diners "quite
often." Most menu items can be modified
to be GF. Alert the server, so Frank can
come to the table to discuss GF options and
modifications. Reservations noting GF are
recommended. ▪ *www.cottageplace.com*

Cowboy Club $$LD
Sedona ▪ *(928) 282-4200*
241 N Highway 89A ▪ *Steakhouse* ▪ Manager Kim reports that the restaurant sees "a
fair amount" of GF diners. She notes that
the kitchen is aware of GF meal preparation. Chicken, sirloin steaks, burgers
without buns, mashed potatoes, salmon,
and shrimp can be GF. Alert a server upon
arrival. ▪ *www.cowboyclub.com*

Diablo Burger   ★ ¢LD
Flagstaff ▪ *(928) 774-3274*
120 N Leroux St ▪ *American* ▪ Manager Eli
reports that any burger can be served on
a GF english muffin and with GF french
fries. Alert the server upon arrival. ▪ *www.
diabloburger.com*

Dragoon Market and Café   ★ ¢S
Dragoon ▪ *(520) 248-9218*
Dragoon Marketplace ▪ *Bakery* ▪ GF
bread is available by the loaf. Baker Debbie
reports that she is "developing" some other
products, including a chocolate chip cook-

ies and lemon bars. They set up a kiosk in
Dragoon Marketplace on Saturdays and
Sundays, but call for the most current
information about where they are located. ▪
www.dragoonmarketplace.mysite.com

Firebirds Wood Fired Grill   ✪ $$$LD
Chandler ▪ *(480) 814-8003*
3435 W Chandler Blvd
Peoria ▪ *(623) 773-0500*
16067 N Arrowhead Fountain Ctr Dr ▪
American ▪ GF menu includes a variety of
salads and a selection of entrées. Examples
are the sirloin, filet mignon, ribs, and the
lobster tail. Both locations report that
servers are trained to alert the chef when
a customer orders from the GF menu. ▪
www.firebirdsrockymountaingrill.com

Heartline Café $$$D
Sedona ▪ *(928) 282-0785*
1610 W State Route 89A ▪ *American* ▪ Bartender John reports that there are several
options for GF diners, including the saffron
slow cooked pork osso buco and the olive
oil poached halibut. Alert a server upon
arrival. John notes that the servers have
"cheat sheets" from which they can read
which items are GF. ▪ *www.heartlinecafe.
com*

Kona Grill   📖
Chandler ▪ *(480) 792-1711*
3111 W Chandler Blvd
Gilbert ▪ *(480) 289-4500*
2224 E Williams Field Rd

La Stalla Cucina Rustica $$$LD
Chandler ▪ *(480) 855-9990*
68 W Buffalo St ▪ *Italian* ▪ Server Frederica reports that although they no longer
have GF pasta, they do offer several GF
entrées, like grilled salmon and grilled
chicken in cream sauce. She recommends
alerting the server upon arrival, and asking
for a manager "if necessary." ▪ *www.lastal-
lacr.com*

Landmark Restaurant, The   ✪ $$LD
Mesa ▪ *(480) 962-4652*
809 W Main St ▪ *American* ▪ GF menu

includes prime rib and Atlantic salmon, as well as chocolate mousse for dessert. Executive Chef Derek reports that all dishes, including sauces, can be modified to be GF. He also recommends alerting the server upon arrival. ▪ *www.landmarkrestaurant. com*

Ling & Louie's Asian Bar & Grill ✪ $LD
Chandler ▪ *(520) 796-7281*
5040 Wild Horse Pass Blvd. ▪ *Asian* ▪ Extensive GF menu includes chicken and seafood, as well as not-so-sizzling platters. Examples include sweet and sour chicken, salmon, and edamame. For dessert, there is a chocolate volcano cake. ▪ *www.lingand-louies.com*

Lone Star Steakhouse & Saloon 📖
Glendale ▪ *(602) 843-7410*
5664 W Bell Rd

Macy's European Coffeehouse ★ ¢S
Flagstaff ▪ *(928) 774-2243*
114 S Beaver St ▪ *Coffee & Café* ▪ GF baked goods are sometimes available. Potential GF items include cheesecake bars and flourless chocolate tortes. ▪ *www. macyscoffee.net*

McGrath's Fish House ✪ $LD
Goodyear ▪ *(623) 547-4688*
1800 N Litchfield Rd
Mesa ▪ *(480) 503-2500*
1610 S Stapley Dr ▪ *Seafood* ▪ GF menu features a large selection of seafood entrees and appetizers, as well as salads and steaks. ▪ *www.mcgrathsfishhouse.com*

Melting Pot, The 📖
Glendale ▪ *(623) 444-4946*
19420 N 59th Ave Ste B113

Mountain Oasis $LD
Flagstaff ▪ *(928) 214-9270*
11 E Aspen Ave ▪ *Global* ▪ Veteran Server Mary Jane reports that GF requests are "really common." Alert a server upon arrival. She notes that the staff has a "cheat sheet" that they can look at if they are unsure which items are GF. Spring rolls, hummus,

and the coconut curry salmon are examples of GF items. Confirm timeliness of this information before dining in. ▪ *www. themenuplease.com/mountainoasis*

Oaxaca Restaurant ✪ $BLD
Sedona ▪ *(928) 282-4179*
321 N Highway 89A ▪ *Mexican* ▪ GF items marked on the menu include the red rock salad, nachos, tacos, and the homemade chicken stew, among other things. For dessert, they offer flan. ▪ *www.oaxacarestaurant.com*

Octagon Café ★ $BLD
Fountain Hills ▪ *(480) 816-8806*
12645 N Saguaro Blvd ▪ *Café* ▪ GF bread is available for sandwiches. The restaurant reports that they can sell entire loaves of GF breads to diners who call in advance.

Outback Steakhouse 📖
Chandler ▪ *(480) 496-8333*
1080 N 54th St
Chandler ▪ *(480) 899-7913*
2520 W Chandler Blvd
Flagstaff ▪ *(928) 774-7630*
2600 E Lucky Ln
Gilbert ▪ *(480) 782-7504*
2687 S Market St
Glendale ▪ *(602) 547-3236*
5605 W Bell Rd
Mesa ▪ *(480) 654-0804*
1650 S Clearview Ave
Mesa ▪ *(480) 615-7667*
1860 E Mckellips Rd
Prescott ▪ *(928) 541-0100*
1951 E. Highway 69
Sierra Vista ▪ *(520) 458-1313*
99 S Highway 92
Surprise ▪ *(623) 544-4687*
14225 W Grand Ave
Tempe ▪ *(480) 491-6064*
1734 E Southern Ave
Yuma ▪ *(928) 376-7711*
328 E 16th St

P.F. Chang's China Bistro 📖
Chandler ▪ *(480) 899-0472*
3255 W Chandler Blvd

Goodyear ▪ (623) 536-3222
14681 W Mcdowell Rd
Mesa ▪ (480) 218-4900
6610 E Superstition Springs Blvd
Peoria ▪ (623) 412-3335
16170 N 83rd Ave
Tempe ▪ (480) 731-4600
740 S Mill Ave Ste 140

Pei Wei Asian Diner   📖

Avondale ▪ (623) 535-9830
1619 N Dysart Rd Ste 101
Chandler ▪ (480) 812-2230
1085 W Queen Creek Rd Ste 1
Chandler ▪ (480) 940-3800
7131 W Ray Rd Ste 3 Bldg 1
Fountain Hills ▪ (480) 837-0926
14835 E Shea Blvd Ste 100
Gilbert ▪ (480) 926-9749
1084 S Gilbert Rd # 601
Glendale ▪ (623) 825-9949
20022 N 67th Ave Ste 100
Mesa ▪ (480) 539-4454
3426 E Baseline Rd Ste 121
Surprise ▪ (623) 546-6868
14155 W Bell Rd Ste 113
Tempe ▪ (480) 333-0014
1825 E Guadalupe Rd Ste F-112

Picazzo's Organic Italian Kitchen
                              ✪★ $$LD

Casa Grande ▪ (520) 836-9188
105 W Florence Blvd
Flagstaff ▪ (928) 226-1000
1300 S Milton Rd
Goodyear ▪ (623) 935-1400
14970 W Indian School Rd
Lake Havasu City ▪ (928) 764-4005
5601 Highway 95 N
Oro Valley ▪ (520) 544-7970
7850 N Oracle Rd
Sedona ▪ (928) 282-4140
1855 W Highway 89A
Surprise ▪ (623) 583-9100
11340 W Bell Rd
Tempe ▪ (480) 831-5823
440 W Warner Rd ▪ Pizza ▪ GF pizza and some GF baked goods like brownies and flatbreads are available at all locations. GF pasta and a full GF menu are available at all locations except Casa Grande and Goodyear, which were about to begin offering the GF menu when this guide was printed. GF menu at other locations includes caprese salad, organic roasted garlic and brie, pear gorgonzola salad, chicken and chorizo pasta, chipotle penne, pizzas, and more. Restaurant recommends specifying GF when ordering, as items may have GF and non-GF variations. ▪ *www.picazzos.com*

Pie Zanos Kitchen   ★ ¢BLD

Glendale ▪ (623) 334-5101
7350 W Bell Rd ▪ Pizza ▪ GF pizza is available in the 9-inch size. GF bagels, a variety of breads, donuts, and several different flavors of cookies are also available. ▪ *www.piezanoskitchen.com*

Roy's   ✪ $$$D

Chandler ▪ (480) 705-7697
7151 W Ray Rd ▪ Hawaiian Fusion ▪ Chef Red reports that the GF menu is very limited, so he always offers to "adapt" items from the regular menu to make them GF. Alert a server upon arrival. Red adds that he is "extremely confident" in his servers, and if they have any questions, they will speak to him directly. The restaurant accommodates several GF diners every day. ▪ *www.roysrestaurant.com*

Shane's Rib Shack   📖

Glendale ▪ (623) 877-7427
9404 W Westgate Blvd

Spinato's Pizzeria   ✪★ $LD

Tempe ▪ (480) 967-0020
227 S Smith Rd ▪ Pizza ▪ GF menu includes pizza with a variety of toppings, salads, and more. GF pizza is available. ▪ *www.spinatospizza.com*

Thee Pitt's Again $LD

Glendale ▪ (602) 996-7488
5558 W Bell Rd ▪ Barbeque ▪ Server Henry reports that they accommodate GF diners "every once in awhile" and that the BBQ sauce is GF. He notes that the fryer is not dedicated GF, so diners should

avoid fried items. He adds that servers have access to an internal list of GF menu items, which is kept in the kitchen. ▪ *www. theepittsagain.com*

Tonto Bar & Grill ✪★ $$$**LD**
Cave Creek ▪ *(480) 488-0698*
5736 E Rancho Manana Blvd ▪ *Modern American* ▪ GF menu includes herbed quail breast, beef tenderloin medallions, and grilled brie polenta. House-made GF bread is available. ▪ *www.tontobarandgrill. com*

Troia's ★ $$$**D**
Sedona ▪ *(928) 282-0123*
1885 W Highway 89A ▪ *Italian* ▪ GF pizza and rice pasta are available. Manager Douglas reports that they also stock GF flour to use for breaded items such as chicken parmesean. Douglas adds that the staff is "very conscious" of customers with "allergies." ▪ *www.troias.com*

Uncle Bear's Grill & Bar ★ $**LD**
Mesa ▪ *(480) 986-2228*
9053 E Baseline Rd
Queen Creek ▪ *(480) 882-3177*
21151 E Rittenhouse Rd
Queen Creek ▪ *(480) 457-8788*
7205 S Power Rd ▪ *American* ▪ GF pizza in the 12-inch size and GF buns for hamburgers are available at all locations. ▪ *www. unclebearsbarandgrill.com*

Water's Edge $$$**D**
Fountain Hills ▪ *(480) 816-3515*
13014 N Saguaro Blvd ▪ *Modern American* ▪ Owner Cindy reports that the restaurant has "several regular GF customers." She notes that almost anything from the menu can be modified to be GF. Alert a server and ask for Chef Josh, who will discuss GF options in detail. ▪ *www.watersedgerestaurant.net*

Yard House 📖
Glendale ▪ *(623) 872-3900*
9401 W Westgate Blvd

Z Pizza ★ ¢**LD**
Chandler ▪ *(480) 855-9792*
2855 W Ray Rd
Chandler ▪ *(480) 722-9792*
7131 W Ray Rd ▪ *Pizza* ▪ GF crusts, sauces, and meats are available for 10-inch pizzas. ▪ *www.zpizza.com*

Z'Tejas Southwestern Grill ✪★ $**LD**
Chandler ▪ *(480) 893-7550*
7221 W Ray Rd
Tempe ▪ *(480) 377-1170*
20 W 6th St ▪ *Southwest* ▪ One-page GF menu includes wild mushroom enchiladas and grilled salmon, along with smoked chicken and black bean salad. Frozen margaritas and GF beer are also available. ▪ *www.ztejas.com*

ARKANSAS

LITTLE ROCK

American Pie Pizza ★ ¢**LD**
North Little Rock ▪ *(501) 753-0081*
4830 N Hills Blvd
North Little Rock ▪ *(501) 758-8800*
9709 Maumelle Blvd ▪ *Pizza* ▪ Both locations carry GF pizza. ▪ *www.american-piepizza.net*

Bonefish Grill 📖
Little Rock ▪ *(501) 228-0356*
11525 Cantrell Rd Ste 901

Brave New Restaurant $$$**LD**
Little Rock ▪ *(501) 663-2677*
2300 Cottondale Ln ▪ *Modern American* ▪ Manager Akku reports that GF diners are welcome and notes that accommodating GF is "not a problem." He adds that they frequently get GF customers and advises communicating clearly with the server regarding GF requests. He adds that the seasoning salt is not GF. ▪ *www.bravenewrestaurant.com*

Cantina Laredo   📖
Little Rock ▪ *(501) 280-0407*
207 N University Ave

Capi's Restaurant $$LD
Little Rock ▪ *(501) 225-9600*
11525 Cantrell Rd ▪ *Fusion* ▪ Manager
Brent reports that the restaurant is "used
to" GF requests. He notes that the kitchen
will do "anything they can" to modify items
to be GF. He recommends alerting the
server, who will notify the kitchen. ▪ *www.*
capisrestaurant.com

Carino's Italian   📖
Little Rock ▪ *(501) 225-3434*
11600 Pleasant Ridge Rd
North Little Rock ▪ *(501) 758-8226*
4221 Warden Rd

Cozymel's   ✪ $$LD
Little Rock ▪ *(501) 954-7100*
10 Shackleford Dr ▪ *Mexican* ▪ GF menu
includes baked tortilla chips, ahi tuna spinach salad with cilantro-lime vinaigrette,
enchiladas with corn tortillas, chipotle
honey glazed salmon, and more. ▪ *www.*
cozymels.com

Izzy's Restaurant   ✪ ¢LD
Little Rock ▪ *(501) 868-4311*
5601 Ranch Dr ▪ *Café* ▪ GF menu includes
appetizers like beef or veggie tamales,
cheese dip with chips, and guacamole with
chips. It also features a wide variety of
soups and salads. ▪ *www.izzyslittlerock.com*

Lilly's Dim Sum, Then Some   ✪★ $LD
Little Rock ▪ *(501) 716-2700*
11121 N Rodney Parham Rd ▪ *Asian* ▪ The
pan-Asian GF menu features Vietnamese
spring rolls and Korean bibim bop with
grilled steak. For dessert, there is coconut
crème brûlée. Co-owner Kathy reports that
all staff members are trained on the GF diet
and on cross-contamination avoidance. GF
soy sauce is available. ▪ *www.lillysdimsum.*
com

Lone Star Steakhouse & Saloon   📖
Little Rock ▪ *(501) 227-8898*
10901 N Rodney Parham Rd

Outback Steakhouse   📖
Little Rock ▪ *(501) 221-7655*
105 Markham Park Dr
North Little Rock ▪ *(501) 771-7799*
4401 Warden Rd

P.F. Chang's China Bistro   📖
Little Rock ▪ *(501) 225-4424*
317 S Shackleford Rd

Pei Wei Asian Diner   📖
Little Rock ▪ *(501) 280-9423*
205 N University Ave

Trio's $$$LD
Little Rock ▪ *(501) 221-3330*
8201 Cantrell Rd ▪ *Fusion* ▪ Restaurant
reports that GF diners can "definitely" be
accommodated. Naturally GF menu items
include chicken enchiladas, some salmon
dishes, and halibut, as well as the flour-
less chocolate mousse cake and crème
brulee for dessert. Confirm timeliness of
this information before dining in. Restau-
rant reports that other menu items can be
modified to be GF. ▪ *www.triosrestaurant.*
com

US Pizza Co.   ★ $L
Little Rock ▪ *(501) 374-5561*
402 Louisiana St ▪ *Pizza* ▪ GF pizza is
available. The restaurant reports that the
kitchen keeps GF pizza separate from
other foods, and that GF pizza is cut with
separate utensils on a clean cutting board. ▪
www.uspizzaco.net

Ya Ya's Euro Bistro $$$LD
Little Rock ▪ *(501) 821-1144*
17711 Chenal Pkwy ▪ *Bistro* ▪ Manager Matt
reports that the restaurant serves GF diners with "increasing" frequency. He notes
that the restaurant has a strict protocol for
flagging orders with "allergies." Ask server
to confer with a chef or manager about the
best GF options, as not all servers are fully
educated in the GF diet. ▪ *www.yiayias.com*

ARKANSAS

ALL OTHER CITIES

Bonefish Grill 📖
Rogers ▪ *(479) 273-0916*
3201 Market St Ste 100

Bordinos ✪★ $$$LD
Fayetteville ▪ *(479) 527-6795*
310 W Dickson St ▪ *Modern American*
▪ GF menu items include salmon, duck
breast, beef tenderloin, and various salads.
GF pasta is available. ▪ *www.bordinos.com*

Brewery, The ★ ¢BLD
Conway ▪ *(501) 327-6278*
2159 Prince St ▪ *Coffee Shop* ▪ GF wraps
and muffins are available. Any sandwich
on the menu can be made with a GF wrap
instead of bread. GF muffins flavors change
daily.

Brewski's Draft Emporium ★ ¢S
Fayetteville ▪ *(479) 973-6969*
408 W Dickson St ▪ *Pub Food* ▪ GF beer is
available.

Carino's Italian 📖
Rogers ▪ *(479) 633-0544*
535 N 46th St

Carrabba's Italian Grill 📖
Rogers ▪ *(479) 273-2962*
3300 Pinnacle Hills Pkwy

Devito's Restaurant $$D
Harrison ▪ *(870) 741-8832*
350 Devitos Loop ▪ *Italian* ▪ Manager
Chris reports that the restaurant serves GF
diners "quite often." Alert a server upon
arrival. Servers are trained to ask the chef
if they have questions about which items
contain gluten. Chris notes that many of
the chicken and seafood dishes can be
easily modified to be GF. Confirm timeliness of this information before dining in. ▪
www.devitosrestaurant.com

Green Room, The ★ ¢S
Fayetteville ▪ *(479) 251-7665*

326 N West Ave ▪ *Pub* ▪ GF beer is available. This is a billiard hall that does not
serve food.

Greenhouse Grille ★ $LD
Fayetteville ▪ *(479) 444-8909*
481 South School Ave. ▪ *Fusion* ▪ Owner
Jeremy reports that all soups and salads are
GF. He adds that other menu items, such
as the free range chicken breast and grilled
vegetable kabobs, are either naturally GF or
can be prepared GF. Confirm timeliness of
this information before dining in. GF beer
is available. ▪ *www.greenhousegrille.com*

Hog Haus Brewing Co. ✪ $$$LD
Fayetteville ▪ *(479) 521-2739*
430 W Dickson St ▪ *Fusion* ▪ GF menu
includes appetizers, salads, bunless burgers,
and entrées. Examples are jalapeno pepper
shrimp, sirloin salad, grilled tuna, and
gouda baked salmon. For dessert, there is a
root beer float. ▪ *www.hoghaus.com*

Outback Steakhouse 📖
Conway ▪ *(501) 548-6220*
2310 Sanders Rd
Fort Smith ▪ *(479) 452-0900*
6800 Rogers Ave
Hot Springs ▪ *(501) 520-5800*
180 Pakis St
Jonesboro ▪ *(870) 910-5600*
906 Southwest Dr Ste C
Rogers ▪ *(479) 936-7660*
4509 W Poplar St
Springdale ▪ *(479) 872-2800*
4808 S Thompson St

Ozark Natural Foods ★ ¢S
Fayetteville ▪ *(479) 521-7558*
1554 N College Ave ▪ *Deli* ▪ Supervisor
Rachel reports that GF brownies, cookies,
pizza dough, and birthday cakes are available. She recommends calling ahead to discuss GF options and place a special order.
Deli is located in the Ozark Natural Foods
Market. ▪ *www.ozarknaturalfoods.com*

P.F. Chang's China Bistro 📖
Rogers ▪ *(479) 621-0491*
2203 Promenade Blvd Ste 13100

Texas Land & Cattle Steak House 📖
Rogers ▪ *(479) 621-0070*
2103 Promenade Blvd

Tiny Tim's Pizza ★ $LD
Fayetteville ▪ *(479) 521-5551*
21 W Mountain St ▪ *Pizza* ▪ GF beer is available. There is no GF pizza.

CALIFORNIA

LOS ANGELES

American Girl Place ★ $$$LD
Los Angeles ▪ *(877) 247-5223*
189 The Grove Dr ▪ *American* ▪ GF pizza and pasta are usually available. Restaurant recommends making reservations at least a few days in advance, especially during summer. They suggest noting GF in reservations so that they have time to prepare for GF diners. Restaurant is family friendly, though it is geared towards young girls.

BabyCakes LA ★ ¢S
Los Angeles ▪ *(213) 623-5555*
130 E 6th St ▪ *Bakery* ▪ A wide variety of GF baked goods is available. GF products include cupcakes, donuts, cookies, brownies, wonderbuns, and different types of bread. Flavors of bread change daily, but possibilities include jalapeno cornbread and chocolate banana bread. ▪ *www.babycakesnyc.com*

Bombay Bite ✪ $LD
Los Angeles ▪ *(310) 824-1046*
1051 Gayley Ave ▪ *Indian* ▪ GF menu is includes chicken vindaloo, saag, tikka masala, lamb vindaloo, and lamb korma. Reservations noting GF are recommended. Upon arrival, alert the server, who will go through GF menu options in detail. ▪ *www.bombaybite.com*

Deano's Gourmet Pizza ★ $$LD
Los Angeles ▪ *(323) 935-6373*
6333 W 3rd St ▪ *Pizza* ▪ GF pizza and pasta are available. GF pizzas can be prepared with any toppings. Restaurant reports a "99.9% GF rule," which means that while they are very careful with GF preparations, there is always a risk of cross-contamination. ▪ *www.deanospizzala.com*

Hugo's Tacos ¢BLD
Los Angeles ▪ *(323) 664-9400*
3300 Glendale Blvd ▪ *Mexican* ▪ Restaurants report that much of their food is naturally GF. They use corn tortillas and do not dredge meats in flour. Manager David at the Glendale Blvd location recommends speaking to a manager about which items are GF. Both locations are taco stands with no indoor seating. For a sit-down meal, see Hugo's, the mother restaurant. ▪ *www.hugostacos.com*

Maggiano's Little Italy ★ $$$LD
Los Angeles ▪ *(323) 965-9665*
189 The Grove Dr Ste Z80 ▪ *Italian* ▪ GF pasta is available. Call individual locations to inquire about additional GF options. ▪ *www.maggianos.com*

Mani's Bakery Café ✪★ $S
Los Angeles ▪ *(323) 938-8800*
519 S Fairfax Ave ▪ *Bakery & Café* ▪ Non-dedicated bakery & café offering several GF baked goods, including cookies, cupcakes, and muffins. For any other GF specialty items, such as lemon vanilla cake or caramelized apple cake, advanced notice of 24 hours is required. GF items marked on the café menu include edamame and a variety of salads. ▪ *www.manisbakery.com*

Napa Valley Grille $$$LD
Los Angeles ▪ *(310) 824-3322*
1100 Glendon Ave ▪ *Italian* ▪ Server Jamie reports that they serve GF diners "all the time," so they are "very used to it." Alert a server upon arrival. Servers are all trained in the GF diet, and they have "good communication" with the chefs. Because the

menu changes every day, servers will be sure to double check with chefs about which items are GF. ▪ *www.napavalleygrille.com*

P.F. Chang's China Bistro   📖
Los Angeles ▪ *(310) 854-6467*
121 N La Cienega Blvd # 117

Pizza Fusion   ★ $$$**LD**
Los Angeles ▪ *(323) 375-3390*
7950 W Sunset Blvd ▪ *Pizza* ▪ GF pizza is available. ▪ *www.pizzafusion.com*

Real Food Daily   ✪★ $**LD**
Los Angeles ▪ *(310) 289-9910*
414 N La Cienega Blvd ▪ *Organic* ▪ GF desserts are available. The restaurant reports that GF diners are accommodated "all the time." They also note that the restaurant staff is very familiar with GF dining. Alert a server upon arrival. When a GF request is rung in by a server, a special note is sent to the kitchen. ▪ *www.realfood.com*

Roy's $$$**D**
Los Angeles ▪ *(213) 488-4994*
800 S Figueroa St ▪ *Hawaiian Fusion* ▪ Sales Manager Aya reports that they have ample experience serving GF diners. She highly recommends reservations noting GF, and notes that it is necessary to alert the server upon arrival. Most servers, she says, will be able to indicate GF items "on the spot," but others will "run and check with the chef." She also notes that the chef is preparing a GF menu for release this year. ▪ *www.roysrestaurant.com*

San Gennarro Café   ★ $$**LD**
Los Angeles ▪ *(310) 476-9696*
140 S Barrington Pl ▪ *Italian* ▪ GF pasta is available. Manager Johnny notes that GF diners are accommodated "all the time," and that the restaurant is regularly featured on GF websites. Reservations noting GF are recommended but not required. ▪ *www.sangennarocafe.com*

Vegan Joint, The   ★ ¢**BLD**
Los Angeles ▪ *(310) 559-1357*

10438 National Blvd ▪ *Vegan* ▪ Owner Rattana reports that they can accommodate GF diners, and she adds that nearly the entire thai section of the menu can be prepared GF. GF soy sauce is available. ▪ *www.theveganjoint.com*

Veggie Grill, The   ✪★ ¢**LD**
Los Angeles ▪ *(323) 822-7575*
8000 W Sunset Blvd ▪ *American* ▪ Co-CEO Kevin reports that the GF menu includes kale, a variety of soups and salads, plus chocolate pudding for dessert. GF pasta is available. Specific GF menu items may vary by location. ▪ *www.veggiegrill.com*

Yard House   📖
Los Angeles ▪ *(213) 745-9273*
800 W Olympic Blvd

Z Pizza   ★ $**LD**
Los Angeles ▪ *(323) 466-6969*
123 N Larchmont Blvd ▪ *Pizza* ▪ GF pizza is available in the 10-inch size. ▪ *www.zpizza.com*

CALIFORNIA
SAN DIEGO

Andre's Restaurant $**LD**
San Diego ▪ *(619) 275-4114*
1235 Morena Blvd ▪ *Cuban* ▪ Co-owner Victor reports that many of the menu items are naturally GF, and others can be prepared GF. He recommends speaking with Jose, Dan, or himself before ordering, so that they can ensure a GF meal. ▪ *www.andresrestaurantsd.com*

Buca di Beppo   📖
San Diego ▪ *(858) 536-2822*
10749 Westview Pkwy
San Diego ▪ *(619) 233-7272*
705 6th Ave

Corvette Diner ✪ ¢LD
San Diego ▪ *(619) 542-1476*
2965 Historic Decatur Road ▪ *American*
▪ Manager Michelle recommends alerting the server upon arrival so that someone can indicate GF menu items. GF options include all burgers and sandwiches without buns, french fries, and the signature dish Dante's Inferno, among other items. Confirm timeliness of this information before dining in. ▪ *www.cohnrestaurants.com*

Cupcakes Squared ★ ¢S
San Diego ▪ *(619) 226-3485*
3772 Voltaire St ▪ *Bakery* ▪ GF cupcakes are available from Thursday to Sunday in flavors such as chocolate almond, lemon, pistacchio, and strawberry. Requests for specific flavors can be accommodated if placed a few days in advance. ▪ *www.cupcakessquared.com*

Extreme Pizza ★ $$LD
San Diego ▪ *(619) 223-4050*
3555 Rosecrans St
San Diego ▪ *(858) 270-2020*
4705 Clairemont Dr ▪ *Pizza* ▪ GF pizza is available. ▪ *www.extremepizza.com*

Fish Market, The $$LD
San Diego ▪ *(619) 232-3474*
750 N Harbor Dr ▪ *Seafood* ▪ Shrimp, oysters, and fish can be made GF by eliminating the sauce. Confirm timeliness of this information before dining in. Managers at all locations note that although they are happy to accommodate GF diners, the kitchens are not GF environments, so cross-contamination may occur. Speaking with a manager upon arrival is recommended. ▪ *www.thefishmarket.com*

Melting Pot, The 📖
San Diego ▪ *(858) 638-1700*
8980 University Center Ln
San Diego ▪ *(619) 234-5554*
901 5th Ave

Old Spaghetti Factory, The 📖
San Diego ▪ *(619) 233-4323*
275 5th Ave

Outback Steakhouse 📖
San Diego ▪ *(619) 294-8998*
1640 Camino Del Rio N Ste 125
San Diego ▪ *(858) 274-6283*
4196 Clairemont Mesa Blvd

P.F. Chang's China Bistro 📖
San Diego ▪ *(858) 458-9007*
4540 La Jolla Village Dr
San Diego ▪ *(619) 260-8484*
7077 Friars Rd

Pei Wei Asian Diner 📖
San Diego ▪ *(619) 321-6670*
1025 Camino De La Reina Ste P-5
San Diego ▪ *(858) 207-2730*
10562 Craftsman Way Ste 190

Pizza Fusion ★ $$$LD
San Diego ▪ *(619) 278-0057*
3827 5th Ave ▪ *Pizza* ▪ GF pizza is available. ▪ *www.pizzafusion.com*

Prado at Balboa Park, The $$$LD
San Diego ▪ *(619) 557-9441*
1549 El Prado ▪ *Global* ▪ The restaurant reports that GF modifications can be made to protein dishes on the regular menu. They also note that several salads can be made GF. Reservations noting GF are recommended. Located inside the House of Hospitality. ▪ *www.cohnrestaurants.com*

Ritual Tavern ✪★ $D
San Diego ▪ *(619) 283-1720*
4095 30th St ▪ *American* ▪ GF items marked on the menu include skirt steak, vegetable sauté, sherpherd's pie, and charcuterie. GF beer is available. ▪ *www.ritualtavern.com*

Roy's ✪★ $$$D
San Diego ▪ *(619) 239-7697*
333 W Harbor Dr
San Diego ▪ *(858) 455-1616*
8670 Genesee Ave ▪ *Hawaiian Fusion* ▪ GF menu varies by location. Brian of the Genesee Avenue location and Candace of the Harbor Drive location report that they frequently serve GF diners. At Genesee Avenue, reservations noting GF are recom-

mended so that the chef receives a ticket from the host stand. At Harbor Drive, just alert the server upon arrival, and the server will tell the chef. GF soy sauce is available at both locations. ▪ *www.roysrestaurant.com*

Sammy's Woodfired Pizza   ✪ $LD
San Diego ▪ *(858) 695-0900*
10785 Scripps Poway Pkwy
San Diego ▪ *(858) 259-6600*
12925 El Camino Real
San Diego ▪ *(619) 298-8222*
1620 Camino De La Reina
San Diego ▪ *(619) 222-3111*
2401 Truxtun Rd Ste 102
San Diego ▪ *(619) 230-8888*
770 4th Ave
San Diego ▪ *(858) 404-9898*
8650 Genesee Ave ▪ *Pizza* ▪ GF menu includes a variety of artisan thin crust and woodfired pizzas, oak roasted chicken breast, a grilled chicken wrap, grilled shrimp salad, beet, walnut with goat cheese salad, and more. ▪ *www.sammyspizza.com*

Station Tavern   ¢LD
San Diego ▪ *(619) 255-0657*
2204 Fern St ▪ *American* ▪ Although they don't have GF buns, they do serve a large number of GF diners, according to Office Manager Lori. She recommends that GF diners order burgers with a side of tater tots or over a salad. ▪ *www.stationtavern.com*

Uno Chicago Grill   📖
San Diego ▪ *(619) 298-1866*
7007 Friars Rd

Urban Solace   ✪ $$LD
San Diego ▪ *(619) 295-6464*
3823 30th St ▪ *Modern American* ▪ GF menu includes pan-seared salmon, the half chicken, steak, a broiled portabella sandwich without bread, and more. ▪ *www.urbansolace.net*

Yard House   📖
San Diego ▪ *(619) 233-9273*
1023 4th Ave

Z Pizza   ★ $LD
San Diego ▪ *(858) 689-9449*
10006 Scripps Ranch Blvd
San Diego ▪ *(858) 675-9300*
11975 Carmel Mountain Rd
San Diego ▪ *(619) 272-0022*
5175 Linda Vista Rd ▪ *Pizza* ▪ GF pizza is available. The Scripps Ranch and Linda Vista locations have a "buy one, get the second for $5" special on Mondays. Confirm timeliness of this information before dining in. ▪ *www.zpizza.com*

CALIFORNIA

SAN FRANCISCO

Alive! Vegetarian Cuisine   ★ $$D
San Francisco ▪ *(415) 923-1052*
1972 Lombard St ▪ *Raw* ▪ Manager Leland reports that the restaurant serves "a lot" of GF diners. There is one menu item served with wheat bread, but most others are naturally GF. GF flatbread made from carrots and sunflower seeds can be substituted for wheat bread. Confirm timeliness of this information before dining in. All servers are GF aware. ▪ *www.aliveveggie.com*

Ana Mandara $$$LD
San Francisco ▪ *(415) 771-6800*
891 Beach St ▪ *Vietnamese* ▪ Manager Khai reports that GF diners are welcome and many menu items are already GF. Alert a server upon arrival. ▪ *www.anamandara.com*

Asia de Cuba   ★ $$$$LD
San Francisco ▪ *(415) 929-2300*
495 Geary St ▪ *Asian & Latin Fusion* ▪ Executive Chef Tom recommends calling ahead to allow the restaurant time to prepare your GF meal. He reports that GF bread and pancakes are available with prior "arrangements." ▪ *www.chinagrillmgt.com*

Betelnut Pejiu Wu   ✪ $**LD**
San Francisco ▪ *(415) 929-8855*
2030 Union St. ▪ *Asian* ▪ GF menu items
include 5-spice garlic edamame, green
papaya shrimp salad, and a Sri Lankan clay
pot with curried fish. ▪ *www.betelnutrestaurant.com*

Bubba Gump Shrimp Co.   📖
San Francisco ▪ *(415) 781-4867*
Pier 39

Buca di Beppo   📖
San Francisco ▪ *(415) 543-7673*
855 Howard St

Café Gratitude   ✪★ $**BLD**
San Francisco ▪ *(415) 683-1346*
1336 9th Ave
San Francisco ▪ *(415) 824-4652*
2400 Harrison St ▪ *Vegetarian* ▪ GF beer,
bread, pasta, cookies, pies, cakes, and more
are available. GF menu items include a
sprouted pumpkin seed and walnut burger
on a sweet onion sunflower bun and buckwheat granola served with almond milk or
coconut yogurt. ▪ *www.cafegratitude.com*

Dosa $$$**LD**
San Francisco ▪ *(415) 441-3672*
1700 Fillmore St
San Francisco ▪ *(415) 642-3672*
995 Valencia St ▪ *Indian* ▪ At both loca-
tions, there is a supplemental "allergy
sheet" showing which items contain wheat,
though it does not list items that contain
gluten. Examples of GF dishes are the
mung masala dosa and the caramelized
onion uttapam. Confirm timeliness of this
information before dining in. ▪ *www.dosasf.
com*

Eagle Pizzeria   ★ $**LD**
San Francisco ▪ *(415) 566-3113*
1712 Taraval St ▪ *Pizza* ▪ GF pizza and beer
are available.

Extreme Pizza   ★ $$**LD**
San Francisco ▪ *(415) 701-9000*
1062 Folsom St
San Francisco ▪ *(415) 929-9900*
1730 Fillmore St
San Francisco ▪ *(415) 929-8234*
1980 Union St
San Francisco ▪ *(415) 661-9300*
3911 Alemany Blvd ▪ *Pizza* ▪ GF pizza is
available. ▪ *www.extremepizza.com*

Gaylord India Restaurant $$$**LD**
San Francisco ▪ *(415) 397-7775*
1 Embarcadero Ctr ▪ *Indian* ▪ Host Emma
notes that they have several GF customers
who dine in regularly. She recommends
alerting her or the server upon arrival.
Servers will ask the chef if they are unsure
of what ingredients are in a specific dish,
but Emma notes that many dishes are natu-
rally GF. ▪ *www.gaylords1.com*

Gracias Madre $**LD**
San Francisco ▪ *(415) 683-1346*
2211 Mission St ▪ *Mexican* ▪ Restaurant
reports that GF diners can be accommo-
dated. GF options include guacamole, en-
chiladas, and tacos. Confirm timeliness of
this information before dining in. ▪ *www.
gracias-madre.comweb*

Greens Restaurant $$$**LD**
San Francisco ▪ *(415) 771-6222*
Fort Mason ▪ *Vegetarian* ▪ Hostess Jessica
reports that all of the servers are "very
knowledgeable" about the GF diet. Alert
the server, who will notify the kitchen.
Jessica also recommends reservations noting GF, as they will allow the restaurant to
prepare more thoroughly. ▪ *www.greensres-
taurant.com*

Ike's Place   ★ ¢**LD**
San Francisco ▪ *(415) 553-6888*
3506 16th St ▪ *Sandwich Shop* ▪ GF bread
is available for sandwiches. ▪ *www.ilikeikes-
place.com*

Kara's Cupcakes   ★ ¢**S**
San Francisco ▪ *(415) 563-2253*
3249 Scott St
San Francisco ▪ *(415) 351-2253*
900 N Point ▪ *Bakery* ▪ GF chocolate
velvet and sweet vanilla cupcakes are
available every day at both locations. The

Scott St location bakes all GF goods, some of which get delivered to North Point. They can make other cupcake flavors GF with advanced notice of one day. ▪ *www. karascupcakes.com*

Kuleto's   ★ $$$**BLD**
San Francisco ▪ *(415) 397-7720*
221 Powell St ▪ *Italian* ▪ GF pasta is available. Manager Hunter notes that GF diners come in "from time to time." He also notes that many of the salad entrées are naturally GF. Alert the server, who will indicate GF options. Reservations noting GF are recommended. ▪ *www.kuletos.com*

Mariposa   100% ¢**S**
San Francisco ▪ *(510) 595-0955*
1 Ferry Building ▪ *Bakery* ▪ Dedicated GF bakery offering tea loaves, bagels, biscotti, brownies, and a large selection of breads. Challah bread is available on Fridays only, and multi-grain bread is available sporadically. Call 24 hours ahead for special requests. ▪ *www.mariposabaking.com*

Maya Restaurant $$**LD**
San Francisco ▪ *(415) 543-2928*
303 2nd St ▪ *Modern Mexican* ▪ Manager Carlos reports that there are a variety of GF menu items. He recommends making reservations noting GF and mentioning the word "allergy" to a manager or chef upon arrival. He notes that all staff members are trained on the GF diet, though they serve GF diners only "sometimes." ▪ *www.mayasf. com*

One Market Restaurant $$$$**LD**
San Francisco ▪ *(415) 777-5577*
1 Market St ▪ *Fusion* ▪ Restaurant reports that GF diners can be accommodated. They note that several seafood and meat dishes are simply wood-grilled, making them easy to modify to be GF. Salads, oysters, and other dishes can also be modified to be GF. Reservations noting GF are recommended. ▪ *www.onemarket.com*

Plant Café Organic, The   ✪ $$**LD**
San Francisco ▪ *(415) 693-9730*

101 California St
San Francisco ▪ *(415) 931-2777*
3352 Steiner St
San Francisco ▪ *(415) 984-1973*
The Embarcadero ▪ *Organic* ▪ GF menu includes soup, shiitake spring rolls, seared scallops with cilantro aioli, griddled calamari, ginger miso quinoa, thai green curry, daily fish specials, and more. While the Pier 3 and Steiner St locations are sit-down restaurants open for lunch and dinner, the California St location closes at 3pm and serves only breakfast and lunch. The GF menu at the California St location is slightly more limited. ▪ *www.theplantcafe. com*

San Francisco Soup Company   ✪ ¢**L**
San Francisco ▪ *(415) 986-3634*
1 California St
San Francisco ▪ *(415) 593-7687*
142 2Nd St
San Francisco ▪ *(415) 834-0472*
221 Montgomery
San Francisco ▪ *(415) 788-7687*
275 Battery St
San Francisco ▪ *(415) 512-7687*
301 Howard St
San Francisco ▪ *(415) 989-7687*
315 California St
San Francisco ▪ *(415) 566-7687*
3251 20Th Ave
San Francisco ▪ *(415) 904-7660*
50 Fremont St
San Francisco ▪ *(415) 397-7687*
50 Post St
San Francisco ▪ *(415) 781-7687*
580 California St
San Francisco ▪ *(415) 512-0472*
845 Market St
San Francisco ▪ *(650) 821-7687*
Airport Terminal 3
San Francisco ▪ *(415) 495-4765*
Bayside Cuisines Food Ct ▪ *Soup* ▪ Soups rotate daily. Check the website for a given day's GF offerings. Most locations also have GF options marked on the board. Some locations, including those in airports, do not have GF options marked on the board, but

they will have a chart of GF options upon request. ▪ *www.sfsoupco.com*

Underdog- the Organic Sausage Joint
★ ¢**LD**

San Francisco ▪ *(415) 665-8881*
1634 Irving St ▪ *Organic* ▪ GF sausages wrapped in lettuce or corn tortillas are available. Restaurant reports that they have GF potato salad, salad dressings, pies, muffins, and pastries.

Zadin
✪★ $$**D**

San Francisco ▪ *(415) 626-2260*
4039 18th St ▪ *Modern Vietnamese* ▪ GF items marked on the menu include Vietnamese rolls, spicy tofu and eggplant, green curry scallops, and more. GF soy sauce is available, as are GF beer and, for dessert, GF brownies. ▪ *www.zadinsf.com*

CALIFORNIA
ALL OTHER CITIES

118 Degrees
★ $**BLD**

Costa Mesa ▪ *(714) 754-0718*
2981 Bristol St ▪ *Raw* ▪ GF beer, raw bread, pasta, pizza, cookies, cake, brownies, and more are available. Executive Chef Jenny reports that the staff is very educated on GF and that almost all dishes are naturally GF. Alert a server upon arrival. ▪ *www. shop118degrees.com*

À Côté
$$**D**

Oakland ▪ *(510) 655-6469*
5478 College Ave ▪ *Modern American* ▪ Manager Daphne reports that they can arrange GF meals by "working off the regular menu" and "adjusting." She notes that the "best way" to get a GF meal is to talk to the server, who will communicate with the chef about which items can be modified to be GF. ▪ *www.acoterestaurant.com*

Aladino's Pizza
★ ¢**LD**

Antioch ▪ *(925) 757-6363*
1324 Sunset Dr ▪ *Pizza* ▪ 12-inch GF pizzas are available with any toppings. Restaurant reports that it will have GF pasta soon.

Amici's East Coast Pizzeria
★ $$$**LD**

Dublin ▪ *(925) 875-1600*
4640 Tassajara Rd
Mountain View ▪ *(650) 961-6666*
790 Castro St
San Jose ▪ *(408) 289-9000*
225 W Santa Clara St
Vacaville ▪ *(707) 451-7777*
1679 E Monte Vista Ave ▪ *Pizza* ▪ GF pizza and beer are available. ▪ *www.amicis.com*

Amigos Grill & Cantina
✪★ $$**LD**

Sonoma ▪ *(707) 939-0743*
19315 Sonoma Highway ▪ *Mexican* ▪ GF menu includes appetizers, salads, soups, an extensive selection of entrées, and desserts like flan and kahlua mousse. GF beer is available. ▪ *www.amigosgrillcantina.com*

Argyle Steakhouse
✪ $$$$**BLD**

Carlsbad ▪ *(760) 603-6800*
7100 Four Seasons Point ▪ *American* ▪ GF menu lists a range of options, from fish and shellfish to meats like wagyu beef. It also details which salads, "enhancers," and sides are GF. Located inside the Four Seasons Resort. ▪ *www.fourseasons.com/aviara/dining_50.html*

Aubrey Rose Tea Room
★ $$$$

La Mesa ▪ *(619) 461-4832*
8362 La Mesa Blvd ▪ *English Tea* ▪ GF finger foods are available for four and five-course teas. Server Pat notes that GF breads and flour are used to make desserts. She advises making a reservation noting GF a few days in advance. ▪ *www.theaubreyrose-tearoom.com*

Azna Gluten Free
100% ¢**S**

Cameron Park ▪ *(530) 677-5810*
2647 Cameron Park Dr ▪ *Bakery* ▪ Dedicated GF bakery and café offering a wide selection of meals and baked goods. Entrées include lasagna and calzones, as

well as mac and cheese. Examples of baked goods are brownies, scones, and cinnamon rolls. ▪ *www.aznaglutenfree.com*

Bella Dolce Bakery ★ ¢S
Santa Barbara ▪ *(805) 962-2253*
113 W De La Guerra St ▪ *Bakery* ▪ Non-dedicated bakery offering cakes, wedding cakes, cookies, and cupcakes by special order. Owner Eileen notes that GF requests are very popular, and she says that advanced notice of three days is required for special orders. ▪ *www.belladolce.com*

Bella Italia $LD
San Gabriel ▪ *(626) 287-5674*
7232 N. Rosemead Blvd ▪ *Italian* ▪ Owner Michael reports that GF diners should ask for him upon arrival. He notes that he is almost always at the restaurant, and he might even be the server. He adds that he serves GF diners "quite often" and is happy to "figure something out" to accommodate GF requests.

Bistro Jeanty $$$LD
Yountville ▪ *(707) 944-0103*
6510 Washington St ▪ *French Bistro* ▪ Manager Bruce notes that GF diners can be accommodated, as there are always at least a couple of menu items that are GF or can be modified to be GF. Alert a server, who will indicate GF options. Reservations noting GF are recommended but not required. ▪ *www.bistrojeanty.com*

Blue Bayou $$$LD
Anaheim ▪ *(714) 781-3463*
1313 S Harbor Blvd ▪ *Cajun & Creole* ▪ Reservationist Virginia reports that they have several GF menu items, including the portobello mushroom with couscous, the five pepper roast New York steak, and the signature Blue Bayou surf and turf (after 4pm only). Located in Disneyland Park.

Bobby G's Pizzeria ★ $LD
Berkeley ▪ *(510) 665-8866*
2072 University Ave ▪ *Pizza* ▪ GF pasta, pizza, and beer are available. GF pizza is

available in the 12-inch size only. ▪ *www. bobbygspizzeria.com*

Boraan ★ $LD
Beverly Hills ▪ *(310) 288-2182*
9036 Burton Way ▪ *Thai* ▪ Owner PJ reports that they are "very conscious" of the GF diet. She explains that they have one regular customer who is "very sensitive," and who taught them how to prepare GF meals. Alert a server upon arrival. The servers are aware of the GF diet and will alert the kitchen to use a fresh wok. GF soy sauce is available. ▪ *www.boraan.com*

Border Grill $$$LD
Santa Monica ▪ *(310) 451-1655*
1445 4th St ▪ *Modern Mexican* ▪ Manager Ron reports that the chefs are able to make GF meals. Alert a server upon arrival, so that the server can notify the chef. Ron adds that there are "a variety of things" on the menu that can be prepared GF. ▪ *www. bordergrill.com*

Borrelli's Pizza ★ $$LD
Encinitas ▪ *(760) 436-1501*
285 N El Camino Real ▪ *Pizza* ▪ GF pizza and pasta are available. Alert the server, who will specify into which dishes GF pasta and pizza can be substituted. ▪ *www. borrellispizza.net*

Bottle Inn, The ★ $$$LD
Hermosa Beach ▪ *(310) 376-9595*
26 22nd St ▪ *Italian* ▪ GF pasta is available. Manager Silvio reports that many menu items are naturally GF. He also notes that there are sporadic nights when GF pasta is not available, so calling ahead is recommended. Reservations noting GF are also recommended. Alert a server upon arrival. ▪ *www.thebottleinn.com*

Brick Oven Restaurant ★ $LD
Poway ▪ *(858) 679-7424*
12222 Poway Rd ▪ *Pizza* ▪ GF pizza is available in the 12-inch size. Ask a staff member to indicate which toppings to avoid. ▪ *www.858brickoven.com*

Bubba Gump Shrimp Co.   📖
Anaheim ▪ *(714) 635-4867*
321 W Katella Ave
Long Beach ▪ *(562) 437-2434*
87 Aquarium Way
Monterey ▪ *(831) 373-1884*
720 Cannery Row
Santa Monica ▪ *(310) 393-0458*
301 Santa Monica Pier
Universal City ▪ *(818) 753-4867*
1000 Universal Studios Blvd

Buca di Beppo   📖
Brea ▪ *(714) 529-6262*
1609 E Imperial Hwy
Campbell ▪ *(408) 377-7722*
1875 S Bascom Ave
Carlsbad ▪ *(760) 479-2533*
1921 Calle Barcelona
Claremont ▪ *(909) 399-3287*
505 W Foothill Blvd
Encino ▪ *(818) 995-3288*
17500 Ventura Blvd
Garden Grove ▪ *(714) 740-2822*
11757 Harbor Blvd
Huntington Beach ▪ *(714) 891-4666*
7979 Center Ave
Irvine ▪ *(714) 665-0800*
13390 Jamboree Rd
Palo Alto ▪ *(650) 329-0665*
643 Emerson St
Pasadena ▪ *(626) 792-7272*
80 W Green St
Redondo Beach ▪ *(310) 540-3246*
1670 S Pacific Coast Hwy
Roseville ▪ *(916) 771-9463*
1212 Galleria Blvd
Sacramento ▪ *(916) 922-6673*
1249 Howe Ave
San Jose ▪ *(408) 226-1444*
925 Blossom Hill Rd
Santa Clarita ▪ *(661) 253-1900*
26940 Theater Dr
Santa Monica ▪ *(310) 587-2782*
1442 2nd St
Thousand Oaks ▪ *(805) 449-3688*
205 N Moorpark Rd
Universal City ▪ *(818) 509-9463*
1000 Universal Studios Blvd

Buckhorn Steak and Roadhouse $$$D
Winters ▪ *(530) 795-4503*
2 Main St ▪ *Steakhouse* ▪ Manager Heath reports that GF diners can just "pick what they want" from the menu, and the restaurant will most likely be able to accommodate them. He notes that nearly the entire menu is naturally GF, and that GF diners are "pretty common." ▪ *www.buckhornsteakhouse.com*

Café Carolina   ★ $LD
Encino ▪ *(818) 881-8600*
17934 Ventura Blvd ▪ *Italian* ▪ GF pasta is available. Owner Giuseppe notes that there are also several GF meat entrées, like the chicken, the fish, and the filet mignon. Confirm timeliness of this information before dining in. Alert a server upon arrival. The servers "know very well" which items are GF. ▪ *www.organiccafecarolina.com*

Cafe Delfini   ★ $$$$D
Santa Monica ▪ *(310) 459-8823*
145 W Channel Rd ▪ *Italian* ▪ GF pasta is available. ▪ *www.caffedelfini.com*

Café Gratitude   ✪★ $BLD
Berkeley ▪ *(510) 725-4418*
1730 Shattuck Ave
Cupertino ▪ *(415) 814-1364*
20955 Stevens Creek Blvd (in Whole Foods)
Healdsburg ▪ *(707) 723-4461*
206 Healdsburg Ave (in The Olive Leaf)
Oakland ▪ *(510) 250-7779*
230 Bay Place (in Whole Foods)
San Rafael ▪ *(415) 578-4928*
2200 4th St ▪ *Vegan* ▪ GF bread, pasta, pizza, and beer are available. For dessert, they have a number of GF options: coconut cream pie, tiramisu, and more. ▪ *www.cafegratitude.com*

Caffé Verbena $$LD
Oakland ▪ *(510) 465-9300*
1111 Broadway ▪ *Italian* ▪ Manager Carly reports that many menu items, like the flatiron steak and some chicken dishes, are naturally GF. Alert a server upon ar-

rival. Carly adds that servers will be able to indicate GF items on the menu. ▪ *www.caffeverbena.com*

California Café $LD
Los Gatos ▪ *(408) 354-8118*
Old Town 50 University Ave
Palo Alto ▪ *(650) 325-2233*
700 Welch Rd
Sacramento ▪ *(916) 925-2233*
1689 Arden Way ▪ *Fusion* ▪ All three locations report that the chefs are "very accommodating" when it comes to GF requests. The Palo Alto location recommends making a reservation noting GF, but the other two locations request only that GF diners alert the server upon arrival. The chef will come to the table to discuss possible GF options. ▪ *www.californiacafe.com*

Carino's Italian   📖
Antioch ▪ *(925) 522-8252*
5799 Lone Tree Way
Chino ▪ *(909) 902-1800*
3801 Grand Ave
Downey ▪ *(562) 803-0108*
12036 Lakewood Blvd
El Centro ▪ *(760) 337-9588*
3203 S Dogwood Rd
Fairfield ▪ *(707) 438-1801*
1640 Gateway Blvd
Gilroy ▪ *(408) 842-3130*
6805 Camino Arroyo
Mira Loma ▪ *(951) 360-9850*
12447 Limonite Ave
Modesto ▪ *(209) 578-9432*
3401 Dale Rd
Palmdale ▪ *(661) 947-9700*
1173 W Rancho Vista Blvd
Rancho Cucamonga ▪ *(909) 646-9985*
12240 Foothill Blvd
Sacramento ▪ *(916) 419-4049*
3860 Truxel Rd
Victorville ▪ *(760) 949-8700*
11920 Amargosa Rd
West Covina ▪ *(626) 966-9878*
147 N Barranca St
Whittier ▪ *(562) 947-3020*
15600 Whittier Blvd

Casa Orinda $$$D
Orinda ▪ *(925) 254-2981*
20 Bryant Way ▪ *American* ▪ Chef Kenneth reports that the restaurant can "easily" accommodate GF diners. He notes that almost any menu item, with the exception of the fried chicken, can be modified to be GF. Confirm timeliness of this information before dining in. Alert a server upon arrival. ▪ *www.casaorinda.net*

Cascal Restaurant   ✪ $$$LD
Mountain View ▪ *(650) 940-9500*
400 Castro St ▪ *Latin American* ▪ GF lists regular menu items that are GF and any modifications that must be made. Reservations noting GF are recommended but not required. ▪ *www.cascalrestaurant.com*

Chez Panisse Restaurant & Café $$$LD
Berkeley ▪ *(510) 548-5049*
1517 Shattuck Ave ▪ *Modern American* ▪ General Manager Jessica reports that GF diners are welcome, and she recommends reservations noting GF. The upstairs restaurant has a fixed menu, but they will specially accommodate GF diners. The downstairs café serves a la carte items only, so GF diners should discuss GF options with the servers. ▪ *www.chezpanisse.com*

Chow Asian Fare   ✪★ $$LD
San Luis Obispo ▪ *(805) 540-5243*
1009 Monterey St ▪ *Asian* ▪ GF menu includes beef, chicken, or tofu over rice noodles and bean sprouts, seafood with rice noodles and coconut broth, tofu with shitake mushrooms, and more. GF soy sauce is available. ▪ *www.chowslo.com*

City Lights Espresso   ★ ¢L
Santa Clara ▪ *(408) 296-0415*
1171 Homestead Rd ▪ *Café* ▪ GF white bread, parmesan bread, and challah bread are available and can be substituted into any sandwich. GF chocolate peanut butter cookies and snicker doodles are also available.

Claire's   ★ $BL
Solana Beach ▪ *(858) 259-8597*

246 N Cedros Ave ■ American ■ GF bread is available. It can be used to make french toast for breakfast or substituted into any sandwich for lunch. GF muffins, cookies, brownies, and more are also available. ■ www.clairesoncedros.com

Clouds Downtown $$$LD
Santa Cruz ■ (831) 429-2000
110 Church St ■ Modern American ■ Chef Nate reports that GF diners are welcome and easy to accommodate. He notes that steaks, gnocchis, and chicken piccata can be made GF, but it is the diner's responsibility to know what he or she can eat. Confirm timeliness of this information before dining in. Alert a server upon arrival. ■ www.cloudsdowntown.com

Cottonwood Restaurant & Bar $$$D
Truckee ■ (530) 587-5711
10142 Rue Hilltop ■ Modern American ■ Executive Chef David reports that he and the kitchen staff are "pretty savvy" about the GF diet, so they have no problems accommodating GF diners. They use only rice flour in the fryer, so even fried items are GF. David recommends alerting the server upon arrival or asking to speak with himself or the sous-chef. ■ www.cottonwoodrestaurant.com

Coyote Bar and Grill $LD
Blairsden ■ (530) 836-2002
8296 Hwy 89 ■ South American ■ Manager Leslie reports that GF diners "rarely" dine at the restaurant. She recommends calling in advance and discussing specific GF options, so that the kitchen can prepare.

Crepes Café   ★ ¢BLD
Menlo Park ■ (650) 473-0506
1195 Merrill St ■ Crêpes ■ GF buckwheat crepes are available. Restaurant can make any crepe dish on the menu with the GF shell. ■ www.crepescafe.com

Cups   ★ ¢S
La Jolla ■ (858) 459-2877
7857 Girard Ave ■ Bakery ■ Bakery reports that one GF cupcake is available daily.

Special orders of two dozen cupcakes or more require advanced notice of two days. GF flavors include limone ricotta, chocolate decadence, chocolate and vanilla, and carrot with almonds and pecans. ■ www.cupslj.com

Cyrus Restaurant $$$$D
Healdsburg ■ (707) 433-3311
29 North St ■ American ■ Chef Chris reports that they have "no problem" accommodating GF guests, who are very common. He notes that many menu items can be modified to be GF. Reservations noting GF are recommended, and advanced notice of one week is preferred. ■ www.cyrusrestaurant.com

Delta King - The Pilothouse ◎★ $$$BLD
Sacramento ■ (916) 441-4440
1000 Front St. ■ Modern American ■ Located aboard the Delta King Riverboat. Manager Charlie reports that most entrées are GF, and GF items are clearly marked on the dinner menu. GF beer and GF chocolate cake are available. ■ www.deltaking.com

Doughboy's Pizzeria   ◎★ $LD
Grover Beach ■ (805) 474-8888
1800 Grand Ave ■ Pizza ■ GF menu includes appetizers and salads. GF pizza is available at the locations listed above. ■ www.doughboyspizzeria.net

Dragonfly $$$LD
Truckee ■ (530) 587-0557
10118 Donner Pass Rd ■ Asian Fusion ■ Chef Billy says they "deal with Celiac all the time" and that GF diners are welcome. Reservations noting GF are highly recommended. Manager Karen adds that all servers are GF aware. ■ www.dragonflycuisine.com

E & O Trading Company $$LD
Larkspur ■ (415) 925-0303
2231 Larkspur Landing Cir
San Jose ■ (408) 938-4100
96 S 1st St ■ Asian Fusion ■ The Larkspur location reports that a few different menu items are naturally GF, while others can

be modified to be GF. Alert a server upon arrival. Servers are GF aware, but they will always double check with the kitchen about which menu items are GF. The San Jose location has an internal GF list that includes fried rice, lemongrass chicken, grilled ahi tuna, and more. The server can bring this list to the table for reference. ▪ *www.eotrading.com*

Extreme Pizza   ★ $$**LD**
Alamo ▪ *(925) 838-1122*
3227 Danville Blvd
Berkeley ▪ *(510) 486-0770*
2352 Shattuck Ave
Berkeley ▪ *(510) 420-0770*
3024 College Ave
Brentwood ▪ *(925) 513-3001*
3120 Balfour Rd
Dublin ▪ *(925) 833-2400*
6599 Dublin Blvd
Folsom ▪ *(916) 984-5000*
25035 Blue Ravine Rd
Fresno ▪ *(559) 440-0120*
6072 S Elm Ave
Granite Bay ▪ *(916) 781-4999*
4060 Douglas Blvd
Hercules ▪ *(510) 964-9990*
3700 San Pablo Ave
La Jolla ▪ *(858) 729-1910*
834 Kline St
Livermore ▪ *(925) 447-9900*
1770 1st St
Long Beach ▪ *(562) 901-9700*
21 The Paseo @ The Pike
Modesto ▪ *(209) 238-0466*
1022 11Th St
Newark ▪ *(510) 742-9200*
5829 Jarvis Ave
Novato ▪ *(415) 898-6575*
104 Vintage Way
Pacifica ▪ *(650) 738-8000*
5430 Coast Hwy
Petaluma ▪ *(707) 763-8100*
3100 Lakeville Hwy
Point Richmond ▪ *(510) 620-1800*
151 Park Pl
Sacramento ▪ *(916) 925-8859*
1140 Exposition Blvd

San Bruno ▪ *(650) 873-6336*
851 Cherry Ave
San Jose ▪ *(408) 293-8008*
30 E Santa Clara St
San Rafael ▪ *(415) 454-6111*
703 4th St
San Ramon ▪ *(925) 244-1000*
164 Sunset Dr
Walnut Creek ▪ *(925) 930-6100*
1630 Cypress St ▪ *Pizza* ▪ GF pizza is available. ▪ *www.extremepizza.com*

Farm Stand   ◑ $$**LD**
El Segundo ▪ *(310) 640-3276*
422 Main St ▪ *Global* ▪ Hostess Aurora reports that GF items on the menu are denoted with an asterisk. For dessert, coconut flan is available. Aurora also notes that it is essential to notify a server of GF requests, so that the server can tell the kitchen to take extra precautions. ▪ *www.farmstand.us*

Fat Mike's Pizza   ★ $**LD**
Elk Grove ▪ *(916) 686-8543*
8970 Grant Line Rd ▪ *Pizza* ▪ GF pizza is available in the 8-inch or 12-inch size. ▪ *www.fatmikespizza.com*

Filippi's Pizza Grotto   ◑★ $**LD**
Napa ▪ *(707) 254-9700*
645 1st St ▪ *Italian* ▪ GF menu includes pasta primavera, spaghetti with pesto, pizzas, and more. GF menu was developed by this location's owner, who is GF, so it is not available at other locations. ▪ *www. realcheesepizza.com*

Fire + Ice   ★ $$**LD**
Anaheim ▪ *(714) 808-9757*
321 W Katella Ave
S Lake Tahoe ▪ *(530) 542-6650*
4100 Lake Tahoe Blvd ▪ *Asian Stir-Fry* ▪ GF pasta is available. Manager Casey at the Anaheim location reports that the restaurant serves GF customers "all the time." Server Renee at the S Lake Tahoe location adds that eight of twelve sauces are GF, and all servers can indicate them. She notes that GF diners who would like their meals cooked on separate cooking surfaces in

the kitchen should inform a server. ▪ *www.fire-ice.com*

Firefly Bistro $$$**D**
South Pasadena ▪ *(626) 441-2443*
1009 El Centro St ▪ *Fusion* ▪ Manager
Gina reports that there are "plenty of options" for GF diners. She notes that all servers are "absolutely" familiar with the GF diet, and they are able to ask the kitchen if they have questions about ingredients. ▪ *www.eatatfirefly.com*

Firefly Grill & Wine Bar $$$**D**
Encinitas ▪ *(760) 635-1066*
251 N El Camino Real ▪ *American* ▪ Owner
Jim reports that the "majority" of the menu is naturally GF, while many other items can be modified to be GF. He notes that they serve GF diners "almost daily," and that all servers are trained on the GF diet. ▪ *www.fireflygrillandwinebar.com*

Fish Market, The $$**LD**
Palo Alto ▪ *(650) 493-8862*
3150 El Camino Real
San Jose ▪ *(408) 269-3474*
1007 Blossom Hill Rd
San Mateo ▪ *(650) 349-3474*
1855 S Norfolk St
Santa Clara ▪ *(408) 246-3474*
3775 El Camino Real
Solana Beach ▪ *(858) 755-2277*
640 Via De La Valle ▪ *Seafood* ▪ Shrimp,
oysters, and fish can be made GF by eliminating the sauce. Confirm timeliness of this information before dining in. Managers at all locations note that although they are happy to accommodate GF diners, the kitchens are not GF environments, so cross-contamination may occur. Speaking with a manager upon arrival is recommended. ▪ *www.thefishmarket.com*

Fit 2B Thai   ✪★ ¢**LD**
Thousand Oaks ▪ *(805) 496-2501*
593 N Moorpark Rd ▪ *Thai* ▪ GF items are
marked on the menu, and GF soy sauce is available. The restaurant recommends alerting the server, who will use a special

button to notify the kitchen of the GF order. ▪ *www.fit2b-thai.com*

Flore Vegan Cuisine   ✪★ $**BLD**
Silverlake ▪ *(323) 953-0611*
3818 W Sunset Blvd ▪ *Vegan* ▪ GF menu
includes griddle cakes, a tofu scramble, crispy kale, edamame, grapefruit and fennel salad, portobello tacos, and more. GF pancakes are available. ▪ *www.florevegan.com*

flourChylde Bakery   ★ ¢**BL**
Old Town Novato ▪ *(415) 893-7700*
850 Grant Ave ▪ *Bakery* ▪ Non-dedicated
bakery offering several GF tortes and wheat-free scones. Calling ahead for scones is advised, as they generally sell out by afternoon. ▪ *www.flourchyld.com*

Fogo De Chao   ★ $$$$**LD**
Beverly Hills ▪ *(310) 289-7755*
133 N La Cienega Blvd ▪ *Brazilian* ▪ GF
cheese bread made with yucca flour is available. ▪ *www.fogodechao.com*

Fresco Cafe & Bakery $**BLD**
Santa Barbara ▪ *(805) 967-6037*
3987 State St ▪ *Café* ▪ Manager Jackie
reports that GF diners should alert the staff member at the register. She notes that the staff is happy to check ingredients to ensure that items are GF. Macaroons are usually available for dessert. ▪ *www.frescosb.com*

Fresh Brothers   ✪★ $**LD**
Manhattan Beach ▪ *(310) 546-4444*
2008 N Sepulveda Blvd
Marina Del Rey ▪ *(310) 823-3800*
4722 1/2 Admiralty Way
Redondo Beach ▪ *(310) 374-5678*
407 N Pacific Coast Hwy ▪ *Pizza* ▪ GF
menu includes bbq chicken pizza, hawaiian pizza, antipasto salad, cobb salad, and more. ▪ *www.freshbrothers.com*

Freshies   ★ $**LD**
S Lake Tahoe ▪ *(530) 542-3630*
3330 Lake Tahoe Blvd ▪ *American* ▪ GF
tamari is available. The restaurant reports that they are accustomed to GF diners, and

that many menu items are naturally GF. Alert a server, who will indicate GF options. ▪ *www.freshiestahoe.com*

Fritto Misto   ★ $LD
Hermosa Beach ▪ *(310) 318-6098*
316 Pier Ave
Santa Monica ▪ *(310) 458-2829*
601 Colorado Ave ▪ *Italian* ▪ GF rice pasta is available. ▪ *www.usmenuguide.com*

Garlic Jim's   ★ $$LD
Burbank ▪ *(818) 556-5467*
2128 N Glenoaks Blvd
Pasadena ▪ *(626) 844-3546*
2982 E Colorado Blvd
Redondo Beach ▪ *(310) 543-5500*
1876 S Pacific Coast Hwy
Simi Valley ▪ *(805) 526-1500*
131 Cochran St Ste D ▪ *Pizza* ▪ GF pizza is available. ▪ *www.garlicjims.com*

Gauchos Village $$$LD
Glendale ▪ *(818) 550-1430*
411 N Brand Blvd ▪ *Brazilian Steakhouse* ▪ Manager Diana reports that most menu items are naturally GF. She also notes that the restaurant is part of a GF society, and that they "frequently" accommodate GF diners. ▪ *www.gauchosvillage.com*

Gluten Not Included   100% ¢S
Escondido ▪ *(760) 432-6100*
2250 S Escondido Blvd ▪ *Bakery & Café* ▪ Dedicated GF bakery offering a wide selection of bread products, including croutons and bread crumbs. GF desserts such as angel food cake, fudge brownies, snicker doodles, ginger bread cookies, and pies are also available. ▪ *www.gnibakery.com*

Goko Café   ¢BLD
Laguna Beach ▪ *(949) 494-4880*
907 S Coast Hwy ▪ *Deli* ▪ Manager BB reports that the restaurant frequently accommodates GF diners. She notes that she is one of two employees in the small café, so she is always there. GF customers can speak to her, and she will make sure appropriate modifications are made. Options include plates with eggs, rice, and hummus,

along with avocado, salads, and vegetarian rice plates. Confirm timeliness of this information before dining in. ▪ *www.gokocafe.com*

Good Chemistry Baking   100% ¢S
Oakland ▪ *(510) 350-7190*
3249 Grand Ave ▪ *Bakery* ▪ Dedicated GF bakery offering a variety of bars, breads, cakes, cookies, cupcakes, muffins, and more. Pizza by the slice and hot sandwiches are also available. ▪ *www.goodchemistrybaking.com*

Goofy's Kitchen $$$$BLD
Anaheim ▪ *(714) 956-6755*
1150 Magic Way ▪ *American* ▪ Reservations noting GF are recommended. Ask the server to speak with the head chef upon arrival, and the chef will come out to discuss GF options. Located inside the Disneyland Hotel.

Green Elephant Gourmet $LD
Palo Alto ▪ *(650) 494-7391*
3950 Middlefield Rd ▪ *Chinese* ▪ Owner Christina reports that GF diners come in to the restaurant "frequently" and that many menu items are GF. She notes that GF diners can bring in their own soy sauce. Alert the server upon arrival. ▪ *www.greenelephantgourmet.com*

Healthy Creations   ✪★ ¢BLD
Encinitas ▪ *(760) 479-0500*
376 N El Camino Real ▪ *Organic* ▪ Baker Mary reports that everything in the bakery case is GF, but the options change frequently. She also notes that though the menu changes monthly, there are always a number of GF options. GF pasta, biscuits, and baked goods are available. ▪ *www.healthycreations.com*

Hugo's Tacos   ¢BLD
Studio City ▪ *(818) 762-7771*
4749 Coldwater Canyon Ave ▪ *Mexican* ▪ Restaurants report that much of their food is naturally GF. They use corn tortillas and do not dredge meats in flour. Manager David at the Glendale Blvd location recom-

mends speaking to a manager about which items are GF. Both locations are taco stands with no indoor seating. For a sit-down meal, see Hugo's, the mother restaurant. ▪ *www.hugostacos.com*

Hugo's   ✪ $BLD
Studio City ▪ *(818) 761-8985*
12851 Riverside Dr
West Hollywood ▪ *(323) 654-3993*
8401 Santa Monica Blvd ▪ *Fusion* ▪ GF menu includes salads with GF dressings, egg frittatas, tamales, tacos on corn tortillas, Asian stir fry, tika masala vegetable patties, black bean chili, portabello stew, shepherd's pie, lentil and rice dishes, and more. ▪ *www.hugosrestaurant.com*

Julian Bakery   ★ ¢S
La Jolla ▪ *(858) 454-1198*
5621 La Jolla Blvd ▪ *Bakery* ▪ Non-dedicated bakery offering GF "Purity Bread." It is baked on Mondays, Tuesdays, and Thursdays, and can be purchased at the storefront or ordered online. ▪ *www.julian-bakery.com*

Juliano's Raw   100% $LD
Santa Monica ▪ *(310) 587-1552*
609 Broadway ▪ *Raw* ▪ Restaurant serving entirely GF and raw cuisine. Sample menu items include green curry pasta, a sundried tomato cheese warp, and truffle cream linguini. GF "pasta" is made with zucchini or kelp. ▪ *www.planetraw.com*

Kara's Cupcakes   ★ $$$$$
Napa ▪ *(707) 258-2253*
610 1st St
Palo Alto ▪ *(650) 326-2253*
855 El Camino Real
San Jose ▪ *(408) 260-2222*
3055 Olin Ave ▪ *Bakery* ▪ GF cupcakes are available in sweet vanilla, chocolate velvet, and vanilla or chocolate coconut. Mini cupcakes are available by preorder, and 6-inch cakes are available at the Palo Alto and San Jose locations. The Palo Alto location also hosts cupcake decorating parties upon request. ▪ *www.karascupcakes.com*

Kitti's Place $LD
Sausalito ▪ *(415) 331-0390*
3001 Bridgeway ▪ *Asian Fusion* ▪ Owner Lisa reports that most dishes are naturally GF. She also notes that everything is made to order and that GF food is "always cooked separately." Alert server upon arrival. ▪ *www.kittisplace.com*

La Biscotteria   ★ ¢S
Redwood City ▪ *(650) 366-2747*
2747 El Camino Real ▪ *Bakery* ▪ Non-dedicated bakery offering GF amaretti cookies. Varieties include amaretti chocolate ganache cookies and amaretti mini chocolate dipped cookies. ▪ *www.labiscotteria.com*

Lawry's The Prime Rib $$$$D
Beverly Hills ▪ *(310) 652-2827*
100 N La Cienega Blvd ▪ *Steakhouse* ▪ Manager Christopher reports that they serve GF diners frequently. He notes that all servers and managers have an allergy list, which includes GF options. If a server does not have that list, Christopher recommends asking to speak to a manager. He warns that salad dressings and some fish dishes are not GF, but the homemade potato chips, shrimp cocktail, iron skillet mushrooms, and prime rib with no au jus are all GF. Confirm timeliness of this information before dining in. ▪ *www.lawrysonline.com*

Le Crumb Bakery   ★ $$$$$
Van Nuys ▪ *(818) 780-3303*
5906 Kester Ave ▪ *Bakery* ▪ GF chocolate and white cakes are available if ordered two days in advance. Cupcakes are also sometimes available.

Left Coast Pizza   ★ $$$LD
Chico ▪ *(530) 892-9000*
800 Bruce Rd ▪ *Pizza* ▪ GF pizza is available. ▪ *www.leftcoastpizza.net*

Lone Star Steakhouse & Saloon   📖
Corona ▪ *(951) 278-4117*
955 Montecito Dr
Laguna Hills ▪ *(949) 951-8687*
24231 Avenida De La Carlota

Lake Elsinore ▪ *(951) 471-2200*
18601 Dexter Ave
Tustin ▪ *(714) 508-8996*
1222 Irvine Blvd

Maggiano's Little Italy　　　★ $$$**LD**
Costa Mesa ▪ *(714) 546-9550*
3333 Bristol St
San Jose ▪ *(408) 423-8973*
3055 Olin Ave
Woodland Hills ▪ *(818) 887-3777*
6100 Topanga Canyon Blvd ▪ *Italian* ▪ GF
pasta is available. Call individual locations
to inquire about additional GF options. ▪
www.maggianos.com

Marin Coffee Roasters　　　★ ¢**BL**
San Anselmo ▪ *(415) 258-9549*
546 San Anselmo Ave ▪ *Coffee House &*
Café ▪ GF ginger cookies, brownies, oat
bars, and pizza are available at the counter.
Manager Chris notes that several GF diners
come in "frequently."

Mary's Pizza Shack　　　★ $$**LD**
Anderson ▪ *(530) 378-1110*
1901 Highway 273
Cloverdale ▪ *(707) 894-8977*
1143 S Cloverdale Blvd
Dixon ▪ *(707) 693-0300*
1460 Ary Ln
Fairfield ▪ *(707) 422-2700*
1500 Oliver Rd
Napa ▪ *(707) 257-3300*
3085 Jefferson St
Novato ▪ *(415) 897-6266*
121 San Marin Dr
Petaluma ▪ *(707) 778-7200*
359 E Washington St
Rohnert Park ▪ *(707) 585-3500*
101 Golf Course Dr
Roseville ▪ *(916) 780-7600*
711 Pleasant Grove Blvd
Santa Rosa ▪ *(707) 573-1100*
3084 Marlow Rd
Santa Rosa ▪ *(707) 538-1888*
535 Summerfield Rd
Santa Rosa ▪ *(707) 571-1959*
615 4th St
Sebastopol ▪ *(707) 829-5800*

790 Gravenstein Hwy N
Sonoma ▪ *(707) 938-3600*
18636 Highway 12
Sonoma ▪ *(707) 938-8300*
8 West Spain St
Vacaville ▪ *(707) 446-7100*
505 Davis St
Walnut Creek ▪ *(925) 938-4800*
2246 Oak Grove Rd
Windsor ▪ *(707) 836-0900*
9010 Brooks Road ▪ *Pizza* ▪ GF pizza is
available in the 12-inch size. There is a limited selection of toppings. ▪ *www.maryspiz-
zashack.com*

Melting Pot, The　　　　📖
Brea ▪ *(714) 671-6000*
375 W Birch St Ste 1
Irvine ▪ *(949) 955-3242*
2646 Dupont Dr
Larkspur ▪ *(415) 461-6358*
125 E Sir Francis Drake Blvd
Pasadena ▪ *(626) 792-1941*
88 W Colorado Blvd
Sacramento ▪ *(916) 443-2347*
814 15th St
San Clemente ▪ *(949) 661-1966*
647 Camino De Los Mares
San Mateo ▪ *(650) 342-6358*
2 N B St
Temecula ▪ *(951) 693-2222*
39738 Winchester Rd
Torrance ▪ *(310) 316-7500*
21525 Hawthorne Blvd
Westlake Village ▪ *(805) 370-8802*
3685 E Thousand Oaks Blvd

Michael's Ristorante　　　★ $$**D**
Moraga ▪ *(925) 376-4300*
1375 Moraga Way ▪ *Mediterranean* ▪
GF pizza and beer are available. Manager
Matthew reports that several menu items
can be modified to be GF. Other items,
such as the ribeye and chicken caprese, are
naturally GF. Confirm timeliness of this
information before dining in. ▪ *www.pen-
ninis.com*

Miner Moe's Pizza　　　★ $**LD**
Nevada City ▪ *(530) 265-0284*

102 Argall Way ▪ Pizza ▪ GF pizza is available in the 12-inch size. ▪ www.miner-moespizza.com

Mission Pizza & Pub ★ $$$LD
Fremont ▪ (510) 651-6858
1572 Washington Blvd ▪ Pizza ▪ GF pizza and beer are available. Manager Joe reports that BBQ chicken and artichokes are not GF, but all other toppings are. He notes that GF diners are served "frequently." ▪ www.missionpizza.com

Moody's Bistro $$$LD
Truckee ▪ (530) 587-8688
10007 Bridge St ▪ Modern American ▪ Chef and Owner Mark reports that most of the menu is naturally GF, and accommodating GF diners is "not a problem at all." Alert the server, who will ask a chef to come out and indicate GF options. ▪ www.moodysbistro.com

Mountain Room Restaurant ✪ $$$$D
Yosemite National Park ▪ (209) 372-1274
Yosemite Lodge At The Falls ▪ Modern American ▪ GF menu includes soups, salads, trout, lamb, the catch of the day, and the rib eye steak. Food and Beverage Manager Carlie notes that the servers and the kitchen staff are aware of the GF diet and can accommodate it. Reservations noting GF are recommended, as it allows the kitchen to prepare in advance. Upon arrival, alert the hostess, who will remind the servers and the kitchen staff. ▪ www.yosemitepark.com

Mustard Seed $$$LD
Davis ▪ (530) 758-5750
222 D St ▪ Modern American ▪ Owner Robin reports that GF diners are welcome and notes that there are naturally GF menu items. GF items include pork chops, duck breasts, and shrimp risotto. Reservations noting GF are recommended. ▪ www.mustardseeddavis.com

Natural Food Works Farmer's Kitchen Café 100% ¢BLD
Davis ▪ (530) 756-1862

624 4th St ▪ Bakery & Café ▪ Bakery and café offering GF breads, buns, bread crumbs, pie crusts, a variety of pastas, and pastries. The café serves GF lunches and dinners, though the menu changes regularly. ▪ www.naturalfoodworks.com

Newport Rib Company ✪★ $$$D
Costa Mesa ▪ (949) 631-2110
2196 Harbor Blvd
Ladera Ranch ▪ (949) 364-9111
27742 Antonio Pkwy
Long Beach ▪ (562) 439-7427
5800 E 2nd St ▪ Barbeque ▪ GF menu is available at all locations and includes baby back ribs, BBQ chicken, hamburgers on a GF bun, and filet mignon. GF buns are available. ▪ www.ribcompany.com

Novo Restaurant & Lounge ✪ $$$LD
San Luis Obispo ▪ (805) 543-3986
726 Higuera St ▪ Global ▪ GF menu includes lettuce wraps, a rice stir fry with prawns, nachos with corn tortillas, the antipasto plate, and shrimp and avocado spring rolls. Manager Steve reports that accommodating GF diners is "no problem at all." ▪ www.novorestaurant.com

Old Spaghetti Factory, The 📖
Concord ▪ (925) 687-5030
1955 Mount Diablo St
Duarte ▪ (626) 358-2115
1431 Buena Vista St
Elk Grove ▪ (916) 478-2400
7727 Laguna Blvd
Fresno ▪ (559) 222-1066
1610 E Shaw Ave
Fullerton ▪ (714) 526-6801
110 E Santa Fe Ave
Newport Beach ▪ (949) 675-8654
2110 Newport Blvd
Rancho Cordova ▪ (916) 985-0822
12401 Folsom Blvd
Rancho Cucamonga ▪ (909) 980-3585
11896 Foothill Blvd
Redlands ▪ (909) 798-7774
1635 Industrial Park Ave
Riverside ▪ (951) 784-4417
3191 Mission Inn Ave

Roseville ▪ *(916) 773-3950*
731 Sunrise Ave
Sacramento ▪ *(916) 443-2862*
1910 J St
San Jose ▪ *(408) 288-7488*
51 N San Pedro St
San Marcos ▪ *(760) 471-0155*
111 N Twin Oaks Valley Rd
Stockton ▪ *(209) 473-3695*
2702 W March Ln

Original Pancake House, The   ★ ¢**BL**
Anaheim ▪ *(714) 535-9815*
1418 E Lincoln Ave
Orange ▪ *(714) 221-8674*
3322 E Chapman Ave
Poway ▪ *(858) 679-0186*
14905 Pomerado Rd
Roseville ▪ *(916) 788-3040*
10000 Fairway Dr
San Jose ▪ *(408) 255-7373*
1366 S De Anza Blvd
San Jose ▪ *(408) 979-0251*
2306 Almaden Rd
Temecula ▪ *(951) 296-9016*
41377 Margarita Rd ▪ Breakfast ▪ GF
pancakes are available. Select locations
may have other GF options as well. Call
an individual location to inquire. ▪ *www.
originalpancakehouse.com*

Outback Steakhouse   📖
Arcadia ▪ *(626) 447-6435*
166 E Huntington Dr
Bakersfield ▪ *(661) 834-7850*
5051 Stockdale Hwy
Brea ▪ *(714) 990-8100*
402 Pointe Dr
Buena Park ▪ *(714) 523-5788*
7575 Beach Blvd
Burbank ▪ *(818) 567-2717*
1761 N Victory Pl
Campbell ▪ *(408) 371-5384*
1887 S Bascom Ave
Chico ▪ *(530) 899-8112*
1990 E 20th St
City Of Industry ▪ *(626) 810-6765*
1418 S Azusa Ave
Corona ▪ *(951) 273-1336*

151 N Mckinley St
Costa Mesa ▪ *(949) 631-8377*
1670 Newport Blvd
Covina ▪ *(626) 812-0488*
1476 N Azusa Ave
Cupertino ▪ *(408) 255-4400*
20630 Valley Green Dr
Daly City ▪ *(650) 756-3691*
371 Gellert Blvd
Dublin ▪ *(925) 833-9335*
6505 Regional St
El Cajon ▪ *(619) 588-4332*
722 Jamacha Rd
Elk Grove ▪ *(916) 714-0141*
7221 Laguna Blvd
Foothill Ranch ▪ *(949) 455-4158*
26652 Portola Pkwy
Fremont ▪ *(510) 252-1595*
5525 Stevenson Blvd
Fresno ▪ *(559) 224-1181*
2765 W Shaw Ave
Garden Grove ▪ *(714) 663-1107*
12001 Harbor Blvd
Glendale ▪ *(818) 244-1136*
146 S Brand Blvd
Gold River ▪ *(916) 635-3603*
2100 Golden Centre Ln
Goleta ▪ *(805) 964-0599*
5690 Calle Real
Irvine ▪ *(949) 651-8760*
15433 Culver Dr
La Mesa ▪ *(619) 466-9795*
5628 Lake Murray Blvd
Laguna Hills ▪ *(949) 829-0683*
25322 Cabot Rd
Lakewood ▪ *(562) 634-0353*
5305 Clark Ave
Long Beach ▪ *(562) 435-0002*
20 W Shoreline Dr
Milpitas ▪ *(408) 263-5400*
1246 Great Mall Dr
Modesto ▪ *(209) 577-2410*
2045 W Briggsmore Ave Ste D
Moreno Valley ▪ *(951) 656-4242*
22680 Centerpoint Dr
National City ▪ *(619) 475-4329*
2980 Plaza Bonita Rd
Newhall ▪ *(661) 287-9630*

25261 The Old Rd
Northridge ▪ *(818) 366-2341*
18711 Devonshire St
Norwalk ▪ *(562) 863-8908*
12850 Norwalk Blvd
Oceanside ▪ *(760) 754-8825*
2485 Vista Way
Ontario ▪ *(909) 484-2999*
4492 Ontario Mills Pkwy
Oxnard ▪ *(805) 988-4329*
2341 Lockwood St
Palm Desert ▪ *(760) 779-9068*
72220 Highway 111
Palmdale ▪ *(661) 274-9607*
1061 W Avenue P
Pinole ▪ *(510) 758-7386*
1361 Fitzgerald Dr
Pittsburg ▪ *(925) 778-3845*
4350 Century Blvd
Pleasant Hill ▪ *(925) 687-2225*
150 Longbrook Way Ste A
Poway ▪ *(858) 486-1563*
14701 Pomerado Rd
Redding ▪ *(530) 226-9394*
910 Dana Dr
Rohnert Park ▪ *(707) 584-7161*
4619 Redwood Dr
Roseville ▪ *(916) 772-6060*
181 N Sunrise Ave
Sacramento ▪ *(916) 927-0806*
1340 Howe Ave
Salinas ▪ *(831) 751-3753*
1401 N Davis Rd
San Bernardino ▪ *(909) 890-0061*
620 E Hospitality Ln
San Jose ▪ *(408) 226-4922*
632 Blossom Hill Rd
San Mateo ▪ *(650) 287-4329*
Sixty-Six 31st Avenue
Sausalito ▪ *(415) 331-6193*
196 Donahue St
Stockton ▪ *(209) 954-9615*
1243 W March Ln
Temecula ▪ *(951) 719-3700*
40275 Winchester Rd
Thousand Oaks ▪ *(805) 381-1590*
137 E Thousand Oaks Blvd
Torrance ▪ *(310) 793-5555*

21880 Hawthorne Blvd
Upland ▪ *(909) 931-1050*
530 N Mountain Ave
Vacaville ▪ *(707) 452-9200*
521 Davis St
Victorville ▪ *(760) 962-1003*
12400B Amargosa Rd
Westminster ▪ *(714) 890-0130*
549 Westminster Mall

P.F. Chang's China Bistro 📖

Anaheim ▪ *(714) 507-2021*
321 W Katella Ave Ste 120
Bakersfield ▪ *(661) 664-8100*
10700 Stockdale Hwy
Burbank ▪ *(818) 391-1070*
201 E Magnolia Blvd Ste 281
Carlsbad ▪ *(760) 795-0595*
5621 Paseo Del Norte
Chino Hills ▪ *(909) 590-8250*
3445 Grand Ave
Chula Vista ▪ *(619) 421-2080*
2015 Birch Rd Ste 1401
Corte Madera ▪ *(415) 413-9890*
301 Corte Madera Town Ctr Spc A
El Segundo ▪ *(310) 607-9062*
2041 Rosecrans Ave Ste 120
Emeryville ▪ *(510) 879-0990*
5633 Bay St
Fremont ▪ *(510) 657-1400*
43316 Christy St
Fresno ▪ *(559) 438-0814*
7894 N Blackstone Ave
Irvine ▪ *(949) 453-1211*
61 Fortune Dr
Long Beach ▪ *(562) 308-1025*
340 S Pine Ave
Mission Viejo ▪ *(949) 364-6661*
800 The Shops At Mission Viejo
Monterey ▪ *(831) 375-0143*
1200 Del Monte Ctr
Newport Beach ▪ *(949) 759-9007*
1145 Newport Center Dr
Palo Alto ▪ *(650) 330-1782*
900 Stanford Shopping Ctr Bldg W
Pasadena ▪ *(626) 356-9760*
260 E Colorado Blvd Ste 201
Pleasanton ▪ *(925) 224-9916*
1330 Stoneridge Mall Rd

Rancho Cucamonga ▪ *(909) 463-4095*
7870 Monticello Ave
Rancho Mirage ▪ *(760) 776-4912*
71800 Highway 111 Ste C104
Riverside ▪ *(951) 689-4020*
3475 Galleria At Tyler
Roseville ▪ *(916) 788-2800*
1180 Galleria Blvd
Sacramento ▪ *(916) 288-0970*
1530 J St Ste 100
San Jose ▪ *(408) 960-2940*
925 Blossom Hill Rd Ste 1515
San Jose ▪ *(408) 961-5250*
98 S 2nd St
Santa Monica ▪ *(310) 395-1912*
326 Wilshire Blvd
Sherman Oaks ▪ *(818) 784-1694*
15301 Ventura Blvd Ste P22
Sunnyvale ▪ *(408) 991-9078*
390 W El Camino Real
Temecula ▪ *(951) 296-6700*
40762 Winchester Rd Ste 400
Thousand Oaks ▪ *(805) 277-5915*
2250 Thousand Oaks Blvd
Torrance ▪ *(310) 793-0590*
3525 W Carson St Ste 166
Walnut Creek ▪ *(925) 979-9070*
1205 Broadway Plz
Woodland Hills ▪ *(818) 340-0491*
21821 Oxnard St

Palermo Ristorante Italiano   ★ $$D

Elk Grove ▪ *(916) 686-1582*
9632 Emerald Oak Dr ▪ *Italian* ▪ Owner
and Chef Giovanni reports that the
restaurant serves GF diners regularly. He
recommends alerting a server upon arrival.
Servers are educated on the GF diet, but if
they have questions, they will ask him. ▪
www.palermo-ristorante.com

Palm Greens Cafe   ★ $BL

Palm Springs ▪ *(760) 864-9900*
611 S Palm Canyon Dr ▪ *Vegetarian* ▪ GF
offerings include pancakes, rice wraps,
salads with GF salad dressings, brownies, muffins, cookies, and more. ▪ *www.
palmgreenscafe.com*

PapaCicio's   ★ ¢LD

Long Beach ▪ *(562) 431-7272*
8185 E Wardlow Rd ▪ *Italian* ▪ GF pizza is
available.

Paulette Macarons   ¢S

Beverly Hills ▪ *(310) 275-0023*
9466 Charleville Blvd ▪ *French* ▪ All
macaroons are naturally GF. Bakery cautions that other, non-GF items are prepared
in the bakery. Calling ahead for large or
specialized orders is recommended. ▪ *www.
paulettemacarons.com*

Pei Wei Asian Diner   📖

Chino Hills ▪ *(909) 393-7472*
4517 Chino Hills Pkwy Ste E
Encinitas ▪ *(760) 635-2888*
1560 Leucadia Blvd Ste A
Huntington Beach ▪ *(714) 230-2050*
7621 Edinger Ave Ste 102
Irvine ▪ *(949) 857-8700*
5781 Alton Pkwy
Lake Forest ▪ *(949) 860-2001*
23632 El Toro Rd
Newport Beach ▪ *(949) 629-1000*
1302 Bison Ave
Pasadena ▪ *(626) 325-9020*
3455 E Foothill Blvd
San Marcos ▪ *(760) 304-7010*
113 S Las Posas Rd Ste 110
Santa Clarita ▪ *(661) 600-0132*
24250 Valencia Blvd
Seal Beach ▪ *(562) 668-5090*
12235 Seal Beach Blvd
Torrance ▪ *(310) 517-9366*
2777 Pacific Coast Hwy
Tustin ▪ *(714) 259-1125*
2695 Park Ave

Peking Wok $$LD

Bonsall ▪ *(760) 724-8078*
5256 S Mission Rd ▪ *Chinese* ▪ Restaurant
reports that they host "a lot of people" who
are GF. They also note that everything
on the menu can be prepared GF. Alert a
server upon arrival. ▪ *www.pekingwokbon-
sall.com*

Pennini's Ristorante Italiano   ★ $$**LD**
Moraga ■ **(925) 376-1515**
1375 Moraga Way ■ *Pizza* ■ GF pizza is available in the medium size. ■ *www.penninis.com*

Peppers Mexicali Café $$**LD**
Pacific Grove ■ **(831) 373-6892**
170 Forest Ave ■ *Latin American* ■ Manager Lisa reports that they have accommodated "several" GF diners in the past. Although all of their marinades contain soy sauce, they can make food such as salmon steaks and chicken breasts to order. Alert the server upon arrival. ■ *www.peppersmexicalicafe.com*

Pica Pica Maize Kitchen   100%★ ¢**BLD**
Napa ■ **(707) 251-3757**
610 1st St ■ *Venezuelan* ■ Kitchen offering a mix-and-match style of GF cuisine. Diners choose one of three cornbreads and a filling. Empanadas are also served. GF beer is available. ■ *www.picapicakitchen.com*

Pizza Cookery, The   ★ $$**LD**
Woodland Hills ■ **(818) 887-4770**
6209 Topanga Canyon Blvd ■ *Pizza* ■ GF pizza and pasta are available. Manager Karen recommends calling ahead, as sometimes only certain pizza sizes are available. ■ *www.pizzacookery.com*

Pizza Fusion   ★ $$$**LD**
Santa Monica ■ **(310) 581-2901**
2901 Ocean Park Blvd
Temecula ■ **(951) 506-8888**
40695 Winchester Rd ■ *Pizza* ■ GF pizza is available. ■ *www.pizzafusion.com*

Pizza Pirate, The   ★ $**LD**
Benicia ■ **(707) 745-1667**
72 Solano Sq ■ *Pizza* ■ GF pizza is available in the personal and small sizes. GF beer is also available.

Pizza Rustica   ★ $$$**LD**
Oakland ■ **(510) 654-1601**
5422 College Ave
Oakland ■ **(510) 339-7878**

6106 La Salle Ave ■ *Pizza* ■ GF pizza available. ■ *www.caferustica.com*

PizzaSalad   ✪★ ¢**LD**
Thousand Oaks ■ **(805) 371-7878**
1655 E Thousand Oaks Blvd ■ *Pizza* ■ GF pizza is available. Manager GJ reports that they have GF soups and salads as well. GF chocolate chip and toffee fudge brownies are available for dessert. ■ *www.pizzasalad.com*

Pizzeria DePaoli   ★ $$**LD**
Windsor ■ **(707) 836-9843**
740 Mcclelland Dr ■ *Italian* ■ GF pizza and pasta are available. There are other GF options, too, like artichoke dips, crab-stuffed mushrooms, chicken piccata, and risottos. ■ *www.pizzeriadepaoli.com*

Prima Ristorante $$$**LD**
Walnut Creek ■ **(925) 935-7780**
1522 N Main St ■ *Italian* ■ Owner and Executive Chef Peter reports that they are happy to prepare GF meals upon request. He notes that "the majority" of the menu is naturally GF, and they can modify other items. The risotto de mare, the polenta with wild mushrooms, and the wood oven roasted game hen are examples of naturally GF meals. Confirm timeliness of this information before dining in. Alert a server upon arrival. ■ *www.primaristorante.com*

Putah Creek Café   ¢**BL**
Winters ■ **(530) 795-2682**
1 Main St ■ *Global* ■ Manager Yvonne reports that there are a large number of GF breakfast options, but fewer GF lunch options. She recommends asking for herself or the kitchen manager, Fred, upon arrival. She and Fred do not work on Tuesdays and Wednesdays, so Yvonne advises coming in on a different day. ■ *www.buckhornsteakhouse.com*

Que SeRAW SeRAW   100% $**BLD**
Burlingame ■ **(650) 400-8590**
1160 Capuchino Ave ■ *Raw* ■ All menu items are GF. Check timeliness of this information. GF pizza, lasagna, and soy

sauce are available, as are GF soups, cinnamon rolls, and pies. Restaurant is mostly deli-style take out, and seating is limited. ■ *www.queserawseraw.com*

Ravens' Restaurant ✪★ $$$BD
Mendocino ■ *(707) 937-5615*
44850 Comptche Ukiah Rd ■ *Vegetarian* ■ GF items marked on the menu include eggplant cannoli and winter squash risotto, among many other things. GF pasta, pizza, and soy sauce are available. Located in the Stanford Inn by the Sea. ■ *www.ravensrestaurant.com*

Red - A Restaurant & Bar $$$$LD
City Of Industry ■ *(626) 854-2509*
1 Industry Hills Pkwy ■ *Fusion* ■ Restaurant reports that its salmon and steak dishes are naturally GF, while other items can be modified to be GF. Confirm timeliness of this information before dining in. Reservations noting GF are recommended. Located at the Pacific Palms Resort. ■ *www.redrestaurant.net*

Redd Rockett's Pizza Port ★ $$$BLD
Anaheim ■ *(714) 781-4000*
1313 S Harbor Blvd ■ *Italian* ■ GF cheese and pepperoni pizzas are available. Located inside the Disneyland Resort.

Rick and Ann's Restaurant ★ $BLD
Berkeley ■ *(510) 649-8538*
2922 Domingo Ave ■ *American* ■ Owner Ann reports that there are options for GF diners. The yukon gold plate is naturally GF, and GF orange rice flour pancakes are available. Confirm timeliness of this information before dining in. Alert a server upon arrival. ■ *www.rickandanns.com*

Robin's Restaurant ✪★ $$LD
Cambria ■ *(805) 927-5007*
4095 Burton Dr ■ *Global* ■ GF menu includes a roasted half chicken, slipper lobster enchiladas, and more. For dessert, they offer crème brulee and chocolate mousse. Owner Shanny reports that all servers are trained on the GF diet, so they can discuss

specific GF options. ■ *www.robinsrestaurant.com*

Romeo Cucina ★ $$LD
Laguna Beach ■ *(949) 497-6627*
249 Broadway St
Laguna Niguel ■ *(949) 831-4131*
28241 Crown Valley Pkwy ■ *Italian* ■ GF pasta is available. ■ *www.romeocucina.com*

Roy's ★ $$$D
Anaheim ■ *(714) 776-7697*
321 W Katella Ave
Newport Beach ■ *(949) 640-7697*
453 Newport Center Dr
Pasadena ■ *(626) 356-4066*
641 E Colorado Blvd
Pebble Beach ■ *(831) 647-7500*
2700 17 Mile Dr
Rancho Mirage ■ *(760) 340-9044*
71959 Highway 111
Woodland Hills ■ *(818) 888-4801*
6363 Topanga Canyon Blvd ■ *Hawaiian Fusion* ■ Triumph spoke to managers or chefs at all locations, and all report that they can accommodate GF diners. GF tamari soy sauce is available at the Rancho Mirage and Woodland Hills locations. Managers at Newport Beach and Woodland Hills note that there is an internal GF list that servers will read to GF diners. Manager Charles at Rancho Mirage reports serving GF diners "often." All restaurants recommend making reservations noting GF and requesting that the server speak to a chef if they have any questions. ■ *www.roysrestaurant.com*

Sage Restaurant $$$LD
Newport Beach ■ *(949) 718-9650*
2531 Eastbluff Dr ■ *Modern American* ■ Manager Francesco reports that GF diners are welcome and recommends reservations noting GF. He reports that they accommodate GF diners on a regular basis and cook GF meals separately. ■ *www.sagerestaurant.com*

Sammy's Woodfired Pizza ✪ $LD
Carlsbad ■ *(760) 438-1212*

5970 Avenida Encinas
La Jolla ▪ *(858) 456-5222*
702 Pearl St
La Mesa ▪ *(619) 460-8555*
8555 Fletcher Pkwy
Palm Desert ▪ *(760) 836-0500*
73595 El Paseo
San Marcos ▪ *(760) 591-4222*
121 S Las Posas Rd
Torrance ▪ *(310) 257-1333*
2575 Pacific Coast Hwy ▪ *Pizza* ▪ GF menu
includes a variety of artisan thin crust and
woodfired pizzas, oak roasted chicken
breast, a grilled chicken wrap, grilled
shrimp salad, beet, walnut with goat cheese
salad, and more. ▪ *www.sammyspizza.com*

San Francisco Soup Company   ⊘ ¢L
Berkeley ▪ *(510) 848-7687*
2512 Bancroft Way
E Palo Alto ▪ *(650) 322-7687*
1950 University Ave
Oakland ▪ *(510) 763-7687*
1300 Clay St ▪ *Soup* ▪ Soups rotate daily.
Check the website for a given day's GF
offerings. Most locations also have GF options marked on the board. Some locations,
including those in airports, do not have GF
options marked on the board, but they will
have a chart of GF options upon request. ▪
www.sfsoupco.com

Satura Cakes   ★ ¢S
Campbell ▪ *(408) 370-2600*
199 E Campbell Ave
Los Altos ▪ *(650) 948-3300*
200 Main St
Palo Alto ▪ *(650) 326-3393*
320 University Ave ▪ *Bakery* ▪ GF chocolate cake is available by the slice at all
locations. Entire GF cakes are available
with advanced notice of at least two days. ▪
www.saturacakes.com

Savory Casual Fare   ★ $$$LD
Encinitas ▪ *(760) 634-5556*
267 N El Camino Real ▪ *Continental*
▪ General Manager John recommends
reservations noting GF. He adds that Chef
Pascal can "customize and create coursed

dinners" for GF diners. GF bread and pasta
are available. For dessert, they offer crème
brûlée and lemon pot de crème. ▪ *www.
savorycasualfare.com*

Scott's Seafood   ⊘ $$$$LD
Folsom ▪ *(916) 989-6711*
9611 Greenback Ln
Sacramento ▪ *(916) 379-5959*
4800 Riverside Blvd
Sacramento ▪ *(916) 489-1822*
545 Munroe St ▪ *Seafood* ▪ GF menu
includes shrimp and crab louies, prawn
skewers, cioppino, lobster tail, filet mignon
with prawns or crab legs, halibut, sesame-
crusted tuna, and more. ▪ *www.scottssea-
food.net*

Sensitive Baker, The   100% ¢S
Culver City ▪ *(310) 815-1800*
10836 1/2 Washington Blvd. ▪ *Bakery*
▪ Dedicated GF bakery offering bread,
bagels, muffins, cakes, cupcakes, cookies,
brownies, and more. ▪ *www.thesensitive-
baker.com*

Slice Pizzeria and Ristorante, The
★ $$LD
Rancho Mirage ▪ *(760) 202-3122*
72775 Dinah Shore Dr ▪ *Pizza* ▪ GF pasta is
available. ▪ *www.theslicepizza.com*

SmoQe BBQ   ★ $LD
Aptos ▪ *(831) 662-2227*
10110 Soquel Dr ▪ *Pizza* ▪ The 12-inch GF
pizza crust can be topped with any avail-
able ingredients. The signature BBQ sauce
is also GF. Manager Toni cautions that
nearly all items are "dusted" with flour due
to the large amounts used in the kitchen, so
cross-contamination is a concern. Alert a
server upon arrival. ▪ *www.smoqe.com*

Sojourner Café   ★ $LD
Santa Barbara ▪ *(805) 965-7922*
134 E Canon Perdido St ▪ *Healthy Ameri-
can* ▪ GF pasta and desserts are available.
Owner Donna reports that they are ac-
commodating GF diners "more and more."
She also notes that some menu items are
naturally GF, while others can be modi-

fied to be GF. Alert a server upon arrival. ▪ www.sojournercafe.com

Sorrento's Italian Restaurant and Pizza
★ $$**LD**

Walnut Creek ▪ **(925) 938-3366**
2064 Treat Blvd ▪ *Pizza* ▪ GF pizza is available. ▪ www.sorrentowalnutcreek.com

SpiritLand Bistro
✪★ $$$**D**

Santa Barbara ▪ **(805) 966-7759**
230 E Victoria St ▪ *Global* ▪ GF menu includes Indian vegetable curry, Japanese crusted halibut, and more. GF pasta and beer are available. GF desserts include lavender and wild flower honey crème brûlée, chocolate cake, and more. Manager Ken advises alerting a server upon arrival. ▪ www.spiritlandbistro.com

Spot, The
$**LD**

Hermosa Beach ▪ **(310) 376-2355**
110 2nd St ▪ *Modern Mexican* ▪ Manager Stacy reports that the staff is knowledgeable about the GF diet and that there are naturally GF menu items. GF diners can view the chef's cookbooks to scan the ingredients. Stacy recommends alerting the server, who will alert the kitchen. ▪ www.worldfamousspot.com

Sprinkles Cupcakes
★ ¢**S**

Beverly Hills ▪ **(310) 274-8765**
9635 Santa Monica Blvd
Newport Beach ▪ **(949) 760-0003**
944 Avocado Ave
Palo Alto ▪ **(650) 323-9300**
393 Stanford Shopping Ctr ▪ *Bakery* ▪ GF red velvet cupcakes are available every day. They are not visible on display, as they are kept behind the counter to avoid cross-contamination. ▪ www.sprinkles.com

Steve's Pizza
★ $**LD**

Davis ▪ **(530) 758-2800**
314 F St
El Dorado Hills ▪ **(916) 939-2100**
3941 Park Dr
Elk Grove ▪ **(916) 683-2200**
9135 W Stockton Blvd
Folsom ▪ **(916) 817-2466**

1016 Riley St
Rancho Cordova ▪ **(916) 851-0749**
3191 Zinfandel Dr
Roseville ▪ **(916) 787-4311**
5080 Foothills Blvd Ste 5
Sacramento ▪ **(916) 920-8600**
813 Howe Ave
Woodland ▪ **(530) 666-2100**
714 Main St ▪ *Pizza* ▪ GF pizza is available in different sizes, depending on the location. Some locations also carry GF brownies. ▪ www.stevespizza.com

StoneFire Grill
✪ $$**LD**

Chatsworth ▪ **(818) 534-3364**
9229 Winnetka Ave
Fountain Valley ▪ **(714) 968-8300**
18727 Brookhurst St
Irvine ▪ **(949) 777-1177**
3966 Barranca Pkwy
Valencia ▪ **(661) 799-8282**
23300 Cinema Dr
West Hills ▪ **(818) 887-4145**
6405 Fallbrook Ave ▪ *American* ▪ Limited GF menu includes "south of the border" salad, "cartwheel" salad, grilled vegetable salad, lemon garlic chicken, pepper garlic tri-tip, and sides. GF menu is a list of select regular menu items with descriptions of how to modify them to be GF. ▪ www.stonefiregrill.com

Storytellers Café
★ $$$**BLD**

Anaheim ▪ **(714) 635-2300**
1600 S Disneyland Dr ▪ *American* ▪ GF pasta, pizzas, and burger buns are available. Manager James reports that GF diners are "very common." He also notes that GF foods are kept in stock at all times. Alert the server, who will bring the chef out to discuss GF options. Reservations noting GF are recommended. Located in the Disneyland hotel.

Sun Power Natural Café
★ $**LD**

Studio City ▪ **(818) 308-7420**
3711 Cahuenga Blvd ▪ *Vegan* ▪ GF items include pizza, kelp noodles, GF buns for burgers, soups, and more. ▪ www.sunpowernatural.com

Sweet Addictions Bakery   ✪ ★ $$$
Montclair ▪ **(909) 624-4650**
4650 Arrow Hwy ▪ *Bakery* ▪ Non-dedi-cated bakery offering GF cakes, brownies, cookies, lemon bars, cream puffs, and more. Owner Annette reports that GF items are available by pre-order only, and there are minimum quantities for orders. She recommends calling at least two weeks in advance, but notes that she will always "squeeze people in" if she can. ▪ *www.sweet-addictions.biz*

Table Café   ¢LD
Larkspur ▪ **(415) 461-6787**
1167 Magnolia Ave ▪ *Global* ▪ GF dosas, a savory Indian pancake, are available. Owner Suzanne reports that dosas are naturally GF. There are ten to fifteen GF dosa fillings, such as salmon, scrambled eggs, curry spiced potatoes, and spinach. Suzanne also notes that all soups and salads are GF. Confirm timeliness of this informa-tion before dining in. Alert the server upon arrival. ▪ *www.table-cafe.com*

Tabu Grill $$$$D
Laguna Beach ▪ **(949) 494-7743**
2892 S Coast Hwy ▪ *Asian Fusion* ▪ Sous-chef Morberto reports that they can make a vegetable stir fry with black thai rice for GF diners. For dessert, they offer flourless chocolate cake. He notes that future menus will "definitely" offer more GF options, as they have been accommodating "a lot more" GF diners "lately." ▪ *www.tabugrill.com*

Three Degrees $$BD
Los Gatos ▪ **(408) 884-1054**
140 S Santa Cruz Ave ▪ *American Region-al* ▪ Restaurant reports that "most entrées are naturally GF." Possible GF items include horseradish crusted salmon, boneless short ribs, and seared ahi tuna. Confirm timeli-ness of this information before dining in. ▪ *www.threedegreesrestaurant.com*

Tillie Gort's Café   ★ $BLD
Pacific Grove ▪ **(831) 373-0335**

111 Central Ave ▪ *American* ▪ GF cakes are available. Sandwiches can be wrapped in corn tortillas. ▪ *www.tilliegortscafe.com*

Tra Vigne   ★ $$$LD
Saint Helena ▪ **(707) 963-4444**
1050 Charter Oak Ave ▪ *Italian* ▪ GF pasta is available with advanced notice of one week. Kitchen manager Jennifer notes that many entrées are naturally GF or can be modified to be GF. Upon arrival, alert the hostess, who will notify the server. The server will then go over GF options in detail. Reservations noting GF should be made at least a week before coming in. ▪ *www.travignerestaurant.com*

Truckee Pizza   ★ ¢L
Truckee ▪ **(530) 587-6300**
12047 Donner Pass Rd ▪ *Pizza* ▪ GF pizza is available in the medium size. ▪ *www.truckeepizzadelivery.com*

Uno Chicago Grill   📖
Antioch ▪ **(925) 522-8554**
4827 Lone Tree Way
Modesto ▪ **(209) 521-8667**
1533 Oakdale Rd

Veggie Grill, The   ✪ ★ ¢LD
El Segundo ▪ **(310) 535-0025**
720 S Allied Way
Irvine ▪ **(949) 509-0009**
4213 Campus Dr
Irvine ▪ **(949) 727-9900**
81 Fortune Dr ▪ *American* ▪ GF menu includes kale, a variety of soups and salads, plus chocolate pudding for dessert. GF pasta is available. Specific items on GF menu may vary by location. ▪ *www.veggiegrill.com*

Vic Stewarts $$$$D
Walnut Creek ▪ **(925) 943-5666**
850 S Broadway ▪ *Steakhouse* ▪ The restaurant reports that they accommodate GF diners "every once in a while." Alert the server, who will ensure that the kitchen is aware of GF requests. Reservations noting GF are recommended. ▪ *www.vicstewarts.com*

Vintage Tea Leaf ★ $$$L
Long Beach ▪ *(562) 435-5589*
969 E Broadway ▪ *Teahouse* ▪ GF scones
are available. ▪ *www.vintagetealeaf.com*

Wente Vineyards Restaurant $$$LD
Livermore ▪ *(925) 456-2450*
5050 Arroyo Rd ▪ *Modern American* ▪
Executive Chef Eric reports that they serve
their "fair share" of GF customers. He
recommends alerting the server, who will
speak to him. He notes that the restaurant
"happily accommodates" GF diners. ▪
www.wentevineyards.com

Willi's Seafood and Raw Bar ✪ $LD
Healdsburg ▪ *(707) 433-9191*
403 Healdsburg Ave ▪ *Seafood* ▪ GF
menu includes ceviches, chicken skewers,
an arugula salad, tuna rolls, melted fondue,
pan roasted shrimp, and more. ▪ *www.
willisseafood.net*

Willi's Wine Bar ✪ $$LD
Santa Rosa ▪ *(707) 526-3096*
4404 Old Redwood Hwy ▪ *American
Regional* ▪ GF menu is the regular menu
notated with GF modifications for each
dish. GF menu includes oysters on the half
shell, tuna tartare, asparagus, calamari
salad, rabbit, pulled duck with polenta, and
lamb chops.

Willow Street Wood-Fired Pizza
✪★ $LD
Los Gatos ▪ *(408) 354-5566*
20 S Santa Cruz Ave
San Jose ▪ *(408) 971-7080*
1072 Willow St
San Jose ▪ *(408) 871-0400*
1554 Saratoga Ave ▪ *Pizza* ▪ Limited GF
menu includes four specialty pizzas and
several GF rice pasta dishes. ▪ *www.wil-
lowstreet.com*

Wilson Creek Winery ✪★ $$$L
Temecula ▪ *(951) 699-9463*
35960 Rancho California Rd ▪ *Fusion* ▪
Limited GF menu includes ratatouille vegetable, cornish hen, Argentine steak, and a
pork porterhouse, among a few salads. GF

beer is available. ▪ *www.wilsoncreekwinery.
com*

Wolfgang Puck's Chinois $$$$LD
Santa Monica ▪ *(310) 392-9025*
2709 Main St ▪ *Chinese Fusion* ▪ Manager
Natalia reports that they can accommodate
GF diners, but it is not something they do
frequently. Alert server, who will consult
with the chef. Reservations noting GF are
strongly recommended. ▪ *www.wolfgang-
puck.com*

Yard House 📖
Brea ▪ *(714) 529-9273*
160 S Brea Blvd
Chino Hills ▪ *(909) 631-2200*
13881 Peyton Dr
Costa Mesa ▪ *(949) 642-0090*
1875 Newport Blvd
Irvine ▪ *(949) 753-9373*
71 Fortune Dr
Long Beach ▪ *(562) 628-0455*
401 Shoreline Village Dr
Newport Beach ▪ *(949) 640-9273*
849 Newport Center Dr
Pasadena ▪ *(626) 577-9273*
330 E Colorado Blvd Ste 230
Rancho Cucamonga ▪ *(909) 646-7116*
12473 N Mainstreet
Rancho Mirage ▪ *(760) 779-1415*
71800 Highway 111
Riverside ▪ *(951) 688-9273*
3775 Tyler St Ste 1A
Temecula ▪ *(951) 296-3116*
40770 Winchester Rd Ste 750

Z Pizza ★ $LD
Aliso Viejo ▪ *(949) 425-0102*
26921 Aliso Creek Rd
Chino Hills ▪ *(909) 631-2224*
3090 Chino Ave
Danville ▪ *(925) 362-4010*
95 Railroad Ave
Fountain Valley ▪ *(714) 444-4260*
18011 Newhope St
Fremont ▪ *(510) 360-9900*
46703 Mission Blvd
Fullerton ▪ *(714) 738-4249*
1981 Sunnycrest Dr # 200

Glendora ▪ *(909) 599-4500*
1365 E Gladstone St
Huntington Beach ▪ *(714) 968-8844*
10035 Adams Ave
Huntington Beach ▪ *(714) 536-3444*
19035 Goldenwest St
La Quinta ▪ *(760) 564-4330*
79024 Highway 111
Ladera Ranch ▪ *(949) 347-8999*
25672 Crown Valley Pkwy
Laguna Beach ▪ *(949) 499-4949*
30902 Coast Hwy
Laguna Niguel ▪ *(949) 481-3948*
32371 Golden Lantern
Long Beach ▪ *(562) 987-4500*
4612 E 2nd St
Newport Beach ▪ *(949) 219-9939*
1616 San Miguel Dr
Newport Beach ▪ *(949) 760-3100*
2549 Eastbluff Dr
Newport Beach ▪ *(949) 723-0707*
3423 Via Lido
Newport Beach ▪ *(949) 715-1117*
7956 E Coast Hwy
Porter Ranch ▪ *(818) 363-2600*
19300 Rinaldi St
Roseville ▪ *(916) 786-9797*
3984 Douglas Blvd
San Juan Capistrano ▪ *(949) 429-8888*
32341 Camino Capistrano
San Pedro ▪ *(310) 831-3728*
28152 S Western Ave
San Ramon ▪ *(925) 328-0525*
3141 Crow Canyon Pl Ste D
Seal Beach ▪ *(562) 493-3440*
12430 Seal Beach Blvd
Seal Beach ▪ *(562) 596-9300*
148 Main St
Upland ▪ *(909) 949-1939*
1943 N Campus Ave Ste C
W Hollywood ▪ *(310) 360-1414*
8869 Santa Monica Blvd
Westlake Village ▪ *(818) 991-4999*
5776 Lindero Canyon Rd
Woodland Hills ▪ *(818) 887-3555*
20040 1/2 Ventura Blvd ▪ *Pizza* ▪ GF pizza
is available. ▪ *www.zpizza.com*

Z'Tejas Southwestern Grill   ✪★ $**LD**
Costa Mesa ▪ *(714) 979-7469*
3333 Bristol St ▪ *Southwest* ▪ One-page
GF menu includes wild mushroom enchiladas and grilled salmon, along with smoked
chicken and black bean salad. Frozen
margaritas and GF beer are also available. ▪
www.ztejas.com

COLORADO

BOULDER

14th Street Bar & Grill   ★ $**LD**
Boulder ▪ *(303) 444-5854*
1400 Pearl St ▪ *Modern American* ▪
Manager Conrad reports that they serve
GF diners "on a daily basis." He notes that
all staff members are aware of naturally
GF menu items, as well as which menu
items can be modified to be GF. For dessert, they offer GF pumpkin bread with
a balsamic drizzle. Confirm timeliness
of this information before dining in. ▪
www.14thstreetboulder.com

Abo's Pizza   ★ $**LD**
Boulder ▪ *(303) 443-1740*
1035 Pearl St
Boulder ▪ *(303) 443-3199*
1110 13Th St
Boulder ▪ *(303) 494-1274*
637 S Broadway St ▪ *Pizza* ▪ GF pizza is
available only at the locations listed. Sizes
and toppings vary by location. ▪ *www.
abospizza.com*

Aji   ✪ $$$**LD**
Boulder ▪ *(303) 442-3464*
1601 Pearl St ▪ *Latin American* ▪ Bartender
Norman explains that the GF menu is a list
of menu items that can be modified to be
GF. Examples are the camarones y chorizo
and the enchiladas with corn tortillas.
Alert a server, who will guide the GF meal

throughout its preparation. ▪ *www.ajires-taurant.com*

Amante Coffee   ★ ⊄S
Boulder ▪ *(303) 546-9999*
1035 Walnut St
Boulder ▪ *(303) 448-9999*
4580 Broadway St ▪ *Coffee Shop* ▪ GF baked goods are available. Options include pumpkin bread, cinnamon coffee cake, and chocolate zucchini bread. ▪ *www.amante-coffee.com*

Black Cat Restaurant $$$D
Boulder ▪ *(303) 444-5500*
1964 13th St ▪ *Organic* ▪ Manager John reports that all staff members are "absolutely" trained on the GF diet. He notes that most of the menu is naturally GF, and that they accommodate GF diners "every night." Alert a server, who will know which menu items are GF. ▪ *www.blackcatboulder.com*

Brasserie Ten Ten   ✪ $LD
Boulder ▪ *(303) 998-1010*
1011 Walnut St ▪ *French* ▪ GF options marked on the menu include the duck confit, hunter style pulled chicken, and milk roasted cauliflower risotto. The server will know whether the item is naturally GF or substitutions must be made. ▪ *www.brasserietenten.com*

Brewing Market   ★ ⊄S
Boulder ▪ *(303) 443-2098*
1918 13Th St
Boulder ▪ *(303) 444-4858*
2525 Arapahoe Ave
Boulder ▪ *(303) 499-1345*
2610 Baseline Rd ▪ *Coffee Shop* ▪ GF baked goods are available. Specific products vary by location, but they generally offer cookies and several different types of bread.

Buchanan's Coffee Pub   ★ ⊄S
Boulder ▪ *(303) 440-0222*
1301 Pennsylvania Ave ▪ *Coffee & Café* ▪ GF pumpkin bread and coffee cakes are available.

Caffé Sole   ★ ⊄S
Boulder ▪ *(303) 499-2985*
637 S Broadway St ▪ *Coffee Shop* ▪ GF cakes and boba bars are available. They offer cake in strudel, chocolate, and pumpkin flavors. ▪ *www.caffesole.com*

Cantina Laredo   📖
Boulder ▪ *(303) 444-2260*
1680 29th St

Carelli's Ristorante Italiano   ✪★ $$LD
Boulder ▪ *(303) 938-9300*
645 30th St ▪ *Italian* ▪ GF bread, pasta, and pizza are available. Other GF menu items include ravioli, steak vesuvio, and seared sea scallops, among other things. ▪ *www.carellis.com*

Casa Alvarez   ✪ $LD
Boulder ▪ *(303) 546-0630*
3161 Walnut St ▪ *Mexican* ▪ GF menu includes garlic mussels and chorizo bean or guacamole dip as appetizers, as well as all of the chilis and many of the enchiladas. ▪ *www.casaalvarezcolorado.com*

Centro Latin Kitchen & Refreshment Palace $LD
Boulder ▪ *(303) 442-7771*
950 Pearl St ▪ *Latin American* ▪ Manager Erin reports that GF diners are welcome and that most menu items are naturally GF. She also notes that the restaurant is planning to have a full GF menu very soon. For now, the GF options include enchiladas, fish, and corn chips. ▪ *www.centrolatinkitchen.com*

Dagabi Cucina   ★ $$D
Boulder ▪ *(303) 786-9004*
3970 Broadway St ▪ *Spanish* ▪ GF pizza and pasta are available. ▪ *www.dagabicucina.com*

Folsom Street Coffee Co.   ★ ⊄S
Boulder ▪ *(303) 440-8808*
1795 Folsom St ▪ *Coffee & Café* ▪ GF specialty items are available, but the options change often. Examples of what may be in stock are chocolate zucchini bread and

cinnamon coffee cake. ▪ www.folsomstreet-coffee.com

Gondolier on Pearl   ✪★ $LD
Boulder ▪ *(303) 443-5015*
1600 Pearl St ▪ *Italian* ▪ GF pasta is available, as are 9-inch GF pizza crusts. Other GF menu items include baked artichoke dip, cream of tomato gorgonzola, chicken or eggplant parmigiana, and more. For dessert, they offer crème brûlée. ▪ www.gondolieronpearl.com

Jax Fish House $$$D
Boulder ▪ *(303) 444-1811*
928 Pearl St ▪ *Seafood* ▪ Restaurant reports that they serve GF diners very frequently, and that everything on the menu is naturally GF or can be made GF. Alert a server upon arrival, as all staff members are trained on the GF diet. ▪ www.jaxfishhouse-boulder.com

Kitchen, The   ★ $$$LD
Boulder ▪ *(303) 544-5973*
1039 Pearl St ▪ *Global* ▪ GF bread is available for sandwiches. Restaurant reports that there are "always several options" for GF diners. They add that they take dietary restrictions seriously and always try to accommodate them. Many any items are naturally GF, and other items can be modified to be GF. ▪ www.thekitchencafe.com

Laudisio Restaurant   ✪★ $$$LD
Boulder ▪ *(303) 442-1300*
1710 29th St Unit 1076 ▪ *Italian* ▪ GF breadsticks, pasta, and beer are available. Manager Tom reports that "10% of customers" are GF. GF menu items include risottos, polenta, pasta with clams and mussels, and pan-roasted pork loin. Tom also notes that they have several protocols to ensure that GF meals are prepared properly. ▪ www.laudisio.com

Leaf Vegetarian Restaurant   ✪★ $LD
Boulder ▪ *(303) 442-1486*
2010 16th St ▪ *Vegetarian* ▪ GF menu includes Jamaican jerk tempeh, raw pasta made with zucchini, and pumpkin curry,

among other things. GF bread is available. For dessert, they offer GF chocolate cake. ▪ www.leafvegetarianrestaurant.com

Logans Espresso Café   ★ ¢S
Boulder ▪ *(303) 443-3600*
3980 Broadway St ▪ *Coffee Shop* ▪ GF pumpkin bread, chocolate zucchini bread, and coffee cake available. The restaurant notes that GF items are sold on a first come, first served basis.

Mad Greens Inspired Eats   ¢L
Boulder ▪ *(720) 496-4157*
1805 29th St ▪ *Sandwich & Soups* ▪ Restaurant reports that there is a large selection of GF salad dressings, including many vinaigrettes like raspberry mint and balsamic, creamy ginger dressing, and lowfat honey mustard. Confirm timeliness of this information before dining in. Restaurant advises building a salad and then asking a staff member to indicate the GF dressings. ▪ www.madgreens.com

Mediterranean, The   ✪ $LD
Boulder ▪ *(303) 444-5335*
1002 Walnut St ▪ *Mediterranean* ▪ GF items marked on the menu include risotto cappesente, pan roasted salmon, and lamb shank. The server will indicate whether the item is naturally GF or whether substitutions must be made. ▪ www.themedboulder.com

O! Pizza   ★ $$LD
Boulder ▪ *(303) 444-9100*
3980 Broadway St ▪ *Pizza* ▪ GF pizza is available in the 12-inch size and can be made with any toppings. The restaurant has limited seating; most orders are prepared for take-out or delivery. ▪ www.o-pizza.com

Organic Dish, The   ✪★ ¢LD
Boulder ▪ *(303) 736-9930*
2690 28th St ▪ *Take-&-Bake* ▪ "Do-it-yourself" style meals consist of prepared foods that must be cooked at home. GF menu changes monthly, but examples of GF options include turkey kielbasa with lentils and tofu with mushrooms and peas

over egg noodles. The GF menu specifies whether an item is naturally GF or must be modified to be GF. GF pasta is available. ▪ *www.theorganicdish.com*

Original Pancake House, The   ★ ¢BL
Boulder ▪ **(303) 449-1575**
2600 Canyon Blvd ▪ *Breakfast* ▪ GF pancakes are available. Other GF options may be available. Call to inquire. ▪ *www. originalpancakehouse.com*

Ozo Coffee Company   ★ ¢S
Boulder ▪ **(303) 440-0233**
5240 Arapahoe Ave ▪ *Coffee & Café* ▪ GF bread and stuffed pockets are available. Bread flavors include pumpkin, lemon poppyseed, and chocolate zucchini. Stuffed pocket varieties include breakfast, florentine, pizza, and curry. ▪ *www.ozocoffee.com*

Page Two   ★ ¢S
Boulder ▪ **(303) 530-3339**
6565 Gunpark Dr ▪ *Coffee & Café* ▪ GF breads, including pumpkin, lemon poppyseed, and chocolate zucchini, are available. GF "breeze bars" are sometimes available as well.

Pei Wei Asian Diner   📖
Boulder ▪ **(720) 479-5570**
1675 29th St Unit 1284

Pekoe Sip House   ★ ¢S
Boulder ▪ **(303) 444-4535**
1125 18th St
Boulder ▪ **(303) 444-5953**
1225 Alpine Ave
Boulder ▪ **(303) 444-4207**
2500 30th St ▪ *Tea Café* ▪ GF bread, cookies, and muffins are available. General Manager Stacie of the Alpine Ave location reports that they have a selection of GF pastries available at each store. ▪ *www. pekoesiphouse.com*

Radda Trattoria   ★ $LD
Boulder ▪ **(303) 442-6100**
1265 Alpine Ave ▪ *Italian* ▪ GF pizza is available. Manager Dan reports that plenty of protein-based dishes can be modified to

be GF. Confirm timeliness of this information before dining in. Alert a server, who will punch in a note to notify the kitchen. ▪ *www.raddatrattoria.com*

Salt Bistro $$$LD
Boulder ▪ **(303) 444-7258**
1047 Pearl St ▪ *Modern American* ▪ Restaurant reports that GF diners can "certainly" be accommodated. They note that several menu items are naturally GF, and the kitchen is very flexible when it comes to modifying dishes for dietary requests. Alert a server, who will discuss GF options in detail. ▪ *www.saltboulderbistro.com*

Saxy's Café   ★ ¢S
Boulder ▪ **(303) 786-8585**
2018 10th St ▪ *Café* ▪ GF pumpkin bread is available. The café also notes that all salads, including the goat cheese apple salad, the prosciutto salad, and the tuna salad, are naturally GF. Confirm timeliness of this information before dining in. ▪ *www. saxyscafe.com*

Sink, The   ★ ¢LD
Boulder ▪ **(303) 444-7465**
1165 13Th St ▪ *American* ▪ Owner Mark reports that they have a "special awareness" of the GF diet because one of the owners and several staff members are GF. He notes that any items with bread or crust, like sandwiches, burgers, and pizza, can be prepared using a GF bread substitution. GF beer is available. ▪ *www.thesink.com*

Sushi Tora   ★ ¢LD
Boulder ▪ **(303) 444-2280**
2014 10th St ▪ *Sushi* ▪ Manager Jake reports that they have a guide to show which menu items are GF or can be made GF. He estimates that "one-third" of the menu items, like the broiled hamachi and the sake leaf marinated cod, are available to GF diners. GF tamari sauce is available. ▪ *www. sushitora.net*

Taj Indian Cuisine $LD
Boulder ▪ **(303) 494-5216**
2630 Baseline Rd ▪ *Indian* ▪ Owner Ka-

mala asks that GF diners speak to her upon arrival. She adds that she knows "exactly" what GF means and can indicate menu items that are GF or can be made GF. She notes that they are educated in cross contamination and careful to avoid it. ▪ *www.tajcolorado.com*

Tokyo Joe's   📖
Boulder ▪ *(303) 443-1555*
2525 Arapahoe Ave

Trident Booksellers and Café   ★ ¢S
Boulder ▪ *(303) 443-3133*
940 Pearl St ▪ *Coffee Shop* ▪ GF breads, including pumpkin bread and chocolate zucchini bread, are available. They sometimes have GF mini-meal bars as well. The coffee shop is also a book shop, and they show independent films outdoors on summer evenings. ▪ *www.tridentcafe.com*

VG Burgers   ★ ¢LD
Boulder ▪ *(303) 440-2400*
1650 Broadway St ▪ *Vegetarian* ▪ GF burger options include the veggie burger and the black bean burger. CEO Tim reports that GF bread, hamburger buns, and pasta are available. ▪ *www.vgburgers.com*

Vic's Again   ★ ¢S
Boulder ▪ *(303) 440-2918*
3305 30th St ▪ *Coffee Shop* ▪ GF granola bars and breads are available. The restaurant recommends calling ahead for GF bread, as it occasionally sells out.

Zolo Grill $$LD
Boulder ▪ *(303) 449-0444*
2525 Arapahoe Ave ▪ *Modern Mexican* ▪ Manager Liz reports that most menu items are GF. She notes that although they discontinued their gluten-free menu because of liability issues, they still have many GF ingredients. Liz notes that the servers are "very well-versed" in GF dining. ▪ *www.zologrill.com*

COLORADO

COLORADO SPRINGS

Biaggi's Ristorante Italiano   📖
Colorado Springs ▪ *(719) 262-9500*
1805 Briargate Pkwy

Borriello Brothers Pizza   ★ $$LD
Colorado Springs ▪ *(719) 884-2020*
215 E Platte Ave
Colorado Springs ▪ *(719) 884-2020*
229 S 8th St
Colorado Springs ▪ *(719) 884-2020*
3240 Centennial Blvd
Colorado Springs ▪ *(719) 884-2020*
4750 Barnes Rd
Colorado Springs ▪ *(719) 884-2020*
5490 Powers Center Pt ▪ *Pizza* ▪ GF pizza is available. ▪ *www.borriellobrothers.com*

Carino's Italian   📖
Colorado Springs ▪ *(719) 622-8041*
3015 New Center Pt

Carrabba's Italian Grill   📖
Colorado Springs ▪ *(719) 527-1126*
2815 Geyser Dr
Colorado Springs ▪ *(719) 264-0401*
7120 Campus Dr

Extreme Pizza   ★ $$LD
Colorado Springs ▪ *(719) 522-1515*
7340 N Academy Blvd ▪ *Pizza* ▪ GF pizza is available. ▪ *www.extremepizza.com*

Garlic Jim's   ★ $$LD
Colorado Springs ▪ *(719) 591-5467*
3735 Bloomington St ▪ *Pizza* ▪ GF pizza is available. The restaurant reports that Garlic Jim's Hot wings, ribs, gourmet cheesecake, and certain flavors of Haagen-Dazs ice cream are also GF. ▪ *www.garlicjims.com*

Gertrude's Restaurant   ★ $$$BLD
Colorado Springs ▪ *(719) 471-0887*
2625 W Colorado Ave ▪ *American* ▪ GF rice pasta is available. All salads are GF, as are the hummus antipasto and other

dishes. Ask the server to indicate GF menu items. ▪ *www.gertrudesrestaurant.com*

Great Harvest Bread Company   ★ ₵S
Colorado Springs ▪ *(719) 528-6442*
12229 Voyager Pkwy
Colorado Springs ▪ *(719) 635-7379*
1466 Garden Of The Gods Rd Ste 148 ▪
Bakery ▪ At the Colorado Springs locations, GF breads, cake bread, muffins, scones, and cookies are available on Tuesdays and Fridays only. Both locations noted that GF items sell out very quickly, but they are able to reserve items for GF diners who call ahead.

Jose Muldoons   ✪ ₵LD
Colorado Springs ▪ *(719) 636-2311*
222 N Tejon St ▪ *Mexican* ▪ GF menu includes appetizers like chili con queso and nachos, as well as entrées like tostadas and fajitas. There are also a variety of GF sides. ▪ *www.josemuldoons.com*

Melting Pot, The   📖
Colorado Springs ▪ *(719) 385-0300*
30 E Pikes Peak Ave Ste A

Outback Steakhouse   📖
Colorado Springs ▪ *(719) 527-8745*
2825 Geyser Dr
Colorado Springs ▪ *(719) 638-7650*
2895 New Center Pt
Colorado Springs ▪ *(719) 590-6283*
7065 Commerce Center Dr

Outside the Breadbox   100%★ ₵S
Colorado Springs ▪ *(719) 633-3434*
2027 W Colorado Ave ▪ *Bakery* ▪ Dedicated GF bakery offering breads, crackers, bagels, cookies, muffins, pizza crust, and cakes. GF items are baked on site every day. The bakery recommends calling 48 hours in advance for special orders. ▪ *www.outsidethebreadbox.com*

P.F. Chang's China Bistro   📖
Colorado Springs ▪ *(719) 593-8580*
1725 Briargate Pkwy

Pei Wei Asian Diner   📖
Colorado Springs ▪ *(719) 260-9922*
7148 N Academy Blvd

Sonterra Southwest Grill   ✪ $$$LD
Colorado Springs ▪ *(719) 471-9222*
28 S Tejon St ▪ *Southwest* ▪ They have extensive GF menus for lunch and dinner. GF menus include prime rib, pork chops, spinach enchiladas, sea bass, housemade flan, and bananas foster. ▪ *www.restauranteur.com/sonterragrillcom*

Wild Ginger Thai Restaurant   ★ $$LD
Colorado Springs ▪ *(719) 634-5025*
3020 W Colorado Ave ▪ *Thai* ▪ Owner Khon reports that almost the entire menu is naturally GF, as they do not use soy sauce in their cooking. She also notes that they accommodate GF diners "daily," so all staff members are familiar with the GF diet. GF rice noodles are available. ▪ *www.wildgingerthai.com*

Zio's   ✪ $LD
Colorado Springs ▪ *(719) 593-9999*
6650 Corporate Dr ▪ *Italian* ▪ GF menu includes salmon caesar salad, chicken piccata, Greek pasta, lemon chicken primavera, shrimp with marinara, ribeye tuscano, grilled sirloin, and more. ▪ *www.zios.com*

COLORADO

DENVER

Abo's Pizza   ★ $LD
Denver ▪ *(303) 722-3434*
303 S Downing St ▪ *Pizza* ▪ GF pizza is available only at the locations listed. Sizes and toppings vary by location. ▪ *www.abospizza.com*

Abrusci's Italiano Ristorante   ✪★ $LD
Denver ▪ *(303) 462-0513*
300 Fillmore St ▪ *Italian* ▪ There are sepa-

rate GF menus for lunch and dinner. Both are extensive, and both include a variety of pastas and entrées. GF bread, pasta, and beer are available. GF pizza is available at the Wheat Ridge location only. The Wheat Ridge location also has a dedicated fryer for GF items. ▪ *www.abruscis.com*

Avenue Grill ✪★ $$$LD
Denver ▪ (303) 861-2820
630 E 17th Ave ▪ *American* ▪ GF menu includes the Avenue burger, the grilled mahi sandwich, and several other items. GF bread is available. ▪ *www.avenuegrill.com*

Beau Jo's Colorado Style Pizza ✪★ $LD
Denver ▪ (303) 758-1519
2710 S Colorado Blvd ▪ *Pizza* ▪ GF pizza is available at all locations. All locations except Steamboat Springs also carry a GF menu that includes the salad bar, sandwiches, appetizers, and GF beer. Call a specific location for details on its GF offerings. ▪ *www.beaujos.com*

Bistro Vendome $$D
Denver ▪ (303) 825-3232
1420 Larimer St ▪ *French Bistro* ▪ Manager Stacy reports that "plenty of dishes" can be modified to be GF. She notes that the chef trains all servers so that they are able to discuss options with GF diners. Alert a server upon arrival. ▪ *www.bistrovendome.com*

Blue Bonnet Mexican Café ✪ ¢LD
Denver ▪ (303) 778-0147
457 S Broadway ▪ *Mexican* ▪ GF menu items include tacos, chimichangas, enchiladas, tamales, and more. All are prepared with white corn tortillas. For dessert, they offer homemade flan and coconut custard. President Gary asks that guests pay careful attention to the GF menu, where all necessary substitutions and instructions are printed. ▪ *www.bluebonnetrestaurant.com*

Bubba Gump Shrimp Co. 📖
Denver ▪ (303) 623-4867
1437 California St

Café Colore ★ ¢LD
Denver ▪ (303) 534-6844
1512 Larimer St ▪ *Italian* ▪ GF pasta and pizza are available. Located in Writer Square. ▪ *www.cafecoloredenver.com*

Capital Grille, The 📖
Denver ▪ (303) 539-2500
1450 Larimer St

City, O' City ★ ¢BLD
Denver ▪ (303) 831-6443
206 E 13th Ave ▪ *Vegetarian* ▪ GF flatbread, pizza, and beer are available. GF desserts change every day, but Manager Sarah confirms that they are always available. Examples include cakes, cupcakes, muffins, and the restaurant's unique scout cookies. ▪ *www.cityocitydenver.com*

Deby's Gluten Free Bakery & Café
100% ¢BLD
Denver ▪ (303) 283-4060
2369 S Trenton Way ▪ *Bakery* ▪ Dedicated GF facility offering over 200 different types of baked goods and "take-&-bake" style meals. Items include chicken pot pie, ravioli, cinnamon rolls, and a variety of breads and muffins. They also offer soups, pizza pockets, chicken nuggets, mini pizzas, bagels, biscuits, pies, cupcakes, and more. Products are available at the storefront or from several retailers around Colorado and beyond. Bakery reports that they will soon begin selling products online as well. ▪ *www.debysglutenfree.com*

Earls $LD
Denver ▪ (303) 595-3275
1600 Glenarm Pl
Denver ▪ (303) 320-3275
201 Columbine St ▪ *Global* ▪ Manager Holly of the Glenarm Place location and Manager Cara of the Columbine Street location report that they serve GF diners "a lot." They note that all meals labeled with an "allergy" are prepared and cooked separately from other foods. Alert a server upon arrival. ▪ *www.earls.ca*

East Side Kosher Deli   ★ $$**BLD**
Denver ▪ *(303) 322-9862*
499 S Elm St ▪ *Deli* ▪ GF bread, pasta,
hamburger buns, and cookies are available.
Owner Marcy reports that they frequently
serve GF diners. Ask for her upon arrival
so she can help you choose an appropriate
dish. GF availability increases during the
Passover season. ▪ *www.eastsidekosherdeli.
com*

Einstein Bros Bagels   ★ ¢**BLD**
Denver ▪ *(303) 639-9717*
2730 S Colorado Blvd ▪ *Sandwich Shop* ▪
GF bagels are available at listed locations
only. ▪ *www.einsteinbros.com*

Extreme Pizza   ★ $$**LD**
Denver ▪ *(303) 398-2500*
250 Steele Street @ 3rd Street ▪ *Pizza* ▪
GF pizza is available. ▪ *www.extremepizza.
com*

Fogo de Chao   ★ $$$$**LD**
Denver ▪ *(303) 623-9600*
1513 Wynkoop St ▪ *Brazilian* ▪ GF cheesebread made with yucca flour is available. ▪
www.fogodechao.com

Fresh Fish Company $$$**LD**
Denver ▪ *(303) 740-9556*
7800 E Hampden Ave ▪ *Seafood* ▪ Manager Sina reports that the chef has put
together a list of non-GF items. This list is
available upon request. Sina notes that all
unlisted items, including the majority of
the fish entrées, are GF. Confirm timeliness of this information before dining in. ▪
www.thefreshfishco.com

Gaia Bistro + Rustic Bakery   ★ ¢**BL**
Denver ▪ *(303) 777-5699*
1551 S Pearl St ▪ *Café* ▪ GF buckwheat
crepes are available. Chef Dacon reports
that "every one of the servers" is educated
on the GF diet, as they serve "quite a few"
GF diners every day. ▪ *www.gaiabistro.com*

Great Harvest Bread Company   ★ ¢**S**
Denver ▪ *(303) 778-8877*
765 S Colorado Blvd ▪ *Bakery* ▪ GF bread

is baked on Wednesdays and available for
sale by Wednesday afternoon each week.
Saturday through Tuesday, GF bread is
available for sale from the freezer. GF
popcorn bars are also available. ▪ *www.
wholegrainheadquarters.com*

Hacienda Colorado   ✪ $$**LD**
Denver ▪ *(303) 756-5700*
4100 E Mexico Ave ▪ *Mexican* ▪ GF menu
includes a selection of enchiladas, tacos,
tostadas, fajitas, and more. For dessert,
they offer cinnamon ice cream. The have
classified their cuisine as "mountain mex,"
or Rocky Mountain Mexican. ▪ *www.haci-
endacolorado.com*

Highland's Garden Cafè   ★ $$$**LD**
Denver ▪ *(303) 458-5920*
3927 W 32nd Ave ▪ *Modern American*
▪ Chef Pat Perry reports that GF bread
and GF pasta are available. She says the
restaurant is making a big effort to offer
GF items, and they are training servers to
guide GF guests through the menu. Alert
a server upon arrival. GF desserts include
pot de crème and crème caramel. ▪ *www.
highlandsgardencafe.com*

India House Restaurant   ✪ $**LD**
Denver ▪ *(303) 595-0680*
1514 Blake St ▪ *Indian* ▪ Owner Ghugi
reports that all of the regular entrées are
naturally GF. Confirm timeliness of this
information before dining in. Ghugi recommends alerting the server upon arrival.
For dessert, they have rice pudding and GF
carrot pudding. ▪ *www.indiahouse.us*

Jax Fish House $$$**D**
Denver ▪ *(303) 292-5767*
1539 17th St ▪ *Seafood* ▪ General Manager
Adam reports that they serve GF diners
"every day" and that everything on the
menu is naturally GF or can be made GF.
Alert a server upon arrival. Adam adds that
all staff members are trained on the GF
diet. ▪ *www.jaxfishhousedenver.com*

Kona Grill   📖
Denver ▪ *(720) 974-1300*
3000 E 1st Ave

La Sandia $$**LD**
Denver ▪ *(303) 373-9100*
8340 Northfield Blvd ▪ *Modern Mexican* ▪
Host Vanessa reports that "almost every-
thing" is naturally GF. She adds that the
servers are "very familiar" with the GF diet,
and any server will be able to indicate GF
items or necessary substitutions. ▪ *www.
modernmexican.com*

Lala's Wine Bar & Pizzeria   ✪ $**LD**
Denver ▪ *(303) 861-9463*
410 E 7th Ave ▪ *Italian* ▪ Extensive GF
menu includes caprese salad, sandwiches
on GF flatbreads, pizza, eggplant parma,
and more. Manager Erin is GF and wrote
the GF menu with help from the head chef.
▪ *www.lalaswinebar.com*

Ling & Louie's Asian Bar & Grill
✪★ $**LD**
Denver ▪ *(303) 623-5464*
1201 16th St
Denver ▪ *(303) 371-4644*
8354 Northfield Blvd ▪ *Asian* ▪ Extensive
GF menu includes chicken and seafood, as
well as "not-so-sizzling" platters. Examples
include sweet and sour chicken, salmon,
and edamame. For dessert, there is a
chocolate volcano cake. GF beer is avail-
able. ▪ *www.lingandlouies.com*

Lola $$$**D**
Denver ▪ *(720) 570-8686*
1575 Boulder St ▪ *Modern Mexican* ▪ Assistant General Manager Patrick reports that
they will "modify any dish" to serve a GF
diner. He notes that over half the menu can
be prepared GF, and since all staff members are trained in the GF diet, the server
can indicate which items are naturally GF
and which require modifications. ▪ *www.
loladenver.com*

Mad Greens Inspired Eats   ¢**L**
Denver ▪ *(720) 496-4158*
1200 Acoma St

Denver ▪ *(720) 468-4173*
1600 Stout St
Denver ▪ *(303) 333-1842*
222 Columbine St ▪ *Sandwich & Soups*
▪ Catering Director Laura of the Stout
St location reports that there is a large
selection of GF salad dressings, including
vinaigrettes like raspberry mint and balsamic, creamy ginger dressing, and lowfat
honey mustard. Confirm timeliness of this
information before dining in. Laura advises
building a salad and then asking a staff
member to indicate the GF dressings. Triumph confirmed that all locations have the
same GF options. ▪ *www.madgreens.com*

Maggiano's Little Italy   ★ $$$**LD**
Denver ▪ *(303) 260-7707*
500 16th St Ste 150 ▪ *Italian* ▪ GF pasta is
available. Call individual locations to in-
quire about additional GF options. ▪ *www.
maggianos.com*

Mercury Café   ★ $$**D**
Denver ▪ *(303) 294-9258*
2199 California St ▪ *Organic* ▪ Manager Georgia reports that they serve GF
pancakes for breakfast on weekends only,
but GF meals can be prepared at any time.
For dessert, they offer GF chocolate cake.
Alert a server upon arrival. All servers are
educated about the GF diet. ▪ *www.mercu-
rycafe.com*

Ninth Door, The   ✪ $**D**
Denver ▪ *(303) 292-2229*
1808 Blake St ▪ *Spanish Tapas* ▪ GF items
marked on the menu include a grilled
shrimp and avocado salad, seared sea scallops with truffled mushroom compote, and
a mixed cheese plate, among other things.
Manager Joanne recommends alerting the
server upon arrival even if ordering from
the items marked as GF. ▪ *www.theninth-
door.com*

Old Spaghetti Factory, The   📖
Denver ▪ *(303) 295-1864*
1215 18th St

Outback Steakhouse
Denver ▪ *(303) 576-6633*
16301 E 40th Ave

P.F. Chang's China Bistro
Denver ▪ *(303) 260-7222*
1415 15th St

Panzano
⊘★ $$$**BLD**
Denver ▪ *(303) 296-3525*
909 17th St ▪ *Italian* ▪ There are separate GF menus for lunch and dinner. GF bread, muffins, and beer are available. Manager Jason adds that they make GF desserts every day, and can make special GF cakes with advanced notice. ▪ *www.panzano-denver.com*

Pei Wei Asian Diner
Denver ▪ *(720) 532-5999*
200 Quebec St Bldg 100 Ste 115
Denver ▪ *(303) 942-3445*
3970 Buchtel Blvd Ste 107

Piatti Locali
★ $$**LD**
Denver ▪ *(303) 321-1919*
190 Saint Paul St ▪ *Italian* ▪ GF pasta is available. Manager Tina reports that staff is trained on GF preparation and GF diners are accommodated "all the time." She notes that the risotto is GF and that many menu items can be modified to be GF. ▪ *www.piatti.com*

Rodizio Grill
★ $$$**LD**
Denver ▪ *(303) 294-9277*
1801 Wynkoop St ▪ *Brazilian Steakhouse* ▪ GF cheese bread is available. Manager Adam reports that most menu items are GF. He notes that there is an internal list of menu items that do contain gluten, which can be made available to customers upon request. ▪ *www.rodiziogrill.com*

Steuben's
⊙ $$**LD**
Denver ▪ *(303) 830-1001*
523 E 17th Ave ▪ *American* ▪ GF menu includes habanero fried corn, deviled eggs, tomato soup, Memphis ribs, grilled salmon, and a breadless chile lime-grilled chicken sandwich. Manager Dave reports that GF clients are served "all the time." He also notes that the restaurant always asks about the severity of a gluten intolerance in order to alert the kitchen. ▪ *www.steubens.com*

Sushi Den
⊙★ $$$**LD**
Denver ▪ *(303) 777-0826*
1487 S Pearl St ▪ *Sushi* ▪ They have a GF sushi menu and a GF entrée menu. GF items include soups, salads, and a wide variety of seafood like octopus, clams, tuna, salmon, and oysters. GF soy sauce is available. ▪ *www.sushiden.net*

Sushi Sasa
★ $$**LD**
Denver ▪ *(303) 433-7272*
2401 15th St ▪ *Sushi* ▪ GF soy sauce is available. Manager Michael reports that only the sashimi is naturally GF, but other items can be modified to be GF. He adds that servers are fairly educated in the GF diet, so alert the server upon arrival. ▪ *www.sushisasadenver.com*

Toast
★ ¢**BL**
Denver ▪ *(303) 322-3493*
222 Columbine St ▪ *Modern American* ▪ GF bread is available for toast, french toast, and sandwiches. Staff members at both restaurants report that they are very accommodating of GF diners and will also modify other menu items. ▪ *www.toastygoodness.com*

Tokyo Joe's
Denver ▪ *(303) 825-0321*
1001 16th St
Denver ▪ *(303) 830-7277*
1360 Grant St
Denver ▪ *(303) 722-7666*
1700 E Evans Ave
Denver ▪ *(720) 213-0580*
2320 S Parker Rd

Tommy's Thai
⊙ ¢**LD**
Denver ▪ *(303) 377-4244*
3410 E Colfax Ave ▪ *Thai* ▪ GF menu is a copy of the takeout menu with GF items highlighted. It includes chicken coconut, shrimp soup, thai beef salad, pad thai,

sweet and sour chicken, catfish, and more. ▪ *www.tommysthaidenver.com*

Udi's Bakery   ★ ¢S
Denver ▪ *(303) 657-1600*
101 E 70th Ave ▪ *Global* ▪ GF sandwich bread, bread loaves,and muffins are available. Manager Torie notes that several salads and dressings are GF, and all sandwiches can be requested on GF bread. She cautions that the café itself is not a GF facility, so there is a risk of cross-contamination. ▪ *www.udisfood.com*

Uno Chicago Grill   📖
Denver ▪ *(303) 371-1555*
16375 E 40th Ave

Vesta Dipping Grill   ✪ $$$D
Denver ▪ *(303) 296-1970*
1822 Blake St ▪ *Modern American* ▪ GF menu is called the "Celiac Menu" and includes jalapeno tuna, pork tenderloin, duck breast, tofu steak, salmon, and lamb. The restaurant reports that they host GF diners "all the time." ▪ *www.vestagrill.com*

Watercourse Bakery   ★ ¢S
Denver ▪ *(303) 318-9843*
214 E 13Th Ave ▪ *Bakery* ▪ Non-dedicated bakery offering GF baked goods such as cupcakes, cookies, cakes, and muffins. At City, O' City, the café next door, GF items are available for buying individually, but at the bakery, they are available by order only. ▪ *www.watercoursefoods.com*

Watercourse Foods   ✪ $BLD
Denver ▪ *(303) 832-7313*
837 E 17th Ave ▪ *Vegetarian* ▪ GF menu options are marked by an asterisk. The restaurant reports that several non-marked items can be modified to be GF, and brown rice can be substituted for pasta. ▪ *www.watercoursefoods.com*

Zengo   ✪★ $$$D
Denver ▪ *(720) 904-0965*
1610 Little Raven St ▪ *Asian & Latin Fusion* ▪ GF menu includes ceviches, sushi, and several meat dishes. The restaurant notes

that GF diners should alert the server, who will alert the kitchen. GF rice noodles are available. ▪ *www.modernmexican.com*

COLORADO

FORT COLLINS

Austin's American Grill   ✪ $LD
Fort Collins ▪ *(970) 224-9691*
100 W Mountain Ave
Fort Collins ▪ *(970) 267-6532*
2815 E Harmony Rd ▪ *American* ▪ Limited GF menu includes salads, bread-free sandwiches, and house favorites like the short smoked wild salmon and the sirloin steak. For dessert, they offer crème brûlée. Marketing Director Lindsey notes that the menu sometimes changes, so call ahead to confirm that a particular item is available. ▪ *www.austinsamericangrill.com*

Beau Jo's Colorado Style Pizza ✪★ $LD
Fort Collins ▪ *(970) 498-8898*
100 N College Ave ▪ *Pizza* ▪ GF pizza is available at all locations. All locations except Steamboat Springs also carry a GF menu that includes the salad bar, sandwiches, appetizers, and GF beer. Call a specific location for details on its GF offerings. ▪ *www.beaujos.com*

Carrabba's Italian Grill   📖
Fort Collins ▪ *(970) 225-6800*
1212 Oakridge Dr

Cuppy's Coffee   ★ ¢BL
Fort Collins ▪ *(970) 232-9778*
353 W Drake Rd ▪ *Coffee House & Café* ▪ GF cookies, pies, cakes, muffins, brownies, and more are available. Manager Krista reports that these items are available "most of the time." She adds that the chef can make GF meals or special desserts upon request. ▪ *www.cuppyscoffeefc.com*

Enzio's Italian Kitchen   ✪ $LD
Fort Collins ▪ *(970) 484-8466*
126 W Mountain Ave ▪ *Italian* ▪ GF menu
includes prosciutto wrapped scallops,
baked cod italiano, and the Tuscan steak
salad, among other things. For dessert, it
offers a GF chocolate torte and spumoni. ▪
www.enzios.com

Everyday Joe's Coffee House   ★ ¢BLD
Fort Collins ▪ *(970) 224-4138*
144 S Mason St ▪ *Coffee House & Café*
▪ GF brownies, pecan bars, and chocolate
chip cookies are available. ▪ *www.everyday-
joes.org*

Great Harvest Bread Company   ★ ¢S
Fort Collins ▪ *(970) 225-0353*
3600 S College Ave
Fort Collins ▪ *(970) 223-8311*
Scotch Pines Village ▪ *Bakery* ▪ At the
Fort Collins locations, GF breads and
cookies are available on Tuesdays and
Thursdays only. Both locations noted that
GF items sell out very quickly, but they are
able to reserve items for GF diners who call
ahead.

Happy Lucky's Teahouse and Treasures
★ ¢S

Fort Collins ▪ *(970) 689-3417*
236 Walnut St ▪ *Tea Café* ▪ GF muffins,
pecan bars, and brownies are available.
GF muffins are almost always available in
chocolate chip, blueberry, and apple cinnamon flavors. Other flavors, like pumpkin,
are available seasonally. ▪ *www.happyluckys.
com*

Mad Greens Inspired Eats   ¢L
Fort Collins ▪ *(970) 372-6216*
2120 E Harmony Rd ▪ *Sandwich & Soups*
▪ Restaurant reports that there is a large
selection of GF salad dressings, including many vinaigrettes like raspberry mint
and balsamic, creamy ginger dressing, and
lowfat honey mustard. Confirm timeliness
of this information before dining in. Restaurant advises building a salad and then
asking a staff member to indicate the GF

dressings. Triumph confirmed that all locations have the same GF options. ▪ *www.
madgreens.com*

Mancino's Grinders & Pizza   ✪★ $$$LD
Fort Collins ▪ *(970) 229-0999*
2601 S Lemay Ave ▪ *Pizza* ▪ GF menu
includes pizza, sandwiches, salads, cookies,
garlic cheese bread, and cinnamon bread. ▪
www.fcmancinos.com

Melting Pot, The   📖
Fort Collins ▪ *(970) 207-0100*
334 E Mountain Ave

Moot House, The   ✪ $$LD
Fort Collins ▪ *(970) 226-2121*
2626 S College Ave ▪ *American* ▪ GF
menu includes artichoke dip, rack of lamb,
Alaskan king crab legs, and filet mignon,
among other things. Marketing Coordinator Lindsey notes that the menu changes
periodically, so call ahead to find out what
GF items are available. ▪ *www.themoot-
house.com*

Mugs Coffee Lounge   ★ ¢BLD
Fort Collins ▪ *(970) 472-6847*
261 S College Ave ▪ *Coffee & Café* ▪ GF
bagels and pita are available. Restaurant
reports that all dishes can be modified to
be GF. ▪ *www.mugscoffeelounge.com*

Nyala Ethiopian Cuisine   ★ $LD
Fort Collins ▪ *(970) 223-6734*
2900 Harvard St ▪ *Ethiopian* ▪ Chef Itag
reports that a GF meal requires advanced
notice of one day, so she can make GF
Ethiopian injera bread. All other menu
selections are naturally GF. Confirm timeliness of this information before dining in. ▪
www.nyalafc.com

Outback Steakhouse   📖
Fort Collins ▪ *(970) 229-0889*
807 E Harmony Rd

Rodizio Grill $$$LD
Fort Collins ▪ *(970) 482-3103*
200 Jefferson St ▪ *Brazilian Steakhouse* ▪
Owner Ryan reports that "only a handful"
of menu items contain gluten. He recom-

mends alerting a server, who will have the manager print a GF list. ▪ *www.rodiziogrill. com*

Suehiro Japanese Restaurant ✪★ $LD
Fort Collins ▪ *(970) 482-3734*
223 Linden St
Fort Collins ▪ *(970) 672-8185*
4431 Corbett Dr ▪ *Japanese* ▪ New GF menu contains items made with GF marinades and GF soy sauce. ▪ *www.suehirofc. com*

Tasty Harmony   ★ $LD
Fort Collins ▪ *(970) 689-3234*
130 South Mason Street ▪ *Vegetarian* ▪ Chef George reports that nearly all menu items can be modified to be GF. He adds that raw items like the hummus and many of the salads are naturally GF. Confirm timeliness of this information before dining in. Alert a server upon arrival and ask him or her to notify the chef. ▪ *www. tastyharmony.com*

Uncle's Pizzeria   ★ $$$LD
Fort Collins ▪ *(970) 224-7100*
1717 S College Ave ▪ *Pizza* ▪ GF pizza is available. The restaurant recommends calling ahead, as GF pizza crusts are made in-house and may not always be available. Advanced notice of 24 hours is needed for large GF orders. ▪ *www.unclespizzeria. homestead.com*

COLORADO

ALL OTHER CITIES

240 Union $$$LD
Lakewood ▪ *(303) 989-3562*
240 Union Blvd ▪ *Modern American* ▪ Manager Michael reports that they are "happy to take care of" GF diners, and he notes that there is a "wide variety" of menu items that can be prepared GF. Alert a serv-

er upon arrival. All servers are educated on the GF diet and can indicate menu items that can be prepared GF. ▪ *www.240union. com*

Abo's Pizza   ★ $LD
Centennial ▪ *(303) 468-4700*
7475 E Arapahoe Rd
Erie ▪ *(303) 828-9777*
720 Austin Ave
Longmont ▪ *(303) 678-0111*
1834 N Main St
Louisville ▪ *(303) 604-9896*
1355 S Boulder Rd
Superior ▪ *(720) 304-6000*
502 Center Dr ▪ *Pizza* ▪ GF pizza is available only at the locations listed. Sizes and toppings vary by location. ▪ *www.abos-pizza.com*

Abrusci's Italiano Ristorante ✪★ $LD
Wheat Ridge ▪ *(303) 232-2424*
3244 Youngfield St ▪ *Italian* ▪ There are separate GF menus for lunch and dinner. Both are extensive, and both include a variety of pastas and entrées. GF bread, pasta, and beer are available. GF pizza is available at the Wheat Ridge location only. The Wheat Ridge location also has a dedicated fryer for GF items. ▪ *www.abruscis.com*

Amicas   ★ $LD
Salida ▪ *(719) 539-5219*
136 E 2nd St ▪ *Pizza* ▪ GF paninis, pizza, and beer are available. Pizzas are available in the 9-inch "lunch" size, while paninis are available in the "full-size." ▪ *www.amicas-salida.com*

Bacco Trattoria   ★ $LD
Littleton ▪ *(303) 979-2665*
10125 W San Juan Way ▪ *Italian* ▪ GF pasta is available with advanced notice. ▪ *www.baccodenver.com*

Beau Jo's Colorado Style Pizza ✪★ $LD
Arvada ▪ *(303) 420-8376*
7805 Wadsworth Blvd
Durango ▪ *(970) 259-9089*
400 S Camino Del Rio Ste B
Evergreen ▪ *(303) 670-2744*

28186 Highway 74
Idaho Springs ▪ *(303) 567-4376*
1517 Miner St
Steamboat Springs ▪ *(970) 870-6401*
704 Lincoln Ave ▪ *Pizza* ▪ GF pizza is available at all locations. All locations except Steamboat Springs also carry a GF menu that includes the salad bar, sandwiches, appetizers, and GF beer. Call a specific location for details on its GF offerings. ▪ *www.beaujos.com*

Biaggi's Ristorante Italiano   📖
Loveland ▪ *(970) 663-0100*
5929 Sky Pond Dr

Bloom $$**LD**
Broomfield ▪ *(720) 887-2800*
1 Flatiron Crossing Dr. ▪ *Modern American* ▪ Marketing Coordinator Julia reports that many menu items are naturally GF. She advises making reservations noting GF and calling ahead to speak with a manager or chef. She also notes that all chefs are trained on the GF diet. ▪ *www.foxrc.com*

Blue Sky Cafe and Juice Bar   ✪★ ¢**BL**
Lakewood ▪ *(303) 216-2670*
14403 W Colfax Ave ▪ *Organic American* ▪ GF muffins are available as a substitute for sandwich bread. GF items marked on the menu include crepes, paninis, omelettes, and melts. Restaurant reports that they often accommodate GF diners. ▪ *www.blueskycafe.biz*

Bonefish Grill   📖
Greenwood Village ▪ *(303) 741-3474*
4948 S Yosemite St
Johnstown ▪ *(970) 663-3474*
4920 Thompson Pkwy
Littleton ▪ *(303) 948-3474*
8100 W Crestline Ave Unit F
Westminster ▪ *(303) 423-3474*
10438 Town Center Dr

Borriello Brothers Pizza   ★ $$**LD**
Fountain ▪ *(719) 884-2020*
5180 Fontaine Blvd
Monument ▪ *(719) 884-2020*
15910 Jackson Creek Pkwy ▪ *Pizza* ▪ GF pizza is available. ▪ *www.borriellobrothers.com*

Brewing Market   ★ ¢**S**
Lafayette ▪ *(720) 890-3993*
2770 Arapahoe Rd
Longmont ▪ *(303) 651-7716*
1520 S Hover St ▪ *Coffee Shop* ▪ GF baked goods are available. Specific products vary by location, but they generally offer cookies and several different types of bread.

Bubba Gump Shrimp Co.   📖
Breckenridge ▪ *(970) 547-9000*
231 South Main St

Buca di Beppo   📖
Broomfield ▪ *(303) 464-7673*
615 Flatiron Marketplace Dr
Littleton ▪ *(303) 738-3287*
7301 S Santa Fe Dr

Bundt Shoppe, The   ★ $**S**
Castle Rock ▪ *(303) 422-8638*
7437 Village Square Dr ▪ *Bakery* ▪ GF bundt cakes are available. Flavors include chocolate chocolate chip, pumpkin spice, raspberry chocolate, key lime, and orange cream pop, among others. Owner Pam recommends calling ahead to order GF bundt cakes, which can be prepared in various sizes. ▪ *www.thebundtshoppe.com*

Buzz Coffee   ★ ¢**S**
Longmont ▪ *(303) 834-9154*
1139 Francis St ▪ *Coffee Shop* ▪ GF chocolate zucchini bread, pumpkin bread, coffee cake, and macaroons are available. ▪ *www.buzz-coffee.com*

Cabin Restaurant & Lounge, The
                                  ✪ $$$**D**
Steamboat Springs ▪ *(970) 871-5550*
2300 Mount Werner Cir ▪ *Steakhouse* ▪ GF items marked on the menu include the Colorado lamb loin and the roasted organic flat iron, as well as the blue Maine mussels, wild salmon tartare, and the soybeans for appetizers. Reservations noting GF are recommended but not required. ▪ *www.steamboatgrand.com*

Café 13   ★ ¢BL
Golden ▪ (303) 278-2225
1301 Arapahoe St ▪ *Café* ▪ GF brown rice
tortillas are available for breakfast entrées
or wraps. They also offer three different
types of GF bread, including chocolate zucchini bread and lemon poppyseed bread. ▪
www.cafe13golden.com

California Café   ✪ $LD
Lone Tree ▪ (303) 649-1111
8505 Park Meadows Center Dr ▪ *American* ▪ GF menu includes calamari, scallops,
cornmeal crusted trout, and filet mignon,
among other things. All of the "trio" options are also GF. Confirm timeliness of
this information before dining in. ▪ *www.
californiacafe.com*

Carino's Italian   📖
Grand Junction ▪ (970) 255-0560
2480 Highway 6 And 50
Greeley ▪ (970) 506-4200
2473 W 28th St
Lakewood ▪ (720) 963-1866
389 S Wadsworth Blvd
Longmont ▪ (303) 485-8077
2033 Ken Pratt Blvd
Loveland ▪ (970) 203-9900
1455 Rocky Mountain Ave
Parker ▪ (303) 841-7103
9355 Crown Crest Blvd
Pueblo ▪ (719) 542-1745
5700 N Elizabeth St

Carrabba's Italian Grill   📖
Aurora ▪ (303) 338-8600
2088 S Abilene St
Louisville ▪ (303) 926-4411
575 S Mccaslin Blvd
Westminster ▪ (303) 940-5620
7401 W 92nd Ave

Colterra Food and Wine $$$LD
Niwot ▪ (303) 652-0777
210 Franklin St ▪ *French & Italian* ▪
Executive Chef Michael reports that they
accommodate GF diners "every day." He
notes that more than half the menu is
naturally GF, and all staff members are

trained about the GF diet. Some examples
of GF options include the ahi tuna steak,
the honey cured long farm pork tenderloin,
and the chocolate decadence or the silky
ganache for dessert. Confirm timeliness of
this information before dining in. ▪ *www.
colterra.com*

Coquette Creperie   ★ ¢LD
Manitou Springs ▪ (719) 685-2420
915 Manitou Ave ▪ *French* ▪ Owner Turu
reports that all crepes are GF. They also
offer GF soups, salads, and quiches. Turu
adds that all items are GF, with the exception of the french bread, which is baked off
the premises. ▪ *www.coquettecreperie.com*

Del Frisco's Double Eagle Steak House
📖
Greenwood Village ▪ (303) 796-0100
8100 E Orchard Rd

Diamond Baking Company   100% ¢S
Longmont ▪ (303) 513-7519
1515 Main St ▪ *Bakery* ▪ Bakery offering
GF cookies, cakes, muffins, brownies, and
more. GF wedding cakes are available. The
bakery is open by appointment only, so call
ahead. ▪ *www.diamondbakingco.com*

Dillon Dam Brewery $$LD
Dillon ▪ (866) 326-6196
100 Little Dam St ▪ *American* ▪ Server
JJ reports that they are very GF aware.
Menu items that can be modified to be GF
include beef, buffalo, and veggie burgers
without buns, along with salads and grilled
mushroom entrées. Confirm timeliness of
this information before dining in. Alert
a server, who will notify the chef. ▪ *www.
dambrewery.com*

Dragonfly Coffee and Tea   ★ ¢S
Louisville ▪ (303) 665-1177
1075 E South Boulder Rd ▪ *Café* ▪ GF tea
breads are available in four or five different flavors, including pumpkin and lemon
poppyseed. Owner Patty reports that GF
diners come in "all the time."

Earls $LD
Lone Tree ▪ (303) 792-3275
8335 Park Meadows Center Dr ▪ *Global*
▪ Manager Ben reports that they serve GF diners at least "three or four times a week." He recommends asking the server to speak with the chef. Many menu items are naturally GF or can be prepared GF, including the dynamite shrimp rolls, the ahi tuna appetizer, and pad thai. Confirm timeliness of this information before dining in. ▪ *www.earls.ca*

Ed's Cantina & Grill   ✪ ¢BLD
Estes Park ▪ (970) 586-2919
390 E Elkhorn Ave ▪ *Mexican* ▪ New GF menu includes a variety of salads, tacos, enchiladas, margarita shrimp, and nachos. Manager Carla advises that the corn tortilla chips, though GF, are fried in a non-dedicated fryer. ▪ *www.edscantina.com*

Einstein Bros Bagels   ★ ¢BLD
Broomfield ▪ (303) 464-9760
5180 W 120th Ave
Highlands Ranch ▪ (303) 683-3344
9385 S Colorado Blvd ▪ *Sandwich Shop* ▪ GF bagels are available at listed locations only. ▪ *www.einsteinbros.com*

Extreme Pizza   ★ $$LD
Westminster ▪ (303) 629-8644
11940 Bradburn Blvd Unit 400 ▪ *Pizza* ▪ GF pizza is available. ▪ *www.extremepizza.com*

Fanelli's Amici's   ★ $LD
Wheat Ridge ▪ (303) 455-5585
4300 Wadsworth Blvd ▪ *Italian* ▪ GF pasta is available.

Fan's Chinese Cuisine   ★ $LD
Longmont ▪ (303) 652-6250
7960 Niwot Rd ▪ *Chinese* ▪ GF soy sauce and rice noodles are available.

Fire Bowl Café   ✪ ¢LD
Centennial ▪ (720) 489-1690
2330 E Arapahoe Rd
Englewood ▪ (303) 799-1690
11435 E Briarwood Ave ▪ *Asian Stir-Fry*
▪ GF menu includes spicy coconut soup, thai seafood tom kha soup, and a variety of salads. It features "Stir Fry Your Way," for which diners choose their own meats, sauces, and starches. The GF sauce options are ginger white wine and yellow curry. ▪ *www.firebowlcafe.com*

Garlic Jim's   ★ $$LD
Highlands Ranch ▪ (303) 346-5467
3982 Red Cedar Dr ▪ *Pizza* ▪ GF pizza is available. The restaurant reports that Garlic Jim's Hot wings, ribs, gourmet cheesecake, and certain flavors of Haagen-Dazs ice cream are also GF. ▪ *www.garlicjims.com*

Global Café at Global Garage   ★ $BLD
Buena Vista ▪ (719) 395-8092
222 Hwy 24 South ▪ *Global* ▪ Chef Tim reports that many menu items are naturally GF, including the ahi tuna, several soups, and prime rib. Confirm timeliness of this information before dining in. GF pasta is available, so all pasta dishes can be made GF. Quite a few dishes come with rice. Alert the server upon arrival, and ask to speak to the chef. ▪ *www.globalgarage.org*

Grandmaison's Chalet Room $$$D
Estes Park ▪ (970) 586-5958
2625 Marys Lake Rd ▪ *Continental* ▪ Manager Lance reports that they serve GF diners "on a weekly basis," and that they are happy to work with GF diners to identify a suitable option. Alert a server, who will notify the chef. Located in the Marys Lake Lodge and Resort. ▪ *www.maryslakelodge.com*

Granny's Gluten-Free Zone   100% ¢S
Loveland ▪ (970) 669-9986
3419 W Eisenhower Blvd ▪ *Bakery* ▪ Dedicated GF grocery store with a wide variety of GF baked goods, including breads, pizza crusts, muffins, cinnamon buns, cookies, and more. Baked goods are brought onto the premises from other bakeries. ▪ *www.grannysglutenfree.com*

Great Harvest Bread Company   ★ ¢S
Longmont ▪ (303) 772-9090

1100 Ken Pratt Blvd ▪ *Bakery* ▪ In Long-mont, GF bread is available on Wednesdays by order only. All locations noted that GF items sell out very quickly, but they are able to reserve items for GF diners who call ahead.

Hacienda Colorado   ✪ $$ LD
Englewood ▪ *(303) 858-8588*
10500 Bierstadt Way
Lakewood ▪ *(303) 932-0272*
5056 S Wadsworth Way
Westminster ▪ *(303) 460-0111*
10422 Town Center Dr ▪ *Mexican* ▪ GF menu includes a selection of enchiladas, ta-cos, tostadas, fajitas, and more. For dessert, they offer cinnamon ice cream. The classify their cuisine as "mountain Mex," or Rocky Mountain Mexican. ▪ *www.haciendacolorado.com*

Highlands Pizza Company   ★ ¢ LD
Aspen ▪ *(970) 920-3747*
133 Prospector Rd ▪ *Pizza* ▪ GF "Signature Thin Crust" pizza is available. ▪ *www.highlandspizzaco.com*

Indochine Cuisine   ✪★ $L
Parker ▪ *(720) 851-8559*
19751 E Mainstreet ▪ *Thai & Vietnamese* ▪ GF items marked on the menu include pad thai, pho ga soup, a variety of curries, ginger jumbo prawns, and more. GF soy sauce is available. ▪ *www.indochine-cuisine.com*

Juicy Lucy's Steakhouse $$ LD
Glenwood Springs ▪ *(970) 945-4619*
308 7th St ▪ *Seafood & Steakhouse* ▪ Manager Lily reports that they serve "a lot of customers" with GF diets. She notes that most of their sauces contain flour, but that the sirloin, salmon, mahi mahi, and other menu items are naturally GF. Confirm timeliness of this information before dining in. Alert a server upon arrival. ▪ *www.juicylucyssteakhouse.com*

Kenosha Steakhouse   ✪ $$ LD
Breckenridge ▪ *(970) 453-7313*
301 S Main St ▪ *Steakhouse* ▪ Manager Tanner reports that they had so many GF customers that the chef printed a new GF menu. It lists all of the regular menu items which are GF or can be made GF. Alert the server, who can get a GF menu from the host stand. ▪ *www.kenoshasteakhouse.com*

La Sandia $$ LD
Lone Tree ▪ *(303) 586-5511*
8419 Park Meadows Center Dr ▪ *Modern Mexican* ▪ Manager Robby reports that nearly all menu items are naturally GF. He also notes that servers are tested daily on which menu items are GF. Alert the server, who will go over GF items from the menu in detail. ▪ *www.modernmexican.com*

Larkspur Restaurant   ✪ $$$$ LD
Vail ▪ *(970) 754-8050*
458 Vail Valley Dr ▪ *Modern American* ▪ GF menu includes lemon risotto, skate wing, and beef carpaccio. GF desserts are also available. ▪ *www.larkspurvail.com*

Lefty's Gourmet Pizza and Ice Cream
                                        ★ $$ LD
Niwot ▪ *(303) 652-3100*
364 2nd Ave ▪ *Italian* ▪ GF pizzas are available in the 12-inch size. GF "lasagna," made with cabbage instead of pasta, is also available. ▪ *www.leftysgourmetpizza.com*

Lone Star Steakhouse & Saloon   📖
Arvada ▪ *(303) 420-7827*
7450 W 52nd Ave
Brighton ▪ *(303) 655-9433*
305 Pavilions Pl
Lakewood ▪ *(303) 237-5727*
11905 W 6th Ave
Littleton ▪ *(303) 932-1718*
4817 S Wadsworth Way
Loveland ▪ *(970) 203-9464*
5330 Stone Creek Cir
Thornton ▪ *(303) 252-0770*
237 E 120th Ave

Loveland Coffee Company   ★ ¢S
Loveland ▪ *(970) 278-1221*
620 E 29th St ▪ *Coffee Shop* ▪ GF muffins are available in a variety of flavors, including chocolate chip, blueberry, apple

cinnamon, and lemon. Flavors change seasonally. ▪ *www.lovelandcoffeeco.com*

Mad Greens Inspired Eats   ¢L
Centennial ▪ **(303) 662-8119**
8283 S Akron St
Greenwood Village ▪ **(720) 259-4441**
4948 S Yosemite St
Lakewood ▪ **(720) 496-4139**
150 S Union Blvd ▪ *Sandwich & Soups*
▪ Restaurant reports that there is a large selection of GF salad dressings, including many vinaigrettes like raspberry mint and balsamic, creamy ginger dressing, and lowfat honey mustard. Confirm timeliness of this information before dining in. Restaurant advises building a salad and then asking a staff member to indicate the GF dressings. Triumph confirmed that all locations have the same GF options. ▪ *www.madgreens.com*

Maggiano's Little Italy   ★ $$$LD
Englewood ▪ **(303) 858-1405**
7401 S Clinton St ▪ *Italian* ▪ GF pasta is available. Call individual locations to inquire about additional GF options. ▪ *www.maggianos.com*

Mahogany Ridge Brewery & Grill
                              ✪ $$$D
Steamboat Springs ▪ **(970) 879-3773**
435 Lincoln Ave ▪ *American* ▪ GF menu includes jumbo sea scallops, maple glazed roasted chicken, yellowfin tuna, pork tenderloin, and more.

Mama Rose's   ★ $$D
Estes Park ▪ **(970) 586-3330**
338 E Elkhorn Ave ▪ *Italian* ▪ GF rice pasta is available for substitution into any pasta dish except lasagna. Restaurant reports that they accommodate GF diners "all the time," and the servers are well-educated on the GF diet. Servers can indicate GF options. ▪ *www.mamarosesrestaurant.com*

Mambo Italiano   ★ $$D
Steamboat Springs ▪ **(970) 870-0500**
521 Lincoln Avenue ▪ *Italian* ▪ Kitchen staffer Vince reports that the everyone is

educated on the GF diet. He adds that they had a "GF 101" training course, so any server will be able to indicate GF items on the menu. GF pasta is usually available, but Vince notes that sometimes their supplier is inconsistent, so call ahead to confirm the availability of this item. ▪ *www.mambos.com*

McGrath's Fish House   ✪ $LD
Lakewood ▪ **(303) 279-3839**
14035 W Colfax Dr ▪ *Seafood* ▪ GF menu features a large selection of seafood entrees and appetizers, as well as salads and steaks. ▪ *www.mcgrathsfishhouse.com*

Melting Pot, The   📖
Littleton ▪ **(303) 794-5666**
2707 W Main St
Louisville ▪ **(303) 666-7777**
732 Main St

Mi Casa Mexican Restaurant   ✪ $$LD
Breckenridge ▪ **(970) 453-2071**
600 S Park Ave ▪ *Mexican* ▪ GF menu includes soups, enchiladas, fish tacos, and pork tamales. Tostitos corn chips are available upon request. Manager Julie notes that the servers are trained to punch GF requests into the computer and alert the kitchen manager. ▪ *www.stormrestaurants.com*

Old Stone Church Restaurant ✪ $$$LD
Castle Rock ▪ **(303) 688-9000**
210 3rd St ▪ *Fusion* ▪ GF menu includes java salmon, pork tenderloin carnitas, and jalapeno catfish, among other things. Manager Steve reports that they accommodate GF diners "every day," so all staff members are GF aware. ▪ *www.oscrestaurant.com*

Original Pancake House, The   ★ ¢BL
Greenwood Village ▪ **(303) 795-0573**
5900 S University Blvd
Greenwood Village ▪ **(303) 224-0093**
8000 E Belleview Ave ▪ *Breakfast* ▪ GF pancakes are available. Select locations may offer other GF options. Call a specific location to inquire. ▪ *www.originalpancakehouse.com*

Outback Steakhouse 📖

Aurora ▪ *(303) 695-9600*
2066 S Abilene St
Aurora ▪ *(720) 889-2965*
6040 S Gun Club Rd Unit G8
Castle Rock ▪ *(303) 814-0099*
4687 Milestone Ln
Centennial ▪ *(303) 792-2903*
10443 E Costilla Ave
Grand Junction ▪ *(970) 257-7550*
2432 Highway 6 And 50
Highlands Ranch ▪ *(303) 791-1500*
15 Springer Dr
Lakewood ▪ *(303) 216-2460*
14295 W Colfax Ave
Littleton ▪ *(303) 932-0315*
8601 W Cross Dr
Longmont ▪ *(303) 684-8149*
1315 Dry Creek Dr
Louisville ▪ *(303) 661-9855*
988 W Dillon Rd
Thornton ▪ *(303) 450-4111*
497 E 120th Ave
Westminster ▪ *(303) 427-2714*
9329 Sheridan Blvd

P.F. Chang's China Bistro 📖

Aurora ▪ *(303) 627-5450*
23902 E Prospect Ave
Broomfield ▪ *(720) 887-6200*
1 Flatiron Cir Ste 500 Bldg 5
Lakewood ▪ *(303) 922-5800*
7210 W Alameda Ave
Littleton ▪ *(303) 790-7744*
8315 Park Meadows Center Dr
Loveland ▪ *(970) 622-9313*
5915 Sky Pond Dr

Pei Wei Asian Diner 📖

Highlands Ranch ▪ *(303) 346-4329*
9352 S Colorado Blvd Ste G-1
Lakewood ▪ *(303) 215-1933*
14255 W Colfax Ave

Poppy's Pizza & Grill   ★ $$$ LD

Estes Park ▪ *(970) 586-8282*
342 E Elkhorn Ave ▪ *Pizza* ▪ Manager Rob
reports that GF diners can order pizza
with zucchini crust. He also notes that the
kitchen can modify most regular menu

items to be GF. He reports that the staff
is "well-educated" on the GF diet. Alert a
server, who will notify the kitchen. ▪ *www.
poppyspizzaandgrill.com*

Posh Pastries Gourmet Bakery ✪★ ¢S

Parker ▪ *(303) 840-1251*
10471 S Parker Rd ▪ *Bakery* ▪ Non-dedicated bakery offering GF quiches, fruit pies,
angel food cakes, and petite fours. Orders
for specific items should be placed at least
48 hours in advance. ▪ *www.poshpastries-
bakery.com*

Rheinlander Bakery   ★ ¢S

Arvada ▪ *(303) 467-1810*
5721 Olde Wadsworth Blvd ▪ *Bakery* ▪
Non-dedicated bakery offering an entire
line of GF products. GF items include
breakfast pastries, dessert pastries, stru-
dels, pies, and more. They also sell GF cake
mixes to take home. ▪ *www.sweetdeliver-
ance.com*

Rock Creek Pizza Dough Co.   ★ $$ LD

Superior ▪ *(303) 499-4100*
1631 Coalton Rd ▪ *Pizza* ▪ GF pizza is available. ▪ *www.rockcreekpizzeria.com*

Sansone's Bistro   ✪ $$$ D

Greenwood Village ▪ *(303) 794-4026*
5969 S University Blvd ▪ *Continental* ▪ GF
menu includes a wide variety of appetizers
and entrées. Examples are cajun seafood
sausage, apple brined duck liver, paella de
mar, and crispy duck confit. For dessert,
they offer their signature Grand Marnier
soufflé. Manager Erica reports that Chef
Robert will suggest additional GF dessert
options if possible. ▪ *www.sansonesbistro.
com*

Stage Coach Inn   ✪★ $$$ LD

Manitou Springs ▪ *(719) 685-9400*
702 Manitou Ave ▪ *American* ▪ GF menu
includes black bean chili, BBQ baby back
ribs, sirloin steak, roasted turkey, and
more. GF beer is available. ▪ *www.stage-
coachinn.com*

Tavern, The $LD
Estes Park ▪ *(970) 586-5958*
2625 Marys Lake Rd ▪ *American* ▪ Manager Lance reports that they serve GF diners "on a weekly basis," and that they are happy to work with GF diners to identify a suitable option. Alert a server, who will communicate with the chef to ensure a GF meal. Located in the Marys Lake Lodge and Resort. ▪ *www.maryslakelodge.com*

Toast   ★ ¢BL
Littleton ▪ *(303) 797-9543*
2700 W Bowles Ave ▪ *Modern American* ▪ GF bread is available for toast, french toast, and sandwiches. Staff members at both restaurants report that they are very accommodating of GF diners and will also modify other menu items. ▪ *www.toasty-goodness.com*

Tokyo Joe's   📖
Aurora ▪ *(303) 627-5485*
23955 E Plaza Ave
Aurora ▪ *(720) 214-2455*
6775 S Cornerstar Way
Centennial ▪ *(303) 656-4392*
6879 S Vine St
Centennial ▪ *(720) 873-6641*
8225 S Chester St
Centennial ▪ *(303) 721-8886*
8727 E Dry Creek Rd
Englewood ▪ *(303) 806-0112*
901 W Hampden Ave
Glendale ▪ *(303) 524-3462*
1000 S Colorado Blvd
Greenwood Village ▪ *(303) 804-0988*
4950 S Yosemite St
Highlands Ranch ▪ *(303) 683-8217*
6642 Timberline Rd
Highlands Ranch ▪ *(303) 791-9222*
9131 S Broadway
Lakewood ▪ *(303) 273-5363*
14227 W Colfax Ave
Lakewood ▪ *(303) 988-1176*
145 Union Blvd
Littleton ▪ *(303) 904-9201*
8501 W Bowles Ave
Louisville ▪ *(303) 926-7100*

1116 W Dillon Rd
Westminster ▪ *(303) 255-4828*
1005 W 120th Ave

Via Toscana   ✪★ $$D
Louisville ▪ *(303) 604-6960*
356 S Mccaslin Blvd ▪ *Italian* ▪ GF menu includes steak sopprafino, veal piccata, mahi bello mahi, and risotto primavera, among other things. GF pasta is available. Manager Sean recommends being specific when speaking to the server about GF requests. ▪ *www.viatoscana.com*

White Chocolate Grill, The   ✪ $$LD
Lone Tree ▪ *(303) 799-4841*
8421 Park Meadows Center Dr ▪ *Modern American* ▪ GF menu includes grilled artichokes and tomato gin soup, among other things, as appetizers. As entrées, it lists a bunless cheeseburger, BBQ baby back ribs, center cut filet, and more. For dessert, it offers molten chocolate soufflé cake. ▪ *www. thewhitechocolategrill.wordpress.com*

Yard House   📖
Lakewood ▪ *(303) 278-9273*
14500 W Colfax Ave Unit 341

CONNECTICUT

Abate Apizza and Seafood Restaurant
                                   ★ $LD
New Haven ▪ *(203) 776-4334*
129 Wooster St ▪ *Pizza* ▪ GF pizza and beer are available.

Amore Baking Company   ★ ¢S
Fairfield ▪ *(203) 292-8475*
1215 Post Rd ▪ *Bakery* ▪ A small selection of GF specialty breads and cookies are available. ▪ *www.biscottidamore.com*

Apizza Pie   ★ $$LD
Norwalk ▪ *(203) 642-3262*

4 New Canaan Ave ▪ Pizza ▪ GF pizza, pastas, and paninis are available. Owner Mike notes the kitchen is very GF aware.

Basil's Pizza   ★ $$LD
Shelton ▪ (203) 926-6848
725 Bridgeport Ave ▪ Pizza ▪ GF pan pizza is available for delivery or take out only. GF pizza is baked on a raised screen and does not touch the oven surface where non-GF pizza is baked. Confirm timeliness of this information before dining in. ▪ *www.basilspizzaandcatering.com*

Bella Napoli   ★ $$LD
Milford ▪ (203) 877-1102
864 Boston Post Rd
Stratford ▪ (203) 375-7700
1112 Barnum Ave ▪ Pizza ▪ GF pizza is available in the small size. ▪ *www.bellanapolionline.com*

Bell'Amici Pizza & Restaurant   ✪★ $$
Guilford ▪ (203) 457-9411
516 Route 80 ▪ Pizza ▪ GF pizza is available, along with GF bread, pasta, and beer. GF menu includes chicken parmigiana, spinach and ricotta ravioli in marinara sauce, and 3 cheese tortellini in alfredo sauce. ▪ *www.bellamicirestaurant.com*

Bertucci's   📖
Avon ▪ (860) 676-1177
380 W Main St
Danbury ▪ (203) 739-0500
98 Newtown Rd
Darien ▪ (203) 655-4299
54 Post Rd
Glastonbury ▪ (860) 633-2225
2882 Main St
Manchester ▪ (860) 648-0730
194 Buckland Hills Dr
Newington ▪ (860) 666-1949
2929 Berlin Tpke
Orange ▪ (203) 799-6828
550 Boston Post Rd
Shelton ▪ (203) 926-6058
768 Bridgeport Ave
Southington ▪ (860) 621-8626
20 Spring St

Waterbury ▪ (203) 755-6224
495 Union St
West Hartford ▪ (860) 231-9571
330 N Main St
Westport ▪ (203) 454-1559
833 Post Rd E

Bobby's Apizza Restaurant   ★ $$LD
North Branford ▪ (203) 484-0773
1179 Foxon Rd ▪ Pizza ▪ GF pizza is available. Manager Joe notes that almost all toppings are GF.

Brendan's at The Elms $$$LD
Ridgefield ▪ (203) 438-9206
500 Main St ▪ New England ▪ Restaurant reports that although there are no specific GF options, GF diners can modify dishes. Alert a server, who will communicate with the chef. The chef "absolutely will accommodate." ▪ *www.brendansattheelms.com*

Bugaboo Creek Steak House   📖
Manchester ▪ (860) 644-6100
1442 Pleasant Valley Rd

Burton's Grill   ✪★ $$LD
South Windsor ▪ (860) 432-4575
100 Evergreen Way ▪ American ▪ GF menu includes grilled stuffed zucchini, chicken and mushroom pasta, and Tuscan brick chicken. GF pasta and buns are available for pasta entrées and burgers. Dessert options include vanilla bean crème brûlée and chocolate torte. ▪ *www.burtonsgrill.com*

Café Cogolulu   ✪ ¢S
Wilton ▪ (203) 544-6000
991 Danbury Rd ▪ Bakery ▪ GF menu includes sandwiches and paninis, soups, gelatos, and dinners to go. Owner Regina emphasizes that all items are made fresh to order. ▪ *www.cogolulucafe.com*

Café Romeo   ✪★ $$BL
New Haven ▪ (203) 865-2233
534 Orange St ▪ Café ▪ GF menu includes pasta salad, prosciutto salad, prosciutto frittata, sausage frittata, tofu scramble, three bean salad, soups, and more. GF pasta is available. ▪ *www.cafe-romeo.com*

Capital Grille, The 📖
Stamford ▪ *(203) 967-0000*
230 Tresser Blvd

Carl Anthony Trattoria ★ $$LD
Monroe ▪ *(203) 268-8486*
477 Main St ▪ *Italian* ▪ GF pizza and pasta are available. Restaurant notes that the staff was recently trained on accommodating GF diners. ▪ *www.carlanthonys.com*

Carrabba's Italian Grill 📖
Manchester ▪ *(860) 643-4100*
31 Redstone Rd

Chuck and Augie's Restaurant ✪★ $LD
Storrs Mansfield ▪ *(860) 486-5633*
233 Glenbrook Rd ▪ *American* ▪ GF menu includes sandwiches and paninis on GF bread, nachos, artichoke dip, caribbean and honey dijon chicken salads with GF dressings, shrimp scampi with GF pasta, and more. GF bread, hamburger buns, pasta, soy sauce, and brownies are available. Located in the student union building on the campus of the University of Connecticut. ▪ *www.chuckandaugies.uconn.edu*

Claire's Corner Copia ✪★ ¢BLD
New Haven ▪ *(203) 562-3888*
1000 Chapel St ▪ *Vegetarian* ▪ GF menu includes stir fries and curries over brown rice, flat bread pizzas, chiles, tostadas, and quesadillas. Directions for ordering dishes GF are included on the GF menu. GF pizza is available, and Chef Claire reports that GF pasta can be made with advanced notice. ▪ *www.clairescornercopia.com*

Cugino's Restaurant ★ $$$LD
Farmington ▪ *(860) 678-9366*
1053 Farmington Ave ▪ *Italian* ▪ GF pasta is available and can be substituted into most pasta dishes. ▪ *www.cuginosrestaurantfarmington.com*

Davinci's Pizza ★ $$LD
Norwalk ▪ *(203) 853-1111*
60 Connecticut Ave ▪ *Pizza* ▪ GF pizza is available. ▪ *www.freshpizzanow.com/davinci*

Dee's One Smart Cookie 100% ¢S
Glastonbury ▪ *(860) 633-8000*
398 Hebron Ave ▪ *Bakery* ▪ Dedicated GF bakery offering muffins, bars, whoopie pies, tarts, and truffles, as well as frozen pasta, pizza, and flatbreads. Owner Dee reports that special orders can be accommodated with advanced notice of one week. ▪ *www.deesonesmartcookie.com*

Divine Treasures ★ $$$$S
Manchester ▪ *(860) 643-2552*
Middle Turnpike West ▪ *Chocolate* ▪ A variety of GF cookies, chocolates, and other dessert items are available. ▪ *www.divine-treasureschocolates.com*

Dolci Lounge ✪★ ¢D
New Haven ▪ *(203) 764-2069*
932 State St ▪ *Italian* ▪ GF items marked on the menu are the sweet potato ravioli with fresh thyme and cavatelli with truffle essence. GF pasta is available. Restaurant reports that many salads can be modified to be GF even though they are not marked on the menu.

Edge of the Woods ★ ¢S
New Haven ▪ *(203) 787-1055*
379 Whalley Ave ▪ *Bakery* ▪ GF chocolate crème bars and slices of GF almond buckwheat cake are almost always available at the bakery. Entire GF cakes can be ordered 48 hours in advance. ▪ *www.edgeofthewoodsmarket.com*

Eggs Up Grill ✪★ ¢BL
Portland ▪ *(860) 342-4968*
1462 Portland Cobalt Rd ▪ *Continental* ▪ Extensive GF breakfast menu includes omelets, egg sandwiches on GF rolls, GF muffins, fresh fruit, and more. GF bread can be used for sandwiches at lunch. ▪ *www.theeggsupgrill.com*

Elephant Trail, The ★ $LD
Avon ▪ *(860) 677-0065*
39 E Main St ▪ *Thai* ▪ GF soy sauce is available. Restaurant reports that nearly all dishes can be modified to be GF. ▪ *www.theelephanttrail.com*

Elizabeth's Bar & Restaurant   ★ $$D
Rocky Hill ▪ *(860) 721-6932*
825 Cromwell Ave ▪ *Italian* ▪ GF rice pasta
is available. ▪ *www.lizrestaurant.com*

Engine No 6 Pizza Co   ★ $LD
Norwich ▪ *(860) 887-3887*
195 W Thames St ▪ *Pizza* ▪ GF pizza, pasta,
lasagna, and breadsticks are available. ▪
www.engineno6pizza.com

Ernie's Pizzeria   ★ $$LD
New Haven ▪ *(203) 387-3362*
1279 Whalley Ave ▪ *Pizza* ▪ GF pizza and
beer are available.

Famous Pizza   ★ $LD
Bethel ▪ *(203) 797-1550*
1 Point Barnum Sq ▪ *Pizza* ▪ GF pizza
is available. Thursdays are "Gluten-Free
Thursdays," and customers can buy GF pizzas at a discounted price. Confirm timeliness of this information before dining in. ▪
www.famouspizzabethel.com

Fitzgerald's Pizza   ★ $LD
Simsbury ▪ *(860) 658-1210*
710 Hopmeadow St ▪ *Pizza* ▪ GF pizza is
available. Restaurant recommends ordering
20-25 minutes in advance so they prepare the pizza. They note that all toppings
except the chicken, eggplant, and meatballs
are GF. Located within Fitzgerald's Foods. ▪
www.fitzgeraldsfoods.com

Flatbread Pizza Company   ★ $LD
Canton ▪ *(860) 693-3314*
The Shoppes At Farmington Valley ▪
Pizza ▪ GF pizza is available in the 8-inch
size. GF beer and desserts are also available. Typical GF desserts are whoopie pies
and brownies. ▪ *www.flatbreadcompany.
com*

Foodworks   ★ ¢BLD
Guilford ▪ *(203) 458-9778*
450 Boston Post Rd
Old Saybrook ▪ *(860) 395-0770*
17 Main St ▪ *Deli* ▪ GF bread is available for
sandwiches at the Guilford location. Muffins and other baked goods, as well as fro-

zen foods, are available at both locations.
The Guilford location has a deli and bakery
that supplies the Old Saybrook location
with GF goods. ▪ *www.food-works.org*

Fountain of Youth   ★ ¢S
Westport ▪ *(203) 259-9378*
1789 Post Rd E ▪ *Bakery* ▪ GF baked goods,
including cookies, cupcakes, and specialty
breads, are available. ▪ *www.fountainofy-
outhwholefoods.com*

Frascati's   ✪★ $$LD
Stamford ▪ *(203) 353-8900*
581 Newfield Ave ▪ *Italian* ▪ GF pasta,
pizza, desserts, and beer are available. GF
menu includes bruschetta, shrimp floren-
tine, and ravioli with marinara sauce. ▪
www.frascatiitalian.com

Fratelli Market   ★ $S
Stamford ▪ *(203) 322-1632*
17 Cedar Heights Rd ▪ *Take-&-Bake* ▪
Fresh GF gnochi and tortellini are avail-
able, as are GF frozen pizzas. GF bread,
cookies, and more are also available. ▪
www.fratellimarketct.com

Georgie's Diner   ✪★ $BLD
West Haven ▪ *(203) 933-1000*
427 Elm St ▪ *American* ▪ GF menu includes
the Waldorf salad, vegan stuffed peppers,
pork chops, chicken parmasean, and the ice
cream sundae. Manager Georgette reports
that the kitchen prepares GF foods sepa-
rately. GF bread is available for sandwiches
and toast. ▪ *www.georgies-diner.com*

Giove's Pizza Kitchen   ★ $$LD
Fairfield ▪ *(203) 254-3772*
246 Post Rd
Shelton ▪ *(203) 225-6000*
494 Bridgeport Ave ▪ *Pizza* ▪ GF pizza
is available. Restaurant's third location in
Trumbull was considering carrying GF
pizza at the time of publication. ▪ *www.
giovespizzakitchen.com*

Grants Restaurant & Bar $$$LD
West Hartford ▪ *(860) 236-1930*
977 Farmington Ave ▪ *Modern Ameri-*

can ■ Manager Grant reports that the executive chef is Celiac, so the restaurant is "fully aware" of GF "issues." He recommends making reservations noting GF and reminding a server upon arrival. ■ *www.billygrant.com*

Heights Pizza   ★ $$**LD**
Darien ■ *(203) 656-3200*
330 Heights Rd ■ *Pizza* ■ GF pizza is available in the small and medium sizes. Any pizza from the regular menu can be ordered GF. Restaurant reports that all GF pizzas are cooked separately, on fresh cookware. ■ *www.heightspizzadarien.com*

Illiano's   ✿★ $$**LD**
Meriden ■ *(203) 634-4000*
510 W Main St
Middletown ■ *(860) 343-9244*
534 Washington St
New London ■ *(860) 447-9390*
929 Bank St ■ *Italian* ■ GF menu at the New London location includes cheese and spinach ravioli, baked ziti, eggplant and chicken parmesan, lasagna, pizzas, and more. The Meriden and Middletown locations do not have GF menus, but GF pizza is available at all locations. ■ *www.illianospizza.com*

Italiano's Restaurant   ★ $$**LD**
Brookfield ■ *(203) 740-2488*
849 Federal Rd ■ *Italian* ■ GF pasta and pizza are available.

It's Only Natural Restaurant   ✿★ $**LD**
Middletown ■ *(860) 346-9210*
386 Main St ■ *Vegetarian* ■ Limited number of GF items marked on the menu include a sweet potato enchilada with mole rojo sauce, vegetable fried rice, and a macrobiotic plate with organic brown rice. GF soy sauce is available. ■ *www.ionrestaurant.com*

Jean-Louis $$$$**LD**
Greenwich ■ *(203) 622-8450*
61 Lewis St ■ *French* ■ Owner and Chef Jean-Louis Gerin recommends reservations noting GF. Chefs and managers are trained on the GF diet, and they'll be happy to accommodate their guests. A possible meal consists of the endive and caviar salad, the red snapper steamed with ginger, and the chocolate mousse. ■ *www.restaurantjean-louis.com*

Joe's American Bar & Grill   ★ $**LD**
Fairfield ■ *(203) 319-1600*
750 Post Rd ■ *American* ■ GF pasta and pizza are available. Both can be prepared in several different ways. GF beer is also available. Manager Doug recommends alerting the server and using the word "allergy." ■ *www.joesamerican.com*

Joe's Pizzeria   ★ $$**LD**
New Canaan ■ *(203) 966-2226*
23 Locust Ave ■ *Pizza* ■ GF pizza and pasta are available.

John Harvard's Brew House $$**LD**
Manchester ■ *(860) 644-2739*
1487 Pleasant Valley Rd ■ *American* ■ Manager David reports that they serve GF diners often. He recommends alerting the server upon arrival. Servers are trained to alert a manager, who in turn speaks to the chef about accommodating GF. He notes that the staff works "as a team to keep you safe." ■ *www.johnharvards.com*

John's Best Pizza & Grille   ★ $**LD**
Westport ■ *(203) 227-7247*
361 Post Rd W ■ *Italian* ■ GF pizza, pasta, cookies, and beer are available. Manager Isho notes that GF diners are "a regular occurrence" at the restaurant. ■ *www.johnsbestwestport.com*

Ken's Corner Breakfast & Lunch ★ ¢**BL**
Glastonbury ■ *(860) 657-9811*
30 Hebron Ave ■ *Sandwich Shop* ■ GF breads are available. Owner Ken notes that breakfast and lunch sandwiches can be made on different types of GF bread, including harvest, oatmeal, rye and white.

Kona Grill   📖
Stamford ■ *(203) 324-5700*
230 Tresser Blvd

La Piastra ★ $LD
Cromwell ▪ *(860) 632-7528*
25 Shunpike Rd ▪ *Italian* ▪ Several GF breads, cookies, raviolis, pizzas, soups, and entrées are available. Owner Lauren notes that the shop also offers several GF specials each month. Meals are available for carry-out only. only. ▪ *www.lapiastra.com*

La Rosticceria ★ ¢S
Guilford ▪ *(203) 458-8885*
500 Village Walk ▪ *Deli* ▪ GF soups and salads such as legume brown rice and tofu casserole, steak salad, and chicken salad are available. GF carrot cupcakes with cream cheese frosting are also available. ▪ *www.guilfordtakeout.com*

Lombardi's II ★ $$LD
Georgetown ▪ *(203) 544-9447*
22 Main St ▪ *Pizza* ▪ GF pizza is available.

Luigi's Apizza ★ $D
North Haven ▪ *(203) 234-9666*
323 Washington Ave ▪ *Pizza* ▪ GF pizza and beer are available. ▪ *www.luigisapizza.com*

Lyman Orchards Apple Barrel ★ ¢BL
Middlefield ▪ *(860) 349-1793*
Route 147 And 157 ▪ *American* ▪ The "eatery" serves breakfast on Saturdays and Sundays only. GF breakfast includes a wide variety of omelets. Confirm timeliness of this information before dining in. Chef George suggests asking for him upon arrival or calling in advance to give him or the chef on duty time to prepare. GF cookies are available from the bakery. ▪ *www.lymanorchards.com*

Mangetout Organic Café ★ ¢BL
New London ▪ *(860) 444-2066*
140 State St ▪ *Café* ▪ GF chocolate tofu pudding and chocolate peanut butter crisp bars are usually available. Manager Sean notes that many items can be modified to be GF, including sandwiches without bread. Many soups are naturally GF. Confirm timeliness of this information before dining in. ▪ *www.mangetoutorganic.com*

Mario's Brick Oven Pizza ★ $$LD
Waterbury ▪ *(203) 575-0485*
1650 Watertown Ave ▪ *Pizza* ▪ GF pizza is available. ▪ *www.mariosbrickovenpizza.com*

Max Amore ☻★ $$$LD
Glastonbury ▪ *(860) 659-2819*
140 Glastonbury Blvd ▪ *Italian* ▪ GF menu includes Toscana salad with GF croutons, shrimp scampi, other pasta dishes, pork chops, salmon, breadless chicken or veal parmesan, and mahi mahi with sweet potato mash. For dessert, they offer a chocolate fudge cake or crème brûlée. GF dinner rolls accompany GF meals. ▪ *www.maxrestaurantgroup.com*

Max Burger ★ $$LD
West Hartford ▪ *(860) 232-3300*
124 Lasalle Rd ▪ *Sandwich Shop* ▪ GF beer and hamburger buns are available. Restaurant reports that all servers are trained in the GF diet. ▪ *www.maxrestaurantgroup.com*

Max Downtown ☻ $$$$LD
Hartford ▪ *(860) 522-2530*
185 Asylum St ▪ *Modern American* ▪ GF menu includes goat cheese salad, grilled ahi tuna, seared jumbo sea scallops, salmon with fennel, artichokes and asparagus, filet mignon, and more. For dessert, a flourless chocolate cake is available. ▪ *www.maxrestaurantgroup.com*

Max's Oyster Bar ☻ $$$LD
West Hartford ▪ *(860) 236-6299*
964 Farmington Ave ▪ *Seafood* ▪ GF menu includes shellfish, sashimi plates, grilled fish with brown rice and root vegetables, steak, and lobster. ▪ *www.maxrestaurantgroup.com*

Melting Pot, The 📖
Darien ▪ *(203) 656-4774*
14 Grove St

Mitchell's Fish Market ☻ $$$LD
Stamford ▪ *(203) 323-3474*
230 Tresser Blvd ▪ *Seafood* ▪ Extensive GF menu includes pan-roasted wild

blue mussels, blackened salmon spinach salad, grilled shrimp and scallop skewers, Shanghai seafood sampler, lobster tail, filet mignon, and live Maine lobster. Mini crème brulee is available for dessert. ■ *www.mitchellsfishmarket.com*

Mocha Coffeehouse ★ ¢BLD
Sandy Hook ■ (203) 364-9200
3 Glen Rd ■ *Coffee House & Café* ■ GF chocolate chip cookies, snickerdoodles, and sugar cookies are available. ■ *www. mochacoffeehouse.com*

Naples Pizza ★ $LD
Farmington ■ (860) 674-8876
838 Farmington Ave ■ *Pizza* ■ GF pizza is available. Restaurant reports that requests for GF pizza are "common." ■ *www. naplespizzact.com*

Nature's Grocer ★ ¢BLD
Vernon ■ (860) 870-0020
81 East St ■ *Bakery & Café* ■ All products baked on the premises are GF. Non-GF items like wraps, which are brought in from outside, are prepared on separate surfaces. GF muffins, cookies, cinnamon buns, and more are available. GF cakes are available for order. Café also houses a grocery store with many GF options. ■ *www. naturesgrocervernon.com*

New Morning Natural and Organic
★ ¢S
Woodbury ■ (203) 263-4868
738 Main St S ■ *Deli & Bakery* ■ GF scones, brownies, and blondies are sometimes available at the deli. Restaurant notes that if customers buy a loaf of GF bread in the store, the deli will make a sandwich on it at a discounted price. ■ *www.newmorn.com*

Ninety Nine Restaurant & Pub 📖
Avon ■ (860) 677-2699
315 W Main St
Bristol ■ (860) 314-9900
827 Pine St
Cromwell ■ (860) 632-2099
36 Shunpike Rd
Dayville ■ (860) 774-3399

1068 Killingly Cmns
Enfield ■ (860) 741-7499
54 Hazard Ave
Glastonbury ■ (860) 652-9699
3025 Main St
Groton ■ (860) 449-9900
117 Long Hill Rd
Norwich ■ (860) 892-1299
5 Salem Tpke
Stratford ■ (203) 378-9997
411 Barnum Avenue Cutoff
Torrington ■ (860) 489-1299
1 S Main St
Vernon ■ (860) 872-1199
295 Hartford Tpke
Wallingford ■ (203) 284-9989
914 N Colony Rd
Waterbury ■ (203) 755-5209
920 Wolcott St

Olde World Apizza ★ $LD
North Haven ■ (203) 287-8820
1957 Whitney Ave ■ *Pizza* ■ GF pizza is available.

Outback Steakhouse 📖
Danbury ■ (203) 790-1124
116 Newtown Rd
Enfield ■ (860) 741-6046
98 Elm St
Manchester ■ (860) 648-2900
170 Hale Rd
New London ■ (860) 447-9205
305 N Frontage Rd
Newington ■ (860) 666-0002
3210 Berlin Tpke
North Haven ■ (203) 985-8282
345 Washington Ave
Orange ■ (203) 795-0700
132 Marsh Hill Rd
Shelton ■ (203) 926-3900
698 Bridgeport Ave
Southington ■ (860) 276-9585
817 Queen St
Wilton ■ (203) 762-0920
14 Danbury Rd

P.F. Chang's China Bistro 📖
Farmington ■ (860) 561-0097
322 Westfarms Mall Spc F226

Stamford ▪ *(203) 363-0434*
230 Tresser Blvd Ste H007

Palmieri's Pizza ★ $LD
Putnam ▪ *(860) 928-1010*
235 Kennedy Dr ▪ *Pizza* ▪ GF pizza is available in the 12-inch size. GF wraps are also available.

Paperback Café, Coffee House & Eatery ✪★ ¢B
Old Saybrook ▪ *(860) 388-9718*
210 Main St ▪ *American* ▪ GF menu includes an open cranberry chicken sandwich on a GF english muffin, an open tuna sandwich on a GF english muffin, mixed vegetables with marinara and parmesan over GF toast, pesto pizza, GF bagel sandwiches, and more.

Penny Lane Pub $$LD
Old Saybrook ▪ *(860) 388-9646*
150 Main St ▪ *American* ▪ Restaurant notes that it can accommodate GF diners. They note that salads, some fish dishes, and vegetable sides are naturally GF, and other menu items can be modified to be GF. Alert a server upon arrival. ▪ *www.pennylanepub.net*

Piccolo Pizza Pasta & Catering ★ $LD
Ridgefield ▪ *(203) 438-8200*
24 Prospect St ▪ *Pizza* ▪ GF pizza and pasta are available. GF pizza is available in the 12-inch size, and rice pasta is available for substitution into any of the regular pasta dishes. Owner Matt is an musician and composer who occasionally plays at the restaurant. ▪ *www.piccolopizzeria.com*

Pizza Pie, A ✪★ $$LD
Norwalk ▪ *(203) 642-3260*
4 New Canaan Ave ▪ *Italian* ▪ GF menu includes spinach and cheese ravioli, pizzas with any toppings except meatballs, and several paninis. Restaurant notes that they serve GF customers "all the time." GF pizza, bread, and pastas are available. Note GF when placing an order.

Pizzetta ★ $D
Mystic ▪ *(860) 536-4443*
7 Water St ▪ *Pizza* ▪ GF pizza is available. ▪ *www.pizzettamystic.com*

Port Coffeehouse ★ ¢BL
Bridgeport ▪ *(203) 345-8885*
2889 Fairfield Ave ▪ *Coffee Shop* ▪ GF baked goods, including cookies, cupcakes, and specialty breads, are available. ▪ *www.portcoffeehouse.com*

Quattro Pazzi ★ $$$LD
Fairfield ▪ *(203) 259-7417*
1599 Post Rd ▪ *Italian* ▪ GF pasta is available. ▪ *www.quattropazzi.com*

Rizzuto's ★ $$LD
Bethel ▪ *(203) 790-4444*
6 Stony Hill Rd
West Hartford ▪ *(860) 232-5000*
111 Memorial Rd
Westport ▪ *(203) 221-1002*
540 Riverside Ave ▪ *Italian* ▪ GF pasta is available. ▪ *www.rizzutos.com*

Rowayton Pizza ★ $LD
Rowayton ▪ *(203) 853-7555*
104 Rowayton Ave ▪ *Pizza* ▪ GF pizza is available. ▪ *www.rowaytonpizza.com*

Shoreline Diner & Vegetarian Enclave ✪ $$BLD
Guilford ▪ *(203) 458-7380*
345 Boston Post Rd ▪ *Global* ▪ Limited GF menu includes only the mediterranean pasta and the curried chicken pilaf. Restaurant reports that other menu items can also be modified to be GF. Alert the server, who will speak with the kitchen about GF requests and discuss which items can be made GF. ▪ *www.shorelinediner.com*

Sweet Harmony Cafe & Bakery ¢L
Middletown ▪ *(860) 344-9646*
158 Broad St ▪ *Bakery & Café* ▪ Co-owner Trang reports that the restaurant is "very GF-friendly." Alert a server upon arrival. Trang notes that all servers are educated on how menu items must be modified to be GF. With advanced notice of one week, she

can make flourless chocolate cake. ▪ *www.sweetharmonycafebakery.com*

Tivoli Pizza & Trattoria   ★ $$**LD**
Danbury ▪ *(203) 748-4821*
79 Newtown Rd ▪ *Pizza* ▪ GF pizza is available. ▪ *www.tivolipizzatrattoria.com*

Toozy Patza Pizza   ★ $**LD**
Wilton ▪ *(203) 544-9500*
991 Danbury Rd ▪ *Pizza* ▪ GF pizza and pasta are available. GF pizza is available in the 12-inch size, and rice pasta is available for substitution into any of the regular pasta dishes. Owner Matt is an musician and composer who occasionally plays at the restaurant. ▪ *www.toozypatzapizza.com*

Toscana Restaurant $$$**LD**
Ridgefield ▪ *(203) 894-8995*
43 Danbury Rd ▪ *Italian* ▪ Restaurant reports that they accommodate GF diners "all the time." GF diners are welcome to bring in their own pasta. The restaurant also notes that chicken or steak can be prepared GF. Alert server upon arrival. Reservations noting GF are recommended. ▪ *www.toscanaridgefield.com*

Uno Chicago Grill   📖
Danbury ▪ *(203) 778-1126*
7 Backus Ave
Milford ▪ *(203) 876-1160*
1061 Boston Post Rd

Vito's By the Park   ★ $$$**LD**
Hartford ▪ *(860) 244-2200*
26 Trumbull St ▪ *Italian* ▪ The restaurant reports that GF pasta is "usually" available. ▪ *www.vitosbythepark.com*

Westfair Pizza & Pasta   ★ $**LD**
Westport ▪ *(203) 259-2299*
1759 Post Rd E ▪ *Pizza* ▪ GF pasta is available. ▪ *www.westfairpizzapasta.com*

Wilton Pizza & Jazzeria   ★ $**LD**
Wilton ▪ *(203) 762-0007*
202 Town Grn ▪ *Pizza* ▪ GF pizza and pasta are available. GF pizza is available in the 12-inch size, and rice pasta is available for substitution into any of the regular pasta

dishes. Owner Matt is an musician and composer who occasionally plays at the restaurant. ▪ *www.wiltonpizza.com*

Wood-n-Tap Bar and Grill   ☺★ $$**LD**
Farmington ▪ *(860) 773-6736*
1274 Farmington Ave
Hartford ▪ *(860) 232-8277*
99 Sisson Ave
Rocky Hill ▪ *(860) 571-9444*
12 Town Line Rd
Southington ▪ *(860) 329-0032*
420 Queen St
Vernon Rockville ▪ *(860) 872-6700*
236 Hartford Tpke ▪ *American* ▪ GF menu includes spinach salad, steak salad, burgers with GF buns, steaks, salmon, Santa Fe chicken, BBQ chicken, and four side dishes. GF hamburger buns and beer are available. ▪ *www.woodntap.com*

DELAWARE

Bella's Cookies   ★ ¢**S**
Milton ▪ *(302) 684-8152*
18572 Coolspring Rd ▪ *Bakery* ▪ Non-dedicated GF bakery offering GF bread, cake, brownies, cookies, and other desserts. GF cookie varieties include chocolate cream filled sandwich cookies, ginger snaps, and more. ▪ *www.bellascookies.com*

Bertucci's   📖
Christiana ▪ *(302) 286-6600*
201 W Main St
Wilmington ▪ *(302) 529-0800*
3596 Concord Pike

Bethany Blues $$$**D**
Bethany Beach ▪ *(302) 537-1500*
6 North Pennsylvania Ave
Lewes ▪ *(302) 644-2500*
18385 Coastal Hwy ▪ *American* ▪ Manager Daniel of the Bethany Beach location

reports that they can "do anything" for GF diners. Manager Stephanie of the Lewes location adds that they serve GF diners "all the time," and all staff members are familiar with GF. Ask for a manager upon arrival. Baby back ribs, mussels, and french fries are just some of the GF items on the menu. Confirm timeliness of this information before dining in. ▪ www.bethanyblues.com

Big Fish Grill on the Riverfront ✪ $$$ LD
Wilmington ▪ (302) 652-3474
720 Justison St ▪ Seafood ▪ GF menu includes grilled charcoal shrimp, goat cheese salad, chopped salad, sirloin steak and shrimp, grilled shrimp, grilled pork chops, filet mignon, a variety of grilled or blackened fish, baked spiced apples, succotash, and sweet potato mashers. ▪ www.bigfish-riverfront.com

Big Fish Grill ✪ $$$ LD
Rehoboth Beach ▪ (302) 227-3474
20298 Coastal Hwy ▪ Seafood ▪ GF menu includes fresh goat cheese salad, greek salad, the fish of the day, Black Angus filet, pork chops, and grilled shrimp. ▪ www.bigfishgrill.com

Bugaboo Creek Steak House 📖
Newark ▪ (302) 283-0615
1323 New Churchmans Rd

Café Azafrán $$$ BLD
Lewes ▪ (302) 644-4446
109 W Market St
Rehoboth Beach ▪ (302) 227-8100
18 Baltimore Ave ▪ Mediterranean ▪ Manager Stephanie reports that all staff members are trained on the GF diet, so GF diners should alert a server upon arrival. Most entrées can be modified to be GF, and the restaurant is "very flexible" when it comes to accommodating GF diners. ▪ www.cafeazafran.com

Captain Pete's Mediterranean Cove $$ D
Fenwick Island ▪ (302) 537-5900
700 Coastal Hwy ▪ Greek ▪ Owner Helen reports that GF diners are welcome and

that many menu items can be modified to be GF. She notes that everything is made to order. Greek salads, rice dishes, and stuffed grape leaves are some examples of GF options. Confirm timeliness of this information before dining in.

Firebirds Wood Fired Grill ✪ $$$ LD
Newark ▪ (302) 366-7577
1225 Churchmans Rd ▪ American ▪ GF menu includes a variety of salads and a selection of entrées. Examples include sirloin, filet mignon, ribs, and lobster tail. Restaurant reports that servers are trained to alert the chef when a customer orders from the GF menu. ▪ www.firebirdsrestaurants.com

Greene Turtle Sports Bar & Grill, The ✪ ¢ LD
Lewes ▪ (302) 644-6840
17388 N Village Main Blvd Unit 21 ▪ American ▪ GF menu includes spinach, artichoke, and jalapeno dip, buffalo chicken wings, roasted chicken, terrapin steak, apple walnut salad, french fries, crab soup, and more. ▪ www.greeneturtle.com

Harry's Savoy Grill $$$ LD
Wilmington ▪ (302) 475-3000
2020 Naamans Rd ▪ American ▪ Company General Manager Kelly reports that over half the menu is naturally GF. She notes that all chefs are trained to prepare GF meals, and all floor staff is trained to serve GF diners. They report accommodating GF diners often. ▪ www.harrys-savoy.com

Harry's Seafood Grill $$$ LD
Wilmington ▪ (302) 777-1500
101 S Market St ▪ Seafood ▪ Company General Manager Kelly reports that over half of the menu is naturally GF. She notes that all chefs are trained to prepare GF meals, and all floor staff members are trained to serve GF diners. Alert a server upon arrival. ▪ www.harrysseafoodgrill.com

Hobos Restaurant & Bar ★ $$$ BLD
Rehoboth Beach ▪ (302) 226-2226
56 Baltimore Ave ▪ American ▪ GF bread, pasta, crackers, and quesadillas are avail-

able. Owner Gretchen notes that she has been "cooking for GF people for 25 years." She notes that the majority of the menu is already GF, but with two days' advanced notice, she can modify her non-GF signature dishes to be GF. She recommends asking for her upon arrival, as she always likes to work with GF customers herself. ▪ *www.myhobos.com*

Iron Hill Brewery & Restaurant
✪★ **$$LD**

Newark ▪ (302) 266-9000
147 E Main St
Wilmington ▪ (302) 472-2739
710 Justison St ▪ *American* ▪ GF menu is available at all locations. It includes sandwiches and burgers without buns, tomato basil soup, baked buffalo wings, and fisherman's stew. GF beer is available. ▪ *www. ironhillbrewery.com*

Kool Bean Bistro, The
$$$BLD

Ocean View ▪ (302) 541-5377
111 Atlantic Ave ▪ *Modern American* ▪ Manager Nancy reports that the restaurant has several regular GF customers. She notes that several fillets, chicken dishes, and meat dishes can be modified to be GF. Confirm timeliness of this information before dining in. She also cautions that GF diners should be prepared to educate servers on the GF diet. Upon arrival, alert a server and ask for a manager. ▪ *www. koolbeanbistro.com*

Lone Star Steakhouse & Saloon
📖

Dover ▪ (302) 736-5836
365 N Dupont Hwy
New Castle ▪ (302) 322-3854
113 S Dupont Hwy

Melting Pot, The
📖

Wilmington ▪ (302) 652-6358
1601 Concord Pike

Outback Steakhouse
📖

Newark ▪ (302) 366-8012
27 Possum Park Mall
Rehoboth Beach ▪ (302) 227-4858
19917 Sea Blossom Blvd

Pizza by Elizabeths
★ **$$LD**

Greenville ▪ (302) 654-4478
3801 Kennett Pike ▪ *Pizza* ▪ GF pizza and beer are available. ▪ *www.pizzabyelizabeths. com*

Restaurant 26
$$$D

Millville ▪ (302) 539-0626
238 Atlantic Ave ▪ *Steakhouse* ▪ Special GF flour is available. Manager Jerry reports that the restaurant has accommodated GF diners in groups of up to 20 people. GF items are not marked on the menu, but the staff is well-trained on GF options. Jerry notes that the menu changes often, so GF diners should alert their servers, who will indicate GF options. ▪ *www.steakhouse26. com*

Soffritto Italian Grill
✪ **$$$LD**

Newark ▪ (302) 455-1101
1130 Kirkwood Hwy ▪ *Italian* ▪ GF menu includes salads, chicken marsala, grilled salmon, filet mignon, and more. Management is knowledgeable about the GF diet and avoiding cross-contamination. ▪ *www. soffrittogrill.com*

Uno Chicago Grill
📖

Dover ▪ (302) 674-5055
1255 N Dupont Hwy

Walter's Steakhouse
$$$D

Wilmington ▪ (302) 652-6780
802 N Union St ▪ *Steakhouse* ▪ Manager Jose reports that the restaurant is "very used" to GF diners, and "careful to avoid cross-contamination." Steaks and baked potatoes are GF. Confirm timeliness of this information before dining in. Jose also recommends reservations noting GF. ▪ *www. walters-steakhouse.com*

DISTRICT OF COLUMBIA

1789 Restaurant $$$$D
Washington ▪ *(202) 965-1789*
1226 36th St NW ▪ *French* ▪ Reservationist
Ashley notes that they accommodate GF
diners "all the time." She recommends reservations noting GF, which give the kitchen
time to prepare. ▪ *www.1789restaurant.com*

Austin Grill   ✪ $LD
Washington ▪ *(202) 393-3776*
750 E St NW ▪ *Tex-Mex* ▪ GF menu includes slow-smoked BBQ ribs, fajitas, tacos
and quesadillas. For dessert, they offer
homemade flan. ▪ *www.austingrill.com*

B. Smith's $$$LD
Washington ▪ *(202) 289-6188*
50 Massachusetts Ave NE ▪ *Modern
American* ▪ Manager Mike reports that
they have "some items" which are GF or
can be prepared GF. He recommends making reservations noting GF and alerting
a server upon arrival. He notes that "the
server will be knowledgeable," and also that
they have an internal GF list which servers
can consult. ▪ *www.bsmith.com*

Bertucci's   📖
Washington ▪ *(202) 463-7733*
1218 Connecticut Ave NW # 1220
Washington ▪ *(202) 296-2600*
2000 Pennsylvania Ave NW

Birch & Barley   ★ $$$D
Washington ▪ *(202) 567-2576*
1337 14th St NW ▪ *Modern American* ▪
Managerial Assistant Lindsay reports that
nearly all menu items can be prepared
GF, and GF flatbreads can be made upon
request. Several different GF beers are
available. Lindsay recommends making
reservations noting GF. ▪ *www.birchand-
barley.com*

Brasserie Beck $$$$LD
Washington ▪ *(202) 408-1717*

1101 K St NW ▪ *Belgian* ▪ Executive Chef
David reports that accommodating GF
diners is "not a problem." He notes that
several menu items, including the beef
carbonade and rockfish, are naturally GF.
Confirm timeliness of this information
before dining in. Alert a server, who will
notify the chef. If necessary, the chef will
come to the table to help choose a GF meal.
▪ *www.beckdc.com*

Buca di Beppo   📖
Washington ▪ *(202) 232-8466*
1825 Connecticut Ave NW

Café Atlantico $$$LD
Washington ▪ *(202) 393-0812*
405 8th St NW ▪ *Fusion* ▪ General Manager Brian reports that the red snapper,
jerk chicken, duck confit, and portobello
mushroom dishes can be prepared GF. He
advises alerting the server, who can provide
a menu listing meals that conform to common dietary restrictions like GF. ▪ *www.
cafeatlantico.com*

CakeLove   ★ ¢S
Washington ▪ *(202) 588-7100*
1506 U St NW ▪ *Bakery* ▪ Non-dedicated
bakery offering GF cakes and cupcakes to
order with advanced notice of at least 4
days. Orders can be placed online for quick
and easy pick-up. ▪ *www.cakelove.com*

Capital Grille, The   📖
Washington ▪ *(202) 737-6200*
601 Pennsylvania Ave NW

Cava Mezze $D
Washington ▪ *(202) 543-9090*
527 8th St SE ▪ *Greek* ▪ Restaurant reports
frequently accommodating GF diners.
Alert a server upon arrival. Many menu
items are naturally GF, such as salads, dips,
omelets and saffron risotto. Confirm timeliness of this information before dining in.
▪ *www.cavamezze.com*

Ceiba $$$LD
Washington ▪ *(202) 393-3983*
701 14th St NW ▪ *Latin American* ▪ Pub-

licist Sue reports that GF items include red snapper vera cruz with tomato sofrito, jumbo shrimp in pineapple salsa, and slow braised pork shank, among others. Confirm timeliness of this information before dining in. She recommends alerting the server upon arrival and, if necessary, asking for Manager Alexandra. ▪ *www.ceibarestaurant.com*

Chop't   ¢LD
Washington ▪ *(202) 955-0665*
1105 1/2 19th St NW
Washington ▪ *(202) 327-2255*
1300 Connecticut Ave NW
Washington ▪ *(202) 783-0007*
618 12Th St NW
Washington ▪ *(202) 347-3225*
730 7th St NW ▪ *Deli* ▪ All restaurants have the same allergy protocol, which includes changing gloves, cleaning all utensils, and cleaning the cooking station. Alert a manager upon arrival to initiate the allergy protocol. Manager Kevin at 7th St offers to make GF salads himself in the back of the restaurant. Restaurants caution that all salad dressings are made in the same facility, and managers recommend ordering olive oil and lemon or vinegar, or taking a look at the ingredient list before ordering. Confirm timeliness of this information before dining in. ▪ *www.choptsalad.com*

ChurchKey   ★ $LD
Washington ▪ *(202) 567-2576*
1337 14th St NW ▪ *Modern American* ▪ Managerial Assistant Lindsay reports that GF flatbreads are available upon request, but she notes that many other menu items cannot be prepared GF. A selection of GF beers is available. ▪ *www.churchkeydc.com*

Clyde's $$LD
Washington ▪ *(202) 333-9180*
3236 M St NW
Washington ▪ *(202) 349-3700*
707 7th St NW ▪ *American* ▪ Both restaurants report that they are accustomed to GF requests. Alert the host upon arrival. He or she will alert the servers and call

a manager over to discuss GF options. ▪ *www.clydes.com*

Comet Ping Pong & Pizza   ★ $LD
Washington ▪ *(202) 364-0404*
5037 Connecticut Ave NW ▪ *Pizza* ▪ GF pizza is available. Manager Jeremy reports that GF diners are served "on a regular basis." They can make any pie with GF crust, and a separate tray is used for GF orders. Jeremy cautions that non-GF items are prepared on the premises, so cross-contamination is always a concern. ▪ *www.cometpingpong.com*

Commissary DC $LD
Washington ▪ *(202) 299-0018*
1443 P St NW ▪ *Modern American* ▪ Manager Josh reports that they accommodate GF diners "fairly easily." He notes that it is restaurant policy to ask arriving guests if they have any dietary restrictions, and that there is an "extensive allergen list" for servers to check which menu items are GF. ▪ *www.commissarydc.com*

DC Coast Restaurant $$$LD
Washington ▪ *(202) 216-5988*
1401 K St NW ▪ *Seafood* ▪ Chef Brendan reports that they serve GF diners "every day," and that all staff members are trained on the GF diet. Alert a server upon arrival. Brendan further notes that calling ahead is "helpful," but not necessary. ▪ *www.dccoast.com*

Dino $$$D
Washington ▪ *(202) 686-2966*
3435 Connecticut Ave NW ▪ *Italian* ▪ Owner and Chef Dean reports that GF options are constantly changing, but they are always available. He notes that they can substitute polenta for pasta, and that all meat and fish dishes can be prepared GF. For dessert, they offer ricotta mousse, among other things. Confirm timeliness of this information before dining in. Dean recommends speaking to a manager to ensure a GF meal. ▪ *www.dino-dc.com*

Ella's Wood Fired Pizza ★ $LD
Washington ▪ (202) 638-3434
901 F St NW ▪ *Pizza* ▪ Any pizza is available on GF crust. For dessert, they offer double chocolate pudding or a selection of ice creams and sorbets. Located a short walk from the National Mall. ▪ *www.ellaspizza.com*

Firefly ✪ $$$BLD
Washington ▪ (202) 861-1310
1310 New Hampshire Ave NW ▪ *Modern American* ▪ Manager Erik reports that there is a new GF menu featuring a mini pot roast with yukon gold mashed potatoes and pan seared sea scallops with black eyed peas. For dessert, GF options include a peanut butter ice cream sandwich, flourless chocolate cake, crumbled peanut praline, and more. Located adjacent to the Hotel Madera. ▪ *www.firefly-dc.com*

Fogo De Chao ★ $$$$LD
Washington ▪ (202) 347-4668
1101 Pennsylvania Ave NW ▪ *Brazilian* ▪ GF cheese bread made with yucca flour is available. ▪ *www.fogodechao.com*

Founding Farmers $$BLD
Washington ▪ (202) 822-8783
1924 Pennsylvania Ave NW ▪ *American* ▪ Manager Nick reports that they take GF requests "very seriously." He recommends making reservations noting GF and asking for him upon arrival. GF options include rotisserie chicken, all fish entrées, and steak. Confirm timeliness of this information before dining in. ▪ *www.wearefoundingfarmers.com*

Greene Turtle Sports Bar & Grill, The ✪ ¢LD
Washington ▪ (202) 637-8889
601 F St NW ▪ *American* ▪ GF menu includes spinach, artichoke, and jalapeno dip, buffalo chicken wings, roasted chicken, terrapin steak, apple walnut salad, french fries, crab soup, and more. ▪ *www.greeneturtle.com*

Grillfish $$LD
Washington ▪ (202) 331-7310
1200 New Hampshire Ave NW ▪ *Seafood* ▪ Veteran Server Elise reports that they serve GF diners "all the time," and she adds that the servers are "very familiar" with the GF diet. All of the grilled fish dishes and the steaks are naturally GF. Confirm timeliness of this information before dining in. ▪ *www.grillfishdc.com*

Heights, The $$LD
Washington ▪ (202) 797-7227
3115 14th St NW ▪ *Modern American* ▪ Manager Ben reports that the restaurant "makes an effort to modify" menu items according to the needs of GF customers. He notes that the dinner menu is probably the easiest to modify to be GF. Alert a server, who will notify a manager. ▪ *www.theheightsdc.com*

Hello Cupcake ★ ¢S
Washington ▪ (202) 861-2253
1361 Connecticut Ave NW ▪ *Bakery* ▪ GF cupcakes are available. A different GF cupcake selection is available every day. Manager Emily reports that GF cupcakes are made first to avoid cross-contamination. She recommends placing special orders 48 hours in advance. ▪ *www.hellocupcakeonline.com*

Jaleo DC ✪ $$$LD
Washington ▪ (202) 628-7949
480 7th St NW ▪ *Tapas* ▪ General Manager Joseph reports that GF menu items include paellas, grilled hangar steak, duck confit, traditional chorizo tapas, and more. He recommends speaking to a manager upon arrival. ▪ *www.jaleo.com*

Java Green Eco Café ✪★ ¢BLD
Washington ▪ (202) 775-8899
1020 19th St NW ▪ *Café* ▪ Limited GF menu includes a tofu mushroom wrap and tofu avocado wrap, along with a few other GF wraps and sandwiches. GF wraps and bread are available. ▪ *www.javagreencafe.com*

Kavanagh's Pizza Pub   ★ $LD
Washington ■ *(202) 337-3132*
2400 Wisconsin Ave NW ■ *Pizza* ■ GF pizza is available in the 10-inch size and can be prepared with any available toppings except meatballs, which are not GF. Co-owner Lee recommends ordering GF pizza with extra sauce. GF beer is also available. ■ *www.kavanaghspizzapub.com*

La Chaumiere $$$LD
Washington ■ *(202) 338-1784*
2813 M St NW ■ *French* ■ Owner Lumé reports that the restaurant serves GF diners "all the time." He suggests noting GF in reservations and speaking to the host or manager about the best GF options. ■ *www.lachaumieredc.com*

Lebanese Taverna   ✪ ¢LD
Washington ■ *(202) 265-8681*
2641 Connecticut Ave. NW ■ *Middle Eastern* ■ GF menu includes lentil soup, lamb shanks, shwarma, chicken and rice, jumbo shrimp, and more. Any dish that normally includes bread can be made GF by substituting rice crackers and vegetables. ■ *www.lebanesetaverna.com*

Legal Sea Foods   📖
Washington ■ *(202) 347-0007*
704 7th St NW

Logan Tavern $LD
Washington ■ *(202) 332-3710*
1423 P St NW ■ *Modern American* ■ Manager Tony reports that the restaurant serves GF diners "all the time." Alert a server, who will ask the kitchen manager or restaurant manager if he or she is unsure of what ingredients are in a certain dish. ■ *www.logantavern.com*

Love Café   ★ $S
Washington ■ *(202) 265-9800*
1501 U St NW ■ *Bakery* ■ Non-dedicated bakery that sometimes has GF cupcakes. Manager Nellie recommends calling ahead to find out what is available. ■ *www.cake-love.com*

Maggiano's Little Italy   ★ $$$LD
Washington ■ *(202) 966-5500*
5333 Wisconsin Ave NW ■ *Italian* ■ GF pasta is available. Call individual locations to inquire about additional GF options. ■ *www.maggianos.com*

Melting Pot, The   📖
Washington ■ *(202) 857-0777*
1220 19th St NW

Mitsitam Native Foods Café   ✪ $L
Washington ■ *(202) 633-7038*
4th St & Independence Ave SW ■ *Native American* ■ Executive Chef Richard reports that there are "signs" on all of the GF items. He notes that staff members are trained on the GF diet, so ask any one of them to confirm whether or not an item is GF. The café is located inside the National Museum of the American Indian.

Old Ebbitt Grill $$$BLD
Washington ■ *(202) 347-4800*
675 15th St NW ■ *American* ■ Manager Christian reports that the restaurant gets "hundreds of allergy requests" every day, many of which come from GF diners. He suggests alerting a server upon arrival. All servers are familiar with the GF diet and will notify the chef. Most menu items, including fish and meats, can be modified to be GF. ■ *www.ebbitt.com*

Oyamel Cocina Mexicana   ✪ $LD
Washington ■ *(202) 628-1005*
401 7th St NW ■ *Mexican* ■ Extensive GF menu includes avocado salad, specialty scallop and snapper ceviches, chicken with poblano mole, and a range of tacos. Certain desserts on the regular menu can be prepared GF. ■ *www.oyamel.com*

Papa Razzi   ★ $$LD
Washington ■ *(202) 298-8000*
1066 Wisconsin Ave NW ■ *Italian* ■ GF pasta and pizza are available. ■ *www.paparazzitrattoria.com*

Pete's New Haven Style Apizza   ★ ¢LD
Washington ■ *(202) 332-7383*

1400 *Irving St NW*
Washington ▪ *(202) 332-7383*
4940 Wisconsin Ave NW ▪ *Pizza* ▪ GF
pizza is available, as are GF pasta and GF
beer. Customers can add toppings of their
choice to the GF pizza. ▪ *www.petesapizza.
com*

Restaurant Nora $$$$D
Washington ▪ *(202) 462-5143*
2132 Florida Ave NW ▪ *Organic American* ▪ Chef Josh reports that many menu
items are naturally GF. He notes that with
advanced notice of at least half a day, the
kitchen can put together several GF options. He recommends making reservations
noting GF and asking for a manager or chef
upon arrival. ▪ *www.noras.com*

Scion Restaurant   ✪ $$LD
Washington ▪ *(202) 833-8899*
2100 P St NW ▪ *American* ▪ GF menu
includes jade vegan curry, wasabi caesar
salad, and smoked salmon on GF rice
crackers. ▪ *www.scionrestaurant.com*

Shanghai Garden   ★ $$LD
Washington ▪ *(202) 362-3000*
4469 Connecticut Ave NW ▪ *Chinese* ▪ GF
soy sauce is available.

Smith & Wollensky $$$$LD
Washington ▪ *(202) 466-1100*
1112 19th St NW ▪ *Steakhouse* ▪ Manager
Dave reports that they serve GF diners
"once in a while." He recommends noting
GF in reservations so that the server will be
made aware in advance. Most steaks can be
prepared GF, and many sides are naturally
GF. Confirm timeliness of this information
before dining in. ▪ *www.smithandwollensky.
com*

Uno Chicago Grill   📖
Washington ▪ *(202) 965-6333*
3211 M St NW
Washington ▪ *(202) 842-0438*
50 Mass Ave NE

Zaytinya   ✪ ¢LD
Washington ▪ *(202) 638-0800*

701 9th St NW ▪ *Mediterranean* ▪ GF
menu includes a variety of mezze, or small
plates. Examples are Syrian lamb and beef
sausage, Ottoman style roasted eggplant,
and goat cheese wrapped in grape leaves. ▪
www.zaytinya.com

Zengo   ✪ $$$LD
Washington ▪ *(202) 393-2929*
781 7th St NW ▪ *Asian & Latin Fusion* ▪
GF menu includes a variety of sushi, small
plates, and large plates. Examples are tuna
tataki salad and chicken tandoori. For
dessert, they offer GF tofu cheesecake and
dulce de leche pudding. Reservations noting GF are recommended. ▪ *www.modern-
mexican.com*

FLORIDA
BOCA RATON

Bonefish Grill   📖
Boca Raton ▪ *(561) 483-4949*
21065 Powerline Rd Ste C-15

Capital Grille, The   📖
Boca Raton ▪ *(561) 368-1077*
6000 Glades Rd

Carrabba's Italian Grill   📖
Boca Raton ▪ *(561) 544-8838*
6909 SW 18th St

Duffy's Sports Grill   ✪ $$LD
Boca Raton ▪ *(561) 869-0552*
21212 Saint Andrews Blvd ▪ *American* ▪
GF menu includes flat iron steak salad
with arugula, burgers without buns, NY
strip steak, baby back ribs, yellowfin tuna,
broiled bay scallops, and a variety of side
dishes. ▪ *www.duffyssportsgrill.com*

First Watch - The Daytime Café   📖
Boca Raton ▪ *(561) 544-8875*
21210 Saint Andrews Blvd Ste 15A

Legal Sea Foods   📖
Boca Raton ▪ *(561) 447-2112*
6000 Glades Rd

Maggiano's Little Italy   ★ $$$**LD**
Boca Raton ▪ *(561) 361-8244*
21090 Saint Andrews Blvd ▪ *Italian* ▪ GF
pasta is available. Call individual locations
to inquire about additional GF options. ▪
www.maggianos.com

Melting Pot, The   📖
Boca Raton ▪ *(561) 997-7472*
5455 N Federal Hwy

Original Pancake House, The   ★ ¢**BL**
Boca Raton ▪ *(561) 395-2303*
7146 Beracasa Way ▪ *Breakfast* ▪ GF
pancakes are available. Select locations
may serve other GF options. Call a specific
location to inquire. ▪ *www.originalpancake-
house.com*

Outback Steakhouse   📖
Boca Raton ▪ *(561) 479-2526*
19595 State Road 7
Boca Raton ▪ *(561) 338-6283*
6030 SW 18th St

P.F. Chang's China Bistro   📖
Boca Raton ▪ *(561) 393-3722*
1400 Glades Rd

Pei Wei Asian Diner   📖
Boca Raton ▪ *(561) 226-0290*
1914 NE 5th Ave
Boca Raton ▪ *(561) 322-1001*
7152 Beracasa Way

Seasons 52   ✪ $$$**LD**
Boca Raton ▪ *(561) 998-9952*
2300 NW Executive Center Dr ▪ *Modern
American* ▪ GF menu includes cedar plank
Atlantic salmon, grilled rack of lamb, and
burgers without buns. Restaurant reports
that some menu items are seasonal. ▪ *www.
seasons52.com*

Stir Crazy   ★ $$**LD**
Boca Raton ▪ *(561) 338-7500*
6000 Glades Rd Ste 1015 ▪ *Asian Stir-Fry*
▪ GF teriyaki, classic Chinese, and thai
BBQ sauces are available. Confirm timeli-

ness of information before dining in. GF
rice noodles are also available. ▪ *www.
stircrazy.com*

FLORIDA

JACKSONVILLE

Bonefish Grill   📖
Jacksonville ▪ *(904) 370-1070*
10950 San Jose Blvd

Brick Restaurant $$**LD**
Jacksonville ▪ *(904) 387-0606*
3585 Saint Johns Ave ▪ *Modern American*
▪ Manager Marshall reports that "everybody knows" how to accommodate GF
diners, as they do it "often." He recommends any of the steak or fish on the menu,
which can almost always be prepared GF.
Confirm timeliness of this information before dining in. Alert a server upon arrival. ▪
www.brickofavondale.com

Buca di Beppo   📖
Jacksonville ▪ *(904) 363-9090*
10334 Southside Blvd

Cantina Laredo   📖
Jacksonville ▪ *(904) 997-6110*
10282 Bistro St

Capital Grille, The   📖
Jacksonville ▪ *(904) 997-9233*
5197 Big Island Dr

Carrabba's Italian Grill   📖
Jacksonville ▪ *(904) 363-2254*
8137 Point Meadows Way
Jacksonville ▪ *(904) 726-9000*
9840 Atlantic Blvd
Jacksonville ▪ *(904) 262-8280*
9965 San Jose Blvd

Lemongrass $$**LD**
Jacksonville ▪ *(904) 645-9911*
9846 Old Baymeadows Rd ▪ *Thai* ▪ The

restaurant reports that they can accommodate GF diners, although it is "not a regular occurrence." Alert a server upon arrival. Reservations noting GF are recommended. ▪ *www.lemongrassjax.com*

Maggiano's Little Italy   ★ $$$LD
Jacksonville ▪ *(904) 380-4360*
10367 Midtown Pkwy ▪ *Italian* ▪ GF pasta is available. Call individual locations to inquire about additional GF options. ▪ *www.maggianos.com*

Melting Pot, The   📖
Jacksonville ▪ *(904) 642-4900*
7860 Gate Pkwy

Mitchell's Fish Market   ✪ $$$LD
Jacksonville ▪ *(904) 645-3474*
5205 Big Island Dr ▪ *Seafood* ▪ Extensive GF menu includes pan-roasted wild blue mussels, blackened salmon spinach salad, grilled shrimp and scallop skewers, Shanghai seafood sampler, lobster tail, filet mignon, and live Maine lobster. Mini crème brulee is available for dessert. ▪ *www.mitchellsfishmarket.com*

Outback Steakhouse   📖
Jacksonville ▪ *(904) 220-5899*
13245 Atlantic Blvd
Jacksonville ▪ *(904) 363-3839*
8145 Point Meadows Way
Jacksonville ▪ *(904) 720-1818*
9400 Atlantic Blvd
Jacksonville ▪ *(904) 268-4329*
9773 San Jose Blvd

P.F. Chang's China Bistro   📖
Jacksonville ▪ *(904) 641-3392*
10281 Midtown Pkwy Ste 137

Roy's   ✪ $$$D
Jacksonville ▪ *(904) 241-7697*
2400 S 3rd St ▪ *Hawaiian Fusion* ▪ GF menu includes blackened ahi tuna, sesame seared shrimp sticks or red grouper, grilled Atlantic salmon, and a filet Hawaiian style. Hostess Ashley recommends alerting the server upon arrival. ▪ *www.roysrestaurant.com*

Tommy's Brick Oven Pizza   ★ ¢LD
Jacksonville ▪ *(904) 565-1999*
4160 Southside Blvd ▪ *Pizza* ▪ GF pizzas are available in the 12-inch size and can be prepared with any toppings. GF beer is available, and there is always at least one GF soup. For dessert, they offer GF cheesecake and brownies. ▪ *www.tbopizza.com*

FLORIDA
NAPLES

Bha! Bha! Persian Bistro $$$LD
Naples ▪ *(239) 594-5557*
847 Vanderbilt Beach Rd ▪ *Persian* ▪ Chef PJ reports that nearly the entire menu is GF, as only meats marinated in soy sauce cannot be prepared GF. Examples of GF items on the menu include the mango ginger shrimp and the spicy kermani beef. Confirm timeliness of this information before dining in. PJ adds that all staff members are "pretty familiar" with the GF diet, so just alert the server upon arrival. ▪ *www.bhabhapersianbistro.com*

Bistro 821   ✪ $$$D
Naples ▪ *(239) 261-5821*
821 5th Ave S ▪ *Bistro* ▪ GF menu includes jumbo prawns, seafood paella, sea bass, rib eye steak, and risottos. Owner Michelle reports that several GF customers are accommodated "on a regular basis." She also notes that everything is made to order. ▪ *www.bistro821.com*

Bonefish Grill   📖
Naples ▪ *(239) 417-1212*
1500 5th Ave S Unit 112

BrickTop's   ✪ $$$LD
Naples ▪ *(239) 596-9112*
5555 Tamiami Trl N ▪ *Seafood & Steakhouse* ▪ GF menu includes rotisserie

chicken, steak frites, ahi tuna salad, and babyback ribs. The signature appetizer, deviled eggs and bacon sausage, is also GF. For dessert, they offer a hot fudge sundae. ▪ *www.westendrestaurants.com*

Buca di Beppo   📖
Naples ▪ *(239) 596-6662*
8860 Tamiami Trl N

Cafe Alessio   ★ $$**LD**
Naples ▪ *(239) 597-7500*
1485 Pine Ridge Rd ▪ *Italian* ▪ GF pasta and pizza are available. ▪ *www.cafealessionaples.com*

Capital Grille, The   📖
Naples ▪ *(239) 254-0604*
9005 Mercato Dr

Carrabba's Italian Grill   📖
Naples ▪ *(239) 774-2965*
12631 Tamiami Trl E
Naples ▪ *(239) 643-7727*
4320 Tamiami Trl N

Chops City Grill   ✪ $$$$**D**
Naples ▪ *(239) 262-4677*
837 5th Ave S ▪ *Seafood & Steakhouse* ▪ GF menu at both locations includes shrimp cocktail, clams on the halfshell, beef satay, sushi, tuna, salads, NY strip steak, grilled chicken breast, and more. ▪ *www.chopscitygrill.com*

First Watch - The Daytime Café   📖
Naples ▪ *(239) 566-7395*
1000 Immokalee Rd Ste 81
Naples ▪ *(239) 213-1709*
13030 Livingston Rd
Naples ▪ *(239) 434-0005*
225 Banyan Blvd Ste 100
Naples ▪ *(239) 304-0746*
7163 Radio Rd

For Goodness Sake Café   ★ ¢**L**
Naples ▪ *(239) 597-0120*
2464 Vanderbilt Beach Rd Ste 528 ▪ *Café* ▪ GF bread and wraps are available for sandwiches. A variety of GF desserts is available. Call ahead to confirm availability, especially at the Bonita Springs location.

Located within the For Goodness Sake Natural Marketplace. ▪ *www.forgoodnesssake123.com*

Melting Pot, The   📖
Naples ▪ *(239) 732-6666*
2950 Tamiami Trl N

Noodles Italian Café & Sushi Bar
                                        ✪★ $$$**LD**
Naples ▪ *(239) 592-0050*
1585 Pine Ridge Rd ▪ *American* ▪ GF menu includes artichoke hearts, shrimp rustica, lamb shanks, and tomato basil soup. Manager Angela reports that the kitchen has "no problem" preparing GF meals. GF rice pasta is available. ▪ *www.noodlescafe.com*

Outback Steakhouse   📖
Naples ▪ *(239) 434-7100*
4910 Tamiami Trl N

P.F. Chang's China Bistro   📖
Naples ▪ *(239) 596-2174*
10840 Tamiami Trl N

Pazzo! Cucina Italiana   ✪★ $$$$**D**
Naples ▪ *(239) 434-8494*
853 5th Ave S ▪ *Italian* ▪ GF menu includes salads, pasta dishes, grilled steak and fish, and more. GF pasta is available. ▪ *www.pazzoitaliancafe.com*

Pei Wei Asian Diner   📖
Naples ▪ *(239) 596-5515*
2355 Vanderbilt Beach Rd Ste 116

Preston's Steak House $$$$**D**
Naples ▪ *(239) 435-1986*
109 9th St S ▪ *Steakhouse* ▪ Manager Jim notes that many menu items can be modified to be GF, including steaks, vegetables, shrimp, and salads. Confirm timeliness of this information before dining in. Upon arrival, alert a server and ask for a manager or chef. Reservations noting GF are required.

Real Seafood Co.   ✪ $$$**LD**
Naples ▪ *(239) 591-3523*
8960 Fontana Del Sol Way ▪ *Seafood* ▪ GF items marked on the menu include little neck clams, smoked salmon sampler,

and crème brûlée. Reservations noting GF are recommended. ▪ *www.realseafoodcorestaurant.com*

Roy's   ✪ $$$D
Naples ▪ *(239) 261-1416*
475 Bayfront Pl ▪ *Hawaiian Fusion* ▪ Triumph contacted a manager at each location and all reported that GF diners can be accommodated. A different GF menu is available at each location. Typically, a chef will come out to speak with GF diners. Reservations noting GF are strongly recommended by all locations. ▪ *www. roysrestaurant.com*

U Food Grill   📖
Naples ▪ *(239) 598-4456*
1201 Piper Blvd

Uno Chicago Grill   📖
Naples ▪ *(239) 566-7866*
2380 Vanderbilt Beach Rd

FLORIDA

ORLANDO

All-Star Sports Resort   ★ $BLD
Orlando ▪ *(407) 939-3463*
1701 W Buena Vista Dr ▪ *American* ▪ GF waffles are available. ▪ *www.disneyworld. disney.go.com*

B-Line Diner $BLD
Orlando ▪ *(407) 345-4460*
9801 International Dr ▪ *American* ▪ Manager Scott reports that GF diners should feel "totally comfortable" because the restaurant has "a lot of experience" accommodating the GF diet. GF bread is available "at times." Located inside the Peabody Hotel. ▪ *www.peabodyorlando.com*

Bonefish Grill   📖
Orlando ▪ *(407) 816-6355*
5463 Orlando Gateway Village Cir

Orlando ▪ *(407) 355-7707*
7830 W Sand Lake Rd

Bubba Gump Shrimp Co.   📖
Orlando ▪ *(407) 903-0044*
6000 Universal Blvd

Buca di Beppo   📖
Orlando ▪ *(407) 859-7844*
8001 S Orange Blossom Trl

Cantina Laredo   📖
Orlando ▪ *(407) 345-0186*
8000 Via Dellagio Way

Capital Grille, The   📖
Orlando ▪ *(407) 370-4392*
9101 International Dr

Capriccio Grill $$$$D
Orlando ▪ *(407) 248-6104*
9801 International Dr ▪ *Italian & Steakhouse* ▪ Restaurant reports that they serve many business travelers who are GF, and they deal with GF requests "a lot." They also note that the chefs are very educated on what is GF and what can be modified to be GF. Reservations noting GF are recommended. ▪ *www.peabodyorlando.com*

Carrabba's Italian Grill   📖
Orlando ▪ *(407) 888-2727*
1001 Sand Lake Rd
Orlando ▪ *(407) 355-7277*
5701 Vineland Rd
Orlando ▪ *(407) 938-0015*
8702 Vineland Ave

Chatham's Place Restaurant $$$$D
Orlando ▪ *(407) 345-2992*
7575 Dr Phillips Blvd ▪ *Modern American* ▪ Maitre d' Maurice reports that they serve GF diners at least "once a week." He notes that all fish entrées, beef dishes, and the rack of lamb can be prepared GF. Confirm timeliness of this information before dining in. Alert a server upon arrival. Servers are very knowledgeable and can indicate GF items. ▪ *www.chathamsplace.com*

Dandelion Communitea Café   ✪ ¢S
Orlando ▪ *(407) 362-1864*
618 N Thornton Ave ▪ *Organic* ▪ GF menu

options include quinoa pilaf, Polynesian bananas and spring greens, along with several GF sides like hummus, tabouli, queso, and black bean dip. GF dessert options are also available. Restaurant reports that one of the founders is GF, so they are very conscious of the diet. ▪ *www.dandelioncommunitea.com*

Ethos Vegan Kitchen ✿ $LD
Orlando ▪ *(407) 228-3898*
1235 N Orange Ave ▪ *Vegetarian* ▪
GF items marked on the menu include edamame, several soups and sandwiches, and all of the side dishes. Co-owner Laina cautions that the Sunday brunch menu has "very limited" GF options. ▪ *www.ethosvegankitchen.com*

First Watch - The Daytime Café 📖
Orlando ▪ *(407) 823-8146*
3402 Technological Ave
Orlando ▪ *(407) 363-5622*
7500 W Sand Lake Rd # A101

Lone Star Steakhouse & Saloon 📖
Orlando ▪ *(407) 827-8225*
8850 Vineland Ave

Maggiano's Little Italy ★ $$$LD
Orlando ▪ *(407) 241-8650*
9101 International Dr Ste 2400 ▪ *Italian*
▪ GF pasta is available. Call individual locations to inquire about additional GF options. ▪ *www.maggianos.com*

Margaritaville ✿★ $$LD
Orlando ▪ *(407) 224-2155*
6000 Universal Blvd ▪ *American* ▪ GF menu items include nachos, sirloin steak, jerk salmon, mushroom cheeseburger with a GF bun, chicken or fish sandwich with a GF bun, and more. For dessert, the "chocolate hurricane," a GF chocolate brownie with whipped cream and chocolate sauce is available. GF beer is available. ▪ *www. margaritavilleorlando.com*

Melting Pot, The 📖
Orlando ▪ *(407) 903-1100*
7549 W Sand Lake Rd

Mia Bella's Scalini Family Restaurant
★ $$LD
Orlando ▪ *(407) 291-9349*
5106 Dr Phillips Blvd ▪ *Pizza* ▪ GF pizza is available. Restaurant cautions that GF diners should call ahead, as GF pizza is very popular. ▪ *www.scalinispizza.com*

Outback Steakhouse 📖
Orlando ▪ *(407) 243-6068*
10749 Narcoossee Rd
Orlando ▪ *(407) 275-9440*
12120 Lake Underhill Rd
Orlando ▪ *(407) 240-6857*
1301 Florida Mall Ave
Orlando ▪ *(407) 292-5111*
4845 S Kirkman Rd
Orlando ▪ *(407) 477-0098*
8195 Vineland Ave
Orlando ▪ *(407) 851-1334*
9333 Airport Blvd

P.F. Chang's China Bistro 📖
Orlando ▪ *(407) 345-2888*
4200 Conroy Rd

Pei Wei Asian Diner 📖
Orlando ▪ *(407) 563-8777*
3011 E Colonial Dr Ste B
Orlando ▪ *(407) 563-9905*
3402 Technological Ave Ste 232
Orlando ▪ *(407) 241-3301*
8015 Turkey Lake Rd Ste 400

Pizza Fusion ★ $$LD
Orlando ▪ *(407) 351-3360*
7563 W Sand Lake Rd ▪ *Pizza* ▪ GF pizza and brownies are available. ▪ *www.pizzafusion.com*

Primo ★ $$$$D
Orlando ▪ *(407) 393-4444*
4040 Central Florida Pkwy ▪ *Modern American* ▪ GF pasta is available by special request and with advanced notice. Chef Edgar notes that accommodating GF diners is "not a problem." Located inside the Grande Lakes Orlando. ▪ *www.primorestaurant.com*

Roy's $$$D
Orlando ■ (407) 352-4844
7760 W Sand Lake Rd ■ Hawaiian Fusion
■ Manager Miguel reports that GF diners are welcome. Alert a server, who will
notify the chef. The chef will come to the
table to discuss GF options. Miguel adds
that because the menu changes so often,
the chef prefers to accommodate each GF
diner individually, rather than limiting all
GF guests to the same predetermined GF
menu. ■ www.roysrestaurant.com

Samba Room $$$D
Orlando ■ (407) 226-0550
7468 W Sand Lake Rd ■ Latin American
■ Manager Stephen reports that GF diners
are welcome. Fresh seafood or vegetable
dishes, steaks, and pork can be prepared
GF. Confirm timeliness of this information
before dining in. Alert a server, who will
notify the kitchen. ■ www.sambaroom.net

Seasons 52   ✪★ $$$LD
Orlando ■ (407) 354-5212
7700 W Sand Lake Rd ■ Modern American ■ GF menu items include a spicy tuna
roll, salads, rainbow trout, rack of lamb,
and burgers without the bun. GF tamari
sauce is available. ■ www.seasons52.com

Uno Chicago Grill   📖
Orlando ■ (407) 827-1212
12553 State Road 535
Orlando ■ (407) 351-8667
8250 International Dr

FLORIDA

SARASOTA

Bonefish Grill   📖
Sarasota ■ (941) 924-9090
3971 S Tamiami Trl

Café Baci $$LD
Sarasota ■ (941) 921-4848
4001 S Tamiami Trl ■ Italian ■ Manager
Roberto reports that the restaurant does
not serve GF diners often. Alert a server
upon arrival. Roberto notes that servers should know what can be modified
to be GF, and if they have a question, he
is available for consult. Grilled fish, veal,
or chicken are a few possible GF options.
Confirm timeliness of this information
before dining in. ■ www.cafebaci.net

Carrabba's Italian Grill   📖
Sarasota ■ (941) 925-7407
1940 Stickney Point Rd
Sarasota ■ (941) 359-1050
2875 University Pkwy

Columbia Restaurant   ✪ $$LD
Sarasota ■ (941) 388-3987
411 Saint Armands Cir ■ Spanish ■ There
is a printed list of GF menu items at all
locations. GF options include the beefsteak
tomato salad, the palomilla, and the queso
fundido. For dessert, they offer flan and
crema catalana. ■ www.columbiarestaurant.
com

First Watch - The Daytime Café   📖
Sarasota ■ (941) 954-1395
1395 Main St
Sarasota ■ (941) 923-6754
8383 S Tamiami Trl

Island Gluten Free Bakery   100%★ ¢S
Sarasota ■ (941) 346-0002
1220 Old Stickney Point Rd ■ Bakery ■
Dedicated GF bakery offering GF bread,
hamburger buns, pizza dough, cookies,
muffins, scones, brownies, key lime pie,
carrot cake, and some frozen meals to go.
The bakery recommends calling in advance
for special orders. ■ www.islandgfbakery.
com

Melting Pot, The   📖
Sarasota ■ (941) 365-2628
1949 Ringling Blvd

Morel Restaurant $$$D
Sarasota ▪ (941) 927-8716
3809 S Tuttle Ave ▪ American ▪ Owner Paula reports that they serve GF diners "all the time." She adds that everything is made to order, so the GF diet is easy to accommodate. She cautions that sauces contain gluten, so GF diners should ask for "no sauce" or request that the chef make a special GF sauce. ▪ *www.morelrestaurant.com*

Ophelia's on the Bay $$$D
Sarasota ▪ (941) 349-2212
9105 Midnight Pass Rd ▪ Modern American ▪ Owner Stanley reports that people "regularly" request GF meals and that all GF dishes are cooked with separate cookware. Call one day in advance for best GF service. ▪ *www.opheliasonthebay.net*

Outback Steakhouse
Sarasota ▪ (941) 351-3711
6390 N Lockwood Ridge Rd
Sarasota ▪ (941) 924-4329
7207 S Tamiami Trl

Roy's ☺ $$$D
Sarasota ▪ (941) 952-0109
2001 Siesta Dr ▪ Hawaiian Fusion ▪ Triumph contacted a manager at each location and all reported that GF diners can be accommodated. A different GF menu is available at each location. Typically, a chef will come out to speak with GF diners. Reservations noting GF are strongly recommended by all locations. ▪ *www.roysrestaurant.com*

FLORIDA

TAMPA

Ballyhoo Grill $LD
Tampa ▪ (813) 926-2149
7604 Ehrlich Rd ▪ Seafood & Steakhouse ▪ Manager Colleen reports that they make everything from scratch, so almost any-

thing can be prepared GF. She cautions that each diner should explain his or her dietary restrictions, because although managers know exactly what ingredients are used in each dish, they may not be "fully educated" on the GF diet. ▪ *www.ballyhooflorida.com*

Bonefish Grill
Tampa ▪ (813) 969-1619
13262 N Dale Mabry Hwy
Tampa ▪ (813) 876-3535
3665 Henderson Blvd

Capital Grille, The
Tampa ▪ (813) 830-9433
2223 N West Shore Blvd

Carrabba's Italian Grill
Tampa ▪ (813) 265-9844
11435 N Dale Mabry Hwy
Tampa ▪ (813) 920-3239
11950 Sheldon Rd
Tampa ▪ (813) 396-4061
5503 West Spruce St.
Tampa ▪ (813) 875-4411
700 N Dale Mabry Hwy

Columbia Café ☺ $LD
Tampa ▪ (813) 229-5511
801 Old Water St ▪ Spanish ▪ The printed list of GF items includes the beefsteak tomato salad and the chicken with yellow rice, as well as the half and half combo with a soup and a salad. Chef Scott advises alerting a server, who will find out what modifications must be made to GF meals. ▪ *www.columbiarestaurant.com*

Columbia Restaurant ☺ $$LD
Tampa ▪ (813) 248-4961
2117 E 7th Ave ▪ Spanish ▪ There is a printed list of GF menu items at all locations. GF options include the beefsteak tomato salad, the palomilla, and the queso fundido. For dessert, they offer flan and crema catalana. ▪ *www.columbiarestaurant.com*

Datz Delicatessen $$BLD
Tampa ▪ (813) 831-7000
2616 S Macdill Ave ▪ Deli ▪ Staff Member George reports that they have "a lot" of GF customers. He notes that servers are

trained to take diet and food intolerance requests very seriously. Many menu items can be modified to be GF. Alert a server, who will go over GF options from the menu. ■ *www.datzdeli.com*

First Watch - The Daytime Café   📖
Tampa ■ (813) 961-4947
13186 N Dale Mabry Hwy
Tampa ■ (813) 975-1718
2726 E Fowler Ave
Tampa ■ (813) 307-9006
520 N Tampa St

J. Christopher's   ¢**BL**
Tampa ■ (813) 908-7023
14366 N Dale Mabry Hwy ■ *Modern American* ■ Owner Bill reports that GF diners are "very welcome." He reports that many egg white omelets, chicken dishes, and vegetable dishes are GF. Confirm timeliness of this information before dining in. He recommends asking a server to indicate GF menu items. ■ *www.jchristophers.com*

Kona Grill   📖
Tampa ■ (813) 877-5938
4134 W Boy Scout Blvd

Lee Roy Selmon's   ✪★ $$**LD**
Tampa ■ (813) 977-3287
17508 Dona Michelle Dr
Tampa ■ (813) 871-3287
4302 W Boy Scout Blvd ■ *American* ■ GF menu includes grilled shrimp salad, burgers without buns, a BBQ chicken plate, and more. GF beer is available. ■ *www.leeroyselmons.com*

Maggiano's Little Italy   ★ $$$**LD**
Tampa ■ (813) 288-9000
203 Westshore Plz ■ *Italian* ■ GF pasta is available. Call individual locations to inquire about additional GF options. ■ *www.maggianos.com*

Melting Pot, The   📖
Tampa ■ (813) 962-6936
13164 N Dale Mabry Hwy

Mitchell's Fish Market   ✪ $$$**LD**
Tampa ■ (813) 289-3663

204 Westshore Plz ■ *Seafood* ■ Extensive GF menu includes pan-roasted wild blue mussels, blackened salmon spinach salad, grilled shrimp and scallop skewers, Shanghai seafood sampler, lobster tail, filet mignon, and live Maine lobster. Mini crème brulee is available for dessert. ■ *www.mitchellsfishmarket.com*

Outback Steakhouse   📖
Tampa ■ (813) 969-4329
11618 N Dale Mabry Hwy
Tampa ■ (813) 920-3100
11950 Sheldon Rd
Tampa ■ (813) 875-4329
3403 Henderson Blvd

P.F. Chang's China Bistro   📖
Tampa ■ (813) 289-8400
219 Westshore Plz

Pei Wei Asian Diner   📖
Tampa ■ (813) 960-2031
12927 N Dale Mabry Hwy
Tampa ■ (813) 207-1190
217 S Dale Mabry Hwy

Rigatoni's Tuscan Oven Restaurant
✪ $$**LD**
Tampa ■ (813) 879-7000
3437 W Kennedy Blvd ■ *Italian* ■ GF menu includes Tuscan chicken pomodoro, seafood paella, and pizza in a bowl. Manager Sunia notes that "several" GF diners come to the restaurant each week. Reservations noting GF are recommended. ■ *www.rigatonisonline.com*

Roy's $$$**D**
Tampa ■ (813) 873-7697
4342 W Boy Scout Blvd ■ *Hawaiian Fusion* ■ Veteran Bartender Richard reports that they welcome GF diners, but he recommends that customers be very specific about their GF needs. Alert a server, who will notify the chef. The chef will "finagle" nearly any GF meal that is desired. ■ *www.roysrestaurant.com*

Viitals   100% ¢**S**
Tampa ■ (813) 443-4567

6605 N Florida Ave ▪ *Bakery & Café* ▪ Bakery and café offering a wide variety of GF lunch items. GF bread, muffins, cakes, and cookies are available. Specialty GF cakes are available with advanced notice. ▪ *www.viitals.com*

FLORIDA

ALL OTHER CITIES

Ballyhoo Grill $$**LD**
Gainesville ▪ *(352) 373-0059*
3700 W University Ave ▪ *Seafood* ▪ Manager Mike reports that they have served several GF diners. Alert a server upon arrival. Mike notes that many servers have been working at the restaurant for years, but he still recommends requesting that the server speak to a manager about GF options.

Better Than Sex Desserts   ★ $S
Key West ▪ *(305) 296-8102*
411 Petronia St ▪ *Desserterie & Bakery* ▪ GF flourless chocolate pie is available. Desserts are entrée-sized and are meant to be shared. ▪ *www.betterthansexkw.com*

Bonefish Grill   📖
Belleair Bluffs ▪ *(727) 518-1230*
2939 West Bay Dr
Bonita Springs ▪ *(239) 390-9208*
26381 S Tamiami Trl Ste 104
Boynton Beach ▪ *(561) 732-1310*
1880 N Congress Ave
Bradenton ▪ *(941) 795-8020*
7456 Cortez Rd W
Brandon ▪ *(813) 571-5553*
1015 Providence Rd
Cape Coral ▪ *(239) 574-1018*
900 SW Pine Island Rd
Clearwater ▪ *(727) 726-1315*
2519 N Mcmullen Booth Rd
Coral Springs ▪ *(954) 509-0405*

1455 N University Dr
Destin ▪ *(850) 650-3161*
4447 Commons Dr E
Fort Myers ▪ *(239) 489-1240*
14261 S Tamiami Trl Ste 1
Ft Lauderdale ▪ *(954) 492-3266*
6282 N Federal Hwy
Gainesville ▪ *(352) 377-8383*
3237 SW 35th Blvd
Jacksonville Beach ▪ *(904) 247-4234*
2400 3rd St S Ste 302B
Kissimmee ▪ *(407) 931-1790*
2699 W Osceola Pkwy
Lake Worth ▪ *(561) 965-2663*
9897 Lake Worth Rd
Lakeland ▪ *(863) 701-9480*
225 W Pipkin Rd
Longwood ▪ *(407) 331-0131*
1761 W State Road 434
Miami ▪ *(786) 293-5713*
12520 SW 120th St
Miami ▪ *(305) 487-6430*
14220 SW 8th St Unit 11
Ocala ▪ *(352) 873-3846*
4701 SW College Rd Unit 1A
Ormond Beach ▪ *(386) 615-7889*
814 S Atlantic Ave
Palm Beach Gardens ▪ *(561) 799-2965*
11650 US Highway 1
Panama City Beach ▪ *(850) 249-0428*
11535 Hutchinson Blvd
Panama City ▪ *(850) 747-9331*
641 W 23rd St
Pensacola ▪ *(850) 471-2324*
5025 N 12Th Ave
Plantation ▪ *(954) 472-3592*
10197 W Sunrise Blvd
St Petersburg ▪ *(727) 344-8600*
2408 Tyrone Blvd N
St Petersburg ▪ *(727) 521-3434*
5062 4th St N
Stuart ▪ *(772) 288-4388*
2283 S Federal Hwy
Tallahassee ▪ *(850) 297-0460*
3491 Thomasville Rd
The Villages ▪ *(352) 674-9292*
3580 Wedgewood Ln
Trinity ▪ *(727) 372-7540*

10750 State Road 54
University Park ▪ (941) 360-3171
8101 Cooper Creek Blvd
Wesley Chapel ▪ (813) 907-8202
1640 Bruce B Downs Blvd
Weston ▪ (954) 389-9273
4545 Weston Rd
Winter Garden ▪ (407) 654-6093
3279 Daniels Rd Ste P-108

Book Lover's Café   ★ ¢LD
Gainesville ▪ (352) 384-0090
505 NW 13Th St ▪ **Vegetarian** ▪ Manager
Rick reports that they frequently accommodate GF diners and that all soups are
GF. Confirm timeliness of this information
before dining in. GF rice bread is available
for sandwiches. This café also houses a
used bookstore. ▪ *www.thebookloverscafe.
com*

Bubba Gump Shrimp Co.   📖
Daytona Beach ▪ (386) 947-8433
250 N Atlantic Ave
Ft Lauderdale ▪ (954) 463-0777
429 S Fort Lauderdale Beach Blvd
Madeira Beach ▪ (727) 397-4867
185 Boardwalk Pl W
Miami ▪ (305) 379-8866
401 Biscayne Blvd

Bubble Room $$LD
Captiva ▪ (239) 472-5558
15001 Captiva Dr ▪ **American Regional** ▪
Manager Julie notes that GF diners come in
"all the time." She reports that several steak
dishes, vegetables, sides, and seafood dishes
can be modified to be GF. Confirm timeliness of this information before dining in.
Upon arrival, alert a server and ask for the
manager. ▪ *www.bubbleroomrestaurant.com*

Buca di Beppo   📖
Brandon ▪ (813) 681-8462
11105 Causeway Blvd
Davie ▪ (954) 577-3287
3355 S University Dr
Maitland ▪ (407) 622-7663
1351 S Orlando Ave
Miami Lakes ▪ (305) 231-3100

15251 NW 67th Ave
Wellington ▪ (561) 790-3287
2025 Wellington Green Dr

Café 118 $$LD
Winter Park ▪ (407) 389-2233
153 E Morse Blvd ▪ **Vegan** ▪ Owner Joseph
reports that nearly the entire menu is GF,
with the exception of two desserts that
contain oat flour. Confirm timeliness of
this information before dining in. He adds
that all staff members are trained on the GF
diet, so GF diners need only alert a server
upon arrival. ▪ *www.cafe118.com*

Café Margaux   ★ $$$LD
Cocoa ▪ (321) 639-8343
220 Brevard Ave ▪ **Modern American** ▪
Owner Alex reports that they accommodate GF diners "very well." He strongly recommends reservations noting GF because
they will be able to prepare more options,
like GF rice pasta, and because they use a
"team service" system, so it's best if servers
are alerted in advance. ▪ *www.cafemargaux.
com*

Cantina Laredo   📖
Fort Myers ▪ (239) 415-4424
5200 Big Pine Way
Hallandale Beach ▪ (954) 457-7662
501 Silks Run
Palm Beach Gardens ▪ (561) 622-1223
4635 Pga Blvd
Sandestin ▪ (850) 654-5649
585 Grand Blvd
Wesley Chapel ▪ (813) 907-3068
2000 Piazza Ave

Capital Grille, The   📖
Fort Lauderdale ▪ (954) 446-2000
2430 E Sunrise Blvd
Miami ▪ (305) 374-4500
444 Brickell Ave
Palm Beach Gardens ▪ (561) 630-4994
11365 Legacy Ave

Carino's Italian   📖
Doral ▪ (305) 403-7919
8240 NW 36th St

Carrabba's Italian Grill 📖

Altamonte Springs ▪ *(407) 788-4222*
931 N State Road 434
Bonita Springs ▪ *(239) 949-0981*
27220 Bay Landing Dr
Boynton Beach ▪ *(561) 734-5152*
1999 N Congress Ave
Bradenton ▪ *(941) 755-7712*
2106 Cortez Rd W
Brandon ▪ *(813) 657-8166*
801 Providence Rd
Brooksville ▪ *(352) 597-9805*
12607 Cortez Blvd
Cape Coral ▪ *(239) 574-2797*
762 SW Pine Island Rd
Clearwater ▪ *(727) 712-0844*
19919 US Highway 19 N
Clermont ▪ *(352) 394-8602*
2240 E Highway 50
Coral Springs ▪ *(954) 345-4600*
2501 N University Dr
Daytona Beach ▪ *(386) 255-3344*
2200 W International Speedway Blvd
Delray Beach ▪ *(561) 266-9393*
335 E Linton Blvd
Fort Myers ▪ *(239) 690-2426*
10075 Gulf Center Dr
Fort Myers ▪ *(239) 433-0877*
12990 S Cleveland Ave
Gainesville ▪ *(352) 692-0083*
3021 SW 34th St
Hialeah ▪ *(305) 816-9131*
18600 NW 87th Ave
Jacksonville Beach ▪ *(904) 249-5550*
9 3rd St N
Kissimmee ▪ *(407) 390-9600*
7890 W Irlo Bronson Hwy
Lakeland ▪ *(863) 646-2518*
4829 S Florida Ave
Lutz ▪ *(813) 926-8212*
16525 Pointe Village Dr
Melbourne ▪ *(321) 253-0991*
7620 N Wickham Rd
Merritt Island ▪ *(321) 453-7045*
60 Palmetto Ave
Miami Beach ▪ *(305) 673-3525*
3921 Collins Ave
North Palm Beach ▪ *(561) 630-7386*

11201 US Highway 1
Ocala ▪ *(352) 867-0240*
2370 SW College Rd
Orange Park ▪ *(904) 278-1077*
1750 Wells Rd
Palm Bay ▪ *(321) 956-1900*
1575 Palm Bay Rd NE
Palm Harbor ▪ *(727) 787-8910*
33983 US Highway 19 N
Panama City Beach ▪ *(850) 230-4522*
13820 Panama City Beach Pkwy
Pensacola ▪ *(850) 438-0073*
311 N 9th Ave
Plant City ▪ *(813) 752-0760*
1205 Townsgate Ct
Plantation ▪ *(954) 423-2214*
1003 S University Dr
Pompano Beach ▪ *(954) 782-2688*
1299 S Federal Hwy
Port Charlotte ▪ *(941) 743-5299*
1811 Tamiami Trl
Port Richey ▪ *(727) 869-4886*
10110 US Highway 19
Port St Lucie ▪ *(772) 344-5897*
1900 SW Fountainview Blvd
Royal Palm Beach ▪ *(561) 793-9980*
11141 Southern Blvd
Sandestin ▪ *(850) 837-1140*
10562 Emerald Coast Pkwy W
South Miami ▪ *(305) 661-2426*
5829 SW 73rd St
St Augustine ▪ *(904) 819-9093*
155 State Road 312 W
St Petersburg ▪ *(727) 897-9375*
1951 4th St N
St Petersburg ▪ *(727) 384-1818*
3530 Tyrone Blvd N
Stuart ▪ *(772) 223-6377*
2700 SE Federal Hwy
Tallahassee ▪ *(850) 297-1100*
2799 Capital Cir NE
Temple Terrace ▪ *(813) 989-3898*
5515 E Fowler Ave
The Villages ▪ *(352) 430-1304*
650 N US Highway 441
University Park ▪ *(941) 355-4116*
5425 University Pkwy
Vero Beach ▪ *(772) 299-5999*

1285 US Highway 1
West Palm Beach ▪ **(561) 615-8900**
2224 Palm Beach Lakes Blvd
Winter Haven ▪ **(863) 293-6635**
700 Third St SW
Winter Springs ▪ **(407) 696-6600**
5820 Red Bug Lake Rd

China Grill at Hilton Ft. Lauderdale Marina
$$$$**BD**
Fort Lauderdale ▪ **(954) 759-9950**
1881 SE 17th St ▪ *Asian Fusion* ▪ Manager Gary notes that they serve GF diners with "no problem at all." He suggests noting GF in reservations, and then confirming with the server upon arrival. Gary notes that a variety of menu items can be modified to be GF. Servers are trained to speak with the chef about these options. ▪ *www.chinagrillmgt.com*

Chops City Grill
✪ $$$$**D**
Bonita Springs ▪ **(239) 992-4677**
8200 Health Center Blvd ▪ *Seafood & Steakhouse* ▪ GF menu at both locations includes shrimp cocktail, clams on the halfshell, beef satay, sushi, tuna, salads, NY strip steak, grilled chicken breast, and more. ▪ *www.chopscitygrill.com*

Columbia Restaurant
✪ $$**LD**
Celebration ▪ **(407) 566-1505**
649 Front St
Clearwater ▪ **(727) 596-8400**
1241 Gulf Blvd
St Augustine ▪ **(904) 824-3341**
98 Saint George St
St Petersburg ▪ **(727) 822-8000**
800 2nd Ave NE ▪ *Spanish* ▪ There is a printed list of GF menu items at all locations. GF options include the beefsteak tomato salad, the palomilla, and the queso fundido. For dessert, they offer flan and crema catalana. ▪ *www.columbiarestaurant.com*

Doc Ford's
$$$**LD**
Sanibel ▪ **(239) 472-8311**
973 Rabbit Rd ▪ *Seafood* ▪ Manager Jean reports that they serve GF diners "all the

time." She recommends alerting a server upon arrival. Servers should know what food is GF, but they will ask the chef if they have questions. She notes that many fish dishes can be modified to be GF. Confirm timeliness of this information before dining in. ▪ *www.docfordssanibel.com*

Duffy's Sports Grill
✪ $$**LD**
Boynton Beach ▪ **(561) 963-3234**
4746 N Congress Ave
Boynton Beach ▪ **(561) 752-4949**
6545 Boynton Beach Blvd
Deerfield Beach ▪ **(954) 429-8820**
401 N Federal Hwy
Delray Beach ▪ **(561) 276-3332**
1750 S Federal Hwy
Ft Lauderdale ▪ **(954) 713-6363**
1804 Cordova Rd
Greenacres ▪ **(561) 642-6388**
6864 Forest Hill Blvd
Jensen Beach ▪ **(772) 692-9123**
4179 NW Federal Hwy
Jupiter ▪ **(561) 743-4405**
185 E Indiantown Rd
Jupiter ▪ **(561) 741-8900**
6791 W Indiantown Rd
North Palm Beach ▪ **(561) 721-2650**
11588 US Highway 1
Palm Beach Gardens ▪ **(561) 493-8381**
4280 Northlake Blvd
Plantation ▪ **(954) 473-0477**
811 S University Dr
Port St Lucie ▪ **(772) 924-3565**
1608 NW Courtyard Cir
Port St Lucie ▪ **(772) 873-8150**
790 SW Saint Lucie West Blvd
Royal Palm Beach ▪ **(561) 792-4045**
11935 Southern Blvd
Stuart ▪ **(772) 221-4899**
1 SW Osceola St
Stuart ▪ **(772) 781-1388**
6431 SE Federal Hwy
West Palm Beach ▪ **(561) 478-8852**
6845 Okeechobee Blvd
West Palm Beach ▪ **(561) 688-1820**
721 Village Blvd ▪ *American* ▪ GF menu includes flat iron steak salad with arugula, burgers without buns, NY strip steak, baby

back ribs, yellowfin tuna, broiled bay scallops, and a variety of side dishes. ▪ *www. duffyssportsgrill.com*

Extreme Pizza   ★ $$LD
Miramar ▪ *(954) 436-9044*
3448 Red Rd ▪ *Pizza* ▪ GF pizza is available. ▪ *www.extremepizza.com*

Felix's $$LD
Ocala ▪ *(352) 629-0339*
917 E Silver Springs Blvd ▪ *American Regional* ▪ The restaurant reports that most items can be modified to be GF. They also note that they have many GF diners who come in "all the time." Reservations noting GF are recommended but not required. ▪ *www.felixsocala.com*

Fiorella Italian Restaurant   ◔★ $$$LD
Lake Worth ▪ *(561) 963-4999*
7008 Charleston Shores Blvd ▪ *Italian* ▪ Extensive GF menu includes pasta dishes with GF spaghetti or penne, seafood, salads, veal, chicken, and more. GF pasta is available. ▪ *www.fiorellarestaurant.com*

First Watch - The Daytime Café   📖
Altamonte Springs ▪ *(407) 682-2315*
249 W State Road 436
Bonita Springs ▪ *(239) 390-0554*
26381 S Tamiami Trl Ste 140
Bradenton ▪ *(941) 792-6071*
7118 Cortez Rd W
Clearwater ▪ *(727) 712-8769*
2569 Countryside Blvd
Fort Myers ▪ *(239) 437-0020*
13211 Mcgregor Blvd
Fort Myers ▪ *(239) 461-9765*
2059 Altamont Ave
Fort Myers ▪ *(239) 274-5551*
7091 College Pkwy
Jupiter ▪ *(561) 746-5960*
6240 W Indiantown Rd
Lakewood Ranch ▪ *(941) 907-6657*
8306 Market St
Longwood ▪ *(407) 774-1830*
2425 W State Road 434
Maitland ▪ *(407) 740-7437*
1221 S Orlando Ave

Palm Harbor ▪ *(727) 789-3447*
35146 US Highway 19 N
Stuart ▪ *(772) 220-4076*
2125 SE Federal Hwy
Sunrise ▪ *(954) 846-1313*
12594 W Sunrise Blvd
Wesley Chapel ▪ *(813) 929-3947*
1648 Bruce B Downs Blvd
Winter Garden ▪ *(407) 654-2826*
3017 Daniels Rd

Fogo De Chao   ★ $$$$LD
Miami Beach ▪ *(305) 672-0011*
836 1st St ▪ *Brazilian* ▪ GF cheese bread made with yucca flour is available. ▪ *www. fogodechao.com*

For Goodness Sake Café   ★ ¢L
Bonita Springs ▪ *(239) 992-5838*
9118 Bonita Beach Rd SE ▪ *Café* ▪ GF bread and wraps are available for sandwiches. A variety of GF desserts is available. Call ahead to confirm availability, especially at the Bonita Springs location. Located within the For Goodness Sake Natural Marketplace. ▪ *www.forgoodness-sake123.com*

Garlic Jim's   ◔★ $$LD
Miami ▪ *(305) 552-0540*
4005 SW 152nd Ave ▪ *Pizza* ▪ GF menu includes specialty pizzas, salads, chicken wings, and ice cream for dessert. Restaurant reports that nearly all pizzas are GF, so GF pizza crust is always available. ▪ *www. garlicjims.com*

Harry's Continental Kitchen $$$BLD
Longboat Key ▪ *(941) 383-0777*
525 Saint Judes Dr ▪ *Continental* ▪ Owner and Chef Harry reports that they are pleased to serve GF diners. Possible GF options include grilled grouper, seafood cobb, braised baby osso buco alla Milanese - veal with risotto, and chili braised short ribs. Confirm timeliness of this information before dining in. He recommends showing a dining card upon arrival. ▪ *www.harryskitchen.com*

Horse and Hounds Restaurant $$LD
Ocala ▪ *(352) 690-6100*
4620 E Silver Springs Blvd
Ocala ▪ *(352) 620-2500*
6998 N US Highway 27 ▪ American ▪
Managers at both locations report that
although GF diners are not frequent, they
can be accommodated. Manager Jay at the
Silver Springs location recommends alerting a server, who will summon a manager
to go over options with GF customers. Lisa
at the Highway 27 location notes that an
allergy button is used to input orders from
customers with any type of food "allergy,"
including GF. This button alerts the kitchen
staff that the food must be prepared separately. ▪ *www.horseandhoundsrestaurant.*
com

Iamsterdam Panini Café   ★ ¢LD
Winter Haven ▪ *(863) 269-8400*
5937 Cypress Gardens Blvd ▪ Café ▪
Owner and Baker Dave reports that GF
bread is available only upon request. He
can prepare GF pizza crusts or bread
loaves, though he advises calling two days
before dining in or picking up. ▪ *www.*
iamsterdamcafe.com

Kona Grill   📖
West Palm Beach ▪ *(561) 253-7900*
700 S Rosemary Ave

Le Bistro   ✪★ $$D
Lighthouse Point ▪ *(954) 946-9240*
4626 N Federal Hwy ▪ French ▪ GF menu
includes grouper en papilotte, seared diver
scallops, steak frites, and slow braised beef
ribs, among others. GF beer is also available, as are GF desserts like crème brûlée
and a rocky road Swiss parfait. ▪ *www.*
lebistrorestaurant.com

Lee Roy Selmon's   ✪★ $$LD
Bradenton ▪ *(941) 798-3287*
6510 Cortez Rd W
Fort Myers ▪ *(239) 690-3287*
5056 Daniels Pkwy
St Petersburg ▪ *(727) 347-5774*
2424 Tyrone Blvd N

University Park ▪ *(941) 360-3287*
8253 Cooper Creek Blvd ▪ American ▪ GF
menu includes grilled shrimp salad, burgers without buns, a BBQ chicken plate, and
more. GF beer is available. ▪ *www.leeroysel-*
mons.com

Liberty Bakery   100% ¢S
Oviedo ▪ *(407) 657-5342*
2781 Wrights Rd ▪ Bakery ▪ Dedicated GF
bakery offering a variety of breads, muffins, cookies, cupcakes, and more. ▪ *www.*
libertybakeryonline.com

Matanzas Innlet Restaurant   ✪★ ¢LD
Saint Augustine ▪ *(904) 461-6824*
8805 A1A S ▪ Seafood ▪ GF menu includes
New England clam chowder, crab cakes,
Alaskan king crab legs, mussels marinara,
and more. GF pizza and pasta are also
available. Owner Joanie is Celiac and is
dedicated to accommodating GF diners. ▪
www.matanzas.biz

Melinda's Café & Catering   ✪★ ¢BL
Holmes Beach ▪ *(941) 778-0411*
5315 Gulf Dr ▪ Café ▪ GF menu includes
a variety of omelets, soups, and salads.
Breakfast sandwiches made with GF bread
are available. Other GF specialty items
include french toast, meatloaf, crab cakes,
muffins, cupcakes, cookies, and more. ▪
www.melindascafe.com

Melting Pot, The   📖
Aventura ▪ *(305) 947-2228*
15700 Biscayne Blvd
Cooper City ▪ *(954) 880-0808*
5834 S Flamingo Rd
Coral Springs ▪ *(954) 755-6368*
10374 W Sample Rd
Destin ▪ *(850) 269-2227*
11394 US Highway 98 W
Fort Myers ▪ *(239) 481-1717*
13251 Mcgregor Blvd
Ft Lauderdale ▪ *(954) 568-1581*
1135 N Federal Hwy
Lake Worth ▪ *(561) 967-1009*
3044 S Military Trl
Longwood ▪ *(407) 862-8773*

1200 Commerce Park Dr
Melbourne ▪ *(321) 433-3040*
2230 Town Center Ave
Miami ▪ *(305) 279-8816*
11520 Sunset Dr
Ocala ▪ *(352) 622-9968*
10 S Magnolia Ave
Oldsmar ▪ *(813) 854-4691*
3689 Tampa Rd
Palm Beach Gardens ▪ *(561) 624-0020*
11811 US Highway 1
Pensacola ▪ *(850) 438-4030*
418 E Gregory St
St Petersburg ▪ *(727) 895-6358*
2221 4th St N
Tallahassee ▪ *(850) 386-7440*
2727 N Monroe St

Mitchell's Fish Market   ✪ $$$**LD**

Sandestin ▪ *(850) 650-2484*
500 Grand Blvd ▪ *Seafood* ▪ Extensive
GF menu includes pan-roasted wild
blue mussels, blackened salmon spinach
salad, grilled shrimp and scallop skewers, Shanghai seafood sampler, lobster tail,
filet mignon, and live Maine lobster. Mini
crème brulee is available for dessert. ▪
www.mitchellsfishmarket.com

Original Pancake House, The   ★ ¢**BL**

Aventura ▪ *(305) 933-1966*
21215 Biscayne Blvd
Delray Beach ▪ *(561) 276-0769*
1840 S Federal Hwy
Fort Lauderdale ▪ *(954) 564-8881*
2851 N Federal Hwy
Palm Beach Gardens ▪ *(561) 721-2213*
4360 Northlake Blvd
Plantation ▪ *(954) 473-2771*
8460 W Broward Blvd
Royal Palm Beach ▪ *(561) 296-0878*
105 S State Road 7
Southwest Ranches ▪ *(954) 272-0825*
6650 Dykes Rd ▪ *Breakfast* ▪ GF pancakes
are available. Select locations may serve
other GF options. Call a specific location to
inquire. ▪ *www.originalpancakehouse.com*

Outback Steakhouse   📖

Altamonte Springs ▪ *(407) 862-1050*

990 N State Road 434
Bonita Springs ▪ *(239) 948-3575*
27230 Bay Landing Dr
Bradenton ▪ *(941) 792-1898*
4402 Cortez Rd W
Bradenton ▪ *(941) 748-7783*
4510 E State Road 64
Brandon ▪ *(813) 684-6283*
2020 W Brandon Blvd
Cape Coral ▪ *(239) 772-5454*
1642 NE Pine Island Rd
Clermont ▪ *(352) 243-0036*
1625 E Highway 50
Coral Springs ▪ *(954) 345-5965*
650 Riverside Dr
Davie ▪ *(954) 430-2223*
14830 Griffin Rd
Daytona Beach ▪ *(386) 253-6283*
1490 W International Speedway Blvd
Delray Beach ▪ *(561) 272-7201*
1300 Linton Blvd
Destin ▪ *(850) 269-1936*
34908 Emerald Coast Pkwy
Fort Lauderdale ▪ *(954) 523-5600*
1801 SE 10th Ave
Fort Lauderdale ▪ *(954) 771-4390*
6201 N Federal Hwy
Fort Myers ▪ *(239) 433-0097*
10045 Gulf Center Dr Ste 120
Fort Myers ▪ *(239) 936-1021*
12995 S Cleveland Ave
Gainesville ▪ *(352) 373-9499*
3536 SW Archer Rd
Inverness ▪ *(352) 637-9292*
2225 Highway 44 W
Islamorada ▪ *(305) 664-3344*
79999 Overseas Hwy
Jacksonville Beach ▪ *(904) 247-7888*
3760 3rd St S
Jupiter ▪ *(561) 743-6283*
103 US Highway 1
Kendall ▪ *(305) 596-6771*
11800 Sherri Ln
Key West ▪ *(305) 292-0667*
3230 N Roosevelt Blvd
Kissimmee ▪ *(407) 931-0033*
3109 W Vine St
Kissimmee ▪ *(407) 396-0017*

7804 W Irlo Bronson Hwy
Lake Worth ▪ (561) 963-7010
6266 Lantana Rd
Lakeland ▪ (863) 858-9468
4208 US 98 North
Lakeland ▪ (863) 648-1019
5255 S Florida Ave
Largo ▪ (727) 538-9499
3690 E Bay Dr
Leesburg ▪ (352) 365-6222
9600 US Highway 441
Lithia ▪ (813) 689-9222
16547 Fishhawk Blvd
Merritt Island ▪ (321) 454-4450
777 E Merritt Island Cswy
Miami ▪ (305) 254-4456
13145 SW 89th Pl
Miami ▪ (305) 262-9766
8255 W Flagler St
Miami Lakes ▪ (305) 558-6868
15490 NW 77th Ct
N Miami Beach ▪ (305) 944-4329
3161 NE 163rd St
New Smyrna Beach ▪ (386) 409-0306
429 E 3rd Ave
Ocala ▪ (352) 237-0022
3215 SW College Rd
Ocala ▪ (352) 236-0041
4899 E Silver Springs Blvd
Orange Park ▪ (904) 269-9091
1775 Wells Rd
Ormond Beach ▪ (386) 676-1550
135 E Granada Blvd
Oviedo ▪ (407) 366-0008
167 E Mitchell Hammock Rd
Palm Bay ▪ (321) 722-0903
4651 Babcock St NE
Palm Coast ▪ (386) 446-6280
45 Plaza Dr
Palm Harbor ▪ (727) 789-6283
31988 US Highway 19 N
Panama City ▪ (850) 784-9649
861 W 23rd St
Pembroke Pines ▪ (954) 981-5300
7841 Pines Blvd
Pensacola ▪ (850) 432-2800
601 E Gregory St
Plant City ▪ (813) 759-4329

1203 Townsgate Ct
Plantation ▪ (954) 370-9956
1823B N Pine Island Rd
Port St Lucie ▪ (772) 873-9990
1950 NW Courtyard Cir
Pt Charlotte ▪ (941) 766-7077
1481 Tamiami Trl
Royal Palm Beach ▪ (561) 795-6663
11101 Southern Blvd
Saint Cloud ▪ (407) 891-2042
4037 13Th St
Sanford ▪ (407) 321-5881
180 Hickman Dr
Sebring ▪ (863) 385-4329
921 US 27
South Miami ▪ (305) 665-8499
5829 SW 73rd St Ste 101
Spring Hill ▪ (352) 592-1028
4905 Commercial Way
St Augustine ▪ (904) 826-4329
245 State Road 312
St Petersburg ▪ (727) 898-2016
1900 4th St N
St Petersburg ▪ (727) 384-4329
4088 Park St N
Stuart ▪ (772) 286-2622
3101 SE Federal Hwy
Tallahassee ▪ (850) 385-1998
1820 Raymond Diehl Rd
Temple Terrace ▪ (813) 980-0755
11308 N 56th St
The Villages ▪ (352) 430-2590
710 N US Highway 441
Trinity ▪ (727) 376-5100
10860 State Road 54
Venice ▪ (941) 497-2700
4220 Tamiami Trl S
Vero Beach ▪ (772) 567-5222
1475 US Highway 1
Viera ▪ (321) 242-8115
6450 N Wickham Rd
Wesley Chapel ▪ (813) 973-7717
5710 Oakley Blvd
West Palm Beach ▪ (561) 625-0793
10933 N Military Trl
West Palm Beach ▪ (561) 683-1011
871 Village Blvd
Winter Haven ▪ (863) 295-9800

170 Cypress Gardens Blvd
Winter Park ▪ **(407) 679-1050**
1927 Aloma Ave
Winter Springs ▪ **(407) 699-0900**
5891 Red Bug Lake Rd

P.F. Chang's China Bistro   📖
Aventura ▪ **(305) 957-1966**
17455 Biscayne Blvd
Fort Myers ▪ **(239) 590-9197**
10081 Gulf Center Dr
Ft Lauderdale ▪ **(954) 565-5877**
2418 E Sunrise Blvd
Miami ▪ **(305) 234-2338**
8888 SW 136th St Ste 100
Miami ▪ **(305) 358-0732**
901 S Miami Ave Ste 104
Palm Beach Gardens ▪ **(561) 691-1610**
3101 Pga Blvd Ste F142
Sandestin ▪ **(850) 269-1806**
640 Grand Blvd
Sunrise ▪ **(954) 845-1113**
1740 Sawgrass Mills Cir
Winter Park ▪ **(407) 622-0188**
436 N Orlando Ave

Pasquale & Sons Pizza Company
                              ★ **$$LD**
Coral Springs ▪ **(954) 510-0707**
5609 Coral Ridge Dr ▪ Pizza ▪ GF pizza is
available. ▪ *www.pasqualeandsons.com*

Pei Wei Asian Diner   📖
Boynton Beach ▪ **(561) 364-1830**
1750 N Congress Ave Ste 700
Kissimmee ▪ **(407) 846-0829**
2501 W Osceola Pkwy
Miami ▪ **(305) 386-8510**
13616 N Kendall Dr
Miami Lakes ▪ **(305) 817-8320**
15519 NW 67th Ave
Pembroke Pines ▪ **(954) 499-8820**
11049 Pines Blvd Ste 424
Plantation ▪ **(954) 308-3720**
522 N Pine Island Rd
St Petersburg ▪ **(727) 347-1351**
1402 66th St N
Stuart ▪ **(772) 219-0466**
2101 SE Federal Hwy
University Park ▪ **(941) 359-8570**

8511 Cooper Creek Blvd
Wellington ▪ **(561) 753-6260**
10610 Bay 10 Forest Hill Blvd
Weston ▪ **(954) 308-7330**
4517 Weston Rd

Pizza Fusion   ★ **$$LD**
Fort Myers ▪ **(239) 337-7979**
12901 Mcgregor Blvd
Ft Lauderdale ▪ **(954) 358-5353**
1013 N Federal Hwy
North Miami ▪ **(305) 405-6700**
14815 Biscayne Blvd
Palm Beach Gardens ▪ **(561) 721-0123**
4783 Pga Blvd
Wellington ▪ **(561) 721-9020**
10160 W Forest Hill Blvd
Weston ▪ **(954) 641-5353**
2378 Weston Rd ▪ Pizza ▪ GF pizza and
brownies are available. ▪ *www.pizzafusion.
com*

Rookery Grill, The   ★ **$BL**
Marco Island ▪ **(239) 394-2511**
400 S Collier Blvd ▪ American ▪ GF bread
and wraps are available. Manager Kathleen
reports that the entire menu is "geared
toward people with allergies," so the chef
can create many GF options. Located in
the Marco Island Resort and Spa. ▪ *www.
marcoislandmarriott.com/rookery.html*

Roy's   ✪ **$$$D**
Bonita Springs ▪ **(239) 498-7697**
26831 S Bay Dr ▪ Hawaiian Fusion ▪ Triumph contacted a manager at each location
and all reported that GF diners can be accommodated. A different GF menu is available at each location. Typically, a chef will
come out to speak with GF diners. Reservations noting GF are strongly recommended
by all locations. ▪ *www.roysrestaurant.com*

Seasons 52   ✪ **$$$LD**
Altamonte Springs ▪ **(407) 767-1252**
463 E Altamonte Dr
Ft Lauderdale ▪ **(954) 537-1052**
2428 E Sunrise Blvd ▪ Modern American
▪ GF menu includes cedar plank Atlantic
salmon, grilled rack of lamb, and burgers

without buns. Restaurant reports that some menu items are seasonal. ▪ *www.seasons52. com*

Seasons 52-Palm Beach Gardens

✪ $$$**LD**

Palm Beach Gardens ▪ *(561) 625-5852*
11611 Ellison Wilson Rd ▪ *Modern American* ▪ GF menu is available. Manager Kimmy reports that GF diners are accommodated "on a regular basis." Alert a server upon arrival. Reservations noting GF are recommended. ▪ *www.seasons52.com*

Shane's Rib Shack

📖

Boynton Beach ▪ *(561) 735-0742*
950 N Congress Ave
Gulf Breeze ▪ *(850) 934-7427*
3707 Gulf Breeze Pkwy
Lakeland ▪ *(863) 686-7427*
1529 Town Center Dr
Royal Palm Beach ▪ *(561) 333-7427*
11051 Southern Blvd
Tallahassee ▪ *(850) 309-7427*
1424 W Tennessee St

Smith & Wollensky

$$$$**LD**

Miami Beach ▪ *(305) 673-2800*
1 Washington Ave ▪ *Steakhouse* ▪ Manager Louis reports that they have served "many" GF diners. He recommends reservations noting GF, which will alert the server, manager, and chef in advance. ▪ *www.smithand-wollensky.com*

Tony's Sushi Japanese Steakhouse $$**LD**

Ocala ▪ *(352) 237-3151*
3405 SW College Rd ▪ *Japanese* ▪ Manager Jane reports that there are a number of naturally GF menu items. She notes that all servers are GF aware. Alert a server and speak to a manager upon arrival. If GF diners bring their own soy sauce, the kitchen is happy to use it in GF meal preparation.

Uno Chicago Grill

📖

Daytona Beach ▪ *(386) 252-8600*
1798 W International Speedway Blvd
Fort Myers ▪ *(239) 693-8667*
9510 Marketplace Rd
Kissimmee ▪ *(407) 396-2755*

5350 W Irlo Bronson Memorial Hwy
Lake Mary ▪ *(407) 444-5666*
901 Currency Cir
Melbourne ▪ *(321) 255-1400*
8260 N Wickham Rd
Winter Garden ▪ *(407) 877-6510*
3167 Daniels Rd

Vertoris Pizza House

✪★ $**D**

Bradenton ▪ *(941) 751-0333*
6830 14th St W ▪ *Pizza* ▪ GF menu includes pizza, spaghetti and meatballs, ravioli, and fettuccini alfredo. For dessert, they offer GF flourless chocolate cake, cheesecake, and tiramisu. GF beer is also available. ▪ *www.vertorispizza.com*

Yard House

📖

Coral Gables ▪ *(305) 447-9273*
320 San Lorenzo Ave
Palm Beach Gardens ▪ *(561) 691-6901*
11701 Lake Victoria Gardens Ave

GEORGIA

ATLANTA

Aja

★ $$$**LD**

Atlanta ▪ *(404) 231-0001*
3500 Lenox Rd NE ▪ *Asian Fusion* ▪ GF soy sauce is sometimes available. Restaurant reports that they serve GF diners "at least once a day." Alert a server upon arrival. Servers are trained to speak with the chef, who will recommend a few GF items. ▪ *www.h2sr.com*

Beleza

¢**D**

Atlanta ▪ *(678) 904-4582*
905 Juniper St ▪ *Brazilian* ▪ Manager Julie reports that GF diners have "a lot of options," and that they accommodate GF customers "at least once a week." Corn tortillas can always be substituted for flour tortillas. Alert a server upon arrival. ▪ *www. sottosottorestaurant.com*

Blue Pointe $$$**LD**
Atlanta ▪ *(404) 237-9070*
3455 Peachtree Rd ▪ *Asian Fusion* ▪
Manager Daniel reports that they serve "so many" GF diners "every night." He notes that there are "a lot of options" for GF diners, who should alert a server upon arrival. He adds that the chef can accommodate GF diners very easily. ▪ *www.buckheadrestaurants.com*

Blue Ridge Grill   ✪ $$$$**LD**
Atlanta ▪ *(404) 233-5030*
1261 W Paces Ferry Rd NW ▪ *Modern American* ▪ GF menu includes iron skillet mussels, tuna tartare, wild Scottish salmon, beet and goat cheese salad, Georgia trout, and more. Alert a server upon arrival. ▪ *www.blueridgegrill.com*

Bluepointe $$$$**D**
Atlanta ▪ *(404) 237-9070*
3455 Peachtree Rd NE ▪ *Seafood* ▪
Manager William reports that the sushi, salads, kobe beef, and duck steak are all GF. Confirm timeliness of this information before dining in. Alert a server, who will notify the kitchen. Also, ask to speak with a manager. Reservations noting GF are recommended. ▪ *www.buckheadrestaurants.com*

Bone's Restaurant $$$$**LD**
Atlanta ▪ *(404) 237-2663*
3130 Piedmont Rd NE ▪ *Seafood & Steakhouse* ▪ Chef Leonard notes that GF diners are accommodated on an almost nightly basis. He also notes that the kitchen takes GF requests "extremely seriously", and that they make every effort to make the GF dining experience "as normal as possible." He reports that most steak and seafood dishes are naturally GF. Confirm timeliness of this information before dining in. Alert a server, who will confer with the kitchen. ▪ *www.bonesrestaurant.com*

BrickTop's   ✪ $$$**LD**
Atlanta ▪ *(404) 841-2212*
3280 Peachtree Rd NE ▪ *Seafood &*
Steakhouse ▪ GF menu includes rotisserie chicken, steak frites, ahi tuna salad, and babyback ribs. The signature appetizer, deviled eggs and bacon sausage, is also GF. For dessert, they offer a hot fudge sundae. ▪ *www.westendrestaurants.com*

Brookhaven Bistro   ¢**BLD**
Atlanta ▪ *(404) 846-2233*
4274 Peachtree Rd NE ▪ *Café* ▪ Owner and Chef Chip reports that GF items are marked on the menu board but not on the printed menus. He notes that with the exception of sandwiches, almost all items in the deli case are GF. Confirm timeliness of this information before dining in. ▪ *www.brookhavenbistro.com*

Buckhead Pizza Co.   ★ $**LD**
Atlanta ▪ *(404) 869-0678*
3324 Peachtree Rd NE ▪ *Pizza* ▪ GF pizza is available in the personal size only. GF desserts like carrot cakes and brownies are available at the Atlanta location only. ▪ *www.buckheadpizzaco.com*

Cantina Taqueria & Tequila Bar $$**LD**
Atlanta ▪ *(404) 892-9292*
3280 Peachtree Rd NW ▪ *Modern Mexican* ▪ Manager Katie reports that salads, fajitas with chicken and vegetables, and corn tortillas are options for GF diners. Confirm timeliness of this information before dining in. Upon arrival, alert a server and ask for a manager or chef. ▪ *www.h2sr.com*

Carrabba's Italian Grill   📖
Atlanta ▪ *(770) 804-0467*
1210 Ashford Crossing
Atlanta ▪ *(770) 437-1444*
2999 Cumberland Blvd SE

Coast $**D**
Atlanta ▪ *(404) 869-0777*
111 W Paces Ferry Rd NW ▪ *Seafood* ▪
Manager Chet reports that GF diners are welcome. He notes that the fish is freshly prepared and can be made to be GF. Confirm timeliness of this information before dining in. He notes that GF diners should

alert a server and ask for a manager. ▪ *www.h2sr.com*

Ecco $D
Atlanta ▪ *(404) 347-9555*
40 7th St NE ▪ *Mediterranean* ▪ Hostess Bethany recommends reservations noting GF, but notes that they are not required. Alert a server upon arrival. Servers are knowledgeable about which menu items are GF. Examples of GF entrées include braised beef short ribs and roasted monk fish, among others. Confirm timeliness of this information before dining in. ▪ *www.ecco-atlanta.com*

Eclipse di Luna   ✪ $LD
Atlanta ▪ *(678) 205-5862*
4505 Ashford Dunwoody Rd NE
Atlanta ▪ *(404) 846-0449*
764 Miami Cir NE ▪ *Spanish Tapas* ▪ GF menus are available at both locations. GF menu items include tomato mozzarella, mussels and chorizo, halibut, carne asada, beef skewars, and roasted scallops. Manager Leana from the Miami Circle location notes that the GF menu tells GF diners how to order. ▪ *www.eclipsediluna.com*

El Taco   ✪ $D
Atlanta ▪ *(404) 873-4656*
1186 N Highland Ave NE ▪ *Tex-Mex* ▪ GF menu includes spicy shrimp ceviche, chili-braised short rib, pork carnitas, mexican chorizo with yuca, cumin-marinated chicken fajitas, chili de arbol steak salad, and flan for dessert.

Figo Pasta   ✪ ★ ¢LD
Atlanta ▪ *(770) 698-0505*
1140 Hammond Dr NE
Atlanta ▪ *(404) 351-9667*
1170 Collier Rd NW Ste B
Atlanta ▪ *(404) 351-3700*
1210 Howell Mill Rd NW
Atlanta ▪ *(404) 586-9250*
1220 Caroline St NE
Atlanta ▪ *(770) 431-4988*
2941 Paces Ferry Rd NE ▪ *Italian* ▪ GF menu includes pasta with choice of any

sauce, as well as chicken, salmon, spinach, caprese, and arugula salads, among other things. GF pasta is available. ▪ *www.figopasta.com*

Fire of Brazil   ★ $$$$LD
Atlanta ▪ *(770) 551-4367*
118 Perimeter Ctr W
Atlanta ▪ *(404) 525-5255*
218 Peachtree St NW ▪ *Brazilian Steakhouse* ▪ GF cheesebread is available. ▪ *www.fireofbrazil.com*

Fogo De Chao   ★ $$$$LD
Atlanta ▪ *(404) 266-9988*
3101 Piedmont Rd ▪ *Brazilian* ▪ GF cheese bread made with yucca flour is available. ▪ *www.fogodechao.com*

Fresh 2 Order   ✪ $LD
Atlanta ▪ *(678) 564-1400*
1260 Cumberland Mall SE
Atlanta ▪ *(404) 503-9999*
3344 Peachtree Rd NE
Atlanta ▪ *(404) 567-8646*
6125 Roswell Rd NE
Atlanta ▪ *(404) 593-2333*
860 Peachtree St NE ▪ *Café* ▪ GF menu includes market, spinach, and mediterranean salads, pork loin, grilled chicken breast, and lime shrimp. ▪ *www.fresh2order.com*

Garrison's Broiler & Tap $$$LD
Atlanta ▪ *(770) 436-0102*
4300 Paces Ferry Rd SE ▪ *American* ▪ Manager Les reports that GF diners should alert a server upon arrival. Servers will go directly to the chef, and, if necessary, a manager will come to the table. Les notes that the steaks, burgers without buns, and salmon with no sauce are GF. Confirm timeliness of this information before dining in. ▪ *www.garrisonsatlanta.com*

Goldfish $$LD
Atlanta ▪ *(770) 671-0100*
4400 Ashford Dunwoody Rd NE ▪ *Global* ▪ Manager Patrick reports that they serve "a lot" of GF diners "all the time." He recommends that GF customers alert their

servers, who can can "steer" them "in the right direction." Servers know the menu "very well," but they always double check with chefs when dealing with GF. Located in Perimeter Mall. ▪ *www.h2sr.comgoldfish*

Graveyard Tavern $D
Atlanta ▪ *(404) 622-8686*
1245 Glenwood Ave SE ▪ American ▪ Sous-Chef D reports that there are GF options available. He notes that several menu items, including any salad, hummus, vegetarian plates, molasses chicken, and risotto with asparagus, can be modified to be GF. Confirm timeliness of this information before dining in. Alert a server, who will indicate GF menu options. ▪ *www.graveyardtavern. com*

Imperial Fez $$$$D
Atlanta ▪ *(404) 351-0870*
2285 Peachtree Rd NE ▪ Moroccan ▪ Owner and Chef Rita reports that she is familiar with the GF diet and happy to serve GF diners. Alert a server, who will notify the chef. On weekdays, GF diners will find something on the menu, and on weekends, Rita will accommodate GF diners by modifying the 5-course dinner. ▪ *www. imperialfez.com*

La Paz $LD
Atlanta ▪ *(770) 801-0020*
2950 New Paces Ferry Rd SE ▪ Mexican ▪ Chef Luis reports that the restaurant gets GF requests "once in awhile." He notes that there are many options for GF diners, including enchiladas on corn tortillas, black bean soup, and grilled meat and fish. Confirm timeliness of this information before dining in. Alert a server and ask him or her to speak to Chef Luis about modifying menu items to be GF. ▪ *www.lapaz.com*

La Tavola Trattoria   ✪ $$$D
Atlanta ▪ *(404) 873-5430*
992 Virginia Ave NE ▪ Italian & Steakhouse ▪ GF menu includes beet and watercress salad, zucchini salad, shrimp risotto, roasted trout, market fish, flat iron

steak, grilled lamb chops with polenta and asparagus, and more.

Legal Sea Foods   📖
Atlanta ▪ *(678) 500-3700*
275 Baker St NW

Maggiano's Little Italy   ★ $$$LD
Atlanta ▪ *(770) 799-1580*
1601 Cumberland Mall SE
Atlanta ▪ *(404) 816-9650*
3368 Peachtree Rd NE
Atlanta ▪ *(770) 804-3313*
4400 Ashford Dunwoody Rd NE ▪ Italian ▪ GF pasta is available. Call individual locations to inquire about additional GF options. ▪ *www.maggianos.com*

Melting Pot, The   📖
Atlanta ▪ *(404) 389-0099*
754 Peachtree St NE

MetroFresh   ✪ $BLD
Atlanta ▪ *(404) 724-0151*
931 Monroe Dr NE ▪ Healthy American ▪ Manager Diane reports that the menu and its marked GF items change daily, but there are always several GF options to choose from. Examples of GF items are mixed field greens with fruit and goat cheese, roasted beet and plum salad, seared trout with spinach, and chilled sweet corn. ▪ *www. metrofreshatl.com*

Metrotainment Bakery   ★ $$$$$
Atlanta ▪ *(404) 873-6307*
1119 Logan Cir NW ▪ Bakery ▪ GF cake options include chocolate cake with fudge frosting and mini chocolate chips, yellow cake with vanilla buttercream, and yellow cake with chocolate buttercream. Manager Keith reports that customers must call at least 48 hours in advance to place an order. ▪ *www.metrobakery.com*

Nan Thai Fine Dining $$$LD
Atlanta ▪ *(404) 870-9933*
1350 Spring St NW ▪ Thai ▪ Manager Yai recommends making reservations noting GF and requesting dishes that require soy sauce in advance, as they are willing to

make modifications if possible. Yai reports that it is necessary to alert a server, who will "make sure with the chef." ▪ *www.nanfinedining.com*

Nava   ✪ $$$**LD**
Atlanta ▪ *(404) 240-1984*
3060 Peachtree Rd NW ▪ *Latin American* ▪ GF menu includes jalapeno giant shrimp, red chile seared scallops, and seared trout with grilled cactus and chipotle brown butter. ▪ *www.buckheadrestaurants.com*

Noche   ¢**D**
Atlanta ▪ *(404) 815-9155*
1000 Virginia Ave NE
Atlanta ▪ *(770) 432-3277*
2850 Paces Ferry Rd SE ▪ *Tapas* ▪ Both locations note that they accommodate GF diners on a regular basis. Menu items that can be modified to be GF include calamari, fried green tomatoes, olives with roasted peppers and almonds, steaks, and chicken and vegetable skewers. Confirm timeliness of this information before dining in. Reservations noting GF are recommended. ▪ *www.h2sr.com*

Outback Steakhouse   📖
Atlanta ▪ *(404) 636-5110*
2145 Lavista Rd NE
Atlanta ▪ *(404) 266-8000*
3850 Roswell Rd

P.F. Chang's China Bistro   📖
Atlanta ▪ *(770) 803-5800*
1624 Cumberland Mall SE Ste Ls108
Atlanta ▪ *(770) 352-0500*
500 Ashwood Pkwy

Park 75   ★ $$$$**BLD**
Atlanta ▪ *(404) 253-3840*
75 14th St NE ▪ *Modern American* ▪ GF bread is available for the restaurant's frequent GF diners. Restaurant recommends discussing GF dessert options when making reservations. The restaurant can make a GF cheesecake, among other things. Located in the Four Seasons Hotel.

Prime $$$**LD**
Atlanta ▪ *(404) 812-0555*
3393 Peachtree Rd NE ▪ *Modern American* ▪ Chef Dan reports that most menu items are naturally GF, and those that are not can be modified to be GF. Most of the sushi is GF, as are the steaks and the veal jus. Alert a server, who will notify the kitchen. Reservations noting GF are recommended. ▪ *www.h2sr.com*

Pure Taqueria   ✪ ¢**LD**
Atlanta ▪ *(404) 522-7873*
300 N Highland Ave NE ▪ *Latin American* ▪ GF menu includes ceviche, mussels, queso fundito, shrimp with chili and lemon, tacos with corn tortillas, fajitas, fish salad, grilled meat, and enchiladas. ▪ *www.puretaqueria.com*

Quinones at Bacchanalia $$$$**D**
Atlanta ▪ *(404) 365-0410*
1198 Howell Mill Rd NW ▪ *American Regional* ▪ Restaurant reports that all meals are made from scratch, so the chef can accommodate any needs or special requests. Reservations noting GF are required at this upscale restaurant. ▪ *www.starprovisions.com*

R. Thomas Deluxe Grill   ★ $**BLD**
Atlanta ▪ *(404) 872-2942*
1812 Peachtree St NW ▪ *Healthy American* ▪ Veteran Server Nina reports that the only non-GF items that do not have GF alternatives are the toast and the sandwich buns. Confirm timeliness of this information before dining in. She adds that the restaurant serves GF diners "every day," and that servers can guide GF customers through the menu. GF pasta is available for substitution, as are corn tortillas. ▪ *www.rthomasdeluxegrill.net*

Real Chow Baby, The   ★ $**LD**
Atlanta ▪ *(770) 405-2464*
1 Galleria Pkwy SE
Atlanta ▪ *(404) 815-4900*
1016 Howell Mill Rd NW ▪ *Asian Stir-Fry* ▪ Manager Ben at Howell Mill reports that

both locations have a list of GF sauces, which customers can carry through the buffet line. Both locations have rice noodles, meats, and vegetables that are GF. GF customers should put white sticks in their bowls to indicate GF to the stir fry cook. ▪ *www.therealchowbaby.com*

Restaurant Eugene $$$$D
Atlanta ▪ *(404) 355-0321*
2277 Peachtree Rd NE ▪ *Modern American* ▪ Restaurant reports that the menu changes frequently, and most menu items are naturally GF. They also note that all dishes are made from scratch. Reservations noting GF are recommended. Alert a server upon arrival. ▪ *www.restauranteugene.com*

Rí-Rá Irish Pub $LD
Atlanta ▪ *(404) 477-1700*
1080 Peachtree St N ▪ *Irish Pub* ▪ Ask for the "Allergen Chart," which has a "Celiac" column. This column contains items that are GF or can be modified to be GF. ▪ *www.rira.com*

Rice Bowl Thai & Sushi $$LD
Atlanta ▪ *(404) 841-2990*
2900 Peachtree Rd NW ▪ *Asian* ▪ Manager Mike reports that the restaurant has served GF customers before, though not very often. He recommends asking for either himself or Paul, the two managers. Both know which dishes are GF or can be modified to be GF. He notes that the curries are naturally GF, and some rice noodle dishes are made without soy sauce. Confirm timeliness of this information before dining in. ▪ *www.ricebowlatlanta.com*

Saba   ✪★ ¢LD
Atlanta ▪ *(404) 377-7786*
1451 Oxford Rd NE ▪ *Italian* ▪ GF menu includes a variety of appetizers, salads, pastas, and side orders. Owner Shane reports that the entire staff is GF aware. GF pasta and beer are available. ▪ *www.saba-restaurant.com*

Sally's Bakery   100% ¢S
Atlanta ▪ *(404) 847-0211*
5920 Roswell Rd NE ▪ *Bakery* ▪ Dedicated GF bakery offering a variety of breads, cookies, english muffins, and "take-&-bake" pizzas. Establishment recommends placing orders for specific items at least one day in advance. ▪ *www.sallysbakery.com*

Seasons 52   ✪★ $$LD
Atlanta ▪ *(404) 846-1552*
3050 Peachtree Rd NW ▪ *Modern American* ▪ GF menu includes a spicy tuna roll with GF tamari, salads, rainbow trout, rack of lamb, and burgers without buns. GF tamari sauce is available. ▪ *www.seasons52.com*

Shane's Rib Shack   📖
Atlanta ▪ *(404) 525-7427*
1221 Caroline St NE
Atlanta ▪ *(770) 399-9010*
123 Perimeter Ctr W
Atlanta ▪ *(770) 951-7211*
3155 Cobb Pkwy
Atlanta ▪ *(404) 231-1742*
3247 Roswell Rd NE

Shaun's Restaurant $$$D
Atlanta ▪ *(404) 577-4358*
1029 Edgewood Ave NE ▪ *Bistro* ▪ Manager Courtney reports that the restaurant serves GF diners often, and they even hold monthly GF dinners at the restaurant. She recommends alerting the server, who will speak with Chef Shaun about GF options. ▪ *www.shaunsrestaurant.com*

Shed at Glenwood, The   ✪ $$$D
Atlanta ▪ *(404) 835-4363*
475 Bill Kennedy Way SE ▪ *American* ▪ GF items marked on the regular menu include a roast beef salad, pan seared free range chicken, and grilled all natural ribeye. Owner Cindy reports that even unmarked items can often be modified to be GF. She also notes that even if ordering from the GF items, it is best to alert the server. ▪ *www.theshedatglenwood.com*

Shout $$$ LD
Atlanta ▪ *(404) 846-2000*
1197 Peachtree St ▪ *Modern American* ▪
Manager Amanda reports that GF diners will typically eat a vegetable plate with
roasted chicken or other simple fare. She
also notes that several menu items can be
modified to be GF, depending on the availability of ingredients. Reservations noting
GF are recommended. ▪ *www.hereto-
serverestaurants.com*

SOHO Restaurant   ✪ $$$ LD
Atlanta ▪ *(770) 801-0069*
4300 Paces Ferry Rd SE ▪ *Modern American* ▪ GF menu includes chicken soup with
tortilla chips, mussels, blackened grouper,
and beef short ribs. Restaurant reports that
they get "a fair amount" of GF diners. ▪
www.sohoatlanta.com

South City Kitchen   ✪ $$$ LD
Atlanta ▪ *(404) 873-7358*
1144 Crescent Ave NE ▪ *Southern* ▪ GF
menu includes Georgia mountain trout,
molasses brined pork chop, Atlantic
salmon, steak, and more. ▪ *www.southci-
tykitchen.com*

Strip $$$ LD
Atlanta ▪ *(404) 385-2005*
245 18th St NW ▪ *Seafood & Steakhouse*
▪ Sous-chef James reports that GF diners
"definitely have some options." He notes
that they are accustomed to accommodating "all types of food allergies." Alert a
server upon arrival. Servers are trained
to go "directly" to the chef and follow a
specific protocol. ▪ *www.h2sr.com*

Twist $$ LD
Atlanta ▪ *(404) 869-1191*
3500 Peachtree Rd NE ▪ *Global* ▪ The restaurant reports that several menu items are
naturally GF. GF options include pork ribs,
beef short steak, garlic and pepper shrimp
satay, paella, and scallops. Confirm timeliness of this information before dining in.
Ask the server to indicate GF menu items.
▪ *www.h2sr.com*

Wildfire   ✪ ★ $$$ LD
Atlanta ▪ *(770) 730-9080*
94 Perimeter Ctr W ▪ *Steakhouse* ▪
GF menu includes a variety of starters,
salads, sides, sandwiches, and entrées. GF
pizza crust, hamburger buns, and beer are
available. For dessert, they offer flourless
chocolate cake, among other things. ▪ *www.
wildfirerestaurant.com*

Wisteria Restaurant   ✪ $$ D
Atlanta ▪ *(404) 525-3363*
471 N Highland Ave NE ▪ *American* ▪ GF
menu includes several seafood dishes, a
vegetable platter, pork tenderloin, and
oysters. Server Allison reports that the GF
menu is very similar to the regular menu,
but with modifications. ▪ *www.wisteria-
atlanta.com*

Woodfire Grill $$$ D
Atlanta ▪ *(404) 347-9055*
1782 Cheshire Bridge Rd NE ▪ *Modern
American* ▪ Manager Rick reports that
the restaurant "deals very well" with GF
requests. He notes that before each shift,
the staff meets to go over the menu items
and potential allergies. He also notes that
most menu items can be modified to be GF.
For a primetime meal, make reservations
noting GF at least a couple of weeks in
advance. ▪ *www.woodfiregrill.com*

GEORGIA

ALL OTHER CITIES

5 Seasons Brewing $$ LD
Alpharetta ▪ *(770) 521-5551*
3655 Old Milton Pkwy
Sandy Springs ▪ *(404) 255-5911*
5600 Roswell Rd ▪ *Modern American* ▪
Manager Jamie at the Alpharetta location
and reservationist Kat at the Sandy Springs
location report that GF diners are welcome,
and they accommodate GF diners often.

They advise making reservations noting GF and alerting the server upon arrival. ▪ *www.5seasonsbrewing.com*

Aqua Terra Bistro $LD
Buford ▪ *(770) 271-3000*
55 E Main St ▪ Bistro ▪ Staffer Christy reports that many items are naturally GF or can be modified to be GF, as the chef does not use flour in many sauces. Servers are GF aware and will accommodate. ▪ *www. aquaterrabistro.com*

Atlantic Seafood Company $$$LD
Alpharetta ▪ *(770) 640-0488*
2345 Mansell Rd ▪ Seafood ▪ Veteran Server Shawn notes that all servers are trained in GF but that newer servers might be less familiar with the diet than more experienced staff members. She does, however, note that the restaurant serves GF diners "all the time." She adds that many menu items can easily be modified to be GF, and recommends reservations noting GF. Ask the server to double check with the kitchen to ensure that menu items are GF. Confirm timeliness of this information before dining in. ▪ *www.atlanticseafoodco. com*

Belly's Pizza   ★ $$LD
Roswell ▪ *(770) 594-8118*
885 Woodstock Rd ▪ Pizza ▪ GF pizza and beer are available. ▪ *www.bellysofroswell. com*

Blue Moon Pizza   ★ $$LD
Marietta ▪ *(770) 984-2444*
2359 Windy Hill Rd SE
Smyrna ▪ *(770) 436-4446*
4600 West Village Pl SE ▪ Pizza ▪ GF pizza, cheesy bread, salads with GF bread, and bruschetta are available. ▪ *www.blue-moonpizzaatl.com*

Bonefish Grill   📖
Alpharetta ▪ *(770) 475-6668*
11705 Jones Bridge Rd
Augusta ▪ *(706) 737-2929*
2911 Washington Rd
Buford ▪ *(678) 546-8240*

3420 Buford Dr Bldg C Ste 590
Macon ▪ *(478) 477-5256*
5080 Riverside Dr Ste 506
Saint Simons Island ▪ *(912) 634-0246*
202 Retreat Vlg # 3
Savannah ▪ *(912) 691-2575*
5500 Abercorn St Ste 44
Snellville ▪ *(678) 344-8945*
1350 Highway 124 N

Buca di Beppo   📖
Alpharetta ▪ *(770) 643-9463*
2335 Mansell Rd

Buckhead Pizza Co.   ★ $LD
Buford ▪ *(770) 932-7820*
3350 Buford Dr
Cumming ▪ *(770) 781-0304*
415 Peachtree Pkwy ▪ Pizza ▪ GF pizza is available in the personal size only. GF desserts like carrot cakes and brownies are available at the Atlanta location only. ▪ *www.buckheadpizzaco.com*

Bugaboo Creek Steak House   📖
Duluth ▪ *(770) 476-1500*
3505 Satellite Blvd
Fayetteville ▪ *(770) 461-2240*
1380 Highway 85 N
Kennesaw ▪ *(770) 919-2200*
840 Ernest W Barrett Pkwy NW
Lithonia ▪ *(678) 526-5000*
2965 Turner Hill Rd
Newnan ▪ *(770) 502-8500*
355 Bullsboro Dr

Café Life   ★ ¢LD
Marietta ▪ *(770) 977-9583*
1453 Roswell Rd ▪ Vegetarian ▪ GF bread is available for sandwiches, and select entrées are GF. Located inside Life Grocery. ▪ *www.lifegrocery.com*

Carino's Italian   📖
Albany ▪ *(229) 439-1022*
3007 Kensington Ct
Columbus ▪ *(706) 317-3343*
3033 Manchester Expy
East Point ▪ *(404) 494-3000*
3330 Camp Creek Pkwy
Lawrenceville ▪ *(678) 847-6300*

1802 N Brown Rd
Warner Robins ▪ *(478) 929-1800*
2707 Watson Blvd

Carpe Diem $$$**LD**
Decatur ▪ *(404) 687-9696*
105 Sycamore Pl ▪ Modern American ▪
Restaurant reports that GF diners are very
welcome. They advise alerting a server
upon arrival and presenting a dining card.
▪ *www.apresdiem.com*

Carrabba's Italian Grill   📖
Athens ▪ *(706) 546-9938*
3194 Atlanta Hwy
Augusta ▪ *(706) 733-0123*
2832 Washington Rd
Columbus ▪ *(706) 494-8144*
5555 Whittlesey Blvd
Douglasville ▪ *(770) 947-0330*
2700 Chapel Hill Rd
Duluth ▪ *(770) 497-4959*
2030 Sugarloaf Cir
Kennesaw ▪ *(770) 499-0338*
1160 Ernest W Barrett Pkwy NW
Macon ▪ *(478) 474-5115*
3913 River Place Dr
Morrow ▪ *(770) 968-3233*
1887 Mount Zion Rd
Peachtree City ▪ *(770) 631-1057*
500 Commerce Dr
Savannah ▪ *(912) 961-7073*
10408 Abercorn St

Chocolate Bar, The   ¢**D**
Decatur ▪ *(404) 378-0630*
201 W Ponce De Leon Ave ▪ Desserterie & Bakery ▪ Manager Jim reports that
though they do not accommodate a lot of
GF diners, they do have several desserts
that are GF or can be modified to be GF,
including the black truffle popcorn, the
oreos and milk soufflé, and the chocolate
pot de crème. He recommends asking for
a manager upon arrival, as that is "safer"
than speaking to a server. ▪ *www.thechoco-
latebardecatur.com*

Crab Shack, The   ¢**LD**
Tybee Island ▪ *(912) 786-9857*

40 Estill Hammock Rd ▪ Seafood ▪ Staffer
Lisa reports that most servers are familiar
with GF. Though they cannot guarantee
that no cross-contamination will occur,
Lisa notes that they can prepare a GF meal.
She suggests previewing the menu online
before coming in. ▪ *www.thecrabshack.com*

Crepe Revolution   ★ ¢**BL**
Smyrna ▪ *(770) 485-7440*
4600 West Village Pl SE ▪ Crêpes ▪ GF
crepes are available. ▪ *www.creperevolution.
com*

Doc Chey's Asian Kitchen   ◉ ¢**LD**
Athens ▪ *(706) 546-0015*
320 E Clayton St ▪ Asian ▪ GF menu
includes thai coconut soup, among other
appetizer options, as well as thai coconut
red curry, the spicy szechuan stir fry, and
the wok fried rice. ▪ *www.doccheys.com*

Earth Fare Market   ★ $**S**
Athens ▪ *(706) 227-1717*
1689 S Lumpkin St
Martinez ▪ *(706) 288-3042*
368 Furys Ferry Rd ▪ Bakery ▪ Bakeries
at both locations have GF breads, cookies, and desserts. Manager Kevin at the
Martinez location recommends asking for
him to answer any GF questions. Liz at the
Athens location notes that GF bread can be
used to make deli sandwiches for customers who are buying an entire loaf. ▪ *www.
earthfare.com*

East West Bistro   ◉ $**LD**
Athens ▪ *(706) 546-9378*
351 E Broad St ▪ Global ▪ GF menu
includes Hawaiian tuna tataki, a vegetable
bowl over GF noodles, grilled chicken,
salmon filet, a hamburger patty with seasonal vegetables, and misto salad. ▪ *www.
eastwestbistro.com*

Figo Pasta   ◉ ★ ¢**LD**
Alpharetta ▪ *(770) 569-1007*
5950 N Point Pkwy
Decatur ▪ *(404) 377-2121*
627 E College Ave ▪ Italian ▪ GF menu
includes pasta with choice of any sauce, as

well as chicken, salmon, spinach, caprese, and arugula salads, among other things. GF pasta is available. ▪ *www.figopasta.com*

Gallery Espresso   ★ ¢S
Savannah ▪ (912) 233-5348
234 Bull St ▪ Coffee & Café ▪ Owner Julianne reports they have at least one GF dessert, usually cheesecake or bundt cake, on the menu everyday. ▪ *www.galleryespresso.com*

Grapes & Hops Bar & Bistro $$LD
Flowery Branch ▪ (770) 965-9145
4856 Hog Mountain Rd ▪ Modern American ▪ Manager Paul reports that servers are generally knowledgeable about the GF diet, but they are trained to confer with the kitchen whenever a customer orders a GF meal. He adds that the filet, the grouper, and the pork chop are examples of naturally GF items. Confirm timeliness of this information before dining in. ▪ *www.grapesandhopsbarandbistro.com*

Grayson House, The   ★ $$$LD
Grayson ▪ (770) 995-3070
516 Grayson Pkwy ▪ Southern ▪ Owner Dot notes that the restaurant has "quite a few" GF customers. Since everything is fresh and made to order, GF requests are not a problem. She can make GF quinoa pasta and cheesecake with pecan crust, as well as other GF specialty items. Reservations noting GF are recommended. ▪ *www.graysonhouse.net*

Hunter House Inn $$$D
Tybee Island ▪ (912) 786-7515
1701 Butler Ave ▪ Steakhouse ▪ Manager Mary reports the restaurant serves "a few" GF diners. She notes that dishes are made to order, and that fish or steak entrées can be modified to be GF. Alert a server, who will communicate with the chef to ensure a safe meal. ▪ *www.hunterhouseinn.com*

J. Christopher's   ★ ¢BL
Marietta ▪ (770) 579-6800
1205 Johnson Ferry Rd ▪ Modern American ▪ GF pancakes are available on week-

days, and GF strada is always available. The strada, a french toast casserole, is made with GF rice bread. ▪ *www.jchristophers.com*

Lavender Asian Bistro   ✪ $LD
Lawrenceville ▪ (770) 982-3887
1195 Scenic Hwy ▪ Chinese & Thai ▪ GF menu is for dining in only and includes pad thai, green curry, and Mongolian beef, among many other items. For take-out, ask about GF options. Hostess Ria reports that over half of the take-out menu is naturally GF. GF soy sauce is available for dining in and take-out. ▪ *www.lavenderasianbistro.com*

Lemon Grass $LD
Marietta ▪ (770) 973-7478
2145 Roswell Rd ▪ Thai ▪ Manager Ginger reports that all of the curry dishes and the pad thai are naturally GF. Confirm timeliness of this information before dining in. She also notes that the chef, who is her brother, is willing to create dishes for GF customers who want something special. Ginger recommends asking for her upon arrival so that she can help choose a GF meal. ▪ *www.lemongrassmarietta.com*

Life Grocery and Café   ✪ $BLD
Marietta ▪ (770) 977-9583
1453 Roswell Rd ▪ Healthy American ▪ Server Julie reports that although the menu changes daily, a selection of WF and GF food is served at the hot and cold bars. She also notes that GF items are indicated in menu descriptions. Examples of past GF items include cake, salads, and vegetable stir-fry. Upon arrival, ask for the chef, or ask the counter-person for GF details. ▪ *www.lifegrocery.com*

Melting Pot, The   📖
Duluth ▪ (770) 623-1290
3610 Satellite Blvd
Kennesaw ▪ (770) 425-1411
2500 Cobb Place Ln NW Ste 800
Roswell ▪ (770) 518-4100
1055 Mansell Rd

Savannah ▪ (912) 349-5676
232 E Broughton St

New Lucky China $LD
Marietta ▪ (770) 565-9666
2960 Shallowford Rd ▪ Chinese ▪ Manager
Chris reports that they serve GF diners, but
he cautions that the staff is not very familiar with the GF diet. He notes that some
customers bring their own GF soy sauce for
the kitchen to cook with. He also notes that
the wok used for cooking is washed after
each usage. ▪ www.newluckychina.com

Oar House Inc., The   ★ $$$LD
Dahlonega ▪ (706) 864-9938
3072 Highway 52 E ▪ American ▪ Res-
taurant reports that the chef prepares GF
items "all the time." Menu items that can
be modified to be GF include the carrot
soup, salmon, crab cakes, steaks, and trout.
For all sandwiches, GF bread is available. ▪
www.theoarhouse.com

Olde Pink House $$$D
Savannah ▪ (912) 232-4286
23 Abercorn St ▪ Southern ▪ Manager
Kristen reports that they serve GF diners
"all the time." She notes that nearly all of
the seafood dishes, including the jumbo sea
scallops and the fish of the day, are naturally GF. Confirm timeliness of this information before dining in. She recommends
alerting a server, who will notify the chef.

Original Pancake House, The   ★ ¢BL
Alpharetta ▪ (678) 393-1355
5530 Windward Pkwy ▪ Breakfast ▪ GF
pancakes are available. ▪ www.originalpan-
cakehouse.com

Outback Steakhouse   📖
Albany ▪ (229) 883-4329
823 N Westover Blvd
Athens ▪ (706) 613-6015
3585 Atlanta Hwy
Augusta ▪ (706) 733-4329
2949 Washington Rd
Austell ▪ (770) 943-8445
2345 E West Connector
Canton ▪ (770) 720-9702

3 Reinhardt College Pkwy
Columbus ▪ (706) 324-6700
5592 Whitesville Rd
Commerce ▪ (706) 423-0022
411 Pottery Factory Dr
Conyers ▪ (770) 483-6268
1188 Dogwood Dr SE
Cumming ▪ (678) 455-7225
1715 Market Place Blvd
Dalton ▪ (706) 277-9600
955 Market St
Douglasville ▪ (770) 949-7000
6331 Douglas Blvd
Dunwoody ▪ (770) 481-0491
1220 Ashford Crossing
Gainesville ▪ (770) 287-1060
655 Dawsonville Hwy
Johns Creek ▪ (770) 442-8775
10955 Jones Bridge Rd Ste 120-124
Kennesaw ▪ (770) 795-0400
810 Ernest W. Barrett Pkwy NE
Macon ▪ (478) 477-1934
3899 Arkwright Rd
Peachtree City ▪ (770) 486-9292
995 N Peachtree Pkwy
Rome ▪ (706) 235-3233
1404 Turner Mccall Blvd SW
Roswell ▪ (770) 998-5630
655 W Crossville Rd
Saint Simons Is ▪ (912) 634-6659
1609 Frederica Rd
Savannah ▪ (912) 920-0555
11196 Abercorn St
Savannah ▪ (912) 232-1611
7 Drayton St
Stockbridge ▪ (770) 507-4198
200 North Park Ct
Stone Mountain ▪ (770) 498-5400
1525 E Park Place Blvd
Suwanee ▪ (770) 614-0092
145 Gwinco Blvd
Valdosta ▪ (229) 242-4329
1824 Club House Dr
Warner Robins ▪ (478) 953-1625
3088 Watson Blvd

P.F. Chang's China Bistro   📖
Alpharetta ▪ (770) 992-3070
7925 N Point Pkwy

Augusta ▪ *(706) 733-0161*
3450 Wrightsboro Rd Ste D215
Buford ▪ *(678) 546-9005*
3333 Buford Dr Ste Va03

Pappasito's Cantina $$**LD**
Marietta ▪ *(770) 541-6100*
2788 Windy Hill Rd SE ▪ *Tex-Mex* ▪ Manager Jenna reports that there are several options for GF diners, including fajitas, rice and beans, enchiladas, and GF chips. Alert a server, who will bring a manager over to discuss GF options. ▪ *www.pappasitos.com*

Pepperoni's   ✪★ $**LD**
Duluth ▪ *(770) 232-0224*
2750 Buford Hwy ▪ *Italian* ▪ GF menu lists almost exclusively GF specialty items. GF pizza, pasta, chicken nuggets, and brownies are available. ▪ *www.pepperonisduluth.com*

Pure Taqueria   ✪ ¢**LD**
Alpharetta ▪ *(678) 240-0023*
103 Roswell St
Woodstock ▪ *(770) 952-7873*
405 Chambers St. ▪ *Latin American* ▪ GF menu includes ceviche, mussels, queso fundito, shrimp with chili and lemon, tacos with corn tortillas, fajitas, fish salad, grilled meat, and enchiladas. ▪ *www.puretaqueria.com*

Ray's Killer Creek $$$$**LD**
Alpharetta ▪ *(770) 649-0064*
1700 Mansell Rd ▪ *American* ▪ Chef Daniel reports that they do not serve GF diners very often, but there are many options for GF diners. He recommends reservations noting GF, so the server is made aware in advance. Servers are fairly educated on the GF diet, but still Daniel suggests asking the server to speak to him about modifying food to be GF.

Ritters Restaurant $$**LD**
Marietta ▪ *(770) 973-1230*
4719 Lower Roswell Rd ▪ *Southern* ▪ The restaurant reports that GF requests are not a problem. Alert a server upon arrival. ▪ *www.rittersrestaurant.net*

Saba   ✪★ ¢**LD**
Decatur ▪ *(404) 377-9266*
350 Mead Rd ▪ *Italian* ▪ GF menu includes a variety of appetizers, salads, pastas, and side orders. Owner Shane reports that the entire staff is GF aware. GF pasta and beer are available. ▪ *www.saba-restaurant.com*

Seasons 52   ✪ $$$**LD**
Dunwoody ▪ *(770) 671-0052*
90 Perimeter Ctr W ▪ *Modern American* ▪ GF menu lists regular menu options that are naturally GF or can be modified to be GF. Manager Jay reports that items are easy to modify, as all dishes are made fresh to order. Reservations noting GF are recommended. ▪ *www.seasons52.com*

Shane's Rib Shack   📖
Alpharetta ▪ *(678) 297-2041*
270 Rucker Rd
Alpharetta ▪ *(770) 569-1988*
4180 Old Milton Pkwy
Athens ▪ *(706) 548-4650*
196 N Milledge Ave
Brunswick ▪ *(912) 264-4227*
315 Village At Glynn Pl
Canton ▪ *(678) 880-1141*
135 Reinhardt College Pkwy
Canton ▪ *(770) 720-8835*
2864 E Cherokee Dr
Canton ▪ *(770) 517-8655*
4504 Old Highway 5
Carrollton ▪ *(770) 830-7427*
1141 Bankhead Hwy
Conyers ▪ *(770) 483-4363*
2890 Highway 212 SW
Covington ▪ *(770) 786-2101*
11162 Highway 142 N
Dacula ▪ *(678) 546-8150*
3465 Braselton Hwy
Eatonton ▪ *(706) 485-3003*
106 Harmony Xing
Ellijay ▪ *(706) 635-7427*
289 Highland Xing
Evans ▪ *(706) 855-8227*
4446 Washington Rd
Flowery Branch ▪ *(770) 965-0123*
5877 Spout Springs Rd

Hinesville ▪ (912) 877-7675
300 W General Screven Way
Kennesaw ▪ (770) 420-3344
400 Ernest W Barrett Pkwy NW
Lawrenceville ▪ (770) 962-1870
4835 Sugarloaf Pkwy
Locust Grove ▪ (678) 583-8186
4980 Bill Gardner Pkwy
Loganville ▪ (770) 554-8200
4743 Atlanta Hwy
Macon ▪ (478) 257-6038
3267 Vineville Ave
Marietta ▪ (678) 290-0053
3894 Due West Rd NW Ste 280
Mcdonough ▪ (770) 898-7878
2136 Highway 155 N
Mcdonough ▪ (678) 583-0011
2788 Highway 81 E
Mcdonough ▪ (678) 583-1998
579 Jonesboro Rd
Newnan ▪ (770) 683-6416
55 Newnan Crossing Byp
Norcross ▪ (770) 416-6606
5770 Peachtree Industrial Blvd
Peachtree City ▪ (678) 364-9700
1261 N Peachtree Pkwy
Rome ▪ (706) 291-6062
315 Riverside Pkwy NE
Savannah ▪ (912) 354-3744
6730 Waters Ave
Smyrna ▪ (678) 213-2640
300 Village Green Cir SE
Snellville ▪ (770) 985-3733
4017 Annistown Rd
St Simons Island ▪ (912) 268-2272
70 Retreat Vlg
Statesboro ▪ (912) 681-4227
1100 Brampton Ave
Suwanee ▪ (770) 886-6657
2609 Peachtree Pkwy
Suwanee ▪ (770) 945-1117
3131 Lawrenceville Suwanee Rd
Winder ▪ (770) 307-1339
108 E May St

Shell House Restaurant $$D

Savannah ▪ (912) 927-3280
8 Gateway Blvd W ▪ Seafood ▪ Manager
Nathan reports that they can accommodate

GF diners. He notes that several chicken
and seafood dishes can be modified to be
GF. Confirm timeliness of this information
before dining in. Upon arrival, ask to speak
with a chef or manager, who will discuss
GF options. ▪ *www.shellhousesav.com*

South City Kitchen ✪ $$$LD

Smyrna ▪ (770) 435-0700
1675 Cumberland Pkwy SE ▪ Southern
▪ GF menu includes Georgia mountain
trout, molasses brined pork chop, Atlantic
salmon, steak, and more. ▪ *www.southcitykitchen.com*

Sugo ✪★ $$D

John's Creek ▪ (770) 817-8000
10305 Medlock Bridge Road
Roswell ▪ (770) 641-9131
408 S Atlanta St
Roswell ▪ (770) 817-4230
625 W Crossville Rd ▪ Italian ▪ GF menu
includes pasta and tomato basil sauce,
grilled pork tenderloin, mozzarella caprese,
and grilled sausages. GF pasta is available.
Owner John reports that the restaurant
"has found a real friend in the GF community." ▪ *www.sugorestaurant.com*

Sweet A'roma Bakery & Café ★ ¢L

Loganville ▪ (770) 559-8382
132 C S Floyd Rd ▪ Bakery & Café ▪ GF
bread is available for sandwiches. For
dessert, GF blond brownies, cakes, cookies, and more are available. Owner Roma
cautions that the bread "goes really fast,"
so always make sure they have some left
before arriving. ▪ *www.sweetaromabakery-cafe.com*

Tam's Backstage $$LD

Cumming ▪ (678) 455-8310
101 School St ▪ American ▪ Manager Vicki
reports that all veggies, grilled chicken
breast, shrimp, and fish dishes can be
modified to be GF. Confirm timeliness of
this information before dining in. Vicki
adds that the kitchen staff is "quite familiar" with GF meal preparation. ▪ *www.tamsbackstage.com*

Union Restaurant, The ✪ $$LD

Milton ▪ (770) 569-7767

14275 Providence Rd ▪ *American* ▪ GF menu includes oven roasted chicken, steak frittes, cobb salad, farmer's beef shortribs, filet mignon, shrimp and grits, and more. ▪ *www.theunionrestaurant.com*

Vinny's on Windward ✪ $$$$LD

Alpharetta ▪ (770) 772-4644

5355 Windward Pkwy ▪ *Modern American* ▪ GF menu consists of regular menu items that can be modified to be GF. It includes rack of lamb, Atlantic salmon, sautéed trout, mussels, and several soups and salads. Hostess Pam reports that chefs are very GF aware. ▪ *www.knowwheretogogh.com/vinnys.html*

Z Pizza ★ $LD

Alpharetta ▪ (678) 205-4471

5315 Windward Pkwy ▪ *Pizza* ▪ GF pizza and sandwiches are available, and the restaurant is expecting to introduce GF pasta in the near future. Desserts such as carrot cake and brownies are sometimes available. ▪ *www.zpizza.com*

HAWAII

HONOLULU

Alan Wong's $$$$D

Honolulu ▪ (808) 949-2526

1857 S King St ▪ *American Regional* ▪ Manager Derek reports that many fish dishes and salads can be modified to be GF upon request. He recommends calling in advance and notifying the head waiter, or "captain," of any GF requirements. ▪ *www.alanwongs.com*

Auntie Pastos $$LD

Honolulu ▪ (808) 523-8855

1099 S Beretania St ▪ *Italian* ▪ Manager Karina reports that the staff members are "very conscious" of the GF diet, and the management team recently attended a seminar on GF dining. Examples of possible GF modifications are replacing pasta with spinach and making eggplant parmesan without breading. ▪ *www.auntiepastos.com*

Bubba Gump Shrimp Co. 📖

Honolulu ▪ (808) 949-4867

1450 Ala Moana Blvd

Buca di Beppo 📖

Honolulu ▪ (808) 591-0800

1030 Auahi St

Duke's Canoe Club $$$BLD

Honolulu ▪ (808) 922-2268

2335 Kalakaua Ave ▪ *Hawaiian - American* ▪ Manager Yvonne notes that the restaurant can "certainly" accommodate GF diners. Chicken, steak and shrimp, shrimp scampi, lobster, and other dishes can be modified to be GF. Confirm timeliness of this information before dining in. Yvonne reports that reservations noting GF are required, as the manager will be able to notify the kitchen and prepare GF options in advance. ▪ *www.dukeswaikiki.com*

Hula Grill Waikiki $$$S

Honolulu ▪ (808) 923-4852

2335 Kalakaua Ave ▪ *American Regional* ▪ Restaurant reports that GF diners can be accommodated. Vegetable stir fries and various fish dishes can be made with GF starch substitutes. The starches in some sauces can be altered upon request. Confirm timeliness of this information before dining in. Alert a server upon arrival. ▪ *www.hulagrillwaikiki.com*

Indigo $$$LD

Honolulu ▪ (808) 521-2900

1121 Nuuanu Ave ▪ *American Regional* ▪ Restaurant reports that the lunch buffet can accommodate GF diners with several salads or other vegetables. For dinner, GF options are limited, as most meals are pre-prepared and pre-seasoned. Alert the server and ask for the manager. Reserva-

tions noting GF are strongly recommended. ▪ *www.indigo-hawaii.com*

La Cucaracha Mexican Bar $$LD
Honolulu ▪ (808) 924-3366
2446 Koa Ave ▪ Mexican ▪ Restaurant
reports limited GF offerings, including
chicken, shrimp, steak, and vegetable fajitas. Confirm timeliness of this information
before dining in. While it may be difficult
to prevent cross-contamination with many
dishes, some can be modified to be GF.

Old Spaghetti Factory, The   📖
Honolulu ▪ (808) 591-2513
1050 Ala Moana Blvd

Outback Steakhouse   📖
Honolulu ▪ (808) 951-6274
1765 Ala Moana Blvd
Honolulu ▪ (808) 396-7576
6650 Kalanianaole Hwy

Roy's   ★ $$$$D
Honolulu ▪ (808) 923-7697
226 Lewers St
Honolulu ▪ (808) 396-7697
6600 Kalanianaole Hwy ▪ *Hawaiian
Fusion* ▪ Triumph contacted a manager
at each location and all reported that GF
diners can be accommodated. The Kalanianaole Hwy and Koloa locations have
allergy cards that GF diners can fill out for
the chef. GF tamari sauce is available at the
Waikoloa location. All locations recommend alerting a server upon arrival, except
the Kalanianaole Hwy location, which recommends making reservations noting GF.
Servers are GF aware, and they are trained
to ask the chef if they have questions. ▪
www.roysrestaurant.com

Yard House   📖
Honolulu ▪ (808) 923-9273
226 Lewers St

Z Pizza   ★ $LD
Honolulu ▪ (808) 596-0066
1200 Ala Moana Blvd ▪ Pizza ▪ GF pizza is
available. ▪ *www.zpizza.com*

HAWAII
ALL OTHER CITIES

Auntie Pastos $$LD
Waipahu ▪ (808) 680-0005
94-673 Kupuohi St ▪ Italian ▪ Manager
Karina reports that the staff members are
"very conscious" of the GF diet, and the
management team recently attended a
seminar on GF dining. Examples of possible GF modifications are replacing pasta
with spinach and making eggplant parmesan without breading. ▪ *www.auntiepastos.
com*

Big Island Grill $BLD
Kailua Kona ▪ (808) 326-1153
75-5702 Kuakini Hwy ▪ *Hawaiian - American* ▪ Manager Janice reports that GF
diners are "nothing new" in the restaurant.
She notes that in the past, they have served
GF stir fries, roast pork without gravy,
and grilled chicken. Confirm timeliness of
this information before dining in. Alert a
server, who can help choose an appropriate
meal.

Bubba Gump Shrimp Co.   📖
Kailua Kona ▪ (808) 331-8442
75-5776 Alii Dr
Lahaina ▪ (808) 661-3111
889 Front St

Down to Earth   ★ ¢BLD
Aiea ▪ (808) 488-1375
98-129 Kaonohi St
Hilo ▪ (808) 935-5515
303 E Makaala St
Kahului ▪ (808) 877-2661
305 Dairy Rd
Kailua ▪ (808) 262-3838
201 Hamakua Dr ▪ *Deli* ▪ Vegetarian deli
inside the Down to Earth market. All locations have a salad bar and hot bar with GF
items. Call ahead to inquire about GF options at various locations. Some items are
marked WF; confirm that these are also GF.

Unlisted locations do not report carrying GF options. ▪ *www.downtoearth.org*

Five Palms Beach Grill $$$$**BLD**
Kihei ▪ *(808) 879-2607*
2960 S Kihei Rd ▪ *American Regional* ▪ Chef Katelyn reports that there are "a lot of different options" for GF diners. She adds that the restaurant is "very GF friendly," and they can almost always "tweak" a dish to make it GF. Alert a server upon arrival. Located at Keawakapu Beach, Maui. ▪ *www.fivepalmsrestaurant.com*

Flatbread Pizza Company   ★ $**LD**
Paia ▪ *(808) 579-8989*
89 Hana Hwy ▪ *Pizza* ▪ GF pizza is available in the 8-inch size. GF beer and desserts are also available. Typical GF desserts are brownies. ▪ *www.flatbreadcompany.com*

Hukilau Lanai $$$**D**
Kapaa ▪ *(808) 822-0600*
520 Aleka Loop ▪ *American* ▪ Manager Krissi reports that they serve GF diners frequently. She notes that there is an "intricate system" for serving customers with food allergies. Many menu items, particularly the fish specials, can be modified to be GF. Located in the Kauai Coast Resort. ▪ *www.hukilaukauai.com*

Kanaka Kava $$**LD**
Kailua Kona ▪ *(808) 883-6260*
75-5803 Alii Drive ▪ *Hawaiian - American* ▪ Owner Zack reports that with the exception of the sweet potato pie crust, everything is naturally GF. He notes that sweet potatoes, kava root, and other traditional Hawaiian fare are GF options. He also notes that all servers are fully aware of dish ingredients, so they can advise GF customers. ▪ *www.kanakakava.com*

Keoki's Paradise $$$**LD**
Koloa ▪ *(808) 742-7534*
2360 Kiahuna Plantation Dr ▪ *Hawaiian - American* ▪ Manager Manette reports that accommodating GF diners is "not a problem," as they have a list of GF options. Many menu items can be modified to be

GF, including sashimi without soy sauce, surf and turf, and Thai-style shrimp sticks. Confirm timeliness of this information before dining in. ▪ *www.keokisparadise.com*

Lahaina Coolers $$$**BLD**
Lahaina ▪ *(808) 661-7082*
180 Dickenson St ▪ *Fusion* ▪ General Manager Josh reports that "the majority of the staff is knowledgeable" about the GF diet. The pork chop, the NY strip, and the black garlic fish are naturally GF. For dessert, GF diners can order the chocolate taco. Confirm timeliness of this information before dining in. ▪ *www.lahainacoolers.com*

Lahaina Grill $$$$**D**
Lahaina ▪ *(808) 667-5117*
127 Lahainaluna Rd ▪ *American Regional* ▪ Restaurant reports that it can accommodate GF requests. Alert a server, who will notify the chef. Many menu items can be modified to be GF. Reservations noting GF are highly recommended. ▪ *www.lahainagrill.com*

Mama's Fish House $$$$**LD**
Paia ▪ *(808) 579-8488*
799 Poho Pl ▪ *American* ▪ Restaurant reports that the chefs are "very accommodating" of dietary requests. They report that many menu items are naturally GF or can be modified to be GF. Alert a server, who will notify the chef. Reservations noting GF are recommended. ▪ *www.mamasfishhouse.com*

Melting Pot, The   📖
Lahaina ▪ *(808) 661-6181*
325 Keawe St

Merriman's $$$$**D**
Kamuela ▪ *(808) 885-6822*
65-1227 Opelo Rd
Koloa ▪ *(808) 742-8385*
2829 Ala Kalani Kaumaka St # G-149
Lahaina ▪ *(808) 669-6400*
1 Bay Club Pl ▪ *Hawaiian - American* ▪ All three locations report that the chefs are very accommodating of GF diners. They note that they serve GF diners on a regular

basis and recommend making reservations noting GF. ▪ *www.merrimanshawaii.com*

Outback Steakhouse 📖

Kailua Kona ▪ *(808) 326-2555*
75-5809 Alii Dr. (coconut Grove Market Place)
Kapolei ▪ *(808) 674-1300*
302 Kamokila Blvd
Kihei ▪ *(808) 879-8400*
281 Piikea Ave
Lahaina ▪ *(808) 665-1822*
325 Keawe St Ste A-201
Waipahu ▪ *(808) 671-7200*
94-810 Ukee St

Papalani Gelato ¢S

Koloa ▪ *(808) 742-2663*
2360 Kiahuna Plantation Dr ▪ *Desserterie & Bakery* ▪ GF brownies, cookies, and chocolates are available, along with over 100 flavors of gelato. They also offer GF gelato sandwiches and cakes. ▪ *www.papalanigelato.com*

Penne Pasta Café ★ $$LD

Lahaina ▪ *(808) 661-6633*
180 Dickenson St ▪ *Italian* ▪ GF pasta is available. Manager Juan reports that they serve "about 14 different GF pastas." All sauces in the restaurant are GF, including alfredo, meat sauce, and vegetables sauces. Confirm timeliness of this information before dining in. ▪ *www.pennepastacafe.com*

Rapanui Island Café $$$D

Kailua Kona ▪ *(808) 329-0511*
75-5695 Alii Dr ▪ *Asian Fusion* ▪ Owner Rich reports that there are many options for GF diners, including pork and shrimp satay with peanut sauce. He recommends asking a server to speak to him about modifying items to be GF.

Roy's ★ $$$$D

Kapolei ▪ *(808) 676-7697*
92-1220 Aliinui Dr
Koloa ▪ *(808) 742-5000*
2360 Kiahuna Plantation Dr
Lahaina ▪ *(808) 669-6999*
4405 Honoapiilani Hwy

Waikoloa ▪ *(808) 886-4321*
250 Waikoloa Beach Dr ▪ *Hawaiian Fusion* ▪ Triumph contacted a manager at each location and all reported that GF diners can be accommodated. The Kalanianaole Hwy and Koloa locations have allergy cards that GF diners can fill out for the chef. GF tamari sauce is available at the Waikoloa location. All locations recommend alerting a server upon arrival, except the Kalanianaole Hwy location, which recommends making reservations noting GF. Servers are GF aware, and they are trained to ask the chef if they have questions. ▪ *www.roysrestaurant.com*

Scotty's Beachside BBQ $$$LD

Kapaa ▪ *(808) 823-8480*
4-1546 Kuhio Hwy. 20062 ▪ *Barbeque* ▪ Manager Britt reports that the hot and mild BBQ sauces are GF, but she notes specifically that the plum sauce is not GF. She further notes that most of the servers are very educated on the ingredients of menu items, but if not, they can ask the kitchen staff. ▪ *www.scottysbbq.com*

Sweet Marie's Hawaii Inc. 100% ¢S

Kapaa ▪ *(808) 823-0227*
4-788 Kuhio Hwy ▪ *Bakery* ▪ Dedicated GF bakery offering a variety of GF baked goods, including cakes, cookies, muffins, brownies, and more. GF muffin and cake mixes, as well as GF pizza dough, are available for shipping. Located in the Activity Warehouse Building. ▪ *www.sweetmarieskauai.com*

Verde New Mexican Restaurant $LD

Kapaa ▪ *(808) 821-1400*
4-1101 Kuhio Hwy ▪ *Modern Mexican* ▪ Owner and Chef Joshua reports that all staff members are trained on the GF diet, and they serve GF diners every day. He advises alerting the server and mentioning the word "allergy." GF options include tacos, enchiladas, and all salsas in the salsa bar. Confirm timeliness of this information before dining in. ▪ *www.verdehawaii.com*

IDAHO

1313 Club ★ ¢BLD
Wallace ▪ *(208) 752-9391*
608 Bank St ▪ *Modern American* ▪ Manager Dean reports that they welcome GF diners and can work with the kitchen to make GF meals. He notes that they have some regular GF customers. GF beer is available. ▪ *www.1313club.com*

Bangkok Cuisine $LD
Sandpoint ▪ *(208) 265-4149*
202 N 2nd Ave ▪ *Thai* ▪ Owner Pat reports that "almost everything" except curries can be modified to be GF. She advises alerting a server upon arrival and notes that all servers should be familiar with GF.

Boise Fry Co. ★ ¢LD
Boise ▪ *(208) 495-3858*
111 S Broadway Ave ▪ *American* ▪ GF french fries are available. Owner Blake reports that most of the sauces are also GF, and that they are "currently working" on a GF hamburger bun, which will be available soon. ▪ *www.boisefrycompany.com*

Bonefish Grill 📖
Boise ▪ *(208) 433-1234*
855 W Broad St Ste 260

Bonsai Bistro & Sushi Bar ✪★ $LD
Coeur d'Alene ▪ *(208) 765-4321*
101 E Sherman Ave ▪ *Asian Fusion* ▪ GF menu includes General Tso's chicken, Mongolian beef, and honey cashew crispy prawns, among other items. GF beer and soy sauce are available. For dessert, they offer white chocolate coconut crème brûlée or homemade green tea ice cream. ▪ *www.bonsaibistro.com*

Carino's Italian 📖
Ammon ▪ *(208) 523-4411*
2833 S 25th E
Boise ▪ *(208) 373-4968*
1700 S Entertainment Ave

Meridian ▪ *(208) 888-7801*
3551 E Fairview Ave
Twin Falls ▪ *(208) 734-4833*
1921 Blue Lakes Blvd N

Cellar, The ✪ $$$D
Ammon ▪ *(208) 525-9300*
3520 E 17th St ▪ *American Regional* ▪ GF menu includes small plates, soups, salads, meats, seafood, and risotto. Examples are veggie style nachos, quinoa portobello, tomato gorgonzola soup, filet mignon, and almond crusted halibut. GF beer is also available. ▪ *www.thecellar.biz*

Globus $$$D
Ketchum ▪ *(208) 726-1301*
291 6th St East ▪ *Asian* ▪ Manager Jodie reports the restaurant serves GF diners "all the time." She notes that servers are well trained in accommodating GF dietary needs, and she recommends alerting the server upon arrival. Dishes that can be modified to be GF include pad thai, fish specials, and more. Confirm timeliness of this information before dining in. ▪ *www.globus-restaurant.com*

Jalapeno's $LD
Boise ▪ *(208) 375-2077*
8799 Franklin Rd
Nampa ▪ *(208) 442-6355*
1921 Caldwell Blvd ▪ *Mexican* ▪ Owner Laeticia reports that the kitchen is trained and GF aware. She notes that several items can be modified to be GF. Calling ahead to note GF is recommended. ▪ *www.jalapenosidaho.com*

Leku Ona $$$LD
Boise ▪ *(208) 345-6665*
117 S 6th St ▪ *Spanish* ▪ Head Chef Ramone recommends calling ahead and asking for him so he can arrange a meal beforehand. Alert a server and ask him or her to communicate with the kitchen about the pre-arranged GF meal. ▪ *www.lekuonaid.com*

Louie's Pizza & Italian Restaurant ★ $LD
Meridian ▪ *(208) 884-5200*

2500 E Fairview Ave ▪ *Italian* ▪ GF pasta and pizza are available. Manager Chris notes that GF requests are common. ▪ *www.louiespizza.com*

McGrath's Fish House   ○ $LD
Boise ▪ (208) 375-6300
1749 S Cole Rd ▪ *Seafood* ▪ GF menu features a large selection of seafood entrees and appetizers, as well as salads and steaks. ▪ *www.mcgrathsfishhouse.com*

Melting Pot, The   📖
Boise ▪ (208) 383-0900
200 N 6th St

Miso Hungry   ★ $$LD
Driggs ▪ (208) 354-8015
165 N Main St ▪ *American Regional* ▪ Manager Marie reports that the restaurant makes "many GF items," and the staff is knowledgeable about GF foods. They can replace soy sauce with a GF white sauce, and all sandwiches, like the Turkey-Cran Pesto with cheese and cucumbers, can be made on GF bread.

Old Spaghetti Factory, The   📖
Boise ▪ (208) 336-2900
610 W Idaho St

Outback Steakhouse   📖
Boise ▪ (208) 323-4230
7189 Overland Rd
Coeur D Alene ▪ (208) 666-1500
1381 N Northwood Center Ct
Idaho Falls ▪ (208) 523-9301
970 Lindsay Blvd
Nampa ▪ (208) 461-4585
2011 W Karcher Rd
Twin Falls ▪ (208) 733-4585
1965 Blue Lakes Blvd N

P.F. Chang's China Bistro   📖
Boise ▪ (208) 342-8100
391 S 8th St

Pier 49 San Francisco Style Sourdough
Pizza   ★ $$LD
Meridian ▪ (208) 888-4961
3665 E Overland Rd
Pocatello ▪ (208) 234-1414

1000 Pocatello Creek Rd ▪ *Pizza* ▪ GF pizza is available. ▪ *www.pier49.com*

Second Avenue Pizza   ★ $LD
Sandpoint ▪ (208) 263-9321
215 S 2nd Ave ▪ *Pizza* ▪ GF pizza is available. Manager Eddie reports that more GF items will be available soon. ▪ *www.secondavenuepizza.com*

Tucanos Brazilian Grill $$LD
Boise ▪ (208) 343-5588
1388 S Entertainment Ave ▪ *Brazilian* ▪ Hostess Kelly reports that there are numerous menu options for GF diners. Alert a hostess or server and ask for the kitchen manager. The kitchen manager will explain GF options in detail. ▪ *www.tucanos.com*

Winger's Grill and Bar   ○ ¢LD
Blackfoot ▪ (208) 785-0774
1215 Parkway Drive
Idaho Falls ▪ (208) 552-5312
2770 S 25th E
Meridian ▪ (208) 888-1030
1701 E Fairview Ave
Moscow ▪ (208) 882-9797
1710 West Pullman Rd
Mountain Home ▪ (208) 587-1212
3150 NE Foothill Ave
Nampa ▪ (208) 442-9464
16250 N Marketplace
Pocatello ▪ (208) 232-0420
696 Yellowstone Ave
Rexburg ▪ (208) 356-4542
469 N 2nd E ▪ *American* ▪ GF menu includes double basted ribs, glazed salmon, quesadillas with corn tortillas, and a variety of salads. ▪ *www.wingers.info*

ILLINOIS

CHICAGO

Adobo Grill   ✪ $$**LD**
Chicago ▪ *(312) 266-7999*
1610 N Wells St
Chicago ▪ *(773) 252-9990*
2005 W Division St ▪ *Modern Mexican*
▪ GF menu varies slightly by location.
Examples of GF menu items are enchiladas,
a grilled half chicken in tamarind, and sautéed tilapia. GF desserts include chocolate
tamal and vanilla flan with caramel sauce. ▪
www.adobogrill.com

Alinea Restaurant $$$$**D**
Chicago ▪ *(312) 867-0110*
1723 N Halsted St ▪ *American* ▪ Reservationist Emily reports that they serve
GF diners "all the time." She notes that
customers will always be asked about food
allergies when making a reservation, and
she recommends noting GF at this time.
Most items on both prix fixe menus can be
easily modified to be GF. ▪ *www.alineares-
taurant.com*

Basil Leaf Café   ★ $$**LD**
Chicago ▪ *(773) 935-3388*
2465 N Clark St ▪ *Italian* ▪ GF pasta is
available. ▪ *www.basilleaf.com*

Ben Pao   ✪★ $$**LD**
Chicago ▪ *(312) 222-1888*
52 W Illinois St ▪ *Chinese* ▪ GF menu includes shanghai ginger chicken, pan-fried
wrinkled beans, ben pao fried rice with
shrimp or chicken, and more. GF soy sauce
and beer are available. GF dessert items
include mango crème brûlée and coconut-
tapioca custard. ▪ *www.benpao.com*

Between Boutique Café & Lounge $**D**
Chicago ▪ *(773) 292-0585*
1324 N Milwaukee Ave ▪ *Asian & Latin
Fusion* ▪ Manager Carl reports serving
GF diners "at least twice a month," and he
notes that they can "absolutely" be accom-

modated. Most items are not breaded, and
the ceviche as a popular GF order. Confirm
timeliness of this information before dining in. Alert a server upon arrival. Servers
generally know which menu items are or
can be modified to be GF, but they are
trained to ask the chef if they are unsure. ▪
www.betweenchicago.com

Big Bowl Restaurant   ✪ $**LD**
Chicago ▪ *(312) 640-8888*
6 E Cedar St
Chicago ▪ *(312) 951-1888*
60 E Ohio St ▪ *Asian* ▪ GF menu includes
thai chicken lettuce wraps as an appetizer, various pad thai dishes and chicken
kung pao as entrées, and two GF desserts,
including the trio of tastes. ▪ *www.bigbowl.
com*

Big Jones $$**LD**
Chicago ▪ *(773) 275-5725*
5347 N Clark St ▪ *Modern American* ▪
Restaurant reports that most menu items
can be modified to be GF, including sauces,
entrées, and sides. They also note that the
corn bread is naturally GF. All staff members are trained on GF dining, so just alert
a server upon arrival. ▪ *www.bigjoneschi-
cago.com*

Bistro 110 $$$$**LD**
Chicago ▪ *(312) 266-3110*
110 E Pearson St ▪ *French Bistro* ▪ The
restaurant reports that "many gluten-free
items are offered," and that GF diners come
in "every day." Either the server will suggest
appropriate dishes, or the chef will come
out to speak with the diner. Reservations
noting GF are recommended. ▪ *www.bistro-
110restaurant.com*

Bistrot Zinc $$$**LD**
Chicago ▪ *(312) 337-1131*
1131 N State St ▪ *French* ▪ Restaurant
owner Casey reports that GF diners are
welcome and advises customers to be
specific about dietary needs. Ask for the
manager upon arrival so that someone will

go over menu options with you. ▪ *www. bistrotzinc.com*

Bleeding Heart Bakery, The   ★ ⊂S
Chicago ▪ *(773) 327-6934*
1955 W Belmont Ave ▪ *Bakery* ▪ Non-dedicated bakery offering GF chocolate chip cookies, cupcakes, and brownies. Manager Aaron cautions that GF cupcakes "move quickly," so call ahead to make sure there are still some available. GF custom chocolate cakes are available for ordering. ▪ *www.thebleedingheartbakery.com*

BOKA $$$D
Chicago ▪ *(312) 337-6070*
1729 N Halsted St ▪ *Fusion* ▪ Manager Tim reports that they accommodate GF diners on a "very regular basis," and all staff members are thoroughly trained on the GF diet. He adds that all menu items are either naturally GF or can be modified to be GF. Alert a server, who will indicate which dishes must be modified, and which modifications must be made. ▪ *www. bokachicago.com*

Boundary, The $LD
Chicago ▪ *(773) 278-1919*
1932 W Division St ▪ *Global* ▪ Restaurant reports that GF diners are "welcome." Restaurant notes that most menu items can be modified to be GF. Upon arrival, alert a server and ask to speak with a manager. ▪ *www.boundarychicago.com*

Brasserie Jo $$$D
Chicago ▪ *(312) 595-0800*
59 W Hubbard St ▪ *French* ▪ Manager Erin reports that the restaurant accommodates GF diners "quite a bit." She notes that dishes can generally be modified to be GF, and that the restaurant has a "pretty fool-proof special request system" in place. Alert a server upon arrival. ▪ *www.brasseriejo.com*

Bristol, The $$D
Chicago ▪ *(773) 862-5555*
2152 N Damen Ave ▪ *Fusion* ▪ Manager Philip reports that GF diners can be accommodated "very easily." He notes that

though the menu changes daily, there are always several options that are naturally GF or can be modified to be GF. Upon arrival, alert the server, who will discuss the evening's GF options with the chef. ▪ *www. thebristolchicago.com*

Bubba Gump Shrimp Co.   📖
Chicago ▪ *(312) 252-4867*
700 E Grand Ave

Buca di Beppo   📖
Chicago ▪ *(312) 396-0001*
521 N Rush St

Café Absinthe $$$D
Chicago ▪ *(773) 278-4488*
954 W North Ave ▪ *Modern American* ▪ Restaurant reports that they receive GF requests "all the time." They note that menu items that can be modified to be GF include the ahi tuna tartar, foie gras, endive and apple salad, Alaskan halibut, sea scallops, and salmon. Alert a server upon arrival, and ask for manager. Reservations noting GF are recommended. ▪ *www. cafeabsinthechicago.com*

Café Ba Ba Reeba   ✪★ $$LD
Chicago ▪ *(773) 935-5000*
2024 N Halsted St ▪ *Spanish Tapas* ▪ GF menu includes paellas, tapas, seared ahi tuna salad, mixed greens salad with beets and goat cheese, chicken skewers, and more. GF bread and desserts such as GF profiteroles are also available. ▪ *www. cafebabareeba.com*

Capital Grille, The   📖
Chicago ▪ *(312) 337-9400*
633 N Saint Clair St

Carnivale $$$LD
Chicago ▪ *(312) 850-5005*
702 West Fulton Market ▪ *Latin American* ▪ Restaurant reports that with advanced notice, they can accommodate GF diners. They note that several dishes on the menu are naturally GF or can be modified to be GF. GF diners should make a reservation, and then upon arrival, talk to the server

about GF options. ▪ *www.carnivalechicago.
com*

Charlie Trotter's $$$$D
Chicago ▪ (773) 248-6228
816 W Armitage Ave ▪ *Modern American*
▪ Chef Chris reports that the kitchen is "extremely flexible" and will create an entirely new dish to satisfy GF requests. The menu changes regularly, but if it has any GF items, a server will discuss them with GF diners. Reservations noting GF are recommended. ▪ *www.charlietrotters.com*

Chicago Diner, The   ✿★ $BLD
Chicago ▪ (773) 935-6696
3411 N Halsted St ▪ *Vegetarian* ▪ GF menu includes nachos, a variety of salads, avocado tostadas, quesadillas, stir fry, and more. Restaurant notes that fried items such as chips are prepared in the same fryer as non-GF items. For dessert, they offer GF cheesecake in various flavors. ▪ *www.veggiediner.com*

Chicago's Pizza   ★ $$LD
Chicago ▪ (773) 348-1700
1919 W Montrose Ave
Chicago ▪ (773) 755-4030
3006 N Sheffield Ave
Chicago ▪ (773) 477-2777
3114 N Lincoln Ave ▪ *Pizza* ▪ GF pizza is available. ▪ *www.chicagos-pizza.com*

China Grill at The Hard Rock Hotel
$$$$BLD
Chicago ▪ (312) 334-6700
230 N Michigan Ave ▪ *Asian Fusion* ▪ Manager Andrea reports that the restaurant serves GF diners "very often." She recommends noting GF in reservations so that the server can prepare in advance. She notes that the Shanghai lobster is naturally GF, and almost all other dishes can be modified to be GF. She offers to have a chef come to the table upon request. ▪ *www.chinagrillmgt.com*

Club Lucky $$$LD
Chicago ▪ (773) 227-2300
1824 W Wabansia Ave ▪ *Italian-American*

▪ GF pasta is available. Restaurant notes that salads, fish dishes, italian sausage, and most meat dishes can be modified to be GF. Confirm timeliness of this information before dining in. Reservations noting GF are recommended. Upon arrival, alert a server, who will notify the kitchen. ▪ *www.clubluckychicago.com*

Cupcake Gallery, The   ★ ¢S
Chicago ▪ (773) 822-2377
1319 W Wilson Ave ▪ *Bakery* ▪ GF cupcakes are available. Owner Darius reports that he can make any of his cupcake flavors GF, but he recommends giving him advanced notice of at least a few days. ▪ *www.cupcakegallery.com*

Dunlays on Clark $$LD
Chicago ▪ (773) 883-6000
2600 N Clark St ▪ *Modern American* ▪ Manager Mark reports that most items are made to order, so modifying menu items to be GF is not a problem. He reports that they "sometimes" host GF diners. Reservations noting GF are recommended. Upon arrival, alert a server and ask to speak with a manager. ▪ *www.dunlaysonclark.com*

Everest $$$$D
Chicago ▪ (312) 663-8920
440 S Lasalle St ▪ *French* ▪ Kitchen manager Mike reports that the restaurant serves GF diners "more and more." Alert a server, who will indicate GF options. Mike also reports that the kitchen can modify most regular menu items to be GF. Reservations noting GF are required. ▪ *www.everestrestaurant.com*

Feast Restaurant + Bar   ✿ $$D
Chicago ▪ (773) 772-7100
1616 N Damen Ave ▪ *American* ▪ GF menu includes chicken tortilla soup, pork chops, blackened fish tacos, sautéed whitefish, and a flourless chocolate decadence cake with raspberry sauce. Restaurant has another Chicago location at 25 E. Delaware Pl, but they do not have a GF menu. ▪ *www.feastrestaurant.com*

Fogo De Chao   ★ $$$$LD
Chicago ▪ (312) 932-9330
661 N Lasalle St ▪ Brazilian ▪ GF cheese
bread made with yucca flour is available. ▪
www.fogodechao.com

Francesca's   ✪★ $$$LD
Chicago ▪ (773) 506-9261
1039 W Bryn Mawr Ave
Chicago ▪ (312) 829-2828
1400 W Taylor St
Chicago ▪ (773) 770-0184
1576 N Milwaukee Ave
Chicago ▪ (773) 281-3310
3311 N Clark St ▪ Italian ▪ GF pasta is
available at all locations. Only the Taylor
St location has a limited GF menu that lists
a few GF pasta preparations. All locations
have several chicken and meat dishes that
can be modified to be GF. Confirm timeliness of this information before dining in. ▪
www.miafrancesca.com

Frankie's Pizzeria & Scaloppine ✪ ¢LD
Chicago ▪ (312) 266-2500
900 N Michigan Ave ▪ Pizza ▪ GF menu
includes calamari, chicken roma, crispy
brick chicken, and the risotto of the day.
GF desserts include chocolate meringue
cookies. The restaurant has two dining
rooms serving different items, so confirm
that GF items are available in a particular
dining room before being seated. ▪ *www.
frankiesscaloppine.com*

Frontera Grill $$$LD
Chicago ▪ (312) 661-1434
445 N Clark St ▪ Modern Mexican ▪
Manager Kevin reports that the restaurant
is "constantly" serving GF diners. He notes
that servers are required to notify the head
chef in the case of any food "allergies." He
recommends noting GF in reservations,
and cautions that fried foods like chips and
chimichangas are not GF because they are
not fried separately. Confirm timeliness of
this information before dining in. ▪ *www.
fronterakitchens.com*

Geja's Café $$$$D
Chicago ▪ (773) 281-9101
340 W Armitage Ave ▪ Fondue ▪ Manager
Adam reports that they serve GF diners "all
the time." He notes that six of eight fondu
dipping sauces are GF, and none of the
seafood or meats are dredged in any sort of
flour. Confirm timeliness of this information before dining in. Adam recommends
noting GF in reservations. Restaurant has
an internal list of GF items that is available to customers upon request. ▪ *www.
gejascafe.com*

Grace O'Malley's $$LD
Chicago ▪ (312) 588-1800
1416 S Michigan Ave ▪ Irish Pub ▪ Executive Chef Daryl reports that he is "certainly" able to accommodate GF diners. He
recommends asking for him upon arrival
so that he can discuss GF options and food
preparation. Dishes that might be modified to be GF include steak salad, chopped
salad, short ribs, and halibut. Confirm
timeliness of this information before dining in. ▪ *www.graceomalleychicago.com*

Handlebar $BD
Chicago ▪ (773) 384-9546
2311 W North Ave ▪ American ▪ Owner
Josh reports that there are extensive GF
options. He notes that GF diners come in
"on a regular basis." GF items include black
bean maduro, ground nut stew, tostadas,
and several sides. Confirm timeliness of
this information before dining in. Alert a
server, who will talk to the kitchen. ▪ *www.
handlebarchicago.com*

Ina's   ★ ¢BL
Chicago ▪ (312) 226-8227
1235 W Randolph St ▪ American ▪ Manager Seana reports that they have GF items
at every meal, but she advises speaking to a
manager before ordering. GF fried chicken
night is the second Wednesday of every
month. GF beer, bread, pasta, and cake
available. ▪ *www.breakfastqueen.com*

Jin Ju $$D
Chicago ▪ *(773) 334-6377*
5203 N Clark St ▪ *Korean* ▪ The manager reports that they have several GF customers. He notes that rice-based dishes with mixed vegetables, spicy chicken, and spicy squid can be modified to be GF. He cautions that it is imperative to alert a server and to be prepared to explain GF to the server. He also recommends asking for the chef or manager.

Joe's Seafood, Prime Steak, and Stone Crab   ✪ $$$$LD
Chicago ▪ *(312) 379-5637*
60 E Grand Ave ▪ *American* ▪ GF menu includes appetizers, soups, salads, and sides. Seafood, steak, and crab dishes are also listed. ▪ *www.joes.net*

Karyn's Cooked   ✪ $LD
Chicago ▪ *(312) 587-1050*
738 N Wells St ▪ *Vegan* ▪ GF items marked on the menu include stuffed eggplant, the raw plate, and the Buddha bowl. GF desserts are available. Alert a server, even if ordering a GF item. ▪ *www.karynraw.com*

Karyn's Raw Café   ✪★ $LD
Chicago ▪ *(312) 255-1590*
1901 N Halsted St ▪ *Raw* ▪ Menu items NOT marked with a star are GF. GF options include dim sum, salads, mango lassie soup, empanadas, zucchini pasta primavera, portobello napoleon, and falafel. GF breadsticks are available. ▪ *www.karynraw.com*

L20 $$$$D
Chicago ▪ *(773) 868-0002*
2300 N Lincoln Park W ▪ *Seafood* ▪ Reservationist Shelby reports that many menu items are naturally GF, as it is a seafood restaurant. She also notes that the menu changes every day, so with reservations, the chef can take GF requests into consideration. Reservations noting GF are highly recommended. ▪ *www.l2orestaurant.com*

Lawry's The Prime Rib   ★ $$$$D
Chicago ▪ *(312) 787-5000*
100 E Ontario St ▪ *Steakhouse* ▪ GF scones, bread, and chocolate raspberry cookies are available. Restaurant recommends noting GF in reservations, as that note will be forwarded to the chef in advance. They note that servers generally know what food is or can be modified to be GF. ▪ *www.lawrysonline.com*

Lou Malnati's $$LD
Chicago ▪ *(773) 395-2400*
1520 N Damen Ave
Chicago ▪ *(773) 762-0800*
3859 W Ogden Ave
Chicago ▪ *(312) 828-9800*
439 N Wells St
Chicago ▪ *(312) 786-1000*
805 S State St
Chicago ▪ *(773) 832-4030*
958 W Wrightwood Ave ▪ *Pizza* ▪ Corporate reports that all locations can do a "crustless" pizza upon request. They also note that most salads are GF when ordered without croutons or tortilla chips. Confirm timeliness of this information before dining in. Alert a manager, who will recommend GF options. ▪ *www.loumalnatis.com*

Luxbar $$LD
Chicago ▪ *(312) 642-3400*
18 E Bellevue Pl ▪ *American* ▪ Manager Michael reports that there are "plenty of items" on the menu that can be modified to be GF. Alert a server upon arrival. Michael notes that because GF diners are "pretty common" at the restaurant, "most servers" are GF aware, and all servers are trained to "let the chef know" as soon as they are alerted of a GF diner. ▪ *www.luxbar.com*

M Henry Chow for Now   ¢BL
Chicago ▪ *(773) 561-1600*
5707 N Clark St ▪ *Modern American* ▪ Manager Eve reports that accommodating GF requests is "no big deal." She reports that most servers know what is GF, but if they do not, they will ask the kitchen. She also notes that several bacon, egg, and potato dishes are GF, while other items can be modified to be GF. Confirm timeliness of

this information before dining in. ▪ *www.mhenry.net*

Maggiano's Little Italy   ★ $$$LD
Chicago ▪ *(312) 644-7700*
516 N Clark St ▪ *Italian* ▪ GF pasta is available. Call individual locations to inquire about additional GF options. ▪ *www.maggianos.com*

Mana Food Bar   ¢D
Chicago ▪ *(773) 342-1742*
1742 W Division St ▪ *Global* ▪ Manager Heather reports that all servers are trained in the GF diet. Alert a server, who will "scoop up" the menu and "mark it off," indicating items that are GF or can be modified to be GF. Heather notes that there are many GF items in the "cold" section of the menu. ▪ *www.manafoodbar.com*

Marcello's, A Father and Son Restaurant   ★ $LD
Chicago ▪ *(773) 252-2620*
2475 N Milwaukee Ave
Chicago ▪ *(312) 654-2550*
645 W North Ave ▪ *Pizza* ▪ GF pizza, pasta, brownies, and apple or berry dessert pizza are available. ▪ *www.marcellos.com*

Melting Pot, The   📖
Chicago ▪ *(312) 573-0011*
609 N Dearborn St

Mercat a la Planxa $$$$BLD
Chicago ▪ *(312) 765-0524*
638 S Michigan Ave ▪ *Spanish* ▪ Manager Jeremy reports that although the restaurant doesn't serve GF diners very often, they can certainly be accommodated. Make reservations noting GF so they can prepare a GF list. ▪ *www.mercatchicago.com*

Mity Nice Bar & Grill   ✪ $LD
Chicago ▪ *(312) 335-4745*
835 N Michigan Ave ▪ *American* ▪ Ask the host or server for a GF menu upon arrival. GF foods are cooked separately from other foods. ▪ *www.leye.com*

Mon Ami Gabi   ✪ $$$D
Chicago ▪ *(773) 348-8886*

2300 N Lincoln Park W ▪ *French* ▪ GF menu includes chicken liver mousse, seared sea scallops, lemon chicken paillard, steak béarnaise, and more. For dessert, chocolate mousse, crème brûlée, and a pear parfait are available. ▪ *www.monamigabi.com*

Nacional 27 $$$D
Chicago ▪ *(312) 664-2727*
325 W Huron St ▪ *Modern Latin* ▪ The restaurant reports that GF options are available, and that many menu items are naturally GF. GF items on the menu include the tequila-marinated chicken, several tapas, ahi tuna, and gaucho barbeque items. Alert a server, who will discuss details more extensively. ▪ *www.nacional27.net*

Naha   ★ $$$$LD
Chicago ▪ *(312) 321-6242*
500 N Clark St ▪ *Fusion* ▪ GF bread and crackers are available. Restaurant reports having accommodated "several" GF diners. They recommend noting GF in reservations and then alerting the server to ensure that he or she specifies GF when sending the order. ▪ *www.naha-chicago.com*

Nine the Steak House $$$$LD
Chicago ▪ *(312) 575-9900*
440 W Randolph St ▪ *Steakhouse* ▪ Manager Octavio reports that GF diners can be accommodated. He notes that servers flag GF orders to alert the kitchen staff to avoid cross-contamination. He further notes that most steaks and seafood are prepared without flour, so they are easy to modify to be GF. Confirm timeliness of information before dining in. ▪ *www.n9ne.com*

North Pond $$$$D
Chicago ▪ *(773) 477-5845*
2610 N Cannon Dr ▪ *Fusion* ▪ Restaurant reports that GF diners can be accommodated "without a problem." Reservations noting GF are highly recommended, so that the server can be informed in advance. Server will discuss GF options with the kitchen, and then indicate options to the diner. ▪ *www.northpondrestaurant.com*

Osteria Via Stato $$LD
Chicago ▪ *(312) 642-8450*
620 N State St ▪ *Italian* ▪ Manager Mo
reports that there are a limited number of
GF items on the menu, but GF diners can
"easily" be accommodated. She notes that
servers have a special alert system for GF
requests. Reservations noting GF are recommended. ▪ *www.osteriaviastato.com*

Outback Steakhouse   📖
Chicago ▪ *(773) 380-0818*
8101 W Higgins Rd

P.F. Chang's China Bistro   📖
Chicago ▪ *(312) 828-9977*
530 N Wabash Ave

Pasta D'Arte Trattoria Italiana   ★ $LD
Chicago ▪ *(773) 763-1181*
6311 N Milwaukee Ave ▪ *Italian* ▪ GF pasta
is available. Examples of GF meals include
risotto pescatora, pasta bolognese, and
sirloin beef stuffed with garlic, parmigiano,
and parsley. All staff members are trained
in the GF diet. ▪ *www.pastadarte.com*

Pasticceria Natalina   ¢S
Chicago ▪ *(773) 989-0662*
5406 N Clark St ▪ *Bakery* ▪ A variety of
naturally GF baked goods, like macaroons
and brittles, are available. Varieties of macaroons include bitter almond, pistachio,
and chocolate hazelnut. Candied oranges
are also available. Owner Nick reports that
the GF goods sometimes run out, especially on Sundays. ▪ *www.p-natalina.com*

Petterino's   ✪ $$$LD
Chicago ▪ *(312) 422-0150*
150 N Dearborn St ▪ *Seafood & Steakhouse* ▪ GF menu includes all steaks,
chicken breasts, different types of potatoes,
and more. Alert a server, who will notify
the chef and ensure proper meal preparation. ▪ *www.leye.com*

R.J. Grunts $LD
Chicago ▪ *(773) 929-5363*
2056 N Lincoln Park W ▪ *American* ▪
Manager Andrea reports that GF diners are

welcome and advises alerting a server upon
arrival, as the restaurant has an "allergy"
procedure which covers GF. She says they
can accommodate GF diners, though they
may have to "improvise" some of the selections. ▪ *www.leye.com*

Ranalli's of Andersonville   ✪ ★ $LD
Chicago ▪ *(773) 334-1300*
1512 W Berwyn Ave ▪ *Italian* ▪ GF menu
includes garlic bread, cheese bread, pizza
bread, and bruschetta for appetizers, as well
as GF croutons and dressings for salads,
sandwiches with GF buns, GF spaghetti or
penne, GF lasagna, and GF pizza. ▪ *www.
ranallispizza.com*

Reza's Restaurant $$$LD
Chicago ▪ *(312) 664-4500*
432 W Ontario St
Chicago ▪ *(773) 561-1898*
5255 N Clark St ▪ *Middle Eastern* ▪ Managers at all locations report serving GF diners often. All recommend asking for a manager upon arrival. Although many servers
are educated on the GF diet, the managers
will know more about which items are GF.
▪ *www.rezasrestaurant.com*

Roy's   ✪ $$$D
Chicago ▪ *(312) 787-7599*
720 N State St ▪ *Hawaiian Fusion* ▪ GF
menu includes a sashimi sampler, seared
tiger shrimp, filet mignon, and sea scallops.
Manager Chris reports that the restaurant
is very comfortable accommodating GF
diners. Alert a server, who will send GF
requests directly to the kitchen. ▪ *www.
roysrestaurant.com*

Scoozi!   ✪ $D
Chicago ▪ *(312) 943-5900*
41 W Huron St ▪ *Italian* ▪ GF menu includes artichoke hearts, filet mignon, and
salmon, among other things. GF menu
changes seasonally, and Chef Jeremy
reports that he expects to have GF pasta
"soon." He adds that they serve GF diners
"very frequently." ▪ *www.leye.com*

Shaw's Crab House ☻ $$$$LD
Chicago ■ (312) 527-2722
21 E Hubbard St ■ Seafood ■ GF menu
includes griddle garlic shrimp, seared
scallops, halibut, salmon, strip steak, crab,
lobster, sushi, and more. Crème brulee is
available for dessert. ■ www.shawscrab-
house.com

Sit Down Café & Sushi Bar, The ☻ ¢LD
Chicago ■ (773) 324-3700
1312 E 53rd St ■ Global ■ Extensive GF
menu includes prosciutto rolls, pizza, and
sandwiches on GF bread, as well as maki
and sashimi rolls. ■ www.thesitdown53.com

Smith & Wollensky ☻ $$$$LD
Chicago ■ (312) 670-9900
318 N State St ■ Steakhouse ■ GF menu
includes tomato and onion salad, ahi tuna
salad, shrimp cobb salad, grilled lamb
chops, lemon basil chicken breast, prime
rib, Scottish salmon, and more. ■ www.
smithandwollensky.com

Swirlz Cupcakes ★ ¢S
Chicago ■ (773) 404-2253
705 W Belden Ave ■ Bakery ■ Non-
dedicated bakery offering GF cupcakes
in flavors that change daily. Possible GF
flavors include red velvet, carrot, chocolate
grasshopper mint, and chocolate chip. Call
ahead to find out which flavors are available on a given day. ■ www.swirlzcupcakes.
com

Takashi $$$$D
Chicago ■ (773) 772-6170
1952 N Damen Ave ■ Japanese ■ Manager
Victoria reports that they serve GF diners about once a week. She recommends
reservations noting GF, so the chef can be
prepared to cook GF food. She notes that
all servers are trained to speak with the
chef about GF dishes. ■ www.takashichi-
cago.com

Tavern on Rush $$$$BLD
Chicago ■ (312) 664-9600
1031 N Rush St ■ Steakhouse ■ Restaurant
reports that they serve several GF diners

each week. Menu items that can be modified to be GF include all steaks, several
salads, grilled vegetables, and most seafood
dishes. Confirm timeliness of this information before dining in. The staff is very
knowledgeable about GF foods. Ask the
server to get a manager or chef, who will
come out and discuss GF options. ■ www.
tavernonrush.com

Taxim $$$D
Chicago ■ (773) 252-1558
1558 N Milwaukee Ave ■ Greek ■ Restaurant reports that GF diners "have been
accommodated" in the past. They note that
GF diners should request all meals to come
without bread and discuss GF options with
a server. ■ www.taximchicago.com

Topolobampo $$$$LD
Chicago ■ (312) 661-1434
445 N Clark St ■ Modern Mexican ■
Manager Kevin reports that they are "very
good about" accommodating GF diners.
He notes that they serve GF diners "quite
often," and he advises alerting the server
upon arrival. Servers must go "directly"
to the chef when they are notified of a GF
diner. ■ www.fronterakitchens.com

Tru Restaurant $$$$D
Chicago ■ (312) 202-0001
676 N Saint Clair St ■ French ■ Chef
Anthony reports that serving GF diners
is "fairly common." He adds that almost
the entire menu is naturally GF or can be
modified to be GF. He recommends making reservations noting GF and alerting the
server when he or she asks about dietary
restrictions. ■ www.trurestaurant.com

Uno Chicago Grill 📖
Chicago ■ (312) 943-4041
49 E Ontario St

Venus ☻ $$D
Chicago ■ (312) 714-1001
820 W Jackson Blvd ■ Mediterranean
■ Extensive GF menu includes marinated portabellos, pork tenderloin kebab,
swordfish shrimp and scallop skewers, and

chicken breast with cheese and spinach, among other things. ▪ *www.venuschicago. com*

Vinci Restaurant   ✪★ $$$D
Chicago ▪ *(312) 266-1199*
1732 N Halsted St ▪ *Italian* ▪ GF menu includes appetizers, pasta dishes, meat courses, and desserts. Examples are carpaccio, duck, and veal saltimbocca. GF pasta is available. For dessert, they offer panna cotta and crème brûlée. ▪ *www.vincichicago. com*

Weber Grill Restaurant   ✪ $$LD
Chicago ▪ *(312) 467-9696*
539 N State St ▪ *American* ▪ Extensive GF menu includes blackened catfish, grilled garlic shrimp, BBQ beef brisket, ribs, and more. For starters, baked onion soup and gulf shrimp cocktail are available. ▪ *www. webergrillrestaurant.com*

Wildfire   ✪★ $$$D
Chicago ▪ *(312) 787-9000*
159 W Erie St ▪ *Steakhouse* ▪ GF menu includes sirloin steak, double stuffed baked potatoes, and oven-baked goat cheese. GF beer, vodka, and sandwich buns are available. ▪ *www.wildfirerestaurant.com*

ILLINOIS

ALL OTHER CITIES

Antico Posto   ✪ $$$LD
Oak Brook ▪ *(630) 586-9200*
118 Oakbrook Ctr ▪ *Italian* ▪ GF menu includes salads, filet mignon, polenta with goat cheese, mussels arrabbiata, brick chicken, and Italian pot roast. Located in the Oakbrook Center Mall. ▪ *www.antico-posto.com*

Apple's Bakery   ★ ¢S
Peoria ▪ *(309) 693-3522*

8412 N Knoxville Ave ▪ *Bakery* ▪ Non-dedicated bakery offering a wide selection of GF products. Pies, cookies, brownies, and breads are available. There is a separate, dedicated GF kitchen where only GF items are prepared. GF baked goods are prepared Monday through Wednesday, but they are sometimes available on other days. ▪ *www. applesbakery.com*

Aurelio's Pizza   ★ ¢LD
Addison ▪ *(630) 889-9560*
1455 W Lake St
Frankfort ▪ *(815) 469-2196*
310 W Lincoln Hwy
Mokena ▪ *(708) 478-0022*
19836 Wolf Rd
New Lenox ▪ *(815) 485-8100*
320 W Maple St ▪ *Pizza* ▪ GF pizza is available in the 6-inch personal size at all locations. Any toppings can be added to the GF crust. GF cookies are sometimes available at Mokena and Frankfurt, while GF beer is available at the Frankfort location only. ▪ *www.aurelios.net*

Bahay Kubo Filipino Asian Cuisine   ★ $BLD
Bourbonnais ▪ *(815) 802-9889*
263 N Convent St ▪ *Asian Fusion* ▪ Owner Arnold reports that the restaurant is "very aware" of Celiac disease and GF dining. GF soy sauce is available. GF buffet nights are offered on the first Tuesday and the third Thursday of every month. Calling ahead to note GF is recommended. ▪ *www.bahayku-bodining.com*

Barraco's Pizzeria   ★ $LD
Evergreen Park ▪ *(708) 424-8182*
3701 W 95th St
Orland Park ▪ *(708) 478-1500*
18040 Wolf Rd
Orland Park ▪ *(708) 444-0661*
7926 W 159th St ▪ *Pizza* ▪ GF pasta is available at all listed locations. At the Wolf Road and Evergreen Park locations, GF pizza is also available. All other locations report that they don't carry GF items. ▪ *www.bar-racos.com*

Biaggi's Ristorante Italiano   📖
Algonquin ▪ *(847) 658-5040*
1524 S Randall Rd
Bloomington ▪ *(309) 661-8322*
1501 N Veterans Pkwy
Champaign ▪ *(217) 356-4300*
2235 S Neil St
Deer Park ▪ *(847) 438-1850*
20560 N Rand Rd
Naperville ▪ *(630) 428-8500*
2752 Show Place Dr

Big Bowl Restaurant   ✪ $LD
Lincolnshire ▪ *(847) 808-8880*
215 Parkway Dr
Schaumburg ▪ *(847) 517-8881*
1950 E Higgins Rd ▪ *Asian* ▪ GF menu
includes thai chicken lettuce wraps as an
appetizer, various pad thai dishes and
chicken kung pao as entrées, and two GF
desserts, including the trio of tastes. ▪ *www.
bigbowl.com*

Bleeding Heart Bakery, The   ★ ¢S
Oak Park ▪ *(708) 358-0559*
1010 North Blvd ▪ *Bakery* ▪ Non-dedicated
bakery offering GF chocolate chip cookies,
cupcakes, and brownies. Manager Aaron
cautions that GF cupcakes "move quickly,"
so call ahead to make sure there are still
some available. GF custom chocolate cakes
are available for ordering. ▪ *www.thebleed-
ingheartbakery.com*

Blind Faith Café $$BLD
Evanston ▪ *(847) 328-6875*
525 Dempster St ▪ *Bakery & Café* ▪ The
restaurant reports that several dishes are
naturally GF. GF dishes include artichoke
hearts and couscous, stuffed avocado,
roasted beet salad, guacamole, and french
fries. Confirm timeliness of this information before dining in. Upon arrival, alert
the server, who will indicate GF options. ▪
www.blindfaithcafe.com

Bonefish Grill   📖
Algonquin ▪ *(847) 658-9268*
1604 S Randall Rd
Schaumburg ▪ *(847) 534-0679*

180 S Roselle Rd
Skokie ▪ *(847) 674-4634*
9310 Skokie Blvd

Buca di Beppo   📖
Lombard ▪ *(630) 932-7673*
90 Yorktown Ctr
Orland Park ▪ *(708) 349-6262*
15350 S 94th Ave
Wheeling ▪ *(847) 808-9898*
604 N Milwaukee Ave

Cab's Wine Bar Bistro $$$D
Glen Ellyn ▪ *(630) 942-9463*
430 N Main St ▪ *Global* ▪ Manager Dave
reports that the restaurant caters to "several
special requests" every day. He notes that
many meat and seafood dishes can be
modified to be GF. Confirm timeliness of
this information before dining in. ▪ *www.
cabsbistro.com*

Capital Grille, The   📖
Lombard ▪ *(630) 627-9800*
87 Yorktown Ctr
Rosemont ▪ *(847) 671-8125*
5340 N River Rd

Capri Restaurant   ★ ¢LD
Rockford ▪ *(815) 965-6341*
313 E State St ▪ *Italian* ▪ GF pasta is available, and cheese lasagna can be prepared
with advanced notice of 24 hours. Other
possible GF options include chicken marsala, chicken parmesan and broiled cod. ▪
www.caprirockford.com

Carrabba's Italian Grill   📖
Naperville ▪ *(630) 355-3234*
944 S Route 59
Woodridge ▪ *(630) 427-0900*
1001 75th St

City Park Grill   ✪★ $$LD
Highland Park ▪ *(847) 432-9111*
1783 Saint Johns Ave ▪ *American* ▪ GF
menu includes cobb salad, roasted chicken,
sautéed tilapia, and baby back ribs. GF
sandwich buns and pastas are available. ▪
www.thecityparkgrill.com

Da Luciano   ✪★ $$D
River Grove ▪ *(708) 453-1000*
8343 W. Grand Ave ▪ *Italian* ▪ Extensive GF menu includes chicken Vesuvio, chicken parmigiana, eggplant parmagiana, mozzarella wedges, and various sauces. GF pizza, pasta, and bread are available. Tiramisu, cannoli, and cupcakes are available for dessert. ▪ *www.dalucianos.com*

Deerfields Bakery   ✪★ ₵S
Buffalo Grove ▪ *(847) 520-0068*
201 N Buffalo Grove Rd
Deerfield ▪ *(847) 520-0068*
813 N Waukegan Rd
Schaumburg ▪ *(847) 520-0068*
25 S Roselle Rd ▪ *Bakery* ▪ GF menu includes cookies, cakes, brownies, baguettes, and stuffing. GF menus are available in stores and online. Calling ahead for specific or large orders is recommended. ▪ *www.deerfieldbakery.com*

Di Pescara   ★ $$$LD
Northbrook ▪ *(847) 498-4321*
2124 Northbrook Ct ▪ *Italian* ▪ GF pasta is available. The restaurant reports that they are able to modify most dishes to be GF. Alert a server upon arrival. ▪ *www.di-pescara.com*

Enzo and Lucia's Ristorante   ★ $$$LD
Long Grove ▪ *(847) 478-8825*
343 Old Mchenry Rd ▪ *Italian* ▪ GF pasta is available. Restaurant also has a wide variety of appetizers, salads, and entrées that can be modified to be GF. ▪ *www.enzoandlucia.com*

Francesca's   ✪★ $$LD
Arlington Heights ▪ *(847) 394-3950*
208 S Arlington Heights Rd
Barrington ▪ *(847) 277-1027*
100 E Station St
Elmhurst ▪ *(630) 279-7970*
174 N York Rd
Forest Park ▪ *(708) 771-3063*
7407 Madison St
Frankfort ▪ *(815) 464-1890*
40 Kansas St

Lake Forest ▪ *(847) 735-9235*
293 E Illinois Rd
Naperville ▪ *(630) 961-2706*
18 W Jefferson Ave
Naperville ▪ *(630) 946-0600*
3124 S Route 59
Northbrook ▪ *(847) 559-0260*
1145 Church St
Palos Park ▪ *(708) 671-1600*
12960 S La Grange Rd
St Charles ▪ *(630) 587-8221*
200 S 2nd St
West Dundee ▪ *(847) 844-7099*
127 W Main St ▪ *Italian* ▪ GF pasta and desserts are available. All locations reported that several chicken, fish, and meat entrées can also be modified to be GF. Confirm timeliness of information before dining in. Alert a server, who will notify the kitchen. ▪ *www.miafrancesca.com*

Gaetano's   ★ $$D
Forest Park ▪ *(708) 366-4010*
7636 Madison St ▪ *Italian* ▪ GF pasta is available. Alert a server, who will inform the kitchen. The kitchen staff members are all trained to prepare GF meals. Gaetano's is named after the head chef at La Piazza (now closed), who runs the Gaetano's kitchen. ▪ *www.gaetanoscafe.com*

Glen Prairie   ✪ $$$BLD
Glen Ellyn ▪ *(630) 613-1250*
1250 Roosevelt Rd ▪ *Modern American* ▪ GF menu includes roasted half chicken, pan seared scallops, and polenta cake. Restaurant notes that servers use a different notation when sending GF orders to the kitchen. ▪ *www.glenprairie.com*

Golden Chef, The   ★ $LD
Wheeling ▪ *(847) 537-7100*
600 S Milwaukee Ave ▪ *Chinese* ▪ Owner Esther reports that she is a nutritionist and is "very familiar" with the GF diet. She suggests asking for her upon arrival. GF soy sauce is available, and Esther notes that almost everything can be made GF. ▪ *www.goldenchefrestaurant.com*

Graziano's Restaurant   ✪★ $LD
Niles ▪ *(847) 647-4096*
5960 W Touhy Ave ▪ *Italian* ▪ The regular
menu mentions the modifications necessary to make items GF. For example, the
grilled chicken avocado wrap can be made
GF by substituting a lettuce wrap. GF pasta
is available, and the menu lists GF sauces. ▪
www.grazianosrestaurant.com

Greco's   ★ $$LD
Willow Springs ▪ *(708) 839-0333*
8850 Archer Ave ▪ *Italian* ▪ GF pasta is
available. Manager Lori recommends call-
ing ahead to confirm availability. ▪ *www.
grecos.ws*

Guardi's Pizza   ★ $D
Tinley Park ▪ *(708) 429-1166*
16711 S. 80th Ave ▪ *Pizza* ▪ GF pizza is
available in the 10-inch size. Any toppings
can be added to the GF crust. ▪ *www.guard-
ispizza.com*

J. Alexander's $$$LD
Northbrook ▪ *(847) 564-3093*
4077 Lake Cook Rd
Oak Brook ▪ *(630) 573-8180*
1410 16th St ▪ *American* ▪ Manager Greg
reports that GF diners are welcome and
notes that the staff is trained on GF. They
cannot guarantee GF products, however,
because they use flour in the kitchen. Thai
barbeque grouper, steaks, pork tenderloin,
baked potatoes, and other fish dishes can
be served GF. Confirm timeliness of this
information before dining in. ▪ *www.jalex-
anders.com*

Johnny's Italian Steakhouse $$LD
Moline ▪ *(309) 736-0100*
1300 River Dr
Peoria ▪ *(309) 692-3887*
5201 W War Memorial Dr ▪ *Steakhouse* ▪
GF items on the menu include lobster and
lobster salad, seafood skewers, and mus-
sels. Confirm timeliness of this information
before dining in. Alert a server, who can
access a list of GF items. ▪ *www.johnnysi-
taliansteakhouse.com*

Julio's Latin Café   ✪ $$LD
Lake Zurich ▪ *(847) 438-3484*
95 S Rand Rd ▪ *South American* ▪ The new
GF menu offers grilled honey balsamic
salmon, calypso chicken, pork tenderloin
with pineapple relish, and enchiladas,
among other entrées. Though there are no
appetizers or desserts on the GF menu,
Manager Denise reports that all servers
are educated on the GF diet and can help
choose items for other courses. ▪ *www.
julioslatincafe.com*

Kona Grill   📖
Lincolnshire ▪ *(847) 955-1210*
940 Milwaukee Ave
Oak Brook ▪ *(630) 515-8395*
3051 Butterfield Rd

L. Woods Restaurant $$$LD
Lincolnwood ▪ *(847) 677-3350*
7110 N Lincoln Ave ▪ *American* ▪ Manager
Terry notes that the restaurant accommo-
dates GF diners "daily." He describes the
restaurant as "more than accommodating,"
and recommends asking for a manager,
who will walk GF customers through the
menu. He also notes that if no GF sauces
or flavorings are available, they will make
something from scratch. ▪ *www.lwoodsres-
taurant.com*

Le Titi de Paris $$LD
Arlington Heights ▪ *(847) 506-0222*
1015 W Dundee Rd ▪ *French* ▪ Owner and
Sous-chef Susan reports that the restaurant
"stops its world" for GF diners. She notes
that the staff is very well versed in GF dining, and even has an employee that is GF.
She reports that soups are thickened with
potato, the salad is GF, and the entrées are
made to order. Confirm timeliness of this
information before dining in. Reservations
noting GF are highly recommended so that
the kitchen and waitstaff can be prepared. ▪
www.letitideparis.com

Little Joe's Famous Pizza & Restaurant
★ $LD
New Lenox ▪ *(815) 463-1099*

1300 N Cedar Rd
Tinley Park ▪ *(708) 532-2240*
7976 167th St ▪ Pizza ▪ GF pasta, pizza, and
beer are available. ▪ *www.littlejoesfamous-pizza.com*

Lou Malnati's $$**LD**

Bloomingdale ▪ *(630) 582-9600*
369 W Army Trail Rd
Buffalo Grove ▪ *(847) 215-7100*
85 S Buffalo Grove Rd
Carol Stream ▪ *(630) 668-7200*
343 E Geneva Rd
Elk Grove Village ▪ *(847) 439-2000*
1050 E Higgins Rd
Elmhurst ▪ *(630) 516-0800*
110 W Park Ave
Evanston ▪ *(847) 328-5400*
1850 Sherman Ave
Geneva ▪ *(630) 208-1600*
1048 Commons Dr
Highland Park ▪ *(847) 266-9000*
1890 1st St
Lake Forest ▪ *(847) 735-1515*
840 S Waukegan Rd
Lake Zurich ▪ *(847) 550-8800*
1225 S Rand Rd
Libertyville ▪ *(847) 362-6070*
1436 S Milwaukee Ave
Lincolnwood ▪ *(847) 673-0800*
6649 N Lincoln Ave
Mount Prospect ▪ *(847) 590-1900*
1504 N Elmhurst Rd
Naperville ▪ *(630) 717-0700*
131 W Jefferson Ave
Naperville ▪ *(630) 904-4222*
2879 W 95th St
Northbrook ▪ *(847) 291-0250*
1326 Shermer Rd
Palatine ▪ *(847) 963-0800*
287 N Northwest Hwy
Park Ridge ▪ *(847) 292-2277*
650 N Northwest Hwy
Schaumburg ▪ *(847) 985-1525*
1 S Roselle Rd
Schaumburg ▪ *(847) 524-1900*
357 S Barrington Rd
Third Lake ▪ *(847) 231-5550*
34500 N US Highway 45

Tinley Park ▪ *(708) 403-9700*
9501 171st St
Village Of Lakewood ▪ *(815) 477-8100*
8515 Redtail Dr
Western Springs ▪ *(708) 246-3400*
4700 Gilbert Ave
Wilmette ▪ *(847) 256-5780*
3223 Lake Ave ▪ Pizza ▪ Corporate reports
that all locations can do a "crustless" pizza
upon request. They also note that most
salads are GF when ordered without croutons or tortilla chips. Confirm timeliness of
this information before dining in. Alert a
manager, who will recommend GF options.
▪ *www.loumalnatis.com*

Maggiano's Little Italy   ★ $$$**LD**

Naperville ▪ *(630) 536-2270*
1847 Freedom Dr
Oak Brook ▪ *(630) 368-0300*
240 Oakbrook Ctr
Schaumburg ▪ *(847) 240-5600*
1901 E Woodfield Rd
Skokie ▪ *(847) 933-9555*
4999 Old Orchard Ctr Ste A28 ▪ Italian
▪ GF pasta is available. Call individual
locations to inquire about additional GF
options. ▪ *www.maggianos.com*

Marcello's   ★ $**LD**

Northbrook ▪ *(847) 498-1500*
1911 Cherry Ln ▪ Pizza ▪ GF pizza, pasta,
brownies, and apple or berry dessert pizzas
are available. ▪ *www.marcellos.com*

Melting Pot, The   📖

Buffalo Grove ▪ *(847) 342-6022*
1205 W Dundee Rd
Downers Grove ▪ *(630) 737-0810*
1205 Butterfield Rd
Naperville ▪ *(630) 717-8301*
4931 S Route 59
Schaumburg ▪ *(847) 843-8970*
255 W Golf Rd

Mississippi Half Step   ✪ $$**LD**

Grafton ▪ *(618) 786-2722*
420 E Main St ▪ American ▪ GF menu is
the regular menu with highlights and notes
about GF items and necessary modifica-

tions. Manager Carla recommends alerting a server upon arrival. ▪ *www.mississippi-halfstep.com*

Mitchell's Fish Market   ✪ $$$ LD
Glenview ▪ (847) 729-3663
2601 Navy Blvd ▪ *Seafood* ▪ Extensive GF menu includes pan-roasted wild blue mussels, blackened salmon spinach salad, grilled shrimp and scallop skewers, Shanghai seafood sampler, lobster tail, filet mignon, and live Maine lobster. Mini crème brulee is available for dessert. ▪ *www.mitchellsfishmarket.com*

Mon Ami Gabi   ✪ $$$ LD
Oak Brook ▪ (630) 472-1900
260 Oakbrook Ctr ▪ *French Bistro* ▪ GF menu includes chicken liver mousse, seared sea scallops, lemon chicken paillard, steak béarnaise, and more. For dessert, chocolate mousse, crème brûlée, and a pear parfait are available. ▪ *www.monamigabi.com*

Monical's Pizza Restaurant   ★ $$ LD
Arcola ▪ (217) 268-4141
528 E Sprinfield
Bloomington ▪ (309) 662-6933
2103 N Veterans Pwy
Bloomington ▪ (309) 662-8502
718 S Eldorado Rd
Bourbonnais ▪ (815) 932-9100
597 William Latham Dr
Canton ▪ (309) 647-1127
135 N 5th Ave
Centralia ▪ (618) 533-2755
1310 N Elm St
Champaign ▪ (217) 356-4243
103 W Kirby Ave
Champaign ▪ (217) 359-3514
205 N Mattis Ave
Charleston ▪ (217) 348-7515
909 18th St
Chillicothe ▪ (309) 274-6721
322 S Plaza Park
Clinton ▪ (217) 935-2919
1044 Jemima St
Danville ▪ (217) 443-3490
1511 N Bowman Avenue Rd
Danville ▪ (217) 446-3111

3542 N Vermilion St
Decatur ▪ (217) 864-2060
2230 S Mount Zion Rd
Decatur ▪ (217) 423-2333
348 W 1st Dr
Decatur ▪ (217) 875-7340
4333 N Prospect St
East Peoria ▪ (309) 698-7075
212 Veterans Dr
El Paso ▪ (309) 527-3663
RR 1 Box 32A
Fairbury ▪ (815) 692-4302
600 W Oak St
Gibson City ▪ (217) 784-4623
314 E 1st St
Gilman ▪ (815) 265-7272
625 US Highway 24 W
Hoopeston ▪ (217) 283-7781
618 W Orange St
Kankakee ▪ (815) 928-8043
1155 W Court St
Mahomet ▪ (217) 586-4242
114 S Lombard St
Manteno ▪ (815) 468-7409
199 Southcreek Dr
Mattoon ▪ (217) 234-6442
815 Broadway Ave
Momence ▪ (815) 472-3342
505 N Dixie Hwy
Monticello ▪ (217) 762-8484
707 W Bridge St
Morton ▪ (309) 284-0709
1067 W Jackson St
Normal ▪ (309) 454-7999
1219 S Main St
Olney ▪ (618) 395-3359
509 N West St
Paris ▪ (217) 465-7684
607 E Jasper St
Paxton ▪ (217) 379-4835
500 W Ottawa Rd
Pekin ▪ (309) 347-7761
111 S Parkway Dr
Peoria ▪ (309) 691-6477
4100 W Willow Knolls Dr
Peoria ▪ (309) 688-0747
4408 N Knoxville Ave
Pontiac ▪ (815) 844-2660

311 US Route 66
Princeton ▪ *(815) 872-0090*
302 S Main St
Rantoul ▪ *(217) 893-1252*
320 E Champaign Ave
Robinson ▪ *(618) 544-3228*
1703 W Main St
Saint Joseph ▪ *(217) 469-7777*
703 N 3rd St
Shelbyville ▪ *(217) 774-4100*
1900 W Main St
Springfield ▪ *(217) 546-7258*
2640 Prairie Crossing Dr
Sullivan ▪ *(217) 728-2373*
402 S Hamilton St
Tilton ▪ *(217) 443-5545*
1628 Georgetown Rd
Tolono ▪ *(217) 485-5711*
102 W Vine St
Tuscola ▪ *(217) 253-4749*
900 S Court St
Urbana ▪ *(217) 367-5781*
2720 Philo Rd
Villa Grove ▪ *(217) 832-2361*
102 N Sycamore St
Washington ▪ *(309) 444-7500*
6 Cherry Tree Shopping Ctr
Watseka ▪ *(815) 432-3714*
1004 E Walnut St
Watseka ▪ *(815) 432-3320*
750 W Walnut St ▪ *Pizza* ▪ GF pizza is available. ▪ *www.monicalspizza.com*

Myron & Phil $$$D
Lincolnwood ▪ *(847) 677-6663*
3900 W Devon Ave ▪ *Steakhouse* ▪ Manager Candy reports that they are serving GF diners "more and more." She notes that the only GF dishes are broiled steak or fish with a side such as a baked potato. Alert a server, who will ask a manager to visit the table. ▪ *www.myronandphils.com*

Nick's Pizza   ★ $LD
Crystal Lake ▪ *(815) 356-5550*
856 Pyott Rd
Elgin ▪ *(847) 531-5550*
990 S Randall Rd ▪ *Pizza* ▪ GF pizza is available. ▪ *www.nickspizzapub.com*

Nirvana Wine & Grillerie   ✪★ $$LD
Vernon Hills ▪ *(847) 918-7828*
701 N Milwaukee Ave ▪ *Global* ▪ Certain menu items are marked "GFA," which stands for "GF alternative available." Server Nikka explains that many of these items are naturally GF, while others are readily modified to be GF. GF crackers and pasta are available. For dessert, they offer flourless chocolate cake. ▪ *www.findmynirvana.com*

Nuovo Italia $$$LD
Addison ▪ *(630) 832-2131*
32 E Lake St ▪ *Italian* ▪ Manager David reports that although the restaurant does not serve GF diners "very often," they can make GF dishes upon request. He recommends asking for him upon arrival, as he is happy to discuss dining options with each individual GF diner. ▪ *www.nuovaitalia.net*

OMG It's Gluten Free   100% ₵BLD
Frankfort ▪ *(815) 469-4900*
19810 S Harlem Ave ▪ *Bakery & Café* ▪ Dedicated GF bakery offering pizza, lasagna, quiche, sandwiches, and more. They also offer a wide variety of baked goods such as breads, cookies, muffins, brownies, scones, and sweet rolls. Meals are available for dining in or carrying out. ▪ *www.omgitsglutenfree.com*

Outback Steakhouse   📖
Bloomingdale ▪ *(630) 582-8914*
166 S Gary Ave
Bloomington ▪ *(309) 663-0455*
1409 N Veterans Pkwy
Buffalo Grove ▪ *(847) 541-4329*
720 W Lake Cook Rd
Calumet City ▪ *(708) 862-0220*
2005 River Oaks Dr
Champaign ▪ *(217) 398-3322*
2402 N Prospect Ave
Crystal Lake ▪ *(815) 479-5161*
4751 Northwest Hwy
Gurnee ▪ *(847) 599-1300*
5642 Northridge Dr
Joliet ▪ *(815) 267-3020*
3241 Chicagoland Cir

Naperville ▪ (630) 778-6290
2855 W Ogden Ave
Orland Park ▪ (708) 633-0900
15608 S Harlem Ave
Rockford ▪ (815) 398-2400
6007 E State St
Schaumburg ▪ (847) 843-8884
216 E Golf Rd
Skokie ▪ (847) 674-7411
5535 Touhy Ave
South Elgin ▪ (847) 717-0100
365 Randall Rd
Springfield ▪ (217) 523-2815
3201 Horizon
Swansea ▪ (618) 235-7000
4390 N Illinois St
Villa Park ▪ (630) 530-0005
100 E Roosevelt Rd Ste 28
Wheaton ▪ (630) 462-8850
50 E Loop Rd

P.F. Chang's China Bistro   📖
Lombard ▪ (630) 652-9977
2361 Fountain Square Dr
Northbrook ▪ (847) 509-8844
1819 Lake Cook Rd
Orland Park ▪ (708) 675-3970
14135 S La Grange Rd
Schaumburg ▪ (847) 610-8000
5 Woodfield Mall Spc D313

Pasta House Co., The   📖
Edwardsville ▪ (618) 655-9955
1097 S State Route 157
Fairview Heights ▪ (618) 222-7144
4660 N Illinois St
Mount Vernon ▪ (618) 244-7400
300 S 44th St
Springfield ▪ (217) 793-2433
2800 SW Plaza Dr

Pinstripes   ☺★ $**LD**
Northbrook ▪ (847) 480-2323
1150 Willow Rd
South Barrington ▪ (847) 844-9300
100 W Higgins Rd ▪ *Bistro* ▪ GF menu
includes soups and salads, as well as a wide
variety of sandwiches, pizzas, and pastas. It
also includes entrées such as beef tenderloin and grilled salmon. GF pasta and

pizza are available with advanced notice of
24 hours. For dessert, they offer flourless
chocolate cake, lemon crème brûlée, and
cheesecake. ▪ *www.pinstripes.com*

Reel Club   ☺★ $$**LD**
Oak Brook ▪ (630) 368-9400
272 Oakbrook Ctr ▪ *Seafood* ▪ GF menu
includes a selection of soups, fish entrées,
and meat dishes. Though there is no GF
soy sauce available, they offer another dip-
ping sauce for the sushi which is GF. GF
bread is available. ▪ *www.leye.com*

Reza's Restaurant $$$**LD**
Oak Brook ▪ (630) 424-9900
40 N Tower Rd ▪ *Middle Eastern* ▪ Managers at all locations report serving GF diners
often. All recommend asking for a manager
upon arrival. Although many servers are
educated on the GF diet, the managers will
know more about which items are GF. ▪
www.rezasrestaurant.com

Roberto's   ★ $$$$**D**
Elmhurst ▪ (630) 279-8474
483 S Spring Rd ▪ *Italian* ▪ GF pizza is
available. ▪ *www.robertosristorante.net*

Rose's Wheat Free Bakery   100% ¢**S**
Evanston ▪ (847) 859-2723
2901 Central St ▪ *Bakery* ▪ Bakery offering a variety of GF breads, pizza crusts,
granola, muffins, cookies, and brownies.
Manager Starr reports that they are certified GF. ▪ *www.rosesbakery.com*

Shaw's Crab House   ☺ $$$$**LD**
Schaumburg ▪ (847) 517-2722
1900 E Higgins Rd ▪ *Seafood* ▪ GF menu
includes griddle garlic shrimp, seared
scallops, halibut, salmon, strip steak, crab,
lobster, sushi, and more. Crème brûlée is
available for dessert. ▪ *www.shawscrab-*
house.com

Singapore Grill   ★ $$**LD**
Loves Park ▪ (815) 636-1888
6390 E Riverside Blvd ▪ *Asian* ▪ GF soy
sauce is available.

South Gate Café $$$**LD**
Lake Forest ▪ *(847) 234-8800*
655 Forest Ave ▪ American ▪ Manager
Tim reports that while GF diners aren't
frequent, they can be accommodated. He
notes that most menu items can be "mixed
and matched" to be GF. Alert a server, as all
staff members are educated on the GF diet
and can recommend GF menu modifications. ▪ *www.southgatecafe.com*

Stashu's Deli & Pizza   ★ $**LD**
Moline ▪ *(309) 797-9449*
4206 44th Ave ▪ Pizza ▪ GF pizza is available with advanced notice of at least thirty
minutes.

Stir Crazy   ★ $$**LD**
Northbrook ▪ *(847) 562-4800*
1186 Northbrook Ct
Oak Brook ▪ *(630) 575-0155*
105 Oakbrook Ctr
Schaumburg ▪ *(847) 330-1200*
5 Woodfield Mall
Warrenville ▪ *(630) 393-4700*
28252 Diehl Rd ▪ Asian Stir-Fry ▪ Triumph
spoke with a manager at each location. All
report that servers are educated about GF
and able to indicate the three GF sauce
options: teriyaki, classic Chinese, and
szechuan. Any of these sauces can be used
on a menu item or at the stir fry market
bar. GF rice noodles are available. ▪ *www.
stircrazy.com*

Sweet Ali's Gluten Free Bakery   100% ¢S
Hinsdale ▪ *(630) 908-7175*
13 W 1st St ▪ Bakery ▪ Dedicated GF bakery offering bread, muffins, cookies, cake,
brownies, and more. Owner Ali reports
that they will add dedicated GF breakfast
and lunch menus in the summer of 2010. ▪
www.sweetalis.com

Uno Chicago Grill   📖
Gurnee ▪ *(847) 856-0000*
6593 Grand Ave
Schaumburg ▪ *(847) 413-0200*
1160 N Plaza Dr

Va Pensiero $$$$**D**
Evanston ▪ *(847) 475-7779*
1566 Oak Ave ▪ Italian ▪ Manager Maureen
reports that GF diners are welcome. She
recommends making reservations noting
GF to allow the kitchen to prepare. Ask
to speak with Jeff, Maureen, or Luis when
calling for GF reservations. ▪ *www.va-p.
com*

Walker Brothers   ★ ¢**BLD**
Arlington Heights ▪ *(847) 392-6600*
825 W Dundee Rd
Glenview ▪ *(847) 724-0220*
1615 Waukegan Rd
Highland Park ▪ *(847) 432-0660*
620 Central Ave
Lake Zurich ▪ *(847) 550-0006*
767 S Rand Rd
Lincolnshire ▪ *(847) 634-2220*
200 Marriott Dr
Wilmette ▪ *(847) 251-6000*
153 Green Bay Rd ▪ Breakfast ▪ GF
pancakes are available, and can be prepared with blueberries or other fruit upon
request. ▪ *www.walkerbros.net*

Weber Grill Restaurant   ✪ $$**LD**
Lombard ▪ *(630) 953-8880*
2331 Fountain Square Dr
Schaumburg ▪ *(847) 413-0800*
1010 N Meacham Rd ▪ American ▪ Extensive GF menu includes blackened catfish,
grilled garlic shrimp, BBQ beef brisket,
ribs, and more. For starters, baked onion
soup and gulf shrimp cocktail are available.
▪ *www.webergrillrestaurant.com*

White Chocolate Grill, The   ✪ $$**LD**
Naperville ▪ *(630) 505-8300*
1803 Freedom Dr ▪ Modern American ▪
GF menu includes grilled artichokes and
tomato gin soup, among other things, as
appetizers. As entrées, it lists a bunless
cheeseburger, BBQ baby back ribs, center
cut filet, and more. For dessert, it offers
molten chocolate soufflé cake. ▪ *www.
thewhitechocolategrill.wordpress.com*

Wildfire   ✪★ $$$LD
Glenview ▪ *(847) 657-6363*
1300 Patriot Blvd
Lincolnshire ▪ *(847) 279-7900*
235 Parkway Dr
Oak Brook ▪ *(630) 586-9000*
232 Oakbrook Ctr
Schaumburg ▪ *(847) 995-0100*
1250 E Higgins Rd ▪ *Steakhouse* ▪ All
locations have the same GF menu, which
includes a variety of starters, salads, sides,
sandwiches, and entrées. GF pizza crust,
hamburger buns, and beer are available.
For dessert, they offer flourless chocolate
cake, among other things. ▪ *www.wildfir-
erestaurant.com*

Winberie's Restaurant & Bar   ✪ $$$LD
Oak Park ▪ *(708) 386-2600*
151 N Oak Park Ave ▪ *American* ▪ GF items
highlighted on the regular menu include
cedar plank salmon, London broil, chicken
marsala, and burgers without buns. ▪ *www.
selectrestaurants.com*

Yard House   📖
Glenview ▪ *(847) 729-9273*
1880 Tower Dr

INDIANA

INDIANAPOLIS

A-2-Z Café   ★ ¢BLD
Indianapolis ▪ *(317) 569-9349*
4705 E 96th St ▪ *American* ▪ GF pasta is
available. Chef Ash reports that GF can be
easily accommodated, as all items are made
in-house and can be modified. Alert a
server upon arrival. ▪ *www.a2zcafe.com*

Adobo Grill   ✪ $$LD
Indianapolis ▪ *(317) 822-9990*
110 E Washington St ▪ *Modern Mexican*
▪ GF menu varies slightly by location.
Examples of GF menu items are enchiladas,

a grilled half chicken in tamarind, and sautéed tilapia. GF desserts include chocolate
tamal and vanilla flan with caramel sauce. ▪
www.adobogrill.com

Bonefish Grill   📖
Indianapolis ▪ *(317) 863-3474*
4501 E 82nd St

Buca di Beppo   📖
Indianapolis ▪ *(317) 632-2822*
35 N Illinois St
Indianapolis ▪ *(317) 842-8666*
6045 E 86th St

Fogo De Chao   ★ $$$$LD
Indianapolis ▪ *(317) 638-4000*
117 E Washington St ▪ *Brazilian* ▪ GF
cheese bread made with yucca flour is
available. ▪ *www.fogodechao.com*

Greek Islands Restaurant, The   ✪ $LD
Indianapolis ▪ *(317) 636-0700*
906 S Meridian St ▪ *Greek* ▪ GF menu
includes tilapia, salmon, chicken souvlaki,
and more. Chef Angela reports that they
are very aware of GF, as a family friend has
Celiac. She adds that all staff members are
trained on the GF diet. ▪ *www.greekisland-
srestaurant.com*

Maggiano's Little Italy   ★ $$$LD
Indianapolis ▪ *(317) 814-0700*
3550 E 86th St ▪ *Italian* ▪ GF pasta is available. Call individual locations to inquire
about additional GF options. ▪ *www.mag-
gianos.com*

Melting Pot, The   📖
Indianapolis ▪ *(317) 841-3601*
5650 E 86th St Ste A

Monical's Pizza Restaurant   ★ $$LD
Indianapolis ▪ *(317) 255-3663*
2635 E 62nd St
Indianapolis ▪ *(317) 870-7722*
6010 W 86th St ▪ *Pizza* ▪ GF pizza is available. ▪ *www.monicalspizza.com*

Old Spaghetti Factory, The   📖
Indianapolis ▪ *(317) 635-6325*
210 S Meridian St

Outback Steakhouse   📖
Indianapolis ▪ *(317) 890-9466*
2315 Post Dr
Indianapolis ▪ *(317) 872-4329*
3454 W 86th St
Indianapolis ▪ *(317) 842-6283*
5771 E 86th St
Indianapolis ▪ *(317) 881-6283*
7525 US 31 S
Indianapolis ▪ *(317) 209-8007*
9140 Rockville Rd

P.F. Chang's China Bistro   📖
Indianapolis ▪ *(317) 974-5747*
49 W Maryland St Ste 226
Indianapolis ▪ *(317) 815-8773*
8601 Keystone Xing

Stir Crazy   ★ $$LD
Indianapolis ▪ *(317) 845-5600*
6020 E 82nd St ▪ *Asian Stir-Fry* ▪ GF
pasta, soy sauce, and teriyaki sauce are
available upon request. Alert a server upon
arrival. ▪ *www.stircrazy.com*

Thai Café   ★ $LD
Indianapolis ▪ *(317) 722-1008*
1041 Broad Ripple Ave ▪ *Thai* ▪ Server
Antel reports that many dishes, like pad
thai and drunken noodles, can be prepared
GF. Confirm timeliness of this information
before dining in. GF soy sauce is available.
Alert a server, who will indicate GF op-
tions. ▪ *www.indythaicafe.com*

Uno Chicago Grill   📖
Indianapolis ▪ *(317) 594-4865*
3716 E 82nd St
Indianapolis ▪ *(317) 791-8667*
4740 E Southport Rd

Weber Grill Restaurant   ✪ $LD
Indianapolis ▪ *(317) 636-7600*
10 N Illinois St ▪ *American* ▪ Extensive GF
menu includes blackened catfish, grilled
garlic shrimp, BBQ beef brisket, ribs, and
more. For starters, baked onion soup and
gulf shrimp cocktail are available. ▪ *www.
webergrillrestaurant.com*

Yats   ¢LD
Indianapolis ▪ *(317) 253-8817*
5463 N College Ave
Indianapolis ▪ *(317) 686-6380*
659 Massachusetts Ave ▪ *Cajun & Creole*
▪ Restaurants note that several chilis and
stews on the menu are naturally GF. Both
locations recommend alerting the server
or cashier, so he or she can indicate GF op-
tions. ▪ *www.yatscajuncreole.com*

INDIANA

ALL OTHER CITIES

Biaggi's Ristorante Italiano   📖
Evansville ▪ *(812) 421-0800*
6401 E Lloyd Expy
Fort Wayne ▪ *(260) 459-6700*
4010 W Jefferson Blvd

Bloomingfoods Deli   ★ ¢BLD
Bloomington ▪ *(812) 333-7312*
316 W 6th St
Bloomington ▪ *(812) 336-5400*
3220 E 3rd St ▪ *Deli* ▪ GF bread is avail-
able for sandwiches, and there are often GF
bakery items. Many "grab-and-go" items
are GF. All GF items are labeled with an
orange "gluten-free" sticker. Located inside
the Bloomingfoods Market. ▪ *www.bloom-
ingfoods.coop*

Bonefish Grill   📖
Evansville ▪ *(812) 401-3474*
6401 E Lloyd Expy
Greenwood ▪ *(317) 884-3992*
1001 N State Road 135
Mishawaka ▪ *(574) 259-2663*
620 W Edison Rd Ste 100

Bristol Bar & Grill $$LD
Jeffersonville ▪ *(812) 218-1995*
700 W Riverside Dr ▪ *American* ▪ Manager Danielle reports that accommodating

GF diners is "not a problem." She notes that there are "several different things" on the menu that are naturally GF, but the chefs can also make a different GF dish upon request. Located inside the Sheraton Louisville Riverside Hotel. ▪ *www.bristolbarandgrille.com*

Buca di Beppo   📖
Greenwood ▪ (317) 884-2822
659 US 31 N

Café Elise $$$$LD
Munster ▪ (219) 836-2233
435 Ridge Rd ▪ American ▪ Owner and Chef Scott notes that the restaurant accommodates GF diners "all the time." He reports that there are only four people on staff, so everyone is GF aware. He adds that most menu items can be modified to be GF.

Carino's Italian   📖
Columbus ▪ (812) 372-2266
870 Creekview Dr
Greenwood ▪ (317) 885-5735
920 US 31 N
Muncie ▪ (765) 284-3196
1101 W Mcgalliard Rd

Carrabba's Italian Grill   📖
Carmel ▪ (317) 575-2200
1235 Keystone Way
Mishawaka ▪ (574) 247-9460
210 W Day Rd
Southport ▪ (317) 881-4008
4690 Southport Crossing Dr

Christo's Family Restaurant $BLD
West Lafayette ▪ (765) 497-3164
1018 Sagamore Pkwy W ▪ American ▪ Manager Blake reports that "a couple people" have dined in GF. He recommends asking for the manager, who will put GF orders through directly to the chef. Limited options include salads, sandwiches without bread, and more. Confirm timeliness of this information before dining in. ▪ *www. christosgrill.com*

Firefly Southern Grill   ✪ $$D
Evansville ▪ (812) 402-2354
6636 Logan Dr ▪ Southern ▪ GF menu in-

cludes grilled or blackened chicken, steaks, salmon, tilapia, or catfish. It also includes a variety of salads and a praline ice cream sandwich for dessert. Manager Michael reports that GF diners come to the restaurant "every so often." He also notes that the kitchen prepares GF dishes on separate surfaces. ▪ *www.fireflysoutherngrill.com*

Hamilton, The $$LD
Noblesville ▪ (317) 770-4545
933 Conner St ▪ American ▪ Owner Vanita reports that the restaurant has "several gluten free customers" who have helped educate the restaurant on GF options. She reports that the restaurant makes its own dressings and all food is cooked to order, so GF requests are easily accommodated. ▪ *www.hamiltonrestaurant.com*

Kona Grill   📖
Carmel ▪ (317) 566-1400
14395 Clay Terrace Blvd

Lennie's   ★ $LD
Bloomington ▪ (812) 323-2112
1795 E 10th St ▪ American ▪ GF pizza is available. The staff learns about the GF diet as part of their training. ▪ *www.bbc. bloomington.com*

Lone Star Steakhouse & Saloon   📖
Anderson ▪ (765) 640-6550
1721 E 60th St
Evansville ▪ (812) 473-5468
943 N Green River Rd
Fort Wayne ▪ (260) 471-5500
5525 Coldwater Rd
Terre Haute ▪ (812) 232-7524
3060 S US Highway 41

Measuring Cup, The   100% ¢S
Fishers ▪ (317) 590-8112
Fishers Farmers Market ▪ Bakery ▪ Dedicated GF bakery offering a wide variety of breads, breakfast items, cookies, cinnamon rolls, cakes, and cupcakes. The menu changes every Sunday, and the bakers bring their products to the Fishers Farmers Market every Saturday during the summer. During other months, customers can

place orders online only. Baker Chris notes that customers can place special orders for items not listed on the menu. ▪ *www.gfmeasuringcup.com*

Melting Pot, The 📖
Greenwood ▪ *(317) 889-0777*
1259 N State Road 135

Mitchell's Fish Market   ✪ $$$ LD
Carmel ▪ *(317) 848-3474*
14311 Clay Terrace Blvd ▪ *Seafood* ▪ Extensive GF menu includes pan-roasted wild blue mussels, blackened salmon spinach salad, grilled shrimp and scallop skewers, Shanghai seafood sampler, lobster tail, filet mignon, and live Maine lobster. Mini crème brulee is available for dessert. ▪ *www.mitchellsfishmarket.com*

Monical's Pizza Restaurant   ★ $$ LD
Avon ▪ *(317) 271-2727*
9271 US 36
Carmel ▪ *(317) 706-0200*
12501 N Meridian St
Delphi ▪ *(765) 564-6670*
1022 S Washington St
Fishers ▪ *(317) 770-8400*
14099 Mundy Dr
Greencastle ▪ *(765) 301-4404*
29 Putnam Plz
Greenwood ▪ *(317) 881-1177*
1675 W Smith Valley Rd
Kentland ▪ *(219) 474-9330*
402 N 7th St
Lafayette ▪ *(765) 448-6066*
3500 State Road 38 E
Monticello ▪ *(574) 583-3550*
912 S Main St
Terre Haute ▪ *(812) 235-4700*
3712 S US 41
West Lafayette ▪ *(765) 464-2885*
3457 Bethel Dr ▪ *Pizza* ▪ GF pizza is available. ▪ *www.monicalspizza.com*

Outback Steakhouse 📖
Bloomington ▪ *(812) 330-1018*
3201 W 3rd St
Clarksville ▪ *(812) 283-4329*
1420 Park Pl

Evansville ▪ *(812) 474-0005*
7201 E Indiana St
Fort Wayne ▪ *(260) 459-9206*
5455 Coventry Ln
Kokomo ▪ *(765) 453-6283*
3730 S Reed Rd
Lafayette ▪ *(765) 449-1790*
3660 State Road 26 E
Merrillville ▪ *(219) 736-8995*
8117 Georgia St
Mishawaka ▪ *(574) 271-2333*
4611 Grape Rd
Muncie ▪ *(765) 284-4329*
3401 N Granville Ave
Terre Haute ▪ *(812) 232-6283*
3700 S US Highway 41

Rí~Rá Irish Pub $ LD
Evansville ▪ *(812) 426-0000*
701-B NW Riverside Dr ▪ *Irish Pub* ▪ Ask for the "Allergen Chart," which has a "Celiac" column. This column contains items that are GF or can be modified to be GF. ▪ *www.rira.com*

Roasted Bean Coffee Company ✪★ ¢ S
Fort Wayne ▪ *(260) 432-5748*
5129 Illinois Rd ▪ *Coffee & Café* ▪ Manager Janet reports that staff is well-educated on GF food. GF options include quiche, hot paninis, wraps, cookies, and pastries. Specify GF when ordering, as there are some non-GF frozen menu items. ▪ *www.roastedbeancoffee.com*

Stir Crazy   ★ $$ LD
Greenwood ▪ *(317) 888-6200*
1251 US Highway 31 N ▪ *Asian Stir-Fry* ▪ Manager Mike reports that they serve "several" GF diners "daily." GF customers can just pick one of three GF sauces and any meat that is not marinated. Mike recommends that GF diners use the stir fry "market," and he notes that GF sauces will sometimes take a few minutes to prepare. GF rice noodles are available. ▪ *www.stircrazy.com*

Third Coast Spice Café   ★ ¢ BLD
Chesterton ▪ *(219) 926-5858*

761 Indian Boundary Rd ▪ Café ▪ GF bread is available for toast in the morning or sandwiches at lunchtime. ▪ *www.thirdcoast-spice.com*

Uno Chicago Grill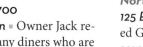
Merrillville ▪ (219) 736-4885
2385 Southlake Mall

Uptown Kitchen ★ $**BLD**
Granger ▪ (574) 968-3030
303 Florence Ave ▪ *Healthy American* ▪ Restaurant reports that there are several GF options on the menu. GF pizza, bread, chocolate chip banana french toast, and oreo cake are available. ▪ *www.uptownkitchen.net*

IOWA

Atlas World Grill $$**LD**
Iowa City ▪ (319) 341-7700
127 Iowa Ave ▪ *American* ▪ Owner Jack reports that they have "many diners who are GF." He notes that the thai salad, the Jamaican chicken, and the salmon are naturally GF. Confirm timeliness of this information before dining in. Alert a server, who will notify a manager. ▪ *www.atlasworldgrill.com*

Aunt Maude's $**LD**
Ames ▪ (515) 233-4136
547 Main St ▪ *Modern American* ▪ Manager Dave reports that accommodating GF diners is "not a problem" and advises alerting a server upon arrival. ▪ *www.auntmaudesames.com*

Biaggi's Ristorante Italiano
Cedar Rapids ▪ (319) 393-6593
320 Collins Rd NE
Davenport ▪ (563) 344-2103
5195 Utica Ridge Rd

West Des Moines ▪ (515) 221-9900
5990 University Ave

Blackstone ✪ $$$**LD**
Iowa City ▪ (319) 338-1770
503 Westbury Dr ▪ *American* ▪ GF menu includes ahi tuna salad, burgers without buns, three berry chicken salad, salmon, steak, and more. ▪ *www.blackstone-ic.com*

Bonefish Grill
West Des Moines ▪ (515) 267-0064
650 S Prairie View Dr Ste 100

Bourbon Street ✪ $$$**D**
Cedar Falls ▪ (319) 266-5285
314 Main St
Grinnell ▪ (641) 236-0334
924 Main St ▪ *American* ▪ Limited GF menu includes sirloin steak, sesame pork with rosemary risotto, Alaskan king crab legs, honey roasted chicken, and foil baked salmon. ▪ *www.barmuda.com/bourbonstreet*

Brown Bottle ✪ $$$**D**
Iowa City ▪ (319) 351-6704
115 E Washington St
North Liberty ▪ (319) 626-3900
125 E Zeller St ▪ *Italian-American* ▪ Limited GF menu includes a chef's salad, shrimp scampi salad, chicken parmesan, chicken florentine, salmon. Prime rib is available on weekends only. ▪ *www.iowacitybrownbottle.com*

Café, The ✪ $$**BLD**
Ames ▪ (515) 292-0100
2616 Northridge Pkwy ▪ *Healthy American* ▪ GF menu includes fish tacos with corn tortillas, halibut, asparagus and prosciutto, ribeye steak, and all sandwiches in lettuce cups instead of with bread. Alert a server upon arrival. ▪ *www.thecafeames.com*

Club Car, The ★ $**LD**
Clive ▪ (515) 226-1729
13435 University Ave ▪ *American* ▪ GF pizzas and pastas are available.

Coach's Pizza ★ $$**LD**
West Des Moines ▪ (515) 223-2233

560 S Prairie View Dr ▪ *Pizza* ▪ GF buffalo wings, pizza, and beer are available. Manager Chanel reports that the staff is GF aware. ▪ *www.coachspizza.com*

Court Avenue Restaurant & Brewing Company   ✪ $$**LD**
Des Moines ▪ **(515) 282-2739**
309 Court Ave ▪ *American* ▪ GF menu includes blackened salmon, lemon scallop salad, chicken marsala, currant pork medallions, and more. Appetizers include wings and a shrimp andouille dish. ▪ *www.courtavebrew.com*

Devotay   ✪ $$$$**LD**
Iowa City ▪ **(319) 354-1001**
117 N Linn St ▪ *Spanish* ▪ New GF menu includes salads, paellas, tapas, and more. For dessert, flourless chocolate torte and crème brûlée are available. ▪ *www.devotay.net*

Fair Grounds Coffee House   ★ ¢**BL**
Iowa City ▪ **(319) 338-2024**
345 S Dubuque St ▪ *Bakery & Café* ▪ GF cakes in a variety of flavors, GF waffles, biscotti, and cookies are available. Cakes are available by preorder only, and they require 2-3 days notice. ▪ *www.fairgroundscoffeehouse.com*

Felix and Oscars   ★ $**LD**
Des Moines ▪ **(515) 278-8887**
4050 Merle Hay Rd
West Des Moines ▪ **(515) 457-1000**
4801 Westown Pkwy ▪ *Italian* ▪ GF pizza and beer are available. Restaurant reports that GF pizza can be made with any toppings, and on Mondays and Tuesdays, GF pizzas are half price. Confirm timeliness of this information before dining in. Manager Katie at the West Des Moines location notes that they sometimes host Celiac groups for dinner. ▪ *www.felixandoscars.com*

Ferrari's Ristorante   ✪ $$**LD**
Cedar Falls ▪ **(319) 277-1385**
1521 Technology Pkwy ▪ *American* ▪ GF menu includes seared scallop salad, Tuscan salad, pan-seared chicken breast, peppercorn encrusted flatiron steak, NY strip steak, and more. ▪ *www.barmuda.com/ferraris*

Givanni's   ★ $$$**D**
Iowa City ▪ **(319) 338-5967**
109 E College St ▪ *Italian-American* ▪ GF pasta is available. Grilled items, such as sea scallops, steak braciole, and colorado lamb chops can be modified to be GF. Alert a server upon arrival. ▪ *www.givannis.net*

Godfather's Pizza   ★ $$**LD**
Davenport ▪ **(563) 359-4418**
3340 E Kimberly Rd
Iowa City ▪ **(319) 354-3312**
531 Highway 1 W
Mason City ▪ **(641) 424-5133**
1703 4th St SE ▪ *Pizza* ▪ GF pizza is available. At the Iowa City and Davenport locations, calling in advance is not necessary. Manager Peggy from Mason City, however, reports that advanced notice of 24 hours is required for GF pizzas. ▪ *www.godfathers.com*

Ground Round   📖
Dubuque ▪ **(563) 556-3540**
50 John F Kennedy Rd

Hickory Park Restaurant Co.   ✪ ¢**LD**
Ames ▪ **(515) 232-8940**
1404 S Duff Ave ▪ *Barbeque* ▪ GF menu includes several burgers without buns, grilled franks, taco salad, and smoked meats. ▪ *www.hickoryparkames.com*

Jiamen Innovative Asian Cuisine   ✪★ $$**LD**
Cedar Rapids ▪ **(319) 294-5889**
5400 Edgewood Rd NE ▪ *Asian Fusion* ▪ GF menu includes wok-fired honey chicken, sweet and sour chicken, Chilean sea bass, and salmon, among other things. GF soy sauce is available. Meals are available for dining in or taking out. ▪ *www.jiamencuisine.com*

Johnny's Italian Steakhouse   ✪ $$$**LD**
Des Moines ▪ **(515) 287-0847**
6800 Fleur Dr

West Des Moines ▪ **(515) 333-5665**
6075 Mills Civic Pkwy ▪ *Italian & Steak-house* ▪ GF menu indicates GF items on the regular menu and includes steaks, the lobster dinner, scampi angelini, and more. Alert a server, who will notify the kitchen staff. ▪ *www.johnnysitaliansteakhouse.com*

King and I Thai Cuisine $**LD**
West Des Moines ▪ **(515) 440-2075**
1821 22nd St ▪ *Thai* ▪ All-purpose Staffer Wan reports that they serve GF customers "a lot." She notes that "anything" can be made GF but adds that many items, like the curries, are naturally GF. Confirm timeliness of this information before dining in. Alert a server, who will ensure that the kitchen prepares a GF meal. ▪ *www.king-and-i-thaicuisine.com*

Lone Star Steakhouse & Saloon   📖
Cedar Rapids ▪ **(319) 393-9648**
4545 1st Ave SE
Waterloo ▪ **(319) 232-3233**
4045 Hammond Ave
West Des Moines ▪ **(515) 223-9606**
1801 22nd St

Motley Cow Café $$$**LD**
Iowa City ▪ **(319) 688-9177**
160 N Linn St ▪ *American* ▪ Manager Kate reports that the restaurant has "quite a few" regular diners with dietary restrictions including GF diners. She notes that chefs are "more than willing" to modify menu items to be GF. Servers are GF aware. Alert a server upon arrival. ▪ *www.motleycow-cafe.com*

Olde Main Brewing Company & Restaurant   ✪ $**LD**
Ames ▪ **(515) 232-0553**
316 Main St ▪ *American* ▪ GF menu includes an angus filet, a fresh salmon filet roasted on a maple plank, and the southwestern steak salad. General Manager Jamie reports that they are happy to accommodate GF diners any time of day. ▪ *www.oldemainbrewing.com*

Outback Steakhouse   📖
Ankeny ▪ **(515) 963-1243**
2410 SE Tones Dr
Cedar Rapids ▪ **(319) 366-6683**
3939 1st Ave SE
Clive ▪ **(515) 221-3309**
10901 University Ave
Coralville ▪ **(319) 354-2755**
945 25th Ave
Davenport ▪ **(563) 386-4711**
1235 E Kimberly Rd
Sioux City ▪ **(712) 276-2242**
4500 Southern Hills Dr

P.F. Chang's China Bistro   📖
West Des Moines ▪ **(515) 457-7772**
110 S Jordan Creek Pkwy

Red Avocado $**LD**
Iowa City ▪ **(319) 351-6088**
521 E Washington St ▪ *Organic* ▪ Manager Katy reports that many menu items are naturally GF or can be made GF by substituting different grains or thickeners. She notes that the restaurant serves many GF diners, and that they almost always have GF truffles for dessert. Alert a server upon arrival. ▪ *www.theredavocado.com*

Sam & Louie's New York Pizzeria
                                    ★ $$**LD**
Council Bluffs ▪ **(712) 256-7712**
1851 Madison Ave ▪ *Pizza* ▪ GF pizza is available. ▪ *www.samandlouiesnyp.com*

Shane's Rib Shack   📖
Clive ▪ **(515) 327-7427**
12695 University Ave

Shanghai Chinese Restaurant $**LD**
Waukee ▪ **(515) 987-3111**
33 NE Carefree Ln ▪ *Chinese* ▪ Owner Hoa reports that they serve GF diners only "once every few months," but they have one regular GF customer. She advises ordering a dish that comes with a white sauce, since they do not carry GF soy sauce. Alert a server upon arrival. ▪ *www.shanghaiwk.com*

Spice Thai Cuisine, The   ✪★ $**LD**
Ames ▪ **(515) 232-0200**

402 Main St ▪ Thai ▪ GF menu includes green curry, lemongrass chicken, pad ka prow duck, and seafood fried rice, among other items. GF soy sauce is available. For dessert, they make a seasonal mango sticky rice. ▪ www.thespiceames.com

KANSAS

4 Olives Wine Bar　　　　　⊘★　$$D
Manhattan ▪ (785) 539-1295
3033 Anderson Ave ▪ *Modern American* ▪ GF menu includes sweat pea and shrimp risotto, sesame-crusted seared ahi tuna, and more. For dessert, they offer a flourless chocolate torte and crème brûlée. GF pasta, soy sauce, and beer are available. ▪ *www.4olives.biz*

Bonefish Grill　　　　　　　📖
Leawood ▪ (913) 239-8856
5021 W 135th St
Wichita ▪ (316) 315-0299
10250 E 13Th St N # 102

Brick Oven Courtyard Grille　　$$D
Topeka ▪ (785) 478-2742
3030 SW Wanamaker Rd ▪ *American* ▪ Manager Mike reports that the restaurant serves GF diners "a lot." Alert a server upon arrival. Although not all servers have an equal knowledge of the GF diet, servers are trained to discuss GF options with the kitchen staff to ensure a GF meal. ▪ *www.brickovencourtyardgrille.com*

Bristol Seafood Grill　　　$$$LD
Leawood ▪ (913) 663-5777
5400 W 119th St ▪ *Seafood* ▪ Manager Pete reports that GF diners are welcome. Many dishes can be modified to be GF, including fish, marsala chicken, scallops, and other

shellfish. Restaurant also features an extensive wine list. ▪ *www.bristolseafoodgrill.com*

Carino's Italian　　　　　　📖
Kansas City ▪ (913) 299-8253
1706 Village West Pkwy
Topeka ▪ (785) 215-8400
6130 SW 6th Ave
Wichita ▪ (316) 636-4411
3213 N Toben St

Carrabba's Italian Grill　　　📖
Overland Park ▪ (913) 385-7811
10586 Metcalf Ln
Wichita ▪ (316) 315-0777
3409 N Rock Rd

Caspian Bistro　　　　　⊘★　$LD
Overland Park ▪ (913) 901-9911
8973 Metcalf Ave ▪ *Persian* ▪ Extensive GF menu includes a wide variety of kabobs made with chicken, lamb, beef, and vegetables, as well as salads, stews, and appetizers. GF bread, beer, and cookies are available. ▪ *www.caspianbistro-ks.com*

Chatters Restaurant & Bar　　★　$LD
Pittsburg ▪ (620) 232-7277
2401 S Rouse St ▪ *American* ▪ GF pasta is available. Manager Callie reports that it is available "most of the time," and she adds that they get "quite a few" GF customers. ▪ *www.mychatters.com*

Essentials Food Store　　　★　$BLD
Concordia ▪ (785) 243-4755
118 W 6th St ▪ *Take-&-Bake* ▪ The soda fountain is no longer open, but a variety of GF "take-&-bake" items are available. The selection includes bread for sandwiches, chips, crackers, donuts, and pizza. Frozen pizzas are available, as are pizza crusts for cooking at home.

First Watch - The Daytime Café　📖
Fairway ▪ (913) 236-7600
2800 W 53rd St
Lawrence ▪ (785) 842-7999
2540 Iowa St
Olathe ▪ (913) 390-6072
15289 W 119th St

Overland Park ▪ (913) 696-1119
12040 Blue Valley Pkwy
Overland Park ▪ (913) 383-2904
7305 W 95th St
Overland Park ▪ (913) 339-6686
9916 College Blvd
Prairie Village ▪ (913) 649-8875
4117 W 83rd St
Shawnee ▪ (913) 631-0888
11112 W 63rd St

Fortune Wok ✪★ $LD
Overland Park ▪ (913) 681-8863
14537 Metcalf Ave
Shawnee Mission ▪ (913) 239-8646
11236 W 135th St ▪ Chinese ▪ Limited GF
menu includes sesame and lemon chicken,
chicken and vegetables, fried rice, and
more. GF soy sauce is also available.

Ingredient Restaurant ✪★ $LD
Lawrence ▪ (785) 832-0100
947 Massachusetts St
Leawood ▪ (913) 948-6800
11563 Ash St ▪ Pizza ▪ GF menu includes
salads with GF dressings and pizza with a
variety of toppings. GF pizza is available. ▪
www.ingredientrestaurant.com

Lemmy's Pizzeria ★ $$LD
Manhattan ▪ (785) 537-4444
600 S 4th St ▪ Pizza ▪ GF pizza, breadsticks, and brownies are available.

Local Burger ✪★ ¢LD
Lawrence ▪ (785) 856-7827
714 Vermont St ▪ American ▪ Owner Hil-
ary reports that almost the entire menu is
GF, and non-GF items are mentioned on
the menu. GF hamburger and hotdog buns,
as well as GF soy sauce and GF cookies, are
available. For dessert, they offer GF peanut
butter balls, chocolate chip cookies, and
more. ▪ www.localburger.com

Lone Star Steakhouse & Saloon 📖
Garden City ▪ (620) 271-0055
2306 E Kansas Ave
Hutchinson ▪ (620) 665-0808
1419 E 11Th Ave

Kansas City ▪ (913) 334-9995
1501 Village West Pkwy

Old Town Pizza ★ $$LD
Overland Park ▪ (913) 897-9242
14850 Metcalf Ave ▪ Pizza ▪ GF pizza is
available. ▪ www.kcoldtownpizza.com

O'Naturals ★ ¢BLD
Wichita ▪ (316) 634-0222
1551 N Rock Rd ▪ Deli ▪ GF wraps can be
used to make almost all sandwiches. GF
soups such as carrot ginger or split pea are
also available about twice per week. ▪ www.
onaturals.com

Outback Steakhouse 📖
Kansas City ▪ (913) 334-2147
1851 Village West Pkwy
Olathe ▪ (913) 780-9222
15430 S Rogers Rd
Overland Park ▪ (913) 894-5115
9501 Quivira Rd
Topeka ▪ (785) 272-3222
5826 SW 21st St
Wichita ▪ (316) 634-6500
2020 N Rock Rd
Wichita ▪ (316) 773-5900
233 S Ridge Rd

P.F. Chang's China Bistro 📖
Wichita ▪ (316) 634-2211
1401 Waterfront Pkwy

Pei Wei Asian Diner 📖
Olathe ▪ (913) 254-7283
15141 W 119th St
Overland Park ▪ (913) 693-9777
9222 Metcalf Ave
Wichita ▪ (316) 729-7285
2441 N Maize Rd Ste 1501

Pizza Fusion ★ $$$LD
Leawood ▪ (913) 685-0033
4800 W 135th St ▪ Pizza ▪ GF pizza is
available. ▪ www.pizzafusion.com

RowHouse Restaurant ★ $$$$D
Topeka ▪ (785) 235-1700
515 SW Van Buren St ▪ American ▪ GF
beer is available. Although the menu
changes weekly, flourless chocolate cake

and crème brulee are often available. ▪ *www.rowhouserestaurant.net*

Spin Pizza ★ $$LD
Olathe ▪ (913) 764-7746
14230 W 119th St
Overland Park ▪ (913) 451-7746
6541 W 119th St ▪ *Pizza* ▪ GF pizza is available. ▪ *www.spinpizza.com*

Via's Pizzeria ★ $LD
Topeka ▪ (785) 215-8421
738 SW Gage Blvd ▪ *Pizza* ▪ GF pizza is available. ▪ *www.viaspizzeria.com*

Yard House 📖
Kansas City ▪ (913) 788-4500
1863 Village West Pkwy

Yia Yia's Euro Bistro ★ $$$LD
Wichita ▪ (316) 634-1000
8115 E 21st St N ▪ *Continental* ▪ GF pizza is available all the time, and GF pasta is usually available. This is the only location that reports having GF specialty items. Manager Tammy cautions, though, that GF pizza and pasta take extra time to prepare. ▪ *www.yiayias.com*

Zio's ✪ $LD
Olathe ▪ (913) 782-2225
11981 S Strang Line Rd ▪ *Italian* ▪ GF menu includes salmon caesar salad, chicken piccata, Greek pasta, lemon chicken primavera, shrimp with marinara, ribeye tuscano, grilled sirloin, and more. ▪ *www.zios.com*

KENTUCKY

LOUISVILLE

Avalon $$LD
Louisville ▪ (502) 454-5336
1314 Bardstown Rd ▪ *American* ▪ Chef Larry reports that several menu items, such as thai meatballs, pork tacos, and deviled eggs, are naturally GF. Confirm timeliness of this information before dining in. He recommends reservations noting GF, and adds that all staff members are "pretty comfortable" with the GF diet. ▪ *www.avalonfresh.com*

Bonefish Grill 📖
Louisville ▪ (502) 412-4666
657 S Hurstbourne Pkwy

Bristol Bar & Grill ✪ $$LD
Louisville ▪ (502) 456-1702
1321 Bardstown Rd
Louisville ▪ (502) 426-0627
300 N Hurstbourne Pkwy
Louisville ▪ (502) 582-1995
614 W Main St ▪ *American* ▪ All locations report that they are able to accommodate GF diners. The Hurstbourne location has a new GF menu that includes all salads, burgers without buns, and a variety of fish, chicken, pork, and steak dishes. ▪ *www.bristolbarandgrille.com*

Buca di Beppo 📖
Louisville ▪ (502) 493-2426
2051 S Hurstbourne Pkwy

Café Bristol $L
Louisville ▪ (502) 634-2723
2035 S 3rd St ▪ *American* ▪ Manager Jamie reports that possible GF items include several salads, the grilled fish of the day, and tuna or chicken salad on a bed of lettuce. Confirm timeliness of this information before dining in. Located inside the J.B. Speed Art Museum. ▪ *www.bristolbarandgrille.com*

Carrabba's Italian Grill 📖
Louisville ▪ (502) 412-2218
617 S Hurstbourne Pkwy

Equus Restaurant $$$D
Louisville ▪ (502) 897-9721
122 Sears Ave ▪ *American Regional* ▪ Manager Elizabeth reports that GF diners are "absolutely" welcome, and the kitchen staff is "well aware" of GF restrictions. GF pasta is available. Most menu items can be modified to be GF, so calling in advance

with specifications is advised. ▪ *www.equus-restaurant.com*

Limestone Restaurant $$$LD
Louisville ▪ *(502) 426-7477*
10001 Forest Green Blvd ▪ *Southern* ▪
Manager Monty reports that they serve GF
guests "pretty frequently," and even some
of their regular customers are GF. He notes
that all staff members are trained on the
GF diet, and servers can indicate GF menu
items. Reservations noting GF are recommended. ▪ *www.limestonerestaurant.com*

Lynn's Paradise Café $BLD
Louisville ▪ *(502) 583-3447*
984 Barret Ave ▪ *American* ▪ Chef Jeremy
reports that they serve GF diners "really
frequently." He adds that "most of the
dishes" can be prepared GF, and he recommends that GF diners come in during less
busy hours. Alert a server upon arrival. ▪
www.lynnsparadisecafe.com

Melting Pot, The   📖
Louisville ▪ *(502) 491-3125*
2045 S Hurstbourne Pkwy

Mitchell's Fish Market   ✪ $$$LD
Louisville ▪ *(502) 412-1818*
4031 Summit Plaza Dr ▪ *Seafood* ▪ Extensive GF menu includes pan-roasted wild
blue mussels, blackened salmon spinach
salad, grilled shrimp and scallop skewers, Shanghai seafood sampler, lobster tail,
filet mignon, and live Maine lobster. Mini
crème brulee is available for dessert. ▪
www.mitchellsfishmarket.com

Napa River Grill $$$LD
Louisville ▪ *(502) 893-0141*
1211 Herr Lane ▪ *American* ▪ Manager
Michelle reports that GF diners regularly
dine at the restaurant. She notes that the
customer "probably knows more" about the
GF diet than the servers, but there is always
a chef on duty who is GF aware. Alert a
server, who will double check menu modifications with the chef. ▪ *www.napariver-louisville.com*

Old Spaghetti Factory, The   📖
Louisville ▪ *(502) 581-1070*
235 W Market St

Outback Steakhouse   📖
Louisville ▪ *(502) 895-4329*
4621 Shelbyville Rd
Louisville ▪ *(502) 964-8383*
6520 Signature Dr
Louisville ▪ *(502) 231-2399*
8101 Bardstown Rd
Louisville ▪ *(502) 426-4329*
9498 Brownsboro Rd

P.F. Chang's China Bistro   📖
Louisville ▪ *(502) 327-7707*
9120 Shelbyville Rd

Porcini $$$D
Louisville ▪ *(502) 894-8686*
2730 Frankfort Ave ▪ *Italian* ▪ Manager
Jenny reports that GF diners are not very
frequent but have "definitely" been accommodated before. She recommends noting
GF in reservations so that the server has
time to speak with the chef about GF menu
modifications. ▪ *www.porcinilouisville.com*

Proof on Main $$BLD
Louisville ▪ *(502) 217-6360*
702 W Main St ▪ *Modern American* ▪
Manager Carter reports that all staff members are "very familiar" with special diets,
and they are particularly trained on the GF
diet. He recommends reservations noting
GF so that the server is notified in advance.
▪ *www.proofonmain.com*

Ramsi's Café on the World $$LD
Louisville ▪ *(502) 451-0700*
1293 Bardstown Rd ▪ *Global* ▪ Restaurant
reports that they accommodate special
diets "on a daily basis." Thai noodle dishes,
chicken, and fish dishes can be modified to
be GF. Confirm timeliness of this information before dining in. All staff members are
trained on the GF diet. Alert a server, who
will notify the kitchen. ▪ *www.ramsiscafe.com*

Rí~Rá Irish Pub $LD
Louisville ▪ *(502) 587-1825*
445 South 4th St ▪ *Irish Pub* ▪ Ask for
the "Allergen Chart," which has a "Celiac"
column. This column contains items that
are GF or can be modified to be GF. ▪ *www.*
rira.com

Shane's Rib Shack   📖
Louisville ▪ *(502) 429-3907*
2420 Lime Kiln Ln Ste G

Sweet Surrender Dessert Café ✪★ ¢S
Louisville ▪ *(502) 899-2008*
1804 Frankfort Ave ▪ *Desserterie &*
Bakery ▪ Non-dedicated bakery offering several GF items, including mocha
concord cake, cheesecake with pecan crust,
and peanut butter chocolate chip cookies.
Restaurant recommends giving advanced
notice of 48 hours. ▪ *www.sweetsurrenderd-*
essertcafe.com

Winston's Restaurant $$$$LD
Louisville ▪ *(502) 456-0980*
3101 Bardstown Rd ▪ *Modern American* ▪
Manager Kevin reports that the restaurant
is "more than able" to accommodate GF
diners. He adds that the chef is very GF
aware. Reservations noting GF are recommended. ▪ *www.sullivan.edu/winstons*

KENTUCKY

ALL OTHER CITIES

Bella Notte   ✪★ $LD
Lexington ▪ *(859) 245-1789*
3715 Nicholasville Rd ▪ *Italian* ▪ GF menu
includes spicy tomato basil soup, salmon
oreganato, the petite Black Angus sampler,
and other items. GF pasta is available, and
there are a variety of pasta dishes on the GF
menu. For dessert, they offer crème brûlée
and vanilla cream custard. ▪ *www.bellalex-*
ington.com

Bonefish Grill   📖
Crescent Springs ▪ *(859) 426-8666*
588 Buttermilk Pike
Lexington ▪ *(859) 233-3474*
2341 Sir Barton Way

Bristol Bar & Grill $$$LD
Prospect ▪ *(502) 292-2585*
6051 Timber Ridge Dr ▪ *American* ▪
Manager Jen reports that all staff members
are trained to handle special diets. In the
kitchen, they have a sheet listing all GF
items. Jen notes that GF items include
several salads, grilled salmon teriyaki, and
steak au poivre. ▪ *www.bristolbarandgrille.*
com

Captain's Quarters $$LD
Harrods Creek ▪ *(502) 228-1651*
5700 Captains Quarters Rd ▪ *American*
▪ Manager Matt reports that the restaurant
accommodates GF diners "at least once
a day." He notes that almost every menu
item can be modified to be GF. Reservations noting GF are recommended. ▪ *www.*
cqriverside.com

Carino's Italian   📖
Frankfort ▪ *(502) 223-4401*
1303 US Highway 127 S
Lexington ▪ *(859) 245-0091*
135 Rojay Dr
Lexington ▪ *(859) 264-1049*
2333 Sir Barton Way

Carrabba's Italian Grill   📖
Crestview Hills ▪ *(859) 344-6163*
2899 Dixie Hwy
Lexington ▪ *(859) 264-8395*
1881 Plaudit Pl

First Watch - The Daytime Café 📖
Covington ▪ *(859) 491-0869*
50 E Rivercenter Blvd
Crestview Hills ▪ *(859) 341-0222*
2762 Town Center Blvd

I Ching Asian Café   ✪ ¢LD
Lexington ▪ *(859) 543-2742*
2312 Sir Barton Way ▪ *Asian* ▪ GF menu
includes crispy shrimp & calamari, drunk-

en noodles, Singapore tomato curry, sweet and sour chicken or shrimp, and more. ▪ *www.ichingcafe.com*

Lone Star Steakhouse & Saloon   📖
Bowling Green ▪ *(270) 796-8880*
2425 Scottsville Rd
Florence ▪ *(859) 647-0600*
7533 Mall Rd

Mainstrasse Village Pub   ★ ¢S
Covington ▪ *(859) 431-5552*
619 Main St ▪ *Pub Food* ▪ GF beer is available. Manager Kurt notes that "numerous" diners order the GF beer. ▪ *www.mainstrassevillagepub.com*

Melting Pot, The   📖
Lexington ▪ *(859) 254-6358*
152 W Tiverton Way

Mitchell's Fish Market   ✪ $$$LD
Newport ▪ *(859) 291-7454*
1 Levee Way ▪ *Seafood* ▪ Extensive GF menu includes pan-roasted wild blue mussels, blackened salmon spinach salad, grilled shrimp and scallop skewers, Shanghai seafood sampler, lobster tail, filet mignon, and live Maine lobster. Mini crème brulee is available for dessert. ▪ *www.mitchellsfishmarket.com*

Outback Steakhouse   📖
Ashland ▪ *(606) 325-4329*
441 River Hill Dr
Bowling Green ▪ *(270) 746-0409*
3260 Scottsville Rd
Crescent Springs ▪ *(859) 331-7222*
2301 Buttermilk Crossings
Erlanger ▪ *(859) 767-1055*
Terminal 3 4th Floor
Lexington ▪ *(859) 272-6283*
127 W Tiverton Way
Lexington ▪ *(859) 263-3770*
1957 Bryant Rd
Paducah ▪ *(270) 442-4111*
3995 Hinkleville Rd
Richmond ▪ *(859) 624-9000*
400 Highland Park Dr

P.F. Chang's China Bistro   📖
Lexington ▪ *(859) 271-1165*
3405 Nicholasville Rd

Pasta House Co., The   📖
Paducah ▪ *(270) 575-1997*
451 Jordan Dr # 1

Stan's Fish Sandwich $LD
St Matthews ▪ *(502) 896-6600*
3729 Lexington Rd ▪ *Seafood* ▪ Manager Leilah reports that the restaurant can accommodate GF diners, as long as they specify GF needs upon arrival. She recommends telling the server that the kitchen should not use flour. Avoid fried foods and burgers, as they are made with bread crumbs. Grilled fish, salads, and balsamic dressing are all GF. Confirm timeliness of this information before dining in. ▪ *www.stansfish.com*

Winger's Grill and Bar   ✪ ¢LD
Lexington ▪ *(859) 271-9464*
240 Canary Road ▪ *American* ▪ GF menu includes double basted ribs, glazed salmon, quesadillas with corn tortillas, and a variety of salads. ▪ *www.wingers.info*

LOUISIANA

Adobe Cantina and Salsa $LD
Hammond ▪ *(985) 419-0027*
1905 W Thomas St ▪ *Mexican* ▪ Manager Uriel reports that they can accommodate GF diners. Some fish and steak dishes are naturally GF, while others can be modified to be GF. Confirm timeliness of this information before dining in. Located in Seville Plaza. ▪ *www.carretarestaurant.com*

Bonefish Grill   📖
Baton Rouge ▪ *(225) 216-1191*
7415 Corporate Blvd

Covington ■ (985) 809-0662
200 River Highlands Blvd
Lafayette ■ (337) 981-0714
1912 Kaliste Saloom Rd

Bubba Gump Shrimp Co.   📖
New Orleans ■ (504) 522-5800
429 Decatur St

Cantina Laredo   📖
Shreveport ■ (318) 798-6363
6535 Youree Dr

Carino's Italian   📖
Alexandria ■ (318) 767-5942
3213 N Macarthur Dr
Lafayette ■ (337) 988-7535
4321 Ambassador Caffery Pkwy
Lake Charles ■ (337) 474-4741
2638 Derek Dr

Carrabba's Italian Grill   📖
Baton Rouge ■ (225) 925-9999
7275 Corporate Blvd
Lafayette ■ (337) 981-6669
2010 Kaliste Saloom Rd
Shreveport ■ (318) 798-6504
1706 E 70th St

Casamentos $LD
New Orleans ■ (504) 895-9761
4330 Magazine St ■ Seafood ■ Manager
CJ notes that the seafood is fried with
corn flour and is GF. He also notes that the
french fries are GF. Confirm timeliness of
this information before dining in. Alert
a server, who will communicate with CJ
directly. ■ www.casamentosrestaurant.com

Commander's Palace $$$$LD
New Orleans ■ (504) 899-8221
1403 Washington Ave ■ American Regional ■ The restaurant reports that GF diners
come in "all the time." All meals are made
to order, so GF requests are not difficult
to accommodate. Reservations noting GF
are recommended, so that the kitchen can
prepare in advance. Upon arrival, alert a
server or ask to speak with a manager. ■
www.commanderspalace.com

Emeril's $$$$LD
New Orleans ■ (504) 528-9393
800 Tchoupitoulas St ■ Seafood ■ Reservationist Danielle reports that while the
restaurant does not often serve GF diners, they "certainly have in the past." She
recommends noting GF in reservations so
that the server will be alerted to the gluten
allergy ahead of time. Servers are trained
to alert the chef when there is a GF diner,
so that the chef can come to the table to
discuss GF options. ■ www.emerils.com

Kona Grill   📖
Baton Rouge ■ (225) 769-0077
10111 Perkins Rowe

**Kosher Cajun New York Deli & Gro-
cery**   ★ ¢LD
Metairie ■ (504) 888-2010
3519 Severn Ave ■ Take-&-Bake ■ GF
breads, chips, frozen pizzas, frozen cakes,
and more are available from the grocery
section. The deli will make customers a
sandwich with purchased loaves of GF
bread, but they do not have GF bread on
hand in the deli. ■ www.koshercajun.com

K-Paul's $$$LD
New Orleans ■ (504) 524-7394
416 Chartres St ■ Cajun & Creole ■ Man-
ager Bill reports that they accommodate
GF diners several times a month. He notes
that if the menu descriptions are not suf-
ficient to determine whether an item is GF,
the server can assist. There is also an "open
kitchen," so servers can ask about any
dishes at any time. ■ www.kpauls.com

La Carreta $LD
Amite ■ (985) 748-9992
122 SW Central Ave
Baton Rouge ■ (225) 334-9940
4065 Government St
Baton Rouge ■ (225) 303-9899
9828 Bluebonnet Blvd
Denham Springs ■ (225) 271-9999
135 Veterans Blvd
Hammond ■ (985) 419-9990
108 NW Railroad Ave

La Place ■ *(985) 651-9991*
107 Carrollwood Dr
Mandeville ■ *(985) 624-2990*
1200 W Causeway Approach ■ *Mexican*
■ Director of Marketing Jane reports that
they are able to serve GF diners. She notes
that a many enchiladas and tacos are naturally GF, as are some of the entrée dinners.
For dessert, they offer flan. Confirm timeliness of this information before dining in. ■
www.carretarestaurant.com

Lone Star Steakhouse & Saloon 📖
Baton Rouge ■ *(225) 754-7827*
1920 Oneal Ln
West Monroe ■ *(318) 388-1954*
108 Basic Dr

Melting Pot, The 📖
Baton Rouge ■ *(225) 928-5677*
5294 Corporate Blvd
New Orleans ■ *(504) 525-3225*
1820 Saint Charles Ave

Muriel's Jackson Square ✪★ $$$LD
New Orleans ■ *(504) 568-1885*
801 Chartres St ■ *American Regional* ■
GF menu includes appetizers, entrées, and
desserts. GF beer is available. Marketing
Director Denise recommends alerting both
a host and a server upon arrival. ■ *www.
muriels.com*

Naked Pizza ★ $LD
New Orleans ■ *(504) 865-0244*
6307 S Miro St ■ *Pizza* ■ GF pizza is available. Manager Mike reports that GF crusts
are made every day in house, and they
occasionally do sell out. He also notes that
the kitchen has a separate station for GF
preparation. ■ *www.nakedpizza.biz*

Napoleon House ¢LD
New Orleans ■ *(504) 524-9752*
500 Chartres St ■ *American Regional* ■
Kitchen Manager Nick reports that a limited number of menu items can be made
GF. He recommends asking for him or
someone else in the kitchen to discuss GF
options. ■ *www.napoleonhouse.com*

Outback Steakhouse 📖
Alexandria ■ *(318) 442-0303*
3217 S Macarthur Dr
Baton Rouge ■ *(225) 927-9488*
2415 S Acadian Thruway
Baton Rouge ■ *(225) 751-1011*
5280 Jones Creek Rd
Bossier City ■ *(318) 742-2400*
2715 Village Ln
Covington ■ *(985) 893-0505*
60 Park Place Dr
Gonzales ■ *(225) 644-3038*
2637 S. Veterans Boulevard
Houma ■ *(985) 580-1800*
1561 Martin Luther King Jr Blvd
Lafayette ■ *(337) 235-4405*
1600 W Pinhook Rd
Lake Charles ■ *(337) 477-3161*
2616 Derek Dr
Marrero ■ *(504) 341-5544*
1601 Barataria Blvd
Metairie ■ *(504) 455-6850*
2746 Severn Ave
Shreveport ■ *(318) 865-0036*
8825 Line Ave
Slidell ■ *(985) 649-4329*
830 E I 10 Service Rd
West Monroe ■ *(318) 387-6700*
305 Constitution Dr

P.F. Chang's China Bistro 📖
Baton Rouge ■ *(225) 216-9044*
7341 Corporate Blvd
Metairie ■ *(504) 828-5288*
3301 Veterans Memorial Blvd Ste 63

Semolina $LD
Metairie ■ *(504) 454-7930*
4436 Veterans Blvd ■ *Italian-American*
■ Manager Adam reports that GF diners
can be accommodated, but there are very
limited GF options. He notes that GF diners generally order the Malibu Salad with
unmarinated chicken breast or the grilled
trout. Confirm timeliness of this information before dining in. ■ *www.semolina.com*

Shane's Rib Shack 📖
Marrero ■ *(504) 324-9701*
1855 Barataria Blvd

Truly Free Bakery and Deli   100% ¢**BLD**
Baton Rouge ▪ *(225) 383-3344*
4321 Perkins Rd ▪ *Deli* ▪ Dedicated GF
bakery offering bread, muffins, cookies, brownies, cupcakes, cakes, and more.
Varieties of bread include banana walnut,
Creole corn, sweet corn, and pumpkin
bread. The deli has GF paninis, pizza, and
wraps, among other things. ▪ *www.truly-
freebakery.com*

MAINE

98 Provence $$$$**D**
Ogunquit ▪ *(207) 646-9898*
262 Shore Rd ▪ *French Country* ▪ Owner
and Chef Pierre reports that he is "very
understanding" of GF diners, and the restaurant serves them "more and more." He
recommends making reservations noting
GF and alerting the server upon arrival.
This should be sufficient, as "everybody is
aware" of the GF diet. ▪ *www.98provence.
com*

Bandaloop   ★ $$$**D**
Kennebunkport ▪ *(207) 967-4994*
2 Dock Sq ▪ *Modern American* ▪ GF rolls
are available. Owner and Chef Scott reports
that there are "plenty of things" on the
menu, and they accommodate GF diners
very frequently. Alert a server upon arrival,
as all staff members are trained to handle
special dietary needs. ▪ *www.bandaloop.biz*

Bibo's Madd Apple Café   ★ $**LD**
Portland ▪ *(207) 774-9698*
23 Forest Ave ▪ *American* ▪ Owner Bobby
reports that the restaurant serves GF
diners "all the time." He reports that the
dinner menu has many items that can be
modified to be GF. GF bread is available

with advanced notice of 24 hours. ▪ *www.
bibosportland.com*

Bugaboo Creek Steak House   📖
Bangor ▪ *(207) 945-5515*
24 Bangor Mall Blvd
South Portland ▪ *(207) 773-5400*
264 Gorham Rd

David's $$$**LD**
Portland ▪ *(207) 773-4340*
22 Monument Sq ▪ *Modern American* ▪
Manager Kim reports that there are "a ton"
of GF options. She adds that they accommodate GF diners "all the time," and she
recommends reservations noting GF. For
dessert, they offer crème brûlée and a
flourless chocolate raspberry torte. ▪ *www.
davidsrestaurant.com*

DiMillo's Floating Restaurant   ☺ $$$**LD**
Portland ▪ *(207) 772-2216*
25 Long Wharf ▪ *Seafood* ▪ GF menu
includes steamed Maine clams, jumbo
shrimp, spinach salad, lobsters steamed
in the shell, grilled salmon, scallops with
no crumbs, and the tuscan ribeye. ▪ *www.
dimillos.com*

Flatbread Pizza Company   ★ $**LD**
Portland ▪ *(207) 772-8777*
72 Commercial St ▪ *Pizza* ▪ GF pizza is
available in the 8-inch size. GF desserts
are also available. Typical GF desserts are
whoopie pies and brownies. ▪ *www.flat-
breadcompany.com*

Frontier Café $**BLD**
Brunswick ▪ *(207) 725-5222*
14 Maine St ▪ *Global* ▪ Restaurant reports
that its menu has several naturally GF op-
tions, namely the soups and entrée salads.
Confirm timeliness of this information
before dining in. ▪ *www.explorefrontier.com*

**Gauchos Churrascaria Brazilian Steak-
house** $$$**D**
Portland ▪ *(207) 774-9460*
100 Commercial St ▪ *Brazilian Steakhouse* ▪ Most menu items are GF. Alert
a server upon arrival. Salads, meats, and

yucca are generally GF. Confirm timeliness of this information before dining in. ▪ *www.gauchosbraziliansteakhouse.com*

Great Impasta, The   ✪★ $LD
Brunswick ▪ **(207) 729-5858**
42 Maine St ▪ *Italian* ▪ The GF menu includes appetizers, risotto with chicken, pesto pizza, and fudge brownies for dessert. ▪ *www.thegreatimpasta.com*

Ground Round   📖
Augusta ▪ **(207) 623-0022**
110 Community Dr
Bangor ▪ **(207) 942-5621**
248 Odlin Rd

Gypsy Sweethearts $$$D
Ogunquit ▪ **(207) 646-7021**
14 Shore Rd ▪ *American Regional* ▪ Chef David reports that they serve GF diners often. He recommends alerting the host upon arrival, and he or she will alert the server. Servers generally know which menu items are or can be modified to be GF, but they will ask the chef if they are unsure. David notes that several menu items are naturally GF, including the sea scallop appetizer, grilled portabello tops, chili rellenos, pork shanks, and more. Confirm timeliness of this information before dining in. ▪ *www.gypsysweethearts.com*

Home Port Inn Restaurant, The $$$D
Lubec ▪ **(800) 457-2077**
45 Main St ▪ *Modern American* ▪ Owner Dave notes that the chef is GF, so the restaurant is "sophisticated in its knowledge" of GF dining. He recommends alerting the server upon arrival and asking for Susanna or Dave. The server will indicate GF options and confer with the chef. ▪ *www.homeportinn.com*

Joshua's $$$D
Wells ▪ **(207) 646-3355**
1637 Post Rd ▪ *American* ▪ Owner Barbara reports that GF diners are "frequently accommodated." GF dishes are not cooked in separate pans, so she notes that it "depends on the degree of the intolerance." Grilled

steaks and fish can be prepared. Confirm timeliness of this information before dining in. Calling ahead to note GF is recommended. ▪ *www.joshuas.biz*

Julie's Ristorante & Provisto   ✪★ $LD
Ogunquit ▪ **(207) 641-2522**
369 Main St ▪ *Italian* ▪ GF pizza, pasta, soy sauce, and beer are available, as are GF bagels, paninis, gnocchi, and ravioli. For dessert, there are GF cookies and muffins. GF specialties change seasonally. GF gift baskets are available with advanced notice. ▪ *www.juliesristorante.com*

Morning Dew Natural Foods   ★ ¢S
Bridgton ▪ **(207) 647-4003**
19 Sandy Creek Rd ▪ *Deli* ▪ Manager Judy reports that GF sandwiches are available at the deli. The deli is located within a larger grocery store, where they offer GF pasta, donuts, bagels, cake mixes, and more. ▪ *www.morningdewnatural.com*

Ninety Nine Restaurant & Pub   📖
Auburn ▪ **(207) 784-9499**
650 Center St
Augusta ▪ **(207) 623-0999**
281 Civic Center Dr
Bangor ▪ **(207) 973-1999**
8 Bangor Mall Blvd
Biddeford ▪ **(207) 283-9999**
444 Alfred St
Topsham ▪ **(207) 725-4999**
24 Topsham Fair Mall Rd

O'Naturals   ✪★ ¢LD
Falmouth ▪ **(207) 781-8889**
240 US Route 1 ▪ *Deli* ▪ GF menu includes wraps, Asian noodles, soups, salads, and brown rice bread for sandwiches. ▪ *www.onaturals.com*

Outback Steakhouse   📖
South Portland ▪ **(207) 761-4400**
147 Western Ave

Pat's Pizza   ★ $LD
Ellsworth ▪ **(207) 667-6011**
396 High St ▪ *Pizza* ▪ GF pizza is available. ▪ *www.patspizzaellsworth.com*

Portland Pie Company ★ $LD
Portland ■ *(207) 772-1231*
51 York St
Scarborough ■ *(207) 510-6999*
400 Expedition Dr
Westbrook ■ *(207) 591-6248*
869 Main St ■ *Pizza* ■ GF pizza is available.
■ *www.portlandpie.com*

Primo $$$$D
Rockland ■ *(207) 596-0770*
2 S Main St ■ *Modern American* ■ Manager
Melissa reports that the kitchen can modify
dishes to be GF. She also notes that with
advanced notice, they can create entirely
new GF dishes. She reports that the managers and chefs have daily meetings to discuss
special requests from diners who have
called ahead, so reservations noting GF are
strongly recommended. ■ *www.primores-taurant.com*

Rí~Rá Irish Pub $LD
Portland ■ *(207) 761-4446*
72 Commercial St ■ *Irish Pub* ■ Ask for
the "Allergen Chart," which has a "Celiac"
column. This column contains items that
are GF or can be modified to be GF. ■ *www.rira.com*

Ricetta's Brick Oven Pizza ★ $LD
Falmouth ■ *(207) 781-3100*
240 US Route 1
South Portland ■ *(207) 775-7400*
29 Western Ave ■ *Pizza* ■ GF pizza is available. ■ *www.ricettas.com*

Sebago Brewing Company ✪ $$LD
Gorham ■ *(207) 839-2337*
29 Elm St
Kennebunk ■ *(207) 985-9855*
67 Portland Rd
Portland ■ *(207) 775-2337*
164 Middle St
Scarborough ■ *(207) 874-2337*
201 Southborough Dr ■ *American* ■ GF
menu includes sesame crusted ahi tuna,
teriyaki grilled chicken, East-West salmon,
burgers without buns, white chicken chili,
and more. ■ *www.sebagobrewing.com*

Silly's ✪★ ¢LD
Portland ■ *(207) 772-0360*
40 Washington Ave ■ *American* ■ GF
items marked on the menu include rice
bowls with chicken or turkey and GF rice
krispie squares. GF pizza is available. There
is a dedicated GF fryer. ■ *www.sillys.com*

Slate's Restaurant $$BLD
Hallowell ■ *(207) 622-9575*
169 Water St ■ *Seafood* ■ Bartender
Jeremy reports that they accommodate GF
diners "all the time." He adds that they can
easily prepare a GF meal, as "everything
is made to order." Jeremy notes that since
there is an open kitchen, GF diners can
speak directly to the cooks. ■ *www.slatesres-taurant.com*

Soakology Foot Sanctuary & Teahouse
★ ¢S
Portland ■ *(207) 879-7625*
30 City Ctr ■ *Café* ■ GF peanut butter
cookies and biscotti are available. Kitchen
Manager Angie is very knowledgeable
about the GF diet and knows which menu
items are GF. Ask for her upon arrival. ■
www.soakology.com

Soup For You ✪ ¢LD
Farmington ■ *(207) 779-0799*
222 Broadway ■ *Soup* ■ GF soups are available. Manager Eddie reports that GF soups
change every day, but there are always a
couple of GF options. The day's GF soups
are indicated on the menu by an asterisk. ■
www.farmington.edu

Stripers Waterfront Seafood Restau-rant $$$LD
Kennebunkport ■ *(207) 967-5333*
127 Ocean Ave ■ *Seafood* ■ Manager Niels
reports that the restaurant serves GF diners on a regular basis. He notes that many
items are GF, and servers know which
items can be modified to be GF. ■ *www.thebreakwaterinn.com*

Sugar House Café ★ ¢B
Rockland ■ *(207) 593-0090*
229 Park St ■ *Café* ■ GF pancakes, cream

of buckwheat, and english muffins are available. GF pancakes can be served with blueberries or cranberries. Restaurant reports that the kitchen is "more than happy" to accommodate GF diners and does so on a regular basis. ▪ *www.mainegold.com*

Thistle Inn, The $$$D
Boothbay Harbor ▪ (207) 633-3541
55 Oak St ▪ *Modern American* ▪ Manager Max reports that the restaurant handles GF requests "all the time." He notes that many dishes on the menu are seafood and meat dishes, so they are naturally GF. Confirm timeliness of information before dining in. Max adds that the kitchen can modify any menu item to be GF. ▪ *www.thethistleinn.com*

Uno Chicago Grill   📖
Bangor ▪ (207) 947-5000
725 Stillwater Ave
S Portland ▪ (207) 780-8667
280 Maine Mall Rd

Wildflours   100% ⊄S
Brunswick ▪ (207) 725-7973
1 Mason St ▪ *Bakery* ▪ Dedicated GF market and bakery offering cookies, bagels, breads, cupcakes, whoopie pies, and more. Cakes are available with advanced notice of 48 hours. GF grocery items like pizza crusts, donuts, and a couple different breads are baked off-site. ▪ *www.wildflours.com*

MARYLAND

BALTIMORE

Austin Grill   ✪ $LD
Baltimore ▪ (410) 534-0606
2400 Boston St
Baltimore ▪ (410) 534-0606
The Can Company 2400 Boston St. ▪
Tex-Mex ▪ GF menu includes slow-smoked

BBQ ribs, fajitas, tacos and quesadillas. For dessert, they offer homemade flan. ▪ *www.austingrill.com*

Bertucci's   📖
Baltimore ▪ (410) 931-0900
8130 Corporate Dr

Blue Hill Tavern $$$LD
Baltimore ▪ (443) 388-9363
938 S Conkling St ▪ *American* ▪ Manager Jessica reports that GF diners are becoming "very popular." She adds that servers have a "verbal list" of GF options that they can recite. It includes the NY strip, chicken, and black cod, among other meats, with substituted sides. ▪ *www.bluehilltavern.com*

Carrabba's Italian Grill   📖
Baltimore ▪ (410) 661-5444
7600 Belair Rd

Donna's Restaurant   ★ $$LD
Baltimore ▪ (410) 328-1962
22 S Greene St ▪ *Mediterranean* ▪ GF pizza is available at listed locations only. ▪ *www.donnas.com*

Fogo De Chao   ★ $$$$LD
Baltimore ▪ (410) 528-9292
600 E Pratt St ▪ *Brazilian* ▪ GF cheese bread made with yucca flour is available. ▪ *www.fogodechao.com*

Gertrude's $$$LD
Baltimore ▪ (410) 889-3399
10 Art Museum Dr ▪ *American* ▪ Manager Paul notes that the staff is "pretty familiar" with the GF diet. He recommends noting GF in reservations. Though not all servers are GF aware, they know to confer with the kitchen staff regarding the best GF options. Located in the Baltimore Museum of Art.

Grano   ★ $D
Baltimore ▪ (443) 869-3429
1031 W 36th St
Baltimore ▪ (443) 438-7521
3547 Chestnut Ave ▪ *Italian* ▪ GF pasta is available. Ask a server which sauces are GF. ▪ *www.granopastabar.com*

Greene Turtle Sports Bar & Grill, The
✪ ¢**LD**

Baltimore ▪ *(410) 691-9802*
1000 Friendship St
Baltimore ▪ *(410) 342-4222*
718 S Broadway # 722 ▪ *American* ▪ GF
menu includes spinach, artichoke, and jalapeno dip, buffalo chicken wings, roasted
chicken, terrapin steak, apple walnut salad,
french fries, crab soup, and more. ▪ *www.*
greeneturtle.com

Helmand, The
$$**LD**

Baltimore ▪ *(410) 752-0311*
806 N Charles St ▪ *Afghan* ▪ Manager
Assad reports that most menu items are
naturally GF. He recommends asking for
him upon arrival and he "will be happy" to
go over the menu with GF diners, indicat-
ing the best GF options. ▪ *www.helmand.*
com

J Paul's
$$$**LD**

Baltimore ▪ *(410) 659-1889*
301 Light St ▪ *American* ▪ GF soups are
sometimes available. Restaurant reports
that they are familiar with the GF diet.
They recommend asking for a manager or
chef, as they are more aware of GF menu
modifications. They note that salads and
protein dishes are options for GF customers. Confirm timeliness of this information
before dining in. ▪ *www.j-pauls.com*

Lebanese Taverna
✪ ¢**LD**

Baltimore ▪ *(410) 244-5533*
719 President St ▪ *Middle Eastern* ▪ GF
menu includes lentil soup, lamb shanks,
shwarma, chicken and rice, jumbo shrimp,
and more. Any dish that normally includes
bread can be made GF by substituting rice
crackers and vegetables. ▪ *www.lebanesetav-*
erna.com

Liquid Earth
★ $$**LD**

Baltimore ▪ *(410) 276-6606*
1626 Aliceanna St ▪ *Healthy American* ▪
GF bread is available for substitution into
all sandwiches. Restaurant also notes that
most items on its raw menu are naturally

GF. They report that GF diners come in
"every so often." ▪ *www.liquidearth.com*

One World Café
✪ $**BLD**

Baltimore ▪ *(410) 235-5777*
100 W University Pkwy ▪ *Café* ▪ GF items
marked on the menu include chili, thai
vegetables in tempe sauce, and organic
tofu. Manager Michelle reports that the
"staff is pretty educated," and servers can
explain the preparation of GF items. ▪
www.one-world-cafe.com

Outback Steakhouse
📖

Baltimore ▪ *(410) 522-7757*
2400 Boston St
Baltimore ▪ *(410) 529-7200*
4215 Ebenezer Rd

P.F. Chang's China Bistro
📖

Baltimore ▪ *(410) 649-2750*
600 E Pratt St Ste 101

Pei Wei Asian Diner
📖

Baltimore ▪ *(410) 435-3290*
6302 York Rd

Pizzazz Tuscan Grill at Pier 5 Hotel
★ $$$**BLD**

Baltimore ▪ *(410) 528-7772*
711 Eastern Ave ▪ *Italian* ▪ Owner Deanna
reports that they serve an "extensive GF
clientele." GF pasta, pizza, and beer are
available at all times, and there is always at
least one GF dessert on the menu. Deanna
adds that all staff members are "very experienced" at accommodating GF diners,
so any server can identify potentially GF
menu items. ▪ *www.pizzazztuscangrille.com*

Roy's
✪ $$$**D**

Baltimore ▪ *(410) 659-0099*
720 Aliceanna St ▪ *Hawaiian Fusion* ▪
Extensive GF menu includes crispy seared
Virginia rockfish, stuffed black tiger
shrimp, and braised beef short ribs, among
other things. There is also a GF prix fixe
menu, which provides a choice of appetiz-
ers and entrées, followed by the melting
hot chocolate soufflé for dessert. The menu

changes seasonally, so items may vary slightly. ▪ *www.roysrestaurant.com*

Sammy's Trattoria ★ $$$LD
Baltimore ▪ *(410) 837-9999*
1200 N Charles St ▪ *Italian* ▪ GF pasta is available. ▪ *www.sammystrattoria.com*

Sascha's $$LD
Baltimore ▪ *(410) 539-8880*
527 N Charles St ▪ *American* ▪ Manager Steve reports that GF diners are "not that rare." He advises reservations noting GF, so that the servers and chefs will be alerted in advance. They will be ready to discuss GF menu modifications. ▪ *www.saschas.com*

Sweet Sin 100% ¢LD
Baltimore ▪ *(410) 366-5777*
123 W 27th St ▪ *Bakery* ▪ Owner Renee reports that her dedicated GF bakery offers "every dessert imaginable." GF treats include cakes, cupcakes, cookies, brownies, muffins, and pies. They also bake fresh GF focaccia bread. ▪ *www.glutenfreedesserts. com*

Uno Chicago Grill 📖
Baltimore ▪ *(410) 625-5900*
201 E Pratt St

Woodberry Kitchen ✪★ $$$D
Baltimore ▪ *(410) 464-8000*
2010 Clipper Park Rd ▪ *Organic American* ▪ GF menu includes deviled eggs, Chesapeake oyster stew, braised short rib with new potatoes, and more. GF desserts include chocolate pudding and blueberry reserves. GF bread, soy sauce, and beer are available. The owner is GF, so all staff members are very educated on the GF diet. ▪ *www.woodberrykitchen.com*

MARYLAND
ALL OTHER CITIES

Austin Grill ✪ $LD
Annapolis ▪ *(410) 571-6688*
2002 Annapolis Mall
Bethesda ▪ *(301) 656-1366*
7278 Woodmont Ave
Rockville ▪ *(301) 838-4281*
36 Maryland Ave
Silver Spring ▪ *(240) 247-8969*
919 Ellsworth Dr ▪ *Tex-Mex* ▪ GF menu includes slow-smoked BBQ ribs, fajitas, tacos and quesadillas. For dessert, they offer homemade flan. ▪ *www.austingrill.com*

Bean Hollow ★ ¢S
Ellicott City ▪ *(410) 465-0233*
8059 Main St ▪ *Coffee Shop* ▪ GF tarts are available.

Bertucci's 📖
Annapolis ▪ *(410) 266-5800*
2207 Forest Dr
Bel Air ▪ *(410) 569-4600*
12 Bel Air South Pkwy
Columbia ▪ *(410) 312-4800*
9081 Snowden River Pkwy
Kensington ▪ *(301) 230-3160*
11301 Rockville Pike
Timonium ▪ *(410) 561-7000*
1818 York Rd

BlueStone ✪ $$$LD
Timonium ▪ *(410) 561-1100*
11 W Aylesbury Rd ▪ *Seafood* ▪ Limited GF dinner menu includes salads, a tuna appetizer, Chilean sea bass, and a filet of beef. Restaurant reports that GF diners are welcome to order from the GF dinner menu during lunch hours, and the chef will use the lunch vegetable as a side instead of the dinner vegetable. ▪ *www.bluestoneonline.net*

Bonefish Grill 📖
Bel Air ▪ *(410) 420-9113*
696 Bel Air Rd
Brandywine ▪ *(301) 782-7604*

15910 Crain Hwy Bldg F
Frederick ▪ *(301) 668-1522*
1305 W 7th St Ste 37
Gaithersburg ▪ *(240) 631-2401*
82 Market St
Glen Burnie ▪ *(410) 553-0299*
6711 Governor Ritchie Hwy Ste 201
Owings Mills ▪ *(410) 654-5500*
10906 Boulevard Circle

Broadway Pizza   ★ $$**LD**
Potomac ▪ *(301) 299-3553*
7965 Tuckerman Ln ▪ Pizza ▪ GF pizza is
available in the 9-inch size. Toppings in-
clude fresh vegetables, chicken, and lamb. ▪
www.broadwaypizzaonline.com

Buca di Beppo   📖
Gaithersburg ▪ *(301) 947-7346*
122 Kentlands Blvd

Bugaboo Creek Steak House   📖
Gaithersburg ▪ *(301) 548-9200*
15710 Shady Grove Rd
Upper Marlboro ▪ *(301) 499-6881*
1100 Capital Centre Blvd

CakeLove   ★ ¢**S**
Oxon Hill ▪ *(301) 686-0340*
160 National Plz
Silver Spring ▪ *(301) 565-2253*
935 Ellsworth Dr ▪ Bakery ▪ Non-dedi-
cated GF bakery offering GF cakes and
cupcakes. All are available to order with
advanced notice of at least 4 days. Orders
can be placed online for quick and easy
pick-up. ▪ *www.cakelove.com*

Capital Grille, The   📖
Chevy Chase ▪ *(301) 718-7812*
5310 Western Ave

Carini's Pizza & Subs   ★ $$**LD**
Stevensville ▪ *(410) 604-2501*
356 Romancoke Rd ▪ Pizza ▪ GF pizza is
available.

Carrabba's Italian Grill   📖
Bowie ▪ *(301) 809-0500*
16431 Governor Bridge Rd
Ellicott City ▪ *(410) 461-5200*
4430 Long Gate Pkwy

Frederick ▪ *(301) 694-6200*
1315 W Patrick St
Germantown ▪ *(240) 686-1100*
19935 Century Blvd
Hunt Valley ▪ *(410) 785-9400*
130 Shawan Rd
Ocean City ▪ *(410) 213-0037*
12728 Ocean Gtwy
Pasadena ▪ *(410) 863-5960*
8030 Ritchie Hwy
Waldorf ▪ *(301) 645-0094*
3754 Crain Hwy

Cava Mezze $**D**
Rockville ▪ *(301) 309-9090*
9713 Traville Gateway Dr ▪ Greek ▪ Restaurant reports frequently accommodating GF diners. Alert a server upon arrival.
Many menu items are naturally GF, such
as salads, dips, omelets and saffron risotto.
Confirm timeliness of this information
before dining in. ▪ *www.cavamezze.com*

Cetrone's Pizza Place   ★ $$**LD**
Bowie ▪ *(301) 805-1500*
13629 Annapolis Rd ▪ Pizza ▪ GF pizza is
available. Pizzas can be ordered with any
of the restaurant's toppings except the beef,
which is not GF. Confirm timeliness of this
information before dining in.

Clustered Spires Pastry Shop   ★ ¢**S**
Frederick ▪ *(301) 662-7446*
285 Montevue Ln ▪ Bakery ▪ Non-dedicat-
ed bakery offering a variety of GF products
by pre-order. GF breads, pastries, cakes,
danishes, cinammon rolls, muffins, and
tarts are available. Manager Janice reports
that on weekends, there may be GF bakery
selections for walk-ins. She recommends
notifying the bakery at least 48 hours in ad-
vance for pick-up orders. ▪ *www.clustered-*
spiresbakery.com

Clyde's $$**LD**
Chevy Chase ▪ *(301) 951-9600*
5441 Wisconsin Ave
Columbia ▪ *(410) 730-2829*
10221 Wincopin Cir ▪ American ▪ Managers at each location note that GF diners

are frequent and the chefs know how to accommodate them. Alert a server, who will confer with the chef about GF menu modifications. ▪ *www.clydes.com*

Comus Inn at Sugarloaf Mountain, The
$$$D

Dickerson ▪ (301) 349-5100
23900 Old Hundred Rd ▪ *Modern American* ▪ Chef Jose reports that the restaurant serves GF diners "about twice a week." He recommends alerting the server, who will speak to the chef about GF options. He also suggests that if GF diners know what they would like when they make their reservation, he is happy to accommodate those requests. ▪ *www.thecomusinn.com*

Donna's Restaurant   ★ $$LD
Columbia ▪ (410) 465-2399
5850 Waterloo Rd ▪ *Mediterranean* ▪ GF pizza is available at listed locations only. ▪ *www.donnas.com*

First Watch - The Daytime Café   📖
Pikesville ▪ (410) 602-1595
1431 Reisterstown Rd
Rockville ▪ (301) 762-0621
100 Gibbs St

Flying Avocado, The   ★ ¢BL
Owings Mills ▪ (443) 471-2600
10210 S Dolfield Rd ▪ *Organic* ▪ GF waffles are available for breakfast before 11am, and GF wraps and breads are available for lunch. ▪ *www.flyingavocado.com*

Freedom Bakery   100% $BL
Severna Park ▪ (410) 975-0261
568 Ritchie Hwy ▪ *Bakery & Café* ▪ Dedicated GF bakery serving sandwiches, pancakes, waffles, cookies, omelets, salads, and breads. The bakery reports that GF birthday cakes are available with advanced notice of at least 48 hours. ▪ *www.thefreedombakery.com*

Giovanni's Restaurant $$$LD
Edgewood ▪ (410) 676-8100
2101 Pulaski Hwy ▪ *Italian* ▪ Manager Dana reports that the restaurant serves GF diners

often, and they have even hosted parties for GF groups. He notes that they are "happy to work around" GF restrictions. While the restaurant does not have GF pasta, Dana welcomes GF customers to bring their own. Alert a server, who will confer with the chef about GF options. ▪ *www.giovannis-rest.com*

Grapeseed $$$D
Bethesda ▪ (301) 986-9592
4865 Cordell Ave ▪ *Modern American* ▪ Manager Ernie reports that GF diners are "accommodated regularly" and recommends reservations noting GF. He reports the sautéed calamari, slow-roasted porkbelly, and quinoa stuffed squash can all be prepared GF. Confirm timeliness of this information before dining in. ▪ *www.grapeseedbistro.com*

Great Sage   ✪★ $LD
Clarksville ▪ (443) 535-9400
5809 Clarksville Square Dr ▪ *Vegetarian* ▪ GF items marked on the menu include herbed quinoa with shiitakes, truffled polenta, and artichoke mushroom paella. GF bread, pasta, and beer are available. For dessert, they offer peanut butter cup cheesecake, apple caramel lasagna, and raw chocolate mousse. ▪ *www.great-sage.com*

Greene Turtle Sports Bar & Grill, The
✪ ¢LD

Aberdeen ▪ (410) 942-4020
1113 Beards Hill Rd
Columbia ▪ (410) 312-5255
8872 Mcgaw Rd
Easton ▪ (410) 763-7303
8249 Teal Dr
Edgewater ▪ (410) 956-1144
3213 Solomons Island Rd Ste A
Frederick ▪ (301) 698-1979
50 Citizens Way
Germantown ▪ (240) 686-1800
19961 Century Blvd
Hagerstown ▪ (301) 745-8800
12818 Shank Farm Way Ste A
Hanover ▪ (410) 799-5001
7556 Teague Rd

La Plata ▪ *(301) 392-9119*
6 Saint Marys Ave
Laurel ▪ *(301) 317-6650*
14150 Baltimore Ave
Mount Airy ▪ *(301) 829-9229*
1604 Ridgeside Dr
Ocean City ▪ *(410) 723-2120*
11601 Coastal Hwy
Ocean City ▪ *(410) 213-1500*
9616 Stephen Decatur Hwy
Prince Frederick ▪ *(410) 414-5030*
98 Solomons Island Rd S
Salisbury ▪ *(410) 860-9991*
2618 N Salisbury Blvd
Towson ▪ *(410) 825-3980*
408 York Rd
Westminster ▪ *(410) 871-1524*
830 Market St ▪ *American* ▪ GF menu includes spinach, artichoke, and jalapeno dip, buffalo chicken wings, roasted chicken, terrapin steak, apple walnut salad, french fries, crab soup, and more. ▪ *www.greene-turtle.com*

Grump's Café   ★ ¢**BLD**
Annapolis ▪ *(410) 267-0229*
117 Hillsmere Dr ▪ *Café* ▪ GF french toast is available. It can be made with GF banana, cranberry, or blueberry bread. ▪ *www.grumpscafe.com*

Harbor House Restaurant $$$**D**
Chestertown ▪ *(410) 778-0669*
23145 Buck Neck Rd ▪ *American Regional* ▪ Chef Robert reports that he will visit the table to ensure that "dietary needs are taken care of." He notes that the crab cakes, the crab imperial, and the filet mignon are GF. For dessert, they offer bananas flambé. Confirm timeliness of this information before dining in. ▪ *www.harborhousewcm.com*

Hunter's Inn, The $$$**LD**
Potomac ▪ *(301) 299-9300*
10123 River Rd ▪ *American* ▪ Manager Cathy reports that the restaurant is familiar with the GF diet. She notes that they have one "regular" who comes in "all the time" and is GF. Alert a server, who will notify

the kitchen. Kitchen staff prepares GF food separately. ▪ *www.thehuntersinn.com*

Italian Market, The   ★ $**LD**
Annapolis ▪ *(410) 224-1330*
126 Defense Hwy
Gambrills ▪ *(410) 721-1080*
2404 Brandermill Blvd ▪ *Italian* ▪ GF pizza is available. Manager Craig at the Annapolis location notes that "many GF diners" come in. Managers at both locations note that pizza is the only thing they can make GF. ▪ *www.theitalianmarket.com*

Jaleo Bethesda   ✪ $$$$**LD**
Bethesda ▪ *(301) 913-0003*
7271 Woodmont Ave ▪ *Tapas* ▪ GF menu includes paellas, a grilled hangar steak tapas, a duck confit tapas, and a traditional chorizo tapas, and more. General Manager Joseph recommends speaking to a manager upon arrival. ▪ *www.jaleo.com*

Lebanese Taverna   ✪ $$**LD**
Bethesda ▪ *(301) 951-8681*
7141 Arlington Rd ▪ *Middle Eastern* ▪ GF menu includes lentil soup, lamb shanks, shwarma, chicken and rice, jumbo shrimp, and more. ▪ *www.lebanesetaverna.com*

Legal Sea Foods   📖
Bethesda ▪ *(301) 469-5900*
7101 Democracy Blvd

Lilit Café   ✪★ ¢**BLD**
Bethesda ▪ *(301) 654-5454*
7921 Old Georgetown Rd ▪ *Café* ▪ Extensive GF menu includes breakfast, sandwiches, appetizers, entrées, and baked goods. GF bread, pizza, beer, and soy sauce are available. For dessert, GF tarts, cupcakes, cookies, and cakes are available. ▪ *www.lilitcafe.com*

Lone Star Steakhouse & Saloon   📖
Lexington Park ▪ *(301) 863-7277*
46590 Corporate Dr
Waldorf ▪ *(301) 870-0949*
11075 Mall Cir

Lures Bar and Grille $$**LD**
Crownsville ▪ *(410) 923-1606*

1397 Generals Hwy ■ American ■ Manager Mike reports that they serve GF diners "quite a bit." Alert a server, as servers are generally aware of what menu items contain gluten, except in the case of daily specials. In any case, Mike notes that servers will always discuss with a manager or chef before placing GF orders. ■ *www.luresbarandgrille.com*

Mamma Lucia   ★ $$**LD**
Bethesda ■ (301) 907-3399
4916 Elm St
College Park ■ (301) 513-0605
4734 Cherry Hill Rd
Elkridge ■ (410) 872-4894
6630 Marie Curie Dr
Frederick ■ (301) 694-2600
1700 Kingfisher Dr
Olney ■ (301) 570-9500
18224 Village Center Dr
Rockville ■ (301) 770-4894
12274 Rockville Pike Ste M
Rockville ■ (301) 762-8805
14921 Shady Grove Rd Unit J
Silver Spring ■ (301) 562-0693
1302 E West Hwy ■ *Italian* ■ GF pizza and pasta are available. The Elkridge, Bethesda, and Shady Grove Rd locations also offer GF beer. ■ *www.mammaluciarestaurants.com*

Melting Pot, The   📖
Annapolis ■ (410) 266-8004
2348 Solomons Island Rd
Columbia ■ (410) 740-9988
10451 Twin Rivers Rd Ste 130
Gaithersburg ■ (301) 519-3638
9021 Gaither Rd
Towson ■ (410) 821-6358
418 York Rd # 420

Mon Ami Gabi   ✪ $$$**LD**
Bethesda ■ (301) 654-1234
7239 Woodmont Ave ■ *French* ■ GF menu includes chicken liver mousse, seared sea scallops, lemon chicken paillard, steak béarnaise, and more. For dessert, chocolate mousse, crème brûlée, and a pear parfait are available. ■ *www.monamigabi.com*

Monocacy Crossing   ✪ $$$**LD**
Frederick ■ (301) 846-4204
4424A Urbana Pike ■ *American* ■ Manager Allie reports that the GF menu is a copy of the regular menu with GF items highlighted. She adds that GF diners come to the restaurant "all the time," and most of the staff is GF aware. Alert a server, who will go over the GF menu in detail. ■ *www.monocacycrossing.com*

Original Pancake House, The   ★ ¢**BL**
Bethesda ■ (301) 986-0285
7700 Wisconsin Ave
Rockville ■ (301) 468-0886
12224 Rockville Pike ■ *Breakfast* ■ GF pancakes are available. Select locations may serve other GF items. Call a specific location to inquire. ■ *www.originalpancakehouse.com*

Outback Steakhouse   📖
Annapolis ■ (410) 266-7229
2207 Forest Dr
Bel Air ■ (410) 893-0110
615 Bel Air Rd
Bowie ■ (301) 464-5800
6868 Race Track Rd
California ■ (301) 863-5530
23415 Three Notch Rd
Ellicott City ■ (410) 480-0472
4420 Long Gate Pkwy
Frederick ■ (301) 662-9584
1007 W Patrick St
Germantown ■ (301) 353-9499
12609 Wisteria Dr
Glen Burnie ■ (410) 863-0045
7744 Governor Ritchie Hwy
Hagerstown ■ (240) 420-6868
240 Railway Ln
Hunt Valley ■ (410) 527-1540
134 Shawan Rd
Hyattsville ■ (301) 853-5959
3500 East West Hwy
La Plata ■ (301) 934-9599
6649 Crain Hwy
Largo ■ (301) 322-6444
9660 Lottsford Ct
Laurel ■ (301) 317-8401

15107 Sweitzer Ln
Ocean City ▪ (410) 213-2595
12741 Ocean Gtwy
Owings Mills ▪ (410) 363-2282
10904 Boulevard Circle
Oxon Hill ▪ (301) 839-4300
6091 Oxon Hill Rd
Prince Frederick ▪ (443) 486-4913
80 Central Square Dr
Salisbury ▪ (410) 341-7355
8245 Dickerson Ln
Silver Spring ▪ (301) 933-4385
13703 Georgia Ave
Waldorf ▪ (301) 645-4120
3020 Crain Hwy

P.F. Chang's China Bistro   📖
Annapolis ▪ (410) 573-2990
307 Sail Pl
Columbia ▪ (410) 730-5344
10300 Little Patuxent Pkwy Ste 3020
Kensington ▪ (301) 230-6933
11301 Rockville Pike Spc 1-4.1
Nottingham ▪ (410) 931-2433
8342 Honeygo Blvd
Towson ▪ (410) 372-5250
825 Dulaney Valley Rd Ste 1161

Pei Wei Asian Diner   📖
Columbia ▪ (410) 423-2550
6478 Dobbin Center Way Ste A

Piccola Roma   ★ $$$D
Annapolis ▪ (410) 268-7898
200 Main St ▪ Italian ▪ GF pasta is available. ▪ *www.piccolaromaannapolis.com*

Planet Pizza and Subs   ★ $$LD
Rockville ▪ (301) 762-9400
819 Hungerford Dr ▪ Pizza ▪ GF pizza is available. Manager Ali reports that the restaurant does its best to accommodate GF diners, and especially during off hours, menu items can be modified to be GF. ▪ *www.planetpizzaandsubs.com*

Rí~Rá Irish Pub $LD
Bethesda ▪ (301) 657-1122
4931 Elm St ▪ Irish Pub ▪ Ask for the "Allergen Chart," which has a "Celiac" column.

This column contains items that are GF or can be modified to be GF. ▪ *www.rira.com*

ROMA'S CAFÉ $$$LD
Cockeysville ▪ (410) 628-6565
10515 York Rd ▪ Italian ▪ Manager Jose reports that the restaurant serves "a few" GF diners. He recommends reservations noting GF, so the kitchen staff can prepare to cook food separately. ▪ *www.romascafe. com*

Roscoe's Neapolitan Pizzeria   ★ $$LD
Takoma Park ▪ (301) 920-0804
7040 Carroll Ave ▪ Italian ▪ GF pizza is available. Any toppings are available on the woodfired GF pizza crust. ▪ *www.roscoespizzeria.com*

Shane's Rib Shack   📖
Laurel ▪ (301) 725-2020
13600 Baltimore Ave

Tenzo Artisan   ✪★ ¢S
Frederick ▪ (410) 302-6233
285 Montevue Ln ▪ Bakery ▪ GF breads, hamburger buns, cookies, pies, cakes, brownies, and more are available. They offer pastries every day, but cakes for special occasions are available upon request. ▪ *www.tenzoartisan.com*

Toppings Pizza Company   ★ $$LD
Frederick ▪ (301) 668-2040
5330 New Design Rd
Hagerstown ▪ (240) 625-9025
11205 John F Kennedy Dr ▪ Pizza ▪ GF pizza is available at both locations. ▪ *www. toppingspizza.com*

Tower Oaks Lodge $$LD
Rockville ▪ (301) 294-0200
2 Preserve Pkwy ▪ American ▪ Chef Caesar reports that GF is the "allergy" they accommodate most frequently. He notes that any steak, fish, or the pork chops can be prepared GF. Confirm timeliness of this information before dining in. Alert a server, as servers are trained to communicate GF requests to the chefs and managers. ▪ *www. toweroakslodge.com*

Uno Chicago Grill   📖

Bowie ▪ (301) 352-5320
4001 Town Center Blvd
Columbia ▪ (410) 964-9945
10300 Little Patuxent Pkwy
Ellicott City ▪ (410) 480-1400
4470 Long Gate Pkwy
Frederick ▪ (301) 668-2512
5449 Urbana Pike
Fruitland ▪ (410) 334-6565
100 E Cedar Ln
Hagerstown ▪ (240) 420-1919
17734 Garland Groh Blvd
Oakland ▪ (301) 387-4866
19746 Garrett Hwy

Vegetable Garden   ★ $LD

Rockville ▪ (301) 468-9301
11618 Rockville Pike ▪ *Vegetarian Chinese*
▪ Manager George reports that WF soy
sauce and GF rice noodles are available.
He also reports that over half of the menu,
including soups and tofu dishes, is GF.
He notes that the restaurant can "always
accommodate" GF diners. ▪ *www.theveg-
etablegarden.com*

Visions Restaurant   ✪★ $LD

Bethesda ▪ (301) 654-3737
4926 Saint Elmo Ave ▪ *American* ▪ GF
menu includes appetizers, salads, entrées,
and desserts. Rice noodles are available for
substitution into any pasta dish. GF soy
sauce is available, as is GF beer. For dessert,
there is a flourless chocolate cake, among
other things. ▪ *www.visionsbethesda.com*

Watermans Seafood Co. $$$LD

Ocean City ▪ (410) 213-1020
12505 Ocean Gtwy ▪ *Seafood* ▪ Cook
Tony reports that GF diners should alert
the server, who will confer with the cooks.
He notes that though the servers are not
familiar with the GF diet, kitchen staff
members are well-trained. He adds that any
fish on the menu can be prepared GF and
recommends that GF diners order broiled
fish. Confirm timeliness of this information
before dining in. ▪ *www.watermansseafood-
company.com*

Wild Orchid, The $$$$LD

Annapolis ▪ (410) 268-8009
909 Bay Ridge Ave ▪ *Modern American*
▪ Manager Dan reports that the restaurant
accommodates GF diners "more often than
you'd think." He advises making reservations noting GF and alerting the server
upon arrival. Many menu items can be
modified to be GF. Crème brûlée and other
custom-made options are available with
advanced notice. ▪ *www.thewildorchidcafe.
com*

MASSACHUSETTS

BOSTON

Bertucci's   📖

Boston ▪ (617) 739-2492
1 Blackfan Cir
Boston ▪ (617) 227-7889
22 Merchants Row
Boston ▪ (617) 236-1030
533 Commonwealth Ave

Brasserie Jo $$$BLD

Boston ▪ (617) 425-3240
120 Huntington Ave ▪ *French* ▪ Maitre d'
Hugo reports that they provide "little pink
forms" to diners with "allergies." GF diners complete the form, and the restaurant
staff will work together to prepare a meal
according to the customer's guidelines. He
notes that GF diners are "very common,"
and the servers are very familiar with the
GF diet. The restaurant is located in the
Colonnade Hotel. ▪ *www.brasseriejoboston.
com*

Burtons Grill   ✪★ $LD

Boston ▪ (617) 236-2236
1363 Boylston St ▪ *American* ▪ Extensive
GF menu includes salads, cheeseburgers on
GF buns, risotto of the day, and jambalaya.

GF hamburger buns are available. ▪ *www.burtonsgrill.com*

Capital Grille, The　📖
Boston ▪ *(617) 262-8900*
359 Newbury St

Charley's　★ $$**LD**
Boston ▪ *(617) 266-3000*
284 Newbury St ▪ *American* ▪ GF pasta and pizza are available. ▪ *www.charleys-restaurant.com*

Chocolate Bar at Café Fleuri　$$$$$
Boston ▪ *(617) 451-1900*
250 Franklin St ▪ *Desserterie & Bakery* ▪ Head pastry chef Jed reports that "a lot" of GF diners have safely dined at the chocolate buffet. He notes that nearly half of the items are GF, including chocolate mousses, the white chocolate strawberry parfait, the cognac torte, and more. He recommends asking for him upon arrival, and he will lead a walk-through of the buffet, indicating GF items. Located inside The Langham Hotel. Open every Saturday, by reservation only.

Elephant Walk, The　✪ $$**LD**
Boston ▪ *(617) 247-1500*
900 Beacon St ▪ *Cambodian & French* ▪ GF menu includes shrimp curry, steak with potato gratin, and more. Most soups and salads are GF. GF desserts like chocolate truffle cake and sorbet are also available. Hands-on GF cooking classes are offered. ▪ *www.elephantwalk.com*

Equal Exchange Café　★ ¢**BLD**
Boston ▪ *(617) 372-8777*
226 Causeway St ▪ *Café* ▪ GF muffins and cookies are delivered fresh on Mondays, Wednesdays, and Fridays; GF coffeecake is delivered on Wednesdays. Manager Adina notes that these items are available all week long, but are freshest on Monday, Wednesday, and Friday afternoons. ▪ *www.equalexchangecafe.com*

Finale Dessert Company　★ $$
Boston ▪ *(617) 423-3184*

1 Columbus Ave ▪ *Desserterie & Bakery* ▪ GF desserts include the flourless dark chocolate decadence cake, the original cheesecake, coconut cream tarts, and a variety of puddings. Confirm timeliness of this information before dining in. Servers are familiar with GF desserts and will be able to indicate GF items. ▪ *www.finaledesserts.com*

Fire + Ice　★ $$**LD**
Boston ▪ *(617) 482-3473*
205 Berkeley St ▪ *Asian Stir-Fry* ▪ GF rice noodles are available. Restaurant Supervisor Luciana reports that it is "very easy" to create a GF meal. Diners pick out their own ingredients, so the meals are flexible. Meals can include vegetables, seafood, poultry, or selections from the salad bar. Luciana also notes that GF diners can request that their food be cooked separately. ▪ *www.fire-ice.com*

Grill 23 & Bar　$$$$**D**
Boston ▪ *(617) 542-2255*
161 Berkeley St ▪ *Modern American* ▪ Chef Mark notes that restaurant staff is very "knowledgeable about allergies," including gluten. He recommends noting GF in reservations and bringing a GF dining card. The menu varies, but chefs can usually modify seafood and steak dishes to be GF. Confirm timeliness of this information before dining in. ▪ *www.grill23.com*

Hamersley's Bistro　$$$$**D**
Boston ▪ *(617) 423-2700*
553 Tremont St ▪ *Modern American* ▪ Manager Erin reports that GF diners are frequent. She notes that waiters are "very knowledgeable" about the GF diet. Many dishes can be modified to be GF. Dessert options include crème brûlée, lemon semi-freddo, meringue, and chocolate mousse. ▪ *www.hamersleysbistro.com*

Ivy　$$**LD**
Boston ▪ *(617) 963-1534*
49 Temple Pl ▪ *Fusion* ▪ Restaurant reports that several GF diners have been accom-

modated in the past. They also note that the chef usually caters to GF diners by making something that is not on the menu. Upon arrival, alert the server, and ask to speak with the chef about GF options. Reservations noting GF are recommended. ▪ *www.ivyrestaurantgroup.com*

Joe's American Bar & Grill $LD
Boston ▪ (617) 367-8700
100 Atlantic Ave
Boston ▪ (617) 536-4200
181 Newbury Street ▪ American ▪ GF pasta and pizza are available. Both can be prepared in several different ways. At each location, a manager recommends alerting the server about the "allergy." ▪ *www.joesamerican.com*

K.O. Prime $$$$BLD
Boston ▪ (617) 772-0202
90 Tremont St ▪ Steakhouse ▪ Manager Mark reports that the restaurant serves GF diners "here and there. " He notes that because they are a steakhouse and have a protein-heavy menu, it is easy to modify dishes to be GF. Alert a server, who will ask a chef if he or she is unsure whether an item is GF. ▪ *www.koprimeboston.com*

Legal Sea Foods   📖
Boston ▪ (617) 568-1888
1 Harborside Dr - Terminal A
Boston ▪ (617) 568-2811
1 Harborside Dr - Terminal B
Boston ▪ (617) 568-2800
1 Harborside Dr - Terminal C
Boston ▪ (617) 266-7775
100 Huntington Ave
Boston ▪ (617) 330-7430
225 Northern Ave
Boston ▪ (617) 742-5300
255 State St
Boston ▪ (617) 426-4444
26 Park Plz
Boston ▪ (617) 266-6800
800 Boylston St

Maggiano's Little Italy   ★ $$$LD
Boston ▪ (617) 542-3456

4 Columbus Ave ▪ Italian ▪ GF pasta is available. Call individual locations to inquire about additional GF options. ▪ *www.maggianos.com*

Melting Pot, The   📖
Boston ▪ (617) 357-7007
76 Arlington St

Nebo Ristorante and Enoteca ✪★ $$D
Boston ▪ (617) 723-6326
90 N Washington St ▪ Italian ▪ Extensive GF menu includes all pasta and pizza dishes from the regular menu. Examples are pasta with homemade sweet sausage, broccoli rabe, and pecorino romano or pizza with fresh ricotta, artichoke hearts, caramelized onions, and mozzarella. For dessert, they offer panna cotta chocolate and nutella pizza. ▪ *www.neborestaurant.com*

P.F. Chang's China Bistro   📖
Boston ▪ (617) 573-0821
8 Park Plz Spc D-6
Boston ▪ (617) 378-9961
Prudential Tower

Papa Razzi   ★ $$LD
Boston ▪ (617) 536-9200
271 Dartmouth St ▪ Italian ▪ GF pasta and pizza are available. ▪ *www.paparazzitrattoria.com*

Skipjack's $$$LD
Boston ▪ (617) 536-3500
199 Clarendon St ▪ Seafood ▪ Manager Emily reports that the staff is "very knowledgeable" about the GF diet. She recommends noting GF in reservations to make the servers aware in advance. Most seafood items can be modified to be GF, and sides such as rice and baked potatoes are available. Confirm timeliness of this information before dining in. ▪ *www.skipjacks.com*

Smith & Wollensky $$$$D
Boston ▪ (617) 423-1112
101 Arlington St ▪ Steakhouse ▪ General Manager Wayne reports that nearly all of the regular menu items, including steaks

and the ahi tuna, are naturally GF or can be prepared GF. He recommends speaking with a manager upon arrival. ▪ *www.smithandwollensky.com*

Stephanie's on Newbury $$$LD
Boston ▪ *(617) 236-0990*
190 Newbury St ▪ *Modern American* ▪ Manager Riley reports that the restaurant accommodates GF diners "every day." He advises alerting the server, who will notify the chef and manager. He also notes that the chefs are happy to speak directly to GF diners. ▪ *www.stephaniesonnewbury.com*

Tremont 647 $$$D
Boston ▪ *(617) 266-4600*
647 Tremont St ▪ *American* ▪ The restaurant notes that the kitchen always accommodates dietary restrictions and will work with GF diners to come up with GF options. Reservations noting GF are recommended. ▪ *www.tremont647.com*

U Food Grill 📖
Boston ▪ *(617) 567-2214*
1 Harborside Dr
Boston ▪ *(857) 254-0082*
201 Brookline Ave
Boston ▪ *(617) 451-0043*
530 Washington St

Uno Chicago Grill 📖
Boston ▪ *(617) 323-9200*
100 Charles Park Rd
Boston ▪ *(617) 424-1697*
280 Huntington Ave
Boston ▪ *(617) 262-4911*
645 Beacon St
Boston ▪ *(617) 267-8554*
731 Boylston St

Wagamama   ★ $LD
Boston ▪ *(617) 742-9242*
1 Faneuil Hall Sq ▪ *Asian* ▪ GF rice noodles are available upon request. A few soups, chilis, and noodle dishes can be modified to be GF. Confirm timeliness of this information before dining in. Manager Zach advises alerting the server, who will notify a manager. ▪ *www.wagamama.us*

MASSACHUSETTS

CAMBRIDGE

Bertucci's 📖
Cambridge ▪ *(617) 864-4748*
21 Brattle St
Cambridge ▪ *(617) 876-2200*
5 Cambridgepark Dr
Cambridge ▪ *(617) 661-8356*
799 Main St

Blue Room $$$D
Cambridge ▪ *(617) 494-9034*
1 Kendall Sq ▪ *Modern American* ▪ Manager Lindsey reports that "most of the menu" is naturally GF, and that they accommodate "a lot" of GF diners. The Scottish salmon with wild rice is just one example a menu item that can be modified to be GF. Alert a server upon arrival. ▪ *www.theblueroom.net*

Casablanca $$$LD
Cambridge ▪ *(617) 876-0999*
40 Brattle St ▪ *Modern American* ▪ Manager Nicole advises alerting a server upon arrival. Many dishes, such as the tuna tapas and certain dips, can be modified to be GF. Confirm timeliness of this information before dining in. ▪ *www.casablanca-restaurant.com*

Elephant Walk, The   ✪ $LD
Cambridge ▪ *(617) 492-6900*
2067 Massachusetts Ave ▪ *Cambodian & French* ▪ GF menu includes shrimp curry, steak with potato gratin, and more. Most soups and salads are GF. GF desserts like chocolate truffle cake and sorbet are also available. Hands-on GF cooking classes are offered. ▪ *www.elephantwalk.com*

Finale Dessert Company $S
Cambridge ▪ *(617) 441-9797*
30 Dunster St ▪ *Desserterie & Bakery* ▪ GF desserts include the flourless dark chocolate decadence cake, the original cheesecake, coconut cream tarts, and a variety of puddings. Confirm timeliness of

this information before dining in. Servers are familiar with GF desserts and will be able to indicate the GF items. ▪ *www.finaledesserts.com*

Fire + Ice $$LD
Cambridge ▪ *(617) 547-9007*
50 Church St ▪ *Asian Stir-Fry* ▪ Restaurant reports that all servers can indicate GF sauce options. They note that meats, seafood, and vegetables can be prepared in the kitchen with a fresh pan, rather than on common cooking surfaces. Alert a server, who will make arrangements with the kitchen. ▪ *www.fire-ice.com*

John Harvard's Brew House $$LD
Cambridge ▪ *(617) 868-3585*
33 Dunster St ▪ *American* ▪ Restaurants report serving GF diners frequently. They recommend alerting a server, who will get a manager or chef if he or she has any questions about GF options. Servers have varying degrees of knowledge regarding the GF diet. ▪ *www.johnharvards.com*

Legal Sea Foods   📖
Cambridge ▪ *(617) 491-9400*
20 University Rd
Cambridge ▪ *(617) 864-3400*
5 Cambridge Ctr

Oxford Spa Café   ¢BL
Cambridge ▪ *(617) 661-6988*
102 Oxford St ▪ *Sandwich Shop* ▪ Manager KC reports that the restaurant is able to accommodate GF diners. Salads, vegetables, and sandwiches without bread can be made GF. KC adds that "staff is trained" on the GF diet and "will know what to do."

P.F. Chang's China Bistro   📖
Cambridge ▪ *(617) 250-9965*
100 Cambridgeside Pl Ste C101

Rialto   ✪★ $$$$D
Cambridge ▪ *(617) 661-5050*
1 Bennett St ▪ *Modern Mediterranean* ▪ GF pasta is available. GF menu includes antipasti from the sea, grilled littlenecks, fisherman's soup, risotto, seared char, and rabbit leg. The restaurant requests that GF diners alert a server of any GF needs. ▪ *www.rialto-restaurant.com*

Stone Hearth Pizza Co.   ✪★ $LD
Cambridge ▪ *(617) 492-1111*
1782 Massachusetts Ave ▪ *Pizza* ▪ GF items marked on the menu include pizza and pasta. For dessert, they ofer hot fudge sundaes and ice cream floats. ▪ *www.stone-hearthpizza.com*

Uno Chicago Grill   📖
Cambridge ▪ *(617) 497-1530*
22 Jfk St

Wagamama   ✪ $LD
Cambridge ▪ *(617) 499-0930*
57 Jfk St ▪ *Asian* ▪ GF rice noodles are available. Manager Tori reports that there are extensive GF options and that GF diners are frequently accommodated. She also notes that a manager will speak with GF diners to ensure that their needs are met. ▪ *www.wagamama.us*

Zing! Pizza   ★ $$LD
Cambridge ▪ *(617) 497-4300*
1923 Massachusetts Ave ▪ *Pizza* ▪ GF pizza is available. Restaurant reports that most of its toppings are also GF. Calling ahead is recommended but not required. ▪ *www.zingpizza.com*

MASSACHUSETTS
ALL OTHER CITIES

Alice's Diner   ✪★ ¢BL
Fall River ▪ *(508) 675-9210*
2663 S Main St ▪ *American* ▪ GF breakfast menu includes waffles, pancakes, and more. GF lunch menu includes hamburgers on GF bread and rotating GF daily specials like fish & chips. ▪ *www.alicesdiner.com*

ALLCANEAT Foods Ltd.   100% ¢BL
Randolph ▪ *(781) 905-1299*

937 N Main St ▪ *Bakery & Café* ▪ Bakery and café serving GF bread, frozen dinners including chicken marsala, steak tips, and meatloaf, as well as salads and sandwiches from the café. GF cookies and cupcakes are available for dessert. ▪ *www.allcaneat.com*

Amanouz Café   ¢BLD
Northampton ▪ *(413) 585-9128*
44 Main St ▪ *Mediterranean* ▪ Veteran Server Jacob reports that the restaurant serves GF diners "a lot." He notes that most salads are GF, and all sandwiches can be ordered on rice instead of with bread. He also notes that many entrées, like the tagines, are GF. Confirm timeliness of this information before dining in. He recommends alerting the server/cashier, who will discuss GF options and ask the chef any questions. ▪ *www.amanouz.com*

Angelo's Pizzeria & Ristorante ★ $$$LD
Stoneham ▪ *(781) 438-8598*
239 Main St ▪ *Italian* ▪ GF pasta, pizza, and beer are available. Owner Angelo notes that acccommodating GF requests is "no problem." Menu items that can be modified to be GF include eggplant dishes, chicken, veal, and several seafood dishes. Upon arrival, alert the server, who will talk to the kitchen. Reservations noting GF are recommended. ▪ *www.angeloristorante.com*

Bacon Street Farm   ★ ¢BLD
Natick ▪ *(508) 653-4851*
100 Bacon St ▪ *Take-&-Bake* ▪ GF bread, cookies, brownies, cookies, and frozen meals are available. Gourmet deli does not make sandwiches, and no seating is available. ▪ *www.baconstreetfarm.com*

Baku's $LD
Amherst ▪ *(413) 253-7202*
197 N Pleasant St ▪ *African* ▪ All menu items are GF, including appetizers, soups, and entrées. Examples of entrees are the sautéed shrimp with onions, curry chicken, and Nigerian stew. Confirm timeliness of this information before dining in. ▪ *www. bakusafricanrestaurant.com*

Bertucci's   📖
Amherst ▪ *(413) 549-1900*
51 E Pleasant St
Andover ▪ *(978) 470-3939*
90 Main St
Beverly ▪ *(978) 927-6866*
27 Enon St
Braintree ▪ *(781) 849-3066*
412 Franklin St
Brockton ▪ *(508) 584-3080*
1285 Belmont St
Canton ▪ *(781) 828-9901*
95 Washington St
Chelmsford ▪ *(978) 250-8800*
14 Littleton Rd
Chestnut Hill ▪ *(617) 965-0022*
300 Boylston St
Chestnut Hill ▪ *(617) 327-0898*
683 Vfw Pkwy
Framingham ▪ *(508) 879-9161*
150 Worcester Rd
Hingham ▪ *(781) 740-4405*
90 Derby St
Holliston ▪ *(508) 429-4571*
414 Washington St
Lexington ▪ *(781) 860-9000*
1777 Massachusetts Ave
Longmeadow ▪ *(413) 567-4900*
674 Bliss Rd
Mansfield ▪ *(508) 261-2371*
280 School St
Marlborough ▪ *(508) 460-0911*
374 Boston Post Rd E
Marlborough ▪ *(508) 485-3636*
601 Donald Lynch Blvd
Medford ▪ *(781) 396-9933*
4054 Mystic Valley Pkwy
Needham ▪ *(781) 449-3777*
1257 Highland Ave
Newton ▪ *(617) 244-4900*
275 Centre St
North Andover ▪ *(978) 685-4498*
435 Andover St
North Attleboro ▪ *(508) 699-2491*
999 S Washington St
Norwood ▪ *(781) 762-4155*
1405 Boston Providence Tpke Ste 1-5
Peabody ▪ *(978) 535-0969*

15 Newbury St
Plymouth ▪ (508) 747-1187
6 Plaza Way
Randolph ▪ (781) 986-8333
55 Mazzeo Dr
Reading ▪ (781) 942-2001
45 Walkers Brook Dr
Swampscott ▪ (781) 581-6588
450 Paradise Rd
Taunton ▪ (508) 880-0222
2 Galleria Mall Dr
Waltham ▪ (781) 684-0650
475 Winter St
Wellesley ▪ (781) 239-0990
380 Washington St
West Springfield ▪ (413) 788-9900
847 Riverdale St
Westborough ▪ (508) 898-3074
160 Turnpike Road Rte 9
Woburn ▪ (781) 933-1440
17 Commerce Way

Beth's Specialty Teas, Bakery, & Café
★ ¢S

Sandwich ▪ (508) 888-7716
16 Jarves St ▪ Bakery & Café ▪ GF cookies,
muffins, and cupcakes are available. Call in
advance to request a particular GF product,
as the GF offerings change frequently. ▪
www.capecodteashop.com

Blue Ginger
★ $$$$LD

Wellesley ▪ (781) 283-5790
583 Washington St ▪ Asian Fusion ▪ Manager Erica reports that both of the signature dishes can be prepared GF. She notes
that they see "a lot" of GF diners "coming
through." Note GF when making reservations, and alert the server upon arrival.
GF fish sauce and GF tamari soy sauce are
available. ▪ www.ming.com/blueginger

Blue Ribbon Bakery, The
100% $S

Marlborough ▪ (508) 317-1767
63 Worster Dr ▪ Bakery ▪ Dedicated GF
bakery offering pizza and pizza crusts, muffins, cookies, waffles, pancakes, brownies,
cakes, and more. Open from 2-5pm. Order
up to 24 hours in advance online. ▪ www.
theblueribbonbakery.com

Boynton Restaurant & Spirits, The
★ $LD

Worcester ▪ (508) 756-5432
117 Highland St ▪ Italian ▪ GF pizza and
chocolate mousse cake are available. ▪
www.boyntonrestaurant.com

British Beer Company Restaurant and Pub, The
✪★ $LD

East Walpole ▪ (508) 668-9909
85 Providence Hwy
Falmouth ▪ (508) 540-9600
263 Grand Ave
Framingham ▪ (508) 879-1776
120 Worcester Rd
Hyannis ▪ (508) 771-1776
412 Main St
Pembroke ▪ (781) 829-6999
15 Columbia Rd
Plymouth ▪ (508) 888-9756
2294 State Rd
Plymouth ▪ (508) 747-1776
6 Middle St
Sandwich ▪ (508) 833-9590
46 Route 6A ▪ American ▪ Extensive GF
menu includes spinach salad, chinese
chicken salad, steak salad, GF wraps,
burgers on GF buns, sweet plum salmon,
turkey tips, pizza, and more. GF beer is also
available. The Plymouth location does not
have a kitchen and thus does not serve the
GF menu; they do, however, serve GF beer.
▪ www.britishbeer.com

Bugaboo Creek Steak House
📖

Braintree ▪ (781) 848-0002
551 John Mahar Hwy
Brockton ▪ (508) 586-9345
540 Westgate Dr
Burlington ▪ (781) 221-3543
43 Middlesex Tpke
Dedham ▪ (781) 407-9890
850 Providence Hwy
Framingham ▪ (508) 370-9001
345 Cochituate Rd
Methuen ▪ (978) 794-9713
90 Pleasant Valley St
Milford ▪ (508) 478-2888
124 Medway Rd

Peabody ▪ *(978) 538-0100*
210 Andover St
Plymouth ▪ *(508) 747-6665*
20 Shops At 5 Way
Seekonk ▪ *(508) 336-2200*
1125 Fall River Ave
Shrewsbury ▪ *(508) 755-6600*
50 Boston Tpke
Watertown ▪ *(617) 924-9000*
617 Arsenal St

Bullfinchs Restaurant   ✪ $$$D
Sudbury ▪ *(978) 443-4094*
730 Boston Post Rd ▪ *American* ▪ GF
menu includes filet mignon, chicken piccata, roasted haddock filet, and a few other
items. Owner Margaret reports that even if
a GF diner prefers something that is not on
the GF menu, the chef will be happy to try
to accommodate. ▪ *www.bullfinchs.com*

Burtons Grill   ✪★ $$$LD
Hingham ▪ *(781) 749-1007*
94 Derby St
North Andover ▪ *(978) 688-5600*
145 Turnpike St ▪ *American* ▪ GF sandwich
buns and pasta are available. Extensive GF
lunch and dinner menus are offered. The
restaurant reports that it frequently accommodates GF diners. ▪ *www.burtonsgrill.com*

BZ's Pizzeria & Mexican   ★ ¢LD
Dennis Port ▪ *(508) 394-6247*
682 Main St ▪ *Pizza* ▪ GF pizza and beer
are available. Any of the pizzas on the
menu can be prepared on GF crust, or
customers can create their own pizzas on
GF crust. Pizzas are available for dining in,
take out, or delivery. ▪ *www.bzspizza.com*

Café Nicholas   ★ $$LD
Newton Center ▪ *(617) 969-1118*
740 Beacon St ▪ *Pizza* ▪ GF pizza and
cookies are available. ▪ *www.cafenicholas.*
com

Capital Grille, The   📖
Burlington ▪ *(781) 505-4130*
10 Wayside Rd
Chestnut Hill ▪ *(617) 928-1400*
250 Boylston St

Carmela's Restaurant at the Colonial Hotel $$D
Gardner ▪ *(978) 630-2322*
625 Betty Spring Rd ▪ *American* ▪ Manager Jason reports that they accommodate
GF diners "every once in awhile." He notes
that many dishes, like steaks and haddock,
can be modified to be GF. Alert a server
upon arrival. If the server cannot answer
questions about GF items, a manager or
chef will come to the table. ▪ *www.colonial-*
hotel.com

Carrabba's Italian Grill   📖
Peabody ▪ *(978) 535-3600*
1A Newbury St
Tyngsboro ▪ *(978) 649-8388*
386 Middlesex Rd
W Springfield ▪ *(413) 733-3960*
955 Riverdale St

Charley's   ★ $$LD
Chestnut Hill ▪ *(617) 964-1200*
199 Boylston St ▪ *American* ▪ GF pasta
and pizza are available. ▪ *www.charleys-*
restaurant.com

Chianti Café   ★ $$$D
Beverly ▪ *(978) 921-2233*
285 Cabot St ▪ *Italian* ▪ Zucchilini, a pasta
made from pure zucchini, is available. Restaurant reports that many menu items can
be modified to be GF. They recommend
bringing in a Spanish language dining card,
as much of the kitchen staff speaks Spanish. They know how to prepare GF meals,
however, and GF diners are welcome. Restaurant is adjacent to their newly-opened
jazz bar.

China Sky   ★ $$LD
Winchester ▪ *(781) 729-6899*
27 Converse Pl ▪ *Chinese* ▪ Manager William reports that GF is the most frequent
allergy request. GF soy sauce is available.
Reservations noting GF are recommended.

Chloe: An American Bistro $LD
Hudson ▪ *(978) 568-1500*
23 Main St ▪ *New England* ▪ Owner Matthew reports that GF diners come in "all

the time." When a GF diner arrives, the server goes through the menu and circles GF dishes. Matthew also notes that the kitchen is "very GF aware." Reservations noting GF are recommended. ■ *www.chloebistro.com*

City Feed and Supply ★ ¢**BLD**
Jamaica Plain ■ *(617) 524-1657*
66A Boylston St
Jamaica Plain ■ *(617) 524-1700*
672 Centre St ■ *Sandwich Shop* ■ At the Centre St location, GF bread is available for sandwiches. At both locations, GF baked goods like cookies and cupcakes are available in the grocery section. Some "take-&-bake" items such as waffles are also available. ■ *www.cityfeedandsupply.com*

Coffee Obsession ★ ¢**S**
Falmouth ■ *(508) 540-2233*
110 Palmer Ave
Woods Hole ■ *(508) 540-8130*
38 Water St ■ *Coffee Shop* ■ GF banana bread and banana muffins are "almost always" available at both locations.

Crown Bakery & Café, The ★ ¢**S**
Worcester ■ *(508) 852-0746*
133 Gold Star Blvd ■ *Bakery & Café* ■ Non-dedicated GF bakery offering GF baked goods like chocolate triangles, three different kinds of jelly rolls, cake, and more. GF options change daily, but Manager Jeanie reports that they will "always" have "something" that is GF. ■ *www.thecrownbakery.com*

David's Tavern on Brown Square $$**D**
Newburyport ■ *(978) 462-8077*
11 Brown Sq ■ *Global* ■ Owner and Chef Steve reports that they accommodate "almost any allergy." There are many grilled steak dishes, like filet mignon, steak tips, and prime rib, on the menu, and they can all be prepared GF. He adds that the restaurant serves GF diners "quite often," so the staff is familiar with the GF diet. ■ *www.davidstavern.com*

Deja Brew Cafe & Pub ★ $**D**
Wendell ■ *(978) 544-2739*
57 A Lockes Village Rd ■ *Italian* ■ GF pizza and pasta are available. Cook Audrey recommends calling ahead to note GF requests, and she adds that the kitchen is very well-educated on GF dining. ■ *www.dejabrewpub.com*

Diesel Café ★ ¢**S**
Somerville ■ *(617) 629-8717*
257 Elm St ■ *Café* ■ Café reports that they are "very sensitive" to GF diners and can accommodate them "without a problem." GF pastries are available, but offerings change daily. Possible GF options include macaroons, bars, brownies, cookies, and salads. Other items can be prepared GF; for example, sandwiches can be served without bread. Upon arrival, alert a server, who will speak with a manager about the day's GF offerings. ■ *www.diesel-cafe.com*

Eastside Grill $$**D**
Northampton ■ *(413) 586-3347*
19 Strong Ave ■ *Modern American* ■ Owner Deborah reports that the staff is very knowledgeable about which menu items are or can be modified to be GF. She notes that all dressings do contain mustard seed, so they may not be GF. ■ *www.eastsidegrill.com*

Elephant Walk, The ☺ $**LD**
Waltham ■ *(781) 899-2244*
663 Main St ■ *Cambodian & French* ■ GF menu includes shrimp curry, steak with potato gratin, and more. Most soups and salads are GF. GF desserts like chocolate truffle cake and sorbet are also available. Hands-on GF cooking classes are offered. ■ *www.elephantwalk.com*

Evo ☺★ $$**BLD**
Worcester ■ *(508) 459-4240*
234 Chandler St ■ *Modern American* ■ Extensive GF menu includes spinach dip, toast, french toast, steak, swordfish, baby spinach salad, and several wraps. GF sand-

wich breads and burger buns are available. ▪ *www.evodining.com*

EVOO Restaurant $$$D
Somerville ▪ *(617) 661-3866*
118 Beacon St ▪ *Modern American* ▪ Server Tim reports that they accommodate GF diners "all the time." He notes that the smoked rabbit cone feet salad and the beef tenderloin are naturally GF, while other items such as the oysters can be modified to be GF. Confirm timeliness of this information before dining in. For dessert, they serve crème brulee. ▪ *www.evoorestaurant. com*

Finale Dessert Company $$
Brookline ▪ *(617) 232-3233*
1306 Beacon St ▪ *Desserterie & Bakery* ▪ GF desserts include the flourless dark chocolate decadence cake, the original cheesecake, coconut cream tarts, and a variety of puddings. Confirm timeliness of this information before dining in. Servers are familiar with GF desserts and will be able to indicate the GF items. ▪ *www. finaledesserts.com*

Fireplace, The   ✪★ $$$LD
Brookline ▪ *(617) 975-1900*
1634 Beacon St ▪ *Modern American* ▪ GF menu includes crumble carrot and fresh thyme risotto, braised beef short ribs, and pan roasted duck, among other things. Owner and Chef Jim reports that they expect to have GF bread and desserts soon. GF beer is available. ▪ *www.fireplacerest. com*

Fitzwilly's $LD
Northampton ▪ *(413) 584-8666*
23 Main St ▪ *American* ▪ Manager Matt reports that GF diners are "very easily" accommodated. Menu items that can be modified to be GF include chicken breast with pico de gallo, seared tuna, and spinach and artichoke hearts. Confirm timeliness of this information before dining in. ▪ *www. fitzwillys.com*

Five Bites Cupcakes   ★ ¢S
Wellesley ▪ *(781) 235-5755*
141 Linden St ▪ *Bakery* ▪ Manager Cathy reports that GF cupcakes are available Wednesday afternoons through Saturday. GF flavors are vanilla, strawberry, and snickerdoodle. Cathy advises that GF cupcakes sometimes sell out, so call ahead to have some set aside. ▪ *www.5bitescupcakes. com*

Flatbread Pizza Company   ★ $LD
Amesbury ▪ *(978) 834-9800*
5 Market Sq
Bedford ▪ *(781) 275-8200*
213 Burlington Rd ▪ *Pizza* ▪ GF pizza is available in the 8-inch size. GF beer and desserts are also available. Typical GF desserts are brownies. ▪ *www.flatbreadcompany.com*

Flayvors of Cook Farm   ★ ¢S
Hadley ▪ *(413) 584-2224*
1 E Hadley Rd ▪ *Ice Cream* ▪ GF ice cream cones are available. The store recommends asking at the counter to find out which ice cream flavors are GF. ▪ *www.cookfarm.com*

Flora $$$D
Arlington ▪ *(781) 641-1664*
190 Massachusetts Ave ▪ *Modern American* ▪ Chef Keith reports that the restaurant gets GF requests "all the time." He notes that several dishes are naturally GF, and many other dishes can be modified to be GF. Alert the server, who will write up a special GF ticket and confer with the kitchen. ▪ *www.florarestaurant.com*

Fresh Side   ✪ $LD
Amherst ▪ *(413) 256-0296*
39 S Pleasant St ▪ *Asian Fusion* ▪ GF menu includes ginger chicken rice, fried rice, shiitake mushroom rice, curry salad with cellophane noodles, thai basil pasta with cellophane noodles, and more. ▪ *www. freshsideamherst.com*

Gibbet Hill Grill   ✪ $$$D
Groton ▪ *(978) 448-2900*
61 Lowell Rd ▪ *American* ▪ GF menu

includes a roasted pork chop, Atlantic halibut, prime rib steak, and several sides. The restaurant reports that the GF menu is an adaptation of the regular menu, and the chefs went over it "with a fine-tooth comb." They also report that GF diners are "always welcome." ▪ *www.gibbethill.com*

Glutenus Minimus   100% ¢**BLD**
Belmont ▪ (617) 484-3550
697 Belmont St ▪ *Bakery* ▪ Dedicated GF bakery offering a wide selection of baked goods, including cookies, cakes, cupcakes, muffins, and holiday specials. They also offer "take-&-bake" mixes for cookies, breas, and pizza crust. ▪ *www.glutenusminimus.com*

Greenwood Food Mart   ★ $**LD**
Wakefield ▪ (781) 245-3663
1117 Main St ▪ *Deli* ▪ GF pizza, beer, and pastries are available. The deli reports that they use a separate oven for GF products. Special GF "two for one" deals are available. Ask for GF products at the counter. ▪ *www.greenwoodfoodmart.com*

Greg's Pizza   ★ $$**LD**
Wilmington ▪ (978) 658-3063
296 Shawsheen Ave ▪ *Pizza* ▪ GF pizza is available. Note GF when placing an order.

Greta's Great Grains   ★ ¢**S**
Newburyport ▪ (978) 465-1709
24 Pleasant St ▪ *Bakery* ▪ Non-dedicated bakery offering GF muffins, cakes, brownies, cookies, and more. Owner Greta reports that "basic items" are always available, but call ahead to ask what other items they have on a given day. ▪ *www.gretas-greatgrains.com*

Grog, The   ◑★ $$**LD**
Newburyport ▪ (978) 465-8008
13 Middle St ▪ *Global* ▪ GF menu includes seared ahi tuna, chicken wings, enchiladas, ribs, lamb tips, salmon roulade, and a New England Fisherman's Bake. GF beer is also available. ▪ *www.thegrog.com*

Hillside Organic Pizza   ★ $$**LD**
Hadley ▪ (413) 585-0003
173 Russell St
South Deerfield ▪ (413) 665-5533
265 Greenfield Rd ▪ *Pizza* ▪ GF pizza, cupcakes, and whoopie pies are available. The Hadley location also carries GF bread for "hotwiches." ▪ *www.hillsidepizza.com*

Jake & Earl's Dixie Barbeque   ◎ $$**LD**
Waltham ▪ (781) 894-4227
220 Moody St ▪ *Barbeque* ▪ GF menu includes buffalo wings, cobb salad, salmon, Memphis style spare ribs, and BBQ pulled chicken. ▪ *www.jakes-bbq.com*

Joe's American Bar & Grill   ★ $**LD**
Braintree ▪ (781) 848-0200
250 Granite St
Dedham ▪ (781) 329-0800
985 Providence Hwy
Framingham ▪ (508) 820-8389
1 Worcester Rd
Franklin ▪ (508) 553-9313
466 King St
Hanover ▪ (781) 878-1234
2087 Washington St
Peabody ▪ (978) 532-9500
210 Andover St
Woburn ▪ (781) 935-7200
311 Mishawum Rd ▪ *American* ▪ GF pasta and pizza are available. Both can be prepared in several different ways. GF beer is available at all locations except Dedham and Woburn. Managers recommend alerting a server and using the word "allergy." ▪ *www.joesamerican.com*

John Harvard's Brew House $$**LD**
Framingham ▪ (508) 875-2337
1 Worcester Rd
Hancock ▪ (413) 738-5500
37 Corey Rd ▪ *American* ▪ Restaurants report serving GF diners frequently. They recommend alerting a server, who will get a manager or chef if he or she has any questions about GF options. Servers have varying degrees of knowledge regarding the GF diet. ▪ *www.johnharvards.com*

Kickass Cupcakes ★ ¢S
Somerville ▪ **(617) 628-2877**
378 Highland Ave ▪ *Bakery* ▪ A daily assortment of GF cupcakes is available. Possible flavors include vanilla with vanilla or chocolate frosting and mojito. Special GF orders can be accommodated with advanced notice of two days. ▪ *www.kickass-cupcakes.com*

Landing, The $$$LD
Marblehead ▪ **(781) 639-1266**
81 Front St ▪ *Modern American* ▪ Server Nick reports that they are accustomed to serving GF diners. He notes that the restaurant can certainly "work something out," and that there are several naturally GF items, such as the grilled salmon, the filet mignon, and the duck. Confirm timeliness of this information before dining in. ▪ *www.thelandingrestaurant.com*

Legal Sea Foods 📖
Braintree ▪ **(781) 356-3070**
250 Granite St
Burlington ▪ **(781) 270-9700**
75 Middlesex Tpke
Chestnut Hill ▪ **(617) 277-0404**
43 Boylston St
Dedham ▪ **(781) 234-6500**
950 Providence Hwy
Framingham ▪ **(508) 766-0600**
50 Worcester Rd
Peabody ▪ **(978) 532-4500**
210 Andover St

Lola's Italian Groceria ✪★ $$$BLD
Natick ▪ **(508) 651-0524**
9 Main St ▪ *Italian* ▪ GF family-style and individual meals are available for "take-&-bake." Meals include eggplant and chicken parmesan, baked ziti with meat sauce, chicken and broccoli pasta, and more. Seating is available, and with advanced notice of one hour, they will heat up a meal for customers to eat on site. ▪ *www.lolasnatick.com*

Max's Tavern ✪★ $$$LD
Springfield ▪ **(413) 746-6299**
1000 W Columbus Ave ▪ *Modern American* ▪ GF menu includes shrimp, oysters, chicken wings, strip steak, salmon, and a chop salad. Restaurant reports that they host GF diners "every once in a while." GF pasta is available. ▪ *www.maxrestaurant-group.com*

Melting Pot, The 📖
Bedford ▪ **(781) 791-0529**
213 Burlington Rd
Framingham ▪ **(508) 875-3115**
92 Worcester Rd

Naked Fish ✪ $$$LD
Billerica ▪ **(978) 663-6500**
15 Middlesex Tpke
Framingham ▪ **(508) 820-9494**
725 Cochituate Rd
Waltham ▪ **(781) 684-0500**
455 Totten Pond Rd ▪ *Seafood* ▪ GF menu includes coconut haddock, orange and balsamic glazed salmon, tuna tartare, sesame encrusted mahi mahi, and chicken and mushroom risotto, among other things. ▪ *www.nakedfish.com*

Naked Oyster Restaurant $$$LD
Hyannis ▪ **(508) 778-6500**
20 Independence Dr ▪ *Modern American* ▪ Restaurant reports that they are a "gluten free-friendly" restaurant. There are several GF entrées and appetizers on the menu. ▪ *www.nakedoyster.com*

Nancy Chang's ✪★ $LD
Worcester ▪ **(508) 752-8899**
372 Chandler St ▪ *Asian* ▪ GF menu includes General Tso's chicken, chicken and shrimp fried rice, tofu curry, beef salad, lemon chicken, lettuce wraps, and more. GF soy sauce is available. ▪ *www.nancychang.com*

Nauset Beach Club Restaurant $$$D
East Orleans ▪ **(508) 255-8547**
222 Main St ▪ *Seafood* ▪ Owner Arthur reports that they have "no problem" serving GF diners, and they do so "frequently." Arthur notes that all of the staff members are "very up to date," and servers can com-

municate with the chef about GF options. ▪
www.nausetbeachclub.com

New Leaf, A   ★ $S
Beverly ▪ *(978) 927-5955*
261 Cabot St
Needham ▪ *(877) 449-6777*
1038 Great Plain Ave ▪ *Take-&-Bake* ▪ GF
"take-&-bake" pizza, frozen bread, snack
bars, pasta, and more are available at the
market. ▪ *www.anewleafvitamins.com*

Ninety Nine Restaurant & Pub   📖
Andover ▪ *(978) 475-8033*
464 Lowell St.
Auburn ▪ *(508) 832-0999*
793 Southbridge St
Billerica ▪ *(978) 663-3999*
160 Lexington Rd
Billerica ▪ *(978) 667-9789*
672 Boston Post Rd
Braintree ▪ *(781) 849-9902*
S Shore Plz
Bridgewater ▪ *(508) 279-2799*
233 Broad St
Canton ▪ *(781) 821-8999*
362 Turnpike St
Centerville ▪ *(508) 790-8995*
1600 Falmouth Rd
Charlestown ▪ *(617) 242-8999*
29 Austin St # 31
Chicopee ▪ *(413) 593-9909*
555 Memorial Dr
Concord ▪ *(978) 369-0300*
13 Commonwealth Ave
Danvers ▪ *(978) 762-8994*
60 Commonwealth Ave
E Wareham ▪ *(508) 295-9909*
3013 Cranberry Hwy
East Longmeadow ▪ *(413) 525-9900*
390 N Main St
East Walpole ▪ *(508) 668-6017*
55 Providence Hwy
Fairhaven ▪ *(508) 992-9951*
34 Sconticut Neck Rd
Fall River ▪ *(508) 673-8999*
404 Pleasant St
Falmouth ▪ *(508) 457-9930*
30 Davis Straits

Fitchburg ▪ *(978) 343-0099*
275 Summer St
Foxboro ▪ *(508) 543-1199*
4 Fisher St
Franklin ▪ *(508) 520-9909*
847 W Central St
Greenfield ▪ *(413) 775-9997*
17 Colrain Rd
Haverhill ▪ *(978) 372-8303*
786 River St
Hingham ▪ *(781) 740-8599*
428 Lincoln St
Holyoke ▪ *(413) 532-9918*
50 Holyoke St
Hudson ▪ *(978) 562-9918*
255 Washington St
Lowell ▪ *(978) 458-9199*
850 Chelmsford St
Lynnfield ▪ *(781) 599-8119*
317 Salem St
Marlborough ▪ *(508) 480-8899*
32 Boston Post Rd W
Mashpee ▪ *(508) 477-9000*
8 Ryans Way
Milford ▪ *(508) 634-1999*
196B E Main St
North Andover ▪ *(978) 683-9999*
267 Chickering Rd
North Attleboro ▪ *(508) 399-9990*
1510 S Washington St
North Dartmouth ▪ *(508) 999-0099*
161 Faunce Corner Mall Rd
Pembroke ▪ *(781) 829-9912*
166 Church St
Pittsfield ▪ *(413) 236-0980*
699 Merrill Rd
Plymouth ▪ *(508) 732-9932*
21 Home Depot Dr
Quincy ▪ *(617) 472-5000*
59 Newport Ave
Revere ▪ *(781) 289-9991*
121 Vfw Pkwy
Rockland ▪ *(781) 871-4178*
2 Accord Park
Salem ▪ *(978) 740-8999*
15 Bridge St
Saugus ▪ *(781) 233-1999*
181 Broadway

Seekonk ■ *(508) 336-9899*
821 Fall River Ave
Somerville ■ *(617) 629-0599*
20 Cummings St
South Easton ■ *(508) 238-2999*
99 Belmont St
Springfield ■ *(413) 731-9999*
1371 Liberty St
Springfield ■ *(413) 273-8999*
1655 Boston Rd
Stoneham ■ *(781) 279-0399*
10 Main St
Taunton ■ *(508) 821-9922*
158 Dean St
Tewksbury ■ *(978) 863-9099*
401 Main St
Waltham ■ *(781) 893-4999*
110 South St
West Springfield ■ *(413) 858-1995*
1053 Riverdale St
West Yarmouth ■ *(508) 862-9990*
14 Berry Ave
Westford ■ *(978) 589-9948*
333 Littleton Rd
Weymouth ■ *(781) 340-9000*
1094 Main St
Wilmington ■ *(978) 657-9694*
144 Lowell St
Woburn ■ *(781) 938-8999*
194 Cambridge Rd
Woburn ■ *(781) 935-7210*
291 Mishawum Rd
Worcester ■ *(508) 792-9997*
11 E Central St
Worcester ■ *(508) 363-3999*
50 Southwest Cutoff
Worcester ■ *(508) 852-2999*
900 W Boylston St

Not Your Average Joe's   ✪ $$**LD**

Acton ■ *(978) 635-0101*
305 Main St
Arlington ■ *(781) 643-1666*
645 Massachusetts Ave
Beverly ■ *(978) 927-8950*
45 Enon St
Burlington ■ *(781) 505-1303*
4 Wayside Rd
Dartmouth ■ *(508) 992-5637*

61 State Rd
Hyannis ■ *(508) 778-1424*
793 Iyannough Rd
Medford ■ *(781) 393-9681*
501 Fellsway
Methuen ■ *(978) 974-0015*
90 Pleasant Valley St
Needham ■ *(781) 453-9300*
109 Chapel St
Newburyport ■ *(978) 462-3808*
1 Market Sq
Norwell ■ *(781) 616-6160*
111 Pond St
Randolph ■ *(781) 961-7200*
16 Mazzeo Dr
Watertown ■ *(617) 926-9229*
55 Main St
Westborough ■ *(508) 986-2350*
291 Turnpike Rd ■ *American* ■ GF menu
includes rosemary-skewered fresh scallops,
fresh salmon filet, cobb salad, NY strip,
grilled chicken breast, and butterscotch
pudding for dessert. ■ *www.notyouraver-
agejoes.com*

Old Jailhouse Tavern   ✪ $$$**LD**

Orleans, Cape Cod ■ *(508) 255-5245*
28 West Rd ■ *New England* ■ GF menu
includes mussels marinara, salads with GF
dressing, oysters, clams, soups, steaks, and
more. ■ *www.jailhousetavern.com*

One Eleven Chophouse   ✪★ $$$**D**

Worcester ■ *(508) 799-4111*
111 Shrewsbury St ■ *American* ■ GF menu
includes beef carpaccio, oysters, firecracker
rolls with no soy sauce, steaks, seafood,
rack of lamb, and more. Dessert options
include GF cheesecake with strawberries, chocolate mousse, and raspberry
crème brûlée. GF beer is also available. ■
www.111chophouse.com

Outback Steakhouse   📖

Auburn ■ *(508) 721-9799*
771 Southbridge St
Bellingham ■ *(508) 966-9333*
275 N Main St
Burlington ■ *(781) 270-9300*
34 Cambridge St

Hanover ▪ *(781) 829-0707*
1775 Washington St
Hyannis ▪ *(508) 778-8787*
1070 Iyannough Rd
Leominster ▪ *(978) 840-3377*
865 Merriam Ave
Lowell ▪ *(978) 934-8700*
28 Reiss Ave
Medford ▪ *(781) 306-1300*
672 Fellsway
Methuen ▪ *(978) 686-1122*
145 Pelham St # 147
Norwood ▪ *(781) 551-8855*
1212 Providence Hwy
Peabody ▪ *(978) 532-4280*
300 Andover St
Quincy ▪ *(617) 769-9494*
227 Parkingway
Randolph ▪ *(781) 961-9778*
45 Mazzeo Dr
Seekonk ▪ *(508) 336-7770*
1301 Fall River Ave
Tyngsboro ▪ *(978) 649-8700*
440 Middlesex Rd
W Springfield ▪ *(413) 746-5700*
1537 Riverdale St
Westborough ▪ *(508) 366-4400*
227 Turnpike Rd

P.F. Chang's China Bistro 📖
Dedham ▪ *(781) 461-6060*
410 Legacy Pl
Natick ▪ *(508) 651-7724*
1245 Worcester St Ste 4008
Peabody ▪ *(978) 326-2410*
210 Andover Street

Papa Razzi ★ $LD
Burlington ▪ *(781) 229-0100*
2 Wall St
Chestnut Hill ▪ *(617) 527-6600*
199 Boylston St
Concord ▪ *(978) 371-0030*
768 Elm St
Framingham ▪ *(508) 848-2300*
155 Worcester Rd
Hanover ▪ *(781) 982-2800*
2087 Washington St
Wellesley ▪ *(781) 235-4747*

16 Washington St ▪ *Italian* ▪ GF pasta and pizza are available at all locations. ▪ *www. paparazzitrattoria.com*

Peaches Bakery & Deli 100% ¢BL
Harvard ▪ *(978) 772-2437*
325 Ayer Rd ▪ *Deli & Bakery* ▪ GF bakery and deli offering many GF options. For breakfast, there are quiches, bagels, toast, english muffins, croissants, and more. For lunch, they offer a variety of sandwiches. For dessert, the wide selection includes cheesecake, muffins, pumpkin cake, cupcakes, and more. There are also "meals on the go." ▪ *www.peachesbakery.com*

Pete's A Place ✪★ ¢LD
Danvers ▪ *(978) 774-5675*
142 Pine St ▪ *Pizza* ▪ GF menu includes chicken tenders, pasta dishes, and sandwiches on GF bread. GF pasta is available. ▪ *www.petes-a-place.com*

Plum Island Grille ★ $$$LD
Newbury ▪ *(978) 463-2290*
2 Plum Island Blvd ▪ *Mediterranean* ▪ Owner and Executive Chef Francis reports that GF diners are "always welcome," and he adds that all staff members are "very well trained" on the GF diet. He notes that the rice noodle bowl and the rack of lamb are naturally GF, as are the flourless chocolate torte and the crème brûlée. Confirm timeliness of this information before dining in. GF beer is available. ▪ *www. plumislandgrille.com*

Prana Café ✪ $BLD
Newton ▪ *(617) 527-7726*
292 Centre St ▪ *Raw & Vegan* ▪ GF menu includes sushi, tostadas, chard-wrapped burritos, and a wide variety of desserts such as lemon merengue pie, coconut pie, chocolate torte, and more. ▪ *www.thepranacafe.com*

Rancho Chico Mexican Restaurant ✪ $LD
Plainville ▪ *(508) 643-2534*
52 Washington St ▪ *Mexican* ▪ Limited GF

menu includes nachos, fajitas, enchiladas, and salads.

Rani Indian Bistro $LD
Brookline ▪ *(617) 734-0400*
1353 Beacon St ▪ *Indian* ▪ Host Arjab reports that "most of the entrées" are naturally GF. He adds that GF diners can choose from chicken, lamb, vegetarian, or seafood dishes, but should be cautious with appetizers, as many are not GF. Confirm timeliness of this information before dining in. ▪ *www.ranibistro.com*

Rawbert's Organic Garden Café
                                        ★ $BLD
Beverly ▪ *(978) 922-0004*
294 Cabot St ▪ *Raw & Vegan* ▪ Chef Robert reports that there are over one hundred GF menu options, which means that almost the entire menu is GF. GF bread and pizza are available. For dessert, they offer GF apple pie, blueberry pie, various cheesecakes, homemade chocolates, brownies, and cookies. ▪ *www.organicgardencafe.com*

Scottish Bakehouse   ★ ¢S
Vineyard Haven ▪ *(508) 693-6633*
977 State Rd ▪ *Bakery* ▪ GF brownies, macaroons, amaretti cookies, cheesecake, and cupcakes are available. The restaurant reports that GF muffins are baked on-site every day.

Scupperjack's $$$LD
Acton ▪ *(978) 263-8327*
3 Nagog Park Route 2A ▪ *American* ▪ Manager Don reports that the restaurant serves GF diners "frequently." He notes that servers are "adept" at accommodating GF customers, and if they are unfamiliar with the GF diet, they will confer with the kitchen staff. ▪ *www.scupperjacks.com*

Siena Italian Grill and Bar   ✪★ $$$LD
Mashpee ▪ *(508) 477-5929*
17 Steeple St ▪ *Italian* ▪ GF menu includes salmon with honey dijon glaze, pan-seared jumbo scallops with citrus-basil pesto, and more. For dessert, they offer flourless chocolate cake. GF pasta is available for

substitution. Located in Mashpee Commons. ▪ *www.siena.us*

Skipjack's $$$LD
Foxboro ▪ *(508) 543-2200*
226 Patriot Pl
Natick ▪ *(508) 628-9900*
1400 Worcester Rd
Newton Highlands ▪ *(617) 964-4244*
55 Needham St ▪ *Seafood* ▪ All locations report that there are several naturally GF menu items, as well as a variety of others that can be modified to be GF. They have GF lists that can be printed upon request. Alert a server, who will notify the chef. Hours and GF options vary by location. ▪ *www.skipjacks.com*

Sole Proprietor, The   ✪★ $$$LD
Worcester ▪ *(508) 798-3474*
118 Highland St ▪ *Seafood* ▪ GF menu includes appetizers, sushi, lunch and dinner fish markets, as well as a variety of other entrées. Desserts on the GF menu include flan, chocolate terrine, cheesecake, and more. GF pasta, soy sauce, and beer are available. ▪ *www.thesole.com*

Spoleto   ★ $$$D
Northampton ▪ *(413) 586-6313*
50 Main St ▪ *Modern American* ▪ GF rice pasta is always available. Chef Collin reports that most servers are educated about the GF diet, so they will be able to find out which sauces are GF. Alert a server, who will communicate with the kitchen. ▪ *www.fundining.com*

Stone Hearth Pizza Co.   ✪★ $LD
Belmont ▪ *(617) 484-1700*
57 Leonard St
Needham ▪ *(781) 433-0600*
974 Great Plain Ave ▪ *Pizza* ▪ GF items marked on the menu include pizza and pasta. For dessert, they ofer hot fudge sundaes and ice cream floats. ▪ *www.stone-hearthpizza.com*

Tavolino   ✪★ $$LD
Foxboro ▪ *(508) 543-6543*
274 Patriot Pl

Westborough ▪ **(508) 366-8600**
33 E Main St ▪ *Italian* ▪ Both locations
have an extensive GF menu that includes
pizzas, salads, antipasti, and carpaccio.
GF pizza and pastas are available. ▪ *www.
tavolinorestaurant.us*

Ten Center $$$**LD**
Newburyport ▪ **(978) 462-6652**
10 Center St ▪ *Italian-American* ▪ Man-
ager Stacy reports that the restaurant
serves GF diners "more often than you
would think." She notes that the restaurant
staff recently attended an allergy training
program that addressed the GF diet. She
recommends reservations noting GF. The
Atlantic cod with parsnips and bok choy
can be prepared GF. Confirm timeliness of
this information before dining in. ▪ *www.
tencenterstreet.com*

True Grounds   ★ ¢**S**
Somerville ▪ **(617) 591-9559**
717 Broadway ▪ *Coffee & Café* ▪ GF
moonpies, raspberry bars, and chocolate
brownies are available. ▪ *www.truegrounds.
com*

Tryst   ✪ $$$**D**
Arlington ▪ **(781) 641-2227**
689 Massachusetts Ave ▪ *Modern American* ▪ GF menu includes an artisan cheese
plate, roasted beet salad, pork sirloin, and
herb-roasted chicken. Cook Shannon
reports that GF diners are "very common"
at the restaurant. ▪ *www.trystrestaurant.com*

Tuscan Grill $$**D**
Waltham ▪ **(781) 891-5486**
361 Moody St ▪ *Italian* ▪ Chef Brian reports
that nearly everything on the menu is GF.
He notes that there is no "hidden gluten"
on the menu, so an educated GF diner
should have no trouble choosing a dish.
Confirm that selections are GF by asking
your server. ▪ *www.tuscangrillwaltham.com*

U Food Grill   📖
Watertown ▪ **(617) 923-7676**
222 Arsenal St

Uno Chicago Grill   📖
Attleboro ▪ **(508) 399-6999**
221 Washington St
Bellingham ▪ **(508) 966-3300**
205 Hartford Ave
Braintree ▪ **(781) 849-8667**
250 Granite St
Burlington ▪ **(781) 229-1300**
75 Middlesex Tpke Ste 1095
Dedham ▪ **(781) 320-0356**
270 Providence Hwy
Framingham ▪ **(508) 620-1816**
70 Worcester Rd
Hanover ▪ **(781) 826-4453**
1799 Washington St
Haverhill ▪ **(978) 556-9595**
30 Cushing Ave
Holyoke ▪ **(413) 534-3000**
50 Holyoke St
Hyannis ▪ **(508) 775-3111**
574 Iyannough Route 132 Rd
Leominster ▪ **(978) 466-7808**
905 Merriam Ave
Millbury ▪ **(508) 581-7866**
70 Worcester Providence Tpke
Newton ▪ **(617) 964-2296**
287 Washington St
Revere ▪ **(781) 289-2330**
210 Squire Rd
Springfield ▪ **(413) 543-6600**
1722 Boston Rd
Springfield ▪ **(413) 733-1300**
820 Hall Of Fame Ave
Sturbridge ▪ **(508) 347-6420**
100 Charlton Rd
Swampscott ▪ **(781) 595-8667**
970 Paradise Rd
Taunton ▪ **(508) 828-9900**
904 County St
Waltham ▪ **(781) 487-7177**
155 Bear Hill Rd
Westborough ▪ **(508) 616-0300**
225 Turnpike Rd
Woburn ▪ **(781) 937-6016**
300 Mishawum Rd
Worcester ▪ **(508) 421-9300**
25 Major Taylor Blvd

Wrentham ■ *(508) 384-3129*
1048 South St

Washington Square Tavern ✪ ★ $$D
Brookline ■ *(617) 232-8989*
714 Washington St ■ *Modern American* ■
GF menu is a list of all regular items that
are naturally GF. Typically, this menu includes salads, steaks, burgers without buns,
lamb, and chicken dishes. GF beer is available. ■ *www.washingtonsquaretavern.com*

Waterstreet Café $LD
Fall River ■ *(508) 672-8748*
36 Water St ■ *American* ■ Owner Jeanne
reports that they are happy to serve GF
diners. She adds that because all meals are
made in house, they can modify almost
anything to be GF. Examples include hummus, falafel, grilled chicken zatar, and the
salmon fillet. Confirm timeliness of this
information before dining in. ■ *www.water-
streetcafe.com*

Wild Willy's ★ ¢LD
Needham ■ *(781) 444-5511*
1257 Highland Ave
Watertown ■ *(617) 926-9700*
46 Arsenal St
Worcester ■ *(508) 459-2088*
317 W Boylston St ■ *American* ■ GF rolls
are available and can be used to make
almost all sandwiches GF. Manager Bob
at the Worcester location reports that they
have been preparing GF food for over a
year. In addition to the GF roll, he reports
that french fries and chicken tenders are
GF. Confirm timeliness of this information
before dining in. ■ *www.wildwillysburgers.
com*

Woodman's Seafood and Grill $$LD
Essex ■ *(978) 768-6057*
121 Main St ■ *Seafood* ■ Manager Lisa
reports that the restaurant is "GF-friendly."
She notes that nearly the entire menu
is GF. For GF orders, there is a separate
"gluten track" in the kitchen, and they use
a separate fryolater. Alert a server, who will
notify the kitchen. ■ *www.woodmans.com*

Yard House 📖
Dedham ■ *(781) 326-4644*
950 Providence Hwy

Zocalo Cocina Mexicana ✪ $$BD
Brighton ■ *(617) 277-5700*
1414 Commonwealth Ave ■ *Mexican* ■ GF
menu includes braised pork with chile
guajillo, jumbo sautéed shrimp with pico
de gallo, chicken, shrimp, or cheese enchiladas, tacos with corn tortillas, and more. ■
www.zocalobrighton.com

MICHIGAN

Amical ✪ $$LD
Traverse City ■ *(231) 941-8888*
229 E Front St ■ *French* ■ GF menu
includes pan seared mahi mahi and the
bourbon glazed pork chop, among other
things. For dessert, they offer raspberry
crème brûlée, caramel apples, flourless
black bottom cake, and coffee custard.
General Manager Jeffrey reports that the
staff is "fully trained" on the GF diet. ■
www.amical.com

Amici's Pizza and the Living Room
★ $$D
Berkley ■ *(248) 544-4100*
3249 12 Mile Rd
Berkley ■ *(248) 544-4100*
3249 Twelve Mile Rd ■ *Pizza* ■ GF pizza
is available and can be prepared with any
toppings. Manager Dave confirmed that GF
pizza crusts are made daily on-site. ■ *www.
amicispizza.com*

Apache Trout Grill ✪ $LD
Traverse City ■ *(231) 947-7079*
13671 S West Bay Shore Dr ■ *Seafood &
Steakhouse* ■ The new GF menu includes
blackened or grilled walleye, mahi mahi,
whitefish, salmon, bacon wrapped shrimp,

and nine layer dip. General Manager Glen reports that in addition, almost any steak, any fish, or any BBQ item can be prepared GF. ▪ *www.apachetroutgrill.com*

Bavarian Inn at Frankenmuth   ✪★ $LD
Frankenmuth ▪ *(989) 652-9941*
713 S Main St ▪ *German* ▪ GF menu includes chicken stir fry, NY strip steak, and more. GF dessert menu includes a cream cheese brownie triangle, chocolate chip cookies, and a variety of take-home products which are available with advanced notice of 3 days. ▪ *www.bavarianinnlodge.com*

Berkley Bistro and Café   ★ ¢BL
Berkley ▪ *(248) 691-4333*
1999 Coolidge Hwy ▪ *Breakfast* ▪ Manager Sherry reports that the chef is well-versed in accommodating GF diners. GF bread is available, and can be used to make french toast or any of the café's sandwiches.

Boathouse Restaurant $$$LD
Traverse City ▪ *(231) 223-4030*
14039 Peninsula Dr ▪ *French* ▪ Executive Chef Eric reports that they serve GF meals "from sun up to sun down." He adds that he is able and happy to prepare meals for GF diners. GF desserts include crème brulee and the chocolate truffle plate. Confirm timeliness of this information before dining in. ▪ *www.boathouseonwestbay.com*

Bombadill's Café   ★ ¢S
Ypsilanti ▪ *(734) 544-5080*
217 W Michigan Ave ▪ *Coffee Shop* ▪ GF chocolate cake is usually available, and GF cupcakes are sometimes available. ▪ *www.bombadills.com*

Bonefish Grill   📖
Grand Rapids ▪ *(616) 949-7861*
1100 East Paris Ave SE Ste 5
Novi ▪ *(248) 347-1635*
43304 W 11 Mile Rd

Boone's Long Lake Inn   ✪ $$$LD
Traverse City ▪ *(231) 946-3991*
7208 Secor Rd ▪ *Seafood & Steakhouse* ▪

GF menu lists regular menu items that can be prepared GF. It includes various steak, pork, chicken, and seafood entrées, as well as shrimp and crab appetizers. ▪ *www.booneslli.com*

Buca di Beppo   📖
Livonia ▪ *(734) 462-6442*
38888 6 Mile Rd
Utica ▪ *(586) 803-9463*
12575 Hall Rd

Buddy's Pizza   ★ $LD
Auburn Hills ▪ *(248) 276-9040*
2612 N Squirrel Rd
Bloomfield Hills ▪ *(248) 645-0300*
3637 W Maple Rd
Dearborn ▪ *(313) 562-5900*
22148 Michigan Ave
Detroit ▪ *(313) 892-9001*
Corner Of East McNichols
Farmington Hills ▪ *(248) 855-4600*
31646 Northwestern Hwy
Grosse Pointe Woods ▪ *(313) 884-7400*
19163 Mack Ave
Livonia ▪ *(734) 261-3550*
33605 Plymouth Rd
Royal Oak ▪ *(248) 549-8000*
32218 Woodward Ave
Warren ▪ *(586) 574-9200*
8100 Old 13 Mile Rd ▪ *Pizza* ▪ GF pizza is available. ▪ *www.buddyspizza.com*

Cameron's Steakhouse $$$$D
Birmingham ▪ *(248) 723-1700*
115 Willits St ▪ *Steakhouse* ▪ Manager Chris reports that there are plenty of naturally GF menu items, such as the seasoned steaks. He notes that all servers are "very knowledgeable" about GF items. ▪ *www.camerons-steakhouse.com*

Capital Grille, The   📖
Troy ▪ *(248) 649-5300*
2800 W Big Beaver Rd

Carino's Italian   📖
Allen Park ▪ *(313) 274-5551*
23075 Outer Dr
Brighton ▪ *(810) 494-5050*
9475 Village Place Blvd

Commerce Township ▪ *(248) 926-5300*
500 Loop Rd
Grand Rapids ▪ *(616) 363-7100*
2183 E Beltline Ave NE
Holland ▪ *(616) 738-5200*
3015 W Shore Dr
Norton Shores ▪ *(231) 798-6363*
5607 Harvey St

Carrabba's Italian Grill 📖

Canton ▪ *(734) 844-7400*
1900 N Haggerty Rd
Grand Rapids ▪ *(616) 940-9865*
4061 28th St SE
Grandville ▪ *(616) 261-3020*
3441 Century Center St SW
Lansing ▪ *(517) 323-8055*
6540 W Saginaw Hwy
Novi ▪ *(248) 735-0400*
43455 W Oaks Dr
Portage ▪ *(269) 381-0607*
5690 S Westnedge Ave
Southgate ▪ *(734) 284-5339*
14805 Dix Toledo Rd
Sterling Heights ▪ *(586) 323-2652*
44695 Schoenherr Rd

Celiac Specialties 100% ¢S

Chesterfield ▪ *(586) 598-8180*
48411 Jefferson Ave
Novi ▪ *(248) 987-2348*
39799 Grand River Ave ▪ *Bakery* ▪ Dedicated GF bakery offering pizza, sandwich bread, pasta, gravies, buns, donuts, granola, cakes, and more. Advanced notice of one day is required for cake orders. Calling ahead is recommended, especially at the Chesterfield location, as it is smaller than the Novi location. ▪ *www.celiacspecialties-shop.com*

Chop House, The ✪ $$$$D

Ann Arbor ▪ *(734) 669-8826*
322 S Main St
Grand Rapids ▪ *(616) 451-6184*
190 Monroe Ave NW ▪ *Steakhouse* ▪ At both locations, GF items are starred on the regular menu. The GF menu at the Grand Rapids location is more extensive, but both locations offer a variety of seafood, filets,

and salads. Both locations report that GF diners should alert a manager about GF requirements. ▪ *www.thechophouserestaurant.com*

Coco Charlotte Gluten-Free Bakery
100% ¢S

Grand Rapids ▪ *(616) 957-3706*
2481 32nd St SE ▪ *Bakery* ▪ Dedicated GF bakery offering pizza crust, buttermilk scones, biscotti, cookies, brownies, muffins, and seasonal pies, as well as breads and rolls. The bakery recommends calling a week in advance for special orders. ▪ *www.coco-charlotte.com*

Crust Pizza & Wine Bar ★ $$LD

Bloomfield Hills ▪ *(248) 855-5855*
6622 Telegraph Rd
Rochester Hills ▪ *(248) 844-8899*
2595 S Rochester Rd ▪ *Pizza* ▪ GF pizza is available. ▪ *www.crustpizza.net*

Earle, The ✪ $$$D

Ann Arbor ▪ *(734) 994-0211*
121 W Washington St ▪ *Modern American* ▪ GF menu includes soups, appetizers, pork tenderloin, mahi mahi, and duck. The restaurant reports that it takes special dietary needs "extremely seriously." Alert a server, who will notify the kitchen. ▪ *www.theearle.com*

Edward's Café & Caterer ★ $$BLD

Northville ▪ *(248) 344-1550*
115 E Main St ▪ *Bakery & Café* ▪ GF cupcakes by the half dozen and flourless chocolate cake are available with advanced notice of 2 days. ▪ *www.edwardscaterer.com*

El Dorado Cadillac Grill $LD

Cadillac ▪ *(231) 779-3663*
7839 E 46 1/2 Rd ▪ *American* ▪ Reservationist Michelle reports that they have accommodated GF diners "many times." She adds that there are "so many options" that it is "too hard" to list them. Located at the Gold Eldorado course. ▪ *www.golfeldorado.com*

Erbelli's ★ $**LD**
Kalamazoo ▪ *(269) 375-0408*
6214 Stadium Dr
Portage ▪ *(269) 327-0200*
8342 Portage Rd ▪ *Italian* ▪ GF pizza is available. Both locations report that servers are trained on GF. ▪ *www.erbellis.com*

Fire Bowl Café ☼ ¢**LD**
Kalamazoo ▪ *(269) 382-0071*
5363 W Main St ▪ *Asian Stir-Fry* ▪ GF menu includes spicy coconut soup, thai seafood tom kah soup, and a variety of salads. It features "Stir Fry Your Way," for which diners choose their own meats, sauces, and starches. GF sauce options are ginger white wine and yellow curry. ▪ *www.firebowlcafe.com*

Firefly $$$**LD**
Traverse City ▪ *(231) 932-1310*
310 Cass St ▪ *Global* ▪ Chef Tim reports that GF diners can be accommodated. Alert a server, who will notify him. Limited GF items include a filet with vegetables and a tuna sushi roll. Confirm timeliness of this information before dining in. ▪ *www.tcfirefly.com*

Frankenmuth Bavarian Inn Restaurant
☼★ $**LD**
Frankenmuth ▪ *(989) 652-9941*
713 S Main St ▪ *American* ▪ GF menu includes chicken stir fry and broiled whitefish, as well as cream cheese brownies and carrot cake for dessert. GF beer is also available. ▪ *www.bavarianinn.com*

G.F. Cucina's 100% ¢**LD**
Sterling Heights ▪ *(586) 276-1200*
37867 Mound Rd ▪ *Italian* ▪ Dedicated GF restaurant offering a wide variety of soups, salads, and entrées. Menu items include lasagna, teriyaki chicken kabobs, and a meatball sub, along with pizzas and calzones. For dessert, they offer cheesecake, peanut butter bars, flourless chocolate cakes, and more. ▪ *www.gfcucinas.com*

Gilly's ☼ $$$**D**
Grand Rapids ▪ *(616) 356-2000*

20 Monroe Ave NW ▪ *Seafood* ▪ GF items highlighted on the menu include oysters, pear and apple salad, Alaskan crab legs, and filet of beef. The restaurant reports that they have GF diners come in "all the time." ▪ *www.thebob.com*

Giulio's Cucina Italiana ★ $$**LD**
Livonia ▪ *(734) 427-9500*
31735 Plymouth Rd ▪ *Italian* ▪ GF pasta, pizza, homemade bread, and beer are available, as is GF flour to coat meats. The chef also makes various GF desserts such as pineapple upside down cake and tiramisu. ▪ *www.giuliositalian.com*

Gluten Free Sensations 100% ¢**S**
Three Rivers ▪ *(877) 458-8360*
53238 Us131 Hwy ▪ *Bakery* ▪ Dedicated GF bakery offering some items for purchase at the storefront. Owner Loretta notes that GF breads, pastas, cereals, and bars are available. She cautions that they sell primarily to larger retail outlets, so the selection in the store is small. ▪ *www.glutenfreesensations.com*

Ground Round 📖
Jackson ▪ *(517) 782-3330*
1051 Boardman Rd
Kalamazoo ▪ *(269) 375-9300*
3939 Stadium Dr
Woodhaven ▪ *(734) 362-8730*
22301 Allen Rd

Guido's Premium Pizza ★ $$**LD**
Okemos ▪ *(517) 347-3030*
1754 Central Park Dr ▪ *Pizza* ▪ GF pizza is available at this location only. ▪ *www.guidospizza.com*

Hanna $$**D**
Traverse City ▪ *(231) 946-8207*
118 Cass St ▪ *Bistro* ▪ Head Chef Carrie reports that although there are very few naturally GF items on the menu, they are happy to "mix and match" to accommodate GF diners. She recommends calling ahead to make a GF reservation and mentioning what sort of meal is preferred (i.e. meat,

fish, vegetarian). ■ *www.hannabistrobar.
com*

Jefferson Market & Cakery　★ $$$$$
Ann Arbor ■ *(734) 665-6666*
609 W Jefferson St ■ *Bakery* ■ Chocolate
flourless cake and cupcakes are available. ■
www.jeffersonmarketandcakery.com

Judson's Steakhouse　✪ $$$D
Grand Rapids ■ *(616) 356-2000*
20 Monroe Ave NW ■ *Steakhouse* ■ Extensive GF menu includes oysters, porterhouse
steak, pear and apple salad, and several
vegetable and potato sides. Restaurant
notes that accommodating GF diners is
"not a problem." ■ *www.thebob.com*

Kona Grill　📖
Troy ■ *(248) 619-9060*
30 E Big Beaver Rd

Lake Street Cafe at Oryana　★ ¢BLD
Traverse City ■ *(231) 947-0191*
260 E 10th St ■ *Organic* ■ GF bread and
rice wraps for sandwiches, as well as selected baked goods like cakes and pies, are
available. Many soups are also GF. ■ *www.
oryana.coop*

Lone Star Steakhouse & Saloon　📖
Battle Creek ■ *(269) 968-6900*
50 Knapp Dr
Bay City ■ *(989) 671-7827*
4107 Wilder Rd
Belleville ■ *(734) 547-0501*
2111 Rawsonville Rd
Dundee ■ *(734) 529-8270*
123 Whitetail Dr
Flint ■ *(810) 233-9240*
G3141 Miller Rd
Jackson ■ *(517) 768-0884*
3510 Oneil Dr
Mt Pleasant ■ *(989) 773-7827*
5768 E Pickard St
Saginaw ■ *(989) 793-7892*
2255 Tittabawassee Rd

M 22 Café　★ $BLD
Arcadia ■ *(231) 889-0290*
17201 Northwood Hwy ■ *American* ■ GF

waffles are available as a toast substitute.
Assorted cakes and muffins are available
as well. Owner reports that he is generally
available to discuss GF options. ■ *www.
m22cafearcadia.com*

Maggiano's Little Italy　★ $$$LD
Troy ■ *(248) 205-1060*
2089 W Big Beaver Rd ■ *Italian* ■ GF pasta
is available. Call individual locations to inquire about additional GF options. ■ *www.
maggianos.com*

Mancino's Grinders & Pizza　★ $LD
Grand Haven ■ *(616) 844-5566*
13040 US 31
Grand Ledge ■ *(517) 627-7799*
914 Charlevoix Dr ■ *Pizza* ■ GF pizza,
bread for grinders, and baked goods are
available. GF baked goods can be ordered
advanced notice of a couple of days.

Marie Catribs　★ $$BLD
Grand Rapids ■ *(616) 454-4020*
1001 Lake Dr SE # 1003 ■ *Deli & Bakery* ■
GF brownies, chocolate raspberry brownies, cakes, puddings, pies, tarts, and bread
for sandwiches is available. ■ *www.mariecatribs.com*

Melting Pot, The　📖
Ann Arbor ■ *(734) 622-0055*
309 S Main St
Grand Rapids ■ *(616) 365-0055*
2090 Celebration Dr NE
Novi ■ *(248) 347-6358*
26425 Novi Rd
Troy ■ *(248) 362-2221*
888 W Big Beaver Rd

Mezze Café & Cabaret　✪ ¢BLD
Grand Rapids ■ *(616) 776-6950*
38 West Fulton St ■ *Global* ■ Extensive GF
menu features a variety of tapas, including baked goat cheese and tomato without
garlic bread, chicken and chorizo skewers,
and hummus. ■ *www.sanchezbistro.com*

Mind Body & Spirits　✪★ $LD
Rochester ■ *(248) 651-3663*
301 S Main St ■ *Organic* ■ GF menu in-

cludes vegetable rolls, tamales, paella, and swordfish and scallop ceviche. GF pasta is available. ▪ *www.mindbodyspirits.com*

Mitchell's Fish Market ✪ $$$**LD**

Birmingham ▪ *(248) 646-3663*
117 Willits St
Lansing ▪ *(517) 482-3474*
2975 Preyde Blvd
Livonia ▪ *(734) 464-3663*
17600 Haggerty Rd
Rochester Hills ▪ *(248) 340-5900*
370 N Adams Rd ▪ *Seafood* ▪ Extensive GF menu includes pan-roasted wild blue mussels, blackened salmon spinach salad, grilled shrimp and scallop skewers, Shanghai seafood sampler, lobster tail, filet mignon, and live Maine lobster. Mini crème brulee is available for dessert. ▪ *www.mitchellsfishmarket.com*

Outback Steakhouse 📖

Ann Arbor ▪ *(734) 662-7400*
3173 Oak Valley Dr
Brighton ▪ *(810) 225-2109*
7873 Conference Center Dr
Canton ▪ *(734) 981-4144*
42871 Ford Rd
Chesterfield ▪ *(586) 948-4329*
27953 23 Mile Rd
Flint ▪ *(810) 720-0979*
4270 Miller Rd
Grand Rapids ▪ *(616) 785-9686*
3475 Alpine Ave NW
Grandville ▪ *(616) 724-2329*
3333 Century Center St SW
Independence ▪ *(248) 620-4329*
6435 Dixie Hwy
Jackson ▪ *(517) 784-7700*
1501 Boardman Rd
Kalamazoo ▪ *(269) 342-4329*
4320 S Westnedge Ave
Kentwood ▪ *(616) 957-7932*
3650 28th St SE
Lansing ▪ *(517) 321-3100*
707 Brookside Dr
Livonia ▪ *(734) 421-0220*
29441 5 Mile Rd
Madison Heights ▪ *(248) 585-2064*

1515 W 14 Mile Rd
Novi ▪ *(248) 347-9201*
48020 Grand River Ave
Okemos ▪ *(517) 381-1704*
4880 Marsh Rd
Rochester Hills ▪ *(248) 650-2521*
1880 S Rochester Rd
Roseville ▪ *(586) 775-4329*
28850 Gratiot Ave
Saginaw ▪ *(989) 797-2319*
2468 Tittabawassee Rd
Shelby Township ▪ *(586) 566-7770*
45170 Schoenherr Rd
Southfield ▪ *(248) 424-9696*
23501 Greenfield Rd
Southgate ▪ *(734) 285-2314*
15765 Eureka Rd
Traverse City ▪ *(231) 935-4329*
3501 Marketplace Cir
W Bloomfield ▪ *(248) 539-1030*
6203 Orchard Lake Rd

P.F. Chang's China Bistro 📖

Clinton Township ▪ *(586) 263-0860*
17390 Hall Rd Unit R-103
Dearborn ▪ *(313) 429-2030*
18900 Michigan Ave Spc R-101
Lansing ▪ *(517) 267-3833*
2425 Lake Lansing Rd
Northville ▪ *(248) 675-0066*
17905 Haggerty Rd
Troy ▪ *(248) 816-8000*
2801 W Big Beaver Rd Ste D112

Paesano Restaurant and Wine Bar
★ $$**LD**

Ann Arbor ▪ *(734) 971-0484*
3411 Washtenaw Ave ▪ *Italian* ▪ Executive Chef Isabella reports that most of the menu is naturally GF. Other items can almost always be modified to be GF, since GF bread, pasta, and pizza are available. The menu changes seasonally, but at least three GF dessert options are usually available. ▪ *www.paesanosannarbor.com*

Panini Press, The ★ ¢**LD**

Berkley ▪ *(248) 547-7377*
28983 Woodward Ave ▪ *Sandwich Shop* ▪ Manager Brad reports that any sandwich

can be made on GF bread. Sandwiches that can be modified to be GF include the tomato mozzarella, roast beef and bell peppers, and tuna and cheddar. ▪ *www.thepaninipress.com*

Pearl's New Orleans Kitchen ✪ $$LD
Elk Rapids ▪ *(231) 264-0530*
617 Ames St ▪ *Cajun & Creole* ▪ GF menu includes jambalaya, tuna, steak, and pork chops, among other things. Manager and Chef JW notes that many GF diners come to the restaurant. ▪ *www.magnumhospitality.com*

Pei Wei Asian Diner 📖
Farmington Hills ▪ *(248) 862-7260*
31367 Orchard Lake Rd
Novi ▪ *(248) 675-0040*
43170 Grand River Ave
Rochester ▪ *(248) 601-1380*
1206 Walton Blvd
Royal Oak ▪ *(248) 837-2420*
30278 Woodward Ave
Sterling Heights ▪ *(586) 566-0362*
13937 Lakeside Cir Ste 113
Troy ▪ *(248) 824-1085*
730 E Big Beaver Rd
Warren ▪ *(586) 834-4020*
5753 E 12 Mile Rd

Piece O' Cake, A ★ ¢S
East Lansing ▪ *(517) 333-6881*
4966 Northwind Dr ▪ *Bakery* ▪ Non-dedicated bakery offering GF graham crackers, bread, pizza, cookies, pies, cakes, and more. GF items are baked on Tuesdays only. ▪ *www.apieceocake.com*

Pisanello's Pizza ★ $LD
Mount Pleasant ▪ *(989) 773-9906*
110 N Main St ▪ *Pizza* ▪ GF pizza is available. Manager Adam cautions that when the pizza goes through the oven, it may come into contact with particles of flour. ▪ *www.pisanellos.net*

Real Seafood Co. ✪★ $$$LD
Ann Arbor ▪ *(734) 769-7738*
341 S Main St ▪ *Seafood* ▪ GF menu includes roasted Atlantic salmon, escargot, clams, and broiled scallops. The restaurant notes that GF diners are accommodated "at least once a day," so the kitchen is very aware of the GF diet. GF pasta is available. ▪ *www.realseafoodcorestaurant.com*

Red Mesa Grill ✪★ $LD
Boyne City ▪ *(231) 582-0049*
117 Water St
Traverse City ▪ *(231) 938-2773*
15445 US Highway 31 N ▪ *Latin American* ▪ GF options include Costa Rican garlic steak, Sonoma tuna, enchiladas, and fajitas. For dessert, they offer cinnamon ice cream. Ask the server for a "Celiac Safe Menu" to see all GF options. GF soy sauce is available. ▪ *www.magnumhospitality.com/red-mesa*

San Chez Bistro ✪ $$$$LD
Grand Rapids ▪ *(616) 774-8272*
38 Fulton St W ▪ *Tapas* ▪ GF menu includes tortillas, stuffed peppers, grilled chicken breast, and scallops with bacon. Restaurant reports that they take allergies "very seriously." ▪ *www.sanchezbistro.com*

Seva ✪★ $LD
Ann Arbor ▪ *(734) 662-1111*
314 E Liberty St ▪ *Vegetarian* ▪ Extensive GF menu includes a variety of alcoholic drinks, salads, and appetizers like baked artichoke-spinach dip, nachos and sweet potato fries. Entrée examples are pasta with soy sausage and cilantro-peanut stir fry. GF brunch options are also available. GF tamari sauce, crackers, pasta and chocolate cake are available. ▪ *www.sevarestaurant.com*

Silvio's Organic Pizza ★ $BLD
Ann Arbor ▪ *(734) 214-6666*
715 N University Ave ▪ *Pizza* ▪ GF pasta and pizza are available. Pizza is available in the 6-inch and 14-inch sizes, while pasta is available for substitution into any pasta dish. For dessert, they offer GF cheesecake and sometimes chocolate mousse. ▪ *www.silviosorganicpizza.com*

Stadium Market   ★ $$LD
Ann Arbor ▪ *(734) 761-9650*
1423 E Stadium Blvd ▪ *Pizza* ▪ GF pizza,
two kinds of beer, bread for sandwiches,
and cheese bread are available. Restaurant
is takeout only.

Stir Crazy   ★ $LD
Auburn Hills ▪ *(248) 454-0400*
4248 Baldwin Rd ▪ *Asian Stir-Fry* ▪
Manager Angie reports that the staff is
trained on the GF diet. She notes that three
different GF sauces are available: teriyaki,
szechuan, and a basic brown sauce. The
"create your own stir-fry" option offers GF
flat rice noodles. She recommends avoiding
fried dishes because of possible cross-contamination. ▪ *www.stircrazy.com*

Sugar Kisses Bakery   ✪★ ¢S
Berkley ▪ *(248) 542-5622*
2688 Coolidge Hwy ▪ *Bakery* ▪ A self-
described "wheat-free pastry shop," they
offer many GF products, which are marked
on the menu. GF options include bread,
cookies, cakes, pies, muffins, brownies, and
more. ▪ *www.sugarkissesbakery.com*

Sweet Lorraine's $$BLD
Livonia ▪ *(734) 953-7480*
17100 N Laurel Park Dr
Southfield ▪ *(248) 559-5985*
29101 Greenfield Rd ▪ *American* ▪ Chef
Paul at the Livonia location reports that
all servers and chefs are GF aware. Still, he
recommends asking for him upon arrival.
Manager Lisa at the Southfield location
reports that they have an internal GF menu
that the server or hostess will give to GF
diners. Most menu items can be modified
to be GF, including maple-cured salmon,
pot roast, and several vegetarian entrées.
Located in the Marriot Hotel. ▪ *www.sweet-
lorraines.com*

Tuscan Bistro   ★ $$LD
Traverse City ▪ *(231) 922-7795*
12930 S West Bay Shore Dr ▪ *Italian* ▪ GF
beer is available. Manager Elizabeth reports

that the kitchen is "very adept" at handling
GF requests. ▪ *www.tuscanbistrotc.com*

Uno Chicago Grill   📖
Bay City ▪ *(989) 684-8667*
2795 Wilder Rd
Birch Run ▪ *(989) 624-8667*
8975 Market Place Dr
Sterling Heights ▪ *(586) 991-0912*
44805 Mound Rd

Wildflours Bakery & Café   ★ ¢S
Northville ▪ *(248) 374-6244*
43053 7 Mile Rd ▪ *Bakery* ▪ GF bread,
pizza dough, lavash, cinnamon chips, and
chocolate raspberry squares are available.

Willy O's Pizza and Grill   ★ $LD
South Haven ▪ *(269) 637-3400*
08960 M 140 ▪ *Pizza* ▪ GF pizza, including specialty blueberry pineapple pizza, is
available.

Zingerman's Roadhouse   ✪ $$LD
Ann Arbor ▪ *(734) 663-3663*
2501 Jackson Ave ▪ *American* ▪ GF menu
features chili & cheddar fries, Eastern
North Carolina pulled pork, grilled free-
range half chicken, and more. GF dessert is
also available. ▪ *www.zingermansroadhouse.
com*

MINNESOTA

MINNEAPOLIS

---

3 Monkey's Pub and Grub   ★ ¢LD
Minneapolis ▪ *(612) 208-0826*
1410 Nicollet Ave ▪ *Pub Food* ▪ GF pasta
and pizza are available. Pizzas are "build
your own," and can be eaten in, taken
out, or prepared for "take-&-bake." GF
pasta options include cheese ravioli. ▪
www.3monkeyspubandgrub.com

Amore Victoria   ★ $$BLD
Minneapolis ▪ *(612) 823-0250*

1601 W Lake St ▪ *Italian* ▪ GF pasta is available. Co-owner Jenna reports that nearly all of the menu can be prepared GF, as everything is made individually and to order. For dessert, they offer a flourless chocolate cake. ▪ *www.amorevictoria.com*

Buca di Beppo 📖
Minneapolis ▪ *(612) 288-0138*
1204 Harmon Pl

Capital Grille, The 📖
Minneapolis ▪ *(612) 692-9000*
801 Hennepin Ave

Chiang Mai Thai ✪★ $LD
Minneapolis ▪ *(612) 827-1606*
3001 Hennepin Ave S ▪ *Thai* ▪ The generous selection of GF menu items includes pad thai, almost all of the curries, and the chicken satay. GF beer, soy sauce, and noodles are available. ▪ *www.chiangmai-thai.com*

Christos Greek Restaurant $LD
Minneapolis ▪ *(612) 871-2111*
2632 Nicollet Ave ▪ *Greek* ▪ Manager Ashley reports that they are "very familiar" with the GF diet. She notes that they used to have a GF menu, so the servers have been trained on which items are naturally GF and which can be modified to be GF. ▪ *www.christos.com*

Common Roots $BLD
Minneapolis ▪ *(612) 871-2360*
2558 Lyndale Ave S ▪ *Café* ▪ Manager Danny reports that although the menu frequently changes, there is always a GF option available. He reports that everything is made from scratch, so dishes from the regular menu are easily modified to be GF. Ask the server at the counter for the day's GF options. ▪ *www.commonrootscafe.com*

Ecopolitan ★ $BLD
Minneapolis ▪ *(612) 874-7336*
2409 Lyndale Ave S ▪ *Raw & Vegan* ▪ GF raw pizza with a buckwheat crust is available. GF raw pasta made with zucchini or carrots is also available. ▪ *www.ecopolitan.com*

Fogo De Chao ★ $$$$LD
Minneapolis ▪ *(612) 338-1344*
645 Hennepin Ave ▪ *Brazilian* ▪ GF cheese bread made with yucca flour is available. ▪ *www.fogodechao.com*

Lucia's $$$LD
Minneapolis ▪ *(612) 825-1572*
1432 W 31st St ▪ *Modern American* ▪ Manager Laurie reports that the restaurant "does their best" to accommodate GF diners. She recommends making reservations noting GF at least one day in advance. She notes that the servers are "extraordinarily well trained" on the GF diet, and if they do not know something, they will ask the kitchen directly. ▪ *www.lucias.com*

Madwoman Gluten Free Bakeshop
100% ¢$
Minneapolis ▪ *(612) 825-6680*
4747 Nicollet Ave ▪ *Bakery* ▪ Dedicated GF bakery offering a variety of breads, paninis, soups, cereals, muffins, and cupcakes. Manager Allie reports that everything in the shop is GF. ▪ *www.madwomanfoods.com*

Manny's Steakhouse $$$$D
Minneapolis ▪ *(612) 339-9900*
825 Marquette Ave South ▪ *Steakhouse* ▪ Hostess Anna reports that all staff members are knowledgeable about the GF diet, as they serve "a fair amount" of GF diners. Although alerting a server should be sufficient, she recommends speaking to a manager "just to be safe." Located in the Foshay Tower at the corner of 9th and Marquette. ▪ *www.mannyssteakhouse.com*

Melting Pot, The 📖
Minneapolis ▪ *(612) 338-9900*
80 S 9th St

Midori's Floating World Café ★ $$LD
Minneapolis ▪ *(612) 721-3011*
2629 East Lake Street ▪ *Japanese* ▪ Owner Midori reports that several menu

items, like the grilled fish dinner, tofu, and many sushi items, can be prepared GF. She notes that most servers are GF aware. WF tamari sauce is available. ▪ *www.floating-worldcafe.com*

Old Spaghetti Factory, The   📖
Minneapolis ▪ *(612) 341-0949*
233 Park Ave

Palomino   ✪ $$$LD
Minneapolis ▪ *(612) 339-3800*
825 Hennepin Ave ▪ *Modern American* ▪ Restaurant reports that there is an "extensive set of options" on the GF menu. ▪ *www.palomino.com*

Pizza Luce   ✪★ $LD
Minneapolis ▪ *(612) 333-7359*
119 N 4th St ▪ *Pizza* ▪ New and extensive GF menu is available seven days a week for pickup, delivery, or dining in. GF pasta, pizza, and beer are available. ▪ *www.pizzaluce.com*

Rice Paper $$LD
Minneapolis ▪ *(612) 926-8650*
2726 W 43rd St ▪ *Vietnamese* ▪ Restaurant reports that GF diners come in "at least twice per week." The staff is "pretty knowledgeable" about what has gluten and what does not. A list of GF items is posted in the kitchen, so servers can remain GF aware. ▪ *www.ricepaperrestaurant.com*

Signature Café and Catering $$LD
Minneapolis ▪ *(612) 378-0237*
130 Southeast Warwick St ▪ *Modern American* ▪ Co-owner Anthony reports that they serve GF diners "every day." He recommends reservations noting GF, and asking to speak with a chef upon arrival. They have many dishes, such as the ratatouille, that can be made GF. Confirm timeliness of this information before dining in. ▪ *www.signaturecafe.net*

Wedge Co-op   ★ ¢BLD
Minneapolis ▪ *(612) 871-3993*
2105 Lyndale Ave S ▪ *Deli & Bakery* ▪ GF bread and soy sauce are available for

deli items like sandwiches and thai red curry mushrooms. GF cookies, pies, cakes, cupcakes, muffins, and brownies are some of the GF desserts available. ▪ *www.wedge.coop*

Zelo   ✪★ $$LD
Minneapolis ▪ *(612) 333-7000*
831 Nicollet Mall ▪ *Italian* ▪ GF menu includes wood grilled portabella mushroom, rice penne with roasted peppers, and pork chops. GF pasta is available. ▪ *www.zelomn.com*

MINNESOTA

ROCHESTER

300 First   ✪ $$$D
Rochester ▪ *(507) 281-2451*
300 1st Ave NW ▪ *Modern American* ▪ GF menu includes soups, salads, and appetizers. In addition, all steaks can be made GF. Restaurant reports that GF diners come in "all the time." Alert a server, who will notify the kitchen. ▪ *www.cccrmg.com/300first.htm*

Backroom Deli, The   ★ ¢BLD
Rochester ▪ *(507) 289-9061*
1001 6th St NW ▪ *Vegan* ▪ GF brown rice wraps are available. The deli reports that most of the salads are also GF. Confirm timeliness of this information before dining in. Ask at the counter about the day's GF soup option. ▪ *www.rochestergoodfood.com*

Bread Baker Company, The   ★ ¢S
Rochester ▪ *(507) 289-7052*
16 17th St NW ▪ *Bakery* ▪ Non-dedicated bakery offering a variety of GF baked goods like pizza crusts, breads, muffins, and cookies. GF products are made once a week on GF bake days, and then frozen for weeklong availability. Calling ahead is

recommended, as some things sell out. ▪ *www.breadbakercompany.com*

Canadian Honker ☺ $**BLD**
Rochester ▪ *(507) 282-6572*
1203 2nd St SW ▪ *American* ▪ Limited GF menu includes egg breakfasts with hashbrowns and sausage, Hawaiian cod with pineapple and salsa, honey mustard chicken, sirloin, and salmon. ▪ *www.canadianhonker.com*

City Café Mixed Grille & Bar ☺ $$**LD**
Rochester ▪ *(507) 289-1949*
216 1st Ave SW ▪ *American* ▪ GF menu includes scallops, tuna, maple roasted chicken breast, filet mignon, flank steak, fresh fish, and chocolate or vanilla crème brulee for dessert. ▪ *www.city-cafe.com*

El Carambas ¢**LD**
Rochester ▪ *(507) 281-3104*
1503 12Th St SE ▪ *Mexican* ▪ Manager Eddie reports that many menu items can be modified to be GF. Enchiladas, fajitas, tacos, and tamales are some examples. Confirm timeliness of this information before dining in. There is an internal list of GF items that chefs, servers, and diners can all refer to. He offers a short tour of the restaurant for GF diners who want to see the kitchen's setup.

Famous Dave's Barbeque $**LD**
Rochester ▪ *(507) 282-4200*
431 16th Ave NW ▪ *Barbeque* ▪ Veteran Server Nicole reports that although the restaurant has discontinued their GF menu, they do have a binder that lists ingredients for all of their dishes. She recommends alerting a server, who can bring over the binder. She notes that many experienced servers know the best options for GF customers, which include chicken breasts, baked potatoes, and warm baked apples. Confirm timeliness of this information before dining in. ▪ *www.famousdaves.com*

Fiesta Café ☺ $$**LD**
Rochester ▪ *(507) 288-1116*
1645 Broadway Ave N ▪ *Mexican* ▪ GF

menu includes fajitas, enchiladas, tortilla soup, and seafood. Other items on the regular menu can also be modified to be GF. Restaurant recommends asking for manager Victorino, who can discuss GF options.

Gluten-Free Cupboard 100% $$**S**
Rochester ▪ *(507) 529-1132*
1833 3rd Ave SE ▪ *Take-&-Bake* ▪ GF shop with several "take-&-bake" meals and baked goods available. "Take-&-bake" pizzas, chicken penne alfredo, chicken pad thai, pasta primavera, lemon basil chicken, and wild salmon meals are available. Muffins, bagels, lemon bars, pumpkin bars, and donuts are also available. ▪ *www.glutenfreecupboard.com*

Michael's Fine Dining ☺ $$$**LD**
Rochester ▪ *(507) 288-2020*
15 S Broadway ▪ *Seafood & Steakhouse* ▪ GF menu includes steak, pork chops, lamb, kebabs, duck, cod, scallops, and more. Crème brulee is available for dessert. ▪ *www.michaelsfinedining.com*

Original Roscoe's Barbecue, The $**LD**
Rochester ▪ *(507) 281-4622*
3456 E Circle Dr NE
Rochester ▪ *(507) 285-0501*
603 4th St SE ▪ *Barbeque* ▪ Both locations report that they are GF friendly. The E Circle Dr location has a list of GF items posted at the front of the restaurant. Both locations use GF BBQ sauce, and all meats, as well as the potato salad, baked beans, and vegetables can be prepared GF. Confirm timeliness of this information before dining in. The E Circle location is open all year round, but the 4th St. location is open from April to September. ▪ *www.roscoesbbq.com*

Outback Steakhouse 📖
Rochester ▪ *(507) 252-1150*
1201 S Broadway

Paradise Pete's ☺★ $$**LD**
Rochester ▪ *(507) 287-8700*
14 17th Ave NW ▪ *American* ▪ GF pizza

is available in the 14-inch size, with any toppings. Manager Matt notes that there are other GF items, most of which are marked on the regular menu. He adds that the owners are working on a GF list, which they hope to release soon.

Redwood Room, The   ✪ $$D
Rochester ▪ *(507) 281-2978*
300 1st Ave NW ▪ *Modern American* ▪ GF menu includes roasted salmon, creamy Cajun sauté, apple cider pork, and tuna. For dessert, there is usually crème brûlée. Chef Hillary reports that "a lot of people" who are GF come to dine in, so all staff members are very familiar with the GF diet. ▪ *www.cccrmg.com/redwoodroom.htm*

Valentino's Pizza   ★ ¢LD
Rochester ▪ *(507) 281-2100*
130 Elton Hills Dr NW ▪ *Pizza* ▪ GF pizza is available in the 7-inch or 10-inch size. ▪ *www.valentinos.com*

Victoria's Italian Cuisine   ✪★ $$LD
Rochester ▪ *(507) 280-6232*
7 1st Ave SW ▪ *Italian* ▪ GF pasta, rolls, and pizza are available. Full GF menu is available upon request. The restaurant reports that GF diners are "frequently" accommodated. ▪ *www.victoriasmn.com*

Zorba's   ✪ ¢LD
Rochester ▪ *(507) 281-1540*
924 7th St NW ▪ *Greek* ▪ GF menu items include beef, lamb, chicken, or pork souvlaki, salmon fillet, Greek chicken, lamb chops, and the shrimp or chicken combo, along with a variety of other dishes.

MINNESOTA
ALL OTHER CITIES

Bello Cucina Italian Restaurant ★ $LD
Fergus Falls ▪ *(218) 998-2221*
106 W Lincoln Ave
Morris ▪ *(320) 585-7000*
506 Atlantic Ave ▪ *Italian* ▪ GF pasta is available. Restaurant reports that GF diners can also eat salads and other modified dishes. They note that calling ahead is advised, since GF pasta takes longer to cook. ▪ *www.bellocucina.com*

Biaggi's Ristorante Italiano   📖
Eden Prairie ▪ *(952) 942-8555*
8251 Flying Cloud Dr
Maple Grove ▪ *(763) 416-2225*
12051 Elm Creek Blvd N

Big Bowl Restaurant   ✪ $LD
Edina ▪ *(952) 928-7888*
3669 Galleria
Minnetonka ▪ *(952) 797-9888*
12649 Wayzata Blvd
Roseville ▪ *(651) 636-7173*
1705 Highway 36 W ▪ *Asian* ▪ GF menu includes thai chicken lettuce wraps as an appetizer, various pad thai dishes and chicken kung pao as entrées, and two GF desserts, including the trio of tastes. ▪ *www.bigbowl.com*

Bittersweet Bakery   100% $S
Eagan ▪ *(651) 686-0112*
2105 Cliff Rd ▪ *Bakery* ▪ Dedicated GF bakery with a variety of breads, bars, cakes, cupcakes, and "take-&-bake" pizzas. Manager Seth reports that the bakery makes all GF products fresh every day. ▪ *www.bittersweetgf.com*

Bubba Gump Shrimp Co.   📖
Bloomington ▪ *(952) 853-6600*
396 S Avenue

Buca di Beppo   📖
Burnsville ▪ *(952) 892-7272*
14300 Burnhaven Dr

Eden Prairie ▪ **(952) 934-9463**
7711 Mitchell Rd
Maple Grove ▪ **(763) 494-3466**
12650 Elm Creek Blvd N
Saint Paul ▪ **(651) 772-4388**
2728 Gannon Rd

Chianti Grill   ✪★ $LD
Burnsville ▪ **(952) 892-7555**
14296 Plymouth Ave
Roseville ▪ **(651) 644-2808**
2050 Snelling Ave ▪ *Italian* ▪ GF menu
includes appetizers, salads, steak, and seafood. GF spaghetti and penne are available
for pasta dishes like spicy chicken penne
and chicken spaghetti al fresco. ▪ *www.
chiantigrill.com*

Christos Greek Restaurant $LD
Minnetonka ▪ **(952) 912-1000**
15600 Highway 7
Saint Paul ▪ **(651) 224-6000**
214 4th St E ▪ *Greek* ▪ Both locations
report that they are familiar with the GF
diet, as they used to have a GF menu. GF
options include the chicken or lamb kabob
and the koupepia. Confirm timeliness of
this information before dining in. ▪ *www.
christos.com*

Ciao Bella   ★ $LD
Bloomington ▪ **(952) 841-1000**
3501 Minnesota Dr ▪ *Italian* ▪ GF pasta
is available. Manager Sarah reports that if
they have the ingredients, they can make
or modify any dish to be GF. Alert a server
upon arrival. ▪ *www.ciaobellamn.com*

Ciatti's Ristorante   ✪★ $$$LD
Saint Cloud ▪ **(320) 257-7900**
2635 W Division St ▪ *Italian* ▪ GF menu
includes antipasti, insulate, pasta, entrées,
sandwiches, bunless burgers, and pizza.
Manager Carrie reports that all servers are
trained on GF foods. GF pasta and pizza
are available. ▪ *www.ciattisristorante.com*

Cooqi Gluten-Free Delights   100% ¢S
Saint Paul ▪ **(651) 645-4433**
2186 Marshall Ave ▪ *Bakery* ▪ Dedicated
GF bakery offering brownies, cookies,

cakes, cupcakes, donuts, muffins, breads,
and more. Bread varieties include sourdough, multigrain, honey molasses, and
honey oat. GF pizza crust is also available
for "take-&-bake." ▪ *www.cooqiglutenfree.
com*

Crumb Gourmet Deli   ★ ¢LD
Eden Prairie ▪ **(952) 934-1717**
7910 Mitchell Rd ▪ *Deli* ▪ GF bread is available. GF soups, cookies, and salads are also
available. A separate toaster, cutting board,
and knives are used for preparing GF products. ▪ *www.crumbgourmetdeli.com*

CurryUp Restaurant & Grocery   ¢LD
Maple Grove ▪ **(763) 416-0473**
13601 Grove Dr ▪ *Indian* ▪ Co-owner Ajay
reports that GF options are always available. He notes that many dishes are naturally GF, such as the dosa and a variety of
vegetable curries. GF desserts include rice
pudding and a special Indian carrot cake
called gajar halwa. Confirm timeliness of
this information before dining in. ▪ *www.
curryupfoods.com*

Doolittles Woodfire Grill   ✪ $$LD
Alexandria ▪ **(320) 759-0885**
4409 Highway 29 S
Eagan ▪ **(651) 452-6627**
2140 Cliff Rd
Golden Valley ▪ **(763) 542-1931**
550 Winnetonka Avenue ▪ *Fusion* ▪ GF
menu notes which dishes are GF and
provides ordering instructions. It includes
prime rib french dip, salads, roasted pork,
grilled chicken breast, and baby red potatoes. ▪ *www.doolittlesrestaurants.com*

Duluth Grill   ✪★ $BLD
Duluth ▪ **(218) 726-1150**
I-35 And 27th Ave W ▪ *American* ▪ GF
menu includes french toast, country fried
steak and eggs, the patty melt on buckwheat bread, and the wild rice meatloaf
dinner. Manager Nick notes that the
kitchen is not entirely GF, but they do the
best they can to separate GF foods from

regular menu items during preparation. GF bread is available. ▪ www.duluthgrill.com

Fishman's Delicatessen and Bakery
★ ¢**BLD**

St. Louis Park ▪ *(952) 926-5611*
4100 Minnetonka Blvd ▪ *Take-&-Bake* ▪ GF muffins, challah bread, cinnamon rugula, chocolate chip cookies, hamantaschen, and more are kept in the frozen section. Manager Stewart notes that he can make sandwiches using GF bread for customers who buy an entire loaf. ▪ *www.fishmanskosher.com*

Fresh and Natural Foods
★ ¢**BLD**

Plymouth ▪ *(763) 559-0754*
4232 Lancaster Ln N
Shoreview ▪ *(651) 203-3663*
1075 Highway 96 W ▪ *Deli* ▪ Deli is located in the Fresh and Natural Foods grocery store. GF sandwiches, soups, pasta, and pizza are available. GF pastries and baked goods are also available. Many GF items are available on a "build your own" or "Grab N Go" basis. ▪ *www.freshandnaturalfoods.com*

Good Earth
$**BLD**

Edina ▪ *(952) 925-1001*
3460 Galleria
Roseville ▪ *(651) 636-0956*
1901 Highway 36 W ▪ *Modern American* ▪ Hostess Samantha of Roseville and Manager Joyce of Edina report that they serve "a lot of people" who are GF. They note that all staff members are trained to accommodate GF diners, and that servers can indicate possible GF menu items. ▪ *www.goodearthmn.com*

Ground Round
📖

Bemidji ▪ *(218) 444-3201*
2200 Paul Bunyan Dr NW
Duluth ▪ *(218) 723-1776*
2102 Maple Grove Rd
Grand Rapids ▪ *(218) 327-8655*
1001 S Pokegama Ave Ste E
Saint Cloud ▪ *(320) 252-7321*
2621 W Division St
Winona ▪ *(507) 452-3390*

405 Highway 14
Worthington ▪ *(507) 376-3043*
1290 Ryans Rd # 1029

Hubbell House, The
✪ $$$**LD**

Mantorville ▪ *(507) 635-2331*
502 N Main St ▪ *American* ▪ GF menu includes smoked pork chops, broiled walleye, raspberry chicken breast, cheddar steak, and more. ▪ *www.hubbellhouserestaurant.com*

Jensen's Supper Club
$$$**D**

Eagan ▪ *(651) 688-7969*
3840 Sibley Memorial Hwy ▪ *Seafood & Steakhouse* ▪ Owner Doran reports that "a lot of people ask" for GF options. He adds that GF requests are easily accommodated, as that they serve a lot of raw and/or simple protein dishes. Alert a server, who will notify the kitchen. ▪ *www.jensenssupperclub.com*

Kona Grill
📖

Eden Prairie ▪ *(952) 941-3262*
11997 Singletree Ln

Leonardo's Pizzeria
★ $$**D**

Mahtomedi ▪ *(651) 777-1200*
3150 Century Ave N ▪ *Pizza* ▪ GF pizza is available. ▪ *www.leonardospizzeria.net*

Liffey, The
✪ $**BLD**

Saint Paul ▪ *(651) 556-1420*
175 7th St W ▪ *Irish* ▪ GF menu includes baked artichoke, Irish cobb salad, sandwiches with no buns, shepherd's pie, and corned beef and cabbage. Manager Cynthia notes that GF diners come in "at least once a week." ▪ *www.theliffey.com*

Napa Valley Grille
$$$**LD**

Bloomington ▪ *(952) 858-9934*
60 E Broadway ▪ *Italian* ▪ Manager Alisha reports that GF diners are "definitely" welcome, and advises alerting both the host and the server upon arrival. Reservations noting GF are recommended but not required. Located in the Mall of America, between Macy's and Nordstrom. ▪ *www.napavalleygrille.com*

Original Pancake House, The   ★ ¢**BL**
Eden Prairie ▪ *(952) 224-9440*
549 Prairie Center Dr
Edina ▪ *(952) 920-4444*
3501 W 70th St
Maple Grove ▪ *(763) 383-0888*
6322 Vinewood Ln
Wayzata ▪ *(952) 475-9151*
901 East Lake St ▪ *Breakfast* ▪ GF pancakes are available. Select locations may serve other GF options. Call a specific location to inquire. ▪ *www.originalpancakehouse.com*

Outback Steakhouse   📖
Bloomington ▪ *(952) 854-1950*
1321 E 78th St
Burnsville ▪ *(952) 892-0700*
2034 County Road 42 W
Coon Rapids ▪ *(763) 792-9159*
8880 Springbrook Dr NW
Hermantown ▪ *(218) 722-2471*
4255 Haines Rd
Inver Grove Heights ▪ *(651) 457-7688*
5723 Bishop Ave
Maplewood ▪ *(651) 748-0661*
1770 Beam Ave
Roseville ▪ *(651) 697-1224*
2181 Snelling Ave N
Woodbury ▪ *(651) 735-3268*
10150 Hudson Rd

P.F. Chang's China Bistro   📖
Edina ▪ *(952) 926-1713*
2700 Southdale Ctr
Maple Grove ▪ *(763) 493-9377*
12071 Elm Creek Blvd N

Park Tavern Bowl   ★ $**BLD**
St Louis Park ▪ *(952) 929-6810*
3401 Louisiana Ave S ▪ *American* ▪ GF pizza available. ▪ *www.parktavern.net*

Pazzaluna Urban Italian Restaurant and Bar   ✪ $$$**LD**
Saint Paul ▪ *(651) 223-7000*
360 Saint Peter St ▪ *Italian* ▪ GF menu includes several risotto options, ahi tuna, sea bass, sirloin, and ribeye, among other things. There is only one copy of the GF menu. ▪ *www.pazzaluna.com*

Pei Wei Asian Diner   📖
Eden Prairie ▪ *(952) 656-1000*
12561 Castlemoor Dr
St Louis Park ▪ *(952) 656-9480*
5330 Cedar Lake Rd S
Woodbury ▪ *(651) 286-3990*
8300 Tamarack Vlg Ste 102

Pizza Luce   ✪★ $**LD**
Saint Paul ▪ *(651) 288-0186*
1183 Selby Ave ▪ *Pizza* ▪ New and extensive GF menu is available seven days a week for pickup, delivery, or dining in. GF pasta, pizza, and beer are available. ▪ *www.pizzaluce.com*

Porterhouse Steaks & Seafood $$$**D**
Lakeville ▪ *(952) 469-2995*
11211 205th St W
Little Canada ▪ *(651) 483-9248*
235 Little Canada Rd E ▪ *Seafood & Steakhouse* ▪ Manager Kevin of the Little Canada location reports that both restaurants have "lots of nice selections" for GF diners, as most of the menu is steaks and seafood. Alert a server upon arrival. ▪ *www.porterhousesteakandseafood.com*

Supatra's Thai Cuisine   ★ $**LD**
Saint Paul ▪ *(651) 222-5859*
967 West 7th St ▪ *Thai* ▪ Owner Supatra reports that they have "a lot of customers" who are GF. She notes that the restaurant has a "big menu" with many naturally GF items. GF beer is available. ▪ *www.supatra.com*

Tasty Asia Take-out   ✪ $**LD**
Wyoming ▪ *(651) 462-1200*
26685 Faxton St ▪ *Asian* ▪ GF menu includes hot and spicy chicken with lemongrass, chicken curry, beef with broccoli, spring rolls, fried rice, and more. For dessert, there is flourless chocolate cake and flan. GF items are available for online ordering. ▪ *www.tastyasia.com*

Timber Lodge Steakhouse   ✪ $$$D
Bloomington ▪ *(952) 881-5509*
7989 Southtown Ctr
Duluth ▪ *(218) 722-2624*
325 Lake Ave S
Maple Grove ▪ *(763) 416-0070*
12635 Elm Creek Blvd
Owatonna ▪ *(507) 444-0303*
4455 West Frontage Rd
St Louis Park ▪ *(952) 345-0505*
6501 Wayzata Blvd ▪ Steakhouse ▪ GF
menu includes prime rib, rainbow trout,
walleye filet, Atlantic salmon, and more. ▪
www.timberlodgesteakhouse.com

Tucci Benucch $$LD
Bloomington ▪ *(952) 853-0200*
114 W Market ▪ *Italian* ▪ Manager Justin
notes that anything except pasta can be
made GF. He reports that all staff members are trained to handle "allergies." He
recommends alerting your server who will
have the chef prepare your meal correctly. ▪
www.leye.com

Twin City Grill $$LD
Bloomington ▪ *(952) 854-0200*
Mall Of America ▪ *Seafood & Steakhouse*
▪ Manager Finesse reports that most menu
items can be made GF. She notes that all
servers are trained to inform the manager
and the chef of "allergies." A server or a
manager will indicate appropriate menu
items. ▪ *www.leye.com*

W.A. Frost & Co. $$$LD
Saint Paul ▪ *(651) 224-5715*
374 Selby Ave ▪ *Modern American* ▪
Chef Wyatt reports that the entire staff is
"absolutely" aware of the GF diet, as they
accommodate it "frequently." The grilled
salmon, the chicken entrée, and the New
York strip steak can all be prepared GF.
Confirm timeliness of this information
before dining in. ▪ *www.wafrost.com*

Wildfire   ✪★ $$$LD
Eden Prairie ▪ *(952) 914-9100*
3020 Eden Prarie Center ▪ *Steakhouse*
▪ GF menu includes a variety of starters,

salads, sides, sandwiches, and entrées. GF
pizza crust, hamburger buns, and beer are
available. For dessert, they offer flourless
chocolate cake, among other things. ▪ *www.*
wildfirerestaurant.com

Z Pizza   ★ $$LD
Saint Paul ▪ *(651) 633-3131*
1607 County Road C W ▪ *Pizza* ▪ GF pizza
is available. ▪ *www.zpizza.com*

Zebra Pizza   ★ $LD
Ramsey ▪ *(763) 323-7303*
14031 Saint Francis Blvd ▪ *Pizza* ▪ GF thin
crust and thick crust pizzas are available.
Any pizza toppings can be added to the 10-
inch GF crusts, which are made in-house.
Carry out and delivery only. GF pizza
crusts are also available for "take-&-bake." ▪
www.zebrapizza.info

MISSISSIPPI

Biaggi's Ristorante Italiano   📖
Ridgeland ▪ *(601) 354-6600*
970 Highland Colony Pkwy

Bonefish Grill   📖
Biloxi ▪ *(228) 388-0009*
2600 Beach Blvd Ste 76
Madison ▪ *(601) 607-3334*
201 Colony Way

Lone Star Steakhouse & Saloon   📖
Jackson ▪ *(601) 957-6026*
6010 I 55 N
Pearl ▪ *(601) 664-1733*
442 Riverwind Dr

Outback Steakhouse   📖
Diberville ▪ *(228) 392-9797*
3586 Sangani Blvd
Hattiesburg ▪ *(601) 264-0771*
103 Carlisle Dr
Jackson ▪ *(601) 977-9040*

6030 I 55 N
Meridian ▪ *(601) 485-3447*
111 S Frontage Rd
Southaven ▪ *(662) 349-7488*
125 Goodman Rd W Ste A
Tupelo ▪ *(662) 842-1734*
1348 N Gloster St

P.F. Chang's China Bistro 📖
Ridgeland ▪ *(601) 605-4282*
910 Highland Colony Pkwy

MISSOURI

KANSAS CITY

American Restaurant, The $$$**D**
Kansas City ▪ *(816) 545-8001*
200 E 25th St ▪ Modern American ▪
Service Director Rene reports that they ac-
commodate GF diners. She advises making
reservations noting GF and giving the staff
at least one day's notice. GF will be noted
on your reservation, but mention it to your
server upon arrival. All staff are trained in
"allergy" procedures. ▪ *www.theamericankc.
com*

Blue Bird Bistro $$**BLD**
Kansas City ▪ *(816) 221-7559*
1700 Summit St ▪ Organic American ▪
Manager Beth reports that there are "some
GF items" on the menu, and they accommodate GF diners "very often." Calling
ahead is recommended. ▪ *www.bluebirdbis-
tro.com*

Bonefish Grill 📖
Kansas City ▪ *(816) 746-8179*
6334 N Lucerne Ave

Buca di Beppo 📖
Kansas City ▪ *(816) 931-6548*
310 W 47th St

Capital Grille, The 📖
Kansas City ▪ *(816) 531-8345*
4740 Jefferson St

Classic Cup Café $$$**BLD**
Kansas City ▪ *(816) 753-1840*
301 W 47th St ▪ Bistro ▪ Senior Chef Labin
reports that the restaurant accommodates
GF diners "regularly, at least once a week."
He also notes that the majority of the staff
goes to culinary classes and is GF aware.
For further questions, ask for Brian the
sous chef, or Mike Turner, the executive
chef. ▪ *www.classiccup.com*

Eden Alley Café   ✪ $**LD**
Kansas City ▪ *(816) 561-5415*
707 W 47th St ▪ Vegetarian ▪ GF items
marked on the menu include garnets and
greens, egg salad on greens, falafel platter,
and baby falafel. Meals are available for
carry out, delivery, and dining in. ▪ *www.
edenalley.com*

First Watch - The Daytime Café 📖
Kansas City ▪ *(816) 931-1054*
1022 Westport Rd

Fogo de Chao   ★ $$$$**LD**
Kansas City ▪ *(816) 931-7700*
222 W 47th St ▪ Brazilian ▪ GF cheese-
bread made with yucca flour is available. ▪
www.fogodechao.com

Grand Street Cafe   ★ $$$**LD**
Kansas City ▪ *(816) 561-8000*
4740 Grand St ▪ Modern American ▪ GF
rolls and pasta are available. ▪ *www.grand-
streetcafe.com*

Ingredient Restaurant   ✪★ $**LD**
Kansas City ▪ *(816) 994-3350*
1111 Main St
Kansas City ▪ *(816) 994-3393*
4807 Jefferson St ▪ Pizza ▪ GF menu
includes salads with GF dressings and pizzas with a variety of toppings. GF pizza is
available. ▪ *www.ingredientrestaurant.com*

Kona Grill 📖
Kansas City ▪ *(816) 931-5888*
444 Ward Pkwy

Lone Star Steakhouse & Saloon   📖
Kansas City ▪ *(816) 505-1771*
6501 NW Barry Rd

LuLu's Thai Noodle Shop   ★ ¢LD
Kansas City ▪ *(816) 474-8424*
333 Southwest Blvd ▪ *Thai* ▪ GF soy sauce
is available. Manager Dennis reports that
GF diners are welcome. ▪ *www.lulusnoo-
dles.com*

Melting Pot, The   📖
Kansas City ▪ *(816) 931-6358*
450 Ward Pkwy

Milano   ★ $$LD
Kansas City ▪ *(816) 398-4825*
2450 Grand Blvd ▪ *Italian* ▪ GF pasta and
pizza are available. Restaurant recommends
reservations noting GF to give them extra
time to prepare the pasta, which takes lon-
ger to cook. Almost all pasta dishes can be
modified to be GF, and the chef will tailor
dishes to accommodate GF diners. ▪ *www.
hyattkc.com*

One More Cup   ★ ¢BL
Kansas City ▪ *(816) 994-3644*
7408 Wornall Rd ▪ *Coffee & Café* ▪ GF
brownies, cookies, vanilla and chocolate
cupcakes, apple cinnamon donut holes, and
pumpkin banana muffins are available. ▪
www.onemorecupkc.com

Outback Steakhouse   📖
Kansas City ▪ *(816) 741-8900*
7006 NW Barry Rd

P.F. Chang's China Bistro   📖
Kansas City ▪ *(816) 931-9988*
102 W 47th St

Peppercorn Duck Club   ✪ $$$$D
Kansas City ▪ *(816) 398-4845*
2345 Mcgee St ▪ *American* ▪ GF menu in-
cludes smoked mozzarella salad, rotisserie
duck, seared strip steak, and horseradish
encrusted filet. The restaurant is located in
the Hyatt Regency Hotel. As the GM of the
hotel is GF, the restaurants within are GF
aware. ▪ *www.thepeppercornduckclub.com*

Skies $$$$D
Kansas City ▪ *(816) 398-4845*
2345 Mcgee St ▪ *Modern American* ▪
Manager Amy reports that the chef can
"specialize any entrée" for GF diners. She
notes that since the manager of the hotel is
GF, the restaurant has had "lots of experi-
ence" with GF dining. Calling ahead to
note GF is recommended. ▪ *www.skieskc.
com*

Spin Pizza   ★ $$LD
Kansas City ▪ *(816) 561-7746*
4950 Main St ▪ *Pizza* ▪ GF pizza and beer
are available. ▪ *www.spinpizza.com*

Waldo Pizza   ✪★ $$LD
Kansas City ▪ *(816) 363-5242*
7433 Broadway St ▪ *Pizza* ▪ GF menu in-
cludes pizza, sandwich breads, cookies, and
cupcakes. Alert the server, who will alert
the kitchen. ▪ *www.waldopizza.net*

MISSOURI

SAINT LOUIS

Atlas Restaurant $$$D
Saint Louis ▪ *(314) 367-6800*
5513 Pershing Ave ▪ *Modern American* ▪
Owner Jean reports that the restaurant is
"very accommodating" to GF diners, who
come in approximately once a week. She
notes that the restaurant generally does not
use flour in sauces or soups. Confirm timeliness of this information before dining
in. Alert the server upon arrival. ▪ *www.
atlasrestaurantstl.com*

Cardwell's at the Plaza $$$$LD
Saint Louis ▪ *(314) 997-8885*
94 Plaza Frontenac ▪ *Modern American* ▪
Manager Katie reports that the restaurant
serves GF diners "quite often." She recommends alerting a server, who will notify the
kitchen and discuss GF options with the

chef. Because the menu changes frequently, it is difficult to tell what types of dishes will be available.She maintains, however, that there will always be GF options. ■ *www.cardwellsattheplaza.com*

City Coffee House & Creperies ★ ¢S
Saint Louis ■ *(314) 862-2489*
36 N Brentwood Blvd ■ *Crêpes* ■ GF buckwheat crepes are available. ■ *www.citycoffeeandcreperie.com*

Clark Street Grill $$$BLD
Saint Louis ■ *(314) 552-5850*
811 Spruce St ■ *Modern American* ■ Manager Lauren reports that although the restaurant does not serve GF diners "on a regular basis," they will make GF items from scratch. She recommends reservations noting GF so that the restaurant can make sure to have a chef available to speak with the GF customer upon arrival. Located inside The Westin St. Louis hotel. ■ *www.clarkstreetgrill.com*

Corner Pub & Grill, The ◑ ¢LD
Saint Louis ■ *(636) 225-1300*
13645 Big Bend Rd ■ *Pub Food* ■ "Hannah's" GF menu includes fried potato skins, BBQ chicken wings, fries, chips, salads with GF dressings, and more. Both locations have a dedicated GF fryer. The menu is named after Owner Brant's daughter, who is GF. ■ *www.cornerpubandgrill.com*

First Watch - The Daytime Café 📖
Saint Louis ■ *(314) 293-1024*
5646 Telegraph Rd

Fitz's American Grill and Bottling Works $LD
Saint Louis ■ *(314) 726-9555*
6605 Delmar Blvd ■ *American* ■ General Manager Tom reports that GF diners should ask to speak with a manager, who will "discuss various options for eliminating gluten" from menu items. Burgers without buns are a popular GF item. Confirm timeliness of this information before dining in. ■ *www.fitzsrootbeer.com*

Herbie's ◑★ $$LD
Saint Louis ■ *(314) 769-9595*
405 N Euclid Ave ■ *American* ■ GF menu includes raspberry duck, spinach and artichoke dip, and shrimp and grits. GF pizza is available. Alert the server, who will direct GF requests to the kitchen. Reservations noting GF are recommended. ■ *www.herbies.com*

Old Spaghetti Factory, The 📖
Saint Louis ■ *(314) 621-0276*
727 N 1st St

Outback Steakhouse 📖
Saint Louis ■ *(314) 843-0777*
5240 S Lindbergh Blvd

P.F. Chang's China Bistro 📖
Saint Louis ■ *(314) 862-2624*
25 The Boulevard Saint Louis

Pasta House Co., The 📖
Saint Louis ■ *(314) 961-6260*
300 Crestwood Plz
Saint Louis ■ *(314) 367-1144*
313 N Euclid Ave
Saint Louis ■ *(314) 894-9161*
6214 S Lindbergh Blvd
Saint Louis ■ *(314) 432-6750*
700 N New Ballas Rd
Saint Louis ■ *(314) 991-2022*
8213 Delmar Blvd
Saint Louis ■ *(314) 638-1240*
9012 Gravois Rd

Pei Wei Asian Diner 📖
Saint Louis ■ *(314) 656-5980*
8885 Ladue Rd Ste 1

Portabella $$$LD
Saint Louis ■ *(314) 725-6588*
15 N Central Ave ■ *Italian* ■ Reservationist Shannon reports that about half of the menu is GF. Alert a server, who will notify the chef. The chef can guide GF diners through the menu. Shannon notes that the restaurant serves "pretty many" GF diners, so the whole staff is knowledgeable about GF. ■ *www.portabellarestaurant.com*

Rooster Crepe.Sandwich.Cafe   ★ ⊄BL
Saint Louis ▪ *(314) 241-8118*
1104 Locust St ▪ Crêpes ▪ GF crepes are
available. ▪ *www.roosterstl.com*

Tony's $$$$D
Saint Louis ▪ *(314) 231-7007*
410 Market St ▪ American ▪ Chef Vince Jr.
reports that accommodating GF diners is
"no problem," and they do it "all the time."
He notes that all servers are "very familiar"
with the GF diet, but adds that it is also ac-
ceptable to ask for him so he can personally
arrange a GF meal. ▪ *www.tonysstlouis.com*

Truffles $$$LD
Saint Louis ▪ *(314) 567-9100*
9202 Clayton Rd ▪ Modern American ▪
Chef Jim reports that the restaurant serves
"a lot" of GF diners. He recommends
avoiding sauces but notes that steaks and
roasted chicken, as well as many potato and
vegetable dishes, are GF. Confirm timeliness of this information before dining in.
The kitchen is very good at accommodating GF requests. Reservations noting GF
are recommended but not required. Alert a
server, who will indicate GF menu items. ▪
www.trufflesinladue.com

Winslow's   ★ $$BLD
Saint Louis ▪ *(314) 725-7559*
7213 Delmar Blvd ▪ American ▪ GF bread
is available, both in the kitchen and for
sale. The restaurant reports that staff is
GF aware, but GF is "not the focus of the
restaurant." ▪ *www.winslowshome.com*

MISSOURI
ALL OTHER CITIES

Andrea's Gluten Free   100% ⊄LD
Chesterfield ▪ *(636) 536-9953*
759 Spirit Of Saint Louis Blvd ▪ Bakery ▪
Dedicated GF bakery offering bread, pasta,
pizza crust, soy sauce, hamburger buns,
and more. For dessert, they make cookies,
cakes, pies, muffins, and brownies, among
other things. Products are available for
pickup at the storefront location or for ordering online. ▪ *www.andreasglutenfree.com*

Annie Gunn's $$$$LD
Chesterfield ▪ *(636) 532-7684*
16806 Chesterfield Airport Rd ▪ Modern
American & Steakhouse ▪ Hostess Michelle reports that GF diners "come in all
the time." Alert a server, who will tell the
chef to modify dishes as necessary. ▪ *www.
smokehousemarket.com*

Big Sky Café $$D
Webster Groves ▪ *(314) 962-5757*
47 S Old Orchard Ave ▪ Modern American
▪ Chef Christine reports that GF diners
are accommodated "at least once every
couple of weeks." She notes that the staff is
knowledgeable about GF. GF items on the
menu include salmon filets, rainbow trout,
vegetable risotto, and sea scallops. Confirm
timeliness of this information before dining in. ▪ *www.allgreatrestaurants.com*

Bristol Seafood Grill-Creve Coeur
$$$LD
Creve Coeur ▪ *(314) 567-0272*
11801 Olive Blvd ▪ Seafood ▪ Manager
Vicky reports that the restaurant has a
handout that indicates "low gluten sugges-
tions," but cannot guarantee a 100% GF
meal. Nearly all items are prepared from
scratch in the kitchen, but particles of flour
may be present. Alert a server, who will
alert the kitchen. ▪ *www.bristolseafoodgrill.
com*

Bristol Seafood Grill-O'Fallon $$$LD
O Fallon ▪ **(636) 625-6350**
2314 Technology Dr ▪ *Seafood* ▪ The
restaurant reports that several menu items,
like oysters, clams, the strawberry salad,
the lobster cobb salad, and filets, can
be made GF. Confirm timeliness of this
information before dining in. Reserva-
tions noting GF are recommended. ▪ *www.
bristolseafoodgrill.com*

Café Napoli   ★ $$$LD
Clayton ▪ **(314) 863-5731**
7754 Forsyth Blvd ▪ *Italian* ▪ GF pasta is
sometimes available. Restaurant notes that
with notice, they can have GF pasta ready
without a lengthy wait. ▪ *www.cafenapoli.
com*

Caito's Sicilian Restaurant & Pizzeria
                          ★ $LD
Chesterfield ▪ **(636) 530-9222**
414 Thf Blvd ▪ *Italian* ▪ GF pizzas, pasta
with red sauce, and rolls are available. The
restaurant reports that GF pizzas are prepared on a separate tray. ▪ *www.caitosres-
taurant.com*

Cantina Laredo   📖
Branson ▪ **(417) 334-6062**
1001 Branson Landing Blvd

Carino's Italian   📖
Joplin ▪ **(417) 206-9090**
137 N Rangeline Rd

Carrabba's Italian Grill   📖
Independence ▪ **(816) 795-9944**
19900 E Valley View Pkwy

Chatters Restaurant & Bar $LD
Webb City ▪ **(417) 673-7639**
1010 S Madison St ▪ *American* ▪ Manager
Stacy reports that they will "do anything"
to accommodate GF diners. She notes that
though they no longer carry GF pasta, they
will prepare GF pasta separately if a diner
brings it from home. She recommends asking for a manager upon arrival and being
specific about GF requests. ▪ *www.mychat-
ters.com*

Cherry Street Grill   ★ $LD
Nevada ▪ **(417) 448-5950**
115 W Cherry St ▪ *American* ▪ GF pasta
is available. The restaurant advises calling
ahead, as they need 45 minutes to prepare
it. ▪ *www.cherrystgrill.com*

Corner Pub & Grill, The   ✪ ¢LD
Chesterfield ▪ **(636) 230-3400**
15824 Fountain Plaza Dr ▪ *Pub Food* ▪
"Hannah's" GF menu includes fried potato
skins, BBQ chicken wings, fries, chips,
salads with GF dressings, and more. Both
locations have a dedicated GF fryer. The
menu is named after Owner Brant's daughter, who is GF. ▪ *www.cornerpubandgrill.
com*

Espinos Mexican Bar & Grill $LD
Chesterfield ▪ **(636) 519-0044**
17409 Chesterfield Airport Rd ▪ *Mexican* ▪
Manager Victor reports that as long as GF
diners alert their servers, they can "always
be accommodated." GF corn tortillas can
be substituted for flour tortillas. ▪ *www.
espinosmexicanbargrill.com*

First Watch - The Daytime Café   📖
Chesterfield ▪ **(636) 530-1401**
120 Hilltown Village Ctr
Clayton ▪ **(314) 863-7330**
8001 Forsyth Blvd
Creve Coeur ▪ **(314) 994-7171**
742 N New Ballas Rd
Des Peres ▪ **(314) 966-3913**
13323 Manchester Rd
Independence ▪ **(816) 795-0814**
19321 E US Highway 40 Ste L
Kirkwood ▪ **(314) 909-7271**
491 S Kirkwood Rd
North Kansas City ▪ **(816) 842-7300**
409 Armour Rd
Saint Peters ▪ **(636) 970-0050**
312 Mid Rivers Ctr
Webster Groves ▪ **(314) 968-9984**
220 W Lockwood Ave

Ground Round   📖
Saint Joseph ▪ **(816) 671-1906**
3708 Frederick Ave

Ingredient Restaurant   ✪ ★ $LD
Columbia ▪ *(573) 442-1502*
304 S 9th St ▪ *Pizza* ▪ GF menu includes
salads with GF dressings and pizzas with a
variety of toppings. GF pizza is available. ▪
www.ingredientrestaurant.com

Lone Star Steakhouse & Saloon   📖
Branson ▪ *(417) 336-5030*
201 S Wildwood Dr
Bridgeton ▪ *(314) 770-1255*
11969 Saint Charles Rock Rd
Columbia ▪ *(573) 814-1225*
3220 Vandiver Dr
Springfield ▪ *(417) 886-2900*
3030 S Campbell Ave

Maggiano's Little Italy   ★ $$$LD
Richmond Heights ▪ *(314) 824-2402*
#2 The Boulevard Saint Louis ▪ *Italian*
▪ GF pasta is available. Call individual
locations to inquire about additional GF
options. ▪ *www.maggianos.com*

Melting Pot, The   📖
Town And Country ▪ *(636) 207-6358*
294 Lamp And Lantern Vlg
University City ▪ *(314) 725-4141*
6683 Delmar Blvd

My Gluten Free Bakery, LLC   100% ¢S
Jefferson City ▪ *(573) 634-3733*
312 W Dunklin St ▪ *Bakery* ▪ Dedicated GF
bakery offering cookies, biscuits, breads,
cheesecakes, white cake, marble cake, muf-
fins, and more. Owner and Baker LaVerne
reports that advanced notice of only one
day is needed for special orders. She rec-
ommends calling ahead to discuss the day's
offerings. ▪ *www.myglutenfreebakery.com*

Nachomama's   ✪ ¢LD
Webster Groves ▪ *(314) 961-9110*
9643 Manchester Rd ▪ *Mexican* ▪ GF items
marked on the menu include tacos, nachos,
rotisserie chicken, chips, and more. ▪ *www.
nachomamas-stl.com*

Old Spaghetti Factory, The   📖
Chesterfield ▪ *(636) 536-9522*
17384 Chesterfield Airport Rd

Original Pancake House, The   ★ ¢BL
Chesterfield ▪ *(636) 536-4044*
17000 Chesterfield Airport Rd ▪ *Break-
fast* ▪ GF pancakes are available. ▪ *www.
originalpancakehouse.com*

Outback Steakhouse   📖
Cape Girardeau ▪ *(573) 335-6889*
101 Cape West Pkwy
Columbia ▪ *(573) 815-0800*
1110 I 70 Dr SW
Ellisville ▪ *(636) 256-4411*
15412 Manchester Rd
Hazelwood ▪ *(314) 830-4200*
7900 N Lindbergh Blvd
Independence ▪ *(816) 795-6790*
20000 E Valley View Pkwy
Joplin ▪ *(417) 625-1156*
3110 E 36th St
Lees Summit ▪ *(816) 246-7555*
1731 NE Douglas St
O Fallon ▪ *(636) 625-4300*
4002 Winghaven Blvd
Osage Beach ▪ *(573) 302-4670*
3930 Highway 54
Saint Charles ▪ *(636) 940-9409*
1620 Country Club Plaza Dr
Springfield ▪ *(417) 890-5900*
3760 S Glenstone Ave

P.F. Chang's China Bistro   📖
Chesterfield ▪ *(636) 532-0215*
1295 Chesterfield Pkwy E

Pasta House Co., The   📖
Arnold ▪ *(636) 296-3330*
921 Arnold Commons Dr
Brentwood ▪ *(314) 292-5000*
2539 S Brentwood Blvd
Cape Girardeau ▪ *(573) 335-4450*
2046 William St
Ellisville ▪ *(636) 227-1970*
15601 Manchester Rd
Farmington ▪ *(573) 760-0026*
931 Valley Creek Dr
Florissant ▪ *(314) 838-7300*
11202 W Florissant Ave
High Ridge ▪ *(636) 677-2711*
4517 Highway 30
Kirkwood ▪ *(314) 909-0054*

11240 Manchester Rd
Maryland Heights ▪ *(314) 878-6676*
12445 Dorsett Rd
O Fallon ▪ *(636) 978-0060*
2558 Highway K
Osage Beach ▪ *(573) 348-2207*
4204 Highway 54
Saint Ann ▪ *(314) 423-8880*
1701 Lambert Int'l Blvd
Saint Peters ▪ *(636) 441-4366*
4095 Veterans Memorial Pkwy
Springfield ▪ *(417) 883-5678*
4109 S National Ave
Union ▪ *(636) 583-4900*
161 Independence Dr

Paul Manno's $$$$D
Chesterfield ▪ *(314) 878-1274*
75 Forum Shopping Ctr ▪ *Italian* ▪ Owner
Paul reports that the wait staff is "GF
aware." He adds that GF diners are welcome to bring in GF pasta. There are 10-12
different GF sauces available. Confirm
timeliness of this information before dining in.

Pei Wei Asian Diner   📖
Creve Coeur ▪ *(314) 656-2004*
11430 Olive Blvd

PJ's Country Bakery   ★ ¢S
Joplin ▪ *(417) 781-5854*
3500 Apricot Dr ▪ *Bakery* ▪ Non-dedicated
bakery offering many varieties of GF bread
(sourdough, cinnamon raisin, fruit breads,
and more), as well as GF dinner rolls,
hamburger buns, pasta, muffins, cakes,
and brownies. Owner PJ reports that GF
items are baked on Mondays only, usually
by order. Place an order during the week
or stop in on Tuesday to see if there are any
leftover GF items.

Remy's Kitchen & Wine Bar $$LD
Clayton ▪ *(314) 726-5757*
222 S Bemiston Ave ▪ *Mediterranean* ▪
The restaurant reports that the kitchen is
"pretty familiar" with GF requests. The
chef makes all dishes from scratch, so GF

modifications are easy. ▪ *www.allgreatres-
taurants.com*

Schlafly Bottleworks   ✪★ $$LD
Maplewood ▪ *(314) 241-2337*
7260 Southwest Ave ▪ *American* ▪ GF
pasta and home-made beer are available.
Kitchen Manager Josh reports that "plenty
of GF diners" come in, and GF items are
marked on the regular menu. Alert a
server, who will notify the chef. ▪ *www.
schlafly.com*

Spin Pizza   ★ $$LD
Lees Summit ▪ *(816) 246-7746*
1808 NW Chipman Rd ▪ *Pizza* ▪ GF pizza
and beer are available. ▪ *www.spinpizza.com*

Stir Crazy   ★ $$LD
Creve Coeur ▪ *(314) 569-9300*
10598 Old Olive Street Rd ▪ *Asian Stir-Fry*
▪ Veteran Bartender Kelly reports that they
serve GF diners "all the time" and "any of
the servers" can help choose a GF meal.
GF customers can pick one of three GF
sauces and any meat that is not marinated.
For meats that are usually marinated, like
steak, advanced notice is recommended.
GF soy sauce and rice noodles are available.
▪ *www.stircrazy.com*

Sunset 44 $$LD
Kirkwood ▪ *(314) 965-6644*
118 W Adams Ave ▪ *Modern American* ▪
Manager Ryan reports that GF diners are
welcome. He explains that the restaurant is
"very accustomed to preparing meals" for
GF diners. He recommends alerting the
server upon arrival. ▪ *www.sunset44.com*

Texas Land & Cattle Steak House 📖
Branson ▪ *(417) 337-8200*
915 Branson Landing Blvd

Waldo Pizza   ✪★ ¢LD
Lees Summit ▪ *(816) 875-2121*
1543 Northeast Douglas St ▪ *Pizza* ▪ GF
menu is extensive. GF breadsticks, pizza,
and bread are available, as are GF cupcakes,
cookies, brownies, and lemonade cake. ▪
www.waldopizza.net

Wild Horse Grill $$$$**LD**
Chesterfield ▪ (636) 532-8750
101 Chesterfield Towne Ctr ▪ *American*
▪ Owner Tony reports that everything
is made "in-house," so GF requests can
be easily accommodated. All servers are
trained to talk with either him or the executive chef in order to determine the best
GF options. ▪ *www.wildhorsegrill.com*

Zio's   ○ $**LD**
Independence ▪ (816) 350-1011
3901 S Bolger Rd
Springfield ▪ (417) 889-1919
1249 E Kingsley St ▪ *Italian* ▪ GF menu
includes salmon caesar salad, chicken piccata, Greek pasta, lemon chicken primavera, shrimp with marinara, ribeye tuscano,
grilled sirloin, and more. ▪ *www.zios.com*

MONTANA

BOZEMAN

BarBQ 3 $**LD**
Bozeman ▪ (406) 587-8789
215 N 7th Ave ▪ *Barbeque* ▪ Becky at the
Belgrade location and Joey at the Bozeman location report that all meats are GF.
The spice rub used on the meats is GF, but
BBQ sauces are not GF. Ask for a manager
upon arrival. Becky notes that most but not
all managers are GF aware. If necessary,
managers can call the Belgrade location to
consult with the chef. ▪ *www.bar3bbq.com*

Carino's Italian   📖
Bozeman ▪ (406) 556-1332
2159 Burke St

Daily Coffee Bar & Bakery, The   ★ ¢**S**
Bozeman ▪ (406) 585-8612
1013 W College St
Bozeman ▪ (406) 585-4574
1203 N Rouse Ave ▪ *Bakery* ▪ GF brownies, peanut butter cookies, and blondies are

available. They also offer chocolate and coconut macaroons and meringues. Though
available at both locations, all GF items are
baked at the North Rouse location. ▪ *www.
tdcbar.com*

John Bozeman's Bistro $$$**LD**
Bozeman ▪ (406) 587-4100
125 W Main St ▪ *American* ▪ Server Rita
reports that all staff is trained to handle GF,
as they have many customers who are GF.
They offer an entrée called the Superfood
Platter, a combination of side dishes, that
is always 100% GF. Confirm timeliness of
this information before dining in. ▪ *www.
johnbozemansbistro.com*

Montana Ale Works   ○★ $**D**
Bozeman ▪ (406) 587-7700
611 E Main St ▪ *American* ▪ The "Gluten
Free Options" list indicates menu items
that are GF. GF bread, hamburger buns,
pasta, soy sauce, and beer are available.
For dessert, they offer flourless chocolate
cake and crème brûlée. ▪ *www.montanaale-
works.com*

Naked Noodle   ★ ¢**LD**
Bozeman ▪ (406) 585-4501
27 South Willson ▪ *Global* ▪ GF rice pasta
is available. GF sauces are listed on a board
in the restaurant. GF options include the
green curry and the lo mein. Restaurant
notes that its staff is educated on GF foods.
▪ *www.nakednoodle.com*

Nova Café, The   ★ ¢**BL**
Bozeman ▪ (406) 587-3973
312 E Main St ▪ *Café* ▪ GF baked goods
like muffins, scones, and cinnamon rolls
are available, as are two types of GF bread.
Baker Kelsey reports that she can also accommodate special orders with advanced
notice of a few days. ▪ *www.thenovacafe.
com*

Oak Street Natural Market Deli   ★ ¢**BLD**
Bozeman ▪ (406) 582-5400
1735 W. Oak St ▪ *Deli* ▪ Small deli offering GF bread, pasta, pizza, cookies, pies,
cakes, and more. GF sandwiches, wraps,

and salads are available. GF cookies include peanut butter, raspberry thumbprint, peanut butter chocolate chip, and hazelnut. Located in the Oak Street Natural market. ▪ *www.oakstreetnaturalmarket.com*

Outback Steakhouse 📖
Bozeman ▪ *(406) 587-5200*
6059 E Valley Center Rd

Over the Tapas ✪ $$**LD**
Bozeman ▪ *(406) 556-8282*
19 S Willson Ave ▪ *Spanish Tapas* ▪ GF items are marked on the dinner menu only, but they are available all day. Options include crispy red potatoes in a creamy tomato-herb sauce, sea salt crusted potatoes served with red and green mojo sauces, sirloin skewers, and bacon-wrapped dates. For dessert, they offer a flourless chocolate tort. ▪ *www.bozemantapas.com*

Sola Café ✪★ ¢**BLD**
Bozeman ▪ *(406) 922-7652*
290 W Kagy Blvd ▪ *Bakery & Café* ▪ GF menu includes salads, paninis, toasted baguette sandwiches, cold sandwiches, rustic pizzas, and entrées. There are GF options for kids, as well as several desserts like blueberry muffins and chocolate chip cookies. Located across from the Museum of the Rockies. ▪ *www.solacafe.com*

Sweet Pea Bakery ✪★ ¢**S**
Bozeman ▪ *(406) 586-8200*
2622 W Main St ▪ *Bakery* ▪ Non-dedicated bakery offering flourless chocolate tortes, GF opera cake, GF cheesecake and key lime torte, among other items. Flourless chocolate tortes are available all the time, but other GF items are available only occasionally. Most GF products can be ordered 72 hours in advance. ▪ *www.sweetpeabakery. net*

MONTANA
ALL OTHER CITIES

BarBQ 3 $**LD**
Belgrade ▪ *(406) 388-9127*
100 S Broadway ▪ *Barbeque* ▪ Becky at the Belgrade location and Joey at the Bozeman location report that all meats are GF. The spice rub used on the meats is GF, but BBQ sauces are not GF. Ask for a manager upon arrival. Becky notes that most but not all managers are GF aware. ▪ *www.bar3bbq. com*

Bert and Ernie's ★ $$**LD**
Helena ▪ *(406) 443-5680*
361 N Last Chance Gulch ▪ *Fusion* ▪ GF soy and szechuan sauces are available. Chef Ernie reports that all soups are made with GF flour. He also notes that GF stir fries with chicken or beef can be prepared, and several chicken and steak dishes can be modified to be GF. Alert a server upon arrival. ▪ *www.bertanderniesofhelena.com*

Biga Pizza ★ $**LD**
Missoula ▪ *(406) 728-2579*
241 W Main St ▪ *Pizza* ▪ GF pizza is available with advanced notice of at least 24 hours. ▪ *www.bigapizza.com*

Carino's Italian 📖
Billings ▪ *(406) 652-9661*
3042 King Ave W
Missoula ▪ *(406) 541-7900*
3630 N Reserve St

Daisy's Deli & Bakery ★ ¢**BL**
Great Falls ▪ *(406) 452-0361*
508 1st Ave N ▪ *Deli & Bakery* ▪ GF bread is available for sandwiches, and loaves of GF bread are available by special order. Nearly all of the soups are GF, and Manager Nicole reports that there are almost always GF cookies or cakes available.

Depot Bar & Restaurant $$**D**
Missoula ▪ *(406) 728-7007*
201 Railroad St W ▪ *American* ▪ Chef John

reports that they use their allergy protocol to ensure GF meals. Nearly any chicken, fish, or beef on the menu can be prepared GF, and they use clean pans to cook GF meals. Confirm timeliness of this information before dining in.

Jade Garden Restaurant $LD
Helena ▪ *(406) 443-8899*
3128 N Montana Ave ▪ *Chinese* ▪ Manager Nicole reports that the kitchen is "accustomed" to dietary requests. She notes that many meat and fish dishes are naturally GF or can be modified to be GF. Confirm timeliness of this information before dining in. Alert a server, who will notify the kitchen. ▪ *www.jadegardenhelena.com*

Jakers Bar and Grill   ✪ $$$LD
Great Falls ▪ *(406) 727-1033*
1500 10th Ave S ▪ *American* ▪ GF menu includes cheeseburgers without buns, BBQ chicken, london broil, sirloin, prime rib, salmon, halibut, and more. Restaurant advises specifying GF, even if ordering off the GF menu, to avoid confusion. ▪ *www.jakers.com*

Montana City Grill $$$D
Montana City ▪ *(406) 449-8890*
1 Jackson Creek Rd ▪ *American* ▪ Kitchen Manager Robby reports that they can easily accommodate GF diners, as everything in the restaurant is made from scratch. Alert a server, who will speak to Robby if he or she has any doubts about what is GF. ▪ *www.montanacitygrill.com*

Mustard Seed Asian Café   ✪★ $LD
Billings ▪ *(406) 259-1400*
1340 15th St W
Missoula ▪ *(406) 542-7333*
2901 Brooks St ▪ *Asian* ▪ The Missoula location has a GF menu, and the Billings location expects to have one soon. Missoula's GF menu includes several halibut dishes, the Singapore beef, and a few tilapia entrées. GF soy sauce is available at both locations. ▪ *www.mustardseedweb.com*

Outback Steakhouse   📖
Billings ▪ *(406) 652-3565*
2001 Overland Ave
Missoula ▪ *(406) 327-6900*
2415 N Reserve St

Penny's Gourmet   ★ ¢LD
Great Falls ▪ *(406) 453-7070*
815 Central Ave ▪ *American* ▪ GF rolls, soups, and raspberry white chocolate chip scones are available.

Staggering Ox   ★ ¢LD
Billings ▪ *(406) 294-6969*
2829 King Ave W
Helena ▪ *(406) 443-1729*
400 Euclid Ave
Missoula ▪ *(406) 542-2206*
1220 SW Higgins Ave ▪ *Café* ▪ GF options vary widely by location. The Helena location has GF pizza and GF bread "almost all of the time," according to Manager Jim. Heidi at the Billings location notes that all of their rice and potato dishes are GF. She also mentions that all staff members are educated about GF. Triumph notes that the staff at the Missoula location was much less knowledgeable about GF than staff at the other two locations. ▪ *www.staggeringox.com*

NEBRASKA

OMAHA

Ahmad's Persian Cuisine $$$LD
Omaha ▪ *(402) 341-9616*
1006 Howard St ▪ *Persian* ▪ Owner Ahmad reports that GF diners are welcome and that the majority of entrées is naturally GF. Alert a server upon arrival. ▪ *www.ahmadscuisine.com*

Biaggi's Ristorante Italiano   📖
Omaha ▪ *(402) 965-9800*
13655 California St

Big Mama's Kitchen & Catering $BLD
Omaha ▪ *(402) 455-6262*
3223 N 45th St Building A ▪ *American* ▪
General Manager Gladys reports that the restaurant is happy to prepare GF dishes. The grilled pork chop and the hamburger without the bun are naturally GF, while other items like the fried catfish can be modified to be GF. Confirm timeliness of this information before dining in. ▪ *www.bigmamaskitchen.com*

Blue Planet Natural Grill   ✪★ ¢BLD
Omaha ▪ *(402) 218-4555*
6307 Center St ▪ *Organic American* ▪
Extensive GF menu includes burgers on GF buns, a variety of pizzas including thai chicken and Hawaiian, and an assortment of GF wraps, sandwiches, and curried soups. ▪ *www.blueplanetnaturalgrill.com*

Bonefish Grill   📖
Omaha ▪ *(402) 391-3474*
120 Regency Pkwy

Carrabba's Italian Grill   📖
Omaha ▪ *(402) 492-9500*
14520 W Maple Rd

Firebirds Wood Fired Grill   ✪ $$$LD
Omaha ▪ *(402) 359-1340*
17415 Chicago St ▪ *American* ▪ GF menu includes a variety of salads and a selection of entrées. Examples include the sirloin, filet mignon, ribs, and lobster tail. Servers are trained to alert the chef when a customer orders from the GF menu. ▪ *www.firebirdsrockymountaingrill.com*

Great Harvest Bread Company   ★ ¢S
Omaha ▪ *(402) 932-0288*
15623 W Dodge Rd
Omaha ▪ *(402) 551-8800*
4910 Underwood Ave ▪ *Bakery* ▪ A variety of GF breads and cookies are available. GF baked goods are made on Tuesdays only, and Baker Elaine recommends ordering ahead, as they sell out quickly. She prefers that customers place all GF orders by the Saturday before the Tuesday baking day. All GF items are baked at the West Dodge

Road location, but they can be delivered to the Underwood Avenue location. ▪ *www.greatharvest.com*

Jam's Bar & Grill $$$LD
Omaha ▪ *(402) 399-8300*
7814 Dodge St ▪ *American* ▪ Manager Todd reports that the restaurant accommodates GF diners on a regular basis. Though the entrée menu changes frequently, portobello mushrooms, agave shrimp tostada, field salad, steak and gorgonzola salad, and many other entrées are GF. Also, minor modifications can be made to make other dishes GF. ▪ *www.jamseats.com*

Johnny's Italian Steakhouse $$$LD
Omaha ▪ *(402) 289-9210*
305 N 170th St ▪ *Steakhouse* ▪ Manager Rafael reports that they have "quite a few" options for GF diners. Many of the salads, steaks, and seafood dishes are naturally GF. Confirm timeliness of this information before dining in. Alert a server, who will ask the kitchen for recommendations. Located at the Village Pointe Shopping Center. ▪ *www.johnnysitaliansteakhouse.com*

Kona Grill   📖
Omaha ▪ *(402) 779-2900*
295 N 170th St

Lazlo's Brewery & Grill   ✪ $$LD
Omaha ▪ *(402) 289-5840*
2425 S 192nd Ave ▪ *American* ▪ GF menu includes most of the appetizers, several salads, almost any burger without the bun, voodoo chicken, rainbow chicken, ribs, steak, and more. ▪ *www.telesis-inc.com*

Lone Star Steakhouse & Saloon   📖
Omaha ▪ *(402) 333-1553*
3040 S 143rd Plz

Mark's Bistro   ✪★ $$LD
Omaha ▪ *(402) 502-2203*
4916 Underwood Ave ▪ *Bistro* ▪ Extensive GF options are marked on the menu. GF crackers are available. Manager Molly reports that the restaurant has "really tried

to focus on GF diners." ▪ *www.marksind-undee.com*

M's Pub   ✪★ $LD
Omaha ▪ *(402) 342-2550*
422 S 11Th St ▪ *American* ▪ Extensive GF menu includes a grilled shrimp marinated in lime and chilies, a variety of burgers, steaks and salads. GF desserts include crème brûlée and a mocha fudge torte. GF pasta available. ▪ *www.mspubomaha.com*

Outback Steakhouse   📖
Omaha ▪ *(402) 697-1199*
2414 S 132nd St
Omaha ▪ *(402) 392-2212*
7605 Cass St

P.F. Chang's China Bistro   📖
Omaha ▪ *(402) 390-6021*
10150 California St

Pasta Amore   ★ $$LD
Omaha ▪ *(402) 391-2585*
11027 Prairie Brook Rd ▪ *Italian* ▪ GF pasta is available and can be substituted into any pasta dish. Verify GF sauces with a server. ▪ *www.pastaamore.net*

Pudgy's Pizza   ★ $$D
Omaha ▪ *(402) 884-7566*
16919 Audrey St ▪ *Pizza* ▪ GF pizza is available. ▪ *www.pudgys.net*

Roja Mexican Grill   ✪ ¢D
Omaha ▪ *(402) 333-7652*
17010 Wright Plz ▪ *Tex-Mex* ▪ GF menu includes nachos and a salsa sampler as appetizers. Examples of GF entrées include quesadillas and a variety of tacos. ▪ *www.rojagrill.com*

Sam & Louie's New York Pizzeria
                                     ★ $$LD
Omaha ▪ *(402) 895-2427*
18010 R Plz
Omaha ▪ *(402) 496-7900*
2062 N 117th Ave
Omaha ▪ *(402) 884-7773*
2418 Cuming St
Omaha ▪ *(402) 965-3858*
541 N 155th Plz

Omaha ▪ *(402) 390-2911*
7641 Cass St ▪ *Pizza* ▪ GF pizza is available. ▪ *www.samandlouiesnyp.com*

Upstream Brewing Company - Legacy
                                     ★ $$LD
Omaha ▪ *(402) 778-0100*
17070 Wright Plz ▪ *American* ▪ Host Supervisor RJ reports that the chef is "always very good" about working with GF customers. Alert a server, who will notify the chef. The chef will come to the table and help choose a GF meal. RJ notes that one item, the pub grilled chicken with shrimp, is naturally GF. Confirm timeliness of this information before dining in. GF beer is available. ▪ *www.upstreambrewing.com*

Upstream Brewing Company - Old Market   ★ $$LD
Omaha ▪ *(402) 344-0200*
514 S 11th St ▪ *American* ▪ Manager Brian reports that all staff members are "very knowledgeable" about the GF diet. He recommends alerting both the host stand and the server, who will go "directly" to the chef. Brian also notes that there are "a lot of moves" they can make to accommodate GF diners. ▪ *www.upstreambrewing.com*

Vincenzo's Ristorante $$$LD
Omaha ▪ *(402) 342-4010*
1207 Harney St
Omaha ▪ *(402) 498-3889*
1818 N 144th St ▪ *Italian* ▪ Taylor at the N 144th St location welcomes GF diners to bring their own GF pasta. Ask a server to speak to the chef about which sauces are GF. Manager Jimmy at the Harney St location reports that the executive chef is "very familiar" with the GF diet, and he recommends asking the server to speak to either him or the chef. Jeannie at the Lincoln location recommends reservations noting GF, so the host can assign an experienced, GF-friendly server to the party. ▪ *www.vincenzos-ne.com*

Vivace   ✪★ $$LD
Omaha ▪ *(402) 342-2050*

1108 Howard St ▪ *Italian* ▪ Manager Becca reports that the new GF menu includes GF pasta prepared with a carbonara, dill pesto, marinara, or caponata sauce. There is also a variety of GF salad and tapas options. GF desserts include crème brûlée and chocolate almond toffee mousse. GF beer is available. ▪ *www.vivaceomaha.com*

NEBRASKA
ALL OTHER CITIES

DISH   ✪ $$LD
Lincoln ▪ *(402) 475-9475*
1100 O St ▪ *American* ▪ GF menu includes appetizers, soups, salads, and entrées. Some examples are clam chowder, a smoked salmon salad, grilled duck breast, and vegetarian shephard's pie. For dessert, they offer crème brûlée and chocolate boudin. ▪ *www.dishdowntown.com*

FireWorks Restaurant   ✪ $$LD
Lincoln ▪ *(402) 434-5644*
5750 S 86th Dr ▪ *American* ▪ GF menu includes the beef brisket sandwich without the bun, prime rib sandwich without bread or au jus, philly cheese steak, roast beef, rotisserie chicken, ribs, steaks, and more. Restaurant adds that they have a special system in place to flag GF orders for the kitchen. ▪ *www.telesis-inc.com*

Las Margaritas   ✪ $LD
Lincoln ▪ *(402) 421-2662*
2700 Jamie Ln ▪ *Mexican* ▪ GF menu includes fajitas, as well as several steak and chicken dishes. Manager Luis reports that these items are available for dining in and take out. He adds that all staff members are knowledgeable about the GF diet, so anyone will be able to assist.

Lazlo's Brewery & Grill   ✪ $$LD
Lincoln ▪ *(402) 434-5636*
210 N 7th St
Lincoln ▪ *(402) 323-8500*
5900 Old Cheney Rd ▪ *American* ▪ GF menu includes the salmon avocado salad, cob salad, burgers without buns, several different steaks, baked beans, and sautéed veggies. ▪ *www.telesis-inc.com*

Lone Star Steakhouse & Saloon   📖
Lincoln ▪ *(402) 489-2100*
200 N 70th St

Mazatlan   ✪ $LD
Lincoln ▪ *(402) 464-7201*
211 N 70th St ▪ *Mexican* ▪ Extensive GF menu includes appetizers, soups, enchiladas, fajitas, tacos, and a variety of chicken, meat, and seafood dishes.

Outback Steakhouse   📖
Bellevue ▪ *(402) 991-9275*
10408 S 15th St
Lincoln ▪ *(402) 465-5050*
633 N 48th St

Oven, The $$LD
Lincoln ▪ *(402) 475-6118*
201 N 8th St ▪ *Indian* ▪ Manager Nawa reports that the restaurant can accommodate GF customers, as many dishes are naturally GF. He or one of the servers will "happily" go over the details of specific recipes to ensure a safe meal. ▪ *www.theoven-lincoln.com*

Sam & Louie's New York Pizzeria
                                           ★ $$LD
Alliance ▪ *(308) 761-1313*
1313 W 3rd St
Bellevue ▪ *(402) 991-3400*
3608 Twin Creek Dr
Blair ▪ *(402) 426-9590*
1995 Ridgeview Rd
Elkhorn ▪ *(402) 575-5500*
2949 N 204th St
Gretna ▪ *(402) 332-0072*
20596 Highway 370
Lincoln ▪ *(402) 475-0777*
1332 P St
Lincoln ▪ *(402) 420-0195*

1501 Pine Lake Rd
Lincoln ▪ (402) 488-4144
4131 Pioneer Woods Dr
Norfolk ▪ (402) 371-0505
2600 W Norfolk Ave
Ralston ▪ (402) 505-9200
5352 S 72nd St ▪ Pizza ▪ GF pizza is available. ▪ www.samandlouiesnyp.com

Sportscasters Bar & Grill   ✪★ ¢**LD**
Lincoln ▪ (402) 466-6679
3048 N 70th St ▪ American ▪ GF menu is available upon request. GF buns are available. Manager Luke reports that the restaurant's owner has Celiac disease, so the staff is "very aware" of GF diners.

Venue Restaurant & Lounge   ✪ $$$**LD**
Lincoln ▪ (402) 488-8368
4111 Pioneer Woods Dr ▪ American ▪ GF items marked on the menu include sea grill skewers, ribeye steak, and blackened ahi tuna. ▪ www.yourvenue.net

Vincenzo's Ristorante $$$**LD**
Lincoln ▪ (402) 435-3889
808 P St ▪ Italian ▪ Taylor at the N 144th St location welcomes GF diners to bring their own GF pasta. Ask a server to speak to the chef about which sauces are GF. Manager Jimmy at the Harney St location reports that the executive chef is "very familiar" with the GF diet, and he recommends asking the server to speak to either him or the chef. Jeannie at the Lincoln location recommends reservations noting GF, so the host can assign an experienced, GF-friendly server to the party. ▪ www.vincenzos-ne. com

NEVADA
LAS VEGAS

B&B Ristorante   ★ $$$$**LD**
Las Vegas ▪ (702) 266-9977
3355 Las Vegas Blvd S ▪ Italian ▪ GF pasta is available. Restaurant is located in The Venetian Hotel. ▪ www.mariobatali.com

Border Grill   ✪ $$$**LD**
Las Vegas ▪ (702) 632-7403
3950 Las Vegas Blvd S ▪ Modern Mexican ▪ GF menu includes sautéed jumbo shrimp, slow roasted pork in banana leaves, and Kobe beef tacos, among other things. For dessert, they offer flourless chocolate truffle cake or flan. Located inside the Mandalay Bay Resort and Casino. ▪ www.bordergrill. com

Buca di Beppo   📖
Las Vegas ▪ (702) 866-2867
412 E Flamingo Rd
Las Vegas ▪ (702) 363-6524
7690 W Lake Mead Blvd

Capital Grille, The   📖
Las Vegas ▪ (702) 932-6631
3200 Las Vegas Blvd S

Carrabba's Italian Grill   📖
Las Vegas ▪ (702) 304-2345
8771 W Charleston Blvd

China Grill $$$$**D**
Las Vegas ▪ (702) 632-7404
3950 Las Vegas Blvd S ▪ Asian Fusion ▪ Maitre d' Linda reports that several menu items can be modified to be GF, including the BBQ salmon and the drunken chicken. Alert a server, who will talk to the chefs about GF requests. He or she will also notify all relevant staff members by punching the GF "alert" button on the computer. ▪ www.chinagrillmgt.com

Craftsteak $$$$**D**
Las Vegas ▪ (702) 891-7318
3799 Las Vegas Blvd S ▪ Steakhouse ▪

Manager Christian reports that all meals are prepared fairly simply, which makes accommodating GF requests easy. He recommends reservations noting GF so that the staff can prepare ahead of time. Located inside the MGM Grand. ▪ *www.mgmgrand.com*

Del Frisco's Double Eagle Steak House
📖

Las Vegas ▪ *(702) 796-0063*
3925 Paradise Rd

Eiffel Tower Restaurant
$$$$LD
Las Vegas ▪ *(702) 948-6937*
3655 Las Vegas Blvd S ▪ *French* ▪ Manager Sharon reports that they can "absolutely" accommodate GF diners. They are accustomed to serving guests with "allergies." She recommends reservations noting GF and advises alerting a server upon arrival. ▪ *www.eiffeltowerrestaurant.com*

El Segundo Sol
✪ $$LD
Las Vegas ▪ *(702) 258-1211*
3200 Las Vegas Blvd S ▪ *Spanish Tapas* ▪ GF menu is available upon request. Manager Sam reports that the restaurant is "very conscious" of GF diners and that chefs can modify several items on the regular menu to be GF. Alert a server, who will discuss GF requests with the kitchen. ▪ *www.elsegundosol.com*

Emeril's New Orleans Fish House
$$$$LD
Las Vegas ▪ *(702) 891-7374*
3799 Las Vegas Blvd S ▪ *Cajun & Creole Seafood* ▪ Reservationist Connie reports that they get GF requests "all the time." They can "absolutely" accommodate GF diners. She recommends reservations noting GF so that the chef can be notified in advance. She also notes that staff members are "highly educated" on the content of the food.

Isla
$$$D
Las Vegas ▪ *(702) 894-7349*
3300 Las Vegas Blvd S ▪ *Mexican* ▪ Manager Tara reports that they accommodate "quite a lot" of GF diners. She notes that

they have corn tortillas, which can be substituted into any of the various tacos on the menu. Other dishes can also be prepared GF. Alert a server, who will indicate GF items on the menu. ▪ *www.modernmexican.com*

Joe's Seafood, Prime Steak, and Stone Crab
✪ $$$$LD
Las Vegas ▪ *(702) 792-9222*
3500 Las Vegas Blvd S ▪ *Seafood & Steakhouse* ▪ GF menu includes a variety of options, including appetizers, soups, salads, and sides. Seafood, steak, and crab dishes are also listed. Manager Dave reports that servers and chefs "use special instructions" to prepare GF meals. ▪ *www.joes.net*

Julian Serrano
$$$$LD
Las Vegas ▪ *(877) 230-2742*
3730 Las Vegas Blvd S ▪ *Spanish* ▪ Hostess Jolan reports that there is a GF list available upon request, but she emphasizes that it is not a menu. Advanced notice is not required, but alert a server upon arrival. Located inside the Aria Resort and Casino.

Kona Grill
📖
Las Vegas ▪ *(702) 547-5552*
750 S Rampart Blvd

Lawry's The Prime Rib
$$$$D
Las Vegas ▪ *(702) 893-2223*
4043 Howard Hughes Pkwy ▪ *Steakhouse* ▪ Manager Wendy reports that they have accommodated several GF diners. She recommends reservations noting GF, so the server will be ready to discuss GF options. Servers have access to an allergen list that includes all non-GF menu items. If servers have questions about modifications to the food, they are trained to ask a manager or chef. ▪ *www.lawrysonline.com*

Le Cirque
$$$$D
Las Vegas ▪ *(702) 425-6502*
3600 Las Vegas Blvd S ▪ *French* ▪ Restaurant reports that they can "easily" accommodate GF requests, but GF diners should make reservations 72 hours in advance.

The hostess will alert the chefs ahead of time. All dishes are made to order, however, so alert a server upon arrival. ▪ *www.bellagio.com*

Lone Star Steakhouse & Saloon 📖
Las Vegas ▪ *(702) 893-0348*
1290 E Flamingo Rd
Las Vegas ▪ *(702) 453-7827*
210 N Nellis Blvd

Maggiano's Little Italy   ★ $$$LD
Las Vegas ▪ *(702) 732-2550*
3200 Las Vegas Blvd S Ste 2144 ▪ *Italian* ▪ GF pasta is available. Call individual locations to inquire about additional GF options. ▪ *www.maggianos.com*

Mark Rich's NY Pizza & Pasta   ★ $$L
Las Vegas ▪ *(702) 898-7424*
11710 W Charleston Blvd
Las Vegas ▪ *(702) 645-3337*
7930 W Tropical Pkwy ▪ *Pizza* ▪ Manager Paul reports that both locations can make "any pie" with GF pizza crust. A different screen is used for GF pizzas, to ensure that they don't come into contact with the regular pizzas. Confirm timeliness of this information before dining in. ▪ *www.markrichnypizza.com*

Melting Pot, The 📖
Las Vegas ▪ *(702) 384-6358*
8704 W Charleston Blvd

Mix $$$$D
Las Vegas ▪ *(702) 632-9500*
3950 Las Vegas Blvd S ▪ *French* ▪ Manager Pascal reports that accommodating GF diners is "not a problem." He recommends making reservations noting GF and then alerting the server upon arrival. He notes that they are "very used to dealing" with GF diners, and that the GF selection will consist of "at least two" of each type of dish. ▪ *www.chinagrillmgt.com*

Mon Ami Gabi   ✪ $$$LD
Las Vegas ▪ *(702) 944-4224*
3655 Las Vegas Blvd S ▪ *French* ▪ GF menu includes chicken liver mousse, seared sea scallops, lemon chicken paillard, steak

béarnaise, and more. For dessert, chocolate mousse, crème brûlée, and a pear parfait are available. Located in the Paris Resort and Casino. ▪ *www.monamigabi.com*

N9ne Steakhouse   ★ $$$$D
Las Vegas ▪ *(702) 942-7777*
4321 W Flamingo Rd ▪ *Steakhouse* ▪ Assistant Banquet Chef Marcus reports that although they don't accommodate GF diners "often," they are happy to provide a GF meal. He recommends reservations noting GF and advises speaking to a chef upon arrival. GF pasta is available. Located in The Palms Hotel. ▪ *www.n9negroup.com*

Nine Fine Irishmen   ✪★ $$$LD
Las Vegas ▪ *(702) 740-6463*
3790 Las Vegas Blvd S ▪ *Irish* ▪ There are separate GF menus for lunch and dinner. GF dinner menu includes stuffed chicken breast, spice grilled pork porterhouse, pan-seared halibut, and a NY strip steak with au jus. GF beer is available. Located inside New York New York Hotel and Casino. ▪ *www.ninefineirishmen.com*

Nobhill Tavern $$$$D
Las Vegas ▪ *(702) 891-7337*
3799 Las Vegas Blvd S ▪ *Seafood & Steakhouse* ▪ Manager Mark reports that the restaurant "occasionally" serves GF diners. He recommends noting GF in reservations. With a advanced notice of a few days, special requests for GF specialty items can be accommodated. All reservations noting allergies are relayed to the server prior to the arrival of the party. All servers are trained on the GF diet and know how menu items must be modified to be GF. ▪ *www.mgmgrand.com*

Olives $$$$LD
Las Vegas ▪ *(702) 693-8181*
3600 Las Vegas Blvd S ▪ *Modern American* ▪ Manager Kendra notes that they get GF requests "all the time." Steaks and fish can be made GF by changing side dishes. Other dishes that can be modified to be GF include garlic broccolini, jumbo sea scal-

lops, crab stuffed arctic char roulade, and arugula risotto. Confirm timeliness of this information before dining in. Located in the Bellagio. ▪ *www.toddenglish.com*

Outback Steakhouse   📖
Las Vegas ▪ (702) 647-1035
1950 N Rainbow Blvd
Las Vegas ▪ (702) 251-7770
3411 Las Vegas Blvd S
Las Vegas ▪ (702) 220-4185
3785 Las Vegas Blvd S Ste 4100
Las Vegas ▪ (702) 898-3801
4141 S Pecos Rd
Las Vegas ▪ (702) 643-3148
7380 Las Vegas Blvd S
Las Vegas ▪ (702) 228-1088
8671 W Sahara Ave
N Las Vegas ▪ (702) 647-4152
2625 W Craig Rd

P.F. Chang's China Bistro   📖
Las Vegas ▪ (702) 968-8885
1095 S Rampart Blvd
Las Vegas ▪ (702) 836-0955
3667 Las Vegas Blvd S
Las Vegas ▪ (702) 792-2207
4165 Paradise Rd

Pei Wei Asian Diner   📖
Las Vegas ▪ (702) 233-4692
10830 W Charleston Blvd Ste 110

Roy's   ✪ $$$D
Las Vegas ▪ (702) 691-2053
620 E Flamingo Rd
Las Vegas ▪ (702) 838-3620
8701 W Charleston Blvd ▪ *Hawaiian Fusion* ▪ GF menus are always available but vary by location. Administrator Helen of Charleston Boulevard and Sous-Chef Ryan of Flamingo Road both report that GF diners are welcome. Servers are trained on the GF diet, and they can always get more information from the kitchen if necessary. ▪ *www.roysrestaurant.com*

Sammy's Woodfired Pizza   ✪ $LD
Las Vegas ▪ (702) 227-6000
6500 W Sahara Ave
Las Vegas ▪ (702) 365-7777

7160 N Durango Dr
Las Vegas ▪ (702) 263-7171
7345 Arroyo Crossing Pkwy
Las Vegas ▪ (702) 638-9500
9516 W Flamingo Rd ▪ *Pizza* ▪ GF menu includes a variety of artisan thin crust and woodfired pizzas, oak roasted chicken breast, a grilled chicken wrap, grilled shrimp salad, beet, walnut with goat cheese salad, and more. ▪ *www.sammyspizza.com*

Smith & Wollensky $$$$LD
Las Vegas ▪ (702) 862-4100
3767 Las Vegas Blvd S ▪ *Steakhouse* ▪ Manager Gina reports that although they have not served "a lot" of GF diners, they certainly know how to accommodate them. She recommends reservations noting GF, so that the server will prepare a list of non-GF items in advance. ▪ *www.smithandwollensky.com*

Stripburger   ¢LD
Las Vegas ▪ (702) 487-7548
3200 Las Vegas Blvd S ▪ *American* ▪ Manager Michael reports that GF diners can be accommodated "without a problem." He notes that any burger can be ordered without the bun. He also notes that servers have a special form for dietary requests, which ensures that the kitchen separates GF food during preparation. ▪ *www.stripburger.com*

Tillerman, The $$$$LD
Las Vegas ▪ (702) 731-4036
2245 E Flamingo Rd ▪ *Seafood & Steakhouse* ▪ Manager Jim notes that the restaurant serves GF diners regularly, and servers are GF aware. Most seafood and steak is GF, and side dishes can be modified to be GF. Alert a server, who will communicate with the kitchen. ▪ *www.tillerman.com*

Trevi $$$LD
Las Vegas ▪ (702) 735-4663
3500 Las Vegas Blvd S ▪ *Italian* ▪ Manager Brandon reports that the restaurant has accommodated GF diners in the past. He adds that there are many GF options,

including the caprese salad, carpaccio, and veal scaloppine. ■ *www.trevi-italian.com*

Verandah $$$$**BLD**
Las Vegas ■ *(702) 632-5000*
3960 Las Vegas Blvd S ■ *Italian-American* ■ Manager Nicole notes that GF diners come in "all the time." The chef is happy to modify regular menu items to be GF. She also reports that if diners call to make reservations noting GF, they can request any dish or even speak with the chef about GF options. ■ *www.fourseasons.com/lasvegas*

Wolfgang Puck Bar & Grill $$$$**LD**
Las Vegas ■ *(702) 891-3000*
3799 Las Vegas Blvd S ■ *Modern American* ■ Manager Drew reports that the restaurant serves GF diners regularly. Alert a server, who will communicate with the chef about how to modify menu items. Most meat and poultry dishes, like the organic half-chicken, can be easily modified to be GF. Confirm timeliness of this information before dining in. Located inside the MGM Grand. ■ *www.mgmgrand.com*

Yard House   📖
Las Vegas ■ *(702) 734-9273*
6593 Las Vegas Blvd S

NEVADA

ALL OTHER CITIES

Big Apple Pizza & Subs   ✪★ $$$**LD**
Sparks ■ *(775) 359-9000*
720 Baring Blvd ■ *Pizza* ■ GF menu includes spaghetti with marinara, baked ziti, shrimp scampi, fettuccine alfredo, pizza, and more. GF pizza and pasta are available. Restaurant recommends calling 24 hours in advance and noting GF in reservations.

Bonefish Grill   📖
Henderson ■ *(702) 228-3474*
10839 S Eastern Ave

Carino's Italian   📖
Reno ■ *(775) 852-8875*
13901 S Virginia St

Carrabba's Italian Grill   📖
Henderson ■ *(702) 990-0650*
10160 S Eastern Ave

Dandelion Deli   ★ ¢**L**
Reno ■ *(775) 322-6100*
1170 S Wells Ave ■ *Deli* ■ Non-dedicated bakery and deli that has a dedicated GF space in the display case. GF muffins, carrot cake, and cupcakes are always available, while GF cookies are occasionally available. GF bread is available for sandwiches, and loaves are available by special order.

Melting Pot, The   📖
Reno ■ *(775) 827-6500*
6950 S Mccarran Blvd

Outback Steakhouse   📖
Henderson ■ *(702) 451-7808*
4423 E Sunset Rd
Laughlin ■ *(702) 298-0419*
1900 S Casino Dr
Reno ■ *(775) 827-5050*
3645 S Virginia St
Sparks ■ *(775) 358-2700*
1805 E Lincoln Way

P.F. Chang's China Bistro   📖
Henderson ■ *(702) 361-3065*
101 S Green Valley Pkwy
Reno ■ *(775) 825-9800*
5180 Kietzke Ln

Pei Wei Asian Diner   📖
Henderson ■ *(702) 837-0861*
10575 S Eastern Ave Ste 100
Henderson ■ *(702) 898-6730*
1311 W Sunset Rd Ste 120

Sammy's Woodfired Pizza   ✪ $**LD**
Henderson ■ *(702) 450-6664*
4300 E Sunset Rd ■ *Pizza* ■ GF menu includes a variety of artisan thin crust and woodfired pizzas, oak roasted chicken

breast, a grilled chicken wrap, grilled shrimp salad, beet, walnut with goat cheese salad, and more. ■ *www.sammyspizza.com*

Winger's Grill and Bar ⚪ ¢LD
Elko ■ (775) 753-7750
1165 E Jennings Way ■ *American* ■ GF menu includes double basted ribs, glazed salmon, quesadillas with corn tortillas, and a variety of salads. ■ *www.wingers.info*

Z Pizza ★ $$LD
Reno ■ (775) 828-6565
4796 Caughlin Pkwy ■ *Pizza* ■ GF pizza is available. The restaurant cautions that they sometimes run out of GF pizza crust. ■ *www.zpizza.com*

NEW HAMPSHIRE

Aladdin's Gourmet Cuisine ¢LD
Salem ■ (603) 893-6969
88 N Broadway ■ *Mediterranean* ■ Hostess Lillian reports that this small family restaurant has "many dishes" which are naturally GF. Examples include hummus, stuffed cabbage and salads. Confirm timeliness of this information before dining in.

All Juiced Up ★ ¢BL
Manchester ■ (603) 518-5000
790 Elm St ■ *Café* ■ Fresh-baked GF bread and muffins are available. GF bread can be used to make most wraps and sandwiches. ■ *www.all-juiced-up.com*

Amigos Mexican Cantina ⚪★ $LD
Merrimack ■ (603) 578-9950
75 Dw Hwy
Milford ■ (603) 673-1500
20 South St ■ *Mexican* ■ Extensive GF menu includes appetizers, entrées, and desserts. GF beer is available, and Owner Mike notes that the restaurant is planning to add GF pasta and hamburger buns. Desserts

include GF carrot cake and flan. ■ *www. amigosmilford.com*

Anello's Gluten Free Café 100% ¢S
Portsmouth ■ (603) 319-8122
41 Congress St ■ *Café* ■ Dedicated GF café offering breakfast sandwiches on GF bagels, quiche, paninis, soups, and more. They also feature GF baked goods like muffins, cupcakes, and desserts like cannolis. Seasonal holiday pies and breads are also available. Confirm timeliness of this information before dining in. ■ *www.anelloscafe. com*

Bertucci's 📖
Manchester ■ (603) 668-6204
1500 S Willow St
Nashua ■ (603) 595-7244
406 Amherst St
Salem ■ (603) 890-3434
99 Rockingham Park Blvd

Blue Mermaid, The ⚪ $$$LD
Portsmouth ■ (603) 427-2583
409 The Hill ■ *Global* ■ GF menu includes spinach salad, paella, seafood tagine, plantain-encrusted cod, Jamaican jerk chicken, and more. Some items marked as GF on the menu need to be modified in order to be GF. Alert a server upon arrival. Servers are trained to notify the kitchen staff, who will make the necessary modifications. Confirm timeliness of this information before dining in. ■ *www.bluemermaid.com*

Brookstone Grille ⚪ $$$LD
Derry ■ (603) 328-9250
14 Route 111 ■ *Modern American* ■ GF menu includes fish and chips, chicken marsala, grilled vegetable sauté, surf and turf, mediterranean shrimp, and sirloin tips. ■ *www.brookstone-park.com*

Bugaboo Creek Steak House 📖
Bedford ■ (603) 625-2975
216 S River Rd
Nashua ■ (603) 881-5816
16 Gusabel Ave
Newington ■ (603) 422-0921
2024 Woodbury Ave

Carrabba's Italian Grill   📖
Bedford ▪ (603) 641-0004
2 Upjohn St

Chatila's Sugar-Free Bakery   ★ ¢S
Salem ▪ (603) 898-5459
254 N Broadway ▪ *Bakery* ▪ GF cheese-cakes, cookies, donuts, muffins, and other pastries are available. GF gift baskets are available for order. Products can be ordered online or picked up in the store, located in the Breckenridge Plaza. ▪ *www.sugarfreebakery.net*

Dining Room at the Bedford Village Inn, The $$$D
Bedford ▪ (800) 852-1166
2 Olde Bedford Way ▪ *Modern American* ▪ Manager Brie reports that the kitchen is "more than willing" to accommodate GF diners. She notes that the kitchen can modify items to be GF. Alert a server, who will relay requests to the kitchen. Reservations noting GF are recommended. ▪ *www.bedfordvillageinn.com*

Dover Natural Food & Café   ★ ¢S
Dover ▪ (603) 749-9999
7 Chestnut St ▪ *Café* ▪ Fresh-baked GF bread for sandwiches, as well as GF soups, cookies, and muffins are available. Located inside the health food market.

Flatbread Pizza Company   ★ $LD
North Conway ▪ (603) 356-4470
2760 White Mountain Hwy
Portsmouth ▪ (603) 436-7888
138 Congress St ▪ *Pizza* ▪ GF pizza is available in the 8-inch size. GF beer and desserts like brownies are also available. ▪ *www.flatbreadcompany.com*

Fratello's Ristorante Italiano   ★ $$$LD
Laconia ▪ (603) 528-2022
799 Union Ave
Lincoln ▪ (603) 745-2022
Kancamagus Hwy
Manchester ▪ (603) 624-2022
155 Dow St ▪ *Italian* ▪ GF pizza, pasta, and lasagna are available. ▪ *www.fratellos.com*

Frontside Grind   ★ ¢S
North Conway Village ▪ (603) 356-3603
2760 White Mountain Hwy ▪ *Coffee & Café* ▪ GF muffins are available in a variety of flavors. Gingerbread whoopie pie is available occasionally. ▪ *www.frontsidecoffee.com*

Garwoods Restaurant & Pub   ✪ $$$LD
Wolfeboro ▪ (603) 569-7788
6 N Main St ▪ *Steakhouse* ▪ GF menu items include spinach salad with scallops, steak tips, nachos, vegetable risotto, filet mignon, and more. ▪ *www.garwoodsrestaurant.com*

Gauchos Churrascaria Brazilian Steakhouse $$$LD
Manchester ▪ (603) 669-9460
62 Lowell St ▪ *Brazilian Steakhouse* ▪ Most menu items are GF. Salads, meats, and yucca are generally GF. Confirm timeliness of this information before dining in. ▪ *www.gauchosbraziliansteakhouse.com*

Italian Farmhouse   ✪★ $D
Plymouth ▪ (603) 536-4536
337 Daniel Webster Hwy ▪ *Italian* ▪ Chef Dennis reports that he started offering printed GF menus due to high demand. He notes that they accommodate GF diners "at least four or five times a week." GF pasta is available.

Joe's American Bar & Grill $LD
Nashua ▪ (603) 891-2060
310 Daniel Webster Hwy ▪ *American* ▪ GF pasta and pizza are available. Both can be prepared in several different ways. GF beer is also available. Manager recommends alerting the server and using the word "allergy." ▪ *www.joesamerican.com*

Juliano's Italian Pizzeria   ✪★ $LD
Derry ▪ (603) 425-7585
121 W Broadway ▪ *Italian* ▪ GF menu includes chicken parmesan with ziti, ziti and broccoli in white wine sauce, lasagna, and cheese pizza. GF pasta and pizza are available. ▪ *www.julianosnh.com*

Las Olas Taqueria   ¢LD

Exeter ▪ (603) 418-8901
30 Portsmouth Ave
Hampton ▪ (603) 967-4880
356 Lafayette Rd ▪ *Mexican* ▪ Owner Matt reports that he is GF himself. He notes that the restaurant serves GF diners "without difficulty." Nearly the entire menu is naturally GF, and that the kitchen takes special precautions when dealing with GF diners. Alert a server upon arrival. ▪ *www. lasolastaqueria.com*

Local Grocer, The   ★ ¢S

North Conway ▪ (603) 356-6068
3358 White Mountain Hwy ▪ *Café* ▪ GF wraps and bread for sandwiches are available. GF soups are also available. The café used to be called "Katrina's" but was sold to different owners.

Luca's Mediterranean Café   ★ $$LD

Keene ▪ (603) 358-3335
10 Central Sq ▪ *Mediterranean* ▪ GF pasta is available and can be substituted into any pasta dish. Manager Laura reports that the staff is "very informed" about the GF diet, and any server can indicate GF pasta sauces or other menu items. There is crème brûlée for dessert. ▪ *www.lucascafe.com*

Lucia's Tavola   ★ $$D

Brookline ▪ (603) 249-9134
181 Route 13 ▪ *Italian* ▪ GF pasta is available. Manager Anne reports that several GF customers dine in regularly. She also notes that certain entrées can be modified to be GF, such as the veal ortolano or chicken cacciatore. ▪ *www.luciastavola.com*

Lui Lui   ✪★ $LD

Nashua ▪ (603) 888-2588
259 Daniel Webster Hwy
West Lebanon ▪ (603) 298-7070
8 Glen Rd ▪ *Italian* ▪ Limited GF menu consists of spaghetti with meat or marinara sauce, cheese pizza, and chicken with broccoli and spaghetti. For dessert, they offer a GF brownie sundae. ▪ *www.luilui.com*

Maples Restaurant $$$D

Durham ▪ (603) 868-7800
17 Newmarket Rd ▪ *Modern American* ▪ Restaurant notes that several menu options are naturally GF. They also note that the chef will accommodate GF requests, as all dishes are made to order. Reservations noting GF are highly recommended. ▪ *www. threechimneysinn.com*

Michael Timothy's $$$LD

Nashua ▪ (603) 595-9334
212 Main St ▪ *Modern American* ▪ Manager Joey reports that the restaurant serves GF diners "regularly." He notes that the kitchen is GF aware and recommends reservations noting GF so that the server will be notified in advance. Although the menu changes regularly, Joey says that there are always items that can be modified to be GF. ▪ *www.michaeltimothys.com*

Ninety Nine Restaurant & Pub   📖

Concord ▪ (603) 224-7399
60 Damante Dr
Dover ▪ (603) 749-9992
8 Hotel Dr
Hooksett ▪ (603) 641-2999
1308 Hooksett Rd
Keene ▪ (603) 355-9990
360 Winchester St
Littleton ▪ (603) 444-7999
687 Meadow St
Londonderry ▪ (603) 421-9902
41 Nh Route 102
Manchester ▪ (603) 641-5999
1685 S Willow St
Nashua ▪ (603) 883-9998
10 Saint Laurent St
North Conway ▪ (603) 356-9909
1920 White Mountain Hwy
Portsmouth ▪ (603) 422-9989
Southgate Plaza
Salem ▪ (603) 893-5596
149 S Broadway
Seabrook ▪ (603) 474-5999
831 Lafayette Rd
Tilton ▪ (603) 286-4994
154 Laconia Rd

West Lebanon ▪ *(603) 298-6991*
10 Benning St

Nonni's Italian Eatery   ✪★ $$**D**
Concord ▪ *(603) 224-0400*
172 N Main St
Hillsborough ▪ *(603) 464-6766*
17 W Main St
New London ▪ *(603) 526-2265*
225 Newport Rd ▪ *Italian* ▪ GF menu includes GF pasta with any sauce, pizza, vegetable lasagna, and eggplant parmesan. GF pasta and pizza are available. ▪ *www.nonnisitalianeatery.com*

Old Salt, The   ✪ $$**LD**
Hampton ▪ *(603) 926-8322*
490 Lafayette Rd ▪ *American Regional* ▪ GF menu includes the lobster salad plate, jumbo shrimp cocktail, broiled sea scallops, and seared steak with gorgonzola cheese. Restaurant reports that it gets at least a few GF customers each week. ▪ *www.oldsaltnh.com*

Outback Steakhouse   📖
Bedford ▪ *(603) 622-8833*
95 S River Rd
Concord ▪ *(603) 226-0300*
22 Loudon Rd
Newington ▪ *(603) 431-5800*
2064 Woodbury Ave

Papagallos Restaurant   ✪ $$**D**
Keene ▪ *(603) 352-9400*
9 Monadnock Hwy ▪ *Italian* ▪ Limited GF menu includes chicken and sausage rustica, grilled chicken florentine, and steak toscano. Manager Tricia suggests "being repetitive" with the server and mentioning the word "allergy," even if ordering from the GF menu. ▪ *www.papagallos.com*

Peterborough Pizza Barn   ★ ¢**LD**
Peterborough ▪ *(603) 924-7119*
71 US Hwy 202 ▪ *Pizza* ▪ GF pizza is available.

Puritan Backroom, The   ✪★ $**LD**
Manchester ▪ *(603) 669-6890*
245 Hooksett Rd ▪ *American* ▪ Extensive GF menu was created by a manager with Celiac disease, and it includes appetizers, salads, side dishes, kids' meals, entrées, and desserts. GF soy sauce and beer are available. ▪ *www.puritanbackroom.com*

Rafferty's Restaurant & Pub   ★ $**LD**
North Conway ▪ *(603) 356-6460*
36 Kearsarge Rd ▪ *American* ▪ GF bread, hamburger buns, hotdog buns, pasta, pizza, and beer are available. They have a dedicated GF fryer and a dedicated GF grill, so they can make nearly any meat or fish dish GF. For dessert, they offer flourless chocolate cake, GF brownies, whoopie pies, and more. ▪ *www.raffspub.com*

Sunflowers   ★ $**LD**
Jaffrey ▪ *(603) 593-3303*
21 Main St ▪ *American* ▪ GF bread and buns are available for sandwiches. GF pasta is available for substitution into any pasta dish. GF beer is also available. They have live music on Sunday evenings starting at 6pm, and they feature new artwork each month. ▪ *www.sunflowerscatering.com*

T-Bones Great American Eatery $$**LD**
Bedford ▪ *(603) 641-6100*
25 S River Rd
Derry ▪ *(603) 434-3200*
39 Crystal Ave
Hudson ▪ *(603) 882-6677*
77 Lowell Rd
Salem ▪ *(603) 893-3444*
311 S Broadway ▪ *American* ▪ At all locations, managers note that GF diners should be specific about what they can eat. All locations also note that many menu items can be modified to be GF. At the Bedford location, the kitchen has a list of menu items that are GF. Alert a server, who will notify the kitchen manager. ▪ *www.t-bones.com*

Uno Chicago Grill   📖
Concord ▪ *(603) 226-8667*
15 Fort Eddy Rd
Dover ▪ *(603) 749-2200*
238 Indian Brook Rd

Nashua ▪ *(603) 888-6980*
304 Daniel Webster Hwy
Nashua ▪ *(603) 886-4132*
593 Amherst St
Tilton ▪ *(603) 286-4079*
122 Laconia Rd

Vito Marcello's Italian Bistro   ★ $$$$D
North Conway ▪ *(603) 356-7000*
1857 White Mountain Hwy ▪ *Italian* ▪ GF pasta and pizza are available. Other GF options include mussels, grilled salmon, sirloin steak, and insalata caprese. ▪ *www.bellinis.com*

Yankee Smokehouse   ✪★ ¢LD
W Ossipee ▪ *(603) 539-7427*
Junction Of Rts 16 And 25 ▪ *Barbeque* ▪ GF menu includes ribs, BBQ chicken, sliced pork, corn on the cob, beans, chili and burgers. Prime rib is available on Saturday night only. For dessert, they offer GF carrot cake. GF beer also available. ▪ *www.yankeesmokehouse.com*

Z Food & Drink $$$LD
Manchester ▪ *(603) 629-9383*
860 Elm St ▪ *American* ▪ The restaurant reports that accommodating GF diners is "no problem," as all dishes are made to order. Many menu items can be modified to be GF, and several steak and chicken dishes are naturally GF. Confirm timeliness of this information before dining in. Reservations noting GF are recommended. ▪ *www.zfoodanddrink.com*

NEW JERSEY

Alfonso's 202   ★ $LD
Flemington ▪ *(908) 237-2700*
482 US Highway 202 ▪ *Italian* ▪ GF pizza and pasta are available.

Aliperti's Ristorante   ✪★ $$LD
Clark ▪ *(732) 381-2300*
1189 Raritan Rd ▪ *Italian* ▪ GF menu includes grilled chicken parmigiana, filet mignon, and fish risotto pescatore, as well as rice pudding or gelato for dessert. GF beer is available. Manager Michael reports that the restaurant is a participating member of GRAP, and that they are happy to serve GF guests. ▪ *www.alipertisrestaurant.com*

Artisan's Brewery & Italian Grill
                   ✪ $$$LD
Toms River ▪ *(732) 244-7566*
1171 Hooper Ave ▪ *American* ▪ GF menu includes shrimp cocktail, chicken parmesan, sesame tuna, burgers without buns, filet mignon with potatoes, brocolli rabe, and more. ▪ *www.artisanstomsriver.com*

Atillio's Pizza   ★ $LD
Tinton Falls ▪ *(732) 922-6760*
4057 Asbury Ave ▪ *Pizza* ▪ GF pizza is available.

Atlantic Bar and Grill $$$$D
S Seaside Park ▪ *(732) 854-1588*
24th & Central Ave ▪ *Seafood & Steakhouse* ▪ Chef Mike reports that serving GF diners is "part of the program" at the restaurant, as they do it many times each night. He adds that servers are "fully knowledgeable" about the GF diet, and they can indicate which items can be prepared GF. Restaurant is closed in January and has limited hours for the rest of winter. ▪ *www.atlanticbarandgrillnj.com*

Backyards Bistro   ★ $LD
Hoboken ▪ *(201) 222-2660*
732 Jefferson St ▪ *Bistro* ▪ GF pasta is available. ▪ *www.backyardsbistro.com*

Bella Vida Garden Café   ★ ¢BLD
West Cape May ▪ *(609) 884-6332*
406 Broadway ▪ *American* ▪ GF pancakes are available for breakfast, while GF bread, wraps, and pasta are available for lunch and dinner. Any sandwich can be prepared on GF bread, and any pasta dish can be made with GF pasta. Manager Jess reports that

there are other items which can also be made GF, so discuss options with a server. ▪ *www.bellavidacafe.com*

Bella Vita Café   ★ $$LD
Freehold ▪ *(732) 866-8484*
3585 Route 9 N ▪ *Italian-American* ▪ GF pizza is available for lunch or dinner. Restaurant hopes to have GF pasta in the near future. ▪ *www.bellavitacafe.com*

Bertucci's   📖
Hazlet ▪ *(732) 264-2422*
2847 Highway 35
Jersey City ▪ *(201) 222-8088*
560 Washington Blvd
Marlton ▪ *(856) 988-8070*
515 Route 73 N
Mount Laurel ▪ *(856) 273-0400*
1220 Nixon Dr
Sicklerville ▪ *(856) 740-9960*
625 Cross Keys Rd
Woodbridge ▪ *(732) 636-8200*
899 Saint George Ave

Blue Bottle Café, The   ✪ $$$LD
Hopewell ▪ *(609) 333-1710*
101 E Broad St ▪ *Modern American* ▪ GF items marked on the menu include sea scallops, pan-seared arctic char, braised veal breast, and asparagus soup. For dessert, they offer fresh fruit pavlova and chocolate hazelnut mousse. Owner Rory reports that GF diners come in "all the time," and he recommends asking the server to notify the chef. ▪ *www.thebluebottlecafe.com*

Bonefish Grill   📖
Brick ▪ *(732) 785-2725*
179 Van Zile Rd
E Brunswick ▪ *(732) 390-0838*
335 State Route 18
Egg Harbor Twp ▪ *(609) 646-2828*
3121 Fire Rd
Green Brook ▪ *(732) 926-8060*
215 Rt 22 E
Iselin ▪ *(732) 634-7695*
625 US Highway 1 S
Marlton ▪ *(856) 396-3122*

500 Route 73 N
Paramus ▪ *(201) 261-2355*
601 From Rd
Pine Brook ▪ *(973) 227-2443*
28 US Highway 46
Secaucus ▪ *(201) 864-3004*
200 Mill Creek Dr
Woodbury ▪ *(856) 848-6261*
1709 Deptford Center Rd

Brothers Moon, The $$$LD
Hopewell ▪ *(609) 333-1330*
7 W Broad St ▪ *Modern American* ▪ Chef Will reports that they serve GF diners every day, and that all staff members are trained on the GF diet. He advises making reservations noting GF and alerting a server upon arrival. Examples of GF items are stilton crusted beef tenderloin, sautéed sea scallops, cardamom-espresso pot de crème, and chocolate mousse. Confirm timeliness of this information before dining in. ▪ *www.brothersmoon.com*

Café Capri   ★ $$LD
Hillsdale ▪ *(201) 664-6422*
343 Broadway ▪ *Italian* ▪ Manager Gary reports that GF diners are "absolutely" welcome and notes that everything is made to order, so GF requests are easy to accommodate. GF rice pasta is sometimes available.

Calabria Restaurant & Pizzeria
                                    ✪★ $$LD
Livingston ▪ *(973) 992-8496*
588 S Livingston Ave ▪ *Italian* ▪ GF menu includes penne vodka, chicken or veal parmigiana, grilled salmon over sautéed spinach, spaghetti and meatballs, pizza, and more. GF pasta and pizza crusts are available. ▪ *www.calabriarestaurant.com*

Capital Grille, The   📖
Cherry Hill ▪ *(856) 665-5252*
2000 Route 38

Carino's Italian   📖
Clifton ▪ *(973) 662-0085*
70 Kingsland Rd
Howell ▪ *(732) 730-0910*
4731 Route 9 N

Carlo's Gourmet Restaurant, Pizzeria and Caterers ✪★ $$LD

Marlboro ▪ (732) 536-6070
326 Route 9 ▪ *Pizza* ▪ GF menu includes appetizers, GF rice rotini and penne, ravioli, pizza, and meat entrées. Restaurant has one smaller location in Manalapan, but only the Marlboro location has GF items. ▪ *www.carlosgourmetpizza.com*

Carmine's Restaurant ★ $$$D

Atlantic City ▪ (609) 572-9300
2801 Pacific Ave ▪ *Italian* ▪ GF pasta is available. Located at the Tropicana Hotel and Casino. ▪ *www.carminesnyc.com*

Carrabba's Italian Grill 📖

Brick ▪ (732) 262-3470
990 Cedarbridge Ave
East Brunswick ▪ (732) 432-8054
335 Route 18
Egg Harbor Township ▪ (609) 407-2580
6725 Black Horse Pike
Green Brook ▪ (732) 424-1200
200 US Highway 22
Maple Shade ▪ (856) 235-5525
500 Route 38 E
Marlton ▪ (856) 988-0581
903 Route 73 S
Middletown ▪ (732) 615-9061
1864 Highway 35
Turnersville ▪ (856) 629-0100
4650 Route 42

Chakra Restaurant ✪ $D

Paramus ▪ (201) 556-1530
144 W State Rt 4 ▪ *Modern American* ▪ Manager Evelyn reports that they have a new GF menu listing a wide variety of entrées, including chicken and fish dishes. ▪ *www.chakrarestaurant.com*

Chambers Walk $LD

Lawrenceville ▪ (609) 896-5995
2667 Main St ▪ *American* ▪ Manager Kristen reports that they have "several people come in regularly" with GF diets. She notes that almost anything can be made GF. Note GF when making reservations, and alert a server upon arrival. ▪ *www.chamberswalk.com*

Charlie Brown's Steakhouse 📖

Brielle ▪ (732) 223-7805
601 Union Ave
Carlstadt ▪ (201) 842-9999
335 Paterson Plank Rd
Chatham ▪ (973) 822-1800
522 Southern Blvd
Clementon ▪ (856) 783-9324
1378 Little Gloucester Rd
Clifton ▪ (973) 471-1400
1296 Van Houten Ave
Denville ▪ (973) 586-3095
167 W Main St
East Windsor ▪ (609) 371-2238
60 Princeton Hightstown Rd
Edison ▪ (732) 494-6135
222 Plainfield Rd
Fairfield ▪ (973) 808-4473
337 Fairfield Rd
Forked River ▪ (609) 242-7306
443 S Main St
Green Brook ▪ (732) 968-9870
171 Route 22 E
Hackettstown ▪ (908) 979-0446
109 Grand Ave
Highland Park ▪ (732) 545-1778
247 Raritan Ave
Hillsborough ▪ (908) 874-6511
381 Route 206
Kingston ▪ (609) 924-7400
4591 Route 27
Lakewood ▪ (732) 367-4818
400 Route 70
Maple Shade ▪ (856) 779-8003
114 E Main St # 116
Matawan ▪ (732) 583-7666
27 Freneau Ave # Rt.79
Millburn ▪ (973) 376-1724
35 Main St
Montclair ▪ (973) 783-9560
50 Upper Montclair Plz
Mt Holly ▪ (609) 265-1100
949 Route 51
Old Tappan ▪ (201) 767-6106
203 Old Tappan Rd
Oradell ▪ (201) 265-0403*

2 Kinderkamack Rd
Phillipsburg ■ *(908) 387-9380*
1603 Springtown Rd
Piscataway ■ *(732) 885-3900*
1776 S Washington Ave
Scotch Plains ■ *(908) 232-3443*
2376 North Ave
Tenafly ■ *(201) 569-5558*
87 County Rd
Tinton Falls ■ *(732) 460-1160*
1202 Sycamore Ave
Toms River ■ *(732) 279-0216*
11 Kettle Creek Rd
Township Of Washington ■ *(201) 666-3080*
95 Linwood Ave
Trenton ■ *(609) 584-0222*
2110 Whitehorse Mercerville Rd
Union ■ *(908) 686-9023*
2501 Route 22 W
Wayne ■ *(973) 686-1901*
1207 Hamburg Tpke
Woodbridge ■ *(732) 636-8550*
300 Woodbridge Ctr Dr
Woodbury ■ *(856) 853-8505*
111 N Broad St

Chimney Rock Inn   ★ $LD
Bound Brook ■ *(732) 469-4600*
800 Thompson Ave
Gillette ■ *(908) 580-1100*
342 Valley Rd ■ American ■ GF pizza and pasta are available. For dessert, GF brownies are available. GF catering trays are available in house or for pick up. ■ *www.chimneyrockinn.com*

Court Street $$$D
Hoboken ■ *(201) 795-4515*
61 6th St ■ American ■ Management reports that GF diners can be accommodated. Make reservations noting GF and alert a server upon arrival. ■ *www.court-street.com*

DeLiteful Foods   ★ ¢BL
Lawrenceville ■ *(609) 586-7122*
4040 Quakerbridge Rd ■ Bakery ■ Dedicated GF market and bakery offering GF items ranging from baguettes and english

muffins to cupcakes. Market contains two adjacent stores, one of which is dedicated GF. ■ *www.delitefulfoods.com*

Dining Room at the Golden Inn, The
$$$D
Avalon ■ *(609) 967-2111*
Oceanfront At 78th St ■ American ■ Chef Bryan reports that there is an internal GF list to which the servers have access. It includes fish, filet mignon, a NY strip steak, and sides. Confirm timeliness of this information before dining in. Bryan notes that the servers are able to "verbalize" GF options. ■ *www.goldeninn.com*

Edison Pizza Restaurant   ★ $$LD
Edison ■ *(732) 985-1733*
2303 Woodbridge Ave ■ Pizza ■ Manager Rob reports that GF pizza is available in the personal size only. GF pizzas are baked on top of aluminum foil and a cut with a designated pizza cutter to ensure that cross-contamination does not occur. ■ *www.edisonpizza.com*

Fontanarosa's Gourmet Specialty Foods   ★ ¢L
Totowa ■ *(973) 942-7784*
86 Lincoln Ave ■ Take-&-Bake ■ GF linguine and ravioli are available for "take-&-bake." ■ *www.fontanarosas.com*

Genteel's Trattoria & Pizzeria   ★ $LD
Skillman ■ *(609) 252-0880*
1378 US Highway 206 ■ Italian ■ GF pizza is available, and GF pasta is available with advanced notice.

Giuseppe's Pizza & Restaurant   ★ $$LD
Cedar Grove ■ *(973) 857-1982*
557 Pompton Ave ■ Pizza ■ GF pizza is available.

Gluten Free Gloriously   100% ¢S
Stirling ■ *(908) 647-7337*
267 Main Ave ■ Bakery ■ Dedicated GF bakery offering pizza, stromboli, pasta, muffins, sugar cookies, cupcakes, and more. ■ *www.glutenfreegloriously.com*

Goodfellows Pizza & Italian ★ ¢LD

Fords ■ *(732) 738-7500*
736 King George Post Rd
Parlin ■ *(732) 707-4455*
3 Johnson Ln ■ *Pizza* ■ GF pizza is available. ■ *www.goodfellowstakeout.com*

Great Harvest Bread Company ★ ¢S

Cherry Hill ■ *(856) 216-0700*
100 Springdale Rd ■ *Bakery* ■ GF white bread, buckwheat bread, banana bread, muffins, scones, and coffee cakes are occasionally available. GF items are baked on Mondays only, and sometimes they run out. ■ *www.greatharvest.com*

Greenhouse Café ★ $BLD

Ship Bottom ■ *(609) 494-7333*
605 Long Beach Blvd ■ *American* ■ GF pasta and pizza are available. Both can be substituted into any dishes, though some specialty pizzas may contain non-GF sauces. GF rolls are available for sandwiches. ■ *www.greenhousecafelbi.com*

Grind House Café ★ ¢B

Haddonfield ■ *(856) 795-8400*
123 Kings Hwy E ■ *Bakery & Café* ■ Manager Devon reports that GF cookies and biscotti are available. He notes that several GF diners come into the bakery each day. ■ *www.grindhousenj.com*

Health Shoppe, The ★ ¢BL

Morristown ■ *(973) 538-9131*
66 Morris St ■ *Deli & Bakery* ■ Extensive GF offerings include fresh-baked focaccia, english muffins, cupcakes, and cookies. Three other locations in New Jersey sell GF specialty items but do not have a bakery or deli. ■ *www.thehealthshoppes.com*

Iron Hill Brewery & Restaurant ☼★ $$LD

Maple Shade ■ *(856) 273-0300*
124 E Kings Hwy ■ *American* ■ GF menu is available at all locations. It includes sandwiches and burgers without buns, tomato basil soup, baked buffalo wings, and fisherman's stew. GF beer is available. ■ *www.ironhillbrewery.com*

It's Greek To Me $$LD

Englewood ■ *(201) 568-0440*
36 E Palisade Ave
Fort Lee ■ *(201) 947-2050*
1611 Palisade Ave
Hoboken ■ *(201) 216-1888*
538 Washington St
Holmdel ■ *(732) 275-0036*
2128 State Route 35
Jersey City ■ *(201) 222-0844*
194 Newark Ave
Livingston ■ *(973) 992-8999*
6230 Town Center Way
Long Branch ■ *(732) 571-0222*
44 Centennial Dr
Ridgewood ■ *(201) 612-2600*
21 E Ridgewood Ave
Westwood ■ *(201) 722-3511*
487 Broadway ■ *Greek* ■ Restaurant reports that many menu items, such as meats, salads, fish, and vegetables, are GF. Confirm timeliness of this information before dining in. Ask for a manager, who will alert the servers and kitchen staff. ■ *www. itsgreektome-taverna.com*

Janice - A Bistro ☼★ $$$BLD

Ho Ho Kus ■ *(201) 445-2666*
23 Sheridan Ave ■ *Italian* ■ GF menu includes duck breast with truffle oil, ribeye steak, and flourless chocolate cake. GF bread is available all day, and GF rice pasta is available for dinner. ■ *www.janiceabistro.com*

Joe's American Bar & Grill ★ $LD

Paramus ■ *(201) 843-8858*
298 Garden State Plz
Short Hills ■ *(973) 379-4444*
1200 Morris Tpke ■ *American* ■ GF pasta and pizza are available. Both can be prepared in several different ways. At each location, a manager recommends alerting the server and using the word "allergy." ■ *www.joesamerican.com*

Joe's Pizzeria & Vittoria Ristorante ★ $$LD

Summit ■ *(908) 522-0615*
101 Springfield Ave ■ *Pizza* ■ GF pizza and

pasta are available. Manager Pam reports that GF diners "frequently stop by." ▪ *www.joespizzasummit.com*

Kona Grill 📖
Iselin ▪ *(732) 750-4400*
511 US Highway 1

La Campagne $$$D
Cherry Hill ▪ *(856) 429-7647*
312 Kresson Rd ▪ *Continental* ▪ Chef Rich reports that they are recognized around the community as a GF friendly restaurant. He reports that there are a "good range" of menu items that can be modified to be GF. Alert a server upon arrival. Reservations noting GF are recommended. ▪ *www.lacampagne.com*

La Riviera Trattoria ✪★ $$LD
Clifton ▪ *(973) 478-4181*
421 Piaget Ave # 27 ▪ *Italian* ▪ GF menu includes appetizers, salads, pasta dishes, meat entrées, and crème brûlée or sorbet for dessert. GF pasta is available. The restaurant recommends noting GF in reservations. ▪ *www.larivieratrattoria.com*

Lake Sea Restaurant ★ $LD
Wayne ▪ *(973) 616-5757*
107 Terhune Dr ▪ *Chinese & Japanese* ▪ GF rice noodles are available. Manager Jeff reports that a GF white sauce can be substituted for soy sauce. He also notes that "twenty percent of the customers" who dine in are GF. He recommends alerting the server, who will accommodate GF requests. ▪ *www.lakesearestaurant.com*

Legal Sea Foods 📖
Paramus ▪ *(201) 843-8483*
1 Garden State Plz
Short Hills ▪ *(973) 467-0089*
1200 Morris Tpke

Little Anthony's Pizzeria & Restaurant ★ $$LD
Vernon ▪ *(973) 764-9800*
530 Route 515 ▪ *Pizza* ▪ GF pizza is available. ▪ *www.littleanthonyspizza.com*

Lone Star Steakhouse & Saloon 📖
Bridgewater ▪ *(908) 526-8177*
970 US Highway 22

Maggiano's Little Italy ★ $$$LD
Bridgewater ▪ *(908) 547-6045*
600 Commons Way
Cherry Hill ▪ *(856) 792-4470*
2000 Route 38 Ste 1180
Hackensack ▪ *(201) 221-2030*
390 Hackensack Ave Spc 70 ▪ *Italian* ▪ GF pasta is available. Call individual locations to inquire about additional GF options. ▪ *www.maggianos.com*

Main Street Trattoria ✪★ $LD
Metuchen ▪ *(732) 205-9080*
413 Main St ▪ *Italian* ▪ GF pizza is available in the 12-inch size and GF pasta are available. GF pizza is available with any toppings, and GF pasta is available with a variety of sauces listed on the GF menu. ▪ *www.mainsttrattoria.com*

Mama's Restaurant & Café Baci ✪★ $$LD
Hackettstown ▪ *(908) 852-2820*
260 Mountain Ave ▪ *Italian* ▪ GF menu is extensive. GF pizza, pasta, bread, and soy sauce are available. For dessert, a variety of GF cookies, cakes, and brownies are available. Owner Thomas reports that all staff members are "highly trained" on the GF diet. ▪ *www.mamascafebaci.com*

Mangia Trattoria ★ $$LD
Glen Rock ▪ *(201) 445-6264*
918 Prospect St ▪ *Italian* ▪ GF pasta, pizza, ravioli, and cheese-stuffed shell pasta are available. Restaurant is also looking into adding GF specialty desserts. ▪ *www.mangiatrattoriaonline.com*

Masina ✪★ $$BLD
Weehawken ▪ *(201) 348-4444*
500 Harbor Blvd ▪ *Italian* ▪ Extensive GF menu includes antipasti, pasta, soup, meat, salad, fried bites, and seafood. GF pasta and beer are available.

Melting Pot, The   📖
Atlantic City ■ (609) 441-1100
2112 Atlantic Ave
Hoboken ■ (201) 222-1440
100 Sinatra Dr
Red Bank ■ (732) 219-0090
2 Bridge Ave
Somerville ■ (908) 575-8010
190 W Main St
Westwood ■ (201) 664-8877
250 Center Ave
Whippany ■ (973) 428-5400
831 Route 10

Miller's Gluten Free Bread Co.   100% ¢L
Butler ■ (973) 291-8190
140 Main St ■ *Bakery & Café* ■ Dedicated GF bakery and café offering bread, pizza, rolls, garlic knots, muffins, and sugar cookie dough. GF café menu includes small pizzas, sandwiches, and more. ■ *www.millersglutenfree.com*

Mirabella Café   ★ $$$LD
Cherry Hill ■ (856) 354-1888
210 E Route 70 ■ *Italian* ■ GF linguine and meat ravioli are available. ■ *www.mirabellacafe.com*

Mom's Bake At Home Pizza   ★ ¢BLD
Medford ■ (609) 654-8885
560 Stokes Rd ■ *Take-&-Bake* ■ GF "take-&-bake" pizza available for pick-up only. ■ *www.momsbakeathome.com*

Napa Valley Grille $$$LD
Paramus ■ (201) 845-5555
Routes 4 And 7 ■ *Modern American* ■ Manager Ginger reports that the restaurant accommodates GF diners "all the time." She notes that many items are naturally GF. Servers are very GF aware and will indicate GF menu items to diners. Reservations noting GF are recommended. ■ *www.napavalleygrille.com*

Natale's   ★ $LD
Waldwick ■ (201) 445-2860
14 W Prospect St ■ *Pizza* ■ GF pizza is available.

Neil's Pizzeria   ★ $$LD
Wayne ■ (973) 305-0405
568 Valley Rd ■ *Pizza* ■ GF pizza is available.

Ninety Nine Restaurant & Pub   📖
Woodbury ■ (856) 251-0099
1440 Almonesson Rd

Original Pancake House, The   ★ ¢BL
Fort Lee ■ (201) 585-0905
1638 Schlosser St
West Caldwell ■ (973) 575-9161
817 Bloomfield Ave
Whippany ■ (973) 515-8552
831 Route 10 ■ *Breakfast* ■ GF pancakes are available. Select locations may serve other GF items. Call a specific location to inquire. ■ *www.originalpancakehouse.com*

Outback Steakhouse   📖
Brick ■ (732) 920-1222
2770 Hooper Ave
Butler ■ (973) 850-3055
1538 Route 23
Cherry Hill ■ (856) 482-1350
230 Lake Dr E
Edgewater ■ (201) 840-9600
539 River Rd
Edison ■ (732) 819-0990
481 US Highway 1
Egg Harbor Township ■ (609) 484-8778
6733 Black Horse Pike
Green Brook ■ (732) 424-0555
98 US Highway 22
Hamilton ■ (609) 581-2444
740 US Highway 130
Ledgewood ■ (973) 927-3030
1070 Route 46
Marlton ■ (856) 983-0921
901 Route 73 S
Middletown ■ (732) 796-0110
740 State Route 35
Old Bridge ■ (732) 525-8899
1397 US Highway 9
Parsippany ■ (973) 257-4888
1300 Route 46
Rochelle Park ■ (201) 843-8445
194 Route 17 N
Secaucus ■ (201) 601-0077

455 Harmon Meadow Blvd
Springfield ▪ (973) 467-9095
901 Mountain Ave
Turnersville ▪ (856) 728-3700
4600 Route 42
Wayne ▪ (973) 305-8383
191 Berdan Ave
Woodbury ▪ (856) 686-5760
1709 Deptford Center Rd

P.F. Chang's China Bistro 📖
Atlantic City ▪ (609) 348-4600
2801 Pacific Ave Unit 101
Freehold ▪ (732) 308-1840
3710 Route 9 Ste 2817
Hackensack ▪ (201) 646-1565
390 Hackensack Ave Ste 50
Marlton ▪ (856) 396-0818
500 Route 73 S Ste G1
Princeton ▪ (609) 799-5163
3545 US Highway 1
West New York ▪ (201) 866-7790
10 Port Imperial Blvd

Papa Razzi ★ $$LD
Paramus ▪ (201) 843-0990
298 Garden State Plz
Short Hills ▪ (973) 467-5544
1200 Morris Tpke ▪ Italian ▪ GF pasta is available at both locations, and GF pizza is available at the Garden State Plaza location. ▪ www.paparazzitrattoria.com

Park & Orchard Restaurant ✪★ $$$LD
E Rutherford ▪ (201) 939-9292
240 Hackensack St ▪ Global ▪ Extensive GF menu includes cheese enchiladas and eggplant stuffed with spinach and mushrooms. GF pasta is available. GF dessert options include chocolate raspberry tart and ultimate chocolate cake. ▪ www.parkandorchard.com

Park Pizza ★ ¢LD
Park Ridge ▪ (201) 391-9393
85 Park Ave ▪ Pizza ▪ Personal-sized GF pizzas are available. GF crusts can be prepared with any available toppings.

Pasta Pomodoro Ristorante Italiano & Catering ✪★ $LD
Voorhees ▪ (856) 782-7430
700 Route 561 ▪ Italian ▪ GF menu items include the blackened chicken sandwich, veal parmigiana, salmon tribeca, and sautéed eggplant in wine sauce. GF pasta, pizza, garlic bread, and desserts are available. The restaurant reports that they have "a million customers" who are GF. ▪ www.pastapomodoronj.com

Pei Wei Asian Diner 📖
Cherry Hill ▪ (856) 792-9260
2050 Route 70 W
Moorestown ▪ (856) 778-0299
400 W Route 38 Ste 8120

Peter Shields Inn $$$$D
Cape May ▪ (609) 884-9090
1301 Beach Ave ▪ Modern American ▪ Innkeeper Bridget notes that GF diners can "definitely" be accommodated. She reports that the servers are all GF aware, and she adds that because all meals are made to order, GF requests are not a problem. Upon arrival, alert a server and ask to speak with a chef about GF options. ▪ www.peter-shieldsinn.com

Peter Wong's Homemade Ice Cream and Asian Café ✪ $LD
Montvale ▪ (201) 391-2797
26 Chestnut Ridge Rd Rm G ▪ Asian ▪ Extensive GF menu includes appetizers, fried rice, rice noodles, and main courses. Examples of GF entrées are sesame chicken with broccoli, thai basil chicken, and snow peas with fresh water chestnuts in brown or white sauce. For dessert, they offer a unique variety of ice cream flavors, including green tea and coconut chip. ▪ www.peterwongsasiancafe.com

Pier House Restaurant $$$BLD
Cape May ▪ (609) 898-0300
1327 Beach Ave ▪ American ▪ Chef George reports that the restaurant serves GF diners "often." He recommends noting GF in reservations, and then alerting a server upon arrival. He notes that servers are generally GF aware, but if they have questions about

the ingredients of a certain dish, they will ask him. He adds that most fish dishes are naturally GF and that there are many options for GF customers. ■ *www.thepier-housecapemay.com*

Pizza and Sandwich Barn ★ $$ LD
Caldwell ■ **(973) 226-9020**
323 Bloomfield Ave ■ *Pizza* ■ GF pizza is available in the 12-inch size, with any toppings. GF sub rolls are available to substitute into any of the sandwiches. Meals can be delivered, picked up, or eaten at the restaurant.

Pizza Fusion ★ $$ LD
Red Bank ■ **(732) 345-1600**
95 Broad St
Ridgewood ■ **(201) 445-9010**
33 Godwin Ave ■ *Pizza* ■ GF pizza and brownies are available. ■ *www.pizzafusion.com*

Plantation Restaurant, The $$$ LD
Harvey Cedars ■ **(609) 494-8191**
7908 Long Beach Blvd ■ *Modern American* ■ Manager Paul reports that GF diners are "very easily" accommodated. He notes that most menu items can be modified to be GF. Reservations noting GF are recommended. Alert a server, who will discuss GF requests with the kitchen. ■ *www.plantationrestaurant.com*

Portuguese Manor $$ LD
Perth Amboy ■ **(732) 826-2233**
310 Elm St ■ *Portuguese* ■ One of the restaurant's two servers, Roy, reports that all staff members are familiar with the GF diet. He notes that the paellas are naturally GF, or he can arrange for the chef to make a GF steak or fish entrée. Confirm timeliness of this information before dining in. ■ *www.portuguesemanorrestaurante.com*

Red Square at The Quarter at Tropicana $$$$ D
Atlantic City ■ **(609) 344-9100**
2801 Pacific Ave ■ *Fusion* ■ General Manager Joe reports that the restaurant serves GF diners often. He recommends reserva-

tions noting GF and offers to speak to GF customers about possible dining options prior to the date of their reservation. He notes that all servers have access to an internal allergen list that includes non-GF menu items. ■ *www.chinagrillmgt.com*

Rí~Rá Irish Pub $ LD
Atlantic City ■ **(609) 348-8600**
The Quarter At The Tropicana ■ *Irish Pub* ■ Ask for the "Allergen Chart," which has a "Celiac" column. This column contains items that are GF or can be modified to be GF. ■ *www.rira.com*

Shelly's Café ★ $$$ LD
Teaneck ■ **(201) 692-0001**
482 Cedar Ln ■ *Vegetarian* ■ GF pizza with any toppings and GF french fries are available. Manager Amir reports that GF orders are "very popular" at the restaurant. He also notes that the kitchen will try to modify other menu items to be GF. ■ *www.shellyscafe.net*

Smithville Inn, The $$$ LD
Galloway ■ **(609) 652-7777**
1 N New York Rd ■ *American* ■ Chef Chris reports that GF diners can be accommodated "no problem." He notes that everything is "fresh and made to order," so he can modify any dish on the menu to be GF. ■ *www.smithvilleinn.com*

Stefano's Ristorante Italiano ★ $$$ LD
Mount Laurel ■ **(856) 778-3663**
3815 Church Rd ■ *Italian* ■ GF pasta, pizza, and cookies are available. Restaurant reports that almost all regular menu items can be modified to be GF. ■ *www.stefanos-ristoranteitaliano.com*

Stein's Bagels and Gourmet Deli ★ ¢ BL
Montvale ■ **(201) 782-0087**
106 Chestnut Ridge Rd ■ *Café* ■ GF rolls and breads are available for sandwiches. Owner Jay also has a freezer of GF foods such as pizza, desserts, individual dinners, pasta, and bagels. He notes that with advanced notice, he can bake pizzas, warm bagels, or cook a fresh GF pasta dish for

GF customers who want to dine in. ▪ *www.steinsbagels.com*

Steve and Cookie's by the Bay　$$$$D
Margate City ▪ (609) 823-1163
9700 Amherst Ave ▪ *Modern American*
▪ Restaurant reports that there are a lot of GF options available. The kitchen is fully versed in GF cooking, and GF diners "frequent" the restaurant. Alert a server, who will discuss GF options. Reservations noting GF are recommended. ▪ *www.steve-andcookies.com*

Sweet Avenue Bake Shop　★ ¢S
Rutherford ▪ (201) 935-2253
153 Park Ave ▪ *Bakery* ▪ Bakery reports that at least one GF cupcake is available every day. Possible GF flavors include chocolate, vanilla, and cotton candy. For special or large orders, advanced notice of at least one week is required. ▪ *www.sweet-avenuebakeshop.com*

Ted's On Main　$$$LD
Medford ▪ (609) 654-7011
20 S Main St ▪ *Modern American* ▪ Owner Ted notes that the restaurant accommodates GF diners "all the time." Servers are trained on GF foods, and GF diners can order salads, butterfish, strip steak, and braised short ribs, among other things. Confirm timeliness of this information before dining in. Alert a server, who will notify the kitchen. ▪ *www.tedsonmain.net*

Tortilla Press Cantina　✪ $$D
Pennsauken ▪ (856) 356-2050
7716 Maple Ave ▪ *Mexican* ▪ GF menu includes empanadas and a variety of seafood, beef, pork, and chicken entrées. All GF fried items are prepared in a dedicated GF fryer. Desserts change daily, but ask a server for GF options. ▪ *www.tortillapress-cantina.com*

Tortilla Press, The　✪ $$LD
Collingswood ▪ (856) 869-3345
703 Haddon Ave ▪ *Mexican* ▪ GF menu includes fajitas, chicken & cheese entomatadas, spicy beef or cheese & onion

enchiladas, and various seafood dishes. Several GF appetizers are also available. ▪ *www.thetortillapress.com*

Toscana's Pizzeria & Restaurant　★ $$LD
Bridgewater ▪ (908) 595-2000
474 Nj-28 ▪ *Pizza* ▪ GF pizza is available. Manager Marco reports that GF pizza is not available on Friday nights.

Uno Chicago Grill　📖
Clifton ▪ (973) 574-1303
426 State Rt 3
Hamilton ▪ (609) 890-0864
225 Sloan Ave
Jersey City ▪ (201) 395-9500
286 Washington St
Maple Shade ▪ (856) 722-5577
2803 Route 73 S
Metuchen ▪ (732) 548-7979
61 US Highway 1
Wayne ▪ (973) 256-0700
57 Route 23
Woodbury ▪ (856) 853-7003
1162 Hurffville Rd

Vesuvio Pizza　★ $LD
Perrineville ▪ (732) 446-1908
221 Millstone Rd ▪ *Italian* ▪ GF pizza and pasta are available. ▪ *www.vesuviosmill-stone.com*

NEW MEXICO
ALBUQUERQUE

Annapurna Ayurvedic Cuisine and Chai House　✪★ ¢BLD
Albuquerque ▪ (505) 262-2424
2201 Silver Ave SE
Albuquerque ▪ (505) 254-2424
7520 4th Street ▪ *Indian* ▪ GF items marked on the menu include traditional Indian dishes such as paneer and dosa. They may also offer a veggie burger on a

GF bun or in a GF wrap, depending on the location. ▪ *www.chaishoppe.com*

Buca di Beppo 📖
Albuquerque ▪ *(505) 872-2822*
6520 Americas Pkwy NE

Great Harvest Bread Company ★ ⊂S
Albuquerque ▪ *(505) 293-8277*
11200 Montgomery Blvd NE ▪ *Bakery* ▪ A variety of GF baked goods are available. While some GF items are baked daily, others are made only on Sundays, Tuesdays, or Thursdays. The bakery follows a GF baking schedule, which is posted online. ▪ *www.ghabq.com*

Just a Bite ★ ⊂S
Albuquerque ▪ *(505) 822-5001*
7900 San Pedro Dr NE ▪ *Bakery* ▪ Non-dedicated bakery that makes GF items by special order only. Baker Ashlea notes that they get "a lot" of GF requests. GF cakes, cupcakes, pies, and cinnamon rolls are available with advanced notice of at least one day. ▪ *www.justabitebakery.com*

Lone Star Steakhouse & Saloon 📖
Albuquerque ▪ *(505) 899-7827*
10019 Coors Blvd NW

Melting Pot, The 📖
Albuquerque ▪ *(505) 843-6358*
2011 Mountain Rd NW

O'Niell's Irish Pub ☯ $$LD
Albuquerque ▪ *(505) 255-6782*
4310 Central Ave SE ▪ *Irish Pub* ▪ Limited GF menu includes salads, chicken kabobs, lemon basil salmon, rib-eye steak, and a smothered chicken breast. ▪ *www.oniells.com*

Outback Steakhouse 📖
Albuquerque ▪ *(505) 890-9713*
10022 Coors Blvd NW
Albuquerque ▪ *(505) 884-8760*
4921 Jefferson St NE

P.F. Chang's China Bistro 📖
Albuquerque ▪ *(505) 344-8282*
4440 The 25 Way NE

Paisano's ☯★ $LD
Albuquerque ▪ *(505) 298-7541*
1935 Eubank Blvd NE ▪ *Italian* ▪ Manager Iggy reports that the GF menu includes "just about everything" that is found on the regular menu. GF garlic bread, pasta, and pizza are available. For dessert, they offer GF molten chocolate cake, GF tiramisu, chocolate mousse, and more. ▪ *www.paisanosabq.com*

Pars Cuisine $$LD
Albuquerque ▪ *(505) 345-5156*
4320 The 25 Way NE ▪ *Persian* ▪ Manager Erica reports that the restaurant can "certainly" accommodate GF diners. She notes that kabobs, basmati rice, stews, cucumbers and hummus, and soups can be prepared GF. Confirm timeliness of this information before dining in. Alert a server, who will discuss GF options with the kitchen. ▪ *www.parscuisine.us*

Pei Wei Asian Diner 📖
Albuquerque ▪ *(505) 897-4811*
10420 Coors Bypass NW Ste 1B
Albuquerque ▪ *(505) 883-1570*
2201 Louisiana Blvd NE Ste G

Pizza 9 ★ $$LD
Albuquerque ▪ *(505) 323-6463*
1716 Eubank Blvd NE
Albuquerque ▪ *(505) 883-6463*
4000 Louisiana Blvd NE
Albuquerque ▪ *(505) 366-6463*
5305 Gibson Blvd SE ▪ *Pizza* ▪ GF pizza is available at all listed locations. ▪ *www.pizzanine.com*

Range Café $BLD
Albuquerque ▪ *(505) 888-1660*
2200 Menaul NE
Albuquerque ▪ *(505) 293-2633*
4401 Wyoming Blvd NE ▪ *American Regional* ▪ GF options are available, but all three locations report that the servers and staff members may not be very knowledgeable about GF. They suggest that GF diners explain their needs thoroughly. Avoid the red chili, as it is made with flour,

and always specify that the meal should be made with corn tortillas. Triumph notes that managers on Wyoming Street and in Bernalillo seemed much more educated about the GF diet. ▪ *www.rangecafe.com*

Texas Land & Cattle Steak House 📖
Albuquerque ▪ *(505) 343-9800*
4949 Pan American Fwy NE

Thai Crystal   ★ $**LD**
Albuquerque ▪ *(505) 244-3344*
109 Gold Ave SW ▪ *Thai* ▪ Restaurant notes that they accommodate GF diners "all the time." GF rice noodles are available. Curries, pad thai, and vegetable dishes are all either naturally GF or can be modified to be GF.

Tucanos Brazilian Grill   ★ $$**LD**
Albuquerque ▪ *(505) 246-9900*
110 Central Ave SW ▪ *Brazilian* ▪ General Manager Scott reports that they serve GF diners "every day." He adds that they accommodate GF customers very well, as the cuisine is mostly "help yourself." Alert a server upon arrival. Staff members can walk customers through the options and indicate GF items. For dessert, they offer crème brulee and New Mexican flan. GF cheese bread is available. ▪ *www.tucanos.com*

Zio's   ☼ $**LD**
Albuquerque ▪ *(505) 792-9222*
10041 Coors Blvd NW ▪ *Italian* ▪ GF menu includes salmon caesar salad, chicken piccata, Greek pasta, lemon chicken primavera, shrimp with marinara, ribeye tuscano, grilled sirloin, and more. ▪ *www.zios.com*

NEW MEXICO
ALL OTHER CITIES

Annapurna Ayurvedic Cuisine and
Chai House   ☼★ ¢**BLD**
Santa Fe ▪ *(505) 988-9688*
905 W Alameda St ▪ *Indian* ▪ GF items marked on the menu include traditional Indian dishes such as paneer and dosa. They may also offer a veggie burger on a GF bun or in a GF wrap, depending on the location. ▪ *www.chaishoppe.com*

Antonio's A Taste of Mexico $**LD**
Taos ▪ *(575) 751-4800*
122 Dona Luz ▪ *Mexican* ▪ Manager Octavio reports that "almost all of the menu" is GF. Menu items that are GF or can be modified to be GF include soups, salads, enchiladas, and shredded pork. Confirm timeliness of this information before dining in. ▪ *www.antoniosoftaos.com*

Blue Corn Café $**LD**
Santa Fe ▪ *(505) 984-1800*
133 W Water St
Santa Fe ▪ *(505) 438-1800*
4056 Cerrillos Rd ▪ *New Mexican* ▪ Manager John Paul at the Southside location and server Jared at the Downtown location report that GF diners are welcome. They accommodate GF diners "very frequently," and they have a variety of naturally GF options, including yellow corn tortillas. ▪ *www.bluecorncafe.com*

Body Café   ☼★ $**BLD**
Santa Fe ▪ *(505) 986-0362*
333 W Cordova Rd ▪ *Healthy American* ▪ GF items marked on the menu include vegetable masala, Asian curry, a collard green burrito, and more. GF apple crumb, ganache, brownies, and carrot cake, among other GF items, are available for dessert. Manager Emily reports that they serve "quite a few" GF customers, so they are

very educated on the GF diet. ▪ *www. bodyofsantafe.com*

Coyote Café $$$$ LD
Santa Fe ▪ **(505) 983-1615**
132 W Water St ▪ *Southwest* ▪ Restaurant notes that GF diners are accommodated "fairly often." They also note that the kitchen is "aware of Celiac" and can modify menu items to be GF. Reservations noting GF are recommended. ▪ *www.coyotecafe. com*

Graham's Grille   ★ $ BLD
Taos ▪ **(575) 751-1350**
106 Paseo Del Pueblo Norte ▪ *American* ▪ GF bread, hamburger buns, pizza, and beer are available. For dessert, they offer a flourless chocolate torte with crème anglais and gelato. Owner and Chef Lesley reports that diners can "custom-make" any of the menu items to be GF, and if they need help, she can offer suggestions. ▪ *www.grahamstaos. com*

Outback Steakhouse   📖
Farmington ▪ **(505) 324-2122**
4921 E Main St
Las Cruces ▪ **(575) 522-1370**
940 N Telshor Blvd
Santa Fe ▪ **(505) 424-6800**
2574 Camino Entrada

Pizza 9   ★ $$ LD
Rio Rancho ▪ **(505) 896-8999**
1751 Rio Rancho Dr SE ▪ *Pizza* ▪ GF pizza is available at all listed locations. ▪ *www. pizzanine.com*

Pranzo Italian Grill   ★ $$$ LD
Santa Fe ▪ **(505) 984-2645**
540 Montezuma Ave ▪ *Italian* ▪ GF brown rice pasta is available. General Manager Kate reports that several other dishes on the menu can be made GF using polenta or risotto. Alert a server, who will discuss all GF options. ▪ *www.pranzo-italiangrill.com*

Range Café $ BLD
Bernalillo ▪ **(505) 867-1700**
925 S Camino Del Pueblo ▪ *American*

Regional ▪ GF options are available, but all three locations report that the servers and staff members may not be very knowledgeable about GF. They suggest that GF diners explain their needs thoroughly. Avoid the red chili, as it is made with flour, and always specify that the meal should be made with corn tortillas. Triumph notes that managers on Wyoming Street and in Bernalillo seemed much more educated about the GF diet. ▪ *www.rangecafe.com*

Uno Chicago Grill   📖
Las Cruces ▪ **(575) 522-8866**
2102 Telshor Ct

NEW YORK

MANHATTAN

Angelica Kitchen   ¢ LD
New York ▪ **(212) 228-2909**
300 E 12th St ▪ *Vegan* ▪ Host Scott reports that they have many naturally GF items on the menu, and each day they try to have "at least one special" that is GF. A GF recipe guide is available upon request. Ask a server for help. ▪ *www.angelicakitchen.com*

Angus McIndoe Restaurant   ★ $$$ LD
New York ▪ **(212) 221-9222**
258 W 44th St ▪ *Modern American* ▪ Manager Ryan reports that they serve a "good amount" of GF diners. He notes that most of the menu is GF or can be made GF. GF pasta is available. ▪ *www.angusmcindoe.com*

Asia de Cuba   ✪ $$$$ LD
New York ▪ **(212) 726-7755**
237 Madison Ave ▪ *Asian & Latin Fusion* ▪ GF menu features roasted lime and garlic duck, grilled chipotle glazed strip steak, and seafood pad Thai "Havana style." ▪ *www.chinagrillmgt.com*

B. Smith's $$$**LD**
New York ▪ *(212) 315-1100*
320 W 46th St ▪ *Modern American* ▪
General Manager John reports that they
can make a roasted chicken breast, grilled
salmon, or "something sautéed" for GF
diners. Confirm timeliness of this information before dining in. John highly recommends making reservations noting GF and
alerting the server upon arrival. He adds
that GF diners are "fairly common" in the
restaurant. ▪ *www.bsmith.com*

BabyCakes NYC   ★ ¢**S**
New York ▪ *(212) 677-5047*
248 Broome St ▪ *Bakery* ▪ Non-dedicated
GF bakery offering only very few non-GF
products. GF items include cupcakes, muffins, crumb cakes, brownies, scones, pies,
and more. Bakery reports that GF products
are "always" in stock. ▪ *www.babycakesnyc.
com*

Bar Breton   ✪ $$$**LD**
New York ▪ *(212) 213-4999*
254 5th Ave ▪ *French* ▪ GF items marked
on the menu include duck leg confit, grilled
salmon, mahi-mahi, pork chops, and more.
▪ *www.chefpiano.com/bar-breton*

Big Booty   ★ ¢**S**
New York ▪ *(212) 414-3056*
261 W 23rd St ▪ *Bakery* ▪ Two types of GF
cheese bread and two types of GF pancakes
are available. Owner Jose reports that he
uses cornmeal, corn flour, and yucca flour
in his GF items. He notes that though GF
cake is not yet available, he hopes it will be
soon. ▪ *www.bigbootybreadco.com*

Bistango   ★ $$**LD**
New York ▪ *(212) 725-8484*
415 3rd Ave ▪ *Italian* ▪ GF pasta and bread
are available. Restaurant reports that nearly
all menu items can be modified to be GF,
including sautéed veal with marsala wine
sauce and braised lamb shank with broccoli
rabe. ▪ *www.bistangonyc.com*

Bloom's Deli   ✪★ $**BLD**
New York ▪ *(212) 922-3663*

350 Lexington Ave ▪ *Deli* ▪ Sizeable GF
menu includes a variety of omelets, pancakes, and french toast for breakfast. GF
sandwiches and salads are available, as are
several entrées such as the chopped steak
and the red snapper. GF desserts include
NY egg creams and creamy rice pudding.
GF bread and hamburger buns are available. ▪ *www.bloomsnewyorkdeli.com*

Blue Smoke   ✪ $$$**LD**
New York ▪ *(212) 447-7733*
116 E 27th St ▪ *Barbeque* ▪ GF menu includes chipotle chicken wings, deviled eggs,
Texas salt & pepper beef ribs, applewood-
smoked chicken, scallops, and filet mignon.
Restaurant reports that GF diners are
accommodated "with no problem." ▪ *www.
bluesmoke.com*

Bonobo's Restaurant   100% ¢**LD**
New York ▪ *(212) 505-1200*
18 E 23rd St ▪ *Vegetarian* ▪ Restaurant
serving only fruits, vegetables, nuts, and
seeds in their natural states. No processed
foods and no gluten are on the premises.
Check timeliness of this information before
dining in. Soups, salads, and nut pates are
menu features. Dessert items include fruit
pies, puddings, and frozen fudge. ▪ *www.
bonobosrestaurant.com*

Bubba Gump Shrimp Co.   📖
New York ▪ *(212) 391-7100*
1501 Broadway

Buddakan $$$**D**
New York ▪ *(212) 989-6699*
75 9th Ave ▪ *Asian Fusion* ▪ Manager Jen-
nessee reports that GF diners are welcome. She notes that servers are trained to
indicate "many GF meal options." Reservations noting GF are recommended. ▪ *www.
buddakannyc.com*

Café 82   ✪★ $**BLD**
New York ▪ *(212) 875-8373*
2282 Broadway ▪ *Café* ▪ GF menu includes sandwiches with GF bread, salads,
salmon, steaks, and burgers with GF buns.
Restaurant notes that it serves GF diners

"all the time." GF bread and hamburger buns are available.

Café Viva Gourmet Pizza　★ $LD
New York ▪ (212) 663-8482
2578 Broadway ▪ Pizza ▪ GF pasta is available.

Cafesol at the 92nd Street Y　★ $BLD
New York ▪ (212) 415-5796
1395 Lexington Ave ▪ Pizza ▪ GF pizza is available. ▪ www.cafesolnyc.com

Candle 79　◎ $$LD
New York ▪ (212) 537-7179
154 E 79th St ▪ Vegetarian ▪ Extensive new GF menu covers everything from starters to desserts. Examples include Moroccan spiced chickpea cake, vegetarian sushi, and salads. ▪ www.candlecafe.com

Candle Café　◎ $LD
New York ▪ (212) 472-0970
1307 3rd Ave ▪ Vegetarian ▪ Extensive GF menu includes ginger miso stir fry, sweet potato and black bean casserole, and Aztec salad. ▪ www.candlecafe.com

Capital Grille, The　📖
New York ▪ (212) 246-0154
120 W 51st St
New York ▪ (212) 953-2000
155 E 42nd St

Carmine's Restaurant　★ $$$LD
New York ▪ (212) 221-3800
200 W 44th St
New York ▪ (212) 362-2200
2450 Broadway ▪ Italian ▪ GF pasta is available. ▪ www.carminesnyc.com

Centrico　$$$D
New York ▪ (212) 431-0700
211 W Broadway ▪ Mexican ▪ Chef Angel reports that nearly the entire menu is GF. He cautions that two dishes are made with flour tortillas, so GF diners should avoid those particular menu items. Alert a server, who will notify the chef. The chef will ensure that a GF meal is prepared. ▪ www.myriadrestaurantgroup.com

Chop't　¢LD
New York ▪ (212) 974-8140
145 W 51st St
New York ▪ (212) 421-2300
165 E 52nd St
New York ▪ (646) 336-5523
24 E 17th St
New York ▪ (212) 750-2467
60 E 56th St ▪ Deli ▪ Restaurants report that they serve GF diners "a fair amount." All restaurants have the same allergy protocol, which includes changing gloves, cleaning all utensils, and cleaning the cooking station. They recommend speaking to a manager upon arrival. Restaurants caution that all salad dressings are made in the same facility, and managers at all locations recommend ordering olive oil and lemon or vinegar on salads. Confirm timeliness of this information before dining in. ▪ www.choptsalad.com

Corton　★ $$$$D
New York ▪ (212) 219-2777
239 W Broadway ▪ American ▪ Maitre d' Susan reports that serving GF diners is "not a problem." She recommends reservations noting GF, so that the staff knows to bring GF canapes instead of wheat flour canapes. She notes that all servers are educated on which menu items can be modified to be GF. GF canapes are available. ▪ www.cortonnyc.com

Del Frisco's Double Eagle Steak House　📖
New York ▪ (212) 575-5129
1221 Avenue Of The Americas

Five Napkin Burger　★ $$LD
New York ▪ (212) 333-4488
2315 Broadway
New York ▪ (212) 757-2277
630 9th Ave ▪ American ▪ GF buns are available for burgers. ▪ www.fivenapkinburger.com

Friedman's Delicatessen　★ $$LD
New York ▪ (212) 929-7100
75 9th Ave ▪ Deli ▪ GF bread and buns

are available for sandwiches and burgers. Restaurant reports that most menu items can be modified to be GF. ▪ *www.friedma-nsdeli.com*

Good Enough to Eat $$BLD
New York ▪ *(212) 496-0163*
483 Amsterdam Ave ▪ *American Regional* ▪ Manager Cary Ann reports that they serve GF diners often. All servers are educated on the GF diet, but she notes that GF customers are welcome to ask for a manager if it makes them more comfortable. She notes that most menu items can be modified to be GF. ▪ *www.goodenough-toeat.com*

Gramercy Tavern $$$D
New York ▪ *(212) 477-0777*
42 E 20th St ▪ *American* ▪ Purchaser Sarah reports that they accommodate GF diners "on a daily basis." Nearly everything on the menu can be modified to be GF, since everything is stored separately and then cooked to order. Sarah recommends alerting the server upon arrival. ▪ *www.gramercytavern.com*

GustOrganics Restaurant & Bar
                               ✪★ $$BLD
New York ▪ *(212) 242-5800*
519 Avenue Of The Americas ▪ *Organic* ▪ GF items marked on the menu include a variety of stews, several different risotto dishes, and more. Select sandwiches can be modified to be GF by substituting a tortilla for bread. GF pizza, pasta, and cookies are available. ▪ *www.gustorganics.com*

Hampton Chutney Company $BLD
New York ▪ *(212) 362-5050*
464 Amsterdam Ave
New York ▪ *(212) 226-9996*
68 Prince St ▪ *Indian* ▪ Manager Brianna of Prince Street and Hostess Kelly of Amsterdam Ave. report that all of the dosas - savory South Indian pancakes made from rice and black lentils - are GF. Fillings can be chosen a la carte or from the many combinations suggested on the menu. Brianna

adds that GF diners can "feel free to play around," since nearly the whole menu is GF. ▪ *www.hamptonchutney.com*

Integral Yoga Natural Foods   ★ $S
New York ▪ *(212) 243-2642*
229 W 13Th St ▪ *Deli & Bakery* ▪ Amy's enchiladas and Amy's pizzas are just two examples of GF menu items. GF bread, pasta, pizza, and soy sauce are available. GF baked goods such as cookies, pies, cakes, muffins, and brownies are also available. ▪ *www.integralyoganaturalfoods.com*

Josie's Restaurant   ★ $$LD
New York ▪ *(212) 490-1558*
565 3rd Ave ▪ *Asian Fusion* ▪ GF tamari sauce available upon request. Restaurant reports that the menu is "very accommodating" of GF diners. ▪ *www.josiesnyc.com*

L'Asso   ★ $LD
New York ▪ *(212) 219-2353*
192 Mott St ▪ *Italian* ▪ GF pizza, pasta, and beer are available. Owner Greg reports that though the GF desserts change weekly, there is always one available. ▪ *www.lassonyc.com*

Lili's 57   ✪★ $LD
New York ▪ *(212) 586-5333*
200 W 57th St ▪ *Asian Fusion* ▪ Extensive GF menu includes chicken satay, tom yum seafood, Saigon rolls, General Tso's chicken, spicy sweet chili shrimp, and cranberry teriyaki grilled chicken. GF soy sauce is available. ▪ *www.lilis57.com*

Lilli and Loo   ✪ $LD
New York ▪ *(212) 421-7800*
792 Lexington Ave ▪ *Asian* ▪ GF menu includes rock shrimp tempura, pork dumplings, green papaya salad, Chilean bass, Manchurian beef, and more. GF soy sauce is available. ▪ *www.lilliandloo.com*

Liquiteria   ★ ¢BLD
New York ▪ *(212) 358-0300*
170 2nd Ave ▪ *Vegetarian* ▪ GF brownies and bars are available. Restaurant reports that all soups, liquid drinks, and add-ons

are also GF. Confirm timeliness of this information before dining in. ■ *www. liquiteria.com*

Luigi's Pizzeria   ★ $$LD
New York ■ *(212) 410-1910*
1701 1st Ave ■ *Pizza* ■ GF pizza is available.

Lumi   ✪★ $$$LD
New York ■ *(212) 570-2335*
963 Lexington Ave ■ *Italian* ■ Extensive GF menu includes grilled salmon, rice-spaghetti marinara, and filet mignon. Manager Gent reports that the restaurant is "very accustomed" to GF diners. GF pasta is available. ■ *www.lumirestaurant.com*

Lupa Osteria Romana   ★ $$$LD
New York ■ *(212) 982-5089*
170 Thompson St ■ *Italian* ■ GF pasta is available. ■ *www.luparestaurant.com*

Macaron Café   ✧S
New York ■ *(212) 564-3525*
161 W 36th St ■ *Bakery* ■ Bakery notes that all macaroons are made with ground almond flour and are therefore GF. Bakery also reports that macaroons are not prepared near any other items that contain gluten. ■ *www.macaroncafe.com*

Maya $$$D
New York ■ *(212) 585-1818*
1191 1st Ave ■ *Mexican* ■ Manager Ciro reports that though they do not serve GF diners frequently, they can accommodate GF requests. He notes that the tuna salad and the mahi mahi are both naturally GF. Confirm timeliness of this information before dining in. Alert a server, who will inform the chef. ■ *www.modernmexican. com*

Mike's Pizzeria & Italian Kitchen
                    ★ $$$LD
New York ■ *(212) 362-0700*
654 Amsterdam Ave ■ *Italian* ■ GF pizza is available. GF penne with pesto or tomato sauce is also available, but it takes 30 minutes to prepare. ■ *www.mikesitaliankitchen. com*

Milk N' Honey NYC   ★ $BLD
New York ■ *(212) 764-4400*
22 W 45th St ■ *Deli* ■ GF pizza is available. GF brownies are available for dessert. ■ *www.milknhoneykosher.com*

Mozzarelli's   ★ $$LD
New York ■ *(212) 475-6777*
38 E 23rd St ■ *Italian* ■ GF pizza, pasta, cookies, and cakes are available. Restaurant reports that there are forty different GF cookie flavors. ■ *www.mozzarellis.com*

Nice Matin   ✪ $$$BLD
New York ■ *(212) 873-6423*
201 W 79th St ■ *French* ■ GF menu is available for lunch and dinner. Manager Ashley reports that reservations noting GF are recommended. ■ *www.nicematinnyc.com*

Nick & Stef's Steakhouse $$$$LD
New York ■ *(212) 563-4444*
9 Penn Plaza ■ *Steakhouse* ■ Chef Steven reports that the restaurant serves GF diners "very often." He recommends asking for him upon arrival, and he will discuss GF options. Steaks, fish, vegetables, and other sides are or can be modified to be GF. Confirm timeliness of this information before dining in. ■ *www.patinagroup.com*

Nizza Restaurant   ✪★ $LD
New York ■ *(212) 956-1800*
630 9th Ave ■ *Italian* ■ GF menu includes pasta pesto, ziti pomodoro, grilled marinated tuna, branzino fillet, and more. GF bread, pasta, pizza, and beer are available. A "crispy chickpea pancake" serves as the GF pizza crust. ■ *www.nizzanyc.com*

Nobu $$$$LD
New York ■ *(212) 219-0500*
105 Hudson St ■ *Asian & Latin Fusion* ■ Manager Hiro reports that the restaurant serves GF diners "a lot." He recommends noting GF in reservations, so that the server will discuss GF options with the diner and the chef. ■ *www.myriadrestaurantgroup.com*

Nussbaum & Wu ★ ¢S
New York ▪ *(212) 280-5344*
2897 Broadway ▪ *Café* ▪ GF pizza, cookies, and cakes are available. ▪ *www.nussbaumwu.com*

O'Lunney's Times Square Pub $$LD
New York ▪ *(212) 840-6688*
145 W 45th St ▪ *Pub Food* ▪ Manager Maureen reports that the restaurant is very GF aware. She notes that the kitchen is "very accommodating" and can prepare GF grilled chicken with garlic and olive oil or white wine, salmon, and several different salads. She cautions that the kitchen is not dedicated GF and advises alerting a server upon arrival. ▪ *www.olunneys.com*

Opus ★ $$$LD
New York ▪ *(212) 772-2220*
1574 2nd Ave ▪ *Italian* ▪ GF pizza, pasta, and other main dishes are available. ▪ *www.opusnewyork.com*

OTTO Enoteca Pizzeria ★ $LD
New York ▪ *(212) 995-9559*
One 5th Ave ▪ *Italian* ▪ GF pasta is available. ▪ *www.ottopizzeria.com*

Outback Steakhouse 📖
New York ▪ *(212) 989-3122*
60 W 23rd St
New York ▪ *(212) 935-6400*
919 3rd Ave

Pala ★ $$LD
New York ▪ *(212) 614-7252*
198 Allen St ▪ *Pizza* ▪ GF pizza, pasta, and beer are available. ▪ *www.pala-ny.com*

Per Se ★ $$$$D
New York ▪ *(212) 823-9335*
10 Columbus Cir ▪ *American* ▪ GF bread is available. The menu changes daily, but dishes can always be prepared GF. Reservations are required and accepted 2 months in advance. The reservationist will ask if there are any allergies or food intolerances. ▪ *www.perseny.com*

Peter's Gourmet Diner ✪★ $$BLD
New York ▪ *(212) 734-9600*
1606 1st Ave ▪ *American* ▪ Extensive GF menu includes egg sandwiches and scrambles, penne rigate with vodka sauce, and chicken marsala. GF pancakes, bread and pasta are available. ▪ *www.petersrestaurant.com*

Petit Café ★ ¢BLD
New York ▪ *(212) 229-0804*
70 Greenwich Ave ▪ *Bakery & Café* ▪ All products baked on the premises are GF, and they are kept separate from non-GF items. GF brownies, english muffins, bagels, pancakes, and french toast are available. Any sandwich on the menu can be prepared with GF bread.

Pizza Bolla ✪★ $$LD
New York ▪ *(212) 786-3300*
102 N End Ave ▪ *Pizza* ▪ GF menu includes garlic bread, chicken parmasean, spaghetti bolognese, and penne melanzane. Manager Alfonso notes that GF diners are served on a regular basis. GF bread, pizza and pasta are available. ▪ *www.pizzabolla.com*

Plum Pomidor ★ $LD
New York ▪ *(212) 781-2222*
4009 Broadway ▪ *Italian-American* ▪ GF rice pasta is available. ▪ *www.plumpomidor.com*

Pure Food and Wine $$$D
New York ▪ *(212) 477-1010*
54 Irving Pl ▪ *Raw* ▪ Chef Neil reports that a "wide array" of menu items are GF, including the signature lasagna, which is made with thin slices of zucchini instad of pasta, and the ravioli, which is made with beets. Confirm timeliness of this information before dining in. He adds that all servers are "well-educated" on the GF diet. Alert a server, who will provide menu guidance. ▪ *www.purefoodandwine.com*

Raw Soul Restaurant and Juice Bar $LD
New York ▪ *(212) 491-5859*
348 W 145th St ▪ *Raw & Vegan* ▪ Owner Lillian reports that nearly all menu items are naturally GF. She notes that they serve GF customers every day, and all staff

members are trained on the GF diet. The pizza, lasagna, and enchiladas can all be GF. Confirm timeliness of this information before dining in. ▪ *www.rawsoul.com*

Rice to Riches　　　　　　　¢S
New York ▪ *(212) 274-0008*
37 Spring St ▪ *Rice Pudding* ▪ Manager Ana notes that there are usually at least fifteen flavors of rice pudding available, and they change daily. Most flavors are GF, but ask at the counter to be sure. Ana reports that the staff is trained on the GF diet. ▪ *www.ricetoriches.com*

Rice　　　　　　　　　　✪ $LD
New York ▪ *(212) 226-5775*
292 Elizabeth St ▪ *Asian* ▪ GF menu consists of modified regular menu items. GF dishes include lemongrass salad, Portuguese soup, kebabs, thai coconut curry, Bhutanese red rice, and more. ▪ *www.riceny.com*

Risotteria　　　　　　　✪★ $LD
New York ▪ *(212) 924-6664*
270 Bleecker St ▪ *Italian* ▪ Extensive GF menu includes a wide variety of GF pizza, risotto and paninis. GF breadsticks, beer and homemade desserts are available. GF pasta specials are available on Tuesdays. A wide variety of GF desserts, including cupcakes, cookies, tiramisu, and pies are available. ▪ *www.risotteria.com*

Ruby Foo's　　　　　　　✪★ $$LD
New York ▪ *(212) 489-5600*
1626 Broadway ▪ *Asian Fusion* ▪ Limited GF menu includes lettuce wraps, pad thai, orange chicken, and chicken fried rice. For dessert, GF brownies and warm crumb cake are available. GF beer is also available. ▪ *www.brguestrestaurants.com*

Sambuca　　　　　　　　✪★ $D
New York ▪ *(212) 787-5656*
20 W 72nd St ▪ *Italian* ▪ GF menu includes pasta dishes with many different sauces. Examples are ricotta and spinach ravioli, pasta primavera broccoli, and pasta with carbonara sauce. GF pizza and beer are also

available, as are GF cakes and brownies for dessert. ▪ *www.sambucanyc.com*

SLICE, The Perfect Food　★ $$LD
New York ▪ *(212) 249-4353*
1413 2nd Ave
New York ▪ *(212) 929-2920*
535 Hudson St ▪ *Pizza* ▪ GF pizza and beer are always available at both locations. Owner Miki advises that customers looking for fast service should order GF pizza in advance, as it usually takes 20-30 minutes to prepare. She also notes that they sometimes offer a GF peanut butter banana cookie. ▪ *www.sliceperfect.com*

S'MAC　　　　　　　　　★ ¢LD
New York ▪ *(212) 358-7912*
345 E 12Th St ▪ *Macaroni & Cheese* ▪ Any macaroni and cheese dish can be made GF. Specify an order for "gluten-free pasta." Breadcrumbs are made from GF cornflakes rather than bread. GF beer is also available. ▪ *www.smacnyc.com*

Smith & Wollensky　　　　$$$$LD
New York ▪ *(212) 753-1530*
49th St & 3rd Ave ▪ *Steakhouse* ▪ Manager Ricardo reports that they do not serve "a lot" of GF diners. He does note, however, that Sean, one of the other managers, if GF and therefore very familiar with the GF diet. He recommends noting GF in reservations and asking for Sean upon arrival. ▪ *www.smithandwollensky.com*

Tramonti　　　　　　　　★ $$LD
New York ▪ *(212) 245-2720*
364 W 46th St ▪ *Italian* ▪ GF pasta is available. Manager Paolo reports that GF pasta can be made with any sauce on the menu.

Trattoria Dellarte　　　　$$$$LD
New York ▪ *(212) 245-9800*
900 7th Ave ▪ *Italian* ▪ Restaurant reports that they can modify many regular menu items to be GF. Examples of dishes that can be modified include antipasto, steaks, and veal dishes. Confirm timeliness of this information before dining in. Reservations noting GF are highly recommended. Ask

for a manager upon arrival. ▪ *www.trattoriadellarte.com*

Tribeca Grill $$$$ LD
New York ▪ *(212) 941-3900*
375 Greenwich St ▪ *Modern American*
▪ Manager Weng reports that the chef is "very accommodating." He notes that many of the protein dishes, such as the chicken, salmon, duck, and venison, are naturally GF. Confirm timeliness of this information before dining in. Alert a server, who will guide GF guests through the menu and notify the chef.

Tu-Lu's Gluten-Free Bakery   100% ¢S
New York ▪ *(212) 777-2227*
338 E 11Th St ▪ *Bakery* ▪ Dedicated GF bakery offering brownies, cookies, coffee cake, and mini cupcakes. Full-sized GF cakes are also available with advanced notice of 48 hours. ▪ *www.tu-lusbakery.com*

Uno Chicago Grill   📖
New York ▪ *(212) 472-5656*
220 E 86th St
New York ▪ *(212) 595-4700*
432 Columbus Ave
New York ▪ *(212) 791-7999*
89 South St

Whole Earth Bakery and Kitchen
✪★   ¢BLD
New York ▪ *(212) 677-7597*
130 Saint Marks Pl ▪ *Bakery & Café* ▪ GF bread, cake, muffins, brownies, pies, and cupcakes are available. Examples of flavors include the signature tofu cupcake and apple pie. GF menu includes all soups, summer rolls, and hummus. ▪ *www.wholeearthbakery.com*

Bazil Restaurant   ✪★ $LD
Rochester ▪ *(585) 697-2006*
1384 Empire Blvd
Rochester ▪ *(585) 427-7420*
749 E Henrietta Rd ▪ *Italian* ▪ GF menu includes chicken parmigiano, grilled trout, and spaghetti pomodoro, among others. GF pasta is available. Lunch is served on weekends only. ▪ *www.bazilrestaurant.com*

Bugaboo Creek Steak House   📖
Rochester ▪ *(585) 292-5800*
935 Jefferson Rd

Carrabba's Italian Grill   📖
Rochester ▪ *(585) 292-6120*
3340 W Henrietta Rd

Donna Marie's Gluten Free Bakery
100% ¢S
Rochester ▪ *(585) 254-0706*
164 Newbury St ▪ *Bakery* ▪ Dedicated GF bakery offering a wide variety of breads, cookies, muffins, cakes, and cupcakes. GF sandwich bread, sandwich rolls, pizza shells, croutons, and bread crumbs are also available. All baked goods are sold wholesale, but they are also offered during limited retail hours at the storefront location. ▪ *www.donnamariesbakery.com*

Eco Bella Bakery   100% $$$$S
Rochester ▪ *(585) 503-2488*
732 South Ave ▪ *Bakery* ▪ Dedicated GF bakery offering a variety of cookies, muffins, brownies, cupcakes, and cakes. Flavors rotate periodically, but they will fill orders for specific flavors if placed in advance. ▪ *www.ecobellabakery.com*

Gusto   ★ ¢BLD
Rochester ▪ *(585) 232-7810*
277 Alexander St ▪ *Italian* ▪ GF pizza is available all day, and GF pasta is available for dinner only. ▪ *www.eatwithgusto.com*

Keenan's Restaurant　　　　○ $$LD
Rochester ▪ *(585) 266-2691*
1010 E Ridge Rd ▪ *American* ▪ GF menu includes grilled chicken sandwich, Cobb salad, and scallops. GF bread is available. Alert a hostess and a server, who will ensure that orders go through to the kitchen with a GF note. ▪ *www.keenansrestaurant. com*

King and I　　　　　　　★ $LD
Rochester ▪ *(585) 427-8090*
1455 E Henrietta Rd ▪ *Thai* ▪ Manager Anh reports that GF diners are welcome and that the staff is very well-educated on GF dining. Ask to speak with Anh or Anthony upon arrival. GF soy sauce is available, so nearly any dish can be prepared GF. ▪ *www. thekingandithaicuisine.com*

Mario's Authentic Italian Restaurant & Catering　　　　　　　○★ $$D
Rochester ▪ *(585) 271-1111*
2740 Monroe Ave ▪ *Italian & Steakhouse* ▪ GF menu includes penne carbonaro, chicken alfredo, and salmon, as well as a variety of steaks. GF pasta is available. Owner Anthony notes that all staff members are trained to handle GF requests. ▪ *www.mariosit.com*

Natural Oasis Café　　　　○ $LD
Rochester ▪ *(585) 325-1831*
288 Monroe Ave ▪ *Vegetarian* ▪ Restaurant reports that the regular menu is almost entirely GF. Non-GF dishes are marked as such. GF items include roasted fennel, lentils, sautéed vegetables, shiitake mushrooms, and more. For dessert, rotating options such as cinnamon-ginger rice pudding are available. ▪ *www.naturaloasisny. com*

Nick's Deli and Catering　　★ $LD
Rochester ▪ *(585) 247-6270*
1098 Chili Coldwater Rd ▪ *Italian* ▪ GF pizza, sliced bread, dinner rolls, sandwich rolls, pasta, and desserts are available. Manager Nick reports that GF lasagna is

also available, as are other frozen entrées. ▪ *www.nicksdeliandpizza.com*

Outback Steakhouse　　　　　📖
Rochester ▪ *(585) 424-6880*
1180 Jefferson Rd
Rochester ▪ *(585) 453-0640*
1954 W Ridge Rd

Portofino Bistro　　　　　★ $LD
Rochester ▪ *(585) 427-0410*
2171 W Henrietta Rd ▪ *Italian* ▪ Owner Dominick reports that one of the restaurant managers is GF, so they "know how to do this." He recommends calling ahead so they can order the "freshest ingredients." GF bread, pasta, pizza, hamburger buns, and cookies are available with advanced notice. ▪ *www.portofinorochester.com*

Ristorante Lucano　　　　★ $$$D
Rochester ▪ *(585) 244-3460*
1815 East Ave ▪ *Italian* ▪ GF pasta available with advanced notice of at least one day.

Salena's Mexican Restaurant　　$$LD
Rochester ▪ *(585) 256-5980*
302 N Goodman St ▪ *Mexican* ▪ Manager Jason reports that the restaurant has "a large group of GF diners" who come in on a regular basis. He notes that all staff members are very GF aware. ▪ *www.salenas.com*

Simply Crepes Café　　　★ ¢BLD
Rochester ▪ *(585) 428-8300*
114 South Ave ▪ *Crêpes* ▪ GF buckwheat crepes are available. The café is located in the Bausch & Lomb Public Library Building. ▪ *www.simplycrepes.com*

NEW YORK

ALL OTHER CITIES

Adam's Fairacre Farms   ★ $$$$
Lake Katrine ▪ *(845) 336-6300*
1560 Ulster Ave
Newburgh ▪ *(845) 569-0303*
1240 Route 300
Poughkeepsie ▪ *(845) 454-4330*
765 Dutchess Tpke ▪ *Bakery* ▪ GF almond
horns, coconut macaroons, and bread are
available at the Kingston location, and
plain cheesecake is available at the Kingston location if ordered in advance. The
Poughkeepsie location carries GF grocery
items and a few GF "take-&-bake" pasta
dinners, but they do not have a bakery. ▪
www.adamsfarms.com

Adam's Rib $LD
Snyder ▪ *(716) 839-3846*
4517 Main St ▪ *American* ▪ Manager Millie
reports that although the GF menu has
been discontinued, the chef is still happy to
serve GF diners. She recommends alerting
a server upon arrival.

Airmont Eats   ★ $LD
Airmont ▪ *(845) 368-1973*
211 Rt 59 ▪ *Pizza* ▪ GF pizza is available in
the 9-inch size, with any toppings. ▪ *www.
airmonteats.wordpress.com*

Aldente Pizzeria   ★ $LD
Rye ▪ *(914) 921-5300*
7 Elm Pl ▪ *Pizza* ▪ GF cheese pizza is available.

Amalfi Restaurant & Pizzeria   ★ $$LD
Glen Cove ▪ *(516) 801-6544*
197 Forest Ave
Port Washington ▪ *(516) 883-4191*
49 Old Shore Rd ▪ *Italian* ▪ GF pizza,
pasta, cookies, and cakes are available. The
Port Washington location also has chicken
fingers and muffins. ▪ *www.amalfipw.com*

American Bounty Restaurant   ★ $$$LD
Hyde Park ▪ *(845) 471-6608*

1946 Campus Dr (Route 9) ▪ *Regional
American* ▪ Located on the campus of the
Culinary Institute of America and run by
its chefs and students. Reservationist Cindy
reports that they have a "special gluten-free
chef" who accommodates GF diners often.
She notes that GF diners should make
reservations over the phone (not online) at
least 4-5 days in advance so that GF bread
will be available. ▪ *www.ciachef.edu/restau-
rants/bounty*

Apple Pie Bakery Café   ★ ¢BL
Hyde Park ▪ *(845) 905-4500*
1946 Campus Dr ▪ *Bakery & Café* ▪ Man-
ger-in-Training Jake reports that the only
available GF pastry is the chocolate excess
cake, which can be ordered in the personal
or large size. He notes that this item is not
prepared in a GF environment. He also
notes that with advanced notice of two
weeks, they can prepare GF treats to order.
Located on the campus of the Culinary Institute of America, and run by the school's
chefs and students. ▪ *www.ciachef.edu*

Aroma Osteria $$$LD
Wappingers Falls ▪ *(845) 298-6790*
114 Old Post Rd ▪ *Italian* ▪ Owner Lucia
reports that they are happy to serve GF
diners. She says that though they do not
keep GF pasta in stock, customers are
welcome to bring their own. The salmon
and pork chop entrées are naturally GF,
and they offer flourless chocolate cake for
dessert. Confirm timeliness of this information before dining in. ▪ *www.aromaoste-
riarestaurant.com*

Aroma Thyme Bistro   ★ $LD
Ellenville ▪ *(845) 647-3000*
165 Canal St ▪ *Modern American* ▪ Co-
owner Jamie reports that nearly the entire
menu is GF. GF entrees include GF pizza
made with rice crust and wild Alaskan
salmon with GF teriyaki sauce. GF desserts
like dark chocolate fudge torte and cheesecake are available. Jamie notes that all servers are "very aware" of GF requirements.

GF pizza and teriyaki sauce are available. ▪ *www.aromathymebistro.com*

Artist's Palate, The   ★ $$**LD**
Poughkeepsie ▪ **(845) 483-8074**
307 Main St ▪ *Fusion* ▪ GF beer, bread, pasta, and soy sauce are available. For dessert, there is GF chocolate cake. Owner Charles reports that though the menu changes every two weeks, there are always naturally GF options and items that can be modified to be GF. ▪ *www.theartistspalate.biz*

Azure Chocolat   100% ¢**S**
Centerport ▪ **(631) 425-1885**
90C Washington Dr ▪ *Chocolate* ▪ Entirely GF environment that produces fresh truffles, "chocolat comforts," and more. Check timeliness of this information before dining in. ▪ *www.azurechocolate.com*

Basillico   ★ $**LD**
Pomona ▪ **(845) 354-1717**
1633 Route 202 ▪ *Pizza* ▪ GF pizza and pasta are available. Hostess Melanie reports that they can make many other items GF as well. Located in the Ramapo Plaza.

Bellizzi   ✪★ $$**LD**
Larchmont ▪ **(914) 833-5800**
1272 Boston Post Rd
Mount Kisco ▪ **(914) 241-1200**
153 E Main St ▪ *Italian* ▪ Extensive GF menu includes a variety of pasta dishes like truffle pasta with wild mushrooms and sundried tomatoes, an array of pizzas, chicken milanese, and chicken and eggplant parmagiana. ▪ *www.bellizzi.us*

Bertucci's   📖
Hauppauge ▪ **(631) 952-2100**
358 Vanderbilt Motor Pkwy
Melville ▪ **(631) 427-9700**
881 Walt Whitman Rd
Westbury ▪ **(516) 683-8800**
795 Merrick Ave

Best Ever Low Carb Cakes, The
                100% $$$$**S**
Massapequa ▪ **(516) 541-3640**
5497 Merrick Rd ▪ *Bakery* ▪ Bakery offering GF cheesecake, mini cakes, mini loaves, mini muffins, cookies, large cakes, and donuts. Manager Linda reports that they bake using almond flour. She also notes that regular sized cakes and cookies must , be ordered two days in advance. Open Thursday through Sunday. ▪ *www.besteverlowcarb.com*

Biaggi's Ristorante Italiano   📖
Victor ▪ **(585) 223-2290**
818 Eastview Mall

Bistro Cassis $$$**LD**
Huntington ▪ **(631) 421-4122**
55B Wall St ▪ *French Bistro* ▪ Server Dana reports that they accommodate "some people" who are GF. She notes that with the exceptions of pasta and breaded items, almost anything on the menu can be prepared GF. Alert a server upon arrival. ▪ *www.bistrocassis.com*

Blue Dragon Café   ★ ¢**LD**
Clayville ▪ **(315) 839-5818**
2269 Oneida St ▪ *Deli* ▪ GF panini bread, wraps, and fresh-baked dessert items are available. Restaurant notes that if customers call ahead to request a specific baked good like apple pie or brownies, they can be easily accommodated.

Bocce Club Pizza   ★ ¢**LD**
Amherst ▪ **(716) 833-1344**
4174 Bailey Ave
E Amherst ▪ **(716) 689-2345**
1614 Hopkins Rd ▪ *Pizza* ▪ GF pizza is available in the 10-inch size. ▪ *www.bocceclub-pizza.com*

Bonefish Grill   📖
Amherst ▪ **(716) 833-6106**
1247 Niagara Falls Blvd
Fayetteville ▪ **(315) 637-0491**
600 Towne Dr
Poughkeepsie ▪ **(845) 432-7507**
2185 South Rd
Victor ▪ **(585) 223-7059**
1002 Eastview Mall

Boulder Creek Steakhouse   ✪ $$$LD
Brooklyn ▪ *(718) 277-0222*
355 Gateway Dr
Hicksville ▪ *(516) 942-7800*
200 N Broadway ▪ *Steakhouse* ▪ GF
menu includes steaks, seafood, mashed
potatoes, chicken, ribs with GF BBQ sauce,
salads with GF dressings, and more. Manager Mike is GF and created the GF menu
himself. At the time of publication, the
Brooklyn location was preparing to offer
the Hicksville location's GF menu. ▪ *www.*
bouldercreeksteakhouses.net

Branding Iron Steakhouse $$D
Ontario ▪ *(315) 524-3963*
6361 Knickerbocker Rd ▪ *Steakhouse*
▪ Owner Diane reports that they serve
GF diners "all the time." She notes that
any chicken dish or steak entrée can be
prepared GF. Alert a server, who will write
GF on the ticket to alert the kitchen. Diane
adds that GF diners will have "no problem
whatsoever" eating at the restaurant.

Broadway Pizzeria   ★ $$LD
Greenlawn ▪ *(631) 261-0828*
60 Broadway ▪ *Pizza* ▪ GF pizza and pasta
are available. Restaurant recommends calling 30 minutes ahead for pizza, but pasta
does not require advanced notice. ▪ *www.*
broadwaycatering.com

Brooks' House of Bar-B-Q   ✪ $LD
Oneonta ▪ *(607) 432-1782*
5560 State Highway 7 ▪ *Barbeque* ▪ Extensive GF menu includes chicken wings,
the St. Louis pork rib dinner, the regular
spare ribs, and more. For dessert, there is
GF tapioca pudding. Owner Ryan reports
that GF items are available "all of the time,"
and there is always an owner or a manager
available to answer questions about preparation. ▪ *www.brooksbbq.com*

Buca di Beppo   📖
Colonie ▪ *(518) 459-2822*
44 Wolf Rd

Bugaboo Creek Steak House   📖
Poughkeepsie ▪ *(845) 297-2200*
1955 South Rd

Buona Sera   ✪★ $LD
Smithtown ▪ *(631) 265-0625*
88 E Main St ▪ *Italian* ▪ GF menu includes
chicken marsala, pasta with clam sauce,
and shrimp fra diavolo. GF pasta, pizza,
and desserts are available. ▪ *www.servey-*
ourfamily.com/buonasera

Café Formaggio   ✪★ $LD
Carle Place ▪ *(516) 333-1718*
307 Old Country Rd ▪ *Italian* ▪ GF menu
includes limoncello chicken, ravioli, and
gnocchi dishes, among other options. GF
bread, pizza, and beer are also available.
For dessert, they offer GF brownies and GF
nutella pizza. ▪ *www.cafeformaggio.com*

Café London $$$LD
Corning ▪ *(607) 962-2345*
69 E Market St ▪ *Modern American* ▪
Manager Brian reports that GF diners
can be accommodated. There are entrée
options and a flourless chocolate cake for
dessert. ▪ *www.cafe-london.com*

Café Pizzazz   ★ $LD
Mohegan Lake ▪ *(914) 743-1055*
1859 E Main St ▪ *Italian* ▪ GF pizza is
available in the personal size. Restaurant
expects to offer GF pasta in the near future.

Café Spiga Pizza & Pasta   ★ $$LD
Mount Sinai ▪ *(631) 331-5554*
176 N Country Rd ▪ *Pizza* ▪ GF pizza and
pasta are available. GF pizza is available in
the 10-inch size only. GF beer is also available. ▪ *www.cafespigapizzapasta.com*

Caffe Baldo   ✪★ $$LD
Wantagh ▪ *(516) 785-4780*
2849 Jerusalem Ave ▪ *Italian* ▪ Extensive
GF menu includes mozzarella sticks, lasagna, gnocchi, chicken, and veal. GF corn
and rice pasta is available. Dessert options
include chocolate cake & pumpkin pie, but
these items change.

Calabria Pizza & Pasta   ★ $$LD
Orangeburg ▪ *(845) 365-2300*
500 Route 303 ▪ Pizza ▪ GF pizza and
pasta are available. Restaurant recommends ordering GF pizzas one half hour in
advance. ▪ *www.calabriapizza.com*

Carrabba's Italian Grill   📖
Amherst ▪ *(716) 833-5003*
1645 Niagara Falls Blvd
Central Islip ▪ *(631) 232-1070*
20 N Research Pl
Fayetteville ▪ *(315) 637-7400*
550 Towne Dr
Latham ▪ *(518) 785-8886*
675 Troy Schenectady Rd
Smithtown ▪ *(631) 265-1304*
730 Smithtown Byp
Staten Island ▪ *(718) 477-9000*
280 Marsh Ave

Casablanca Coffee Co.   ★ ¢S
Poughkeepsie ▪ *(845) 454-4440*
11 Marist Dr ▪ Coffee & Café ▪ GF muffins
and wraps are available, and sometimes
dessert items like brownies and cake are
also available. ▪ *www.casablancacoffee-
house.com*

Charlie Brown's Steakhouse   📖
Commack ▪ *(631) 462-4206*
88 Veterans Memorial Hwy
Fishkill ▪ *(845) 896-2666*
18 Westage Dr Ste 22
Holtsville ▪ *(631) 289-3320*
45 Middle Ave
Middletown ▪ *(845) 342-0601*
505 Schutt Road Ext
Mohegan Lake ▪ *(914) 528-0074*
1745 E Main St
New Hyde Park ▪ *(516) 294-7320*
2349 Jericho Tpke
Staten Island ▪ *(718) 983-6846*
1001 Goethals Rd N
Yonkers ▪ *(914) 779-7227*
1820 Central Park Ave

Charlotte's Restaurant & Catering
                              ★ $$$D
Millbrook ▪ *(845) 677-5888*

4258 Route 44 ▪ Modern American ▪
Owner Alicia reports that though the menu
changes daily, the chefs will always accommodate GF diners with "tailor-made"
meals. She recommends reservations noting GF. Alert a server upon arrival. ▪ *www.
charlottesny.com*

Ciao Restaurant   ✪★ $$LD
Eastchester ▪ *(914) 779-4646*
5-7 John Albanese Pl ▪ Italian ▪ GF menu
includes pastas, risotto dishes, pizza, steak,
and pork chops. GF pasta, pizza, and beer
are available. ▪ *www.ciaoeastchester.com*

Circus Café   ✪★ $LD
Saratoga Springs ▪ *(518) 583-1106*
392 Broadway ▪ American ▪ Extensive GF
menu includes starters, sandwiches, salads,
entrées, and signature dishes. Desserts
on the GF menu include a chocolate lava
cake, cotton candy, and mango gelato. GF
bread, pasta, and beer are available. ▪ *www.
circuscafe.com*

Comfort   ★ $LD
Hastings On Hudson ▪ *(914) 478-0666*
583 Warburton Ave ▪ Global ▪ Chef Dan
reports that GF pasta is "almost always"
available. GF desserts like chocolate cake
and brownies are also available. ▪ *www.
comfortrestaurant.net*

Cool Fish Grille & Wine $$$$D
Syosset ▪ *(516) 921-3250*
6800 Jericho Tpke ▪ Seafood ▪ Manager
Edy reports that they are able to accommodate GF diners. Several fish dishes
and several entrées can be made GF, but
advanced notice is required, as fish are
normally seared using flour. Confirm
timeliness of this information before dining in. Reservations noting GF are strongly
recommended.

Crabtree's Kittle House   ★ $$$$LD
Chappaqua ▪ *(914) 666-8044*
11 Kittle Rd ▪ Modern American ▪ Partner
Glenn reports that over half the menu is
GF or can be made GF. He adds that all
sauces are made with GF thickeners, and

all staff members are trained on the GF diet. Examples of GF items include Chatham cod and a loin of free range Colorado lamb. Confirm timeliness of this information before dining in. GF beer is available. ▪ *www.kittlehouse.com*

Curly's Bar & Grill   ✪★ $$$LD
Lackawanna ▪ *(716) 824-9716*
647 Ridge Rd ▪ *American* ▪ GF menu includes mussels, salads, pizza, cioppino, steak, chicken, and more. GF muffins, pasta, and pizza are available. For dessert, "chocolate mousse in a bag," crème brûlée, Swiss roll, and GF chocolate chip cookies are available. Restaurant recommends ordering the chocolate chip cookies upon arrival, as they are baked fresh and take about half an hour to make. ▪ *www. curlysgrill.com*

Davinci's   ★ $$$LD
Island Park ▪ *(516) 889-3939*
118 Long Beach Rd ▪ *Italian* ▪ GF pizza is available.

D'Cocco's   ★ $BLD
Oceanside ▪ *(516) 766-3938*
3573 Long Beach Rd ▪ *Italian* ▪ GF pasta and pizza are available. ▪ *www.dcoccos.com*

Deanna's Pizzeria and Restaurant
                                                ★ $$LD
New Rochelle ▪ *(914) 636-5960*
1284 North Ave ▪ *Pizza* ▪ GF pizza and pasta are available. ▪ *www.deannaspizza. com*

El Loco Mexican Café   ✪ $LD
Albany ▪ *(518) 436-1855*
465 Madison Ave ▪ *Tex-Mex* ▪ GF menu includes corn tortilla chips with salsa, chili, chipotle quesadillas, chicken enchiladas, and spinach enchiladas, as well as pork tamales. ▪ *www.ellocomexicancafe.com*

Elegante Restaurant   ★ $LD
Lynbrook ▪ *(516) 596-1600*
88 Atlantic Ave. ▪ *Pizza* ▪ GF pizza and pasta are available every day. They can be

prepared with any sauce or toppings. ▪ *www.elegantepizzeria.com*

Enzo's Antichi Sapori Restaurant ★ $LD
Armonk ▪ *(914) 273-4186*
111 Bedford Rd ▪ *Italian* ▪ GF pizza, pasta, crackers, and cookies are available. ▪ *www. enzosofarmonk.com*

Epstein's Kosher Deli   ✪★ $BLD
Hartsdale ▪ *(914) 428-5320*
385 N Central Ave ▪ *Deli* ▪ Extensive GF menu includes appetizers, salads, sandwiches, entrées, and desserts. Examples are the chopped steak, the roast turkey sandwich, and the pepper steak over rice. GF bread is available. ▪ *www.epsteinsdeli.com*

Escoffier Restaurant   ★ $$$$LD
Hyde Park ▪ *(845) 471-6608*
1946 Campus Dr ▪ *French* ▪ GF bread is available with advanced notice of at least a few days. Located on the Culinary Institute of America's campus and run by its chefs and students. ▪ *www.ciachef.edu*

Fifth Season   ✪★ $$$D
Port Jefferson ▪ *(631) 477-8500*
34 E Broadway ▪ *Modern American* ▪ GF menu items include asparagus salad, shrimp fettuccine, pan-seared duck breast, arctic char, and rice pudding for dessert. GF brown rice pasta and beer are also available. ▪ *www.thefifth-season.com*

Fire + Ice $$LD
West Nyack ▪ *(845) 358-3473*
4532 Palisades Center Dr ▪ *Asian Stir-Fry* ▪ Hostess Saith reports that they accommodate "a lot" of GF diners. She notes that several sauces are GF, and all of the ingredients are posted for customers to read. She adds that upon request, they are able to prepare GF meals on separate cooking surfaces in the back. ▪ *www.fire-ice.com*

Forestview Restaurant   ★ $BLD
Depew ▪ *(716) 656-8760*
4781 Transit Rd ▪ *American* ▪ GF pancakes are available. ▪ *www.forestviewrestaurant. com*

Frantoni's Pizzeria & Ristorante ★ $$LD
East Meadow ▪ *(516) 794-8831*
1928 Hempstead Tpke
Williston Park ▪ *(516) 747-3413*
66 Hillside Ave ▪ *Italian* ▪ GF pizza and pasta are available. Pizza can be prepared with any toppings, and pasta can be prepared with a variety of sauces. General Manager Peter reports that all GF items are kept separate from non-GF items to reduce the risk of cross contamination. ▪ *www.frantonis.com*

Gaudino's Brooklyn Pizza ★ $LD
Ronkonkoma ▪ *(631) 736-3957*
1021 Portion Rd ▪ *Pizza* ▪ GF pizza and pasta are available.

Ghenet Brooklyn ★ $$LD
Brooklyn ▪ *(718) 230-4475*
348 Douglass St ▪ *Ethiopian* ▪ GF injera bread is available with advanced notice of one day. GF injera is made of teff only. ▪ *www.ghenet.com*

Gianni Mazia's ★ $LD
Clarence ▪ *(716) 759-2803*
10325 Main St ▪ *Italian-American* ▪ GF pizza and chicken wings are available. Restaurant reports that they use a separate fryer for GF chicken wings. ▪ *www.maziaspizza.com*

Ginger Man $$$LD
Albany ▪ *(518) 427-5963*
234 Western Ave ▪ *Italian-American* ▪ Bartender Stephanie notes that GF diners are "pretty common" at the restaurant. She reports that cheese plates, charcuterie platters, and short ribs, as well as meat and seafood dishes, are GF or can be modified to be GF. Confirm timeliness of this information before dining in. Alert a server, who will speak with the chef about GF offerings. ▪ *www.albanygingerman.com*

Gino's Pizza ★ $$LD
Flushing ▪ *(718) 886-3411*
2519 Parsons Blvd
Great Neck ▪ *(516) 487-1122*
60 Middle Neck Rd ▪ *Pizza* ▪ GF pizza is available.

Golden Duck Restaurant ★ $LD
Williamsville ▪ *(716) 639-8888*
1840 Maple Rd ▪ *Chinese* ▪ GF soy sauce is available. ▪ *www.goldenduckrestaurant.com*

Golden Phoenix ✪★ $LD
Fairport ▪ *(585) 223-4539*
7323 Pittsford Palmyra Rd ▪ *Chinese* ▪ Extensive GF menu features chicken, beef, shrimp, and eggplant curries, noodle soups, fried rice, and more. GF soy sauce is available. ▪ *www.goldenphoenixchinese.com*

Golden Wok Café ✪ $LD
Ardsley ▪ *(914) 693-2110*
875 Saw Mill River Rd ▪ *Chinese* ▪ Extensive GF menu includes pork, beef, seafood, poultry, and vegetable dishes. It also lists noodle and rice dishes, as well as chef's specialties, which include filet mignon, fried squid, and chicken with crispy walnut.

Gourmet Café $$LD
Glens Falls ▪ *(518) 761-0864*
185 Glen St ▪ *Deli* ▪ Restaurant reports that GF soups are available, as are other GF options like salads with grilled chicken or vegetables. They welcome GF diners to bring in their own GF bread or pasta. ▪ *www.downtowngourmet.com*

Grande Centrale $$$D
Congers ▪ *(845) 267-3442*
17 N Rockland Ave ▪ *Continental* ▪ Veteran Server Amanda reports that "most of the meals on the menu" can be prepared GF. She notes that "everything is made fresh," and all staff members have served "at least a couple of people" who have requested GF meals. Alert a server, who will indicate GF items. ▪ *www.grandecentrale.com*

Ground Round 📖
Brookhaven ▪ *(631) 286-1512*
2647 Montauk Hwy
Johnson City ▪ *(607) 231-2020*
214 Reynolds Rd

Plattsburgh ▪ (518) 561-2897
32 Smithfield Blvd
Riverhead ▪ (631) 591-2933
1077 Old Country Rd

Halstead Avenue Bistro   ✪★ $$LD
Harrison ▪ (914) 777-1181
123 Halstead Ave ▪ American ▪ GF menu
includes sautéed shrimp, seared sea scallops, coconut crusted halibut, and more.
GF beer, bread, pasta, and hamburger buns
are available. GF dessert options include
flourless chocolate cake with white chocolate mousse, caramelized apple cheesecake
with fresh whipped cream, and more. ▪
www.halsteadbistro.com

Hampton Chutney Company $LD
Amagansett ▪ (631) 267-3131
Amagansett Sq ▪ Indian ▪ Manager Katy
reports that all of the dosas - savory South
Indian pancakes made from rice and black
lentils - are GF. She also reports that the
uttapams - like dosas, but thicker - are GF.
Fillings can be chosen a la carte or from
the many combinations suggested on the
menu. ▪ www.hamptonchutney.com

Harry's Harbour Place Grill $$$LD
Buffalo ▪ (716) 874-5400
2192 Niagara St ▪ American ▪ Manager
Claudia reports that the restaurant serves
GF diners "often" and has always successfully accommodated them. She recommends alerting the server and asking the
server to speak with the chef about GF
options. ▪ www.harrysharbour.com

Heights Bistro & Bar, The   ✪★ $$LD
Yorktown Heights ▪ (914) 962-3777
334 Underhill Ave ▪ Modern American ▪
Extensive GF menu includes pork chops,
sea scallops, and a variety of salads. GF
pasta is available. ▪ www.theheightsbistro.
com

Highlands $$D
Altamont ▪ (518) 872-1938
1670 Berne Altamont Rd ▪ Italian ▪
Manager Michelle reports that all of the
staff members are "really knowledgeable"

about GF. Chef Sheena is especially aware,
and she uses cornstarch to thicken both
her sauces and soups. Confirm timeliness
of this information before dining in. GF
vodka is available. ▪ www.highlandsrestau-
rant.com

Hunki's Kosher Pizza   ★ $$LD
Plainview ▪ (516) 870-0435
131 Central Park Rd ▪ Pizza ▪ GF pizza is
available. ▪ www.hunkispizza.com

Il Barilotto $$$LD
Fishkill ▪ (845) 897-4300
1113 Main St ▪ Italian ▪ Manager Scott notes
that GF diners come in "quite a bit." He
notes that several menu items can be modified to be GF, and the risotto of the day is
almost always naturally GF. Alert a server
upon arrival. ▪ www.ilbarilottorestaurant.
com

Il Capuccino   ✪★ $$$D
Sag Harbor ▪ (631) 725-2747
30 Madison St ▪ Italian ▪ GF menu items
include mozzarella and tomato with pesto,
pasta with calamari sauce, shrimp fra
diavolo, and pasta with roasted pistacchio
alfredo sauce. GF pasta is available. ▪ www.
ilcapuccino.com

Ilio Dipaolo's Restaurant   ✪★ $$LD
Blasdell ▪ (716) 825-3675
3785 S Park Ave ▪ Italian ▪ GF menu
includes grilled steaks, pork chops and
chicken. The "Friday Only" special is baked
haddock in a white wine, lemon, and
basil sauce. GF pasta is available. ▪ www.
iliodipaolos.com

Irises Café & Wine Bar   ✪★ $$LD
Plattsburgh ▪ (518) 566-7000
20 City Hall Place ▪ Fusion ▪ GF menu
includes sesame encrusted sashimi grade
tuna, grilled filet mignon, and a petite
salmon filet. GF soy sauce is available. For
dessert, GF brownies are available for the
warm chocolate brownie soufflé. They also
have GF cheesecake. Owner Carol reports that all staff members are trained by
GFRAP. ▪ www.irisescafe.com

Joan's GF Great Bakes　　100% ¢S
North Bellmore ▪ *(516) 804-5600*
1905 Bellmore Ave ▪ *Bakery* ▪ Dedicated
GF bakery offering pizza, bagels, corn
bread, english muffins, rolls, and cookies.
Owner Joan reports that many GF customers frequent the bakery. She also notes that
menu items are frozen and available to take
home. ▪ *www.gfgreatbakes.com*

Joe and Pat's Pizzeria　　★ $$LD
Staten Island ▪ *(718) 981-0887*
1758 Victory Blvd ▪ *Pizza* ▪ GF pizza and
pasta are available.

Joe Willys Fish Shack　　★ $$$LD
Fishkill ▪ *(845) 765-0234*
10 Old Route 9 W ▪ *Seafood* ▪ GF ziti is
available. Owner Joe reports that almost
everything on the menu can be modified to
be GF, including broiled salmon, shrimp,
bay scallops, and the zuppa de pesce. Alert
a server upon arrival. ▪ *www.joewillysfish-
shack.com*

Joey B's　　$$$D
Fairport ▪ *(585) 377-9030*
400 Packetts Lndg ▪ *American* ▪ Manager
Joe reports that the restaurant serves GF
diners "every night." He notes that all menu
items can be modified to be GF, including desserts and dessert sauces. He further
notes that servers are well trained on the
GF diet. ▪ *www.joeybsrestaurant.com*

John Harvard's Brew House　　$$LD
Lake Grove ▪ *(631) 979-2739*
2093 Smith Haven Plz ▪ *American* ▪ Manager Eric reports that the restaurant serves
GF diners "sometimes." He notes that
most salads can be made GF, but cautions
that dressings are not made on site and
may contain gluten. He also recommends
ordering chicken or steak dishes without
seasoning, as the seasoning is not GF. Confirm timeliness of this information before
dining in. ▪ *www.johnharvards.com*

Jo-Sef Gluten Free　　100% $S
Brooklyn ▪ *(718) 599-0707*
194 S 8th St ▪ *Bakery* ▪ This dedicated GF

bakery, founded when the owners' son
was diagnosed with celiac disease, offers a
variety of GF cookies - including sandwich
cookies, square cookies, and animal cookies. ▪ *www.josefsglutenfree.com*

Judean Hills Pizza　　★ $LD
Bronx ▪ *(718) 432-8320*
5677 Riverdale Ave ▪ *Pizza* ▪ GF pizza is
available. Manager Jordan recommends
ordering in advance.

Karma Road　　¢BLD
New Paltz ▪ *(845) 255-1099*
11 Main St ▪ *Vegetarian* ▪ Owner Jen
reports that almost everything in the deli
case is GF. She notes that any sandwich
can be made with rice tortillas instead of
bread, and that most of the soups are GF.
Confirm timeliness of this information
before dining in. Jen adds that the staff is
"really knowledgeable" about the GF diet,
so it is easy to get help choosing a GF meal.
▪ *www.karmaroad.net*

KD's Fish Fry　　✪★ ¢LD
Ballston Spa ▪ *(518) 583-9677*
418 Geyser Rd ▪ *Seafood* ▪ KD's considers
itself an "Allergy Free Zone," and it has an
"Allergy Free Menu" which includes GF
items such as calamari, fried clams, and
fried shrimp. GF bread, pasta, pizza, and
baked goods are available. Chef Dawn is
GF, and she has trained her staff accordingly. The kitchen has two dedicated GF
fryers. ▪ *www.kdsfishfry.com*

Kilpatrick's Publick House　　$$LD
Ithaca ▪ *(607) 277-8900*
118 N Tioga St ▪ *Irish Pub* ▪ Restaurant
reports that they have "some" GF options.
They report that most salads including the
spinach, lentil, and house salads, are GF.
They also note that a few other entrées,
such as the scallops, can be modified to be
GF. Alert a server, who will discuss GF options with the chef. ▪ *www.kilpatrickspub.
com*

King and I, The　　$$LD
Amherst ▪ *(716) 839-2950*

2188 Kensington Ave ■ *Thai* ■ Server My reports that "practically all" of the menu items are GF, and that they accommodate GF diners "pretty often." She notes that there are at least two GF appetizers every day. Alert a server upon arrival. ■ *www.kingandibuffalo.com*

Kozy Shack Gluten Free Kiosk at Citi Field   100% ¢S
Flushing ■
126th St & Roosevelt Ave ■ *American* ■ Kozy Shack GF snacks are available. Hot dogs and hamburgers on GF buns are also available, as is GF beer. This is a kiosk located inside Citi Field during Mets games.

La Capannina Ristorante   ★ $$LD
Holtsville ■ (631) 569-4524
173 Morris Ave ■ *Pizza* ■ GF pizza is available in the 12-inch size. GF pasta is also available. Only the listed location has GF items. ■ *www.lacapanninapizza.com*

La Famiglia Pizza & Pasta   ★ $$LD
Katonah ■ (914) 232-8027
280 Katonah Ave ■ *Pizza* ■ GF pizza is available all the time, except on Fridays and Saturdays from 5:30-7:30pm. Restaurant has another location at Cross River, but only the Katonah location has GF pizza. ■ *www.lafamigliapizza.net*

La Fontanella   ★ $$$LD
Tappan ■ (845) 398-3400
5254 Rt 303 ■ *Italian* ■ GF pasta is available.

La Pizzeria   ★ $$LD
Great Neck ■ (516) 466-5114
114 Middle Neck Rd ■ *Pizza* ■ GF pizza is available in the 12-inch size. ■ *www.lapizzeriany.com*

La Tee Da   ★ $$$D
Buffalo ■ (716) 881-4500
206 Allen St ■ *Italian* ■ GF pasta is available. Flourless chocolate torte, crème brûlée, and rice pudding are available for dessert.

Le Metro Bakery & Café $$$BLD
Williamsville ■ (716) 634-0726
5110 Main St ■ *Bakery & Café* ■ Manager David reports that GF diners are "not irregular" in the restaurant. The signature black bean and chicken chili is GF, as are many of the soups, which change daily. Most dishes must be slightly modified to be GF, but David notes that these modifications are "easy enough." ■ *www.lemetrobuffalo.com*

Le Pavillon $$$D
Poughkeepsie ■ (845) 473-2525
230 Salt Point Tpke ■ *French* ■ The restaurant reports that many dishes are naturally GF. All sauces are GF, as they are made with rice flour. Confirm timeliness of this information before dining in. GF soufflés are available for dessert. Reservations noting GF are recommended. ■ *www.lepavillonrestaurant.com*

Legal Sea Foods   📖
Garden City ■ (516) 248-4600
630 Old Country Rd
Huntington Station ■ (631) 271-9777
160 Walt Whitman Rd
White Plains ■ (914) 390-9600
5 Mamaroneck Ave

Leo's Pizza   ★ $LD
Victor ■ (585) 924-1480
7387 State Route 96 ■ *Pizza* ■ GF pizza, "bombers," and calzones are available every day. GF chicken wings and fries are served on Tuesdays and Wednesdays only. ■ *www.leospizzaonline.com*

Little Bake Shop, The   ★ ¢S
Valley Cottage ■ (845) 268-5511
491 Kings Hwy ■ *Bakery* ■ GF macaroons, sandwich bread, rolls, cookies, focaccia breads, and cupcakes are available. Calling at least 48 hours in advance for special requests is recommended.

Little Hen Specialties   100% ¢S
Maine ■ (607) 323-5026
2635 N Route 26 ■ *Bakery* ■ Bakery offering several kinds of GF bread, macaroons, snickerdoodles, cookies, brownies, and

bunny cakes. Owner DJ reports that special orders can be accommodated with advanced notice of at least 24 hours. ▪ *www.littlehenspecialties.com*

Lost Dog Café, The   ✪★ $$LD
Binghamton ▪ *(607) 771-6063*
222 Water St ▪ *American* ▪ GF menu includes Greek chicken, bacon bourbon NY strip steak, sesame ginger salmon, the "Aye Chihuahua" salad with blackened chicken, beans, and tortilla strips, among other things. GF rice noodles and rice crackers are available as starch substitutes. ▪ *www.lostdogcafe.net*

Luigi's Pizzeria   ★ $$LD
Bronxville ▪ *(914) 776-1251*
843 Bronx River Rd ▪ *Pizza* ▪ GF pizza is available.

Mama's Italian Restaurant   ✪★ $$LD
Oakdale ▪ *(631) 567-0909*
1352 Montauk Hwy ▪ *Italian* ▪ Extensive GF menu includes appetizers, soups, salads, and a kids' menu. GF pasta is available and can be served with a wide variety of sauces. Mini GF pizzas are also available. Examples of GF entrées are veal piccata, chicken marsala, and flounder parmigiana. They also have GF specials, which change weekly. ▪ *www.mamas-restaurant.com*

Mangia Ristorante & Caffe   ★ $$$LD
Orchard Park ▪ *(716) 662-9467*
4264 N Buffalo Rd ▪ *Italian* ▪ GF pasta is available. The restaurant reports that they regularly serve GF diners. Alert a server, who will notify the kitchen. ▪ *www.mangia-ristorante.com*

Mangino's Ristorante   ★ $$$D
Saratoga Springs ▪ *(518) 584-5599*
149 Route 9P ▪ *Italian* ▪ GF rice pasta is available. ▪ *www.manginos.com*

Maria's Mexican Restaurant $LD
Webster ▪ *(585) 872-1237*
75 W Main St ▪ *Mexican* ▪ Manager Valerie reports that many GF diners frequent the restaurant. She notes that tacos, enchiladas, tostadas, guacamole, chile, and quesadillas can be prepared GF. Confirm timeliness of this information before dining in. She also cautions that there is a minimal amount of cross-contamination in the kitchen.

Maud's Tavern   ✪★ $$LD
Hastings On Hudson ▪ *(914) 478-2326*
149 Southside Ave ▪ *Modern American* ▪ GF menu includes a roasted half chicken, sautéed shrimp in lemon white wine sauce, and fusilli with mushrooms and tomatoes. Shepherd's Pie, rice, and french fries can be made GF with advanced notice of at least 24 hours. GF pasta is available. ▪ *www.maudstavern.com*

Maxie's Supper Club and Oyster Bar
$$D
Ithaca ▪ *(607) 272-4136*
635 W State St ▪ *Modern American* ▪ Manager Rachel reports that "most of the things on the menu" can be modified to be GF. She lists the jambalaya, BBQ tofu, and any salad without croutons as just a few examples. Alert a server upon arrival. Rachel notes that the servers will "definitely" be able to "navigate the menu," as they are required to take a test on menu ingredients before starting work. ▪ *www.maxies.com*

McKenzie's Bar & Grill $$LD
Hamburg ▪ *(716) 627-9752*
4151 Lake Shore Rd ▪ *Modern American* ▪ Manager Mary reports that they serve GF diners "occasionally." Roasted chicken, capri salad, porterhouse steak, grilled shrimp, chicken caesar without croutons, and sandwiches without rolls are GF. Confirm timeliness of this information before dining in. Alert a server upon arrival, and ask for a manager to indicate GF options. ▪ *www.mckenziesbarandgrill.com*

Melting Pot, The   📖
Albany ▪ *(518) 862-1292*
1 Crossgates Mall Rd
Buffalo ▪ *(716) 685-6358*
1 Walden Galleria
Farmingdale ▪ *(631) 752-4242*

2377 Broadhollow Rd
White Plains ▪ *(914) 993-6358*
30 Mamaroneck Ave

Moosewood Restaurant ★ $$LD
Ithaca ▪ *(607) 273-9610*
215 N Cayuga St ▪ *Global* ▪ Co-owner
Laura reports that the restaurant has "hundreds of recipes that can be modified to be
GF." She notes that GF diners should alert
a server and ask the server to communicate
with the cooks. GF soy sauce is available. ▪
www.moosewoodrestaurant.com

Mr. Miceli Pizzeria & Italian Restaurant
★ $$$LD
Rockville Centre ▪ *(516) 764-7701*
19 N Park Ave ▪ *Italian* ▪ GF pasta, pizza,
and garlic knots are available. Owner Luca
reports that he is GF, so his restaurant is
dedicated to serving GF diners. ▪ *www.*
mrmiceli.com

Mulberry Cafe LLC ★ $$$LD
Lackawanna ▪ *(716) 822-4292*
64 Jackson Ave ▪ *Italian* ▪ GF pasta is
available. ▪ *www.mulberrybuffalo.net*

My Dad's Cookies 100% $$$
Nanuet ▪ *(917) 653-0580*
119 Rockland Ctr ▪ *Bakery* ▪ Dedicated GF
bakery offering cookies, cakes, and brownies. Orders can be placed online only. ▪
www.mydadscookies.com

My Goodness! Deli & Café ★ ¢BLD
Pound Ridge ▪ *(914) 764-3431*
78 Westchester Ave ▪ *Sandwich Shop* ▪ GF
bread is available for sandwiches and paninis. GF ice cream cones are available for ice
cream. ▪ *www.mygoodnessdeliandcafe.com*

My Tomato Pie ★ $LD
Amherst ▪ *(716) 838-0969*
3085 Sheridan Dr ▪ *Italian* ▪ GF pasta and
pizza are available. ▪ *www.mytomatopie.*
com

Natural Village Café ★ $$BLD
Brooklyn ▪ *(347) 417-6424*
2 Avenue I ▪ *Organic* ▪ Owner Nina
reports that the restaurant "specializes" in

GF foods, and the staff is trained on the
GF diet. GF pizza, pasta, and cookies are
available. She notes that several salads,
fish dishes, and soups from the menu are
naturally GF. Alert a server, who will go
over GF options in detail. ▪ *www.naturalvil-*
lagecafe.com

Near & Natural ★ ¢BLD
Bedford ▪ *(914) 205-3545*
1 Court Rd ▪ *Café* ▪ GF bread and rolls are
available and served as sandwiches in the
café. Located inside the Near & Natural
Market. ▪ *www.nearandnatural.com*

Nevaèh Cuisine ✪★ $BLD
Pleasantville ▪ *(914) 495-3440*
146 Bedford Rd ▪ *Healthy American* ▪ GF
items marked on the menu include wraps
prepared on rice paper, falafel, turkey burgers, lentil salad, banana bread, and macaroons. Chef Charles reports that nearly
the entire menu is GF, but if diners have
questions, they should ask for him. GF
brownies are available for dessert. ▪ *www.*
nevaehcuisine.com

New World Home Cooking ✪★ $$D
Saugerties ▪ *(845) 246-0900*
1411 Route 212 ▪ *Café* ▪ GF menu includes a
smoked chickpea cake, tamales, wings, salads, and entrées like thai green curry stew,
mushroom risotto, and round sandwiches.
GF pasta is available. For dessert, they offer
GF chocolate cake with raspberry filling. ▪
www.ricorlando.com

Ninety Nine Restaurant & Pub 📖
Albany ▪ *(518) 452-1999*
1470 Western Ave
Clifton Park ▪ *(518) 348-1499*
306 Clifton Park Ctr Rd
Colonie ▪ *(518) 446-9909*
107 Wolf Rd
Kingston ▪ *(845) 336-4399*
53 Massa Dr
New Hartford ▪ *(315) 736-9699*
8675 Clinton St
Plattsburgh ▪ *(518) 566-9900*
446 Route 3

Queensbury ▪ (518) 798-0699
578 Aviation Rd
Rotterdam ▪ (518) 374-7799
93 W Campbell Rd
Saratoga Springs ▪ (518) 584-9906
3073 Route 50

Nirchi's Pizza ★ ¢LD
Binghamton ▪ (607) 723-8474
166 Water St
Binghamton ▪ (607) 231-6561
219 Main St
Binghamton ▪ (607) 722-8756
907 Front St
Binghamton ▪ (607) 722-6331
954 Front St
Conklin ▪ (607) 775-3822
1023 Conklin Rd
Vestal ▪ (607) 729-5131
Vestal Parkway E ▪ Pizza ▪ GF pizza is
available at the listed locations only. ▪ www.
nirchis.com

Noodle Pudding ★ $$D
Brooklyn ▪ (718) 625-3737
38 Henry St ▪ Italian ▪ GF pasta is available.

Nunzio's Pizza and Deli ★ $LD
Saratoga Springs ▪ (518) 584-3840
119 Clinton St ▪ Pizza ▪ GF pizza and pasta
are available, as is GF bread for sandwiches.
Select entrées, such as spaghetti with meatballs and eggplant parmesan, can also be
made GF. Confirm timeliness of this information before dining in. GF pizza requires
advanced notice of one hour.

Old Red Mill Inn ★ $$$LD
Williamsville ▪ (716) 633-7878
8326 Main St ▪ American ▪ GF chocolate
cake is available. Manager Dan reports that
GF is his "number one dietary request."
Swordfish, broiled haddock, shrimp, and
steaks can be served GF. Dan notes that if
the restaurant is not busy, the chef will be
happy to make a GF sauce. Alert a server,
who will notify the kitchen. ▪ www.redmil-
linn.com

Olives Greek Taverna $LD
Pittsford ▪ (585) 381-3990
50 State St ▪ Greek ▪ Manager Cary reports that GF diners come in "all the time,"
and the servers are "well aware" of the GF
diet. She notes that because the restaurant
is small, it is easy to make everyone aware
of GF dining needs. ▪ www.shotsnapped.
com

Original Pancake House, The ★ ¢BL
Amherst ▪ (716) 691-8219
2075 Niagara Falls Blvd
Orchard Park ▪ (716) 674-3344
3019 Union Rd
Williamsville ▪ (716) 634-1025
5479 Main St ▪ Breakfast ▪ GF pancakes
are available. Select locations may serve
other GF options. Call a specific location to
inquire. ▪ www.originalpancakehouse.com

Outback Steakhouse 📖
Amherst ▪ (716) 833-6067
1551 Niagara Falls Blvd
Bayside ▪ (718) 819-0908
2348 Bell Blvd
Blasdell ▪ (716) 823-2020
3670 Mckinley Pkwy
Brooklyn ▪ (718) 837-7200
1475 86th St
Clifton Park ▪ (518) 348-1900
610 Old Route 146
Colonie ▪ (518) 482-4863
145 Wolf Rd
Commack ▪ (631) 864-7400
216 Jericho Tpke
East Setauket ▪ (631) 474-8700
5040 Nesconset Hwy
Elmhurst ▪ (718) 760-7200
8801 Queens Blvd
Glens Falls ▪ (518) 792-4014
925 State Route 9
Holbrook ▪ (631) 585-0404
325 Main St
Horseheads ▪ (607) 795-1224
200 Colonial Dr
Huntington ▪ (631) 547-6675
839 New York Ave
Island Park ▪ (516) 897-8989

3939 Long Beach Rd
Lindenhurst ■ *(631) 957-2600*
612 Wellwood Ave
Liverpool ■ *(315) 622-1559*
3946 State Route 31
Merrick ■ *(516) 377-7761*
2124 Merrick Mall
Middletown ■ *(845) 695-1913*
25 Crystal Run Xing
Monroe ■ *(845) 782-6389*
215 Larkin Dr
New Hartford ■ *(315) 736-0010*
8655 Clinton St
Staten Island ■ *(718) 761-3907*
280 Marsh Ave
Suffern ■ *(845) 368-3800*
30 Indian Rock
Syracuse ■ *(315) 445-2121*
3112 Erie Blvd E
Vestal ■ *(607) 766-9915*
3140 Vestal Pkwy E
Wappingers Falls ■ *(845) 298-6753*
1510 Route 9
West Nyack ■ *(845) 353-0707*
4242 Palisades Center Dr
Westbury ■ *(516) 334-0518*
1067 Old Country Rd
White Plains ■ *(914) 684-1397*
60 S Broadway
Yonkers ■ *(914) 337-3244*
1703 Central Park Ave

Oysterman's Restaurant & Pub
　　　　　　　　　✪★ **$$LD**
Sayville ■ *(631) 589-7775*
45 Foster Ave ■ *Seafood* ■ GF menu
includes the angler's seafood combo, veal
saltimbocca over rice pasta, and almond
crusted filet of salmon, among other
things. Examples of GF desserts include
rice pudding and homemade GF brownies.
GF beer, bread, and soy sauce are available.
■ *www.oystermans.com*

P.F. Chang's China Bistro　📖
Albany ■ *(518) 454-0040*
131 Colonie Ctr Spc 305
Buffalo ■ *(716) 706-0791*
1 Galleria Dr # Th131

Victor ■ *(585) 223-2410*
820 Eastview Mall
Westbury ■ *(516) 222-9200*
1504 Old Country Rd # B9A
White Plains ■ *(914) 997-6100*
125 Westchester Ave Spc D315

P.S. Restaurant & Luxury Lounge　**$$$D**
Vestal ■ *(607) 770-0056*
100 Rano Blvd ■ **Continental** ■ Manager
Sylvana reports that GF meals are available
and that many menu items are "flexible for
GF preparation." She reports that many of
the thai items are naturally GF, as are other
beef, chicken, shrimp, and stir-fry dishes.
Reservations noting GF are recommended.
■ *www.psrestaurant.com*

Papa Razzi　　　　　　★ **$$LD**
Westbury ■ *(516) 877-7744*
1500 Jericho Tpke ■ **Italian** ■ GF pasta and
pizza are available. In addition, Manager
Michael reports that they are a scratch
kitchen, so they can make "anything that a
customer is looking for." ■ *www.paparaz-
zitrattoria.com*

Patricia's of Tremont　　★ **$LD**
Bronx ■ *(718) 918-1800*
3883 E Tremont Ave ■ **Italian** ■ GF pizza
and pasta are available. Manager Tony reports that the kitchen uses separate utensils
and is "extremely thorough" when dealing
with GF requests. ■ *www.patriciasoftrem-
ont.com*

Peter Pratt's Inn　　　　　**$$$D**
Yorktown Heights ■ *(914) 962-4090*
673 Croton Heights Rd ■ **American** ■ Chef
Nick reports that the restaurant serves GF
diners "every day, all the time." He notes
that everyone on staff is "very aware" of
the GF diet, and he recommends alerting
a server upon arrival. Servers know which
menu items can be made GF. Nick also
notes that a majority of menu items are
naturally GF. ■ *www.prattsinn.com*

Phuket Thai Cuisine　　　　**$LD**
Webster ■ *(585) 671-8410*
2122 Empire Blvd ■ **Thai** ■ Owner Sim

reports that she serves many GF diners on a regular basis. She takes customers' orders herself, and she is very GF aware. She recommends alerting her upon arrival, so she can alert the chef and help choose an appropriate meal. ▪ *www.phuketthaicuisine. info*

Pizza 2000   ★ $LD
Harrison ▪ *(914) 835-8000*
337 Halstead Ave ▪ *Pizza* ▪ GF pizza is available in the 9-inch and 12-inch sizes. GF pizza can be prepared with any toppings. GF pasta is also available and can be substituted into any pasta dish on the menu. Meals are available for dining in, taking out, and delivery. ▪ *www.pizza2000. net*

Pizza Bistro   ❂★ $LD
Massapequa Park ▪ *(516) 797-4747*
4952 Merrick Rd ▪ *Italian* ▪ GF menu includes pizza, pasta, gyros, and cheesecake for dessert. Monday nights are GF nights, where GF diners can order a salad, a GF pasta dish, coffee, and cheesecake for a fixed price. GF pasta and pizza are available. ▪ *www.pizzabistrony.com*

Pizza Bono Ristorante   ★ ¢LD
Plattsburgh ▪ *(518) 561-8541*
93 Margaret St ▪ *Pizza* ▪ GF pizza is available in the 12-inch size, with any toppings. Located in downtown Plattsburgh, just blocks from the SUNY campus.

Pizza Gourmet   ★ $LD
Mamaroneck ▪ *(914) 777-1056*
597 E Boston Post Rd ▪ *Pizza* ▪ GF pizza is available in the personal size, with any toppings. GF pasta is also available, but shipments are rare.

Pizza Pious   ★ $LD
Woodmere ▪ *(516) 295-2050*
1063 Broadway ▪ *Pizza* ▪ GF pizza is available by the pie only. Owner Leo reports that other items, including salads, soups, and vegetable rolls, can be modified to be GF. Upon arrival, alert a server, who will discuss GF requests with the kitchen.

Pizza Pizzazz   ★ $$LD
Shrub Oak ▪ *(914) 245-6400*
966 E Main St ▪ *Pizza* ▪ GF pizza is available.

Pizza Plant Restaurant   ❂★ $$D
Williamsville ▪ *(716) 632-0800*
8020 Transit Rd ▪ *Pizza* ▪ GF pasta, pizza, lasagna, breaded chicken fingers, burgers with GF buns, and beer are available. GF menu is available only on Wednesdays after 4 pm. ▪ *www.pizzaplant.com*

Plum Tomatoes Pizzeria & Restaurant   ★ $LD
Mineola ▪ *(516) 248-6390*
230 Old Country Rd
Rockaway Park ▪ *(718) 474-1775*
420 Beach 129th St ▪ *Pizza* ▪ GF pizza, pasta, beer, and cookies are available at the Mineola location. The Rockaway Park location has GF pizza and pasta, but no beer or cookies. ▪ *www.plumtomatoespizzarest.com*

Posa Posa   ★ $LD
Nanuet ▪ *(845) 623-7050*
121 Rockland Ctr ▪ *Italian* ▪ GF pizza and pasta are available. Manager John reports that many other entrées can be prepared GF, like most of the veal, chicken, beef, and seafood dishes. ▪ *www.posaposa.com*

Prince Umberto's Pizza   ★ $LD
Franklin Square ▪ *(516) 872-9049*
721 Franklin Ave ▪ *Pizza* ▪ GF pizza and pasta are available. ▪ *www.princeumberto. com*

Putrino's Pizza   ★ ¢LD
Owego ▪ *(607) 687-5985*
941 Rt 17 C ▪ *Pizza* ▪ GF pizza is available.

Ravenous $LD
Saratoga Springs ▪ *(518) 581-0560*
21 Phila St ▪ *Crêpes* ▪ Owner Fran reports that although they do not have GF crepes, they can serve some of their crepe fillings in a bowl. He also notes that their french fries are fried in a separate fryer and are GF. Confirm timeliness of this information before dining in. Alert a server, who will

discuss GF options. They are trained to look in the recipe book if they do not know what is in a certain dish. ▪ www.ravenouscrepes.com

Ray's Café ✪★ $LD
Rye Brook ▪ (914) 937-0747
176 S Ridge St ▪ Chinese ▪ GF menu includes chicken and broccoli, basil broccoli, eggplant dishes, fried rice, and more. GF soy sauce is available.

Red Bar & Restaurant ★ $$$$LD
Huntington ▪ (631) 673-0304
417 New York Ave ▪ Modern American ▪ GF pasta is available. ▪ www.redrestaurantli.com

Rice ✪ ¢LD
Brooklyn ▪ (718) 858-2700
166 Dekalb Ave
Brooklyn ▪ (718) 222-9880
81 Washington St ▪ Asian ▪ GF menu consists of modified regular menu items. The menu features rice dishes from around the world. It includes lemongrass salad, Portuguese soup, kebabs, thai coconut curry, Bhutanese red rice, and more. ▪ www.riceny.com

Ristorante Caterina de Medici ★ $$$LD
Hyde Park ▪ (845) 471-6608
1946 Campus Dr ▪ Italian ▪ Manager Charles reports that the restaurant employs a baker who has written a GF cookbook. GF bread, desserts, and pastries are available with advanced notice of several days. He recommends making reservations noting GF in order to alert the bakers and kitchen staff. Located on the Culinary Institute of America's campus and run by its chefs and students. ▪ www.ciachef.edu/restaurants/caterina

Rocco's Pizzeria ★ $LD
Mahopac ▪ (845) 621-1215
559 Route 6N ▪ Pizza ▪ GF pizza is available. Call ahead to confirm availability as sometimes they sell out.

Rock Da Pasta ✪★ $LD
New Paltz ▪ (845) 255-1144
62 Main St ▪ Pasta ▪ GF bread, brown rice pasta, pizza, and beer are available. GF bread and pizza are always homemade. Pizza varieties include classics like Cheese and Pepperoni, as well as experimental recipes such as Chicken Pesto with Artichoke and "The Ramble," which features onions, peppers, sun-dried tomatoes, fennel, artichoke hearts, broccoli florets, and garlic. They also offer a variety of GF desserts, including brownies and apple crumble. All GF items are cooked in dedicated GF pots and pans. Their "jamming atmosphere" comes partially from the connected "grassroots tech café" Slash Root, which has live music performances and open mic events every Thursday night. ▪ www.rockdapasta.com

Roma Pizza ★ $LD
Oxford ▪ (607) 843-6555
2 Main St
Sidney ▪ (607) 563-8888
25 Union St ▪ Pizza ▪ GF pizza is available.

Roycroft Inn $$$LD
East Aurora ▪ (716) 652-5552
40 S Grove St ▪ American ▪ Manager Leah reports that the restaurant has several "regulars" who are GF. She notes that servers and kitchen staff are well trained on the GF diet, and there is an annotated menu that describes how regular menu items can be modified to be GF. ▪ www.roycroftinn.com

Santa Fe Restaurant ✪ $D
Tivoli ▪ (845) 757-4100
52 Broadway ▪ Modern Mexican ▪ The restaurant has one copy of a GF menu that is almost the same as the regular menu. The restaurant reports that almost the entire menu is naturally GF. Alert a server upon arrival. ▪ www.santafetivoli.com

Satelite Pizza ★ $$LD
Bayport ▪ (631) 472-3800
799 Montauk Hwy ▪ Pizza ▪ GF pizza is available. ▪ www.satelitepizza.com

Scarsdale Pizza Station   ★ $$LD
Scarsdale ■ *(914) 723-4700*
844 Scarsdale Ave ■ *Pizza* ■ GF pizza is
available by the pie. Individual slices are
not available.

Season's Restaurant   ✪ $$$LD
Somers ■ *(914) 276-0600*
289 Route 100 ■ *Modern American* ■ GF
menu includes a warm arugula salad, a
warm goat cheese salad, grilled salmon
with mango salsa, pesto shrimp, and more.
For dessert, chocolate mousse is available. ■
www.seasonsatsomers.com

Shane's Rib Shack   📖
Clifton Park ■ *(518) 615-0555*
7 Southside Dr

**Sherry Lynn's Gluten Free
Bakery & Café**   100% $BLD
Latham ■ *(518) 786-7700*
836 Troy Schenectady Rd ■ *Café* ■
Family-run, dedicated GF café offering
a wide variety of items, including french
toast, pizza, pasta, sandwiches, and baked
goods. Featured desserts include cherry
cheesecake with a graham cracker crust
and hot apple pie. There are extensive,
separate menus for breakfast and sandwiches, as well as one for appetizers, pizza,
and pasta. There is also a kids' GF menu.
The bakery & café periodically hosts all-
you-can-eat GF buffets. ■ *www.sherrylynns-
glutenfree.com*

Shimon's Kosher Pizza   ★ ¢LD
Flushing ■ *(718) 793-1491*
7124 Main St ■ *Pizza* ■ GF pizza is available.

Shogun Hibachi Steak & Seafood ★ $D
Williamsville ■ *(716) 631-8899*
7590 Transit Rd ■ *Japanese* ■ GF soy sauce
is available. Restaurant reports serving
GF diners frequently and notes that most
menu items are naturally GF. ■ *www.ichi-
shogun.com*

Silver Lake Pizzeria   ★ $$LD
West Harrison ■ *(914) 328-2326*
79 Lake St ■ *Pizza* ■ GF pizza is available.

Simply Crepes Café   ★ ¢BLD
Canandaigua ■ *(585) 394-9090*
101 S Main St
Pittsford ■ *(585) 383-8310*
7 Schoen Pl ■ *Crêpes* ■ GF buckwheat
crepes are available. Owner Pierre reports
that all staff members are GF aware, and
they can ensure a GF meal. Examples of GF
entrées include a turkey gouda crepe and a
reuben crepe. Most dessert crepes are avail-
able GF. ■ *www.simplycrepes.com*

Smoking Sloe's   ✪ $$$LD
Northport ■ *(631) 651-8812*
847 Fort Salonga Rd ■ *Barbeque* ■ Extensive GF menu includes baby back ribs,
BBQ chicken, andouille sausage with sautéed onions, and "Celiwiches" with pork,
chicken, or brisket. GF brownies are available for dessert. Restaurant reports that
certain GF dishes, like the "Mac Daddy"
(GF mac n' cheese) and "Free Birds" (GF
chicken wings) have been given special
names to avoid confusion in the kitchen.
They recommend using those names when
placing orders. ■ *www.smokingsloes.com*

Soul Dog   ★ ¢LD
Poughkeepsie ■ *(845) 454-3254*
107 Main St ■ *American* ■ GF hot dog buns,
kaiser rolls, and sliced breads are available.

Owner Jenny reports that nearly the entire menu is GF. She notes that it is important to alert a server so that the kitchen can take the proper steps to prevent cross-contamination. ▪ *www.souldog.biz*

Sparrow Tavern, The   ★ $$**LD**
Astoria ▪ **(718) 606-2260**
2401 29th St ▪ *American* ▪ GF beer is available. ▪ *www.thesparrowtavern.com*

Speedy Greens   ✪★ $**LD**
Cicero ▪ **(315) 752-0333**
8169 Brewerton Rd ▪ *Organic* ▪ GF items marked on the menu include vegetable brown rice, greens and feta quiche, and veggie pad thai. GF pasta and cookies are available. Restaurant reports that it serves "several" GF diners. ▪ *www.rnholistic.com*

Spice of India $$**LD**
Nyack ▪ **(845) 353-3663**
125 Main St ▪ *Indian* ▪ Restaurant reports that curry dishes, tandoori entrées, soups, salads and some desserts are GF. Confirm timeliness of this information before dining in. Restaurant recommends alerting a server, who will guide GF diners "through any hidden spots." ▪ *www.spiceofindianyack.com*

St. Andrew's Café   ★ $**LD**
Hyde Park ▪ **(845) 471-6608**
1946 Campus Dr ▪ *Modern American* ▪ Reservationist Linda reports that the restaurant is equipped to accommodate GF diners. She recommends making reservations noting GF so that the chefs know ahead of time. GF bread is available. ▪ *www.ciachef.edu*

Stir Crazy   ★ $**LD**
West Nyack ▪ **(845) 727-2002**
4422 Palisades Center Dr ▪ *Asian Stir-Fry* ▪ Teriyaki, szechuan, and thai BBQ are GF sauce options. GF rice noodles are also available. ▪ *www.stircrazy.com*

Suzanne Fine Regional Cuisine $$$**D**
Lodi ▪ **(607) 582-7545**
9013 Route 414 ▪ *American Regional* ▪

Owner Bob notes that the restaurant has "quite a few" GF customers. He notes that they try to have "a couple" of GF options for each course. He also notes that the further in advance the restaurant knows about GF requests, the better. Reservations noting GF are strongly recommended. ▪ *www.suzannefrc.com*

Sweet Karma Desserts   ★ $$$$$
East Meadow ▪ **(516) 794-4478**
550 E Meadow Ave ▪ *Bakery* ▪ Non-dedicated bakery offering GF pastries, cookies, cupcakes, and cakes. Cookies are available in different flavors each day, and cakes can be ordered in advance. GF pizza crusts are also available. ▪ *www.sweetkarmadesserts.com*

Symeon's Greek Restaurant   ✪ $$**LD**
Yorkville ▪ **(315) 736-4074**
4941 Commercial Dr ▪ *Greek* ▪ Extensive GF menu includes dips, a gyro platter, a mixed grill, lamb chops, chicken florentine, and more. ▪ *www.symeons.com*

T & J Pizza and Pasta   ★ $**LD**
Port Chester ▪ **(914) 939-4134**
223 Westchester Ave ▪ *Pizza* ▪ GF pizza is available in the 12-inch size. GF pizza is served in the pizzeria only. T & J Villaggio Trattoria, which is located next door, does not serve GF items. ▪ *www.tandjs.net*

Tantalus Restaurant $$**LD**
East Aurora ▪ **(716) 652-0341**
634 Main St ▪ *Global* ▪ Hostess Linda notes that all servers are GF aware, as they get "a lot of requests" for it. Alert the staff upon arrival.

Three Dogs Gluten-Free Bakery 100% ¢**S**
Briarcliff Manor ▪ **(914) 762-2121**
510 N State Rd ▪ *Bakery* ▪ Dedicated GF bakery offering a wide variety of GF baked goods. Some items, like bread, muffins, scones, and cookies, are available every day, while others can be requested by calling ahead. Gluten is not allowed on the premises. ▪ *www.threedogsgfbakery.com*

Tiger Lily Café ¢LD

Port Jefferson ▪ *(631) 476-7080*
156 E Main St ▪ Café ▪ Manager Fiona
reports that although the restaurant does
not carry GF bread, most of the sandwiches
can be converted to salads, and most
dressings are GF. She further reports that
the restaurant is trying to make more GF
specials, available daily. Confirm timeliness
of this information before dining in. She
notes that either she or an owner is always
working, and recommends asking for one
of them upon arrival. ▪ *www.tigerlilycafe.
com*

Tuiello's Pizza House & Restaurant
★ $$LD

Nyack ▪ *(845) 358-5440*
76 Main St ▪ Pizza ▪ GF pizza is available.

Tuttoriso Restaurant and Café
✪★ $BLD

Staten Island ▪ *(718) 273-7644*
36 Richmond Ter ▪ *Italian* ▪ The extensive
GF menu features lasagna, paninis, pizza,
heroes, french toast, pancakes, and more.
GF beer, soy sauce, and hamburger buns
are available, as are GF baked goods like
cookies and brownies. All GF items are
prepared in a dedicated GF kitchen. Owner
Helen reports that all servers are "trained
and sensitized to dietary needs." ▪ *www.
tuttorisocafe.com*

Umami Café ★ $D

Croton On Hudson ▪ *(914) 271-5555*
325 S Riverside Ave ▪ *Fusion* ▪ GF pasta is
available. GF pasta can be substituted into
any pasta dish. Restaurant also notes that
most menu items can be modified to be
GF by removing sauces or substituting veg-
etables for starches. Confirm timeliness of
this information before dining in. ▪ *www.
umamicafe.com*

Uno Chicago Grill 📖

Albany ▪ *(518) 869-3100*
120 Washington Avenue Ext
Bayside ▪ *(718) 279-4900*
3902 Bell Blvd

Bronx ▪ *(718) 824-8667*
71 Metropolitan Oval
Brooklyn ▪ *(718) 748-8667*
9201 4th Ave
Central Valley ▪ *(845) 783-6560*
20 Centre Dr
Fayetteville ▪ *(315) 637-8667*
520 Towne Dr
Forest Hills ▪ *(718) 793-6700*
10716 70th Rd
Henrietta ▪ *(585) 272-8667*
1000 Hylan Dr
Latham ▪ *(518) 782-7166*
601 Troy Schenectady Rd
Liverpool ▪ *(315) 622-0718*
3974 State Route 31
Long Island City ▪ *(718) 706-8800*
3711 35th Ave
New Hartford ▪ *(315) 736-8323*
8645 Clinton St
Poughkeepsie ▪ *(845) 452-4930*
842A Main St
Queensbury ▪ *(518) 792-5399*
880 State Route 9
Saratoga Springs ▪ *(518) 587-4270*
3008 Route 50
Syracuse ▪ *(315) 466-8667*
9558 Carousel Ctr
Vestal ▪ *(607) 770-7000*
2503 Vestal Pkwy
Victor ▪ *(585) 223-6100*
7724 Victor Pittsford Rd
Wappingers Falls ▪ *(845) 297-6770*
1794 South Rd
Webster ▪ *(585) 872-4760*
931 Holt Rd
White Plains ▪ *(914) 684-7040*
14 Martine Ave
Yonkers ▪ *(914) 779-7515*
2650 Central Park Ave

V Spot, The ✪ $LD

Brooklyn ▪ *(718) 622-2275*
156 5th Ave ▪ Vegan ▪ GF items high-
lighted on the menu include raw nori rolls,
jicama salad, summer rolls, pad thai, and
portobello spinach tacos. Manager Greg
reports that many GF diners frequent the
restaurant. ▪ *www.thevspotcafe.com*

Via Pizza   ★ $$**LD**
East Setauket ▪ *(631) 689-9540*
205 Route 25 A ▪ *Pizza* ▪ GF pizza is available.

Victor's Pizza Restaurant   ★ $$**LD**
New City ▪ *(845) 639-0454*
68 N Main St ▪ *Pizza* ▪ GF pizza is available.

Villa Italian Specialties   ★ $**LD**
East Hampton ▪ *(631) 324-5110*
7 Railroad Ave ▪ *Italian* ▪ GF pizza is available. Manager Francesco reports that during the summer, GF dinners such as eggplant parmasean and chicken parmasean are available. Confirm timeliness of this information before dining in. Upon arrival, alert a server, who will notify the kitchen. ▪ *www.villaitalianspecialties.com*

Villa Milano   ★ $$**LD**
Manhasset ▪ *(516) 365-3441*
168 Plandome Rd ▪ *Italian* ▪ GF pizza is available. Call 20 minutes in advance for a GF pie.

Villa Monte   ★ $$**LD**
Staten Island ▪ *(718) 668-0486*
170 New Dorp Ln ▪ *Pizza* ▪ GF pizza is available. Restaurant has three other locations on Staten Island, but the New Dorp Lane location is the only one with GF pizza. ▪ *www.villamontepizza.com*

Villa Nova E   ★ $$$**LD**
Pelham ▪ *(914) 748-1444*
6 1st St ▪ *Italian* ▪ GF pizza and pasta are available. Manager Ernie reports that almost any other menu item can be modified to be GF. Ask for him upon arrival. Also alert a server, who will send GF requests to the kitchen. ▪ *www.villanovae.com*

Vin-Chet Pastry Shop   ★ ¢**S**
Amherst ▪ *(716) 839-0871*
2178 Kensington Ave ▪ *Bakery* ▪ GF bread, pizza crust, hamburger rolls, cookies, brownies, and cake are available on Saturdays by pre-order only. The restaurant

recommends calling at least one day in advance. ▪ *www.vinchet.com*

Western Door, The $$$$**D**
Niagara Falls ▪ *(716) 278-3211*
310 4th St ▪ *Steakhouse* ▪ Chef Andrew reports that most of the menu is naturally GF. Items that are GF or can be modified to be GF include steaks, surf and turf, sea bass, salmon, and shrimp. Alert a server upon arrival. Reservations noting GF are recommended.

Wheatfields Restaurant & Bar ✪ $$**LD**
Clifton Park ▪ *(518) 383-4444*
54 Crossing Blvd
Saratoga Springs ▪ *(518) 587-0534*
440 Broadway ▪ *Italian* ▪ GF menu includes pasta, pizza, steamed mussels, beet and goat cheese salad, pan-seared scallops, and Atlantic salmon. GF pasta and pizza are available. Cheesecake, crème brulee, and chocolate mousse are available for dessert. ▪ *www.wheatfields.com*

Whole in the Wall   ✪ $$**LD**
Binghamton ▪ *(607) 722-5138*
43 S Washington St ▪ *Organic American* ▪ Extensive GF menu includes shrimp scampi, black bean chili, and mushroom soup. Manager Brian reports that the restaurant "sees GF diners all the time" and is accustomed to making GF modifications. ▪ *www.wholeinthewall.com*

Yorktown Pizza & Pasta   ★ $**LD**
Yorktown Heights ▪ *(914) 962-0096*
2013 Crompond Rd ▪ *Pizza* ▪ GF pizza is available. Manager Joe reports that they can also prepare other GF items, like grilled chicken and salads. Confirm timeliness of this information before dining in.

NORTH CAROLINA

ASHEVILLE

Bonefish Grill   📖
Asheville ■ *(828) 298-6530*
105 River Hills Rd

Carrabba's Italian Grill   📖
Asheville ■ *(828) 281-2300*
10 Buckstone Pl

Corner Kitchen, The $$$**BLD**
Asheville ■ *(828) 274-2439*
3 Boston Way ■ *American* ■ Manager
Tracy reports that GF diners are welcome.
Alert a server, who will alert the kitchen.
All kitchen staff has been trained on
the GF diet. Meat and fish dishes can be
modified to be GF. Confirm timeliness of
this information before dining in. ■ *www.
thecornerkitchen.com*

Doc Chey's Asian Kitchen   ✪★ ¢**LD**
Asheville ■ *(828) 252-8220*
37 Biltmore Ave ■ *Asian* ■ GF menu in-
cludes thai fried rice, Indian curry, tomato
ginger noodles, and Vietnamese prawn
salad, among other things. GF rice noodles
are available. Manager Tyler recommends
alerting a server, who can assure that the
GF meal is prepared properly. ■ *www.doc-
cheys.com*

Earth Fare Market   ★ ¢**S**
Asheville ■ *(828) 210-0100*
1856 Hendersonville Rd
Asheville ■ *(828) 253-7656*
66 Westgate Pkwy ■ *Bakery* ■ GF desserts
like carrot cake, cupcakes, and brownies
are available. Crème brûlée is also available.
The bakery is located inside the Earth Fare
Market. ■ *www.earthfare.com*

Flying Frog Café $$$**D**
Asheville ■ *(828) 254-9411*
1 Battery Park Ave ■ *German & Indian* ■
Chef Jesse reports that they accommodate
GF diners very frequently, and all serv-
ers are "well-trained" on the GF diet. Two

of the owners are GF themselves, so the
restaurant is "pretty sensitive" to GF needs.
Alert a server, who will indicate GF options
and notify the kitchen. ■ *www.flyingfrog-
cafe.com*

Greenlife Grocery   ★ ¢**S**
Asheville ■ *(828) 254-5440*
70 Merrimon Ave ■ *Deli* ■ Deli manager
Sean reports that there are GF soups and
salads available. GF bread is available for
sandwiches. GF desserts include chocolate
soufflé cake, pot de crème, Swedish cream,
and more. Located within the Greenlife
Grocery store. ■ *www.greenlifegrocery.com*

Laughing Seed Café   ✪ $**LD**
Asheville ■ *(828) 252-3445*
40 Wall St ■ *Vegetarian* ■ GF menu includes pomegranate grilled tempeh, whole
grain risotto, thai panang seitan curry, an
Indian thali plate, and more. ■ *www.laugh-
ingseed.com*

Mamacitas   ¢**LD**
Asheville ■ *(828) 255-8080*
77A Biltmore Ave ■ *Mexican* ■ Manager
James reports that the restaurant serves GF
diners "all the time." He notes that there is
very little hidden flour in their food, and
that the walk-through style of the restaurant allows GF diners to see their food
before they order. He recommends alerting
a server, who will indicate GF options.
Corn tortillas can be substituted for flour
tortillas, and most toppings are GF. Confirm timeliness of this information before
dining in. ■ *www.mamacitasgrill.com*

Mela $**LD**
Asheville ■ *(828) 225-8880*
70 N Lexington Ave ■ *Indian* ■ Manager
Amanda reports that GF diners are "pretty
safe" at the restaurant. She notes that all
servers are GF aware, and the restaurant
has an internal list of the few menu items
(mostly naan breads) that are not GF. ■
www.melaasheville.com

Noodle Shop, The   ★ $**LD**
Asheville ■ *(828) 250-9898*

3 SW Pack Sq ▪ *Asian Fusion* ▪ GF rice noodles are available. Manager Alan reports that most of the servers are veterans, so they will be able to indicate which sauces are GF.

Outback Steakhouse   📖
Asheville ▪ *(828) 252-4510*
30 Tunnel Rd

P.F. Chang's China Bistro   📖
Asheville ▪ *(828) 681-2975*
26 Schenck Pkwy

Piazza   ★ $LD
Asheville ▪ *(828) 298-7224*
4 Olde Eastwood Vil Blvd ▪ *Pizza* ▪ GF pasta and pizza are available. Owner Reza notes that nearly all entrées on the menu are GF. For dessert, they offer chocolate mousse and coconut macaroons. ▪ *www.piazzaeast.com*

Posana Café   100% $BLD
Asheville ▪ *(828) 505-3969*
1 Biltmore Ave ▪ *American* ▪ All menus are entirely GF. GF bread, pasta, beer, soy sauce, and hamburger buns are available, as are GF desserts like pies, cakes, and brownies. Some examples are campfire s'mores with sp'ice cream and spice chocolate pots de crème with cinnamon sauce. ▪ *www.posanacafe.com*

Rezaz $$LD
Asheville ▪ *(828) 277-1510*
28 Hendersonville Rd ▪ *Mediterranean* ▪ Manager John reports that the kitchen is "remarkable" at accommodating GF requests. Alert a server, who will ensure that any desired dish is prepared GF. John notes that reservations noting GF are always helpful. ▪ *www.rezaz.com*

Vinnie's   ★ $D
Asheville ▪ *(828) 253-1077*
641 Merrimon Ave ▪ *Italian* ▪ GF pasta is available. Manager Chris reports that GF diners "are always welcome." ▪ *www.vinniesitalian.com*

West End Bakery   ★ ¢S
Asheville ▪ *(828) 252-9378*
757 Haywood Rd ▪ *Bakery & Café* ▪ Non-dedicated bakery offering GF bread, muffins, cookies, cakes, and cupcakes. Homemade GF soups and salads are also available. Co-owner Krista advises calling ahead to order GF items, especially desserts. ▪ *www.westendbakery.com*

World's Best Carrot Cake   ★ $$$$$
Asheville ▪ *(828) 658-0809*
175 Weaverville Hwy ▪ *Bakery* ▪ GF carrot cake is available in regular and chocolate flavors. Cakes for special occasions can be ordered in advance. ▪ *www.worldsbestcarrotcake.com*

NORTH CAROLINA

CHARLOTTE

Aria Tuscan Grill $$$LD
Charlotte ▪ *(704) 376-8880*
100 N Tryon St ▪ *Italian* ▪ Manager Hope recommends alerting the staff upon arrival. She reports that the entire staff is trained to handle "allergies," and the chefs can always "create something" special. ▪ *www.dineatpietown.com*

Blue Restaurant & Bar   ✪★ $$$D
Charlotte ▪ *(704) 927-2583*
214 N Tryon St ▪ *Mediterranean* ▪ GF items marked on the regular menu include the duo of wild boar, yellow fin tuna, and grilled ribeye, among other things. GF beer and cake are available. ▪ *www.bluerestaurantandbar.com*

Bonefish Grill   📖
Charlotte ▪ *(704) 541-6659*
7520 Pineville Matthews Rd

BrickTop's   ✪ $$$LD
Charlotte ▪ *(704) 364-6255*

6401 Morrison Blvd ▪ Seafood & Steakhouse ▪ GF menu includes rotisserie
chicken, steak frites, ahi tuna salad, and
babyback ribs. The signature appetizer,
deviled eggs and bacon sausage, is also GF.
For dessert, they offer a hot fudge sundae. ▪
www.westendrestaurants.com

Capital Grille, The   📖
Charlotte ▪ (704) 348-1400
201 N Tryon St

Carrabba's Italian Grill   📖
Charlotte ▪ (704) 377-2458
1520 South Blvd

Del Frisco's Double Eagle Steak House
                                          📖
Charlotte ▪ (704) 552-5502
4725 Piedmont Row Dr

Earth Fare Market   ★ ¢S
Charlotte ▪ (704) 926-1201
12235 N Community House Rd
Charlotte ▪ (704) 749-5042
721 Governor Morrison St ▪ Bakery ▪ GF
desserts like chocolate and regular carrot cake are available. GF bread is also
available. Some other GF options may be
available, depending on the location. The
bakery is located inside the Earth Fare
Market. ▪ www.earthfare.com

Encore Bistro & Bar   ✪ $$$LD
Charlotte ▪ (704) 341-3651
9824 Rea Rd ▪ Bistro ▪ GF menu includes
chicken & bacon corn chowder, salt and
pepper tuna, ribs, and espresso coriander
crusted pork tenderloin, among other
things. ▪ www.encorebistro.com

Firebirds Wood Fired Grill   ✪ $$$LD
Charlotte ▪ (704) 366-3655
3920 Sharon Rd
Charlotte ▪ (704) 295-1919
6801 Northlake Mall Dr
Charlotte ▪ (704) 752-7979
7716 Rea Rd ▪ American ▪ GF menu
includes a variety of salads and a selection
of entrées. Examples include sirloin, filet
mignon, ribs, and lobster tail. All locations

report that servers are trained to alert the
chef when a customer orders from the GF
menu. ▪ www.firebirdsrockymountaingrill.
com

Harper's Restaurant   ✪ $$LD
Charlotte ▪ (704) 366-6688
6518 Fairview Rd ▪ American ▪ GF menu
is extensive. Restaurant notes that all items
are prepared from scratch, so GF diners are
easily accommodated. ▪ www.harpersres-
taurants.com

La Paz $LD
Charlotte ▪ (704) 372-4168
1910 South Blvd ▪ Mexican ▪ Manager
Trace reports that the restaurant serves
GF diners frequently. He notes that the
100% corn chips are fried in their own
fryer, making them GF. He further notes
that while most servers are knowledgeable
about the restaurant's GF offerings, diners
are welcome to ask for a manager. ▪ www.
lapaz.com

Maggiano's Little Italy   ★ $$$LD
Charlotte ▪ (704) 916-2300
4400 Sharon Rd ▪ Italian ▪ GF pasta is
available. Call individual locations to inquire about additional GF options. ▪ www.
maggianos.com

Melting Pot, The   📖
Charlotte ▪ (704) 548-2432
230 E W T Harris Blvd
Charlotte ▪ (704) 334-4400
901 S Kings Dr

New South Kitchen & Bar $$LD
Charlotte ▪ (704) 541-9990
8140 Providence Rd ▪ American ▪ Owner
and chef Chris reports that nearly all menu
items are GF or can be made GF. Alert a
server upon arrival and mention the word
"allergy." All servers are trained to handle
food "allergies," so they will provide menu
guidance. GF desserts include crème brûlée
and sorbet. ▪ www.newsouthkitchen.com

Original Pancake House, The   ★ ¢BL
Charlotte ▪ (704) 553-8364

4736 Sharon Rd
Charlotte ▪ (704) 372-7099
915 Charlottetowne Ave ▪ Breakfast ▪
GF pancakes are available. Select locations may serve other GF items. Call a specific location to inquire. ▪ www.originalpancakehouse.com

Outback Steakhouse   📖
Charlotte ▪ (704) 598-7727
1015 Chancellor Park Dr
Charlotte ▪ (704) 333-0505
1412 East Blvd Ste A
Charlotte ▪ (704) 759-9575
8338 Pineville Matthews Rd

P.F. Chang's China Bistro   📖
Charlotte ▪ (704) 598-1927
10325 Perimeter Pkwy
Charlotte ▪ (704) 552-6644
6809 Phillips Place Ct Ste F

Pei Wei Asian Diner   📖
Charlotte ▪ (704) 543-1121
13855 Conlan Cir Ste J

Rí~Rá Irish Pub $LD
Charlotte ▪ (704) 333-5554
208 N Tryon St ▪ Irish Pub ▪ Ask for the "Allergen Chart," which has a "Celiac" column. This column contains items that are GF or can be modified to be GF. ▪ www.rira.com

Shane's Rib Shack   📖
Charlotte ▪ (704) 503-3113
440 Mccullough Dr
Charlotte ▪ (704) 509-6553
9330 Center Lake Dr

Texas Land & Cattle Steak House   📖
Charlotte ▪ (704) 503-3830
517 University Center Blvd

Bella Monica Italian Restaurant
✪ ★ $LD
Raleigh ▪ (919) 881-9778
3121-103 Edwards Mill Rd ▪ Italian ▪ GF menu includes a variety of salads, sausage parmigiana, stuffed shells, and more. GF pizza and flatbreads are available, as are GF desserts such as chocolate amore and mascarpone panna cotta. Manager John notes that they also have GF specials not listed on the menu. ▪ www.bellamonica.com

Bombay Kitchen $LD
Raleigh ▪ (919) 862-0506
6016 Falls Of Neuse Rd ▪ Indian ▪ The manager reports that she can accommodate GF diners "with no problem at all." She notes that lentil bread, rice cakes, several soups, and most entrées are naturally GF. Alert a server upon arrival. ▪ www.bombaykitchen.com

Bonefish Grill   📖
Raleigh ▪ (919) 782-5127
4421 Six Forks Rd Ste 122

Carino's Italian   📖
Durham ▪ (919) 405-1316
6709 Fayetteville Rd
Raleigh ▪ (919) 806-5524
8101 Brier Creek Pkwy

Carrabba's Italian Grill   📖
Durham ▪ (919) 401-5950
5312 New Hope Commons Extension
Raleigh ▪ (919) 871-0001
4821 Capital Blvd

Earth Fare Market   ★ ¢S
Raleigh ▪ (919) 433-1390
10341 Moncreiffe Rd ▪ Bakery ▪ GF breads, granola, cookies, s'mores cups, and more are available. The bakery does not make GF items in house, but they receive shipments of GF items twice monthly. The bakery

is located inside the Earth Fare Market. ▪ *www.earthfare.com*

Elmo's Diner   ¢**BLD**
Durham ▪ *(919) 416-3823*
776 9th St ▪ *American* ▪ Manager Mica of Carrboro and Manager Dan of Durham report that GF diners can be accommodated. Both note that it is best to alert a server upon arrival and to ask to speak with a manager for "more specific recommendations." Both also note that cross-contamination can be a concern, since all food is prepared on the same surfaces. ▪ *www.elmosdiner.com*

Firebirds Wood Fired Grill   ✪ $$$**LD**
Durham ▪ *(919) 544-6332*
8030 Renaissance Pkwy
Raleigh ▪ *(919) 788-8778*
4350 Lassiter At North Hills Ave ▪ *American* ▪ GF menu includes a variety of salads and a selection of entrées. Examples include sirloin, filet mignon, ribs, and lobster tail. Both locations report that servers are trained to alert the chef when a customer orders from the GF menu. ▪ *www.firebirdsrockymountaingrill.com*

Francesca's Dessert Caffe   ★ $$$$**S**
Durham ▪ *(919) 286-4177*
706B 9th St ▪ *Bakery & Café* ▪ GF chocolate raspberry decadence and mocha mousse, two flourless chocolate cakes, are available on a regular basis. These cakes can be bought whole or by the slice. ▪ *www.francescasdessertcaffe.com*

Lone Star Steakhouse & Saloon   📖
Durham ▪ *(919) 401-4800*
5307 New Hope Commons Extension
Raleigh ▪ *(919) 781-8400*
6512 Glenwood Ave

Maggiano's Little Italy   ★ $$**LD**
Durham ▪ *(919) 572-0070*
8030 Renaissance Pkwy ▪ *Italian* ▪ GF pasta is available. Call individual locations to inquire about additional GF options. ▪ *www.maggianos.com*

Melting Pot, The   📖
Durham ▪ *(919) 544-6358*
7011 Fayetteville Rd
Raleigh ▪ *(919) 878-0477*
3100 Wake Forest Rd

Mo's Diner   ★ $$**D**
Raleigh ▪ *(919) 856-9938*
306 E Hargett St ▪ *American* ▪ Owner Holly reports that nearly all menu items can be prepared GF. Some examples are the rack of lamb, pork tenderloin, and spicy shrimp and scallops. Confirm timeliness of this information before dining in. For dessert, they offer GF chocolate cake and various flavors of cheesecake. ▪ *www.mosdiner.net*

Outback Steakhouse   📖
Durham ▪ *(919) 493-2202*
3500 Mount Moriah Rd
Raleigh ▪ *(919) 790-0990*
3105 Capital Blvd
Raleigh ▪ *(919) 846-3848*
7500 Creedmoor Rd

P.F. Chang's China Bistro   📖
Durham ▪ *(919) 294-3131*
6801 Fayetteville Rd
Raleigh ▪ *(919) 787-7754*
4325 Glenwood Ave Ste 2089

Pei Wei Asian Diner   📖
Raleigh ▪ *(919) 484-4113*
10251 Little Briar Creek Ln Ste 112
Raleigh ▪ *(919) 227-3810*
4408 Falls Of Neuse Rd

Rockfish Seafood Grill   ✪ $**LD**
Durham ▪ *(919) 544-9220*
8030 Renaissance Pkwy ▪ *Seafood* ▪ Extensive GF menu includes ribs, salmon salad, chicken caesar and a variety of seafood dishes. ▪ *www.rockfishseafood.com*

Rosie's Plate   100% $**BLD**
Raleigh ▪ *(919) 833-0505*
701 N Person St ▪ *Deli* ▪ Dedicated GF deli offering chicken quesadillas, pork and portobello kebobs, and roasted veggie lasagna. Restaurant reports that only about half of

its menu is available on any given day, so specific orders should be placed one day in advance. Call ahead for pick up or delivery. ▪ *www.rosiesplate.com*

Shane's Rib Shack 📖
Raleigh ▪ *(919) 850-9900*
5811 Poyner Village Pkwy

Twisted Noodles ★ $LD
Durham ▪ *(919) 489-9888*
4201 University Dr ▪ *Thai* ▪ Veteran Server Pranee reports that many menu items are naturally GF. The restaurant uses a "thin" soy sauce that is reportedly GF. She recommends alerting a server upon arrival, but cautions that not all servers are familiar with the GF diet. Ask the server to speak with the chef. GF customers should order their food without oyster sauce and without hoisin sauce. Confirm timeliness of this information before dining in. ▪ *www.twistednoodles.com*

Z Pizza ★ $LD
Raleigh ▪ *(919) 844-0065*
9630 Falls Of Neuse Rd ▪ *Pizza* ▪ GF pizza is available. ▪ *www.zpizza.com*

NORTH CAROLINA
ALL OTHER CITIES

Bento Box ★ $LD
Wilmington ▪ *(910) 509-0774*
1121 Military Cutoff Rd Ste L ▪ *Japanese* ▪ GF soy sauce is available, as are GF soy sheets, which can be used instead of seaweed in the restaurant's "signature" rolls. Restaurant reports that it is one of the only establishments in North Carolina carrying GF soy sheets. ▪ *www.bentoboxsushi.com*

Biaggi's Ristorante Italiano 📖
Cary ▪ *(919) 468-7229*
1060 Darrington Dr

Bonefish Grill 📖
Cary ▪ *(919) 677-1347*
2060 Renaissance Park Pl
Greensboro ▪ *(336) 851-8900*
2100 Koury Blvd
Matthews ▪ *(704) 845-8001*
10056 E Independence Blvd
Southern Pines ▪ *(910) 692-1131*
190 Partner Cir
Wilmington ▪ *(910) 313-1885*
4719 New Centre Dr Ste K
Winston Salem ▪ *(336) 724-4518*
300 S Stratford Rd

Bub O'Malley's ★ ¢S
Chapel Hill ▪ *(919) 942-6903*
157 E Rosemary St ▪ *Pub Food* ▪ GF beer is available.

Buca di Beppo 📖
Pineville ▪ *(704) 542-5146*
10915 Carolina Place Pkwy

Carino's Italian 📖
Kannapolis ▪ *(704) 782-9612*
2235 Roxie St NE

Carrabba's Italian Grill 📖
Apex ▪ *(919) 387-6336*
1201 Haddon Hall Dr
Arden ▪ *(828) 654-8411*
332 Rockwood Rd
Cary ▪ *(919) 467-9901*
1148 Kildaire Farm Rd
Concord ▪ *(704) 979-3224*
7900 Lyles Ln NW
Fayetteville ▪ *(910) 486-9300*
4209 Sycamore Dairy Rd
Greensboro ▪ *(336) 218-0623*
1653 New Garden Rd
Greensboro ▪ *(336) 323-6069*
3200 High Point Rd
Hickory ▪ *(828) 322-9032*
1954 13Th Avenue Dr SE
Huntersville ▪ *(704) 895-3080*
16408 Northcross Dr
Matthews ▪ *(704) 844-0464*
10400 E Independence Blvd
Wilmington ▪ *(910) 794-9094*
15 Van Campen Blvd

Winston Salem ▪ *(336) 831-0580*
587 S Stratford Rd

Chatham's Street Café   ✪★ $$LD
Cary ▪ *(919) 380-1193*
140 E Chatham St ▪ *American Regional*
▪ GF items marked on the menu include soups, sandwiches on GF bread, salads, steaks, shrimp and grits, and shrimp and rice. GF bread is available. ▪ *www.chatham-streetcafe.com*

Colington Café, The $$$D
Kill Devil Hills ▪ *(252) 480-1123*
1029 Colington Rd ▪ *American* ▪ Chef Jeff reports that "plenty of people" request GF meals. He advises alerting a server and recommends being specific about GF needs. He also notes that all staff members are well-versed in menu ingredients. ▪ *www.colingtoncafe.com*

Earth Fare Market   ★ ¢S
Boone ▪ *(828) 263-8138*
178 W King St
Greensboro ▪ *(336) 369-0190*
2965 Battleground Ave ▪ *Bakery* ▪ GF breads are available at the bakery. Customers can buy loaves of GF bread, then have the bakery cut it and make sandwiches from it. ▪ *www.earthfare.com*

Elmo's Diner   ¢BLD
Carrboro ▪ *(919) 929-2909*
200 N Greensboro St ▪ *American* ▪ Manager Mica of Carrboro and Manager Dan of Durham report that GF diners can be accommodated. Both note that it is best to alert a server upon arrival and to ask to speak with a manager for "more specific recommendations." Both also note that cross-contamination can be a concern, since all food is prepared on the same surfaces. ▪ *www.elmosdiner.com*

Firebirds Wood Fired Grill   ✪ $$$LD
Winston Salem ▪ *(336) 659-3973*
1215 Creekshire Way ▪ *American* ▪ GF menu includes a variety of salads and a selection of entrées. Examples include sirloin, filet mignon, ribs, and lobster tail. Both

locations report that servers are trained to alert the chef when a customer orders from the GF menu. ▪ *www.firebirdsrockymoun-taingrill.com*

Harper's Restaurant   ✪ $LD
Greensboro ▪ *(336) 299-8850*
601 Friendly Center Rd
Pineville ▪ *(704) 541-5255*
11059 Carolina Place Pkwy ▪ *American* ▪ GF menu includes starters, salads, sides, and entrées such as hickory grilled sirloin, Texas beef brisket, and slow smoked Danish baby back ribs. ▪ *www.harpersrestau-rants.com*

Kelly's Outer Banks Restaurant and Tavern $$$D
Nags Head ▪ *(252) 441-4116*
2316 S Croatan Hwy ▪ *American Regional* ▪ Restaurant reports that GF diners must call ahead to speak with a chef. The chef will arrange for a GF meal to be available at the time of the reservation. They note that they have little experience serving GF diners. ▪ *www.kellysrestaurant.com*

Lone Star Steakhouse & Saloon   📖
Arden ▪ *(828) 684-5506*
341 Rockwood Rd
Clayton ▪ *(919) 359-6201*
13049 US 70 Business Hwy W
Fayetteville ▪ *(910) 867-2222*
1800 Skibo Rd
Greensboro ▪ *(336) 855-1228*
3025 High Point Rd
Jacksonville ▪ *(910) 938-3700*
408 Western Blvd
Knightdale ▪ *(919) 217-7070*
6601 Knightdale Blvd
Monroe ▪ *(704) 291-2525*
2841 W Highway 74
Mooresville ▪ *(704) 799-3262*
668 River Hwy
Mount Airy ▪ *(336) 789-0142*
1905 Woodland Dr
Pineville ▪ *(704) 543-1922*
10610 Centrum Pkwy Ste A
Roanoke Rapids ▪ *(252) 537-7481*
270 Premier Blvd

Rocky Mount ▪ (252) 451-7827
920 N Wesleyan Blvd
Salisbury ▪ (704) 647-9991
215 Bendix Dr
Southern Pines ▪ (910) 693-8080
10820 S US Highway 15 501
Statesville ▪ (704) 871-2929
700 Sullivan Rd
Winston Salem ▪ (336) 760-9720
504 Hanes Mall Blvd

Melting Pot, The   📖
Greensboro ▪ (336) 545-6233
2924 Battleground Ave
Wilmington ▪ (910) 256-1187
885 Town Center Dr

New Town Bistro and Bar   ★ $$**LD**
Winston Salem ▪ (336) 659-8062
420 Jonestown Rd ▪ American ▪ Owner
Kyle reports that the restaurant "has done
some GF dinners." The chef will speak with
GF diners. Kyle notes that patrons should
allow extra time when a GF item is being
prepared. Shrimp grits may be made GF,
and GF pasta is available. ▪ *www.newtown-
bistro.com*

Outback Steakhouse   📖
Blowing Rock ▪ (828) 295-6283
PO Box 365
Burlington ▪ (336) 586-0330
2735 Longpine Rd
Cary ▪ (919) 460-1770
1289 Kildaire Farm Rd
Fayetteville ▪ (910) 487-9200
505 N Mcpherson Church Rd
Garner ▪ (919) 329-9211
845 US Highway 70 W
Gastonia ▪ (704) 866-4533
501 N New Hope Rd
Goldsboro ▪ (919) 751-9991
2617 N Park Dr
Greensboro ▪ (336) 282-6283
1611 Westover Ter
Greensboro ▪ (336) 294-5456
2105 Four Seasons Blvd
Greenville ▪ (252) 321-8444
606 Greenville Blvd SW
Hendersonville ▪ (828) 692-1109

250 Mitchelle Dr
Hickory ▪ (828) 328-6283
1435 13Th Avenue Dr SE
High Point ▪ (336) 885-6283
260 E Parris Ave
Huntersville ▪ (704) 895-1888
16400 Northcross Dr
Jacksonville ▪ (910) 938-8900
1045 Western Blvd
Lumberton ▪ (910) 735-0888
223 Wintergreen Dr
Matthews ▪ (704) 845-2222
9623 E Independence Blvd
Morehead City ▪ (252) 247-6283
4937 Arendell St
Nags Head ▪ (252) 441-3981
5220 S Croatan Hwy
New Bern ▪ (252) 672-9394
111 Howell Rd
Rocky Mount ▪ (252) 451-7800
210 Gateway Blvd
Salisbury ▪ (704) 637-1980
1020 E Innes St
Smithfield ▪ (919) 989-3056
911 Industrial Park Dr
Southern Pines ▪ (910) 695-7000
100 Southern Rd
Statesville ▪ (704) 838-1818
979 Folger Dr
Wilmington ▪ (910) 791-5335
302 S College Rd
Winston Salem ▪ (336) 760-4329
505 Highland Oaks Dr

P.F. Chang's China Bistro   📖
Greensboro ▪ (336) 291-1302
3338 W Friendly Ave

Pamlico Jacks Restaurant $$**D**
Nags Head ▪ (252) 441-2637
6708 S. Croatan Hwy. ▪ Modern American ▪ General Manager Tom reports that
they are happy to accommodate GF diners,
but their GF options change daily. They will
always have a GF entrée available, and they
will usually have a GF dessert available. ▪
www.pamlicojacks.com

Pei Wei Asian Diner

Cary ▪ **(919) 337-0050**
1107 Walnut St

Phil's BBQ Pit $**LD**

Black Mountain ▪ **(828) 669-3606**
701 Nc Highway 9 ▪ *Barbeque* ▪ Manager
Travis reports that they have one GF diner
who "comes in regularly." He notes that
there is an open kitchen and that customers
can hear their orders being called, which
helps to prevent misunderstandings about
GF. The BBQ sauce is GF.

Shane's Rib Shack

Greensboro ▪ **(336) 272-4696**
1410 Westover Ter
Greensboro ▪ **(336) 292-7272**
4217 W Wendover Ave Ste A

Stoney Knob Café $**LD**

Weaverville ▪ **(828) 645-3309**
337 Merrimon Ave ▪ *Modern American*
▪ Restaurant reports that they serve GF
diners "often." Alert a server upon arrival.
While not all servers are equally trained on
the GF diet, they are trained to confer with
the chef about GF options. They note that
every GF order gets an allergy flag so that
the kitchen knows to use separate preparation utensils. The popular shrimp saganaki
and the paella can be modified to be GF.
Confirm timeliness of this information before dining in. ▪ *www.stoneyknobcafe.com*

T. DiStefano's Bakery and Coffee Shop
                                        ★ $$

Burlington ▪ **(336) 447-4606**
2280 S Church St ▪ *Coffee & Café* ▪ GF
cakes, cookies and brownies are available
with advanced notice of 24 hours. This location is the only one that reports making
GF items.

Texas Land & Cattle Steak House

Concord ▪ **(704) 510-0021**
7779 Lyles Ln NW
Winston Salem ▪ **(336) 760-9066**
1110 Creekshire Way

Top of the Hill $$$**LD**

Chapel Hill ▪ **(919) 929-8676**
100 E Franklin St ▪ *American* ▪ Manager
Griffin reports that most menu items can
be modified to be GF. Alert a server upon
arrival. Servers are knowledgeable about
the GF diet, so they can recommend the
best and safest dishes. ▪ *www.topofthehill-
restaurant.com*

Twisted Noodles   ¢**LD**

Chapel Hill ▪ **(919) 933-9933**
1800 E Franklin St ▪ *Thai* ▪ Manager Vijay
reports that the restaurant can accommodate GF diners. Alert a server upon arrival.
All servers are GF aware and will specifically note GF when sending orders to the
kitchen. Vijay also notes that most dishes
are GF if they are cooked without soy
sauce. Confirm timeliness of this information before dining in. ▪ *www.twisted-
noodles.com*

Xios $$**LD**

Apex ▪ **(919) 363-5288**
800 W Williams St ▪ *Greek* ▪ Restaurant
reports that GF diners can "certainly" be
accommodated. GF items on the menu
include lamb chicken, shrimp souvlaki, and
several spreads. Alert a server upon arrival.
▪ *www.xioscafe.com*

Z Pizza   ★ ¢**LD**

Cary ▪ **(919) 465-9009**
96 Cornerstone Dr ▪ *Pizza* ▪ GF crusts,
sauces, and meats are available for 10 inch
pizzas. ▪ *www.zpizza.com*

Zoez Pizza Subs & More   ★ $$**LD**

Reidsville ▪ **(336) 616-0978**
1627 Freeway Dr ▪ *Pizza* ▪ GF pizza is
available.

NORTH DAKOTA

Carino's Italian 📖
Bismarck ▪ (701) 258-5655
1601 W Century Ave
Fargo ▪ (701) 282-2922
4410 17th Ave SW

Dempsey's Public House ★ ¢D
Fargo ▪ (701) 235-5913
226 Broadway N ▪ Pub Food ▪ GF beer
is available. Manager Naomi reports that
though GF food options are limited, the
restaurant is willing to "work with" GF
diners. Possible GF meals include sandwich
meat over a bed of lettuce and vegetables. ▪
www.dempseyspublichouse.com

Doolittles Woodfire Grill $$LD
Fargo ▪ (701) 478-2200
2112 25th St S ▪ Fusion ▪ GF menu notes
which dishes are GF and provides ordering
instructions. GF menu includes prime rib
french dip, roasted pork, grilled chicken
breast, and baby red potatoes. ▪ www.doo-
littlesrestaurants.com

Ground Round 📖
Bismarck ▪ (701) 223-0000
526 S 3rd St
Fargo ▪ (701) 280-2288
2902 13Th Ave S
Grand Forks ▪ (701) 775-4646
2800 32nd Ave S
Minot ▪ (701) 838-3500
2110 Burdick Expy E

HoDo Restaurant ★ $$$D
Fargo ▪ (701) 478-1000
101 Broadway N ▪ Fusion ▪ Sous-chef Josh
reports that they can "certainly" accommodate GF diners. He explains that the menu
is "broken down" so that they can easily
substitute GF items into dishes. GF crackers are available for the cheese plate. GF
beer is available. ▪ www.hoteldonaldson.com

Kic Bac Bar & Grill ★ ¢LD
Cogswell ▪ (701) 724-3619
255 4th Ave ▪ American ▪ GF beer is available. Owner Teresa reports that they also
have a limited selection of GF entrées to
choose from. Alert a server, who will suggest GF options.

Lone Star Steakhouse & Saloon 📖
Fargo ▪ (701) 282-6642
4328 13Th Ave S

Nine Dragons Restaurant ★ ¢LD
Fargo ▪ (701) 232-2411
4525 17th Ave S ▪ Chinese ▪ GF soy sauce
is available. Restaurant has an internal
list of GF options that they let GF customers use. Potential GF options include
chow mein, fried rice, green pepper steak,
chicken with mushrooms or peapods, and
chicken with cashews. Confirm timeliness of this information before dining in. ▪
www.9dragonsrestaurant.com

Oakes American Legion ★ $LD
Oakes ▪ (701) 742-2411
22 N 5th St ▪ American ▪ GF beer is available.

Roost ★ $D
Ashley ▪ (701) 288-3228
118 1st Ave NW ▪ American ▪ GF beer is
available.

Seven Fires Grill ★ $LD
Hankinson ▪ (800) 325-6825
16849 102nd St SE ▪ American ▪ GF beer is
available in the lounge. Lounge reports that
diners can bring the beer to their dining
table from the lounge, or they can order
from a server in the restaurant. ▪ www.
dakotamagic.com

Speck's Bar ★ $D
Fargo ▪ (701) 232-0202
2611 Main Ave ▪ American ▪ GF beer is
sometimes available.

Spitfire Bar & Grill ★ $$LD
West Fargo ▪ (701) 478-8667
1660 13Th Ave E ▪ American ▪ GF beer is

available. ▪ *www.spitfirebarandgrillfargo.
com*

Timber Lodge Steakhouse   ✪ $$$D
Fargo ▪ *(701) 282-8990*
1111 38th St SW ▪ *Steakhouse* ▪ GF menu
includes prime rib, rainbow trout, walleye
filet, Atlantic salmon, and more. ▪ *www.
timberlodgesteakhouse.com*

Twisted Bakery, The   ★ ¢S
Dickinson ▪ *(701) 483-4726*
1470 East Villard Street ▪ *Bakery* ▪ Non-
dedicated bakery offering a wide variety
of GF products, including baked goods,
frozen items, and dry mixes. Examples
include a pie crust mix, a pizza crust mix,
banana chocolate chip muffins, and molas-
ses cookies. ▪ *www.qualityglutenfree.com*

Xtreme Pizza Kitchen   ★ $LD
Fargo ▪ *(701) 298-0420*
1404 33rd St SW ▪ *Pizza* ▪ GF pizza is
available for delivery, take out, and dining
in. Any of the restaurant's numerous top-
pings can be added to the GF crust. The
homemade GF crust can also be purchased
for "take-&-bake." ▪ *www.xtremepizza-
kitchen.com*

OHIO

CINCINNATI

Blue Point Grill $$$LD
Cleveland ▪ *(216) 875-7827*
700 W Saint Clair Ave ▪ *Seafood* ▪ Chef
Mark reports that they see a lot of customers with "every kind of allergy." He notes
that about half of the menu is naturally GF,
while other items can be prepared GF. They
offer a flourless chocolate torte for dessert.
Confirm timeliness of this information
before dining in. ▪ *www.bluepointgrille.com*

Bonefish Grill   📖
Cincinnati ▪ *(513) 321-5222*
2737 Madison Rd
Cleveland ▪ *(216) 520-2606*
6150 Rockside Pl

Buca di Beppo   📖
Cincinnati ▪ *(513) 396-7673*
2635 Edmondson Rd

Carrabba's Italian Grill   📖
Cincinnati ▪ *(513) 233-0999*
7500 Beechmont Ave

Fire Food and Drink $$$LD
Cleveland ▪ *(216) 921-3473*
13220 Shaker Sq ▪ *Modern American* ▪
Chef Jeremy reports that they serve GF
diners regularly. He notes that most sauces
and proteins are GF, as they are prepared
without flour. He recommends alerting a
server upon arrival. Servers will speak with
the chef if they have any questions about
GF modifications. ▪ *www.firefoodanddrink.
com*

First Watch - The Daytime Café 📖
Cincinnati ▪ *(513) 489-6849*
11301 Montgomery Rd
Cincinnati ▪ *(513) 531-7430*
2692 Madison Rd
Cincinnati ▪ *(513) 721-4744*
700 Walnut St
Cincinnati ▪ *(513) 231-4620*
7625 Beechmont Ave
Cincinnati ▪ *(513) 891-0088*
8118 Montgomery Rd

Forkable Feast, A   ★ ¢LD
Cincinnati ▪ *(513) 871-8646*
3363 Madison Rd ▪ *Deli* ▪ GF bread for
sandwiches, bagels, pizza, beer, cheesecake,
blondies, and cupcakes are available. ▪
www.aforkablefeast.com

Maggiano's Little Italy   ★ $$$LD
Cincinnati ▪ *(513) 794-0670*
7875 Montgomery Rd ▪ *Italian* ▪ GF pasta
is available. Call individual locations to inquire about additional GF options. ▪ *www.
maggianos.com*

Melting Pot, The   📖
Cincinnati ▪ *(513) 530-5501*
11023 Montgomery Rd
Cleveland ▪ *(440) 356-8900*
3111 Westgate

Momocho $$D
Cleveland ▪ *(216) 694-2122*
1835 Fulton Rd ▪ *Modern Mexican* ▪
Manager Eric reports that they serve GF
diners "all the time." Alert a server upon
arrival. Most servers are trained on the GF
diet, but Eric notes that if they have any
questions, they will speak to the chef. He
recommends the pecan and pumpkin seed
crusted trout with a tarragon dressing,
which the chef makes a special GF sauce
for when serving GF diners. Confirm timeliness of this information before dining in.
▪ *www.momocho.com*

Outback Steakhouse   📖
Cincinnati ▪ *(513) 671-8200*
11790 Springfield Pike
Cincinnati ▪ *(513) 662-4900*
6168 Glenway Ave
Cincinnati ▪ *(513) 624-8181*
7731 5 Mile Rd
Cincinnati ▪ *(513) 793-5566*
8240 Montgomery Rd
Cincinnati ▪ *(513) 245-0900*
9880 Colerain Ave

P.F. Chang's China Bistro   📖
Cincinnati ▪ *(513) 531-4567*
2633 Edmondson Rd

Uno Chicago Grill   📖
Cincinnati ▪ *(513) 231-5357*
7578 Beechmont Ave

OHIO

COLUMBUS

Alana's Food and Wine $$$D
Columbus ▪ *(614) 294-6783*
2333 N High St ▪ *Modern American* ▪
Manager Kevin reports that the chef will
modify any menu item to be GF. He recommends making reservations noting GF and
providing "specifics" in advance. He adds
that the staff has a "keen understanding" of
the GF diet, and they are happy to accommodate it. ▪ *www.alanas.com*

Bon Vie $$LD
Columbus ▪ *(614) 416-0463*
4089 The Strand E ▪ *French Bistro* ▪ Chef
Allen reports that they can accommodate
GF diners without a problem. He notes
that chefs and servers are well-equipped to
handle GF diners, as "a dozen or so" come
in each week. Alert the server, who will
notify the chef. ▪ *www.bon-vie.com*

Bonefish Grill   📖
Columbus ▪ *(614) 436-0286*
1930 Polaris Pkwy

Buca di Beppo   📖
Columbus ▪ *(614) 621-3287*
343 N Front St

Cameron's American Bistro   ✪ $$D
Columbus ▪ *(614) 885-3663*
2185 W Dublin Granville Rd ▪ *Modern
American* ▪ GF menu includes sautéed
calamari, a variety of salads, steak frites,
hoisin glazed salmon, and roasted Indiana
duck with a honey chili glaze, among other
things. All sauces are thickened with cornstarch. Confirm timeliness of this information before dining in. GF desserts include
crème brûlée and lemon gratin. ▪ *www.
cameronsamericanbistro.com*

Cantina Laredo   📖
Columbus ▪ *(614) 781-1139*
8791 Lyra Dr

Cap City Fine Diner ⊛ $$LD
Columbus ▪ (614) 291-3663
1299 Olentangy River Rd
Columbus ▪ (614) 478-9999
1301 Stoneridge Dr ▪ American ▪ Extensive
GF menu includes salads and sandwiches,
as well as large plates like pan seared
salmon and balsamic chicken. For dessert,
they offer crème brûlée and upside down
banana cream pie. ▪ www.capcityfinediner.
com

Carrabba's Italian Grill 📖
Columbus ▪ (614) 880-2426
8460 Lyra Dr

Columbus Brewing Company $$LD
Columbus ▪ (614) 464-2739
525 Short St ▪ Fusion ▪ Chef Brian reports
that they accommodate GF diners "all
the time," and that servers are "definitely"
informed about the GF diet. He notes that
they can modify many menu items to be
GF. For dessert, they offer crème brûlée
and banana cream pie without the graham
crackers. ▪ www.columbusbrewingco.com

Columbus Fish Market ⊛ $$$LD
Columbus ▪ (614) 291-3474
1245 Olentangy River Road
Columbus ▪ (614) 410-3474
40 Hutchinson Avenue ▪ Seafood ▪
Extensive GF menu includes New Orleans
"Voodoo" BBQ shrimp, seared Hawaiian
ahi tuna, oysters, cedar plank salmon, San
Francisco cioppino, the "Fish Market" trio,
and Chilean sea bass. Vanilla bean crème
brulee is available for dessert. ▪ www.
columbusfishmarket.com

Faculty Club ⊛ $LD
Columbus ▪ (614) 292-2262
181 S Oval Dr ▪ American ▪ Catering
Manager Liz reports that the menu changes
quarterly, but there are always GF options
available. The restaurant is accessible only
to members of Ohio State University's
Faculty Club and their guests. Dinner is
served on Thursdays only. ▪ www.ohio-
statefacultyclub.com

First Watch - The Daytime Café 📖
Columbus ▪ (614) 846-2738
2103 Polaris Pkwy
Columbus ▪ (614) 538-9866
3144 Kingsdale Ctr
Columbus ▪ (614) 475-8512
4770 Morse Rd
Columbus ▪ (614) 228-7554
496 S High St

Giuseppe's Ritrovo ★ $$LD
Columbus ▪ (614) 235-4300
2268 E Main St ▪ Italian ▪ GF pasta is available. ▪ www.giuseppesritrovo.com

Lindey's Restaurant $$$LD
Columbus ▪ (614) 228-4343
169 E Beck St ▪ Bistro ▪ Chef John reports
that the staff is "very familiar" with the
GF diet, as they serve GF diners "at least a
couple of times a night." He notes that any
unseasoned steaks can be prepared GF,
and for dessert, GF diners can order crème
brûlée without the cookie. Confirm timeliness of this information before dining in. ▪
www.lindeys.com

Lone Star Steakhouse & Saloon 📖
Columbus ▪ (614) 853-1000
1620 Georgesville Square Dr

M ⊛ $$$D
Columbus ▪ (614) 629-0000
2 Miranova Pl ▪ Modern American ▪ Manager Amanda reports that GF diners are
welcome and that the chef can prepare GF
meals. GF menu items are "always available," and the kitchen is GF aware. Reservations noting GF are highly recommended. ▪
www.matmiranova.com

Martini ⊛ $$$D
Columbus ▪ (614) 224-8259
445 N High St ▪ Italian ▪ GF menu includes a rack of lamb, veal martini, chicken
piccata, and antipasto. Hostess Samantha
reports that they get "quite a few" GF diners. ▪ www.martinimodernitalian.com

Melting Pot, The 📖
Columbus ▪ (614) 476-5500
4014 Townsfair Way

Mitchell's Fish Market ✪ $$$LD
Columbus ▪ (614) 291-3474
1245 Olentangy River Rd
Columbus ▪ (614) 410-3474
40 Hutchinson Ave ▪ Seafood ▪ Extensive GF menu includes pan-roasted wild blue mussels, blackened salmon spinach salad, grilled shrimp and scallop skewers, Shanghai seafood sampler, lobster tail, filet mignon, and live Maine lobster. Mini crème brulee is available for dessert. ▪ www.mitchellsfishmarket.com

Mitchell's Ocean Club $$$$D
Columbus ▪ (614) 416-2582
4002 Easton Sta ▪ Seafood & Steakhouse ▪ Manager Kirk reports that GF diners come in "all the time." The chef is aware of Celiac disease and different ways to accommodate it. Upon request, a manager will stop by the table and speak about GF options. ▪ www.mitchellsoceanclub.com

Mitchell's Steakhouse $$$$D
Columbus ▪ (614) 888-2467
1408 Polaris Pkwy
Columbus ▪ (614) 621-2333
45 N 3rd St ▪ Steakhouse ▪ Both locations report that GF diners are "absolutely" welcome. Bartender Mark of the 3rd St location and Server Molly of the Polaris Parkway location recommend alerting a server upon arrival. They note that servers are trained on the GF diet, but they can also get information from the chefs. ▪ www.mitchellssteakhouse.com

Molly Woo's Asian Bistro ✪ $LD
Columbus ▪ (614) 985-9667
1500 Polaris Pkwy ▪ Asian Fusion ▪ GF menu includes various sushi & maki rolls, black pepper steak, firecracker shrimp, and the thai seafood medley, among other things. ▪ www.mollywoos.com

Outback Steakhouse 📖
Columbus ▪ (614) 326-1605

2704 Bethel Rd
Columbus ▪ (614) 755-9926
6000 E Main St

P.F. Chang's China Bistro 📖
Columbus ▪ (614) 416-4100
4040 Townsfair Way

Pattycake Bakery ★ ¢S
Columbus ▪ (614) 784-2253
3009 N High St ▪ Bakery ▪ GF items are always available, though not every GF item is available all the time. GF buckeye bars, cheesecake, truffles, cookies, and cupcakes are some of the items that may be available. Special orders should be placed 48 hours in advance. ▪ www.pattycakeveganbakery.com

Pei Wei Asian Diner 📖
Columbus ▪ (614) 985-4845
2050 Polaris Pkwy
Columbus ▪ (614) 418-9825
4155 Morse Xing

Pistacia Vera ✪ ¢S
Columbus ▪ (614) 220-9070
541 S 3rd St ▪ Desserterie & Bakery ▪ Non-dedicated bakery offering GF nougat, toffees, flourless chocolate cake, meringues, macaroons, and truffles. Manager Kelly reports that all GF items are marked on the tags, and that the staff is very GF aware. ▪ www.pistachiosweets.com

Shane's Rib Shack 📖
Columbus ▪ (614) 436-9600
1522 Gemini Pl

Smith & Wollensky $$$$LD
Columbus ▪ (614) 416-2400
4145 The Strand ▪ Steakhouse ▪ Manager Brian reports that they serve GF diners "once in a while." He notes that the restaurant has an internal allergy listnoting which menu items are and are not GF. He recommends reservations noting GF, so that the server can have the allergy list ready beforehand. ▪ www.smithandwollensky.com

Z Pizza ★ $$LD
Columbus ▪ (614) 299-3289

945 N High St ▪ Pizza ▪ GF pizza is available. ▪ *www.zpizza.com*

OHIO

ALL OTHER CITIES

Altieri's Pizza   ✪★ ₵LD
Stow ▪ *(330) 686-6860*
3291 Kent Rd ▪ Pizza ▪ GF items are marked on the menu. GF pizza and pasta are available. Meals are available for carry out only. ▪ *www.altierispizza.com*

Avalanche Pizza   ★ $$LD
Athens ▪ *(740) 594-4664*
329 E State St ▪ Pizza ▪ GF pizza is available. ▪ *www.avalanchepizza.net*

Biaggi's Ristorante Italiano   📖
Perrysburg ▪ *(419) 872-6100*
1320 Levis Commons Blvd

Bistro of Green   ✪★ $$$LD
Uniontown ▪ *(330) 896-1434*
3459 Massillon Rd ▪ Modern American ▪ GF menu includes steamed mussels, shrimp and feta, Santa Fe chicken salad, and chicken and asparagus alfredo. GF pasta is available. ▪ *www.thebistroofgreen.com*

Bonefish Grill   📖
Dayton ▪ *(937) 428-0082*
2818 Miamisburg Centerville Rd
Dublin ▪ *(614) 789-3474*
5712 Frantz Rd
West Chester ▪ *(513) 755-2303*
7710 Voice Of America Center Dr

Buca di Beppo   📖
Strongsville ▪ *(440) 846-6262*
16677 Southpark Ctr
Westlake ▪ *(440) 356-2276*
23575 Detroit Rd
Worthington ▪ *(614) 848-8466*
60 E Wilson Bridge Rd

Cabin Club Steakhouse, The $$$$LD
Westlake ▪ *(440) 899-7111*
30651 Detroit Rd ▪ Steakhouse ▪ Manager Sherry reports that they serve GF diners "very often." She notes that there are internal lists of all non-GF foods posted in the kitchen. All servers are trained on which menu items are the best options for GF diners, and they will ask a chef if they are unsure whether or not a menu item is GF. ▪ *www.hrcleveland.com*

Carrabba's Italian Grill   📖
Brooklyn ▪ *(216) 898-5790*
5030 Tiedeman Rd
Canton ▪ *(330) 966-2426*
6560 Strip Ave NW
Hilliard ▪ *(614) 771-1653*
3949 Trueman Blvd
Mason ▪ *(513) 339-0900*
5152 Merten Dr
Maumee ▪ *(419) 861-2200*
3405 Briarfield Blvd
Poland ▪ *(330) 629-2356*
1320 Boardman Poland Rd
Washington Township ▪ *(937) 438-9690*
900 Miamisburg Centerville Rd
Westlake ▪ *(440) 250-0880*
25054 Sperry Dr

Coppertop Baking Company   100% ₵S
Strongsville ▪ *(440) 342-1244*
20621 Royalton Rd ▪ Bakery ▪ Dedicated GF bakery offering a wide array of options, including pizza, pasta, hamburger buns, muffins, brownies, cakes, cookies, and more. The menu is updated and expanded at the beginning of each month.

Eat 'n Park   📖
Austintown ▪ *(330) 779-0410*
5451 Mahoning Ave
Boardman ▪ *(330) 758-1307*
8051 Market St
Cuyahoga Falls ▪ *(330) 923-4111*
200 Howe Ave
Elyria ▪ *(440) 324-3286*
1524 W River Rd N
Medina ▪ *(330) 723-6390*
1007 N Court St

Mentor ■ (440) 255-5300
7061 Chillicothe Rd
Parma ■ (216) 459-1517
2075 Snow Rd
Saint Clairsville ■ (740) 695-5507
50620 Valley Frontage Rd
Steubenville ■ (740) 266-6643
100 Mall Dr
Streetsboro ■ (330) 422-1601
9436 State Route 14
Warren ■ (330) 372-6610
2057 Wal Mart Dr NE
Willoughby ■ (440) 943-1050
6035 Som Center Rd

First Watch - The Daytime Café   📖
Dayton ■ (937) 435-3127
2824 Miamisburg Centerville Rd
Dublin ■ (614) 799-2774
6768 Perimeter Loop Rd
Fairborn ■ (937) 431-9150
2614A Colonel Glenn Hwy
Fairlawn ■ (330) 835-4076
3265 W Market St
Hilliard ■ (614) 876-4957
3800 Fishinger Blvd
Kettering ■ (937) 643-4077
4105 W Town And Country Rd
Mayfield Heights ■ (440) 684-1825
1431 Som Center Rd
Rocky River ■ (440) 333-3529
19340 Detroit Rd
Springdale ■ (513) 671-1740
80 W Kemper Rd
University Heights ■ (216) 321-1075
13950 Cedar Dr
West Chester ■ (513) 942-5100
9233 Floer Dr
Westlake ■ (440) 808-1082
168 Market St
Worthington ■ (614) 431-9040
116 Worthington Mall

Galaxy Restaurant, The $$**LD**
Wadsworth ■ (330) 334-3663
201 Park Center Dr ■ American ■ Chef Jeff
reports that they serve GF diners "regularly." All chefs are trained in GF cooking,
and all dishes are made from scratch. He

recommends asking the server to speak to
the kitchen staff about the best GF options.
■ www.thegalaxyrestaurant.com

Gluten-Free Bakeree, The   100% $$$
Bay Village ■ (216) 408-3070
29261 Inverness Dr ■ Bakery ■ Dedicated
GF bakery offering cookies, cakes, breads,
pizzas, and more. Everything is made to
order. Orders can be placed by phone or
online, and they must be placed at least 24
hours in advance. ■ www.glutenfreebakeree.
com

Gregory's Family Restaurant   ✪★ ¢**BL**
Canton ■ (330) 477-1296
2835 Whipple Ave NW ■ American ■ GF
menu features all day breakfast, including
pancakes. Owner Jean reports that they are
"ready to serve GF at any time." She notes
that many of the soups are GF, as are certain desserts such as rice pudding, peanut
butter cookies, and chocolate walnut cookies. ■ www.JeanniesCatering.com

Ground Round   📖
Toledo ■ (419) 478-5663
5806 Telegraph Rd

Holiday Baking Company Gluten-Free
Bakery   100% ¢**S**
Worthington ■ (614) 846-9300
1000 High St ■ Bakery ■ Dedicated GF
bakery offering "everyday staples" like
breads, buns, and crusts, as well as sweets
like cakes, muffins, and cookies. GF pastas
are also available. ■ www.holidaybaking-
company.com

Kathy's Creations   100% ¢**S**
Alliance ■ (330) 821-8183
2010 Crestview Ave ■ Bakery ■ Dedicated
GF bakery offering a wide selection of
baked goods, including hotdog buns, hamburger buns, muffins, cookies, cakes, pies,
and brownies. A variety of GF breads are
also available. ■ www.kathyscreationsbakery.
com

Kona Bistro   ✪★ $$**LD**
Oxford ■ (513) 523-0686

31 W High St ▪ American ▪ GF menu includes grilled salmon with honey pomegranate drizzle, coconut-crusted tilapia, sugar spiced organic tofu, grilled flatiron steak, and jambalaya, as well as peanut butter and nutella mousse for dessert. GF pasta and bread for sandwiches are also available. ▪ www.konabistro.com

Lone Star Steakhouse & Saloon 📖
Canton ▪ (330) 492-9777
4801 Dressler Rd NW
Dayton ▪ (937) 291-0711
251 N Springboro Pike
Dayton ▪ (937) 890-2100
6868 Miller Ln
Mason ▪ (513) 459-9191
9890 Escort Dr
Middletown ▪ (513) 424-7827
6780 Roosevelt Pkwy
Niles ▪ (330) 544-7000
5555 Youngstown Warren Rd
North Olmsted ▪ (440) 777-6522
24941 Country Club Blvd
Springfield ▪ (937) 324-8580
1661 W 1st St
Toledo ▪ (419) 861-7827
5640 Airport Hwy

Maggiano's Little Italy   ★ $$$ LD
Beachwood ▪ (216) 755-3000
26300 Cedar Rd Ste 1103 ▪ *Italian* ▪ GF pasta is available. Call individual locations to inquire about additional GF options. ▪ www.maggianos.com

Manchu Café   ✪★ $ LD
North Canton ▪ (330) 494-5889
5528 Dressler Rd NW ▪ *Chinese* ▪ GF menu includes cashew chicken, sweet and sour pork, General Tso's chicken, pepper steak, and rice noodles with pork, chicken, or shrimp. GF soy sauce and baked goods like peanut butter cookies are available. ▪ www.manchucafe.com

Melting Pot, The   📖
Dayton ▪ (937) 567-8888
453 Miamisburg Centerville Rd
Lyndhurst ▪ (216) 381-2700

24741 Cedar Rd
Sylvania ▪ (419) 885-6358
5839 Monroe St

Mitchell's Fish Market   ✪ $$$ LD
West Chester ▪ (513) 779-5292
9456 Water Front Dr
Woodmere ▪ (216) 765-3474
28601 Chagrin Blvd ▪ *Seafood* ▪ Extensive GF menu includes pan-roasted wild blue mussels, blackened salmon spinach salad, grilled shrimp and scallop skewers, Shanghai seafood sampler, lobster tail, filet mignon, and live Maine lobster. Mini crème brulee is available for dessert. ▪ www.mitchellsfishmarket.com

Mustard Seed Market & Café ✪★ $$ LD
Akron ▪ (330) 666-7333
3885 W Market St ▪ *American* ▪ GF menu items include spinach salad with strawberries, pizza, wraps, stir fry, bison burgers, and more. GF pizza, buns, and beer are available. Located in the Mustard Seed Market. ▪ www.mustardseedmarket.com

Old Spaghetti Factory, The   📖
Fairfield ▪ (513) 942-6620
6320 S Gilmore Rd

Olde Harbor Inn, The $$$ LD
Akron ▪ (330) 644-1664
562 Portage Lakes Dr ▪ *Seafood* ▪ Manager Steve reports that they serve GF diners "quite often." He recommends reservations noting GF, so that the servers and chefs can prepare in advance. Most menu items can be modified to be GF. ▪ www.theoldeharborinn.com

Organic Bliss Gluten Free Bakery
                                100% ¢ S
Toledo ▪ (419) 517-7799
3723 King Rd ▪ *Bakery* ▪ Dedicated GF bakery offering pizza crust, breads, cupcakes, cookies and many other treats. Baker Christie recommends ordering special orders 2-3 days in advance. ▪ www.organicblissmarket.com

Original Gino's Pizza   ★ $$LD
Maumee ▪ (419) 897-4466
449 W Dussel Dr
Northwood ▪ (419) 690-4466
2670 Woodville Rd
Perrysburg ▪ (419) 874-9170
26597 Dixie Hwy
Toledo ▪ (419) 269-4466
1280 W Alexis Rd
Toledo ▪ (419) 472-3567
3981 Monroe St
Toledo ▪ (419) 843-3567
5307 Monroe St ▪ Pizza ▪ GF pizza is available. GF baked goods are also available at selected locations. Call specific locations to inquire. ▪ www.originalginos.com

Original Pancake House, The   ★ ¢BL
Fairview Park ▪ (440) 333-5515
3000 Westgate
Woodmere ▪ (216) 292-7777
28700 Chagrin Blvd ▪ Breakfast ▪ GF pancakes are available. Select locations may serve other GF options. Call a specific location to inquire. ▪ www.originalpancakehouse.com

Outback Steakhouse   📖
Canton ▪ (330) 493-9515
4303 Whipple Ave NW
Centerville ▪ (937) 434-6522
101 E Alex Bell Rd
Copley ▪ (330) 665-4849
110 Montrose West Ave
Cuyahoga Falls ▪ (330) 928-9550
738 Howe Ave
Dayton ▪ (937) 454-1585
6800 Miller Ln
Findlay ▪ (419) 424-1510
930 Interstate Dr
Hilliard ▪ (614) 777-5433
1735 Hilliard Rome Rd
Independence ▪ (216) 520-3544
6100 Rockside Pl
Lyndhurst ▪ (440) 449-8557
5708 Mayfield Rd
Macedonia ▪ (330) 468-5032
8250 Macedonia Commons Blvd
Mason ▪ (513) 754-0601

2512 Kings Center Ct
Maumee ▪ (419) 891-3621
401 W Dussel Dr
Mentor ▪ (440) 205-9505
8595 Market St
Niles ▪ (330) 544-6774
5555 Youngstown Warren Rd
Ontario ▪ (419) 747-5646
820 N Lexington Springmill Rd
Parma ▪ (440) 842-6114
6950 Ridge Rd
Saint Clairsville ▪ (740) 699-0737
50575 Valley Frontage Rd
Sandusky ▪ (419) 609-9226
4920 Milan Rd
Toledo ▪ (419) 841-2313
5200 Monroe St
Troy ▪ (937) 332-7811
1801 Towne Park Dr
Westlake ▪ (440) 892-3445
24900 Sperry Dr
Youngstown ▪ (330) 629-2775
7000 Tiffany S

P.F. Chang's China Bistro   📖
Beachwood ▪ (216) 292-1411
26001 Chagrin Blvd
Dayton ▪ (937) 428-6085
2626 Miamisburg Centerville Rd
Dublin ▪ (614) 726-0070
6135 Parkcenter Cir
Fairlawn ▪ (330) 869-0560
3265 W Market St Ste 100A
Maumee ▪ (419) 878-8490
2300 Village Dr W Ste 140
West Chester ▪ (513) 779-5555
9435 Civic Centre Blvd

Pei Wei Asian Diner   📖
Dublin ▪ (614) 726-4190
7571 Sawmill Rd

Real Seafood Co.   ✪ $$$LD
Toledo ▪ (419) 697-5427
22 Main St ▪ Seafood ▪ GF menu includes stuffed salmon, friend gulf shrimp, fettuccine alfredo, and filet mignon. GF pasta is available. ▪ www.realseafoodcorestaurant.com

Sandy Chanty Seafood Restaurant
★ $$LD

Geneva On The Lake ▪ *(440) 415-1080*
5457 Lake Rd E ▪ *Seafood* ▪ GF bread, pasta, and beer are available. The restaurant will specially prepare GF sauces. Some GF options include lobster over rice pasta and crab patteze in a blanket of salmon served in a lobster sauce. ▪ *www.sandychanty.com*

Sinfully Gluten-Free
100% ¢S

Miamisburg ▪ *(937) 866-3000*
79 S Main St ▪ *Bakery & Café* ▪ Dedicated GF restaurant offering pizza, breads, shortbreads, brownies, cakes, and cookies. Manager Heather reports that baked goods rotate daily, so call a couple of days in advance to order something specific. ▪ *www.sinfullygf.com*

Soup Pot, The
✪★ ¢S

Solon ▪ *(440) 248-0996*
34376 Aurora Rd ▪ *Soup* ▪ The wide variety of GF options includes several soups, paninis, salads, and sweets. GF bread is available, as are GF chocolate chip cookies and GF cinnamon rolls. ▪ *www.thesouppot.com*

Stir Crazy
★ $$LD

Lyndhurst ▪ *(216) 381-7600*
25385 Cedar Rd ▪ *Asian Stir-Fry* ▪ Manager Michelle reports that they serve GF diners "very often." GF customers can just pick one of three GF sauces and any meat that is not marinated. Michelle recommends that GF diners use the stir fry "market," and she notes that GF sauces will sometimes take a few minutes to prepare. GF rice noodles are available. ▪ *www.stircrazy.com*

Sweet Shalom Tea Room
$$$$

Sylvania ▪ *(419) 297-9919*
8216 Erie St ▪ *Teahouse* ▪ Owner Kris reports that they serve GF diners "all the time." She recommends reservations noting GF, so the kitchen will have time to prepare. They will look at the current menu, "work with it," and "adapt it" to accommodate the GF diet. There are two seatings for tea, one at 11am and one at 2pm. ▪ *www.sweetshalomtearoom.com*

Tommy's PCR
✪★ ¢BLD

North Ridgeville ▪ *(440) 327-1212*
34441 Center Ridge Rd ▪ *American* ▪ GF menu includes ribs, nachos, chicken wings, and chicken fingers. GF pizza and beer are available, as are GF cheesy breadsticks and cinnamon sticks for dessert. ▪ *www.tommyspcr.com*

Tommy's Pizza and Chicken
✪★ ¢LD

Seven Hills ▪ *(216) 520-8888*
7729 Broadview Rd
Strongsville ▪ *(440) 878-9999*
17664 Pearl Rd ▪ *Italian-American* ▪ GF pizza is available in the 12-inch size, cooked or on a "take-&-bake" basis. GF breadsticks and cheesy garlic breadsticks are also available, and there are chicken wings on the GF menu. ▪ *www.tommyspizzaandchicken.com*

Tree Huggers Café
✪★ ¢LD

Berea ▪ *(440) 342-4901*
1330 W Bagley Rd Unit 1 ▪ *Organic* ▪ GF menu includes a cranberry walnut salad, "giant armadillo" fresh spinach salad, dandelion soup, rice bowls, grilled eggplant panini, lemon chicken panini, ground chicken burger, and more. An assortment of GF baked goods are also available. ▪ *www.treehuggerscafe.com*

Uno Chicago Grill
📖

Dayton ▪ *(937) 910-8000*
126 N Main St
Dublin ▪ *(614) 793-8300*
5930 Britton Pkwy
Pickerington ▪ *(614) 501-1900*
1720 Hill Rd N
West Chester ▪ *(513) 942-6646*
9246 Schulze Dr

OKLAHOMA

OKLAHOMA CITY

Beatnix Café, The   ¢BL
Oklahoma City ▪ (405) 604-0211
136 NW 13Th St ▪ Coffee House & Café
▪ Manager Dave notes that GF diners are
welcome to bring their own GF bread for
sandwiches. He recommends the chicken
or tuna salad, which can be put on a
sandwich or over a bed of greens. Confirm timeliness of this information before
dining in. He further suggests speaking to
Chef Bonnie upon arrival and asking that
everything be sanitized to prevent cross-
contamination. ▪ www.thebeatnixcafe.com

Bricktown Brewery $LD
Oklahoma City ▪ (405) 232-2739
1 N Oklahoma Ave ▪ American ▪ Manager
Heather reports that GF diners are welcome and that many menu items can be
modified to be GF, like the Caesar salad
without croutons, cheese nachos, and any
bbq items. Confirm timeliness of this information before dining in. ▪ www.bricktown-
brewery.com

Cafe do Brasil   ★ ¢LD
Oklahoma City ▪ (405) 525-9779
440 NW 11Th St ▪ Brazilian ▪ GF cheese
bread is available. Restaurant reports that
most menu items are naturally GF. Servers are educated on which menu items are
GF. Examples of GF dishes include the
traditional Brazilian feijoada, chicken and
shrimp with coconut milk and cashews,
and breakfast scrambles. Confirm timeliness of this information before dining in. ▪
www.cafedobrazilokc.com

Cantina Laredo   📖
Oklahoma City ▪ (405) 840-1051
1901 NW Expressway 1069-A

Carino's Italian   📖
Oklahoma City ▪ (405) 752-0087
2905 W Memorial Rd

Oklahoma City ▪ (405) 632-4600
7900 S Walker Ave

Coffy's Café   100% ¢BLD
Oklahoma City ▪ (405) 604-8796
1739 NW 16th St ▪ Bakery & Café ▪ Bakery
and café offering a large and varied GF
menu. GF bread is available for french toast
in the morning or sandwiches at lunchtime.
GF pizza is also available, as are GF cakes,
pies, and pastries. ▪ www.coffyscafe.org

Deep Fork Grill $$$$LD
Oklahoma City ▪ (405) 848-7678
5418 N Western Ave ▪ Seafood & Steakhouse ▪ Manager Christie reports that the
restaurant has "several regulars" who are
GF, and that it is "very easy" for them to
accommodate GF diners. She notes that the
chef is very sensitive to the GF diet, and he
has an internal list of GF items to recommend. She advises reservations noting GF,
so that the staff can prepare ahead of time.
▪ www.deepforkgrill.com

Mantel Wine Bar & Bistro, The $$$$LD
Oklahoma City ▪ (405) 236-8040
201 E Sheridan Ave ▪ Modern American
▪ General Manager Lorin recommends
reservations noting GF. There are many
menu items that naturally GF or can
be prepared GF, including soups, a variety
of risotto dishes, a prime filet of beef, duck
breast, Atlantic salmon, and more. ▪ www.
themantelokc.com

Melting Pot, The   📖
Oklahoma City ▪ (405) 235-1000
4 E Sheridan Ave

Outback Steakhouse   📖
Oklahoma City ▪ (405) 686-0918
2219 SW 74th St
Oklahoma City ▪ (405) 840-5030
4144 N.W. Expressway

P.F. Chang's China Bistro   📖
Oklahoma City ▪ (405) 748-4003
13700 N Pennsylvania Ave

Paseo Grill $$LD
Oklahoma City ▪ (405) 601-1079

2909 Paseo ▪ *Modern American* ▪ Manager Leslie reports that the restaurant has several menu items, including grilled salmon, steaks, mashed potatoes with sour cream, and some side dishes, that can be modified to be GF. Confirm timeliness of this information before dining in. Leslie notes that everything is prepared fresh, so GF requests are easily accommodated. ▪ *www.paseogrill.com*

Pearl's Lakeside $LD
Oklahoma City ▪ *(405) 748-6113*
9201 Lake Hefner Pkwy ▪ *American Regional* ▪ Manager Brad reports that they accommodate GF diners "on a regular basis." He notes that all fish dishes, pepper tuna, oysters, and enchiladas are among the menu items that can be modified to be GF. Confirm timeliness of this information before dining in.

Pei Wei Asian Diner   📖
Oklahoma City ▪ *(405) 767-9001*
1841 Belle Isle Blvd

Red Prime Steak   ✪ $$$$D
Oklahoma City ▪ *(405) 232-2626*
504 North Broadway ▪ *Steakhouse* ▪ Manager Dennis reports that the restaurant serves GF diners "at least once a week." If reservations noting GF are made, the restaurant will prepare a list of GF items. This list includes steaks, beef tamales, salads, beef carpaccio, salmon, tilapia, and more. Confirm timeliness of this information before dining in. ▪ *www.redprimesteak.com*

Sage $LD
Oklahoma City ▪ *(405) 232-7243*
228 NE 2nd St ▪ *Modern American* ▪ Manager Patrick reports that all salads and several appetizers can be made GF, and over half the menu is entrée salads. Confirm timeliness of this information before dining in. He also notes that GF diners come in "all the time." Alert a server upon arrival. Patrick adds that the staff is GF aware and can assist GF diners. ▪ *www.sageokc.com*

Zio's   ✪ $LD
Oklahoma City ▪ *(405) 278-8888*
12 E California Ave
Oklahoma City ▪ *(405) 680-9999*
2035 S Meridian Ave ▪ *Italian* ▪ GF menu includes salmon caesar salad, chicken piccata, Greek pasta, lemon chicken primavera, shrimp with marinara, ribeye tuscano, grilled sirloin, and more. ▪ *www.zios.com*

OKLAHOMA

TULSA

Bodean Seafood Restaurant $$$LD
Tulsa ▪ *(918) 749-1407*
3376 E 51st St ▪ *Seafood* ▪ Executive Chef Tim reports that "almost anything" on the menu can be modified to be GF. He recommends alerting the server upon arrival and notes that making reservations noting GF will help, though it is not required. ▪ *www.bodean.net*

Brookside by Day   ¢BLD
Tulsa ▪ *(918) 745-9989*
3313 S Peoria Ave ▪ *American* ▪ Manager Karen reports that the restaurant "assumes that anyone with an allergy knows what they can and can't eat." She advises alerting the server upon arrival but notes that deciding what to eat is "the customer's responsibility."

Carino's Italian   📖
Tulsa ▪ *(918) 270-2000*
6364 E 41st St
Tulsa ▪ *(918) 298-7010*
9718 Riverside Pkwy

Carlee's Gluten Free   100% $S
Tulsa ▪ *(918) 398-3828*
1502 E 15th St ▪ *Bakery* ▪ Dedicated GF bakery offering zucchini muffins, pound cake, pumpkin rolls, sandwich bread, and

granola bars. Manager Lee reports that all baked goods are made to order. GF orders can be placed online or by phone. ▪ *www.carleesglutenfree.com*

Carrabba's Italian Grill 📖
Tulsa ▪ *(918) 254-8888*
11021 E 71st St

First Watch - The Daytime Café 📖
Tulsa ▪ *(918) 296-9960*
8178 S Lewis Ave

Kilkenny's Irish Pub ✪ $$LD
Tulsa ▪ *(918) 582-8282*
1413 E 15th St ▪ *Irish* ▪ Manager Marilyn reports that the extensive GF menu includes variations of regular menu items. She also notes that GF diners are accommodated "all the time." ▪ *www.tulsairishpub.com*

Lone Star Steakhouse & Saloon 📖
Tulsa ▪ *(918) 748-8500*
3915 E 51st St
Tulsa ▪ *(918) 294-0732*
7110 S 101st East Ave

Michael Fusco's Riverside Grill
✪★ $$$LD
Tulsa ▪ *(918) 394-2433*
9912 Riverside Drive ▪ *American* ▪ GF items marked on the menu include all salads without croutons, linguine with clam sauce, shrimp and lobster bisque, and many more. For dessert, they offer GF bread pudding, chocolate cake, or crème brûlée. GF bread, hamburger buns, pasta, beer, and soy sauce are available. ▪ *www.michaelfuscosriversidegrill.com*

More Than Noodles ★ ¢LD
Tulsa ▪ *(918) 299-5900*
9635 Riverside Pkwy ▪ *Pasta* ▪ Owner Rebecca reports that GF rice noodles can be used in any dish on the menu. She also notes that all sauces are GF except for the beef stroganoff. ▪ *www.morethannoodles.com*

Outback Steakhouse 📖
Tulsa ▪ *(918) 627-1992*
4723 S Yale Ave

Tulsa ▪ *(918) 254-4741*
9006 E 71st St
Tulsa ▪ *(918) 299-0069*
9710 Riverside Pkwy

P.F. Chang's China Bistro 📖
Tulsa ▪ *(918) 747-6555*
1978 E 21st St

Pei Wei Asian Diner 📖
Tulsa ▪ *(918) 749-6083*
3535 S Peoria Ave
Tulsa ▪ *(918) 497-1015*
5954 S Yale Ave

Zio's ✪ $LD
Tulsa ▪ *(918) 250-5999*
7111 S Mingo Rd
Tulsa ▪ *(918) 298-9880*
8112 S Lewis Ave ▪ *Italian* ▪ GF menu includes salmon caesar salad, chicken piccata, Greek pasta, lemon chicken primavera, shrimp with marinara, ribeye tuscano, grilled sirloin, and more. ▪ *www.zios.com*

OKLAHOMA
ALL OTHER CITIES

Blu Fine Wine & Food ✪ $LD
Norman ▪ *(405) 360-4258*
201 S Crawford Ave ▪ *Seafood* ▪ Extensive GF menu lists many items from the regular menu that can be prepared GF, and it includes instructions on how to order them. Manager John reports that the restaurant is "quite familiar" with GF diners. ▪ *www.blufinewineandfood.com*

Bonefish Grill 📖
Broken Arrow ▪ *(918) 252-3474*
4651 W Kenosha St

Carino's Italian 📖
Norman ▪ *(405) 447-5000*
970 Ed Noble Dr

Yukon ▪ *(405) 350-0756*
1608 Garth Brooks Blvd

Chelino's Mexican Restaurant $**LD**
Edmond ▪ *(405) 340-3620*
1512 S Boulevard ▪ *Mexican* ▪ Manager
Caesar reports that they serve GF diners
regularly. He recommends asking for him
upon arrival, so he can discuss the "many"
GF options. ▪ *www.chelinosmexicanrestau-*
rant.com

Eischen's Bar $**LD**
Okarche ▪ *(405) 263-9939*
108 South 2Nd ▪ *Pub Food* ▪ Veteran
Server Kathleen reports that they serve a
fair amount of GF customers. She notes
that the nachos are among the limited GF
selections. Confirm timeliness of this information before dining in.

Freebirds on the Fly   ¢**LD**
Norman ▪ *(405) 364-7736*
746 Asp Ave ▪ *Latin American* ▪ Although
the website has a list of non-GF items,
this information may not apply to every
location. Manager Carl reports that the restaurant does not serve GF customers very
often. He notes that the contents of a burrito could be served in a bowl, without a
tortilla. They also have corn tortillas, which
the website indicates are GF. Confirm timeliness of this information before dining in.
▪ *www.freebirds.com*

Gina & Guiseppe's   ✪★ $**LD**
Jenks ▪ *(918) 296-0111*
400 Riverwalk Ter ▪ *Italian* ▪ GF pasta and
pizza are available. Menu items that can
be prepared GF are marked on the menu.
They include all salads and house pasta. ▪
www.gngitalian.com

Lone Star Steakhouse & Saloon   📖
Broken Arrow ▪ *(918) 355-1133*
101 E Albany St
Lawton ▪ *(580) 248-8785*
5374 NW Cache Rd
Owasso ▪ *(918) 274-3500*
9013 N 121st East Ave

Melting Pot, The   📖
Jenks ▪ *(918) 299-8000*
300 Riverwalk Ter

Outback Steakhouse   📖
Edmond ▪ *(405) 359-7432*
3600 S Broadway
Lawton ▪ *(580) 536-6550*
7206 NW Cache Rd
Norman ▪ *(405) 447-6770*
860 N Interstate Dr

Pei Wei Asian Diner   📖
Broken Arrow ▪ *(918) 250-8557*
4609 W Kenosha St
Edmond ▪ *(405) 341-6850*
1141 E 2nd St Ste 100-A
Norman ▪ *(405) 364-1690*
1500 24th Ave NW

Pink Elephant Café   ★ $**LD**
Norman ▪ *(405) 307-8449*
301 E Main St ▪ *American* ▪ GF quiche
is available. Several salads can also be
prepared GF. Hostess Grace reports that
specials change daily, but they are often GF
or can be modified to be GF.

Rodney's Pizza Place   ★ $**LD**
Purcell ▪ *(405) 527-7373*
2234 N Green Ave ▪ *Pizza* ▪ GF pizza is
available with any toppings. Restaurant
reports that "not many" GF diners come in,
so asking for a manager who can discuss
GF details is advised. ▪ *www.rodneyspiz-*
zaplace.com

OREGON

EUGENE

Adam's Sustainable Table   ✪★ $$**D**
Eugene ▪ *(541) 344-6948*
30 E Broadway ▪ *Healthy American* ▪ The
"Dietary Menu" indicates GF items. GF
items marked on the menu include dates
and bacon, fresh Pacific halibut, smoked

surata tofu, andouille stuffed pork tender-loin, and more. Couscous and GF flatbread are brought in from the adjacent Moroccan restaurant. ▪ *www.thesustainabletable.com*

Cozmic Pizza ★ $$$**LD**

Eugene ▪ **(541) 338-9333**
199 W 8th Ave ▪ *Pizza* ▪ GF pizza is usually available. ▪ *www.cozmicpizza.com*

Evergreen Indian Cuisine $**LD**

Eugene ▪ **(541) 343-7944**
1525 Franklin Blvd ▪ *Indian* ▪ Owner Meeraali reports that everything except the bread is GF or can be prepared GF. She notes that many of the curries, soups, and other Indian dishes are GF. Confirm timeliness of this information before dining in. Managers and chefs are trained in the GF diet. ▪ *www.evergreenindianrestaurant.com*

Go Healthy Café ✪★ ¢**S**

Eugene ▪ **(541) 683-3164**
3802 W 11Th Ave ▪ *Healthy American* ▪ GF menu includes burrito bowls, teriyaki chicken bowls, broccoli and cheese, turkey guacamole sandwiches, and avocado salad. ▪ *www.gohealthycafe.com*

Holy Donuts! ★ ¢**B**

Eugene ▪ **(541) 510-6635**
1437 Willamette Aly ▪ *Bakery* ▪ Baker Kelly reports that they offer GF options every day. Examples of GF items include blueberry cobbler, "sconuts," and donuts. She cautions that only 24 GF donuts are made per day, and they are made first thing in the morning. Special orders can be filled only if they are placed by 3 PM the day before.

Lok Yaun Restaurant ✪ ¢**LD**

Eugene ▪ **(541) 345-7448**
2360 W 11Th Ave ▪ *Chinese* ▪ GF menu is available upon request. Manager Wing reports that they accommodate "a lot of GF diners." ▪ *www.lokyaunrestaurant.com*

McGrath's Fish House ✪ $**LD**

Eugene ▪ **(541) 342-6404**
1036 Valley River Way ▪ *Seafood* ▪ GF menu features a large selection of seafood entrees and appetizers, as well as salads and steaks. ▪ *www.mcgrathsfishhouse.com*

Original Pancake House, The ★ ¢**BL**

Eugene ▪ **(541) 343-7523**
782 E Broadway ▪ *Breakfast* ▪ GF pancakes are available. Select locations may serve other GF items. Call a specific location to inquire. ▪ *www.originalpancakehouse.com*

P.F. Chang's China Bistro 📖

Eugene ▪ **(541) 225-2015**
124 Coburg Rd

Papa's Pizza Parlor ✪★ $$**LD**

Eugene ▪ **(541) 485-5555**
1577 Coburg Rd
Eugene ▪ **(541) 485-5555**
1700 W 11Th Ave ▪ *Pizza* ▪ GF menu includes an extensive list of GF pizzas. GF beer is also available. ▪ *www.papaspizza.net*

Sweet Life Patisserie ★ ¢**S**

Eugene ▪ **(541) 683-5676**
755 Monroe St ▪ *Bakery* ▪ Non-dedicated GF bakery offering GF cookies and brownies in assorted flavors. They always carry crème brûlée and chocolate mousse, which are naturally GF. GF cakes are available by special order only. ▪ *www.sweetlifedesserts.com*

OREGON

PORTLAND

¡Oba! Restaurante ✪ $$$**D**

Portland ▪ **(503) 228-6161**
555 NW 12th Ave ▪ *Spanish* ▪ GF menu offers options such as Cuban pulled flank steak, a mesquite grilled wild salmon fillet, and cumin-coriander crusted Misty Isle N.Y. steak. ▪ *www.obarestaurant.com*

Acapulco's Southwest Gold ☉ ¢LD
Portland ▪ (503) 244-0771
7800 SW Capitol Hwy ▪ *Mexican* ▪ GF
menu includes tacos, fajitas, enchiladas,
and huevos rancheros. Manager Mick
specifies that almost anything can be made
GF, as they use corn tortillas.

Andina Restaurant ☉ $$LD
Portland ▪ (503) 228-9535
1314 NW Glisan St ▪ *Peruvian* ▪ There are
separate GF menus for lunch, dinner, and
dessert. Sample GF entrées are seared yellowfin tuna sprinkled with black pepper
and orange zest, in addition to a double
rack of lamb. Extensive GF dessert menu
includes handmade truffles, goat cheese
and lemon cake, and chocolate cinnamon
cake. ▪ *www.andinarestaurant.com*

Bellagios Pizza ☉★ $$LD
Portland ▪ (503) 221-0110
1742 SW Jefferson St
Portland ▪ (503) 230-2900
8112 SE 13th St.
Portland ▪ (503) 244-1737
9055 SW Barbur Blvd ▪ *Pizza* ▪ GF menu
includes a variety of pizzas, salads, and
appetizers. There is a GF "build your own
pizza" option, and GF pizza dough is available for "take-&-bake." GF pizza is available
in the 10-inch size only. ▪ *www.bellagio-
spizza.com*

Blossoming Lotus ☉★ $LD
Portland ▪ (503) 228-0048
1713 NE 15th Ave ▪ *Raw & Vegan* ▪ GF
items marked on the menu include raw
pizza, salads, wraps, and entrées like pasta
fagioli and the southwestern bowl. GF rice
pasta, cookies, and beer are available. ▪
www.blpdx.com

Carafe Parisian Bistro $$LD
Portland ▪ (503) 248-0004
200 SW Market St ▪ *Bistro* ▪ Bartender
Stacy reports that all staff members are
"really familiar" with the GF diet, since
they accommodate GF diners "at least
three or four times a week." She notes that

the chefs can modify many menu items to
be GF. Alert a server upon arrival. ▪ *www.
carafebistro.com*

Coffee Plant 100% ¢S
Portland ▪ (503) 293-3280
5911 SW Corbett Ave
Portland ▪ (503) 295-1227
724 SW Washington St ▪ *Coffee House &
Café* ▪ GF café offering muffins, cookies,
scones, and more, as well as GF bread for
sandwiches. For breads, order 48 hours in
advance. ▪ *www.coffeeplant.net*

Corbett Fish House ★ $LD
Portland ▪ (503) 246-4434
5901 SW Corbett Ave ▪ *Seafood* ▪ Restaurant reports that "almost the whole menu"
is GF. All fish is breaded with rice flour,
and corn tortillas are available for the fish
tacos. GF sandwich buns are also available.
▪ *www.corbettfishhouse.com*

Francis Restaurant ★ $BL
Portland ▪ (503) 288-8299
2338 NE Alberta St ▪ *American* ▪ GF items
marked on the menu include hash, biscuits
and gravy, tofu scrambles, oat pancakes,
and sausage, as well as soups and salads.
Manager Danny reports that accommodating GF diners is "a normal occurrence" at
the restaurant. GF biscuits and pancakes
are available. ▪ *www.francisrestaurant.com*

Fratelli Cucina $$D
Portland ▪ (503) 241-8800
1230 NW Hoyt St ▪ *Italian* ▪ Manager
Tim reports that the "staff is fantastic" at
handling GF requests. All components of
a dish are listed on the menu, to make determining GF dishes easier. Alert a server
upon arrival. ▪ *www.fratellicucina.com*

Hawthorne Fish House ★ $$LD
Portland ▪ (503) 548-4434
4343 SE Hawthorne Blvd ▪ *Seafood* ▪
Manager John reports that "almost the
whole menu" is GF. All fish is breaded with
rice flour, and corn tortillas are available
for the fish tacos. GF sandwich buns are
also available. ▪ *www.corbettfishhouse.com*

Jo Bar and Rotisserie $$LD
Portland ▪ *(503) 222-0048*
705 NW 23rd Ave ▪ *American* ▪ Manager
Lisa reports that they have started accommodating GF diners more and more. She
notes that servers are "pretty saavy" about
GF options, and they can take GF diners
on a "walk through" of the menu, which
has several naturally GF items. It also has
other items that can be modified to be GF.
▪ *www.papahaydn.com*

Keana's Kandyland Restaurant & Bak-
ery   ★ ¢S
Portland ▪ *(503) 719-5131*
5314 SE Milwaukie Ave ▪ *Desserterie &*
Bakery ▪ Non-dedicated bakery offering
GF loaf breads, bagels, croissants, pizza
crust, foccacia bread, chocolates, cookies,
pies, and cheese cakes. The breakfast and
lunch restaurant attached to the bakery
serves GF pancakes, crepes, and other GF
items. Denise notes that noitce of one day
is required for special orders.

Mama Mia Trattoria   ★ $$D
Portland ▪ *(503) 295-6464*
439 SW 2nd Ave ▪ *Italian* ▪ GF pasta is
available. The restaurant reports that GF
diners are accommodated on a regular basis. They also note that GF food is prepared
in a separate area. ▪ *www.mamamiatrat-*
toria.com

Melting Pot, The   📖
Portland ▪ *(503) 517-8960*
Sw 6th Avenue And Main St

Mississippi Pizza Pub, The   ★ $$$LD
Portland ▪ *(503) 288-3231*
3552 N Mississippi Ave ▪ *Pizza* ▪ GF pizza
is available. The restaurant reports that the
GF pizza is "very popular." ▪ *www.mississip-*
pipizza.com

Mother's Bistro & Bar $$BLD
Portland ▪ *(503) 464-1122*
212 SW Stark St ▪ *Italian* ▪ Manager Pia reports that the restaurant can accommodate
GF diners "without difficulty." She notes
that salads, breakfast scrambles, vegan

stir-fry, and the hummus/Greek salad
combo are all GF, and other dishes can be
modified to be GF. Confirm timeliness of
this information before dining in. Alert a
server, who will notify the kitchen. ▪ *www.*
mothersbistro.com

New Cascadia Traditional   100% ¢S
Portland ▪ *(503) 546-4901*
1700 SE 6th Ave ▪ *Bakery* ▪ Bakery offering a large selection of GF baked goods.
Different types of breads, cookies, pies,
cakes, and muffins are available, as are
pizzas and brownies. Bakery's products are
also sold at the Portland Farmers Market. ▪
www.newcascadiatraditional.com

Old Spaghetti Factory, The   📖
Portland ▪ *(503) 222-5375*
0715 SW Bancroft St

Old Wives' Tale   ✪★ ¢BLD
Portland ▪ *(503) 238-0470*
1300 E Burnside St ▪ *Modern American*
▪ Much of the menu is GF, and GF bread
is available for sandwiches. GF desserts
marked on the regular dessert menu include a coconut almond brownie, pumpkin
pudding, and a chocolate raspberry loaf. ▪
www.oldwivestalesrestaurant.com

Original Pancake House, The   ★ ¢BL
Portland ▪ *(503) 246-9007*
8601 SW 24th Ave ▪ *Breakfast* ▪ GF
pancakes are available. Select locations
may serve other GF options. Call a specific
location to inquire. ▪ *www.originalpancake-*
house.com

Outback Steakhouse   📖
Portland ▪ *(503) 643-8007*
11146 SW Barnes Rd
Portland ▪ *(503) 775-8977*
9500 SE 82nd Ave

P.F. Chang's China Bistro   📖
Portland ▪ *(503) 432-4000*
1139 NW Couch St
Portland ▪ *(503) 430-3020*
7463 SW Bridgeport Rd

Papa G's   ☺ $**LD**
Portland ▪ *(503) 235-0244*
2314 SE Division St ▪ *Organic* ▪ The
entrees rotate daily, but all GF items are
marked on the menu. Restaurant reports
that GF is "one of their big things." Examples of GF menu items include 3 bean
chili, macaroni salad, blueberry yogurt,
tacos, and vegetable and tofu curry. ▪ *www.
papagees.com*

Papa Haydn $$**LD**
Portland ▪ *(503) 232-9440*
5829 SE Milwaukie Ave
Portland ▪ *(503) 228-7317*
701 NW 23rd Ave ▪ *American Regional* ▪
Managers at both locations note that many
entrées are naturally GF or can be modified
to be GF. Both locations also noted that
servers are "well-versed" in GF foods. Manager Lisa from the 23rd Ave location noted
that most dishes are made from scratch, so
GF requests are easy to accommodate. The
Milwaukie Ave menu notes GF desserts
with an asterisk. Reservations noting GF
are recommended. ▪ *www.papahaydn.com*

Papa's Pizza Parlor   ☺★ $$**LD**
Portland ▪ *(503) 251-5555*
16321 SE Stark St ▪ *Pizza* ▪ GF menu
includes an extensive list of GF pizzas. GF
beer is also available. ▪ *www.papaspizza.net*

Park Kitchen $**LD**
Portland ▪ *(503) 223-7275*
422 NW 8th Ave ▪ *Modern American &
Steakhouse* ▪ General Manager Anna
reports that the restaurant is very GF
friendly. She says that many menu items
are naturally GF, while others can be made
GF. She recommends alerting a server, who
can indicate appropriate menu items. ▪
www.parkkitchen.com

Pastini Pastaria   ★ ¢**LD**
Portland ▪ *(503) 288-4300*
1426 NE Broadway
Portland ▪ *(503) 595-1205*
1506 NW 23rd Ave
Portland ▪ *(503) 595-6400*

2027 SE Division St
Portland ▪ *(503) 863-5188*
911 SW Taylor At 9th Avenue ▪ *Italian* ▪
GF pasta is available. It can be used in any
pasta dish except for those that are pre-
baked, like lasagna or manicotti. ▪ *www.
pastini.com*

Picazzo's Organic Italian Kitchen
                                ☺★ $$**LD**
Portland ▪ *(503) 238-7255*
8000 SE 13Th Ave ▪ *Pizza* ▪ GF menu includes avocado pasta, insalata caprese, and
an organic hummus platter, among many
other things. Kitchen manager Josh reports
that they cater "extensively" to the GF community. GF pizza and pasta are available. ▪
www.picazzos.com

Piece of Cake Bakery   ★ ¢**S**
Portland ▪ *(503) 234-9445*
8306 SE 17th Ave ▪ *Bakery* ▪ Non-
dedicated bakery offering GF cakes in a
wide selection of flavors, including carrot,
chocolate raspberry, and double chocolate.
GF cookies, bundts, and mini loaves are
also available. GF wedding cakes are available for order. ▪ *www.pieceofcakebakery.net*

Por Que No Tacqueria   ¢**LD**
Portland ▪ *(503) 467-4149*
3524 N Mississippi Ave
Portland ▪ *(503) 954-3138*
4635 SE Hawthorne Blvd ▪ *Mexican* ▪
Both locations report serving GF diners "all
the time." Manager Bridget at the Mississippi Ave location notes that all servers are
well educated on the GF diet and the ingredients of the food. If they have any questions, they will ask a manager. While flour
tortillas are available upon request, corn
tortillas are used as a default, and meats
are dredged in cornmeal rather than flour.
Confirm timeliness of this information
before dining in. ▪ *www.porquenotacos.com*

Seasons & Regions Seafood Grill
                                ☺ $$**BLD**
Portland ▪ *(503) 244-6400*
6660 SW Capitol Hwy ▪ *Global* ▪ GF

menu includes honey ginger lime salmon salad, thai red curry scallops and gulf shrimp, and soy ginger chicken stir fry, among many other things. Dining in and take out options are available. ▪ *www.seasonsandregions.com*

Slappy Cakes ★ ¢BL
Portland ▪ *(503) 477-4805*
4246 SE Belmont St ▪ *American* ▪ GF pancakes are available. They can be ordered off the menu or selected for the "make your own pancakes" option. Ask the server what other menu items can be prepared GF. ▪ *www.slappycakes.com*

Soluna Grill $$D
Portland ▪ *(971) 222-3433*
4440 NE Fremont St ▪ *Modern American* ▪ Owner and Chef Dan reports that nearly the entire menu is naturally GF. He adds that GF diners come in to the restaurant at least once a month. Upon arrival, ask a server to indicate GF menu options, or ask for Dan. Reservations noting GF are recommended. ▪ *www.solunagrill.com*

TeaZone & Camellia Lounge, The ★ ¢BLD
Portland ▪ *(503) 221-2130*
510 NW 11Th Ave ▪ *Teahouse* ▪ GF bread and hamburger buns are available, so any cold sandwich or panini can be prepared GF. Most soups are also GF, as are desserts like scones, earl grey truffles, cookies, and some of the bubble teas. Ask a server which items are GF, as sweets are GF on a rotational basis. ▪ *www.teazone.com*

Three Degrees $$$BD
Portland ▪ *(503) 295-6166*
1510 SW Harbor Way ▪ *American Regional* ▪ Manager Stuart reports that "all of the staff is educated on gluten" and GF dining. Most sauces and gravies do not contain flour. Grilled white prawns, farm-raised ruby trout, and braised lamb shanks are among the menu items that can be modified to be GF. Confirm timeliness of information before dining in. ▪ *www.threedegreesrestaurant.com*

Three Square Grill ✪ $$D
Portland ▪ *(503) 244-4467*
6320 SW Capitol Hwy ▪ *Modern American* ▪ GF items marked on the menu include crab bisque, a spring vegetable platter, roast vegetable hash, garlic fries, and pork loin. Owner David reports that the restaurant accommodates GF diners on a regular basis. ▪ *www.threesquare.com*

Typhoon! ✪★ $BLD
Portland ▪ *(503) 243-7557*
2310 NW Everett St
Portland ▪ *(503) 224-8285*
410 SW Broadway ▪ *Thai* ▪ There are separate GF menus for lunch and dinner, and both are extensive. They include starters, soups, salads, noodle dishes, rice dishes, main courses, and more. Examples of main courses are pineapple curry, cashew chicken, and Buddha's feast. GF noodles are available. ▪ *www.typhoonrestaurants.com*

Vindalho $$D
Portland ▪ *(503) 467-4550*
2038 SE Clinton St ▪ *Indian* ▪ Chef April reports that nearly everything on the menu is naturally GF. She notes that all of the sauces are thickened with coconut milk or yogurt rather than flour, and any dish can be served with rice instead of naan. Confirm timeliness of this information before dining in. ▪ *www.vindalho.com*

Ya Hala Lebanese Cuisine ¢LD
Portland ▪ *(503) 256-4484*
8005 SE Stark St ▪ *Mediterranean* ▪ Manager Lisa reports that they are able to accommodate GF diners. Kabob dishes served with rice, hummus served with cucumber, and baba ganoush are naturally GF. Confirm timeliness of this information before dining in. ▪ *www.yahalarestaurant.com*

OREGON

ALL OTHER CITIES

Angeline's Bakery ★ ¢BL
Sisters ■ *(541) 549-9122*
121 W Main St ■ *Bakery & Café* ■ Non-dedicated bakery offering GF enchiladas, quiche crust, muffins, brownies, cookies, scones, and cupcakes. The bakery cautions that cross contamination may occur, as it is not a dedicated facility and all products are baked in common ovens. ■ *www.angelines-bakery.com*

Bellagios Pizza ✪★ $$LD
Beaverton ■ *(503) 466-2070*
16265 NW Cornell Rd
Clackamas ■ *(503) 698-6699*
12050 SE Sunnyside Rd
Gresham ■ *(503) 465-8000*
862 NW Burnside Rd
Lake Oswego ■ *(503) 635-8700*
1235 Mcvey Ave
Oregon City ■ *(503) 518-5000*
19735 Trails End Hwy
Tigard ■ *(503) 639-1500*
10115 SW Nimbus Ave
Tualatin ■ *(503) 691-7841*
8835 SW Tualatin Sherwood Rd
West Linn ■ *(503) 557-1406*
1880 Willamette Falls Dr
Wilsonville ■ *(503) 682-3400*
29702-G SW Town Center Loop W ■ *Pizza* ■ GF menu includes a variety of pizzas, salads, and appetizers. There is a GF "build your own pizza" option, and GF pizza dough is available for "take-&-bake." GF pizza is available in the 10-inch size only. ■ *www.bellagiospizza.com*

Bentley's Grill $$LD
Salem ■ *(503) 779-1660*
291 Liberty St SE ■ *American* ■ Hostess Haley reports that the kitchen will make any dish GF upon request. She notes that they have served GF customers in the past, and recommends alerting a server, who will ask the chef to discuss GF options. ■ *www.bentleysgrill.com*

Big River Restaurant and Bar $$$LD
Corvallis ■ *(541) 757-0694*
101 NW Jackson Ave ■ *American Regional* ■ Manager Carol reports that they accommodate GF diners "a lot." She notes that they have several risotto dishes and a pan seared halibut that are naturally GF, while other selections can be prepared GF. GF desserts include crème brûlée and the flourless chocolate raspberry sin. ■ *www.bigriverrest.com*

Bob's Red Mill Whole Grain Store & Visitors Center ★ ¢BL
Milwaukie ■ *(503) 607-6455*
5000 SE International Way ■ *Deli* ■ GF pancakes are available for breakfast, and GF bread is available for sandwiches. Restaurant notes that bread is baked in the same oven as non-GF bread. Although there is no dedicated GF grill, when the restaurant is less busy, they can clean a grill to make GF pancakes or other items. ■ *www.bobsredmill.com*

Calapooia Brewing Co. ★ ¢LD
Albany ■ *(541) 928-1931*
140 NE Hill St ■ *Pub Food* ■ GF cupcakes are available during the week, but are usually sold out by the weekend. ■ *www.calapooiabrewing.com*

Carino's Italian 📖
Bend ■ *(541) 318-6300*
63455 N Highway 97

China Delight Restaurant ★ $LD
Corvallis ■ *(541) 753-3753*
325 NW 2nd St ■ *Chinese* ■ GF soy sauce is available. Restaurant reports that some dishes on the menu can be made GF. Alert a server, who will know which dishes can be modified to be GF. ■ *www.chinadelight-corvallis.com*

Ciddici's ★ $LD
Albany ■ *(541) 928-2536*

133 5th Ave SE ▪ *Pizza* ▪ GF pizza is available. ▪ *www.ciddicipizza.com*

Clarke's Restaurant $$$D
Lake Oswego ▪ *(503) 636-2667*
455 2nd St ▪ *Modern American* ▪ Chef John reports that GF diners are accommodated "on a regular basis." He notes that naturally GF menu items include grilled Alaskan salmon, lobster and shrimp risotto, cod, steak, and grilled pork tenderloin. Alert a server, who will discuss GF options with the kitchen. Reservations noting GF are recommended. ▪ *www.clarkesrestaurant. net*

Dundee Bistro $LD
Dundee ▪ *(503) 554-1650*
100A SW 7th St ▪ *Modern American* ▪ Manager Scott reports that they serve GF diners "all the time." He notes that the kitchen is very accommodating of GF requests. Menu items like the pork loin, salads, chicken, and clam chowder can be modified to be GF. Because the menu changes almost daily, GF diners should alert the server, who will discuss GF menu options with the kitchen. ▪ *www.dundeebistro.com*

Evergreen Indian Cuisine $LD
Corvallis ▪ *(541) 754-7944*
136 SW 3rd St ▪ *Indian* ▪ Owner Meeraali reports that everything except the bread is GF or can be prepared GF. She notes that many of the curries, soups, and other Indian dishes are GF. Confirm timeliness of this information before dining in. Managers and chefs are trained in the GF diet. ▪ *www.evergreenindianrestaurant.com*

Extreme Pizza   ★ $$LD
Hillsboro ▪ *(503) 645-4200*
1888 NW 188th Ave @ Cornell ▪ *Pizza* ▪ GF pizza is available. ▪ *www.extremepizza. com*

FireWorks Restaurant & Bar   ★ $$LD
Corvallis ▪ *(541) 754-6958*
1115 SE 3rd St ▪ *Modern American* ▪ GF pizza is available. Restaurant reports that many sauces are thickened with rice flour instead of wheat flour. They note that in addition to pizzas, there are many menu items that are or can be modified to be GF. Alert a server, who will know the ingredients of each dish and help figure out the best options for GF diners. ▪ *www.fireworksvenue.com*

Garlic Jim's   ✪★ $LD
Beaverton ▪ *(503) 645-3400*
12480 SW Walker Rd
Beaverton ▪ *(503) 601-5467*
8410 SW Nimbus Ave
Clackamas ▪ *(503) 496-5467*
10219 SE Sunnyside Rd
Salem ▪ *(503) 779-2722*
4555 Liberty Rd S ▪ *Pizza* ▪ GF pizza is available in the large size only. GF menu also includes salads and hot wings. All locations report that GF cheesecake is also available. ▪ *www.garlicjims.com*

Giuseppe's Ristorante   ★ $$D
Bend ▪ *(541) 389-8899*
932 NW Bond St ▪ *Italian* ▪ GF pasta is available. ▪ *www.giuseppesofbend.com*

Greenleaf Restaurant   ✪ $BLD
Ashland ▪ *(541) 482-2808*
49 N Main St ▪ *Mediterranean* ▪ GF menu includes Greek salad, snapper polermo, wild salmon, and hummus, among other things. According to Owner Daniel, items not listed on the GF menu can sometimes be modified to be GF. ▪ *www.greenleafrestaurant.com*

JP's at Cannon Beach   ✪ $$$LD
Cannon Beach ▪ *(503) 436-0908*
240 North Hemlock St ▪ *Continental* ▪ GF menu includes halibut noisette, feta chicken breast, and a stuffed filet mignon. For dessert, they offer GF sugar free cheesecake, a South American lime tart, and coconut milk ice cream balls. ▪ *www. jpsatcannonbeach.com*

Living Earth Bakery   100% ¢S
Corvallis ▪ *(541) 738-2591*
363 SW Jefferson Ave ▪ *Bakery* ▪ Bakery

offering GF bread, pizza crusts, cookies, brownies, cakes, and cinnamon rolls. Special orders must be placed at least 48 hours in advance. ▪ *www.livingearthbakery.com*

Marco Polo Global Restaurant ✪ $LD
Salem ▪ *(503) 364-4833*
210 Liberty St SE ▪ Chinese ▪ GF menu includes pesto and cream cheese filled mushrooms, garlic green beans with beef, and sweet and sour salmon. The restaurant reports that they regularly accommodate GF diners. ▪ *www.mpologlobal.com*

McGrath's Fish House ✪ $LD
Beaverton ▪ *(503) 646-1881*
3211 SW Cedar Hills Blvd
Bend ▪ *(541) 388-4555*
3118 N Hwy 97
Corvallis ▪ *(541) 752-3474*
350 Circle Blvd
Medford ▪ *(541) 732-1732*
68 E Stewart Ave
Milwaukie ▪ *(503) 653-8070*
11050 SE Oak St
Salem ▪ *(503) 362-0736*
350 Chemeketa NE
Salem ▪ *(503) 485-3086*
3805 Center St NE ▪ Seafood ▪ GF menu features a large selection of seafood entrees and appetizers, as well as salads and steaks. ▪ *www.mcgrathsfishhouse.com*

Monteaux's Public House ✪ $LD
Beaverton ▪ *(503) 439-9942*
16165 SW Regatta Ln ▪ American ▪ GF items marked on the menu include the prawn and avocado martini, shrimp pinchos, chicken schnitzel, and the wild salmon caesar. Owner Larry reports that the restaurant hosts "a lot of people" who are GF. He recommends alerting a server upon arrival. ▪ *www.monteauxs.com*

Nature's Corner Café & Market
✪★ ¢LD
Florence ▪ *(541) 997-0900*
185 Highway 101 ▪ American ▪ GF items are marked on the regular menu. GF bread and pancakes are available. The restaurant

shares space with a food store offering many GF "take-&-bake" options. ▪ *www.naturescornercafe.com*

Nearly Normal's ✪ ¢BLD
Corvallis ▪ *(541) 753-0791*
109 NW 15th St ▪ Modern Mexican ▪ GF menu includes corn tortillas and burgers without buns, as well as several vegetable and tofu dishes. ▪ *www.nearlynormals.com*

Oceana Natural Foods Cooperative ¢L
Newport ▪ *(541) 265-8285*
159 SE 2nd St ▪ Deli ▪ Manager Linda reports that there are usually GF options available in the deli. She notes that all foods have "ingredient cards," so diners can easily read what does and does not contain gluten. Call ahead to ask about GF options of the day. ▪ *www.oceanafoods.org*

Old Spaghetti Factory, The 📖
Clackamas ▪ *(503) 653-7949*
12725 SE 93rd Ave
Hillsboro ▪ *(503) 617-7614*
18925 NW Tanasbourne Dr

Original Pancake House, The ★ ¢BL
Bend ▪ *(541) 317-0380*
1025 SW Donovan Ave
Redmond ▪ *(541) 316-2515*
3030 SW 6th St ▪ Breakfast ▪ GF pancakes are available. Select locations may serve other GF items. Call a specific location to inquire. ▪ *www.originalpancakehouse.com*

Outback Steakhouse 📖
Bend ▪ *(541) 383-8104*
1180 SE 3rd St
Gresham ▪ *(503) 674-5340*
2424 SE Burnside Rd
Medford ▪ *(541) 732-0997*
3613 Crater Lake Hwy
Salem ▪ *(503) 399-3700*
2285 Lancaster Dr NE
Springfield ▪ *(541) 746-7700*
3463 Hutton St
Tualatin ▪ *(503) 885-0410*
8665 SW Tualatin Sherwood Rd

P.F. Chang's China Bistro   📖
Hillsboro ▪ *(503) 533-4580*
19320 NW Emma Way

Papa's Pizza Parlor   ✪★ $$**LD**
Beaverton ▪ *(503) 531-7220*
15700 NW Blueridge St
Corvallis ▪ *(541) 757-2727*
1030 SW 3rd St
Springfield ▪ *(541) 485-5555*
4011 Main St ▪ *Pizza* ▪ GF menu includes
an extensive list of GF pizzas. GF beer is
also available. ▪ *www.papaspizza.net*

Pastini Pastaria   ★   ¢**LD**
Beaverton ▪ *(503) 619-2241*
3487 SW Cedar Hills Blvd
Bend ▪ *(541) 749-1060*
375 SW Powerhouse Dr
Corvallis ▪ *(541) 257-2579*
1580 NW 9th St
Tigard ▪ *(503) 718-2300*
7307 SW Bridgeport Rd ▪ *Italian* ▪ GF
pasta is available. It can be used in any
pasta dish except for those that are pre-
baked, like lasagna or manicotti. ▪ *www.
pastini.com*

Pizza Garden   ★ $$**LD**
Nehalem ▪ *(503) 368-7675*
35815 Hwy 101 N ▪ *Pizza* ▪ GF pizza is
available. Manager Jeannie reports that the
restaurant has "quite a following" of GF
diners from all over the area.

R.R. Thompson House B&B   ★   ¢**B**
Carlton ▪ *(503) 852-6236*
517 North Kutch St ▪ *Breakfast* ▪ For
guests at the bed and breakfast, GF breakfasts are available. They include pancakes,
french toast, omelets, and fresh fruit. ▪
www.rrthompsonhouse.com

Tidal Raves $$**LD**
Depoe Bay ▪ *(541) 765-2995*
279 U.S. Hwy 101 ▪ *Seafood* ▪ Restaurant
reports that they have "many" GF diners.
They have a list of ingredients for each
dish, which is available upon request.
Menu items that can be modified to be GF
include calamari, vegetarian black beans,

and fish tacos. Confirm timeliness of this
information before dining in.

Typhoon!   ✪★ $**LD**
Beaverton ▪ *(503) 644-8010*
12600 SW Crescent St
Bend ▪ *(541) 385-8885*
148 NW Bond Street
Gresham ▪ *(503) 669-9995*
543 NW 12th St ▪ *Thai* ▪ There are sepa-
rate GF menus for lunch and dinner, and
both are extensive. They include starters,
soups, salads, noodle dishes, rice dishes,
main courses, and more. Examples of
main courses are pineapple curry, cashew
chicken, and Buddha's feast. GF noodles
are available. ▪ *www.typhoonrestaurants.
com*

Vine, The   ✪★ $$**LD**
Grants Pass ▪ *(541) 479-8463*
1610 Allen Creek Rd ▪ *Fusion* ▪ Among
the numerous GF options marked on the
menu are a sun-dried tomato pesto torte,
calamari, and paninis. GF bread is available
for burgers and sandwiches, and GF pasta
is available for substitution into any pasta
dish. GF pizza is also available. For dessert,
there is a GF chocolate ganache. ▪ *www.
wix.com/foodie19/the-vine-restaurant*

White Rabbit Bakery   ✪★   ¢**S**
Aurora ▪ *(503) 267-9044*
21368 Highway 99E NE ▪ *Bakery* ▪ Baker
Emily notes that a variety of GF baked
goods are marked on the menu. GF
sandwiches, muffins, cookies, bars, scones,
cupcakes, and more are available. She cautions that all baked goods are made in the
same kitchen, but she also notes that the
bakery has "never had an issue" with cross-
contamination.

Winger's Grill and Bar   ✪   ¢**LD**
Klamath Falls ▪ *(541) 273-9464*
3430 Washburn Way
Ontario ▪ *(541) 881-0062*
1255 SE 1st Ct ▪ *American* ▪ GF menu
includes double basted ribs, glazed salmon,

quesadillas with corn tortillas, and a variety of salads. ■ www.wingers.info

Woodsman, The   ⒸBLD
Philomath ■ **(541) 929-4500**
529 Main St ■ *Thai* ■ Manager Patty reports that GF diners are accommodated "all the time." She reports that most dishes can modified to be GF.

Zao Noodle Bar   ★ $LD
Lake Oswego ■ **(503) 620-6500**
7237 SW Bridgeport Rd ■ *Asian Noodles* ■ The only GF dish is pad thai. No other sauces are GF. ■ www.zaonoodle.com

Zia Southwest Cuisine $BLD
Corvallis ■ **(541) 757-9427**
121 SW 3rd St ■ *American Regional* ■ Manager Diego reports that most of menu is naturally GF. He notes that the enchiladas and burritos can be made with corn tortillas, and both soups are GF. He also reports that the buffet table has many GF options. Confirm timeliness of this information before dining in. Alert a server, who will indicate GF menu items. ■ www.ziaswcuisine.com

Zydeco Kitchen & Cocktails   Ⓧ $$$D
Bend ■ **(541) 312-2899**
1085 SE 3rd St ■ *Modern American* ■ GF menu is available upon request. Manager Shari reports that the goal of the GF menu is to "make GF diners feel like regular diners." She reports that the staff is very educated and GF aware. Reservations noting GF are recommended. Flourless chocolate cake is available for dessert. ■ www.zydecokitchen.com

PENNSYLVANIA
PHILADELPHIA

Amada   Ⓒ $$LD
Philadelphia ■ **(215) 625-2450**
217 Chestnut St ■ *Tapas* ■ Extensive GF menu includes tortillas espanolas, a variety of charcuteries and cheeses, clams and chorizo, seafood dishes, pork and white beans, and more. Alert a server, who will present the GF menu. ■ www.amadarestaurant.com

Amis Trattoria $$$$D
Philadelphia ■ **(215) 732-2647**
412 S 13Th St ■ *Italian* ■ Restaurant notes that everything is made to order, so accommodating GF requests is not a problem. They also note that "quite a few" regulars are GF. They report that their main chef won an award for GF cooking, so there are many options that the kitchen can prepare for GF diners. Reservations noting GF are recommended but not required. ■ www.amisphilly.com

Barclay Prime $$$$D
Philadelphia ■ **(215) 732-7560**
237 S 18th St ■ *Steakhouse* ■ General Manager Michele reports that the "majority" of menu items are GF. She recommends noting GF when making a reservation and alerting the server, so that a manager can "walk you through the menu." ■ www.starr-restaurant.com

Bindi Restaurant $$$D
Philadelphia ■ **(215) 922-6061**
105 S 13th St ■ *Indian* ■ Manager Valerie reports that nearly the entire menu is GF. She also notes that GF diners come in "all the time." Many dishes are lentil based, and so they are naturally GF. Upon arrival, ask to speak with a manager or chef, who will indicate non-GF menu items. ■ www.bindibyob.com

Bliss $$$LD
Philadelphia ■ **(215) 731-1100**

220 S Broad St ▪ Asian Fusion ▪ Owner Chris reports that they serve GF customers "all the time." He notes that if a diner makes a reservation noting GF, he will be sure to have at least two GF menu items to choose from. He adds that it is also possible to have a GF meal prepared without prior notice. ▪ www.bliss-restaurant.com

Buca di Beppo   📖
Philadelphia ▪ (215) 545-2818
258 S 15th St

Buddakan   ✪ $$$LD
Philadelphia ▪ (215) 574-9440
325 Chestnut St ▪ Asian Fusion ▪ GF menu items include Asian seasoned salad, crab fried rice, Singapore noodles, Japanese cod, and sesame crusted tuna. Most items are slight modifications of regular menu items. ▪ www.buddakan.com

Bugaboo Creek Steak House   📖
Philadelphia ▪ (215) 281-3700
601 Franklin Mills Cir

Cantina Laredo   📖
Philadelphia ▪ (215) 492-1160
8500 Essington Ave

Capital Grille, The   📖
Philadelphia ▪ (215) 545-9588
1338 Chestnut St

Chifa   ✪ $$$LD
Philadelphia ▪ (215) 925-5555
707 Chestnut St ▪ Asian & Latin Fusion ▪ GF menu includes fluke, medai, and tuna ceviches, chicken and saffron rice, duck and lobster buns, rice curry, rack of lamb, and more. GF desserts are not listed on the menu, but banana passion fruit mousse with coconut meringue can be made GF upon request. Confirm timeliness of this information before dining in. ▪ www.chifarestaurant.com

Cupcake Wonderland, A   ★ ¢S
Philadelphia ▪ (267) 968-6604
1620 Montrose St ▪ Bakery ▪ Non-dedicated bakery offering GF cakes and cupcakes. Items are available by order only, and

orders can be placed via email only. ▪ www.acupcakewonderland.com

Del Frisco's Double Eagle Steak House   📖
Philadelphia ▪ (215) 246-0533
1426 Chestnut St

Distrito Restaurant   ✪ $LD
Philadelphia ▪ (215) 222-1657
3945 Chestnut St ▪ Latin American ▪ GF menu includes flatbreads with mushrooms, short ribs, and ham, as well as guacamole, tacos, chop salad with walnuts and apples, ceviches, and more. ▪ www.distritorestaurant.com

Fogo De Chao   ★ $$$$LD
Philadelphia ▪ (215) 636-9700
1337 Chestnut St ▪ Brazilian ▪ GF cheese bread made with yucca flour is available. ▪ www.fogodechao.com

Giorgio on Pine   ★ $$LD
Philadelphia ▪ (215) 545-6265
1328 Pine St ▪ Italian ▪ GF pasta and pizza are available. Restaurant reports that they always try to have one GF dessert available. At the time of publication, restaurant was working on a complete GF menu. ▪ www.giorgioonpine.com

Horizon's Café $$D
Philadelphia ▪ (215) 923-6117
611 S 7th St ▪ Vegan ▪ Owner Kate reports that they are "very accustomed to accommodating" GF diners. She notes that all staff members are trained to guide GF guests through the menu, indicating items that are naturally GF or items that can be prepared GF. ▪ www.horizonsphiladelphia.com

James   ★ $$$D
Philadelphia ▪ (215) 629-4980
824 S 8th St ▪ Modern American ▪ GF pasta is available. Restaurant reports that most of the menu is GF, and all servers are GF aware. ▪ www.jameson8th.com

Legal Sea Foods 📖
Philadelphia ▪ *(267) 295-9300*
Philadelphia Int'l Airport

Lolita $$$D
Philadelphia ▪ *(215) 546-7100*
106 S 13th St ▪ *Modern Mexican* ▪ All appetizers and entrées are naturally GF. Confirm timeliness of this information before dining in. For dessert, there is one GF item: a flourless chocolate cake. All servers are trained on the GF diet and knowledgeable about the menu, so alert a server upon arrival. ▪ *www.lolitabyob.com*

Long's Gourmet Chinese ★ $LD
Philadelphia ▪ *(215) 496-9928*
2018 Hamilton St ▪ *Chinese* ▪ GF soy sauce is available. Manager Fon reports that most menu items can be made GF. She recommends asking for her upon arrival, as she can discuss GF options with diners.

Maggiano's Little Italy ★ $$$LD
Philadelphia ▪ *(215) 567-2020*
1201 Filbert St ▪ *Italian* ▪ GF pasta is available. Call individual locations to inquire about additional GF options. ▪ *www.maggianos.com*

Marigold Kitchen $$$D
Philadelphia ▪ *(215) 222-3699*
502 S 45th St ▪ *Modern American* ▪ Manager Nina reports that GF diners are "frequently" accommodated. She notes that most of the menu is naturally GF, and other dishes can be modified to be GF. She adds that servers can usually indicate GF menu items, and if they cannot, they will ask a manager. ▪ *www.marigoldkitchenbyob.com*

Matyson $$$LD
Philadelphia ▪ *(215) 564-2925*
37 S 19th St ▪ *Modern American* ▪ Manager Zack reports that GF diners are welcome and "very easily accommodated." He recommends making reservations noting GF and alerting a server upon arrival. Many menu items are naturally GF and the kitchen is capable of modifying other dishes to be GF. ▪ *www.matyson.com*

Melting Pot, The 📖
Philadelphia ▪ *(215) 922-7002*
1219 Filbert St

Mom's Bake At Home Pizza ★ $BLD
Philadelphia ▪ *(215) 247-7878*
219 E Willow Grove Ave
Philadelphia ▪ *(215) 487-2440*
4452 Main St # 54 ▪ *Take-&-Bake* ▪ GF "take-&-bake" pizza is available for pick-up only. ▪ *www.momsbakeathome.com*

Morimoto $$$$LD
Philadelphia ▪ *(215) 413-9070*
723 Chestnut St ▪ *Japanese* ▪ Hostess Jessica recommends reservations noting GF, as they will give them a chance to prepare. She notes that all staff members are very educated about the GF diet, so servers will be able to indicate GF menu items. For prime time reservations, call at least two weeks in advance. ▪ *www.morimotorestaurant.com*

My Thai $$D
Philadelphia ▪ *(215) 985-1878*
2200 South St ▪ *Thai* ▪ Manager Idd reports that they serve GF diners "all the time" and that there are "several" menu items that are GF. Alert a server, who will indicate "exactly" which menu items are not GF.

Ninety Nine Restaurant & Pub 📖
Philadelphia ▪ *(215) 464-9099*
9183 Roosevelt Blvd

Osteria $$$D
Philadelphia ▪ *(215) 763-0920*
640 N Broad St ▪ *Italian* ▪ Hostess Jaclyn reports that all servers are "extremely familiar" with the GF diet. She notes that "plenty of people" come in to request GF meals, and she adds that they typically choose a slightly modified entrée off the menu or bring their own pasta to be prepared with any sauce on the menu. ▪ *www.osteriaphilly.com*

Paradiso Restaurant & Wine Bar
★ $$LD

Philadelphia ▪ *(215) 271-2066*
1627 E Passyunk Ave ▪ *Italian* ▪ Chef Lynn
reports that the menu is seasonal, but almost any entrée can be prepared GF upon
request. GF pasta is available, though it is
not on the menu. Alert a server, who will
indicate GF items. ▪ *www.paradisophilly.
com*

Pei Wei Asian Diner   📖
Philadelphia ▪ *(215) 594-8230*
4040 City Ave Ste 2 Spc 2

Pod   ★ $$LD
Philadelphia ▪ *(215) 387-1803*
3636 Sansom St ▪ *Asian* ▪ GF soy sauce is
available. The restaurant reports that many
of the menu items can be modified to be
GF. Alert a server upon arrival. ▪ *www.
podrestaurant.com*

Roy's   ✪ $$$D
Philadelphia ▪ *(215) 988-1814*
124 South 15th St. ▪ *Hawaiian Fusion* ▪
Limited GF menu includes pan seared
Atlantic salmon, beef short ribs, and pan
seared chicken breast. Administrator Naomi reports that servers are trained to ask
guests if they have any "dietary restrictions"
when they first approach the table, and to
notify the chef immediately if the response
is affirmative. ▪ *www.roysrestaurant.com*

Sazon Restaurant and Café $LD
Philadelphia ▪ *(215) 763-2500*
941 Spring Garden St ▪ *Venezuelan* ▪
Manager Robert reports that GF diners should alert the server upon arrival.
The server will speak to Chef Judy, who
is happy to prepare GF meals. GF desserts include a variety of hot chocolates
and truffles, egg custard, different flavors
of flan, and a rice pudding drink. ▪ *www.
sazonrestaurant.com*

Smith & Wollensky $$$$LD
Philadelphia ▪ *(215) 545-1700*
210 W Rittenhouse Sq ▪ *Steakhouse* ▪ Assistant General Manager Lane reports that
most of the regular menu is GF. She notes
that the split pea soup, salad without crou-

tons, Berkshire Farm pork porterhouse,
and dry-aged bone-in ribeye are all GF,
as are the trio of crème brulee, fresh fruit,
and root beer float. Confirm timeliness of
this information before dining in. ▪ *www.
smithandwollensky.com*

Supper $$$LD
Philadelphia ▪ *(215) 592-8180*
926 South St ▪ *Global* ▪ Manager Sue
notes that the restaurant serves GF diners
"all the time." She reports that many menu
items can be modified to be GF. She highly
recommends reservations noting GF, so
servers can prepare in advance. ▪ *www.sup-
perphilly.com*

Sweet Freedom Bakery   100% ¢S
Philadelphia ▪ *(215) 545-1899*
1424 South St ▪ *Bakery* ▪ Dedicated GF
bakery offering an extensive menu of cookies, muffins, and loaves. Daily specials are
available as listed on the website. ▪ *www.
sweetfreedombakery.com*

Tinto   ✪ $$$D
Philadelphia ▪ *(215) 665-9150*
116 S 20th St ▪ *Spanish* ▪ GF menu is a
version of the regular menu that includes
cheese plates, charcuterie, fish, tapas, and
more. ▪ *www.tintorestaurant.com*

Tre Scalini $$$D
Philadelphia ▪ *(215) 551-3870*
1533 S 11Th St ▪ *Italian* ▪ Chef Franca
reports that the restaurant gets "a lot" of
GF diners. She recommends that GF diners
choose a meat or fish dish from the menu
and alert the server that the meal must be
prepared GF. The server will tell the kitch-
en. Confirm timeliness of this information
before dining in. Reservations noting GF
are recommended. ▪ *www.trescalinirestau-
rant.com*

Ugly Moose, The   ★ $$D
Philadelphia ▪ *(215) 482-2739*
443 Shurs Ln ▪ *Pub Food* ▪ Owner JP notes
that many menu items can be modified to
be GF. He reports that the kitchen "always"
accommodates GF diners. Alert a server

upon arrival. GF beer is available. ▪ *www. theuglymoose.com*

Uno Chicago Grill   📖
Philadelphia ▪ *(215) 632-5577*
789 Franklin Mills Cir

White Dog Café $$$**LD**
Philadelphia ▪ *(215) 386-9224*
3420 Sansom St ▪ *Modern American* ▪
Manager Michael reports that the restaurant serves GF diners "on a regular basis." He recommends making reservations noting GF and alerting the server upon arrival. GF orders print in red so that the kitchen staff knows to avoid any sort of cross-contamination. Menu options include filet mignon, crispy seared sea trout, and an heirloom apple salad. Confirm timeliness of this information before dining in. ▪ *www.whitedog.com*

PENNSYLVANIA

PITTSBURGH

Buca di Beppo   📖
Pittsburgh ▪ *(412) 471-9463*
3 E Station Square Dr
Pittsburgh ▪ *(412) 788-8444*
6600 Robinson Center Dr

Calabria's Restaurant   ★ $$$**LD**
Pittsburgh ▪ *(412) 885-1030*
3107 Library Rd ▪ *Italian* ▪ GF pasta is available with advanced notice of one day. ▪ *www.calabrias.biz*

Capital Grille, The   📖
Pittsburgh ▪ *(412) 338-9100*
301 5th Ave

Carino's Italian   📖
Pittsburgh ▪ *(412) 788-8813*
1000 Sutherland Dr

Double Wide Grill $**LD**
Pittsburgh ▪ *(412) 390-1111*

2339 E Carson St ▪ *American* ▪ Wheat-free menu includes tofu with chimichurri sauce, New York strip steak, and BBQ St. Louis Ribs. Restaurant reports that servers are "top-notch trained" to serve GF customers. Confirm that WF dishes are also GF before ordering. ▪ *www.doublewidegrill.com*

Eat 'n Park   📖
Pittsburgh ▪ *(412) 787-8556*
100 Park Manor Dr
Pittsburgh ▪ *(412) 766-6764*
1002 Ohio River Blvd
Pittsburgh ▪ *(412) 242-3700*
11746 Frankstown Rd
Pittsburgh ▪ *(412) 561-7894*
1300 Banksville Rd
Pittsburgh ▪ *(412) 243-5530*
1605 S Braddock Ave
Pittsburgh ▪ *(412) 422-7203*
1816 Murray Ave
Pittsburgh ▪ *(412) 561-4944*
2874 W Liberty Ave
Pittsburgh ▪ *(412) 854-4855*
301 S Hills Vlg
Pittsburgh ▪ *(412) 882-0258*
5100 Clairton Blvd
Pittsburgh ▪ *(412) 366-6220*
7370 Mcknight Rd
Pittsburgh ▪ *(412) 364-1211*
7671 Mcknight Rd

First Watch - The Daytime Café   📖
Pittsburgh ▪ *(412) 787-1049*
215 Settlers Ridge Center Dr

Gluuteny   100% ¢**S**
Pittsburgh ▪ *(412) 521-4890*
1923 Murray Ave ▪ *Bakery* ▪ Dedicated GF bakery offering bread, cupcakes, brownies, muffins, cookies, cakes, and party platters. Advanced notice of one day is required for special orders, such as cakes or party platters. ▪ *www.gluuteny.com*

Lone Star Steakhouse & Saloon   📖
Pittsburgh ▪ *(412) 494-9990*
120 Andrew Dr

Mandy's Pizza   ★ $**LD**
Pittsburgh ▪ *(412) 931-1120*

512 Perry Hwy ■ Pizza ■ GF pizza and pasta are available. ■ www.mandyspizza.com

Melting Pot, The   📖
Pittsburgh ■ (412) 261-3477
125 W Station Square Dr

Mitchell's Fish Market   ✪ $$$**LD**
Pittsburgh ■ (412) 571-3474
1500 Washington Rd ■ Seafood ■ Extensive GF menu includes pan-roasted wild blue mussels, blackened salmon spinach salad, grilled shrimp and scallop skewers, Shanghai seafood sampler, lobster tail, filet mignon, and live Maine lobster. Mini crème brulee is available for dessert. ■ www.mitchellsfishmarket.com

Monterey Bay Fish Grotto   ★ $$$$**D**
Pittsburgh ■ (412) 481-4414
1411 Grandview Ave ■ Seafood ■ GF tapioca rolls are available, as is GF flour for dredging meats and making crabcakes. For dessert, the "steaming chocolate latte," a flourless soufflé cake served in a cappuccino cup, is available. Restaurant recommends reservations noting GF. ■ www.montereybayfishgrotto.com

Original Pancake House, The   ★ ¢**BL**
Pittsburgh ■ (412) 279-1442
2229 Swallow Hill Rd
Pittsburgh ■ (412) 358-9622
8600 McKnight Rd ■ Breakfast ■ GF pancakes are available. Select locations may serve other GF options. Call a specific location to inquire. ■ www.originalpancakehouse.com

Outback Steakhouse   📖
Pittsburgh ■ (412) 833-4211
25 Mcmurray Rd
Pittsburgh ■ (412) 635-5255
9395 Mcknight Rd

P.F. Chang's China Bistro   📖
Pittsburgh ■ (412) 464-0640
148 Bridge St
Pittsburgh ■ (412) 788-2901
1600 Settlers Ridge Center Dr

PENNSYLVANIA
ALL OTHER CITIES

1 North Front Street Café and Books
                                    100% ¢**BL**
Philipsburg ■ (814) 342-3113
1 N Front St ■ Coffee & Café ■ Owner is GF and has organized the entire café around GF dining. Extensive GF offerings include egg sandwiches, bagels, soups, cinnamon buns, danishes, carrot cake, cookies, and more. GF pizza is available every Friday. ■ www.1northfrontstreet.com

A.J.'s Club Soda   ★ $$
Peckville ■ (570) 383-7632
1017 Main St ■ Pub Food ■ GF bread, soy sauce, pizza, and beer are available. Other dishes, like steaks and wings, can be modified to be GF. Confirm timeliness of this information before dining in. Owner A.J. notes that all kitchen staff are GF aware because one of them is GF. ■ www.mybeer-buzz-ajclubsoda.blogspot.com

Alfredo's Pizza   ★ $**LD**
Broomall ■ (610) 355-9424
2900 W Chester Pike ■ Pizza ■ GF pizza is available in the personal size only. ■ www.alfredos-pizza.com

Arpeggio $$**LD**
Spring House ■ (215) 646-5055
542 Spring House Vlg Ctr ■ Mediterranean ■ Manager Missy reports that GF ordering guidelines and options are available on the restaurant's website. She notes that all kitchen staff and servers are GF aware. GF orders are marked with a special button that alerts chefs to use different utensils to prevent cross-contamination. ■ www.arpeggiobyob.com

Austin's Restaurant & Bar   ✪★ $$**LD**
Drexel Hill ■ (610) 678-5500
5037-37 Township Line Rd. ■ American ■ GF menu includes Cajun shrimp soup, Monterey ranch salad, filet mignon, baby

back ribs, and pasta dishes with brown rice instead of pasta. For dessert, a hot banana with caramel is available. GF beer is also served. ▪ *www.jbdawsons.com*

Baggataway Tavern   ★ $$D
West Conshohocken ▪ *(610) 834-8085*
31 N Front St ▪ *Pub Food* ▪ Bartender Keith reports that GF diners are welcome, and they should be prepared to ask a staff member what can be prepared GF. Keith recommends speaking to himself or Manager Stew. GF beer is available. ▪ *www. baggtav.com*

Basically Burgers   ★ ¢LD
Doylestown ▪ *(215) 345-8502*
12 W State St ▪ *American* ▪ Manager Jason reports that GF hamburger buns are available. He adds that the restaurant has "several" GF diners "who are regulars," and that fried items can be prepared in fresh oil. ▪ *www.basicallyburgers.com*

Bella Tori at the Mansion $$$D
Langhorne ▪ *(215) 702-9600*
321 S Bellevue Ave ▪ *Italian* ▪ Manager Ryan reports that they are "very good about accommodating" GF diners. Mention GF when making a reservation, and alert a server upon arrival. ▪ *www.bellatori. com*

Bertucci's   📖
Bryn Mawr ▪ *(610) 519-1940*
761 W Lancaster Ave # 763
Glen Mills ▪ *(610) 358-0127*
501 Byers Dr
Huntingdon Valley ▪ *(215) 322-2200*
2190 County Line Rd
Langhorne ▪ *(215) 752-9200*
675 Middletown Blvd
Norristown ▪ *(610) 630-1890*
711 S Trooper Rd
Plymouth Meeting ▪ *(610) 397-0650*
500 W Germantown Pike
Springfield ▪ *(610) 543-8079*
965 Baltimore Pike
Warrington ▪ *(215) 918-1590*
855 Easton Rd

Wayne ▪ *(610) 293-1700*
523 W Lancaster Ave

Bona Terra Restaurant $$$$D
Sharpsburg ▪ *(412) 781-8210*
908 Main St ▪ *Organic* ▪ Open for dinner Tuesday through Saturday only. Manager Andrew reports that "everything is made in-house" and the chefs are "happy" to accommodate GF diners. Bisques and bean soups, tofu and vegetable dishes, and polenta cakes can be modified to be GF. Confirm timeliness of this information before dining in. ▪ *www.bonaterrapgh.com*

Bonefish Grill   📖
Exton ▪ *(610) 524-1010*
460 W Lincoln Hwy
Newtown Square ▪ *(610) 355-1784*
4889 West Chester Pike
Whitehall ▪ *(610) 264-3476*
901 Lehigh Lifestyle Ctr
Willow Grove ▪ *(215) 659-5854*
1015 Easton Rd

Brothers Pizza West Chester   ★ $LD
West Chester ▪ *(610) 431-1000*
670 Downingtown Pike ▪ *Pizza* ▪ GF pizza is available. Owner Bill reports that all staff are trained to handle GF pizza properly. Located in Bradford Plaza. ▪ *www.brother- spizzawestchester.com*

Buca di Beppo   📖
Exton ▪ *(610) 524-9939*
300 Main St
Whitehall ▪ *(610) 264-3389*
714 Grape St
Wyomissing ▪ *(610) 374-3482*
2745 Papermill Rd

Café Monterosso   ★ $$LD
Yardley ▪ *(215) 295-1311*
93 Makefield Rd ▪ *Italian* ▪ GF pizza and pasta are available for substitution into any of the regular pizza or pasta dishes. For dessert, they offer GF brownies, cakes, cheesecakes, and cookies. Owner and Chef Dave reports that there is a special area for GF meal preparation. ▪ *www.cafemonter- osso.com*

Caileigh's $$$D
Uniontown ▪ (724) 437-9463
105 E Fayette St ▪ Modern American ▪ Supervisor Samantha reports that GF diners are accommodated "on a regular basis." She notes that most menu items are naturally GF, and others can be modified to be GF. Reservations noting GF are recommended. Alert a server upon arrival. ▪ www.caileighs.com

California Café   ★ $LD
King Of Prussia ▪ (610) 354-8686
160 N Gulph Rd ▪ Fusion ▪ GF pasta is sometimes available. Sous-chef Steve reports that "many" GF diners come to the restaurant. He notes that there are some naturally GF items on the menu. He also notes that the kitchen can modify several menu items to be GF, or just make up their own GF dishes. ▪ www.californiacafe.com

Carino's Italian   ☐
Monroeville ▪ (412) 856-1780
145 Mall Circle Dr

Carrabba's Italian Grill   ☐
Bensalem ▪ (215) 245-3555
3210 Tillman Dr
Easton ▪ (610) 258-5326
2471 Park Ave
Frazer ▪ (610) 725-1901
245 Lancaster Ave
Lancaster ▪ (717) 560-6756
100 N Pointe Blvd
Mechanicsburg ▪ (717) 795-9200
5250 Carlisle Pike
Springfield ▪ (610) 544-0517
1250 Baltimore Pike
West Chester ▪ (610) 358-0156
102 Painters Xing
Willow Grove ▪ (215) 659-3950
2575 Maryland Rd

Charlie Brown's Steakhouse   ☐
Allentown ▪ (610) 437-1070
1908 Walbert Ave
Bloomsburg ▪ (570) 389-7880
181 Columbia Mall Dr
Harrisburg ▪ (717) 558-8449

3523 Union Deposit Rd
Langhorne ▪ (215) 757-8830
735 Middletown Blvd
Springfield ▪ (610) 604-7410
1001 Baltimore Pike
York ▪ (717) 751-6989
2860 Whiteford Rd

Eat 'n Park   ☐
Altoona ▪ (814) 943-4070
Eatnpark
Beaver Falls ▪ (724) 847-7275
500 Chippewa Town Ctr
Belle Vernon ▪ (724) 930-7470
1675 Broad Ave
Bethel Park ▪ (412) 835-4011
5220 Library Rd
Bridgeville ▪ (412) 221-8800
1197 Washington Pike
Butler ▪ (724) 282-7674
114 Clearview Cir
Butler ▪ (724) 287-0153
214 New Castle Rd
Canonsburg ▪ (724) 941-8261
3528 Washington Rd
Clarion ▪ (814) 227-2188
35 Perkins Rd
Dubois ▪ (814) 375-8622
1355 Bee Line Hwy
Erie ▪ (814) 838-9125
2519 W 12Th St
Erie ▪ (814) 866-3970
7355 Peach St
Etna ▪ (412) 487-4870
930 Butler St
Franklin ▪ (814) 432-3352
553 Allegheny Blvd
Gibsonia ▪ (724) 443-7280
5143 Route 8
Greensburg ▪ (724) 837-2759
5277 Route 30
Grove City ▪ (724) 748-5911
1911 Leesburg Road
Harrisburg ▪ (717) 986-9194
4641 Lindle Rd
Hermitage ▪ (724) 342-1383
2270 E State St
Homestead ▪ (412) 464-7275
245 Waterfront Dr E

Indiana ▪ (724) 465-2301
2675 Oakland Ave
Irwin ▪ (724) 864-8031
8891 Route 30
Johnstown ▪ (814) 266-5714
1461 Scalp Ave
Johnstown ▪ (814) 255-7711
1900 Minno Dr
Lancaster ▪ (717) 390-2212
1683 Oregon Pike
Latrobe ▪ (724) 532-1966
520 Mountain Laurel Plz
Mars ▪ (724) 776-4460
19085 Perry Hwy
Mc Kees Rocks ▪ (412) 331-2881
300 Chartiers Ave
Mckeesport ▪ (412) 664-9148
805 Lysle Blvd
Monaca ▪ (724) 770-0644
120 Wagner Rd
Monongahela ▪ (724) 258-4654
1250 W Main St
Monroeville ▪ (412) 373-8760
3987 Monroeville Blvd
Moon Twp ▪ (412) 264-7201
9516 University Blvd
Murrysville ▪ (724) 327-7270
4584 William Penn Hwy
Natrona Hts ▪ (724) 224-2442
1626 Broadview Blvd
New Castle ▪ (724) 654-2311
100 W Washington St
New Cumberland ▪ (717) 774-5004
146 Sheraton Dr
New Kensington ▪ (724) 335-3361
380 Freeport St
New Stanton ▪ (724) 925-1060
PO Box 223
North Versailles ▪ (412) 816-2006
299 Lincoln Hwy
Sewickley ▪ (412) 741-4650
201 Ohio River Blvd
Somerset ▪ (814) 443-4579
926 N Center Ave
State College ▪ (814) 231-8558
1617 N Atherton St
Tarentum ▪ (724) 275-1014
3005 Pittsburgh Mills Blvd

Uniontown ▪ (724) 439-0440
519 W Main St
Washington ▪ (724) 229-7333
320 Oak Spring Rd
Washington ▪ (724) 222-7110
875 W Chestnut St
Wexford ▪ (724) 940-3270
2650 Brandt School Rd
York ▪ (717) 751-4891
145 Memory Ln

Ferrara's　　　　　　　　　✪★　$**LD**
Sharon ▪ (724) 347-1247
1208 Hall Ave ▪ Italian ▪ Extensive GF menu includes appetizers, pasta dishes, specialty pizzas, and sandwiches. GF pasta, pizza crust, and bread are available. Restaurant reports that over a third of their clientele is GF. ▪ www.ferraraatasteofitaly.com

First Watch - The Daytime Café　　📖
Cranberry Township ▪ (724) 741-0581
20424 Route 19

Gamble Mill Restaurant　　　$$$**LD**
Bellefonte ▪ (814) 355-7764
160 Dunlap St ▪ Modern American ▪ Restaurant reports that most entrées can be made GF. Steaks, vegetable substitutions for starches, and fish dishes can be made GF. Confirm timeliness of this information before dining in. Reservations noting GF are recommended. ▪ www.gamblemill.com

Good Eatz Green Café　　　✪★　¢**BLD**
West Reading ▪ (610) 670-4885
701 Penn Ave ▪ Healthy American ▪ GF items marked on the menu include pancakes, frittatas, ahi tuna, a turkey wrap, and a grilled reuben. GF sandwich breads, bagels, pizza, and pasta are available. The restaurant reports that GF diners make up a large part of their clientele, so GF options are extensive. ▪ www.goodeatzgreencafe.com

Grandma's Grotto　　　　✪★　$$$**LD**
Horsham ▪ (215) 675-4700
986 Easton Rd ▪ Italian ▪ GF menu includes caprese salad, mussel soup, garlic bread, bruschetta, penne vodka, fettucine

alfredo, chicken parmesan, veal with pro-sciutto and mushrooms, pizza, and more. Owner John reports that GF menu items are made fresh every day. GF pasta and bread are available. ▪ *www.grandmasgrotto. com*

Ground Round   📖
Coraopolis ▪ *(412) 269-0644*
5980 University Blvd
Greensburg ▪ *(724) 836-1550*
960 E Pittsburgh St

Gullifty's   ✪★ $LD
Rosemont ▪ *(610) 525-1851*
1149 Lancaster Ave ▪ *American* ▪ GF menu includes a Gran Marnier filet, Green God-dess tuna, grilled salmon, burgers without buns, and about 12 salad options. GF beer is available. ▪ *www.gulliftys.com*

Hershey Grill   ★ $$$$LD
Hershey ▪ *(717) 520-5656*
446 W Chocolate Ave ▪ *American* ▪ GF pasta is always available. Many of the soups are naturally GF. ▪ *www.hersheylodge.com*

Iron Hill Brewery & Restaurant
                                    ✪★ $$LD
Lancaster ▪ *(717) 291-9800*
781 Harrisburg Ave
Media ▪ *(610) 627-9000*
30 E State St
North Wales ▪ *(267) 708-2000*
1460 Bethlehem Pike
Phoenixville ▪ *(610) 983-9333*
130 Bridge St
West Chester ▪ *(610) 738-9600*
3 W Gay St ▪ *American* ▪ GF menu is available at all locations. It includes sand-wiches and burgers without buns, tomato basil soup, baked buffalo wings, and fisher-man's stew. GF beer is available. ▪ *www. ironhillbrewery.com*

Isaac Newton's $LD
Newtown ▪ *(215) 860-5100*
18 S State St ▪ *American* ▪ Manager Aaron reports that they have discontinued the GF beer, but they can still accommodate GF diners and do so frequently. Though GF menu items are not marked, the server should be able to indicate them. ▪ *www. isaacnewtons.com*

Isaac's Famous Grilled Sandwiches
                                    ★ ¢LD
Ephrata ▪ *(717) 733-7777*
120 N Reading Rd
Exton ▪ *(484) 875-5825*
630 W Uwchlan Ave
Hanover ▪ *(717) 646-0289*
1412 Baltimore St
Harrisburg ▪ *(717) 541-1111*
2900 Linglestown Rd
Harrisburg ▪ *(717) 920-5757*
421 Friendship Rd
Hummelstown ▪ *(717) 533-9665*
100 Lucy Ave
Lancaster ▪ *(717) 560-7774*
1559 Manheim Pike
Lancaster ▪ *(717) 393-1199*
245 Centerville Rd
Lancaster ▪ *(717) 394-5544*
25 N Queen St
Lancaster ▪ *(717) 393-6067*
565 Greenfield Rd
Lemoyne ▪ *(717) 731-9545*
1200 Market St
Lititz ▪ *(717) 625-1181*
4 Crosswinds Dr
Mechanicsburg ▪ *(717) 766-1111*
4940 Ritter Road (Rossmoyne Business Center)
Mechanicsburg ▪ *(717) 795-1925*
6520 Carlisle Pike
Reading ▪ *(610) 376-9354*
94 Commerce Dr
Strasburg ▪ *(717) 687-7699*
226 Gap Rd
York ▪ *(717) 854-2292*
2159 White St
York ▪ *(717) 747-5564*
235 Pauline Dr
York ▪ *(717) 751-0515*
2960 Whiteford Road ▪ *Sandwich & Soups* ▪ GF flatbread is available for sand-wiches, or for purchase by the dozen. ▪ *www.isaacsdeli.com*

J.B. Dawson's Restaurant & Bar ✪ $$LD
Drexel Hill ▪ *(610) 853-0700*
5037 Township Line Rd # 37
Lancaster ▪ *(717) 399-3996*
491 Park City Ctr
Langhorne ▪ *(215) 702-8119*
92 N Flowers Mill Rd ▪ *American* ▪ GF
menu includes slow roasted baby back
ribs and several steaks. The fresh salmon
and tilapia entrées are also GF. Any pasta
dish can be prepared with brown rice
rather than pasta, and most salads can be
modified to be GF. For dessert, there is hot
banana caramel crunch without the crunch
and a hot fudge sundae. ▪ *www.jbdawsons.
com*

Jessica's Bagel Bin & Deli ✪★ ¢BL
Hamlin ▪ *(570) 689-7797*
RR 590 ▪ *Deli* ▪ GF menu is a flyer that lists
all GF items and includes breads, sandwiches, crackers, ice cream cones, cereals,
pretzels, and pasta. The restaurant reports
that it hosts "many" GF diners. GF pies are
available with advanced notice of at least
24 hours.

Jules Thin Crust Pizza ★ $$LD
Doylestown ▪ *(215) 345-8537*
78 S Main St
Newtown ▪ *(215) 579-0111*
300 N Sycamore St ▪ *Pizza* ▪ GF pizza is
available. ▪ *www.julesthincrust.com*

Kabuki $$LD
Peckville ▪ *(570) 383-3888*
1574 Main St ▪ *Japanese* ▪ Veteran Server
Gita reports that the restaurant has a few
regulars who are GF and bring their own
GF soy sauce to the restaurant. All GF diners are welcome to do the same. Gita notes
that most sushi is GF, but she cautions that
not all employees are GF aware.

Lamberti's Cucina $LD
Feasterville ▪ *(215) 355-6266*
1045 St Rd & Bustleton Pike ▪ *Italian* ▪
Manager Vidalia reports that the kitchen
can modify several menu items to be GF.
She notes that grilled chicken, vegetables,

pasta dishes, and all of the sauces can be
modified to be GF. Confirm timeliness of
this information before dining in. ▪ *www.
lambertis.com*

Legal Sea Foods 📖
King Of Prussia ▪ *(610) 265-5566*
690 W Dekalb Pike

Lone Star Steakhouse & Saloon 📖
Easton ▪ *(610) 252-1180*
20 Kunkle Dr
Johnstown ▪ *(814) 262-0707*
510 Galleria Dr
King Of Prussia ▪ *(610) 265-2370*
153 S Gulph Rd
Mars ▪ *(724) 779-4441*
926 Sheraton Dr
West Mifflin ▪ *(412) 655-1986*
6111 Mountain View Dr
Whitehall ▪ *(610) 432-0939*
1410 Grape St
Wilkes Barre ▪ *(570) 826-7080*
805 Kidder St

Maggiano's Little Italy ★ $$$LD
King Of Prussia ▪ *(610) 992-3333*
160 N Gulph Rd ▪ *Italian* ▪ GF pasta is
available. Call individual locations to inquire about additional GF options. ▪ *www.
maggianos.com*

Main Line Pizza ★ $$LD
Wayne ▪ *(610) 687-4008*
233 E Lancaster Ave ▪ *Pizza* ▪ GF pizza is
available. The restaurant reports that GF
pizzas are requested "often." ▪ *www.main-
linepizza.com*

Mamma D's Italian Restaurant ✪★ $LD
Pipersville ▪ *(215) 766-9468*
6637 Easton Rd ▪ *Global* ▪ GF menu includes fried calamari with rice flour, grilled
chicken parmigiana, penne pasta with basil
pesto, and more. For dessert, there is a GF
chocolate truffle tort. GF diners should
always ask about other GF specials, as some
may not be listed. GF pasta and beer are
available. ▪ *www.mammadesiato.com*

Margaret Kuo's ★ $$LD
Malvern ▪ (610) 647-5488
190 Lancaster Ave
Media ▪ (610) 566-4110
1067 W Baltimore Pike
Wayne ▪ (610) 688-7200
175 E Lancaster Ave ▪ Chinese & Japanese ▪ General Manager Paul of the Wayne location reports that "most, but not all" of the menu items can be made GF because GF soy sauce is available. Confirm timeliness of this information before dining in. He recommends alerting the server and the manager upon arrival, and notes that all staff members are trained on the GF diet. The State St location in Media does not carry GF soy sauce. ▪ www.margaretkuo. com

Melting Pot, The 📖
Bethlehem ▪ (484) 241-4939
1 E Broad St
Harrisburg ▪ (717) 564-6358
3350 Paxton St
King Of Prussia ▪ (610) 265-7195
150 Allendale Rd
Warrington ▪ (215) 343-0895
751 Easton Rd

Miller's Smorgasbord ✪ $$$BLD
Ronks ▪ (717) 687-8853
2811 Lincoln Hwy E ▪ American ▪ GF menu is included in the "Food Sensitivities Booklet," which covers allergies as well as GF. Alert a server upon arrival. ▪ www. millerssmorgasbord.com

Mitchell's Fish Market ✪ $$$LD
Homestead ▪ (412) 476-8844
185 Waterfront Dr W ▪ Seafood ▪ Extensive GF menu includes pan-roasted wild blue mussels, blackened salmon spinach salad, grilled shrimp and scallop skewers, Shanghai seafood sampler, lobster tail, filet mignon, and live Maine lobster. Mini crème brulee is available for dessert. ▪ www.mitchellsfishmarket.com

Mom's Bake At Home Pizza ★ $$BLD
Devon ▪ (610) 254-0580

896 Lancaster Ave
Downingtown ▪ (610) 466-0999
3617 Old Lincoln Hwy
Glenmoore ▪ (610) 458-1022
Rts 100 And 401
Havertown ▪ (610) 446-1995
28 W Eagle Rd
Newtown ▪ (215) 968-5054
19 S State St
Newtown Square ▪ (610) 356-4099
4007 West Chester Pike
Sellersville ▪ (215) 794-1977
1301 Fairhill Rd ▪ Take-&-Bake ▪ GF "take-&-bake" pizza is available for pick-up. Restaurants report that they can bake the pizza, but it takes an additional 15 minutes. ▪ www.momsbakeathome.com

Mom's Coffee Pot ✿★ ¢BL
Gettysburg ▪ (717) 337-9034
65 W Middle St ▪ Coffee & Café ▪ GF menu includes sandwiches, salads, breakfast foods, and more. The restaurant just began baking GF bread, and often Owner Mary bakes GF dessert items.

Monterey Bay Fish Grotto ★ $$$$D
Monroeville ▪ (412) 374-8530
146 Mall Circle Dr ▪ Seafood ▪ GF tapioca rolls are available, as is GF flour for dredging meats and making crabcakes. Manager Tom reports that the restaurant is "hyperconcerned" with working around customers' allergies. He recommends the "steaming chocolate latte," a flourless chocolate soufflé cake served in a cappuccino cup, for dessert. Note GF in reservations in order to get GF rolls for the table. ▪ www.montereybayfishgrotto.com

Ninety Nine Restaurant & Pub 📖
Audubon ▪ (610) 635-0799
675 Shannondell Blvd
Trevose ▪ (215) 355-9099
3617 Horizon Blvd
Warrington ▪ (215) 343-8099
500 Easton Rd

Outback Steakhouse 📖
Allentown ▪ (610) 437-7117

3100 W Tilghman St
Altoona ▪ (814) 941-0555
100 Sheraton Dr
Bensalem ▪ (215) 633-8228
3240 Tillman Dr
Bethlehem ▪ (610) 814-5860
3200 Emrick Blvd
Conshohocken ▪ (610) 828-8931
322 Ridge Pike
Erie ▪ (814) 864-8513
2076 Interchange Rd
Frazer ▪ (610) 407-9444
675 Lancaster Ave
Glen Mills ▪ (610) 558-0644
561 Glen Eagle Sq
Harrisburg ▪ (717) 564-5082
3527 Union Deposit Rd
Jamison ▪ (215) 918-2633
2520 York Rd
Jenkintown ▪ (215) 886-5120
610 Old York Rd
Lancaster ▪ (717) 569-4500
100 N Pointe Blvd
Mechanicsburg ▪ (717) 795-9909
25 Gateway Dr
Monroeville ▪ (412) 374-8646
3000 Mosside Blvd
Montgomeryville ▪ (215) 855-1060
411 Doylestown Rd
Moon Township ▪ (412) 809-0120
1400 Market Place Blvd
Royersford ▪ (610) 792-4300
22 Anchor Pkwy
Springfield ▪ (610) 544-9889
1162 Baltimore Pike
State College ▪ (814) 861-7801
1905 Waddle Rd
Washington ▪ (724) 222-3524
460 Washington Rd
Wayne ▪ (610) 687-6023
299 E Swedesford Rd
Wilkes Barre ▪ (570) 823-7731
547 Arena Hub Plz
Wyomissing ▪ (610) 376-9910
1101 Woodland Rd
York ▪ (717) 757-4363
2496 E Market St

P.F. Chang's China Bistro   📖
Collegeville ▪ (610) 489-0110
10 Town Center Dr
Glen Mills ▪ (610) 545-3030
983 Baltimore Pike
Plymouth Meeting ▪ (610) 567-0226
510 W Germantown Pike
Warrington ▪ (215) 918-3340
721 Easton Rd

Pasta Lorenzo   ★ $$LD
Uniontown ▪ (724) 437-4440
100 Wayland Smith Dr ▪ Italian ▪ GF
pasta, pizza, and beer are available. ▪ *www.
pastalorenzo.com*

Pazzo Ristorante   ★ $$$$D
Mount Lebanon ▪ (412) 341-5555
1535 Washington Rd ▪ Italian ▪ Manager
Mario reports that "all servers are knowledgeable" about the GF diet and which
menu items are GF. He notes that they have
"more than thirty options" for GF diners.
GF breadsticks and GF beer are available.
Mario cautions that they frequently run out
of GF breadsticks. ▪ *www.pazzopittsburgh.
com*

Pei Wei Asian Diner   📖
Springfield ▪ (610) 549-9060
950 Baltimore Pike

Piazza Sorrento   ✪★ $LD
Hershey ▪ (717) 835-1919
16 Briarcrest Sq ▪ Italian ▪ GF pizza, pasta,
rolls, and beer are available. GF menu
includes a variety of pasta dishes and sandwiches. For dessert, they offer GF tiramisu
and crème brûlée. ▪ *www.piazzasorrento.
com*

Pizza Fusion   ★ $$LD
Gibsonia ▪ (724) 502-4160
5513 William Flynn Hwy ▪ Pizza ▪ GF pizza
and brownies are available. ▪ *www.pizzafu-
sion.com*

Pop Pop's Pizza & Pasta   ★ $$LD
Warminster ▪ (215) 441-8217
216 W Street Rd ▪ Pizza ▪ GF pizza is available.

Prince Street Café   ★ ¢**BLD**
Lancaster ▪ *(717) 397-1505*
15 N Prince St ▪ *Café* ▪ GF bread is available in two flavors: regular and cinnamon raisin. Any sandwich can be prepared on GF bread, and the kitchen will put foil over the grill before cooking a GF meal. ▪ *www.princestreetcafe.com*

Relish   ✪★ $$**LD**
Allentown ▪ *(610) 351-6126*
4686 Broadway ▪ *Modern American* ▪ GF items marked on the menu include mango tilapia, flat iron steak, shrimp scampi with angel hair pasta, and pizza. Manager Brian notes that the restaurant hosts GF diners "all the time." ▪ *www.eatrelish.net*

Roman Delight   ★ $$**LD**
Warminster ▪ *(215) 957-6465*
225 E St Rd ▪ *Italian* ▪ GF pizza, pasta, and beer are available. Manager John reports that a GF insert is included with the menu upon request. He notes that the restaurant is "accustomed" to dealing with GF diners. ▪ *www.romandelightwarminster.com*

Sal's Brick Oven Pizza   ★ $$$**LD**
Bethlehem ▪ *(610) 317-0400*
313 S New St ▪ *Pizza* ▪ GF pasta is sometimes available. Restaurant reports that GF diners are welcome to bring their own GF pasta or their own GF beer.

Smiler's Grill & Bar $$**LD**
Dickson City ▪ *(570) 383-0041*
600 Main St ▪ *American* ▪ Restaurant reports that they have accommodated GF diners in the past. They note that several chicken dishes, salads, and burgers can be modified to be GF. Confirm timeliness of this information before dining in. Upon arrival, ask to speak to a chef, who can discuss GF options.

Soba $$$**D**
Shadyside ▪ *(412) 362-5656*
5847 Ellsworth Ave ▪ *Asian Fusion* ▪ General Manager Ryan reports that there are "very few things" that cannot be prepared GF. He notes that they serve GF diners "all

the time," but it is "very important" to alert a server upon arrival. He suggests following up with the server upon delivery of the food. ▪ *www.bigburrito.com/soba*

Sunset Café   ✪ $$**D**
Greensburg ▪ *(724) 834-9903*
302 S Urania Ave ▪ *Modern American* ▪ GF menu includes tuscan tuna, NY strip steak, polenta with sausage, sautéed sweet peppers, and crème brulee. Alert a server upon arrival. Manager Ron reports that the staff is trained on the GF diet. ▪ *www.sunsetcafepa.com*

Sweet Christine's Gluten Free Confections   100% ¢**S**
Kennett Square ▪ *(610) 444-5542*
132 W State St ▪ *Bakery & Café* ▪ Dedicated GF bakery offering GF muffins, donuts, cookies, breads, cakes, and pizzelles. Calling ahead for special requests is recommended. ▪ *www.sweetchristinesglutenfree.com*

Tango $**LD**
Bryn Mawr ▪ *(610) 526-9500*
39 Morris Ave ▪ *Modern American* ▪ Manager Chris reports that GF diners are welcome. She says that a number of entrées and appetizers either are GF or can be made GF. She notes that all servers are knowledgeable about the GF diet, as GF diners are "fairly frequent." ▪ *www.tastetango.com*

Tavern, The $$**D**
State College ▪ *(814) 238-6116*
220 E College Ave ▪ *American* ▪ Manager Ben reports that "a number of entrées" can be made GF. He recommends alerting any staff member upon arrival so that the staff can communicate with the kitchen. Though the menu changes daily, they always offer chocolate mousse and GF parfaits for dessert. Confirm timeliness of this information before dining in. ▪ *www.thetavern.com*

Unique Desserts   ★ $**S**
West Reading ▪ *(610) 372-7879*
530 Grape St ▪ *Bakery* ▪ GF cookies and

cakes are available. Manager Ann-Louise reports that items are available by order only. She recommends calling ten days in advance to ensure that the bakery has time to prepare. ▪ *www.uniquedesserts.biz*

Uno Chicago Grill   📖
Altoona ▪ *(814) 941-8667*
206 E Plank Rd
Bensalem ▪ *(215) 322-6003*
801 Neshaminy Mall
Conshohocken ▪ *(610) 825-3050*
1009 Ridge Pike
Cranberry Township ▪ *(724) 772-1711*
1294 Freedom Rd
Dickson City ▪ *(570) 307-4200*
3905 Commerce Blvd
Exton ▪ *(610) 280-4555*
8 N Pottstown Pike
Homestead ▪ *(412) 462-8667*
205 Waterfront Dr E
Langhorne ▪ *(215) 741-6100*
198 N Buckstown Rd
North Wales ▪ *(215) 283-9760*
1100 Bethlehem Pike
Warrington ▪ *(215) 491-1212*
1661 Easton Rd

Virago   ★ ¢S
Lansdale ▪ *(215) 412-7071*
620 S Broad St ▪ *Bakery* ▪ Non-dedicated bakery offering GF cupcakes, lunches, "take-&-bake" pizzas, cakes, pastries, cookies, and rolls. Manager Joe reports that the bakery is very careful to separate GF ingredients from non-GF ingredients. Notice of at least a few days is required for special orders. ▪ *www.viragobakingcompany.com*

Woodside's Grille $$$**LD**
Sewickley ▪ *(724) 934-3000*
1600 Stone Mansion Dr ▪ *Global* ▪ Chef Robert reports that the restaurant "deals with Celiacs all the time." He notes that GF diners can ask for him, and he will discuss creative GF options with them. Reservations noting GF are recommended but not required. ▪ *www.stonemansionrestaurant.com*

Z Pizza   ★ $$**LD**
Mechanicsburg ▪ *(717) 691-1112*
6416 Carlisle Pike ▪ *Pizza* ▪ GF pizza is available. ▪ *www.zpizza.com*

RHODE ISLAND

PROVIDENCE

Capital Grille, The   📖
Providence ▪ *(401) 521-5600*
1 Union Sta

Fire + Ice $$**LD**
Providence ▪ *(401) 270-4040*
48 Providence Pl ▪ *Asian Stir-Fry* ▪ GF sauces are available. Restaurant notes that servers have access to an internal list of GF ingredients. They add that GF meals can be prepared separately in the kitchen, instead of on common cooking surfaces. Alert the server, who will make arrangements. ▪ *www.fire-ice.com*

Joe's American Bar & Grill $**LD**
Providence ▪ *(401) 270-4737*
148 Providence Pl ▪ *American* ▪ GF pasta and pizza are available. Both can be prepared in several different ways. The manager recommends alerting the server and using the word "allergy." ▪ *www.joesamerican.com*

Kabob and Curry   ✪ $**LD**
Providence ▪ *(401) 273-8844*
261 Thayer St ▪ *Indian* ▪ Extensive GF menu includes curries, soups, chickpea masala, tandoori shrimp, and more. ▪ *www.kabobandcurry.com*

Melting Pot, The   📖
Providence ▪ *(401) 865-6670*
199 Providence Pl

Pot Au Feu $$$**LD**
Providence ▪ *(401) 273-8953*
44 Custom House St ▪ *French Bistro* ▪

Manager Dale recommends making reservations noting GF and alerting a server upon arrival. He also notes that the chef has won an award for his GF recipes. ▪ *www.potaufeuri.com*

Rí~Rá Irish Pub $**LD**
Providence ▪ *(401) 272-1953*
50 Exchange Terr ▪ *Irish Pub* ▪ Ask for the "Allergen Chart," which has a "Celiac" column. This column contains items that are GF or can be modified to be GF. ▪ *www.rira.com*

Twist on Angell   ✪★ $$**LD**
Providence ▪ *(401) 831-4500*
500 Angell St ▪ *Modern American* ▪ GF menu includes clam soup, buffalo chicken tenders, and lemon pepper shrimp. Manager Jeff reports that they are a "certified GF restaurant." He also notes that the kitchen is designed to separate GF foods from non-GF foods. GF pasta and pizza are available. ▪ *www.pinellimarrarestaurants.com*

Union Station Brewery $$**LD**
Providence ▪ *(401) 274-2739*
36 Exchange Ter ▪ *American* ▪ Kitchen manager Juan reports that GF diners are becoming more common in the restaurant. Alert a server, who will notify him or the chef on duty. Juan notes that many menu items can be modified to be GF, the salads and protein dishes in particular. Confirm timeliness of this information before dining in. ▪ *www.johnharvards.com*

Uno Chicago Grill   📖
Providence ▪ *(401) 270-4866*
82 Providence Pl

Walter's Restaurant   ✪★ $$$**D**
Providence ▪ *(401) 273-2652*
286 Atwells Ave ▪ *Italian* ▪ GF menu includes duck breast, salmon, haddock, foie gras, and wild boar pappardelle. Manager Carmella reports that GF diners come in "all the time" because the restaurant is so well-versed on GF dining. GF pasta is available. ▪ *www.chefwalter.com*

Waterplace   ✪★ $$$**LD**
Providence ▪ *(401) 272-1040*
1 Finance Way ▪ *Modern American* ▪ GF menu includes hummus, a BBQ chopped chicken salad, and the Big Fat Greek sandwich without bread, among other things. For dessert, they offer flourless chocolate cake. Manager Juan reports that the GF menu is updated each time they change the regular menu. GF pasta and beer are available. ▪ *www.waterplaceri.com*

RHODE ISLAND
ALL OTHER CITIES

Bertucci's   📖
Warwick ▪ *(401) 732-4343*
1946 Post Rd

Bugaboo Creek Steak House   📖
Warwick ▪ *(401) 781-1400*
30 Jefferson Blvd

Carrabba's Italian Grill   📖
Warwick ▪ *(401) 827-8880*
1350 Bald Hill Rd

Cucina Mista   ★ $$$**D**
East Greenwich ▪ *(401) 398-2900*
455 Main St ▪ *Italian & Steakhouse* ▪ GF pasta is available. ▪ *www.cucinamista.com*

Cucina Twist   ✪★ $$**D**
S Kingstown ▪ *(401) 789-5300*
2095 Kingstown Rd ▪ *Italian* ▪ GF menu offers an entrée selection of meats and seafood, as well as a list of GF sauces. It also lists appetizers and sides. GF pizza is available. ▪ *www.pinellimarrarestaurants.com*

Cucina   ✪★ $$$**D**
North Smithfield ▪ *(401) 767-2444*
900 Victory Hwy ▪ *Italian* ▪ GF items marked on the menu include pizza, pasta, salads, chicken, steaks, and seafood. Restaurant recommends specifying GF in your

order, and servers will alert the chefs. GF pizza and pasta are available. ▪ *www.pinellimarrarestaurants.com*

Encore   ✪★ $$$D
North Providence ▪ *(401) 726-4400*
1058 Charles St ▪ *Italian* ▪ GF menu includes soups, salads, sweet chips, pizzas with toppings such as roast peppers, goat cheese, meatballs, brie, and walnuts, pasta bowls with seafood, sausage with mixed vegetables, several preparations of veal and chicken, salmon, steak, and more. GF pizza and pasta are available. ▪ *www.encorenprov.com*

Garden Grille Café, The   ✪★ $D
Pawtucket ▪ *(401) 726-2826*
727 East Ave ▪ *Global* ▪ GF items marked on the menu include mac and cheese, grilled sweet potatoes, nachos, Bhudda bowls, cakes, cookies, cupcakes, and mousse. The restaurant reports that there is also a different GF special every night. GF pasta and bread are available. ▪ *www.gardengrillecafe.com*

Grille on Main, The   ✪★ $$LD
E Greenwich ▪ *(401) 885-2200*
50 Main St ▪ *Modern American* ▪ Extensive GF menu includes a variety of salads, starters, pizzas, sandwiches, and entrées. GF pizza, rice bread, and rice wraps are available, as is a selection of GF beer. ▪ *www.pinellimarrarestaurants.com*

Ground Round   📖
Pawtucket ▪ *(401) 724-5522*
2 George St

Il Piccolo   ★ $$LD
Johnston ▪ *(401) 421-9843*
1450 Atwood Ave ▪ *Italian* ▪ GF pasta is available. Owner Monica notes that most other menu items can also be modified to be GF, including chicken, beef, and seafood dishes.

Legal Sea Foods   📖
Warwick ▪ *(401) 732-3663*
2099 Post Rd

Ninety Nine Restaurant & Pub   📖
Cranston ▪ *(401) 463-9993*
1171 New London Ave
Newport ▪ *(401) 849-9969*
199 Connell Hwy
Westerly ▪ *(401) 348-8299*
7 Airport Rd

Outback Steakhouse   📖
E Greenwich ▪ *(401) 886-4543*
1000 Division St

Papa Razzi   ★ $$LD
Cranston ▪ *(401) 942-2900*
1 Paparazzi Way ▪ *Italian* ▪ GF pasta and pizza are available. ▪ *www.paparazzitrattoria.com*

Pinelli's Cucina   ✪★ $$LD
Slatersville ▪ *(401) 767-2444*
900 Victory Hwy ▪ *Italian* ▪ GF items marked on the menu include penne pink vodka, scrod filet stuffed with baby shrimp, steak florentine, and chicken marsala. GF pizza and pasta are available. Alert the server, who will alert the kitchen. ▪ *www.pinellimarrarestaurants.com*

Post Office Café   ✪★ $$D
E Greenwich ▪ *(401) 885-4444*
11 Main St ▪ *Italian* ▪ GF menu includes entrées such as grilled sirloin gorgonzola, grilled chicken polermo, and harvest pork. GF pizza and pasta are available. ▪ *www.pinellimarrarestaurants.com*

Rasoi Restaurant   ✪★ $LD
Pawtucket ▪ *(401) 728-5500*
727 East Ave ▪ *Indian* ▪ Among the many GF items marked on the menu are lentil soup, chicken korma, vegetable mango curry, and tawa fish. For dessert, there is GF chocolate molten cake. GF beer is available. They have a dedicated GF buffet brunch on Saturday mornings. ▪ *www.rasoi-restaurant.com*

Twist   ✪★ $$LD
Warwick ▪ *(401) 734-4440*
336 Bald Hill Rd ▪ *Modern American* ▪ Extensive GF menu includes a variety of

starters, salads, entrées, sandwiches, and pizzas. GF bread and pizzas are available. ▪ www.pinellimarrarestaurants.com

Uno Chicago Grill 📖
Smithfield ▪ *(401) 233-4570*
371 Putnam Pike
Warwick ▪ *(401) 738-5610*
399 Bald Hill Rd

Wright's Farm Restaurant $LD
Harrisville ▪ *(401) 769-2856*
84 Inman Rd ▪ *American* ▪ There are three GF items available: chicken, french fries, and a dry salad. Though none of the salad dressings are GF, customers are welcome to bring their own. Confirm timeliness of this information before dining in. Servers have access to a list of GF items, so they can confirm upon request. ▪ *www.wrightsfarm. com*

SOUTH CAROLINA

Black Marlin Bayside Grill, The $$LD
Hilton Head Island ▪ *(843) 785-4950*
86 Helmsman Way ▪ *Seafood* ▪ Manager Jill reports that "plenty of seafood options" and steaks can be prepared GF. They can always provide rice pilaf on the side, as they have done "several times" for GF diners. Alert the server, who will act as a liaison to the chef. ▪ *www.blackmarlinhhi.com*

Bonefish Grill 📖
Columbia ▪ *(803) 407-1599*
1260 Bower Pkwy Ste A1
Columbia ▪ *(803) 787-6200*
4708 Forest Dr
Greenville ▪ *(864) 297-5142*
1515 Woodruff Rd
Hilton Head ▪ *(843) 341-3772*
890 William Hilton Pkwy Ste 74
Myrtle Beach ▪ *(843) 497-5294*

7401 N Kings Hwy
North Myrtle Beach ▪ *(843) 280-6638*
103 Highway 17 S
Surfside Beach ▪ *(843) 215-4374*
8703 Highway 17 Byp S Ste L

Bubba Gump Shrimp Co. 📖
Charleston ▪ *(843) 723-5665*
99 S Market St

Carrabba's Italian Grill 📖
Columbia ▪ *(803) 865-5688*
200 Graces Way
Columbia ▪ *(803) 407-1811*
370 Columbiana Dr
Greenville ▪ *(864) 213-9494*
1022A Woodruff Rd
Hilton Head Island ▪ *(843) 785-5007*
14 Folly Field Rd
Mt Pleasant ▪ *(843) 849-9126*
2668 Highway 17 N
Murrells Inlet ▪ *(843) 652-3800*
511 Courtfield Dr
Myrtle Beach ▪ *(843) 467-2600*
6803 N Kings Hwy
North Charleston ▪ *(843) 824-0404*
2150 Northwoods Blvd
North Myrtle Beach ▪ *(843) 281-9222*
1015 Highway 17 N

Crave Kitchen & Cocktails ✪ $$$D
Mount Pleasant ▪ *(843) 884-1177*
1968 Riviera Dr ▪ *American* ▪ GF menu includes seared bass, bouillabaisse, sirloin steak, and mussels. GF menu is not available for weekend brunches. Manager JC reports that they server GF diners "all the time." ▪ *www.cravemtp.com*

Dragon Palace ✪ $LD
Charleston ▪ *(843) 388-8823*
162 Seven Farms Dr ▪ *Chinese* ▪ GF menu includes General Tso's chicken, Mongolian beef, Buddha's feast, and more. Manager Teresa reports that GF items are marked on the to-go menu, but not on the regular menu. ▪ *www.dragonpalacesc.com*

Earth Fare Market ★ ⊄S
Charleston ▪ *(843) 769-4800*
74 Folly Road Blvd

Columbia ■ (803) 799-0048
3312B Devine St
Greenville ■ (864) 527-4220
3620 Pelham Rd
Rock Hill ■ (803) 327-1030
725 Cherry Rd ■ Bakery ■ Flourless chocolate cake and other GF baked goods are
available. The bakeries are located inside of
the Earth Fare Markets. ■ www.earthfare.
com

Fat Hen Restaurant ✪ $$D
Johns Island ■ (843) 559-9090
3140 Maybank Hwy ■ French Country
■ GF items marked on the menu include
duck confit, coq au vin, flouder, and salmon bearnaise. Restaurant notes that they are
"very GF friendly." ■ www.thefathen.com

Gina's Pizza & Italian Gourmet ★ ¢LD
Irmo ■ (803) 781-7800
107 N Royal Tower Dr ■ Italian ■ GF pizza
is available.

Harper's Restaurant ✪ $$LD
Columbia ■ (803) 252-2222
700 Harden St ■ American ■ GF menu includes chipotle chili roasted chicken salad,
hickory grilled sirloin, slow-cooked pulled
port BBQ, and slow-smoked Danish baby
back ribs. ■ www.harpersrestaurants.com

Melting Pot, The 📖
Columbia ■ (803) 731-8500
1410 Colonial Life Blvd W
Greenville ■ (864) 297-5035
475 Haywood Rd Ste 5
Myrtle Beach ■ (843) 692-9003
5001 N Kings Hwy Ste 104

Monster Pizza ★ ¢LD
Bluffton ■ (843) 757-6466
142 Burnt Church Rd
Bluffton ■ (843) 705-3434
30 William Pope Dr ■ Pizza ■ GF pizza,
beer, cakes, brownies, and cookies are
available. GF pasta is available at the Okatie
location only. ■ www.monsterpizzasc.com

Mustard Seed ✪★ $LD
Charleston ■ (843) 762-0072

1970 Maybank Hwy
Mount Pleasant ■ (843) 849-0500
1036 Chuck Dawley Blvd
Summerville ■ (843) 821-7101
101 N Main St ■ American ■ GF menu includes hummus, mussels, gazpacho, scallop
salad, mushroom risotto, and pasta dishes
with GF rice noodles. All three locations
have the same GF menu. ■ www.dinewith-
sal.com

Oak Steakhouse $$$D
Charleston ■ (843) 722-4220
17 Broad St ■ Steakhouse ■ Restaurant
reports that they are "100% able to accommodate" GF diners. The kitchen can prepare several dishes GF. Restaurant has accommodated entire GF parties in the past.
Reservations noting GF are recommended.
■ www.oaksteakhouserestaurant.com

Outback Steakhouse 📖
Aiken ■ (803) 644-4031
160 Aiken Mall Dr
Anderson ■ (864) 261-6283
110 Interstate Blvd
Beaufort ■ (843) 379-6283
2113 Boundary St
Bluffton ■ (843) 757-9888
100 Buckwalter Pkwy
Charleston ■ (843) 763-8999
1890 Sam Rittenberg Blvd
Columbia ■ (803) 732-3771
252 Harbison Blvd Ste F
Columbia ■ (803) 788-9800
7611 Two Notch Rd
Easley ■ (864) 855-7897
125 Southern Center Way
Florence ■ (843) 679-0055
110 Dunbarton Dr
Gaffney ■ (864) 902-0026
945 Factory Shops Blvd
Greenville ■ (864) 676-0360
21 Orchard Park Dr
Greenwood ■ (864) 223-6283
454 Bypass 72 NW
Hilton Head ■ (843) 681-4329
20 Hatton Pl
Mt Pleasant ■ (843) 849-9456

715 Johnnie Dodds Blvd
Murrells Inlet ▪ (843) 651-0080
3270 S Highway 17
Myrtle Beach ▪ (843) 236-8787
4650 Factory Stores Blvd
Myrtle Beach ▪ (843) 449-5888
7025 N Kings Hwy
North Charleston ▪ (843) 569-3600
7643 Rivers Ave
North Myrtle Beach ▪ (843) 280-4855
1721 Highway 17 N
Rock Hill ▪ (803) 329-6283
1319 River Run Ct
Spartanburg ▪ (864) 574-4329
1646 J.B. White Sr Blvd
Sumter ▪ (803) 469-4329
2480 Broad St

P.F. Chang's China Bistro 📖
Greenville ▪ (864) 297-0589
1127 Woodruff Rd
Myrtle Beach ▪ (843) 839-9470
1190 Farrow Pkwy

Red Bowl Asian Bistro ✪ $LD
Fort Mill ▪ (803) 802-5666
845 Stockbridge Dr ▪ Asian ▪ Extensive
GF menu includes the shrimp summer roll,
tom ka kai soup, and beef with spinach in
a white sauce, among other things. ▪ www.
redbowltegacay.com

Shane's Rib Shack 📖
Florence ▪ (843) 679-3503
1940 Hoffmeyer Rd Ste B

Travinia Italian Kitchen ★ $$LD
Aiken ▪ (803) 642-9642
470 Fabian Dr
Columbia ▪ (803) 419-9313
101 Sparkleberry Xing
Greenville ▪ (864) 458-8188
1625 Woodruff Rd
Lexington ▪ (803) 957-2422
5074 Sunset Blvd
Myrtle Beach ▪ (843) 233-8500
4011 Deville St ▪ Italian ▪ GF menu is available at all locations and includes fettuccini
alfredo, pasta with chicken and mushrooms, sausage and peppers rustica, classic

spaghetti bolognese, chicken scaloppini,
chicken piccata, and veal marsala. GF pasta
is available. ▪ www.traviniaitaliankitchen.
com

Uno Chicago Grill 📖
Lexington ▪ (803) 359-3888
5304 Sunset Blvd

SOUTH DAKOTA

Beau Jo's Colorado Style Pizza ✪★ $LD
Rapid City ▪ (605) 716-1033
2520 West Main St ▪ Pizza ▪ GF pizza
is available at all locations. All locations
except Steamboat Springs also carry a GF
menu that includes the salad bar, sandwiches, appetizers, and GF beer. Call a specific location for details on its GF offerings.
▪ www.beaujos.com

Buffaloberries ★ ¢L
Sioux Falls ▪ (605) 271-8280
309 S Phillips Ave ▪ Café ▪ GF pizza,
bread, pumpkin muffins, brownies, and
more are available. Owner Karen notes
that with very few exceptions, items on the
menu are GF or can be modified to be GF.
▪ www.buffaloberries.com

Bully Blends Coffee & Tea Shop ★ ¢BLD
Rapid City ▪ (605) 342-3559
410 5th St ▪ Coffee & Café ▪ GF beer is
available from 11am to close. GF cheesecake brownies and soups are sometimes
available. ▪ www.bullyblends.com

Carino's Italian 📖
Sioux Falls ▪ (605) 361-7222
2310 S Louise Ave

Ground Round 📖
Sioux Falls ▪ (605) 334-8995
1301 W 41st St

Jim's Tap ★ ¢S
Brookings ▪ (605) 692-2833
309 Main Ave ▪ *Pub Food* ▪ GF beer is available.

Lintz Brother's Pizza ★ ¢D
Hermosa ▪ (605) 255-4808
14287 Sd Highway 36 ▪ *Pizza* ▪ GF pizza is available in the 10-inch size. Any available toppings can be put on the GF crust. A selection of GF beer is also available.

Lone Star Steakhouse & Saloon 📖
Sioux Falls ▪ (605) 331-3648
1801 W 41st St

Meadowood Lanes ★ ¢LD
Rapid City ▪ (605) 343-0923
3809 Sturgis Rd ▪ *American* ▪ GF beer is available.

Monkey's Bar & Grill ★ ¢S
Dell Rapids ▪ (605) 428-6000
313 N Garfield Ave ▪ *Pub Food* ▪ GF beer is available.

Original Pancake House, The ★ ¢BL
Sioux Falls ▪ (605) 271-7222
2713 W 41st St ▪ *Breakfast* ▪ GF pancakes and crepes are available. ▪ *www.original-pancakehouse.com*

Outback Steakhouse 📖
Rapid City ▪ (605) 341-1192
665 E Disk Dr
Sioux Falls ▪ (605) 362-7266
2411 S Carolyn Ave

Pirates Table ✪ $$$D
Rapid City ▪ (605) 341-4842
3550 Sturgis Rd ▪ *American* ▪ GF menu includes the shrimp cocktail, chilled relish tray, ribeye steak, top sirloin steak, chicken cordon bleu, burgers without buns, wild salmon filet, halibut steak, mahi-mahi, and more.

Sanaa's Gourmet ✪ ¢LD
Sioux Falls ▪ (605) 275-2516
401 E 8th St ▪ *Mediterranean* ▪ GF menu includes Mediterranean calzones, beef kabobs, and chicken on a bed of saffron rice.

GF bread and pizza are available. ▪ *www.sanaasgourmet.com*

Timber Lodge Steakhouse ✪ $$$D
Sioux Falls ▪ (605) 361-8899
3509 W 41st St ▪ *Steakhouse* ▪ GF menu includes prime rib, rainbow trout, walleye filet, Atlantic salmon, and more. ▪ *www.timberlodgesteakhouse.com*

Wooly Mammoth Family Fun ★ $$BLD
Hot Springs ▪ (605) 745-6414
1403 Highway 18 Byp ▪ *American* ▪ GF beer is available.

TENNESSEE

KNOXVILLE

Bonefish Grill 📖
Knoxville ▪ (865) 966-9777
11395 Parkside Dr
Knoxville ▪ (865) 558-5743
6604 Kingston Pike

Carino's Italian 📖
Knoxville ▪ (865) 671-1900
210 Lovell Rd

Carrabba's Italian Grill 📖
Knoxville ▪ (865) 692-2223
324 N Peters Rd

Earth Fare Market ★ ¢S
Knoxville ▪ (865) 777-3837
10903 Parkside Dr ▪ *Bakery* ▪ Chef Ashley reports that each day, there is a table with GF brownies, cookies, pound cakes, and mint-squares. She also makes a variety of other GF baked goods that change daily. She recommends calling ahead for the best selection of GF products, and she can accommodate special orders with advanced notice. ▪ *www.earthfare.com*

Gluten-Free Goodies 100% ¢BL
Knoxville ▪ (865) 602-2000
5211 Kingston Pike ▪ *Bakery & Café* ▪

Dedicated GF bakery and café offering
bread, pasta, cookies, pies, cakes, cupcakes,
muffins, brownies, and more. Sample meals
include french toast, biscuits with gravy,
and homemade chicken salad on bread or
on top of a salad. ▪ *www.glu10freegoodies.*
com

Melting Pot, The   📖
Knoxville ▪ *(865) 971-5400*
111 N Central St

Outback Steakhouse   📖
Knoxville ▪ *(865) 281-0999*
314 Merchant Dr Ste A
Knoxville ▪ *(865) 539-2540*
330 N Peters Rd
Knoxville ▪ *(865) 932-0636*
7400 Sawyer Ln

P.F. Chang's China Bistro   📖
Knoxville ▪ *(865) 212-5514*
6741 Kingston Pike

Pei Wei Asian Diner   📖
Knoxville ▪ *(865) 966-1610*
11301 Parkside Dr Ste 1200

Pizza Kitchen, The   ★ ¢LD
Knoxville ▪ *(865) 531-1422*
9411 S Northshore Dr ▪ *Pizza* ▪ GF pizza
and beer are available. Other menu items,
like chicken strips, can also be made GF.
Owner Travis reports that they "generally"
have GF products "seven days a week." ▪
www.thepizzakitchen.net

Roman's Pizza   ★ $$LD
Knoxville ▪ *(865) 539-1784*
179 N Seven Oaks Dr ▪ *Pizza* ▪ GF pizza,
pasta, stromboli, calzones, and desserts
like carrot cake are available. Call at least
2 hours ahead of time for the GF pizza. ▪
www.romans-pizza.com

TENNESSEE
NASHVILLE

Aquarium Restaurant $$LD
Nashville ▪ *(615) 514-3474*
516 Opry Mills Dr ▪ *Seafood* ▪ General
Manager Bill reports that they accommodate GF requests "every day." He notes that
nearly all of the GF diners are children, so
the staff treats items prepared GF especially
carefully. All GF items are cooked separately, and GF fried foods are prepared in
clean oil.

BrickTop's   ✪ $$$LD
Nashville ▪ *(615) 298-1000*
3000 West End Ave ▪ *Seafood & Steak-
house* ▪ GF menu includes rotisserie
chicken, steak frites, ahi tuna salad, and
babyback ribs. The signature appetizer,
deviled eggs and bacon sausage, is also GF.
For dessert, they offer a hot fudge sundae. ▪
www.westendrestaurants.com

Cantina Laredo   📖
Nashville ▪ *(615) 259-9282*
592 12Th Ave S

Carrabba's Italian Grill   📖
Nashville ▪ *(615) 463-3000*
2101 Green Hills Village Dr

Chappy's on Church $$$LD
Nashville ▪ *(615) 322-9932*
1721 Church St ▪ *Cajun & Creole Seafood*
▪ Manager Starr reports that GF diners are
"absolutely" welcome, and they serve many
GF customers. She recommends alerting a
server upon arrival. All staff members are
knowledgeable about specialty diets and
can "steer" GF diners through the menu. ▪
www.chappys.com

Demo's Restaurant   ✪ $LD
Nashville ▪ *(615) 256-4655*
300 Commerce St ▪ *American* ▪ Limited
GF menu includes salads, steaks, seafood,
blackened chicken stuffed potato, baked

potato, broccoli, hashbrowns, and spinach.
▪ *www.demosrestaurants.com*

Maggiano's Little Italy   ★ $$$**LD**
Nashville ▪ *(615) 514-0270*
3106 West End Ave ▪ *Italian* ▪ GF pasta is
available. Call individual locations to in-
quire about additional GF options. ▪ *www.*
maggianos.com

Melting Pot, The   📖
Nashville ▪ *(615) 742-4970*
166 2nd Ave N

Old Spaghetti Factory, The   📖
Nashville ▪ *(615) 254-9010*
160 2nd Ave N

Outback Steakhouse   📖
Nashville ▪ *(615) 385-3440*
3212 West End Ave

P.F. Chang's China Bistro   📖
Nashville ▪ *(615) 329-8901*
2525 West End Ave Ste 2535

Pei Wei Asian Diner   📖
Nashville ▪ *(615) 514-3230*
4017 Hillsboro Pike Ste 301

Sole Mio   ★ $$$**LD**
Nashville ▪ *(615) 256-4013*
311 3rd Ave S ▪ *Italian* ▪ Owner Debra
reports that they can prepare many items
GF, including chicken, fish, and veal dishes.
They use clean pots, pans, and preparation
spaces for GF items. Debra advises calling
ahead, and notes that with notice, they can
make GF pasta. ▪ *www.solemionash.com*

Sunset Grill $$**LD**
Nashville ▪ *(615) 386-3663*
2001 Belcourt Ave ▪ *Modern American* ▪
Veteran server Chris reports that the chefs
are "very willing to work with" GF diners.
He says that although they accommodate
GF diners only "a couple times a month,"
they are able to modify many items to be
GF. Alert a server upon arrival. ▪ *www.*
sunsetgrill.com

TENNESSEE
ALL OTHER CITIES

Bonefish Grill   📖
Chattanooga ▪ *(423) 892-3175*
2115 Gunbarrel Rd
Collierville ▪ *(901) 854-5822*
4680 Merchants Park Cir Ste 200
Cordova ▪ *(901) 753-2220*
1250 N Germantown Pkwy Ste 118
Franklin ▪ *(615) 771-1025*
3010A Mallory Ln
Murfreesboro ▪ *(615) 217-1883*
505 N Thompson Ln

Bubba Gump Shrimp Co.   📖
Gatlinburg ▪ *(865) 430-3034*
900 Parkway

Buca di Beppo   📖
Franklin ▪ *(615) 778-1321*
1722 Galleria Blvd

Carino's Italian   📖
Johnson City ▪ *(423) 952-0790*
1902 N Roan St
Pigeon Forge ▪ *(865) 868-0790*
2425 Parkway

Carrabba's Italian Grill   📖
Chattanooga ▪ *(423) 894-9970*
2040 Hamilton Place Blvd
Collierville ▪ *(901) 854-0200*
4600 Merchants Park Cir
Franklin ▪ *(615) 778-9111*
553 Cool Springs Blvd
Hendersonville ▪ *(615) 822-7100*
202 N Anderson Ln
Johnson City ▪ *(423) 232-2858*
175 Marketplace Dr
Memphis ▪ *(901) 685-9900*
5110 Poplar Ave
Murfreesboro ▪ *(615) 890-6693*
544 N Thompson Ln

Couture Cakes & Confections by
Bountiful Harvest   ✪ ★ ¢**S**
Hixson ▪ *(423) 876-1922*
5228 Hixson Pike ▪ *Bakery* ▪ Everything

baked in-house is GF. They offer GF bread, cookies, pies, cakes, muffins, brownies, and more. Co-owner Andrew reports that they have "limited" pre-made items each day. Orders must be placed in advance. ▪ *www.abountifulharvest.com*

Demo's Restaurant   ✪ $**LD**
Hendersonville ▪ *(615) 824-9097*
161 Indian Lake Blvd
Lebanon ▪ *(615) 443-4600*
130 Legends Dr
Murfreesboro ▪ *(615) 895-3701*
1115 NW Broad St ▪ *American* ▪ Limited GF menu includes salads, steaks, seafood, blackened chicken stuffed potato, baked potato, broccoli, hashbrowns, and spinach. ▪ *www.demosrestaurants.com*

Easy Seafood Company $$$**LD**
Chattanooga ▪ *(423) 266-1121*
203 Broad St ▪ *Seafood* ▪ Chef Erik reports that they have accommodated GF requests "for many customers." He advises calling ahead to note GF. Several dishes are GF, including steak au poivre, salmon with wild mushrooms, and jumbo shrimp wrapped in prosciutto. Confirm timeliness of this information before dining in. ▪ *www.easyseafood.com*

Firebirds Wood Fired Grill   ✪ $$$**LD**
Bartlett ▪ *(901) 379-1300*
8470 US Highway 64
Collierville ▪ *(901) 850-1603*
The Ave Carriage Crossing ▪ *American* ▪ GF menu includes a variety of salads and a selection of entrées. Examples are sirloin, filet mignon, ribs, and lobster tail. Both locations report that servers are trained to alert the chef when a customer orders from the GF menu. ▪ *www.firebirdsrockymountaingrill.com*

Five Oaks County Club   ★ $$**LD**
Lebanon ▪ *(615) 444-2784*
5 Oaks Blvd. ▪ *American* ▪ GF beer is available. Manager Kelly, who is GF, notes that she eats at the restaurant all the time. Grilled chicken, steak, salads, hamburg-

ers without buns, some soups, and several sides can be modified to be GF. Alert the server upon arrival.

Garlic Jim's   ✪★ $$**LD**
Franklin ▪ *(615) 791-5461*
4115 Mallory Ln ▪ *Pizza* ▪ New GF menu includes GF pizza, salads, and wings. ▪ *www.garlicjims.com*

Lone Star Steakhouse & Saloon   📖
Elizabethton ▪ *(423) 543-1313*
1361 Hwy 19 E Bypass
Jackson ▪ *(731) 668-0088*
2116 Emporium Dr

Matteo's Pizzeria   ★ $**LD**
Brentwood ▪ *(615) 661-5811*
1800 Carouthers Pkwy ▪ *Pizza* ▪ GF pizza is available. ▪ *www.matteospizza.com*

Melting Pot, The   📖
Chattanooga ▪ *(423) 893-5237*
2553 Lifestyle Way
Memphis ▪ *(901) 380-9500*
2828 Wolfcreek Pkwy

Outback Steakhouse   📖
Brentwood ▪ *(615) 661-9150*
8005 Moores Ln
Chattanooga ▪ *(423) 899-2600*
2120 Hamilton Place Blvd
Chattanooga ▪ *(423) 870-0980*
501A Northgate Mall
Clarksville ▪ *(931) 552-2900*
2790 Wilma Rudolph Blvd
Cleveland ▪ *(423) 339-1630*
536 Paul Huff Pkwy NW
Cookeville ▪ *(931) 372-2145*
1390 Interstate Dr
Cordova ▪ *(901) 751-9800*
1110 N Germantown Pkwy
Hermitage ▪ *(615) 885-6677*
5582 Old Hickory Blvd
Jackson ▪ *(731) 664-9000*
194 Stonebrook Pl
Johnson City ▪ *(423) 283-9222*
3101 Browns Mill Rd
Lebanon ▪ *(615) 444-7193*
1125 Franklin Rd
Madison ▪ *(615) 868-0477*

1560 Gallatin Pike N
Memphis ▪ *(901) 728-5100*
2255 Union Ave
Murfreesboro ▪ *(615) 849-9200*
1968 Old Fort Pkwy
Oak Ridge ▪ *(865) 220-0783*
402 S Illinois Ave
Sevierville ▪ *(865) 429-3085*
611 Parkway

P.F. Chang's China Bistro   📖

Chattanooga ▪ *(423) 242-0045*
2110 Hamilton Place Blvd
Franklin ▪ *(615) 503-9640*
439 Cool Springs Blvd
Memphis ▪ *(901) 818-3889*
1181 Ridgeway Rd

Pei Wei Asian Diner   📖

Brentwood ▪ *(615) 514-4990*
101 Creekside Xing Ste 1800
Cordova ▪ *(901) 382-1822*
2257 N Germantown Pkwy
Memphis ▪ *(901) 722-3780*
1680 Union Ave Ste 109
Memphis ▪ *(901) 761-9226*
540 S Mendenhall Rd Ste 9
Murfreesboro ▪ *(615) 896-3886*
1911 Medical Center Pkwy Ste A

Shane's Rib Shack   📖

Cleveland ▪ *(423) 476-5970*
4484 Frontage Rd NW
Franklin ▪ *(615) 591-8626*
3046 Columbia Ave
Hendersonville ▪ *(615) 264-2597*
203 N Anderson Ln

St. John's Restaurant & Meeting Place
$$$D

Chattanooga ▪ *(423) 266-4400*
1278 Market St ▪ *Modern American* ▪ Chef
Joshua reports that they serve GF diners
every day. He notes that over half the menu
is naturally GF or can be made GF, and all
staff members are trained on the GF diet.
He further notes that advanced notice
is not required, but it is helpful. ▪ *www.
stjohnsrestaurant.com*

Whipped Cupcakes   ★ ¢S

Chattanooga ▪ *(423) 305-7755*
149 River St ▪ *Bakery* ▪ GF chocolate
cupcakes with vanilla icing are available on
Friday and Saturdays only.

Winger's Grill and Bar   ✪ ¢LD

Manchester ▪ *(931) 728-5065*
138 Relco Drive ▪ *American* ▪ GF menu
includes double basted ribs, glazed salmon,
quesadillas with corn tortillas, and a variety
of salads. ▪ *www.wingers.info*

TEXAS

AUSTIN

Austin's Pizza   ★ $LD

Austin ▪ *(512) 795-8888*
10900 Research Blvd
Austin ▪ *(512) 795-8888*
1600 W 35th St
Austin ▪ *(512) 795-8888*
1817 S Lamar Blvd
Austin ▪ *(512) 795-8888*
2324 Guadalupe St
Austin ▪ *(512) 795-8888*
3601 W William Cannon Dr
Austin ▪ *(512) 795-8888*
3637 Far West Blvd
Austin ▪ *(512) 795-8888*
7301 Ranch Rd 620 N ▪ *Pizza* ▪ GF pizza
is available in the 10-inch size. ▪ *www.
austinspizza.com*

Beets Living Food Café   ★ $BLD

Austin ▪ *(512) 477-2338*
1611 W 5th St ▪ *Café* ▪ GF sprouted almond
sunflower flatbread is available. Restaurant
reports that almost all menu items are
naturally GF. They recommend alerting
a server, who will know the few items to
avoid. ▪ *www.beetscafe.com*

Brick Oven Restaurant   ✪★ $LD

Austin ▪ *(512) 345-6181*

10710 Research Blvd
Austin ▪ *(512) 477-7006*
1209 Red River St
Austin ▪ *(512) 292-3939*
9911 Brodie Ln ▪ Italian ▪ GF menu at the
Brodie Ln location includes shrimp picatta,
fettuccine with basil pesto cream sauce,
pasta rustica, pizzas, and more. The Red
River and Research Blvd locations do not
have GF menus, but they do have GF pizza,
pasta, selected desserts such as brownies
and carrot cake, and sometimes beer. ▪
www.brickovenrestaurant.com

Buca di Beppo   📖
Austin ▪ *(512) 342-8462*
3612 Tudor Blvd

Cantina Laredo   📖
Austin ▪ *(512) 542-9670*
201 W 3rd St

Carino's Italian   📖
Austin ▪ *(512) 506-8181*
11620 N Fm 620
Austin ▪ *(512) 989-6464*
12901 N I-35 Service Rd
Austin ▪ *(512) 292-1658*
9500 S Ih 35 Ste B

Carrabba's Italian Grill   📖
Austin ▪ *(512) 345-8232*
11590 Research Blvd
Austin ▪ *(512) 419-1220*
6406 N I H 35

Casa de Luz   ✪ $LD
Austin ▪ *(512) 476-2535*
1701 Toomey Rd ▪ Organic ▪ GF menu is
fixed-plate and changes for every meal.
Restaurant reports that the rare non-GF
menu item is always marked as such.
Sample meals include tamales and sushi. ▪
www.casadeluz.org

Clay Pit, The $$LD
Austin ▪ *(512) 322-5131*
1601 Guadalupe St ▪ Indian ▪ Manager
Linda reports that most menu items are
naturally GF. The restaurant has an internal
list of items that are not GF, and GF cus-

tomers can ask their server to see that list.
Servers are GF aware. ▪ *www.claypit.com*

CraigO's Pizza and Pasta   ★ $LD
Austin ▪ *(512) 282-7499*
11215 S Ih 35
Austin ▪ *(512) 323-0660*
2222 And North Mopac
Austin ▪ *(512) 891-7200*
4970 Hwy 290 ▪ Pizza ▪ GF pizza is available. ▪ *www.craigospizzaandpasta.com*

Eastside Café   ✪ $$LD
Austin ▪ *(512) 476-5858*
2113 Manor Rd ▪ American ▪ GF menu
includes a Greek chicken salad, a poblano
chicken sandwich without a bun, skewered
pork tenderloin, and eggs benedict without
the english muffin. ▪ *www.eastsidecafeaus-
tin.com*

Fire Bowl Café   ✪ ¢LD
Austin ▪ *(512) 795-8998*
9828 Great Hills Trl ▪ Asian Stir-Fry ▪
GF menu includes spicy coconut soup,
thai seafood tom kah soup, and a variety
of salads. It features "Stir Fry Your Way,"
for which diners choose their own meats,
sauces, and starches. GF sauce options are
ginger white wine and yellow curry. ▪ *www.
firebowlcafe.com*

Fogo De Chao   ★ $$$$LD
Austin ▪ *(512) 472-0220*
309 E 3rd St ▪ Brazilian ▪ GF cheese bread
made with yucca flour is available. ▪ *www.
fogodechao.com*

Food 4 Fitness Café   ¢BLD
Austin ▪ *(512) 472-1674*
1112 N Lamar Blvd ▪ Organic ▪ Manager
Sarah reports that the café has several GF
options, including kale salads, quinoa salads, meat entrées with quinoa on the side,
and raw desserts. She recommends asking
for her, Cath, or Emily, but she also notes
that all ingredients are marked in the deli
cases. Located in Castle Hill Specialized
Fitness. ▪ *www.food4fitness.com*

Guero's Taco Bar ✪ ¢LD
Austin ▪ (512) 447-7688
1412 S Congress Ave ▪ Mexican ▪ GF menu includes chalupas, fajitas, enchiladas, grilled steak, and tamales. The rice has trace elements of gluten, so all GF entrées must be ordered without rice. ▪ www.guerostacobar.com

Hula Hut ✪ $LD
Austin ▪ (512) 476-4852
3825 Lake Austin Blvd ▪ Hawaiian Fusion ▪ GF menu includes guacamole salad, black beans, the Hula Hut burger with no bun, grilled salmon, the Hula Hut chop salad, and flan for dessert. ▪ www.hulahut.com

Jade Leaves Tea House ★ $S
Austin ▪ (512) 687-0569
3110 Guadalupe St ▪ Tea Café ▪ GF tamari is used to make stir fry dishes, and GF brownies are available. Restaurant reports that many items are naturally GF. Some GF options include pad thai, soups, salads. Confirm timeliness of this information before dining in. ▪ www.jadeleaves.net

Jasper's $$$LD
Austin ▪ (512) 832-8012
11506 Century Oaks Ter ▪ American ▪ Reservationist Lane reports that they are "familiar" with the GF diet. She recommends calling one hour in advance so that the chef can have a GF option ready. ▪ www.kentrathbun.com

Ka-Prow Pan Asian Bistro ¢LD
Austin ▪ (512) 990-2111
1200 W Howard Ln ▪ Asian ▪ Manager Opart reports that WF entrées and appetizers are marked on the menu. Alert a server, who will specially note GF on the order ticket that goes to the kitchen. ▪ www.kaprowleaf.com

Kobe Japanese Steakhouse ★ $$$LD
Austin ▪ (512) 288-7333
13492 Research Blvd ▪ Japanese ▪ Head Server Becky reports that GF soy sauce is available, so nearly all dishes can be made GF. All servers are trained on the GF diet, so they can help to ensure a GF meal. Becky cautions, however, that GF meals will not be cooked on the Tepanyaki grill; instead, they will be prepared in the kitchen. ▪ www.kobeaustin.com

Kona Grill 📖
Austin ▪ (512) 835-5900
11410 Century Oaks Ter

Maggiano's Little Italy ★ $$$LD
Austin ▪ (512) 501-7870
10910 Domain Dr ▪ Italian ▪ GF pasta is available. Call individual locations to inquire about additional GF options. ▪ www.maggianos.com

Matt's El Rancho Mexican Restaurant
$$LD
Austin ▪ (512) 462-9333
2613 S Lamar Blvd ▪ Mexican ▪ Manager Billy reports that the restaurant serves GF diners "every day," and they are very familiar with the GF diet. The chips are fried in a dedicated GF fryer, and all meats can be prepared GF. Confirm timeliness of this information before dining in. ▪ www.mattselrancho.com

Maudie's Hacienda ✪ ¢BLD
Austin ▪ (512) 280-8700
9911 Brodie Ln ▪ Tex-Mex ▪ GF menu includes guacamole salad, tortilla bean dip, fajita salad, beef, chicken, or shrimp fajitas, enchilada platters, and more. Restaurant notes that they are "very conscious" of the GF diet. ▪ www.maudies.com

Maudie's Milagro ✪ ¢BLD
Austin ▪ (512) 306-8080
3801 N Capital Of Texas Hwy ▪ Tex-Mex ▪ GF menu includes guacamole salad, tortilla bean dip, fajita salad, beef, chicken, or shrimp fajitas, enchilada platters, and more. Restaurant notes that the only two non-GF sauces are the chili con carne and the poblano sauces. ▪ www.maudies.com

Maudie's Too ✪ $BLD
Austin ▪ (512) 440-8088
1212 S Lamar Blvd ▪ Tex-Mex ▪ GF menu

includes soups, salads, bean dips, fajitas, and corn tortillas. Manager Jorge reports that they accommodate GF diners "regularly" and that the kitchen is accustomed to these requests. ▪ *www.maudies.com*

Maudie's   ✪ $$**BLD**
Austin ▪ *(512) 832-0900*
10205 N Lamar Blvd
Austin ▪ *(512) 473-3740*
2608 W 7th St ▪ *Tex-Mex* ▪ GF menu includes enchiladas, fajitas, nachos, tacos, and more. Request GF chips for the table. ▪ *www.maudies.com*

Melting Pot, The   📖
Austin ▪ *(512) 401-2424*
13343 Research Blvd
Austin ▪ *(512) 401-2424*
305 E 3rd St

Mother's Café & Garden   ¢**LD**
Austin ▪ *(512) 451-3994*
4215 Duval St ▪ *Vegetarian* ▪ A WF menu is available, and they are working on a GF menu. Restaurant reports that the staff is required to notify a manager before entering an order with a GF request. All managers are knowledgeable about Celiac disease and are GF aware. ▪ *www.mother-scafeaustin.com*

Mr. Natural   ✪★ ¢**BLD**
Austin ▪ *(512) 477-5228*
1901 E Cesar Chavez St
Austin ▪ *(512) 916-9223*
2414A S Lamar Blvd ▪ *Vegetarian* ▪ GF items marked on the menu include tamales, several omelets, crispy tacos, and various types of migas. GF bread, pies, cakes, muffins, brownies, and cookies are available, though they may have to be specially ordered. ▪ *www.mrnatural-austin.com*

North by Northwest Restaurant & Brewery   ✪ $$**LD**
Austin ▪ *(512) 467-6969*
10010 Capital Of Texas Hwy N ▪ *American* ▪ GF menu includes the jumbo shrimp cocktail as a starter, a selection of salads, and entrées like the NXNW chicken,

grilled duck breast, and smoked pork tenderloin. ▪ *www.nxnwbrew.com*

Outback Steakhouse   📖
Austin ▪ *(512) 343-6333*
11600 Research Blvd
Austin ▪ *(512) 383-8024*
4211 S Lamar Blvd

P.F. Chang's China Bistro   📖
Austin ▪ *(512) 231-0208*
10114 Jollyville Rd
Austin ▪ *(512) 457-8300*
201 San Jacinto Blvd

Pei Wei Asian Diner   📖
Austin ▪ *(512) 382-3860*
1000 E 41st St
Austin ▪ *(512) 691-3060*
12901 N I-35 Service Road Nb Building 15
Austin ▪ *(512) 996-0095*
13429 N Highway 183
Austin ▪ *(512) 382-2990*
4200 S Lamar Blvd

People's Pharmacy   ★ ¢**BLD**
Austin ▪ *(512) 219-9499*
13860 US 183 N
Austin ▪ *(512) 444-8866*
3801 S Lamar Blvd
Austin ▪ *(512) 459-9090*
4018 N Lamar Blvd
Austin ▪ *(512) 327-8877*
4201 Westbank Dr ▪ *Deli & Bakery* ▪ Health food store and pharmacy offering various GF items like burritos, bread, donuts, and muffins. Selection varies by location. ▪ *www.peoplesrx.com*

Roy's   ✪ $$$**D**
Austin ▪ *(512) 391-1500*
340 E 2nd St ▪ *Hawaiian Fusion* ▪ Limited GF menu includes a few appetizers like sushi rolls and meals, including the scallop risotto. Chef Jason reports that they are "absolutely" able to accommodate GF diners, and if the items on the GF menu are not appealing, he will "build any dish." ▪ *www.roysrestaurant.com*

Talk House　　　　　　　100% $BL
Austin ▪ (512) 828-7404
1221 W 6th St ▪ Café ▪ "Living" café serving GF salads, sandwiches, and pizza. GF bread and pizza are available. Meals area available for dining in or take out. ▪ www.borboletagourmet.com

Tam Deli & Café　　　　　　　¢LD
Austin ▪ (512) 834-6458
8222 N Lamar Blvd ▪ Vietnamese ▪ Owner Tam reports that there are "quite a few" GF dishes on the menu. Much of the time, they use rice flour rather than wheat flour. Confirm timeliness of this information before dining in. Ask to speak with a manager upon arrival.

Texas Land & Cattle Steak House　📖
Austin ▪ (512) 330-0030
1101 S Mo Pac Expy
Austin ▪ (512) 258-3733
14010 N Highway 183
Austin ▪ (512) 442-6448
5510 S Ih 35 Ste C
Austin ▪ (512) 451-6555
6007 N Ih 35

Wild Wood Art Café　　　　100% ¢S
Austin ▪ (512) 327-9660
3663 Bee Caves Rd ▪ Café ▪ Café offering an extensive GF menu. Options include sandwiches, tamales, and enchiladas. They also offer GF cookies, cakes, muffins, and breads by the loaf. Owner Andrew reports that the menu changes periodically, but that diners can get a good idea of what is served by looking online. ▪ www.wildwoodartcafe.com

Zen Japanese Food Fast　　　¢LD
Austin ▪ (512) 444-8081
1303 S Congress Ave
Austin ▪ (512) 451-4811
2900 W Anderson Ln
Austin ▪ (512) 300-2633
3423 Guadalupe St ▪ Japanese ▪ There are two GF sauces: shiro-miso sauce and green curry sauce. These can be substituted into any dish on the menu, and the fully trained kitchen staff will use clean woks and utensils to cook GF meals. Confirm timeliness of this information before dining in. GF rice noodles are available. ▪ www.eatzen.com

Z'Tejas Southwestern Grill　✪★ $LD
Austin ▪ (512) 388-7772
10525 W Parmer Ln
Austin ▪ (512) 478-5355
1110 W 6th St
Austin ▪ (512) 346-3506
9400 A Arboretum Blvd ▪ Southwest ▪ One-page GF menu includes wild mushroom enchiladas and grilled salmon, along with smoked chicken and black bean salad. Frozen margaritas and GF beer are also available. ▪ www.ztejas.com

TEXAS

DALLAS

Banana Leaf Thai Cuisine　　　$LD
Dallas ▪ (972) 713-0123
17370 Preston Rd ▪ Thai ▪ Manager Kathy reports that they have "quite a few" GF diners. Many dishes, like the fried rice dishes, can be prepared GF. ▪ www.thaibananaleaf.com

Blue Mesa Grill　　　　　　✪ $LD
Dallas ▪ (214) 378-8686
7700 W Northwest Hwy ▪ Southwest ▪ Ask for the "Nutritional Brochure," which contains a list of GF items and advice on GF ordering. GF options include red chili crusted salmon, painted desert soup, guacamole, and queso blanco. For dessert, they offer flan. ▪ www.bluemesagrill.com

Buca di Beppo　　　　　　📖
Dallas ▪ (214) 361-8462
7843 Park Ln

Cantina Laredo   📖
Dallas ▪ *(214) 350-5227*
165 Inwood Village
Dallas ▪ *(469) 828-4818*
17808 Dallas Pkwy
Dallas ▪ *(214) 821-5785*
2031 Abrams Rd
Dallas ▪ *(214) 265-1610*
6025 Royal Ln Ste 250

Capital Grille, The   📖
Dallas ▪ *(214) 303-0500*
500 Crescent Ct

Del Frisco's Double Eagle Steak House
📖
Dallas ▪ *(972) 490-9000*
5251 Spring Valley Rd

Extreme Pizza   ★ $$**LD**
Dallas ▪ *(214) 363-2464*
6112 Luther Ln ▪ *Pizza* ▪ GF pizza is available. ▪ *www.extremepizza.com*

Kona Grill   📖
Dallas ▪ *(214) 369-7600*
8687 N Central Expy

Kozy Kitchen, The   ✪★ $$$**BL**
Dallas ▪ *(214) 219-5044*
4433 Mckinney Ave ▪ *Café* ▪ Items marked on the menu with an asterisk cannot be made GF. Extensive GF menu includes pan seared scallops, buffalo nachos, chicken marsala, a grass-fed burger plate, filet mignon, and more. GF breakfast menu includes pancakes, GF toast, and breakfast tacos. GF buns, bread, and an array of desserts such as carrot cake, German chocolate cake, and "Oh My God" cake are available. ▪ *www.thekozy.net*

Lawry's The Prime Rib $$$$**D**
Dallas ▪ *(972) 503-6688*
14655 Dallas Pkwy ▪ *Steakhouse* ▪ Chef Mike reports that the restaurant serves GF diners "all the time." He notes that there is an internal "allergy" list, which includes GF options. He recommends alerting a server, who will bring a chef or manager to the table. Crème brulee is available for dessert. ▪ *www.lawrysonline.com*

Maggiano's Little Italy   ★ $$$**LD**
Dallas ▪ *(214) 360-0707*
8687 N Central Expy Ste 205 ▪ *Italian* ▪ GF pasta is available. Call individual locations to inquire about additional GF options. ▪ *www.maggianos.com*

Melting Pot, The   📖
Dallas ▪ *(972) 960-7027*
4900 Belt Line Rd

Outback Steakhouse   📖
Dallas ▪ *(972) 783-0397*
9049 Vantage Point Dr

P.F. Chang's China Bistro   📖
Dallas ▪ *(972) 818-3336*
18323 Dallas Pkwy
Dallas ▪ *(214) 265-8669*
225 Northpark Ctr

Pappas Bros. Steakhouse $$$$**D**
Dallas ▪ *(214) 366-2000*
10477 Lombardy Ln ▪ *Steakhouse* ▪ Manager Matthew reports that GF diners have come to the restaurant, and he notes that many menu items, especially the steaks and seafood, can be modified to be GF. He recommends reservations noting GF so that the host will notify the server. Servers will notify the kitchen. ▪ *www.pappasbros.com*

Pappasito's Cantina $$**LD**
Dallas ▪ *(214) 350-1970*
10433 Lombardy Ln ▪ *Tex-Mex* ▪ Manager Bucky reports that because everything is made from scratch, there are "tons of options" for GF diners. Alert a server, who will get the floor manager. The floor manager will speak to GF diners before discussing options with the kitchen manager. ▪ *www.pappasitos.com*

Pei Wei Asian Diner   📖
Dallas ▪ *(214) 765-0030*
11700 Preston Rd Ste A
Dallas ▪ *(972) 985-0090*
18204 Preston Rd Ste E1
Dallas ▪ *(214) 965-0007*

2222 Mckinney Ave Ste 100
Dallas ▪ (214) 219-0000
3001 Knox St Ste 100
Dallas ▪ (972) 764-0844
4801 Beltline Road
Dallas ▪ (214) 765-9911
8305 Westchester Dr

Rockfish Seafood Grill　　　　　✪ $LD
Dallas ▪ (214) 363-7722
11611 Preston Road
Dallas ▪ (214) 823-8444
5331 E Mockingbird Ln ▪ Seafood ▪ Extensive GF menu includes ribs, salmon salad, chicken caesar and a variety of seafood dishes. ▪ www.rockfishseafood.com

Sprinkles Cupcakes　　　　　★ ¢S
Dallas ▪ (214) 369-0004
4020 Villanova St ▪ Bakery ▪ GF red velvet cupcakes are available every day. They are not visible on display, as they are kept behind the counter to avoid cross-contamination. ▪ www.sprinkles.com

Texas Land & Cattle Steak House　　📖
Dallas ▪ (214) 353-8000
10250 Technology Blvd W
Dallas ▪ (214) 526-4664
3130 Lemmon Ave

U Food Grill　　　　　　　　　📖
Dallas ▪ (972) 586-0380
3200 E Airfield Dr
Dallas ▪ (214) 879-1450
5201 Harry Hines Blvd

York Street　　　　　　　　$$$D
Dallas ▪ (214) 826-0968
6047 Lewis St ▪ Seafood ▪ Manager Fana reports that they serve "a lot" of GF diners, and they are "very aware" of the GF diet. Alert a server, as "any server" will be able to indicate GF items on the menu, which changes daily. Reservations noting GF are recommended. ▪ www.yorkstreetdallas.com

TEXAS
HOUSTON

Buca di Beppo　　　　　　　　📖
Houston ▪ (713) 665-2822
5192 Buffalo Speedway

Cantina Laredo　　　　　　　📖
Houston ▪ (713) 952-3287
11129 Westheimer Rd

Capital Grille, The　　　　　📖
Houston ▪ (713) 623-4600
5365 Westheimer Rd

Carino's Italian　　　　　　📖
Houston ▪ (281) 458-4424
5921 E Sam Houston Pkwy N

Carrabba's Italian Grill　　　📖
Houston ▪ (713) 464-6595
11339 Katy Fwy
Houston ▪ (713) 468-0868
1399 S Voss Rd
Houston ▪ (713) 522-3131
3115 Kirby Dr
Houston ▪ (281) 397-8255
5440 Fm 1960 Rd W
Houston ▪ (281) 859-9700
7540 Highway 6 N

Del Frisco's Double Eagle Steak House
　　　　　　　　　　　　　　　📖
Houston ▪ (713) 355-2600
5061 Westheimer Rd

Dessert Gallery　　　　★ $$$$LD
Houston ▪ (713) 622-0007
1616 Post Oak Blvd
Houston ▪ (713) 522-9999
3600 Kirby Dr Ste D ▪ Desserterie & Bakery ▪ GF peanut butter truffles, chocolate mousse cake, and lemon meringue mousse cake are available. ▪ www.dessertgallery.com

Fogo De Chao　　　　　★ $$$$LD
Houston ▪ (713) 978-6500
8250 Westheimer Rd ▪ Brazilian ▪ GF cheese bread made with yucca flour is available. ▪ www.fogodechao.com

Goode Company Seafood   ✪ $$$LD
Houston ▪ (713) 464-7933
10211 Katy Fwy
Houston ▪ (713) 523-7154
2621 Westpark Dr ▪ Seafood ▪ GF menu
includes fresh-shucked oysters, shrimp
cocktail, salads, pan-fried fish in about 12
different varieties, and more. ▪ www.goode-
company.com

Goode Company Texas BBQ   ★ $LD
Houston ▪ (832) 678-3562
20102 Northwest Frwy
Houston ▪ (713) 522-2530
5109 Kirby Dr
Houston ▪ (713) 464-1901
8911 Katy Fwy ▪ Barbeque ▪ GF beer is
available. Manager Bray from the Kirby
Drive location reports that at all locations,
a manager can provide a hand-out listing
GF items. Manager Lupe from the Katy
Freeway location reports that "there aren't
a lot" of GF diners who come in, but if they
do, the restaurant is happy to accommodate
them. ▪ www.goodecompany.com

Gourmet India   ✪ $LD
Houston ▪ (281) 493-5435
13155 Westheimer Rd ▪ Indian ▪ Extensive
GF menu includes a variety of appetizers, tandoori specialties with a modified
marinade, seafood dishes, chicken specialties, lamb specialties, and more. Desserts
include a homemade milk dumpling and
carrot halwa, among others. ▪ www.gour-
metindiahouston.com

Kona Grill   📖
Houston ▪ (713) 877-9191
5061 Westheimer Rd

Maggiano's Little Italy   ★ $$$LD
Houston ▪ (713) 961-2700
2019 Post Oak Blvd ▪ Italian ▪ GF pasta is
available. Call individual locations to inquire about additional GF options. ▪ www.
maggianos.com

Melting Pot, The   📖
Houston ▪ (713) 532-5011
6100 Westheimer Rd

Mockingbird Bistro $$$$LD
Houston ▪ (713) 533-0200
1985 Welch St ▪ Modern American ▪
Reservationist Monica reports that they
accommodate GF diners "every day." She
notes that several seafood, meat, and
poultry items are naturally GF or can be
modified to be GF. Confirm timeliness of
this information before dining in. Alert a
server, who will discuss GF options with
the kitchen. Reservations noting GF are
recommended. ▪ www.mockingbirdbistro.
com

Outback Steakhouse   📖
Houston ▪ (713) 978-6283
10001 Westheimer Rd
Houston ▪ (281) 464-8455
12130 Dickinson Rd
Houston ▪ (281) 587-0044
4 Fm 1960 Rd W
Houston ▪ (281) 580-4329
5710 Fm 1960 Rd W
Houston ▪ (281) 859-9413
7070 Highway 6 N
Houston ▪ (713) 218-0760
8731 West Loop S # 610

P.F. Chang's China Bistro   📖
Houston ▪ (281) 920-3553
11685 Westheimer Rd
Houston ▪ (281) 571-4050
18250 Tomball Pkwy
Houston ▪ (713) 627-7220
4094 Westheimer Rd

Pappas Bros. Steakhouse $$$$D
Houston ▪ (713) 780-7352
5839 Westheimer Rd ▪ Steakhouse ▪
Manager Pete reports that GF diners are
"absolutely" welcome and advises making
reservations noting GF. He notes that the
staff's GF knowledge is "extensive" and that
there is a special label servers use to notify
the kitchen. ▪ www.pappasbros.com

Pappas Seafood House $$$LD
Houston ▪ (281) 999-9928
11301 I-45 N @ Aldine Bender
Houston ▪ (713) 453-3265

12010 I-10 E
Houston ▪ (713) 522-4595
3001 S Shepherd Dr @ Alabama
Houston ▪ (713) 784-4729
6894 Hwy 59 S
Houston ▪ (713) 641-0318
6945 I-45 @ Woodbridge ▪ Seafood ▪
Triumph contacted a manager at each location. In all cases, GF diners were advised
to notify servers that they have an "allergy."
The server will summon a manager, who
will advise GF diners. Restaurants also note
that it is the diner's responsibility to know
what he or she cannot eat. ▪ www.pappas-
seafood.com

Pappasito's Cantina $$ LD
Houston ▪ (713) 468-1913
10409 I-10 W At Sam Houston Tollway
Houston ▪ (713) 455-8378
11831 I-10 E At Federal Rd
Houston ▪ (713) 462-0246
13070 Highway 290
Houston ▪ (281) 565-9797
13750 Southwest Frwy
Houston ▪ (281) 821-4500
15280 I-45 N At Airtex
Houston ▪ (713) 668-5756
2515 S Loop W At S Main
Houston ▪ (713) 520-5066
2536 Richmond Ave
Houston ▪ (281) 821-2266
3950 S Terminal Rd
Houston ▪ (713) 784-5253
6445 Richmond Ave
Houston ▪ (281) 893-5030
7050 Fm 1960 Rd W
Houston ▪ (281) 657-6157
7800 Airport Blvd ▪ Tex-Mex ▪ Triumph
spoke with a manager at each location,
and all reported having served GF diners
before. All locations recommend alerting a
server upon arrival. All servers are trained
to alert a manager, who will communicate
with the kitchen staff. The S Terminal restaurant is located in the food court of the
George Bush Airport, and manager Rachel
recommends alerting the cashier upon arrival. ▪ www.pappasitos.com

Pei Wei Asian Diner   📖
Houston ▪ (713) 353-7366
1005 Waugh Dr Ste A
Houston ▪ (281) 571-4990
12020 Fm 1960 Rd W
Houston ▪ (281) 506-3500
14008 Memorial Dr Ste A
Houston ▪ (713) 785-1620
1413 S Voss Rd Ste A
Houston ▪ (713) 661-0900
5110 Buffalo Speedway # 100
Houston ▪ (281) 885-5430
5203 Fm 1960 Rd W Ste E

Rioja Tapas   ✪ $$$ LD
Houston ▪ (281) 531-5569
11920 Westheimer Rd ▪ Spanish ▪ GF
menu includes paellas, lamb dishes, chick-
en dishes, and other items. Manager Luis
notes that they accommodate "a bunch" of
GF diners on a regular basis. ▪ www.riojar-
estaurant.com

Rockfish Seafood Grill   ✪ $ LD
Houston ▪ (281) 558-7380
11805 Westheimer Rd
Houston ▪ (281) 587-2900
5500 FM 1960 Rd W ▪ Seafood ▪ Extensive GF menu includes ribs, salmon salad,
chicken caesar and a variety of seafood
dishes. ▪ www.rockfishseafood.com

Ruggles Green   ✪★ $ LD
Houston ▪ (713) 533-0777
2311 W Alabama St ▪ Organic ▪ GF menu
includes pizzas, quinoa spaghetti, and
several salads. Hostess Dakota reports that
they have "tons" of GF customers. ▪ www.
rugglesgreen.com

Smith & Wollensky $$$$ LD
Houston ▪ (713) 621-7555
4007 Westheimer ▪ Steakhouse ▪ Manager Melissa reports that they serve GF diners
"often." She recommends reservations noting GF, so the reservationist will alert the
server in advance. All servers are familiar
with the GF diet, but they are trained to ask
the chef if they are unsure of something. ▪
www.smithandwollensky.com

Taco Milagro   ✪ ¢**LD**
Houston ▪ *(713) 522-1999*
2555 Kirby Dr ▪ *Mexican* ▪ The menu lists
the very few items which are not GF. The
tacos, the tamales, and nearly all of the
main plates can be prepared GF. There is
a bar with specialty margaritas and more
than 50 premium tequilas. ▪ *www.taco-
milagro.com*

T'afia $$$**D**
Houston ▪ *(713) 524-6922*
3701 Travis St ▪ *Modern American* ▪ Man-
ager Tino reports that the restaurant serves
GF diners "all the time." He recommends
making reservations noting GF, and then
alerting a server, who will speak to the chef
about GF options. He notes that the menu
changes daily, but there are always dishes
that can be modified to be GF. ▪ *www.tafia.
com*

Texas Land & Cattle Steak House 📖
Houston ▪ *(281) 922-6333*
11900 Dickinson Rd
Houston ▪ *(281) 679-9900*
12313 Katy Fwy
Houston ▪ *(281) 469-3838*
8015 Fm 1960 Rd W

Yard House   📖
Houston ▪ *(713) 461-9273*
800 W Sam Houston Pkwy N

Yia Yia Mary's $$**LD**
Houston ▪ *(713) 840-8665*
4747 San Felipe St ▪ *Greek* ▪ Manager
Amanda reports that most of the menu is
naturally GF, and GF diners are "accommodated often." Alert a server, who will notify
a manager. The manager will discuss GF
options with the customer. ▪ *www.yiayia-
marys.com*

Zio's   ✪ $**LD**
Houston ▪ *(281) 872-5333*
14915 North Fwy ▪ *Italian* ▪ GF menu
includes salmon caesar salad, chicken piccata, Greek pasta, lemon chicken primavera, shrimp with marinara, ribeye tuscano,
grilled sirloin, and more. ▪ *www.zios.com*

TEXAS

SAN ANTONIO

Aldaco's Mexican Cuisine   ✪ $**LD**
San Antonio ▪ *(210) 222-0561*
100 Hoefgen Ave ▪ *Mexican* ▪ GF menu
features ribeye steak, chicken breast with
cilantro sauce, and different types of fajitas.
▪ *www.aldacos.net*

Asia Kitchen   ✪ $**LD**
San Antonio ▪ *(210) 673-0662*
1739 SW Loop 410 ▪ *Thai* ▪ Items that can
be prepared GF are marked on the menu.
GF options include pad thai, ka pao,
various curries and thai fried rice. Alert a
server that the item must be prepared GF. ▪
www.asia-kitchen.com

Auden's Kitchen $**LD**
San Antonio ▪ *(210) 494-0070*
700 E Sonterra Blvd ▪ *American* ▪ Sous-
chef Crockett reports that they accommodate GF diners "every single day." There is
always one GF soup available, and there are
"a number of" entrées that are either naturally GF or can be prepared GF. All servers
are trained to accommodate GF diners, so
alert a server upon arrival. ▪ *www.auden-
skitchen.com*

Beto's Comida Latina   ✪★ ¢**LD**
San Antonio ▪ *(210) 930-9393*
8142 Broadway St ▪ *Latin American* ▪
GF menu includes tacos and quesadillas, among other things. Owner Cheryl
reports that nearly all soups and salads are
naturally GF. GF beer is available. ▪ *www.
betoscomidalatina.com*

Biga on the Banks $$$**D**
San Antonio ▪ *(210) 225-0722*
203 S Saint Marys St ▪ *Modern American*
▪ Restaurant reports that they accom-
modate "quite a few" customers who are
GF. Make reservations noting GF. Alert a
server, who will notify a manager and a

chef. The chef will indicate GF options. ▪ *www.biga.com*

Bistro Vatel $$$LD
San Antonio ▪ *(210) 828-3141*
218 E Olmos Dr ▪ *French Bistro* ▪ Manager Ray reports that they can accommodate GF diners, as the chef will modify any dish upon request. Alert a server upon arrival. ▪ *www.bistrovatel.com*

Carino's Italian   📖
San Antonio ▪ *(210) 493-9998*
1301 N Fm 1604 W

Carrabba's Italian Grill   📖
San Antonio ▪ *(210) 694-4191*
12507 Interstate Hwy 10 W

Ciao2   ★ $$$D
San Antonio ▪ *(210) 481-7031*
20626 Stone Oak Pkwy ▪ *Italian* ▪ GF pasta is available with advanced notice of 24 hours. ▪ *www.bistrovatel.com*

Cove, The   ✪ ¢LD
San Antonio ▪ *(210) 227-2683*
606 W Cypress St ▪ *Organic American* ▪ GF items are marked with a star on the regular menu. The chefs are trained to treat GF requests with care. Alert a server upon arrival. ▪ *www.thecove.us*

Fire Bowl Café   ✪ ¢LD
San Antonio ▪ *(210) 829-0887*
255 E Basse Rd ▪ *Asian Stir-Fry* ▪ GF menu includes spicy coconut soup, thai seafood tom kha soup, and a variety of salads. It features "Stir Fry Your Way," for which diners choose their own meats, sauces, and starches. GF sauce options are ginger white wine and yellow curry. ▪ *www.firebowlcafe.com*

Fire Hut Grill & Bar   ★ $LD
San Antonio ▪ *(210) 491-4209*
1742 N Loop 1604 E ▪ *Asian Stir-Fry* ▪ GF pasta and beer are available. GF dishes include pad thai or a fresh stir fry plate with tofu or chicken. A sign listing GF sauces is posted, and it includes the spiciest option,

Tiger Cry. For dessert, they offer tapioca pudding. ▪ *www.firehutgrill.com*

Fogo de Chao   ★ $$$$LD
San Antonio ▪ *(210) 227-1700*
849 E Commerce St ▪ *Brazilian* ▪ GF cheesebread made with yucca flour is available. ▪ *www.fogodechao.com*

Kona Grill   📖
San Antonio ▪ *(210) 877-5355*
15900 La Cantera Pwy

Little Aussie Bakery & Café   100% ¢BL
San Antonio ▪ *(210) 826-7877*
3610 Avenue B ▪ *Bakery & Café* ▪ Dedicated GF bakery and café offering garlic bread, pasta, sandwiches, quiches, pizzas, and more. They have a kids' menu and various cakes for dessert. ▪ *www.thelittleaussiebakery.com*

Maggiano's Little Italy   ★ $$$LD
San Antonio ▪ *(210) 451-6000*
17603 Ih 10 W ▪ *Italian* ▪ GF pasta is available. Call individual locations to inquire about additional GF options. ▪ *www.maggianos.com*

Melting Pot, The   📖
San Antonio ▪ *(210) 479-6358*
14855 Blanco Rd

Outback Steakhouse   📖
San Antonio ▪ *(210) 696-4329*
12511 I-10 W
San Antonio ▪ *(210) 490-7316*
16080 San Pedro Ave
San Antonio ▪ *(210) 509-4329*
5552 NW Loop 410

P.F. Chang's China Bistro   📖
San Antonio ▪ *(210) 507-6500*
15900 La Cantera Pkwy Ste 1100 Bldg #
San Antonio ▪ *(210) 507-1000*
255 E Basse Rd Ste 1200

Paloma Blanca Mexican Cuisine   ✪ $LD
San Antonio ▪ *(210) 822-6151*
5800 Broadway St ▪ *Mexican* ▪ Extensive GF menu includes a variety of enchiladas, tacos, chicken, and squab dishes. Ask the

hostess for the "Celiac menu." ▪ *www.palo-mablanca.net*

Pam's Patio Kitchen ★ $LD
San Antonio ▪ *(210) 492-1359*
11826 Wurzbach Rd ▪ *Deli* ▪ Owner David reports that GF diners are "a big part of the business." GF pizza is available. Bean and cheese nachos, chalupas, all dressings, and many soups are GF. ▪ *www.pamspatio.com*

Pappasito's Cantina $$LD
San Antonio ▪ *(210) 691-8974*
10501 I-10 West ▪ *Tex-Mex* ▪ Manager Susan reports that they are "so familiar" with GF diners that they can certainly accommodate them at any time. Alert a server, who will bring over the floor manager to discuss GF options and notify the kitchen manager. ▪ *www.pappasitos.com*

Pei Wei Asian Diner 📖
San Antonio ▪ *(210) 561-5600*
11267 Huebner Rd
San Antonio ▪ *(210) 523-0040*
11398 Bandera Rd Ste 101 Bldg 1
San Antonio ▪ *(210) 507-9160*
1802 N Loop 1604 E Ste 101
San Antonio ▪ *(210) 507-5520*
430 W Loop 1604 N Ste 101
San Antonio ▪ *(210) 507-3600*
999 E Basse Rd Ste 199

Shiraz Restaurant $$D
San Antonio ▪ *(210) 829-5050*
4230 McCullough Ave ▪ *Persian* ▪ Manager Rashin reports that all staff members are trained on the GF diet, and they will "steer" GF diners away from the few items that are not GF. There are several GF entrées, and for dessert, there is rice flour pudding, a rice noodle dessert, and saffron ice cream. Confirm timeliness of this information before dining in. ▪ *www.dineatshiraz.com*

Texas Land & Cattle Steak House 📖
San Antonio ▪ *(210) 222-2263*
201 N Saint Marys
San Antonio ▪ *(210) 342-4477*
60 NE Loop 410

San Antonio ▪ *(210) 699-8744*
9911 IH 10 W

Yard House 📖
San Antonio ▪ *(210) 691-0033*
15900 La Cantera Pkwy

Zio's ✪ $LD
San Antonio ▪ *(210) 697-7222*
12858 W Interstate 10
San Antonio ▪ *(210) 495-7722*
18030 N US Highway 281 ▪ *Italian* ▪ GF menu includes salmon caesar salad, chicken piccata, Greek pasta, lemon chicken primavera, shrimp with marinara, ribeye tuscano, grilled sirloin, and more. ▪ *www.zios.com*

TEXAS
ALL OTHER CITIES

Austin's Pizza ★ $LD
Cedar Park ▪ *(512) 795-8888*
2800 E Whitestone Blvd
Pflugerville ▪ *(512) 795-8888*
15424 Farm-To-Market 1825
Round Rock ▪ *(512) 795-8888*
3750 Gattis School Rd
West Lake Hills ▪ *(512) 795-8888*
3638 Bee Cave Rd ▪ *Pizza* ▪ GF pizza is available in the 10-inch size. ▪ *www.austinspizza.com*

Bavarian Grill ✪ $$LD
Plano ▪ *(972) 881-0705*
221 W Parker Rd ▪ *German* ▪ GF menu includes smoked salmon on green salad, applewood smoked chicken breast, and trout. ▪ *www.bavariangrill.com*

Blue Mesa Grill ✪ $LD
Addison ▪ *(972) 934-0165*
5100 Beltline Rd
Fort Worth ▪ *(817) 332-6372*
1600 S University Dr
Plano ▪ *(214) 387-4407*

8200 Dallas Pkwy
Southlake ▪ *(817) 416-0055*
1586 E Southlake Blvd ▪ *Southwest* ▪
Ask for the "Nutritional Brochure," which
contains a list of GF items and advice on
GF ordering. GF options include red chili
crusted salmon, painted desert soup, guacamole, and queso blanco. For dessert, they
offer flan. ▪ *www.bluemesagrill.com*

Buca di Beppo   📖

Frisco ▪ *(972) 668-3287*
8580 State Highway 121
Shenandoah ▪ *(936) 321-6262*
19075 I-45 S
Southlake ▪ *(817) 749-6262*
2701 E State Highway 114

Cakes by Monica   100% $$$$$

Pasadena ▪ *(281) 998-1658*
5005 Anthony Ln ▪ *Bakery* ▪ Dedicated
GF bakery offering cakes, cookies, brownies, pies, and more. Items are available by
phone or email order only. Orders must be
placed at least 4 days in advance. ▪ *www.
monicasgfcakes.com*

Cantina Laredo   📖

Addison ▪ *(972) 458-0962*
4546 Belt Line Rd
Dfw Airport ▪ *(972) 973-4267*
3200 E Airfield Dr
Frisco ▪ *(214) 618-9860*
1125 Legacy Dr
Ft Worth ▪ *(817) 810-0773*
530 Throckmorton St
Grapevine ▪ *(817) 358-0505*
4020 William D Tate Ave Ste 208
Lewisville ▪ *(972) 315-8100*
2225 S Stemmons Fwy

Carino's Italian   📖

Abilene ▪ *(325) 698-4950*
4157 Buffalo Gap Rd
Amarillo ▪ *(806) 468-9375*
8400 I-40 W
Baytown ▪ *(281) 421-7077*
7017 Garth Rd
Beaumont ▪ *(409) 842-1919*
3805 Interstate 10 S

El Paso ▪ *(915) 778-7771*
1201 Airway Blvd
El Paso ▪ *(915) 581-7042*
675 Sunland Park Dr
Ft Worth ▪ *(817) 346-4456*
5900 S Hulen St
Humble ▪ *(281) 812-6127*
7069 Fm 1960 Rd E
Hurst ▪ *(817) 503-8917*
2175 Precinct Line Rd
Jersey Village ▪ *(281) 970-1554*
19820 Northwest Fwy
Katy ▪ *(281) 398-5646*
21875 Katy Fwy
Longview ▪ *(903) 236-9654*
411 E Loop 281 Ste B
Lubbock ▪ *(806) 798-0944*
6821 Slide Rd
Midland ▪ *(432) 520-7600*
4711 W Loop 250 N
Missouri City ▪ *(281) 261-2630*
5750 Highway 6
New Braunfels ▪ *(830) 609-1141*
1304 E Common St
Odessa ▪ *(432) 362-4426*
5111 E 42nd St
Pearland ▪ *(713) 436-0090*
3050 Silverlake Village Dr
Round Rock ▪ *(512) 238-8288*
2600 Ih 35 N
San Angelo ▪ *(325) 655-8744*
1407 Knickerbocker Rd
San Marcos ▪ *(512) 393-5060*
1207 Ih 35 S
Sherman ▪ *(903) 813-8595*
306 W US Highway 82
Sunset Valley ▪ *(512) 899-0572*
5601 Brodie Ln
Texarkana ▪ *(903) 223-8655*
3402 Saint Michael Dr
Tyler ▪ *(903) 534-8280*
1723 W Southwest Loop 323
Wichita Falls ▪ *(940) 691-8900*
4330 Kell Blvd

Caro's Mexican Restaurant $$LD

Fort Worth ▪ *(817) 924-9977*
3505 Blue Bonnet Cir ▪ *Mexican* ▪ Owner
John reports that GF diners are welcome

and notes that there are several GF items available on the menu. He also notes that the staff is "very familiar" with GF diners. ▪ www.caros.biz

Carrabba's Italian Grill   📖
Beaumont ▪ *(409) 842-5561*
1550 Ih 10 S
Grapevine ▪ *(817) 410-8461*
1701 Cross Roads Dr
Hurst ▪ *(817) 595-3345*
1101 Melbourne Rd
Kingwood ▪ *(281) 358-5580*
750 Kingwood Dr
Plano ▪ *(972) 516-9900*
3400 N Central Expy
Spring ▪ *(281) 367-9423*
25665 Interstate 45 N
Sugar Land ▪ *(281) 980-4433*
2335 Highway 6
Webster ▪ *(281) 338-0574*
502 W Bay Area Blvd

Classic Café at Roanoke, The $$$LD
Roanoke ▪ *(817) 430-8185*
504 N Oak St ▪ *American* ▪ Manager Francis reports that GF diners are welcome and that they accommodate GF guests "all the time." He advises making reservations noting GF. ▪ www.theclassiccafe.com

CraigO's Pizza and Pasta   ★ $LD
Georgetown ▪ *(512) 869-7499*
1015 W University Ave
San Marcos ▪ *(512) 558-2220*
690 Center Point Rd ▪ *Pizza* ▪ GF pizza is available. ▪ www.craigospizzaandpasta.com

Del Frisco's Double Eagle Steak House   📖

Fort Worth ▪ *(817) 877-3999*
812 Main St

Fire Bowl Café   ✪ ¢LD
Round Rock ▪ *(512) 248-2695*
150 Sundance Pkwy
Sunset Valley ▪ *(512) 899-8998*
5601 Brodie Ln ▪ *Asian Stir-Fry* ▪ GF menu includes spicy coconut soup, thai seafood tom kah soup, and a variety of salads. It features "Stir Fry Your Way," for which

diners choose their own meats, sauces, and starches. GF sauce options are ginger white wine and yellow curry. ▪ www.firebowlcafe.com

Fogo De Chao   ★ $$$$LD
Addison ▪ *(972) 503-7300*
4300 Belt Line Rd ▪ *Brazilian* ▪ GF cheese bread made with yucca flour is available. ▪ www.fogodechao.com

Fresco's Cocina Mexicana   ✪ $$LD
Burleson ▪ *(817) 426-9990*
112 S Main St
Watauga ▪ *(817) 498-6370*
7432 Denton Hwy ▪ *Mexican* ▪ GF menu includes cheese and guacamole appetizers, Mexican salad, ribeye and brisket fajitas, tamales, and more. Restaurant recommends calling 48 hours in advance if you want GF chips or taco shells. ▪ www.frescos-mexicanfood.com

Garliq   ★ ¢LD
Southlake ▪ *(817) 337-9100*
250 Randol Mill Ave ▪ *Italian* ▪ GF pasta and pizza are available. ▪ www.garliqpasta.com

Gristmill River Restaurant & Bar $$$LD
New Braunfels ▪ *(830) 625-0684*
1287 Gruene Rd ▪ *American* ▪ Manager Tim reports that the restaurant serves "a few gluten-free diners each week." He notes that the restaurant has an internal, electronic list of items that are or can be modified to be GF, and he recommends asking for that list and alerting a manager upon arrival. He cites steaks, salads, and ribs as popular dishes among the restaurant's GF clientele. Confirm timeliness of this information before dining in. ▪ www.gristmillrestaurant.com

Jasper's $$$LD
Plano ▪ *(512) 832-8012*
7161 Bishop Rd
The Woodlands ▪ *(281) 298-6600*
9595 Six Pines Dr ▪ *American* ▪ Manager Dustin of the Plano location reports that GF diners are "absolutely" welcome.

He notes that they see "quite a few" GF customers, and that several menu items are naturally GF. Manager Patrick confirms this information for the location in The Woodlands and adds that the servers are trained on the GF diet. ▪ *www.kentrathbun. com*

Java Dive Organic Café   ✪ ★ ¢**BL**
Lakeway ▪ *(512) 266-5885*
1607 Ranch Road 620 N ▪ *Organic* ▪ Extensive GF menu includes quesadillas, falafel, paninis, bagels, and more. For weekend brunch, it offers banana bread french toast, waffles, and pancakes, among other options. A wide variety of GF specialty items, including bread, is available. ▪ *www. javadivecafe.com*

Kona Grill   📖
Sugar Land ▪ *(281) 242-7000*
16535 Southwest Fwy

La Trattoria   ★ $$$**BLD**
Alpine ▪ *(432) 837-2200*
901 E Holland Ave ▪ *Italian* ▪ GF pasta is available. Owner Keith reports that the kitchen can prepare GF pasta at any time, but it will take more time than most other dishes. Call ahead so that they can prepare the pasta beforehand. ▪ *www.latrattoriacafe. com*

Loretta's Finest $$$**LD**
Schertz ▪ *(210) 945-8700*
858 Farm To Market 78 ▪ *American Regional* ▪ Restaurant reports that the whole menu, with the exception of the bread, is GF. The menu includes fried chicken, sautéed chicken breast, catfish, tilapia and shrimp, as well as cabbage, greens, okra and tomatoes, and fried okra and gumbo. Alert a server upon arrival.

Maggiano's Little Italy   ★ $$$**LD**
Plano ▪ *(972) 781-0776*
6001 W Park Blvd ▪ *Italian* ▪ GF pasta is available. Call individual locations to inquire about additional GF options. ▪ *www. maggianos.com*

Melting Pot, The   📖
Arlington ▪ *(817) 469-1444*
4000 Five Points Dr
Shenandoah ▪ *(936) 271-7416*
19075 Interstate 45 S

Olive Branch Pizza   ★ ¢**LD**
Denton ▪ *(940) 566-2239*
1776 Teasley Ln ▪ *Pizza* ▪ GF pizza is available with advanced notice of at least one day.

Outback Steakhouse   📖
Abilene ▪ *(325) 692-7177*
4142 Ridgemont Dr
Addison ▪ *(972) 392-0972*
15180 Addison Rd
Amarillo ▪ *(806) 352-4032*
7101 I-40 W
Arlington ▪ *(817) 557-5959*
1151 W I-20
Baytown ▪ *(281) 421-9001*
5218 I-10 East
Beaumont ▪ *(409) 842-6699*
2060 I-10 South
Burleson ▪ *(817) 447-8216*
13265 South Fwy
College Station ▪ *(979) 764-4329*
2102 Texas Ave S
Conroe ▪ *(936) 760-4329*
808 Interstate 45 N
Corpus Christi ▪ *(361) 814-6283*
4221 S Padre Island Dr
Denton ▪ *(940) 320-5373*
300 I-35 S.
Desoto ▪ *(972) 228-8748*
1101 N I 35 E
El Paso ▪ *(915) 592-5063*
11875 Gateway Blvd W
Fort Worth ▪ *(817) 370-7800*
4608 Bryant Irvin Rd
Frisco ▪ *(972) 668-6955*
9382 State Highway 121
Garland ▪ *(972) 495-3699*
4902 N George Bush Hwy
Grapevine ▪ *(817) 329-4949*
1031 W State Highway 114
Humble ▪ *(281) 446-4329*
9753 Fm 1960 Bypass Rd W

Hurst ■ *(817) 285-0004*
701 Airport Fwy
Irving ■ *(972) 399-1477*
3510 W Airport Fwy
Katy ■ *(281) 492-2225*
20455 Katy Fwy
Killeen ■ *(254) 699-4164*
2701 E Central Texas Expy
Lewisville ■ *(972) 315-5772*
2211 S Stemmons Fwy
Longview ■ *(903) 663-6373*
501 E Loop 281
Lubbock ■ *(806) 788-0035*
4015 S Loop 289
Lufkin ■ *(936) 634-4616*
2206 S 1st St
Mcallen ■ *(956) 618-0577*
1109 E Business Highway 83
Mesquite ■ *(972) 686-0555*
3903 Towne Crossing Blvd
Midland ■ *(432) 684-1152*
2314 W Loop 250 N
Plano ■ *(972) 516-4100*
1509 N. Central Expwy
Round Rock ■ *(512) 733-6828*
1651 South I-35
San Angelo ■ *(325) 224-2796*
4505 Sherwood Way
San Marcos ■ *(512) 353-2500*
4205 I-35 South
Selma ■ *(210) 945-8100*
8131 Agora Pkwy
Shenandoah ■ *(936) 321-9106*
18326 I-45 South
Sugar Land ■ *(281) 980-4329*
15253 S.W. Freeway
Texarkana ■ *(903) 831-4252*
3209 Mall Dr
Tyler ■ *(903) 509-8193*
5704 S Broadway Ave
Waco ■ *(254) 772-5449*
4500 Franklin Ave
Webster ■ *(281) 338-6283*
481 W Bay Area Blvd

P.F. Chang's China Bistro 📖

Allen ■ *(972) 390-1040*
915 W Bethany Dr
Arlington ■ *(817) 375-8690*

215 E I-20 Hwy
El Paso ■ *(915) 845-0166*
760 Sunland Park Dr
Ft Worth ■ *(817) 840-2450*
400 Throckmorton St
Grapevine ■ *(817) 421-6658*
650 W Highway 114
Mcallen ■ *(956) 664-1516*
3100 E Expressway 83
Sugar Land ■ *(281) 313-8650*
2120 Lone Star Dr
The Woodlands ■ *(281) 203-6350*
1201 Lake Woodlands Dr Ste 301

Pappas Grill $$LD

Meadows Place ■ *(281) 277-9292*
12000 Hwy 59 S ■ Steakhouse ■ Manager
Justine reports that GF diners are welcome
and advises alerting a server upon arrival.
She reports that the restaurant is "used to"
GF diners. They use separate cookware
for GF food, and managers stop by a GF
diner's table to ensure that GF needs are
met. ■ *www.pappasgrillhouston.com*

Pappas Seafood House $$LD

Humble ■ *(281) 446-7707*
20410 Hwy 59 N @ Fm 1960
Webster ■ *(281) 332-7546*
19991 I-45 S ■ Seafood ■ Triumph contacted a manager at each location. Both
advised alerting the server and using the
word "allergy." Servers will notify both the
floor manager and the kitchen manager,
and a server or manager will indicate GF
options. ■ *www.pappasseafood.com*

Pappasito's Cantina $$LD

Arlington ■ *(817) 795-3535*
321 West Road to Six Flags
Fort Worth ■ *(817) 877-5546*
2704 West Fwy
Humble ■ *(281) 540-8664*
10005 Fm 1960
Richardson ■ *(972) 480-8595*
723 S Central Expy
Sugar Land ■ *(281) 565-9797*
13750 Southwest Fwy ■ Tex-Mex ■ Triumph contacted a manager at each location. All managers advised alerting the

server and using the word "allergy." Servers will notify both the floor manager and the kitchen manager. A manager will indicate GF options. ▪ *www.pappasitos.com*

Pei Wei Asian Diner 📖
Allen ▪ *(469) 675-2266*
1008 W Mcdermott Dr Ste 100
Amarillo ▪ *(806) 352-5632*
3350 S Soncy Rd Ste 194
Arlington ▪ *(817) 299-8687*
2100 N Collins St Ste 120
Arlington ▪ *(817) 466-4545*
4133 S Cooper St Ste 307
Beaumont ▪ *(409) 866-0620*
3050 Dowlen Rd Ste N
Bee Cave ▪ *(512) 263-8565*
12913 Galleria Circle Suite 101
Carrollton ▪ *(972) 407-0056*
3412 E Hebron Pkwy Ste 100
College Station ▪ *(979) 260-1209*
980A University Dr E # 4
Denton ▪ *(940) 380-9303*
1931 S Loop 288 Ste 130
El Paso ▪ *(915) 591-2006*
1325 George Dieter Dr Spc H2
El Paso ▪ *(915) 581-8540*
7500 N Mesa St Ste 101
Fort Worth ▪ *(817) 806-9950*
2600 W 7th St Ste 101
Fort Worth ▪ *(817) 294-0808*
5900 Overton Ridge Blvd Ste 130
Garland ▪ *(972) 202-5490*
4170 Lavon Dr
Highland Village ▪ *(972) 317-8809*
3090 Fm 407 Ste 306
Irving ▪ *(972) 373-8000*
7600 N Macarthur Blvd Ste 102
Katy ▪ *(281) 392-1410*
1590 S Mason Rd Ste A
Kingwood ▪ *(281) 318-2877*
702 Kingwood Dr
Lewisville ▪ *(469) 948-9000*
713 Hebron Pkwy Ste 200
Lubbock ▪ *(806) 792-4896*
4210 82nd St Ste 230
Mckinney ▪ *(972) 548-9843*
3000 S Central Expy
Pasadena ▪ *(281) 487-2226*

5932 Fairmont Pkwy Ste 150
Pearland ▪ *(713) 436-3840*
11302 Broadway St Ste 102
Plano ▪ *(972) 202-5380*
601 W 15th St Ste 101
Plano ▪ *(469) 362-8288*
8412 Preston Rd Ste 400
Round Rock ▪ *(512) 863-4087*
200 University Blvd Ste 100
Shenandoah ▪ *(936) 271-9217*
19075 I H 45 S Ste 480
Southlake ▪ *(817) 722-0070*
1582 E Southlake Blvd
Sugar Land ▪ *(281) 240-1931*
16101 Kensington Dr
Waco ▪ *(254) 772-0190*
4300A W Waco Dr Ste 1
Watauga ▪ *(817) 605-0145*
7620 Denton Hwy Ste 632
Webster ▪ *(281) 554-9876*
19411 Gulf Fwy

Reata Restaurant ✪ $$$$LD
Alpine ▪ *(432) 837-9232*
203 N 5th St
Fort Worth ▪ *(817) 336-1009*
310 Houston St ▪ *American Regional* ▪ GF menu at the Fort Worth location includes bacon-wrapped shrimp, smoked quail, boar ribs, salads, tortilla soup, pan-seared tenderloin, veal, buffalo ribeye, stuffed salmon, and more. The Alpine location does not have a GF menu, but manager Abraham reports that GF diners can be accommodated. He recommends noting GF in reservations in order to alert the chefs ahead of time. ▪ *www.reata.net*

Rio Mamba ✪ $$LD
Colleyville ▪ *(817) 354-3124*
5150 Highway 121
Fort Worth ▪ *(817) 423-3124*
6125 SW Loop 820 ▪ Tex-Mex ▪ Extensive GF menu features five pages of options, including fajitas, grilled chipotle chicken and tacos. ▪ *www.riomambo.com*

Rockfish Seafood Grill ✪ $LD
Arlington ▪ *(817) 419-9988*
3785 S Cooper St

Ft Worth ▪ *(817) 738-3474*
3050 S Hulen St
Highland Village ▪ *(972) 317-7744*
4061 Barton Creek
Las Colinas ▪ *(214) 574-4111*
7400 N Macarthur Blvd
Lubbock ▪ *(806) 780-7625*
6253 Slide Rd
Mckinney ▪ *(972) 542-2223*
2780 S Central Expy
Plano ▪ *(972) 599-2190*
4701 W Park Blvd
Richardson ▪ *(972) 267-8979*
7639 Campbell Rd
Southlake ▪ *(817) 442-0131*
228 State St
The Woodlands ▪ *(281) 419-3474*
1201 Lake Woodlands Dr ▪ *Seafood* ▪
Extensive GF menu includes ribs, salmon
salad, chicken caesar and a variety of seafood dishes. ▪ *www.rockfishseafood.com*

Roy's   ✪ $$$D
Plano ▪ *(972) 473-6263*
2840 Dallas Pkwy ▪ *Hawaiian Fusion* ▪
GF menu includes filet mignon, shiitake
stuffed chicken, and beef short ribs. Server
Jordan reports that learning about the GF
diet is "a big part" of the training program,
as they accommodate GF diners fairly frequently. ▪ *www.roysrestaurant.com*

Saltgrass Steak House $$$LD
Galveston ▪ *(409) 762-4261*
1502 Seawall Blvd
Pearland ▪ *(713) 436-0799*
3251 Silverlake Village Dr ▪ *Steakhouse* ▪
Manager Robert at the Galveston location
and Manager Alvin at the Pearland location advise that GF guests should ask for a
manager to guide them through the menu.
Manager Robert adds that servers may not
be familiar with the GF diet because they
serve GF diners "maybe multiple times
a month." He notes that all steaks, most
chicken dishes, and the salmon can be
prepared GF. ▪ *www.saltgrass.com*

Sublime Bakery   ✪★ ¢S
Fort Worth ▪ *(817) 570-9630*

5512 Bellaire Dr S ▪ *Bakery* ▪ Non-dedicated bakery offering a variety of GF products, including sugar cookies, lemon glaze
cheesecake, and custom cakes. All bakery
items are available by order only. ▪ *www.
sublimebakery.com*

Sugarless DeLite   ★ ¢S
Richardson ▪ *(972) 644-2000*
1389 W Campbell Rd ▪ *Bakery* ▪ Non-dedicated bakery with extensive GF offerings.
They offer GF cheesecake, chocolate chip
cookies, brownies, and crackers. All GF
items are baked fresh every day. ▪ *www.
sugarlessdelite.com*

Texas Land & Cattle Steak House   📖
Arlington ▪ *(817) 461-1500*
2009 E Copeland Rd
Bedford ▪ *(817) 318-1811*
1813 Highway 121
Frisco ▪ *(972) 668-2832*
3191 Preston Rd
Garland ▪ *(972) 203-1333*
4881 Bass Pro Dr
Hickory Creek ▪ *(940) 497-4550*
8398 S Stemmons Fwy
Killeen ▪ *(254) 699-5500*
3403 E Central Texas Expy
Lubbock ▪ *(806) 791-0555*
7202 Indiana Ave
Plano ▪ *(972) 578-8707*
3945 N Central Expy
Richardson ▪ *(972) 705-9700*
812 S Central Expy
Stafford ▪ *(281) 494-8844*
12710 Southwest Fwy

Uno Chicago Grill   📖
Fort Worth ▪ *(817) 885-8667*
300 Houston St

Wildfire $$$LD
Georgetown ▪ *(512) 869-3473*
812 S Austin Ave ▪ *American* ▪ Manager
Billy reports the restaurant serves GF diners "all the time." He recommends alerting
a server upon arrival, as most servers are
well versed in the GF diet. If, however, a
server seems not to know about the GF

diet, ask for Billy, who will be happy to discuss GF options. ▪ *www.wildfiretexas.com*

Yao Fuzi   ★ $$D

Plano ▪ *(214) 473-9267*
4757 W Park Blvd ▪ *Asian Fusion* ▪ GF
soy sauce is available. Restaurant reports
that most of the menu can be modified to
be GF. Alert a server upon arrival. ▪ *www.
yaofuzi.com*

Zen Japanese Food Fast   ¢LD

Sunset Valley ▪ *(512) 899-2222*
5207 Brodie Ln ▪ *Japanese* ▪ There are
two GF sauces: shiro-miso sauce and green
curry sauce. These can be substituted into
any dish on the menu, and the fully trained
kitchen staff will use clean woks and utensils to cook GF meals. Confirm timeliness
of this information before dining in. GF
rice noodles are available. ▪ *www.eatzen.
com*

Zeste Café & Market   ✪★ $$$LD

South Padre Island ▪ *(956) 761-5555*
3508 Padre Blvd ▪ *Mediterranean* ▪ GF
menu includes urban crusted lamb chop,
empanadas with sautéed mushrooms,
roasted chicken breast, quiche, hummus
and GF crackers, garlic cream spinach, rice
pilaf, thai-style mushrooms, and more.
Macaroons, chocolate truffles, and other
GF desserts are also available. GF crackers
are available.

Zio's   ✪ $LD

Ft Worth ▪ *(817) 232-3632*
6631 Fossil Bluff Dr
Georgetown ▪ *(512) 869-6600*
1007 W University Ave
Humble ▪ *(281) 540-7787*
20380 Highway 59 N
Live Oak ▪ *(210) 637-7787*
7824 Pat Booker Rd
Webster ▪ *(281) 338-7800*
820 W Bay Area Blvd ▪ *Italian* ▪ GF menu
includes salmon caesar salad, chicken piccata, Greek pasta, lemon chicken primavera, shrimp with marinara, ribeye tuscano,
grilled sirloin, and more. ▪ *www.zios.com*

UTAH

SALT LAKE CITY

Biaggi's Ristorante Italiano   📖

Salt Lake City ▪ *(801) 596-7222*
194 S 400 W

Blossom Fine Foods - Gluten Free Bakery   ★ ¢S

Salt Lake City ▪ *(801) 746-4454*
902 East Logan Ave ▪ *Bakery* ▪ Non-dedicated bakery that is primarily wholesale,
but opens to the public on Thursdays and
Fridays. GF cookies, cakes, muffins, brownies, and more are available. The signature
chocolate torte is GF, as are some of the
carrot cakes, cheesecakes, marble cream
cheese brownies, and other items. ▪ *www.
blossomfinefoods.com*

Bombay House $D

Salt Lake City ▪ *(801) 581-0222*
2731 Parley's Way ▪ *Indian* ▪ Manager
Singh reports that "lots of people" who are
GF dine in. He notes that with the exception of the samosas and naan bread, almost
everything is naturally GF. Confirm timeliness of this information before dining in.
Alert a server, and if the server is not GF
aware, ask him or her to speak to Singh
about GF options. ▪ *www.bombayhouse.
com*

Buca di Beppo   📖

Salt Lake City ▪ *(801) 575-6262*
202 W 300 S

Dodo Restaurant, The $$LD

Salt Lake City ▪ *(801) 486-2473*
1355 E 2100 S ▪ *Fusion* ▪ Restaurant reports
that the kitchen has an internal list of all
menu items that can be modified to be GF.
GF items include salads, wings, hummus
and vegetables, salmon, ahi steaks, and the
dessert flan. Confirm timeliness of this information before dining in. Alert a server,
who will indicate GF menu items. ▪ *www.
thedodo.net*

House of Bread   ★ ¢S
Salt Lake City ■ *(801) 466-1758*
2005 E 2700 S ■ *Bakery & Café* ■ GF
bread is available by the loaf on Saturday
afternoons only. The bakery notes that
sandwiches can be made from GF bread,
but GF customers will be charged for, and
get to take home, the whole GF loaf. Special orders can be placed for a large number
of loaves. ■ *www.houseofbread.com*

Lone Star Steakhouse & Saloon   📖
Salt Lake City ■ *(801) 466-1968*
1206 E 2100 S

Mazza   ✪★ $$LD
Salt Lake City ■ *(801) 484-9259*
1515 S 1500 E
Salt Lake City ■ *(801) 521-4572*
912 E 900 S ■ *Middle Eastern* ■ Chef Janin
of the 900 St location reports that the new
menus at both locations indicate GF items.
She notes that the rice and lentils, hummus, baba ganooj, and chicken shawarma
are all GF. GF beer is available. ■ *www.
mazzacafe.com*

Melting Pot, The   📖
Salt Lake City ■ *(801) 521-6358*
340 S Main St

Old Spaghetti Factory, The   📖
Salt Lake City ■ *(801) 521-0424*
189 Trolley Sq

Olio Ristorante $$$BLD
Salt Lake City ■ *(801) 401-2000*
150 W 500 S ■ *Italian* ■ Manager Paul
reports that he can accommodate GF diners, but only with some advanced notice.
Common GF dishes include salads or
simply-seasoned chicken and seafood
dishes. Located in the Sheraton Hotel. ■
www.starwoodhotels.com/sheraton

Original Pancake House, The   ★ ¢BL
Salt Lake City ■ *(801) 484-7200*
790 E 2100 S ■ *Breakfast* ■ GF pancakes
are available. Select locations may serve
other GF items. Call a specific location to
inquire. ■ *www.originalpancakehouse.com*

P.F. Chang's China Bistro   📖
Salt Lake City ■ *(801) 539-0500*
174 W 300 S

Pei Wei Asian Diner   📖
Salt Lake City ■ *(801) 907-2030*
1028 E 2100 S Ste 3

Pier 49 San Francisco Style Sourdough
Pizza   ★ $$LD
Salt Lake City ■ *(801) 364-2974*
238 S Main St ■ *Pizza* ■ GF pizza is available. ■ *www.pier49.com*

Red Rock Brewing $$LD
Salt Lake City ■ *(801) 521-7446*
254 S 200 W ■ *American* ■ Chef Eric reports that diners ask for GF meals "at least
once a day." He adds that several menu
items can be prepared GF. For example,
the steak, rice, mashed potatoes, and
salads are GF. He can make seafood dishes
without breading. Confirm timeliness of
this information before dining in. Alert a
server, who will notify the kitchen. ■ *www.
redrockbrewing.com*

Rodizio Grill   ✪ $$$LD
Salt Lake City ■ *(801) 220-0500*
600 S 700 E Trolley Sq ■ *Brazilian Steakhouse* ■ The restaurant offers a printed
description of which items on the menu
contain gluten. People regularly come in
specifically for the GF options. Alert a
server, who will discuss GF options and
notify the chef. ■ *www.rodiziogrill.com*

Sage's Café   ✪★ $BLD
Salt Lake City ■ *(801) 322-3790*
473 E 300 S ■ *Vegetarian* ■ The "Sensitivity Menu" lists "gluten-free alternative"
menu items, including tacos vegetarianos,
pesto brown rice risotto, and mushroom
stroganoff. For dessert, it lists rum-infused
bananas, as well as shakes, floats, and
smoothies. GF soy sauce, beer, and cookies
are available. ■ *www.sagescafe.com*

Thaifoon   ✪ $LD
Salt Lake City ■ *(801) 456-8424*
The Gateway, 7 N 400 W ■ *Thai* ■ GF

menu includes blackened ahi, chicken lettuce wrap, edamame, miso soup, the chopstick chicken salad, and chicken stir-fry. Manager Chelaine reports that the kitchen staff is "very knowledgeable" about GF cooking. ▪ *www.thaifoon.com*

Tucanos Brazilian Grill $$LD
Salt Lake City ▪ *(801) 456-2550*
162 S 400 W ▪ *Brazilian* ▪ Veteran Server Carly reports that they serve many GF diners. She notes that there is an internal list of non-GF items, which can be provided to customers upon request. She recommends speaking to a server, who will ask a manager if he or she has any questions. ▪ *www.tucanos.com*

Vertical Diner   ★ ¢LD
Salt Lake City ▪ *(801) 484-8378*
2280 S West Temple ▪ *American* ▪ Server David reports that all staff members are "pretty dialed in" to the GF diet, as they serve GF customers "daily." The sunshine burger on a corn tortilla is naturally GF. GF pancakes, biscuits, and gravy are available all day. ▪ *www.verticaldiner.com*

Z'Tejas Southwestern Grill   ✪★ $LD
Salt Lake City ▪ *(801) 456-0450*
191 S Rio Grande ▪ *Southwest* ▪ One-page GF menu includes wild mushroom enchiladas and grilled salmon, along with smoked chicken and black bean salad. Frozen margaritas and GF beer are also available. ▪ *www.ztejas.com*

UTAH

ALL OTHER CITIES

350 Main Brasserie   ✪ $$$D
Park City ▪ *(435) 649-3140*
350 Main St ▪ *Global* ▪ Extensive GF menu includes eggplant salad, lobster bisque, grilled trout, and pork tenderloin. Reser-

vations noting GF are recommended. ▪ *www.350main.com*

Bangkok Garden   ★ ¢LD
Ogden ▪ *(801) 621-4049*
2426 Grant Ave ▪ *Asian Fusion* ▪ GF soy sauce and noodles are available. Restaurant reports that most menu items can be prepared GF. They also recommend discussing GF options with the server. ▪ *www.bangkokgardenthaicuisine.com*

Blind Dog Restaurant   ★ $$D
Park City ▪ *(435) 655-0800*
1781 Sidewinder Dr ▪ *Modern American* ▪ GF pasta is available with advanced notice. Make reservations noting GF, as GF items may take longer to prepare. ▪ *www.blind-doggrill.com*

Bombay House $D
Provo ▪ *(801) 373-6677*
463 N University Ave ▪ *Indian* ▪ Manager Singh reports that "lots of people" who are GF dine in. He notes that with the exception of the samosas and naan bread, almost everything is naturally GF. Confirm timeliness of this information before dining in. Alert a server, and if the server is not GF aware, ask him or her to speak to Singh about GF options. ▪ *www.bombayhouse.com*

Buca di Beppo   📖
Midvale ▪ *(801) 561-9463*
935 Fort Union Blvd

Cafe Terigo $$$LD
Park City ▪ *(435) 645-9555*
424 Main St ▪ *French & Italian* ▪ Chef Ed reports that he has been serving GF customers "for several years." Certain menu items, such as filet mignon, grilled fish, and scallop risotto, can be prepared GF. Confirm timeliness of this information before dining in. ▪ *www.cafeterigo.com*

Carino's Italian   📖
Sandy ▪ *(801) 553-2580*
10585 S State St

West Jordan ▪ *(801) 282-8591*
7191 Plaza Center Dr

Carrabba's Italian Grill   📖
Orem ▪ *(801) 765-1222*
683 E University Pkwy

Chimayo $$$$D
Park City ▪ *(435) 649-6222*
368 Main St ▪ *Southwest* ▪ Restaurant reports that many people request GF meals, so they are "accustomed" to GF diners. They note that all entrées are made to order. A server or manager will speak with GF diners to ensure that their requests are met. Reservations noting GF are recommended. ▪ *www.chimayorestaurant.com*

China Lily   ★ ¢LD
Lindon ▪ *(801) 796-9666*
133 S State St ▪ *Chinese* ▪ GF soy sauce is available. Owner Sylvia reports that all menu items except those that are deep fried can be prepared GF. Confirm timeliness of this information before dining in. ▪ *www.chinalilylindon.com*

Gecko's Mexican Grill   ¢LD
S Jordan ▪ *(801) 253-8668*
781 W 10600 S Jordan Pky ▪ *Mexican* ▪ Owner Frank reports that they accommodate "a lot of customers" who are GF. Some sauces are thickened with cornstarch instead of flour. Most employees and all cooks are trained on the GF diet. Alert a server upon arrival or ask for Frank.

Grub Steak Restaurant $$$$LD
Park City ▪ *(435) 649-8060*
2200 Sidewinder Dr ▪ *Steakhouse* ▪ Manager Jessica reports that they have a "very GF friendly" menu. All steaks, potatoes, creamed spinach without bread crumbs, chicken, and jumbo prawns are GF. Confirm timeliness of this information before dining in. Jessica notes that they are very careful with regard to allergies, and servers will put a special note on GF orders going to the kitchen. ▪ *www.grubsteakrestaurant.com*

Lone Star Steakhouse & Saloon   📖
Centerville ▪ *(801) 294-8300*
111 S Frontage Rd
Layton ▪ *(801) 593-9823*
820 N Main St
Midvale ▪ *(801) 568-2600*
7176 S 900 E

Maddox Ranch House $$$LD
Perry ▪ *(435) 723-8545*
1900 S Highway 89 ▪ *Steakhouse* ▪ Manager Linda reports that nearly all meats and fish can be prepared GF. She notes that the brown gravy is thickened with corn starch and that all salads are naturally GF. Confirm timeliness of this information before dining in. All servers are trained on the GF diet, and they accommodate GF diners "all the time." ▪ *www.maddoxfinefood.com*

Madeline's Steakhouse & Grill   ✪ $$$LD
S Jordan ▪ *(801) 446-6639*
1133 W 10600 S Jordan Parkway ▪ *Steakhouse* ▪ GF menu includes flat iron steaks, baby back ribs, grilled halibut, and broccoli cheese soup. Manager Brian reports that they accommodate a lot of requests for GF meals. ▪ *www.madelinessteakhouse.com*

Mandarin   ✪★ $D
Bountiful ▪ *(801) 298-2406*
348 E 900 N ▪ *Chinese* ▪ GF menu includes cashew chicken or vegetable, curry chicken or beef, Mongolian beef, and tropical Thai chicken, halibut, or tofu, among other selections. GF soy sauce is available. Among the GF desserts are ginger ice cream and raspberry vanilla bean crème brûlée. ▪ *www.mandarinutah.com*

McGrath's Fish House   ✪ $LD
Layton ▪ *(801) 771-3474*
908 N Main St
Sandy ▪ *(801) 571-1905*
10590 S State St ▪ *Seafood* ▪ GF menu features a large selection of seafood entrees and appetizers, as well as salads and steaks. ▪ *www.mcgrathsfishhouse.com*

Old Spaghetti Factory, The   📖
Orem ▪ *(801) 224-6199*

575 E University Pkwy
Taylorsville ▪ (801) 966-2765
5718 S 1900 W

Outback Steakhouse 📖
Layton ▪ (801) 779-9394
1664 N 1200 W
Orem ▪ (801) 764-0552
372 E 1300 S
Sandy ▪ (801) 566-9394
7770 S 1300 E
St George ▪ (435) 674-7788
250 Red Cliffs Dr Ste 40

P.F. Chang's China Bistro 📖
Orem ▪ (801) 426-0900
575 E University Pkwy Ste A20

Pei Wei Asian Diner 📖
Midvale ▪ (801) 601-3170
1148 Fort Union Blvd Unit 162
Sandy ▪ (801) 601-1990
10373 S State St
West Bountiful ▪ (801) 294-0929
71 N 500 W Ste A

Red Rock Brewing $$**LD**
Park City ▪ (435) 575-0295
1640 Redstone Center Dr ▪ American ▪
Manager Chantel reports that the staff is
"absolutely" trained on the GF diet. She
recommends alerting the server upon ar-
rival, as they accommodate GF diners "a
lot" and can help choose a GF meal. ▪ www.
redrockbrewing.com

Rodizio Grill ★ $$$**LD**
American Fork ▪ (801) 763-4946
749 W 100 N ▪ Brazilian Steakhouse ▪
Manager Mike reports that they can accommodate GF diners. Most of the menu,
including cheesebread, polenta, and meats,
is GF or can be modified to be GF. Alert a
server, who will get a manager. There is a
list of non-GF items that GF diners must be
sure to avoid. GF cheesebread is available. ▪
www.rodiziogrill.com

Roosters Brewing Company ☺ $$**LD**
Layton ▪ (801) 774-9330
748 Heritage Park Blvd

Ogden ▪ (801) 627-6171
253 Historic 25th St ▪ American ▪ The GF
menu lists modified regular menu items
and includes chicken wings, ahi spring
salad, and fish tacos. Both locations report
that GF orders are rung in with a special
note to the kitchen. ▪ www.roostersbrew-
ingco.com

Spaghetti Mama's ★ $**LD**
Sandy ▪ (801) 676-0662
75 E 9400 S ▪ Italian ▪ GF pasta is avail-
able. ▪ www.spaghettimamas.com

Tucanos Brazilian Grill $$**LD**
Provo ▪ (801) 224-4774
4801 N University Ave ▪ Brazilian ▪
Manager Paul reports that they serve GF
diners "all the time." He notes that there is
an internal list of non-GF items, which can
be provided to customers upon request. He
recommends speaking to a server, who will
ask a manager if he or she has any questions. ▪ www.tucanos.com

Union Grill $**LD**
Ogden ▪ (801) 621-2830
2501 Wall Ave ▪ American ▪ Manager
Annette reports that most items must be
modified to be GF. For example, GF diners
can order fajitas with no tortilla, or filet mignon without sauce. BBQ ribs are naturally
GF. Confirm timeliness of this information
before dining in. Annette notes that servers
have lists of GF items at all service stations.
Alert a server upon arrival. Located in the
south end of Union Station. ▪ www.union-
grillogden.com

Winger's Grill and Bar ☺ ¢**LD**
American Fork ▪ (801) 492-1350
784 E State Rd
Bountiful ▪ (801) 295-4884
530 West 500 S
Brigham City ▪ (435) 723-3910
855 West 1100 S
Cedar City ▪ (435) 867-1700
1555 W Regency Rd
Clearfield ▪ (801) 779-3322
743 N Main St

Draper ▪ *(801) 501-9979*
12458 S Minuteman Dr
Kaysville ▪ *(801) 497-0303*
260 W 200 N
Lehi ▪ *(801) 766-6116*
380 N 850 E
Logan ▪ *(435) 752-3252*
2281 N Main St
Midvale ▪ *(801) 233-8763*
7269 S Union Park Ave
Murray ▪ *(801) 685-8889*
4790 S State St
N Ogden ▪ *(801) 737-4700*
360 E 2600 N
Ogden ▪ *(801) 479-1104*
4649 Harrison Blvd
Orem ▪ *(801) 221-4511*
610 State St
Provo ▪ *(801) 812-2141*
1200 S Provo Towne Ctr
Richfield ▪ *(435) 896-8595*
1080 West 1350 S
Riverton ▪ *(801) 254-8001*
3816 W 13400 S
Spanish Fork ▪ *(801) 798-9585*
592 N Kirby Ln
St George ▪ *(435) 688-1181*
188 S River Rd
Tooele ▪ *(435) 882-1441*
1211 N Mail
Vernal ▪ *(435) 781-1923*
1797 W 1000 S
W Jordan ▪ *(801) 567-9799*
9175 S Redwood Rd
West Valley ▪ *(801) 969-9464*
3671 S 2700 W ▪ *American* ▪ GF menu
includes double basted ribs, glazed salmon,
quesadillas with corn tortillas, and a variety
of salads. ▪ *www.wingers.info*

Zoom $$$$D

Park City ▪ *(435) 649-9108*
660 Main St ▪ *American* ▪ Manager Steve
reports that they have served "quite a few"
GF diners. He notes that there is an internal list of menu items that can be modified
to be GF, and he recommends asking a
server for the "gluten-free list" upon arrival. If servers are unsure of ingredients,

they are trained to ask the chef. ▪ *www.*
zoomparkcity.com

VERMONT

American Flatbread   ★ $D

Burlington ▪ *(802) 861-2999*
115 Saint Paul St
Middlebury ▪ *(802) 388-3300*
137 Maple St
Waitsfield ▪ *(802) 496-8856*
46 Lareau Rd ▪ *American* ▪ GF flatbread
pizza is available. Marketing Director
Megan reports that they carry a frozen GF
crust, which they can top and bake upon
request. Special desserts like crème brulee
are sometimes available. ▪ *www.american-*
flatbread.com

Blue Moon Café $$$D

Stowe ▪ *(802) 253-7006*
35 School St ▪ *Modern American* ▪ Hostess
Veronica reports that everything is made
to order, and only a few dishes cannot be
prepared GF. She notes that they serve GF
diners at least "once or twice a week," so the
servers are GF aware. Alert the hostess and
server, who will alert the rest of the staff. ▪
www.bluemoonstowe.com

Butler's Restaurant & Tavern $$$BLD

Essex Junction ▪ *(802) 764-1489*
70 Essex Way ▪ *American* ▪ Director Chris
reports that the restaurant is "very familiar"
with the GF diet. He notes that the kitchen
is flexible and can modify many menu
items to be GF. He recommends reservations noting GF, so that the server knows to
speak to a chef about GF options. Restaurant is run by teachers and interns of the
New England Culinary Institute. Located
inside the Essex Culinary Resort and Spa. ▪
www.vtculinaryresort.com

Café & Bakery at Healthy Living ★ ¢S
S Burlington ▪ (802) 863-2569
222 Dorset St ▪ *Healthy American* ▪ GF muffins, brownies, cakes, and more are available. Supervisor Shelby that they accommodate "a lot of people" with GF requests. ▪ *www.healthylivingmarket.com*

Ground Round 📖
South Burlington ▪ (802) 862-1122
1633 Williston Rd

Hemingway's $$$$D
Killington ▪ (802) 422-3886
4988 US Rt 4 ▪ *Modern American* ▪ GF bread and desserts are available. Manager Ted reports that most items on the menu are naturally GF, and the restaurant "constantly" hosts GF diners. Alert a server, who will indicate GF options. Reservations noting GF are recommended but not required. ▪ *www.hemingwaysrestaurant.com*

Ice House, The $$$$LD
Burlington ▪ (802) 864-1800
171 Battery St ▪ *Modern American* ▪ Manager Mike reports that GF diners are welcome "for sure." He suggests alerting a hostess and a server, who will speak to the chef. Many dishes can be prepared GF, including prime cuts of steak and seafood. Confirm timeliness of this information before dining in.

Jeff's Restaurant ★ $$$LD
Saint Albans ▪ (802) 524-6135
65 N Main St ▪ *Seafood* ▪ GF pasta is available, and GF crackers are sometimes available. ▪ *www.jeffsmaineseafoodrestaurant.com*

Kismet ★ ¢BL
Montpelier ▪ (802) 223-8646
207 Barre St ▪ *Healthy American* ▪ GF buckwheat crepes and bread are available. Ask about other GF options, as the restaurant may offer other things. ▪ *www.kismetkitchen.com*

Madera's Restaurante Mexicano and Cantina ✪ $LD
Burlington ▪ (802) 657-3377
#3 Main St Landing ▪ *Mexican* ▪ Manager Jenna reports that the WF menu is GF "to the best of our knowledge." It includes ceviches and salads, as well as house specials like fajitas, enchiladas, and various fish and meat dishes. Manager Josh reports that servers "know all about" the GF diet, and they accommodate GF diners "pretty often." All fried items are prepared in shared oil. ▪ *www.maderasvt.com*

Main Street Grill & Bar $$LD
Montpelier ▪ (802) 223-3188
118 Main St ▪ *American* ▪ Manager Steven reports that they frequently accommodate GF diners. He recommends reservations noting GF so the staff can discuss GF options beforehand. He notes that the chef is "very flexible," and usually has four or five dishes that he can modify to be GF. Run by the teachers and students of the New England Culinary Institute. ▪ *www.necidining.com*

Michael's on the Hill $$$D
Waterbury Center ▪ (802) 244-7476
4182 Stowe-Waterbury Rd ▪ *Continental* ▪ Owner Laura reports that they are accustomed to serving GF diners, as they do so every day. She notes that all staff members are trained on the GF diet, and she recommends making reservations noting GF. For dessert, they serve a GF chocolate torte and chocolate fondue. ▪ *www.michaelsonthehill.com*

Ninety Nine Restaurant & Pub 📖
Brattleboro ▪ (802) 251-0899
1184 Putney Rd
Rutland ▪ (802) 775-9288
315 S Main St
Williston ▪ (802) 879-9901
11 Taft Corners Shopping Ctr

Outback Steakhouse 📖
South Burlington ▪ (802) 862-0003
150 Dorset St

Rí~Rá Irish Pub $LD
Burlington ▪ (802) 860-9401

123 Church St ▪ Irish Pub ▪ Ask for the "Allergen Chart," which has a "Celiac" column. This column contains items that are GF or can be modified to be GF. ▪ www.rira.com

Simon Pearce Restaurant $$$ **LD**
Quechee ▪ (802) 295-1470
1760 Main St ▪ Modern American ▪ Manager Deanna reports that the kitchen is "very accommodating." The beef carpaccio, arugula salad, strawberry and spinach salad, venison meatloaf, and mascarpone polenta are possible GF options. Servers are given sheets detailing GF foods, and they will indicate GF options upon request. Reservations noting GF are recommended. ▪ www.simonpearce.com

Single Pebble, A   ★ $$ **LD**
Burlington ▪ (802) 865-5200
133 Bank St ▪ Chinese ▪ GF soy sauce is available. Restaurant reports that most dishes can be prepared GF. Servers are well trained in accommodating GF diners. ▪ www.asinglepebble.com

Souza's   ★ $$$$ **D**
Burlington ▪ (802) 864-2433
55 Main St ▪ Brazilian ▪ Chef Mattias notes that most meats are seasoned only with garlic and salt, so GF diners are "easily" accommodated. Alert a server, who will notify the kitchen. GF cheese bread made with yucca flour is available. ▪ www.souzas. org

Stone Soup   ★ $ **LD**
Burlington ▪ (802) 862-7616
211 College St ▪ Soup ▪ GF soups, stews, rices, and salads are available, and the restaurant bakes GF muffins fresh on Saturdays.

Uno Chicago Grill   📖
S Burlington ▪ (802) 865-4000
1330 Shelburne Rd

West Meadow Farm Bakery   100% ¢ **S**
Essex Junction ▪ (802) 878-1646
34 Park St ▪ Bakery ▪ Dedicated GF bakery offering bread, pizza, and hamburger buns, as well as a wide variety of baked goods such as cookies, pies, brownies, and cakes. ▪ www.westmeadowfarmbakery.com

Windjammer, The $$$ **LD**
S Burlington ▪ (802) 862-6585
1076 Williston Rd ▪ Seafood & Steakhouse ▪ Manager Carrie reports that "a lot" of GF diners come in. She notes that there are many options for GF diners, and the staff is very well educated on the GF diet. Ask a server about the GF options. ▪ www. windjammerrestaurant.com

VIRGINIA

ARLINGTON / ALEXANDRIA

219, The $$$ **LD**
Alexandria ▪ (703) 549-1141
219 King St ▪ French ▪ Manager Patty reports that GF diners are "very welcome" at the restaurant. She notes that the sole, ribs, salmon, cassoulet, seafood au gratin, chicken breast with shrimp scampi, steak, and lamb can be modified to be GF. Confirm timeliness of this information before dining in. Alert a server, who will notify the kitchen. ▪ www.219restaurant.com

American Flatbread   ★ $ **D**
Arlington ▪ (703) 243-9465
1025 N Fillmore St ▪ American ▪ GF flatbread pizza is available. Marketing Director Megan reports that they carry a frozen GF crust, which they can top and bake upon request. Special desserts like crème brulee are sometimes available. ▪ www.americanflatbread.com

Austin Grill   ✪ $ **LD**
Alexandria ▪ (703) 684-8969
801 King St ▪ Tex-Mex ▪ GF menu includes slow-smoked BBQ ribs, fajitas, tacos and quesadillas. For dessert, they offer homemade flan. ▪ www.austingrill.com

Bertucci's   📖
Alexandria ▪ (703) 548-8500
725 King St
Arlington ▪ (703) 528-9177
2800 Clarendon Blvd

Buzz   ★ ¢S
Alexandria ▪ (703) 600-2899
901 Slaters Ln ▪ *Bakery & Café* ▪ Non-dedicated bakery offering GF cupcakes, brownies, muffins, crème brûlée, and ice cream. All items are freshly made every day. Bakery recommends calling in advance, as they sometimes sell out of particular items. ▪ *www.buzzonslaters.com*

CakeLove   ★ ¢S
Arlington ▪ (703) 933-0099
4150 Campbell Ave ▪ *Bakery* ▪ Non-dedicated bakery offering GF cakes and cupcakes to order with advanced notice of at least 4 days. Orders can be placed online for quick and easy pick-up. ▪ *www.cakelove. com*

Carlyle   ✪ $$LD
Arlington ▪ (703) 931-0777
4000 Campbell Ave ▪ *American* ▪ The "low-gluten" menu features the chicken grill, New Orleans shrimp, and roast pork tenderloin. For dessert, there is a flourless chocolate macadamia nut waffle. The menu is "low-gluten" rather than GF because the items are prepared in the same kitchen as non-GF items. ▪ *www.greatamericanrestaurants.com*

Chop't   ¢LD
Arlington ▪ (703) 875-2888
1735 N Lynn St ▪ *Deli* ▪ Manager Val reports that they are trained to accommodate GF diners. Alert the "chopper" upon arrival, and he or she will call a manager. The manager will prepare a GF salad with a clean surface and clean utensils. All managers are knowledgeable about which salad items and toppings are GF. ▪ *www. choptsalad.com*

Clyde's $LD
Alexandria ▪ (703) 820-8300

1700 N Beauregard St ▪ *American* ▪ Staff members are trained to handle "allergies" of all kinds. Alert a server, who will communicate with the chefs and managers. A server or manager will indicate GF options. ▪ *www.clydes.com*

Dairy Godmother, The   ¢S
Alexandria ▪ (703) 683-7767
2310 Mount Vernon Ave ▪ *Frozen Custard* ▪ Restaurant reports that most custards and sorbets are GF. Always check with a staff member to ensure that the flavor is GF and a clean spoon is used. ▪ *www.thedairygodmother.com*

Gadsby's Tavern $$$LD
Alexandria ▪ (703) 548-1288
138 N Royal St ▪ *American* ▪ Chef Frank reports that they can accommodate GF diners, as they have a scratch kitchen and everything can be modified. He notes, however, that most sauces are premade and are not GF. Alert a server, and be specific about GF restrictions. The server will notify the kitchen. ▪ *www.gadsbystavernrestaurant.com*

Great Harvest Bread Company   ★ ¢S
Alexandria ▪ (703) 671-8678
1711 Centre Plz ▪ *Bakery* ▪ GF bread is baked every other Tuesday. GF muffins and scones are made by special order only. The Burke and Lorton locations have discontinued all GF products. ▪ *www.alexandriagreatharvest.com*

Jaleo Crystal City   ✪ $$$LD
Arlington ▪ (703) 413-8181
2250 Crystal Dr Ste A ▪ *Tapas* ▪ GF menu items include paellas, grilled hangar steak tapas, duck confit tapas, and a traditional chorizo tapas, and more. General Manager Joseph recommends speaking to a manager upon arrival. ▪ *www.jaleo.com*

La Bergerie   ★ $$$$LD
Alexandria ▪ (703) 683-1007
218 N Lee St ▪ *French* ▪ Owner Laurent reports that they accommodate GF diners. The menu changes seasonally, but the fresh

fish of the day and the baby rack of lamb can be prepared GF. Confirm timeliness of this information before dining in. GF bread, pasta, soy sauce, pies, and cakes are available. Located on the 2nd floor of the Crilley Warehouse. ▪ *www.labergerie.com*

Lebanese Taverna   ✪ ¢**LD**
Arlington ▪ *(703) 415-8681*
1101 S Joyce St
Arlington ▪ *(703) 241-8681*
5900 Washington Blvd ▪ *Middle Eastern* ▪ GF menu includes lentil soup, lamb shanks, shwarma, chicken and rice, jumbo shrimp, and more. Any dish that normally includes bread can be made GF by substituting rice crackers and vegetables. ▪ *www.lebanesetaverna.com*

Legal Sea Foods   📖
Arlington ▪ *(703) 415-1200*
2301 Jefferson Davis Hwy

Lone Star Steakhouse & Saloon   📖
Alexandria ▪ *(703) 823-7827*
3141 Duke St

Lost Dog Café, The   ★ $**LD**
Arlington ▪ *(703) 553-7770*
2920 Columbia Pike
Arlington ▪ *(703) 237-1552*
5876 Washington Blvd ▪ *Deli* ▪ GF pizza and beer are available. ▪ *www.lostdogcafe.com*

Melting Pot, The   📖
Arlington ▪ *(703) 243-4490*
1110 N Glebe Rd

Outback Steakhouse   📖
Alexandria ▪ *(703) 768-1063*
6804 Richmond Hwy
Arlington ▪ *(703) 527-0063*
4821 1st St N

P.F. Chang's China Bistro   📖
Arlington ▪ *(703) 527-0955*
901 N Glebe Rd

Peking Duck Restaurant   ★ $**LD**
Alexandria ▪ *(703) 768-2774*
7531 Richmond Hwy ▪ *Chinese* ▪ Owner Peter reports that GF items include curry

chicken, shrimp pepperada, and moo goo gai pan. GF soy sauce is available, so many other menu items can be modified to be GF. For dessert, they offer lychee nuts and taffy strawberries. ▪ *www.pekingduck.com*

Rí~Rá Irish Pub $**LD**
Arlington ▪ *(703) 248-9888*
2915 Wilson Blvd ▪ *Irish Pub* ▪ Ask for the "Allergen Chart," which has a "Celiac" column. This column contains items that are GF or can be modified to be GF. ▪ *www.rira.com*

Rustico   ★ $$$**LD**
Alexandria ▪ *(703) 224-5051*
827 Slaters Ln ▪ *Modern American* ▪ GF pizza is available. Manager Jason reports that salads, eggplant, and chicken dishes can also be made GF. He cautions that the kitchen works with a lot of flour, and cross-contamination is always a risk. ▪ *www.rusticorestaurant.com*

Shane's Rib Shack   📖
Alexandria ▪ *(703) 660-6288*
7698 Richmond Hwy

Z Pizza   ★ $$**LD**
Alexandria ▪ *(703) 660-8443*
6328C Richmond Hwy ▪ *Pizza* ▪ GF pizza is available. ▪ *www.zpizza.com*

Z Pizza   ★ $**LD**
Alexandria ▪ *(703) 600-1193*
3217 Duke St ▪ *Pizza* ▪ GF pizza is available. ▪ *www.zpizza.com*

VIRGINIA

RICHMOND

Bertucci's   📖
Richmond ▪ *(804) 360-1252*
11721 W Broad St

Can Can Brasserie $$$**LD**
Richmond ■ *(804) 358-7274*
3120 W Cary St ■ *French* ■ Owner Chris
reports that the restaurant serves GF diners frequently, and that servers are "very
well trained" on the GF diet. He notes that
the menu contains all fresh and seasonal
foods, making it easy to modify items to
be GF. Alert the hostess and server, who
will notify the kitchen. Items that can be
prepared GF include cranberry stuffed
trout and hanger steak. Confirm timeliness
of this information before dining in. Mint
chocolate crème brûlée is available for dessert. ■ *www.cancanbrasserie.com*

Carrabba's Italian Grill   📖
Richmond ■ *(804) 794-1771*
11450 Midlothian Tpke

Extreme Pizza   ★ $$**LD**
Richmond ■ *(804) 359-2030*
941 W Broad St ■ *Pizza* ■ GF pizza is available. ■ *www.extremepizza.com*

Firebirds Wood Fired Grill   ✪ $$$**LD**
Richmond ■ *(804) 440-0000*
11448 Belvedere Vista Ln
Richmond ■ *(804) 364-9744*
11800 W Broad St ■ *American* ■ GF menu
includes a variety of salads and a selection
of entrées. Examples include sirloin, filet
mignon, ribs, and lobster tail. All locations
report that servers are trained to alert the
chef when a customer orders from the GF
menu. ■ *www.firebirdsrockymountaingrill.*
com

Ichiban   ★ $**LD**
Richmond ■ *(804) 750-2380*
10490 Ridgefield Pkwy ■ *Japanese* ■ Manager Angela reports that many menu items
can be modified to be GF. She also notes
that GF diners come in "all the time." GF
soy sauce is available. ■ *www.ichibanjapane-*
secuisine.com

Lone Star Steakhouse & Saloon   📖
Richmond ■ *(804) 272-0391*
10456 Midlothian Tpke

Richmond ■ *(804) 747-8783*
8099 W Broad St Ste A

Maggiano's Little Italy   ★ $$$**LD**
Richmond ■ *(804) 253-0900*
11800 W Broad St ■ *Italian* ■ GF pasta is
available. Call individual locations to inquire about additional GF options. ■ *www.*
maggianos.com

Melting Pot, The   📖
Richmond ■ *(804) 741-3120*
9704 Gayton Rd

Nile Ethiopian Restaurant   ★ $$**LD**
Richmond ■ *(804) 225-5544*
309 N Laurel St ■ *Ethiopian* ■ Manager Be-
nyam reports that everything on the menu
is GF, except for desserts. He recommends
any meat or vegetarian dish. GF diners
can ask servers about GF options, just to
confirm. ■ *www.nilerichmond.com*

Old Original Bookbinder's $$$**D**
Richmond ■ *(804) 643-6900*
2306 E Cary St ■ *Seafood & Steakhouse*
■ The restaurant reports that they can accommodate GF diners. They note that fish
and meat selections can be prepared simply
with herbs, sea salt, and lemon juice.
Confirm timeliness of this information
before dining in. Reservations noting GF
are recommended. ■ *www.bookbindersrich-*
mond.com

Outback Steakhouse   📖
Richmond ■ *(804) 272-4500*
2063 Huguenot Rd
Richmond ■ *(804) 527-0583*
7917 W Broad St

P.F. Chang's China Bistro   📖
Richmond ■ *(804) 253-0492*
9212 Stony Point Pkwy

Positive Vibe Café $**LD**
Richmond ■ *(804) 560-9622*
2825 Hathaway Rd ■ *American* ■ Host
Max reports that there are several GF
items, like spinach dip, burgers without
buns, and the spinach tacos. Confirm timeliness of this information before dining in.

He notes that servers have access to a list of all GF items, and they accommodate "a fair amount" of GF diners. ▪ *www.positivevibe-cafe.com*

Tara Thai ✪ $LD
Richmond ▪ *(804) 360-0001*
11800 W Broad St ▪ *Thai* ▪ GF menu includes pad thai, papaya salad, beef salad, mussels, mint chicken, and other seafood dishes. ▪ *www.tarathairichmond.com*

Thai Diner Too ✪ $LD
Richmond ▪ *(804) 353-9514*
3028 W Cary St ▪ *Thai* ▪ GF menu includes pad ping curry, chicken satay with peanut sauce, masaman curry, rama, and sticky rice with mango for dessert.

VIRGINIA

VIRGINIA BEACH

Bonefish Grill 📖
Virginia Beach ▪ *(757) 306-3323*
3333 Virginia Blvd Suite 41

Burton's Grill ✪ $LD
Virginia Beach ▪ *(757) 422-8970*
741 First Colonial Rd ▪ *American* ▪ There are separate GF menus for lunch and dinner. Both are extensive and include appetizers, entrées, and desserts like vanilla bean crème brûlée and a warmed chocolate torte. ▪ *www.burtonsgrill.com*

Carrabba's Italian Grill 📖
Virginia Beach ▪ *(757) 631-0856*
739 Lynnhaven Pkwy

Lone Star Steakhouse & Saloon 📖
Virginia Beach ▪ *(757) 463-2879*
2712 North Mall Dr

Melting Pot, The 📖
Virginia Beach ▪ *(757) 425-3463*
1564 Laskin Rd

Outback Steakhouse 📖
Virginia Beach ▪ *(757) 563-8034*
1113 Nimmo Pkwy
Virginia Beach ▪ *(757) 523-4832*
1255 Fordham Dr
Virginia Beach ▪ *(757) 422-5796*
1757 Laskin Rd

P.F. Chang's China Bistro 📖
Virginia Beach ▪ *(757) 473-9028*
4551 Virginia Beach Blvd

Swan Terrace Restaurant $$$BLD
Virginia Beach ▪ *(757) 366-5777*
5641 Indian River Rd ▪ *American* ▪ Manager Cordell reports that they accommodate GF diners, and the kitchen is "conscious of" GF diners. Sauces made with flour can be modified to be GF, and filets are always GF. Confirm timeliness of this information before dining in. Cordell recommends reservations noting GF. ▪ *www.foundersinn.com*

Uno Chicago Grill 📖
Virginia Beach ▪ *(757) 306-9101*
1005 Lynnhaven Mall Loop

Z Pizza ★ $LD
Virginia Beach ▪ *(757) 368-9090*
3376 Princess Anne Rd ▪ *Pizza* ▪ GF pizza is available. ▪ *www.zpizza.com*

VIRGINIA

ALL OTHER CITIES

3 Fellers Bakery 100% ¢S
Goochland ▪ *(804) 556-0671*
3041 River Rd W ▪ *Bakery* ▪ Dedicated GF bakery offering an array of pastries, cakes, cupcakes, brownies, mini cheesecakes, fruit tortes, cookie dough, and cookies. Owner Susan reports that they are certified GF. Calling ahead for special requests is recommended. ▪ *www.3fellersbakery.com*

456 FISH $$$D
Norfolk ▪ *(757) 625-4444*
456 Granby St ▪ *Seafood* ▪ Manager
Ronnie reports that most menu items are
naturally GF. GF items like pan-seared
grouper in spicy Creole sauce, blackened
tuna, and stuffed baked squash topped with
mozzarella are included. Confirm timeli-
ness of this information before dining in. ▪
www.456fish.com

99 Main Restaurant   ◐ $$$D
Newport News ▪ *(757) 599-9885*
99 Main St ▪ *Continental* ▪ GF menu
includes appetizers, soups, salads, and
chef's specialties. Examples are roasted
oysters, beef tenderloin, a rack of lamb,
and NY strip rossini. For dessert, they
offer pomegranate crème brûlée. ▪
www.99mainrestaurant.com

Alexander's Restaurant $$$D
Roanoke ▪ *(540) 982-6983*
105 S Jefferson St ▪ *American Regional*
▪ Owner Bridget reports that the entire
staff is "well-trained" on the GF diet. Alert
a server, who will indicate menu items
that are GF or can be modified to be GF.
Reservations noting GF are recommended.
▪ *www.alexandersva.com*

American Flatbread   ★ $D
Ashburn ▪ *(703) 723-7003*
43170 Southern Walk Plz ▪ *American* ▪
GF flatbread pizza is available. Marketing
Director Megan reports that they carry a
frozen GF crust, which they can top and
bake upon request. Special desserts like
crème brulee are sometimes available. ▪
www.americanflatbread.com

AnnaB's Gluten Free Bakery   100% $S
Ashland ▪ *(804) 491-9288*
Hanover County ▪ *Bakery* ▪ Dedicated
GF bakery offering bagels, hamburger
buns, breads, pies, cakes, cookies, donuts,
muffins, brownies, and more. All items are
made to order, in small batches. Items not
listed on the menu may be available upon

request. Orders can be placed online only. ▪
www.annabglutenfree.com

Argia's   ★ $$LD
Falls Church ▪ *(703) 534-1033*
124 N Washington St ▪ *Italian* ▪ GF pasta
is available. Owner and Chef Amy recommends "emphasizing" to the server that the
meal must be GF. ▪ *www.argias.com*

Artie's $LD
Fairfax ▪ *(703) 273-7600*
3260 Old Lee Hwy ▪ *American* ▪ Reservationist Chelsea reports that the "low-
gluten" menu includes a variety of salads,
cheddar cheeseburgers without buns, and
hickory barbeque burgers without buns.
The menu is "low-gluten" rather than GF
because the items are prepared in the same
kitchen as non-GF items. Chelsea notes,
however, that "at least two or three people
per day" come to the restaurant for its
"low-gluten" menu. ▪ *www.greatamerican-
restaurants.com*

Austin Grill   ✪ $LD
Springfield ▪ *(703) 644-3111*
8430A Old Keene Mill Rd ▪ *Tex-Mex* ▪ GF
menu includes slow-smoked BBQ ribs,
fajitas, tacos and quesadillas. For dessert,
they offer homemade flan. ▪ *www.austin-
grill.com*

Bertucci's   📖
Gainesville ▪ *(571) 248-6397*
8114 Stonewall Shops Sq
Herndon ▪ *(703) 787-6500*
13195 Parcher Ave
Springfield ▪ *(703) 313-6700*
6525 Frontier Dr
Vienna ▪ *(703) 893-5200*
1934 Old Gallows Rd

Big Bowl Restaurant   ✪ $LD
Reston ▪ *(703) 787-8852*
11915 Democracy Dr ▪ *Asian* ▪ GF menu
includes thai chicken lettuce wraps as an
appetizer, various pad thai dishes and
chicken kung pao as entrées, and two GF
desserts, including the trio of tastes. ▪ *www.
bigbowl.com*

Bizou $LD
Charlottesville ▪ *(434) 977-1818*
119 W Main St ▪ *American* ▪ Manager
Mundo reports that they have "a couple of
regular customers" who are GF. The staff is
very educated and can accommodate GF
diners. Mundo emphasizes that there are
GF meals on both the lunch and dinner
menus. They have an open kitchen, so GF
diners can speak to the chef directly.

Blackstone Grill $$D
Christiansburg ▪ *(540) 381-0303*
420 Peppers Ferry Rd NW ▪ *Seafood &*
Steakhouse ▪ The restaurant notes that GF
diners come in "frequently." They report
that salmon, tuna, pork chops, chicken,
and any of the steaks can be prepared GF.
Confirm timeliness of this information before dining in. Alert a server upon arrival.
Reservations noting GF are recommended.
▪ *www.blackstonegrillva.com*

Blue Iguana $$$LD
Fairfax ▪ *(703) 502-8108*
12727 Shoppes Ln ▪ *American* ▪ Manager David reports that all food is made
to order, and accommodating GF diners
is "relatively common." He notes that all
kitchen staff members are certified to pro-
duce GF meals. He further reports that GF
diners should "pick their protein" and the
kitchen will prepare a suitable dish. ▪ *www.*
blueiguana.net

Bonefish Grill   📖
Broadlands ▪ *(703) 723-8246*
43135 Broadlands Center Plz Ste 137
Centreville ▪ *(703) 815-7427*
6315 Multiplex Dr
Charlottesville ▪ *(434) 975-3474*
269 Connor Dr
Fairfax ▪ *(703) 378-4970*
13005 Lee Jackson Hwy Ste J
Fredericksburg ▪ *(540) 548-1984*
1779 Carl D Silver Pkwy
Gainesville ▪ *(703) 753-2597*
7611 Somerset Crossing Dr
Kingstowne ▪ *(703) 971-3202*
5920 Kingstowne Towne Ctr Ste 110

Midlothian ▪ *(804) 639-2747*
6081 Harbour Park Dr
Newport News ▪ *(757) 269-0002*
340 Oyster Point Rd Ste 106
Williamsburg ▪ *(757) 229-3474*
5212 Monticello Ave

Bray Bistro $$$S
Williamsburg ▪ *(757) 253-1703*
1010 Kingsmill Rd ▪ *American Regional*
▪ Chef Justin reports that GF diners are
becoming more common at the restaurant.
He recommends noting GF in reservations
and asking to speak with the chef, who
will go over the menu with GF customers.
Located at Kingsmill Resort & Spa, the
restaurant is open only for Friday buffet-
style dinners and Sunday brunches. ▪ *www.*
kingsmill.com

Brooklyn Pizza   ★ $LD
Sterling ▪ *(703) 433-1313*
22000 Dulles Retail Plz ▪ *Pizza* ▪ GF pizza
is available.

Byrd & Baldwin Brothers Steakhouse,
The $$$$D
Norfolk ▪ *(757) 222-9191*
116 Brooke Ave ▪ *Steakhouse* ▪ General
Manager Bill reports that all staff members
are trained on the GF diet. He adds that
over half of the menu, including all chop-
house items, is naturally GF. For dessert,
they have flourless chocolate cake, crème
brûlée, and Mexican chocolate mousse.
Confirm timeliness of this information
before dining in. ▪ *www.byrdbaldwin.com*

C&O Restaurant $$$D
Charlottesville ▪ *(434) 971-7044*
515 E Water St ▪ *French Provincial* ▪ Chef
Eric reports that GF diners are accommodated regularly and "all of the staff is
very knowledgeable." The menu changes
regularly, so calling ahead is recommended. Dishes that can be modified to be GF
include squash and tomato soups, smoked
dates stuffed with mascarpone cheese, and
a three bird roast with root vegetable gratin. Confirm timeliness of this information

before dining in. ▪ *www.candorestaurant. com*

CakeLove   ★ ⊊S
McLean ▪ *(703) 442-4880*
1961 Chain Bridge Rd ▪ *Bakery* ▪ Non-dedicated bakery offering GF cakes and cupcakes to order with advanced notice of at least 4 days. Orders can be placed online for quick and easy pick-up. ▪ *www.cakelove. com*

Camp Critter at Great Wolf Lodge Grand Mound $$LD
Williamsburg ▪ *(757) 229-9700*
549 E Rochambeau Dr ▪ *American* ▪ Chef Tracy reports that the restaurant is "well versed" in accommodating their frequent GF diners. Alert a server upon arrival, and ask to speak with a chef or supervisor, any of whom will discuss GF options with customers. ▪ *www.greatwolf.com*

Capital Grille, The   📖
McLean ▪ *(703) 448-3900*
1861 International Dr

Carolina Cupcakery   ✪★ ⊊S
Chesapeake ▪ *(757) 204-4775*
237 Carmichael Way ▪ *Bakery* ▪ Non-dedicated bakery offering a variety of sweets, including cupcakes, cakes, lemon bars, brownies, cookies, and more. Dinner rolls and cheddar rolls are also available. Located at Edinburgh Commons. ▪ *www. carolinacupcakery.com*

Carrabba's Italian Grill   📖
Centreville ▪ *(703) 266-9755*
5805 Trinity Pkwy
Chesapeake ▪ *(757) 382-0337*
1217 Battlefield Blvd N
Fredericksburg ▪ *(540) 548-1122*
1951 Carl D Silver Pkwy
Newport News ▪ *(757) 269-4917*
12363 Hornsby Ln
Reston ▪ *(703) 464-7909*
12192 Sunset Hills Rd
Roanoke ▪ *(540) 265-0961*
4802 Valley View Blvd NW
Williamsburg ▪ *(757) 564-3696*

2500 Richmond Rd
Woodbridge ▪ *(703) 583-7300*
13870 Foulger Sq

Chima Brazilian Steakhouse $$$$LD
Vienna ▪ *(703) 639-3080*
8010 Towers Crescent Dr ▪ *Brazilian Steakhouse* ▪ Manager Fernando reports that GF diners are welcome. He notes that all meat varieties and thirty-nine of the salad bar items are GF. The cheese bread, however, is not GF. Fernando suggests asking to speak with a manager for a detailed description of GF options. . ▪ *www.chima.cc*

Choices by Shawn   ✪★ $BLD
Fairfax ▪ *(703) 385-5433*
3950 Chain Bridge Rd ▪ *Healthy American* ▪ GF items marked on the menu include mussels in white wine, stuffed avocados, and NY strip steak with Creole spice rub. For dessert, they offer GF carrot cake, fudge cake, and more. GF bread and pasta are available, as are GF cookies. ▪ *www.choicesbyshawn.com*

Clyde's $LD
Reston ▪ *(703) 787-6601*
11905 Market St
Vienna ▪ *(703) 734-1901*
8332 Leesburg Pike ▪ *American* ▪ Staff members at both locations are trained to handle "allergies" of all kinds. Alert a server, who will notify the chefs and managers. The server or manager will indicate GF options. ▪ *www.clydes.com*

Coastal Flats $$LD
Fairfax ▪ *(571) 522-6300*
11901 Grand Commons Ave
McLean ▪ *(703) 356-1440*
7860L Tysons Corner Ctr ▪ *American* ▪ The "low-gluten" menu includes warm goat cheese and spiced pecan salad, sautéed shrimp and creamy grit cakes, as well as other seafood and steak options. For dessert, there is a warm flourless chocolate waffle. Management reports that the menu is "low-gluten" instead of GF because items are prepared in the same kitchen as non-

GF items. ▪ *www.greatamericanrestaurants.com*

Cranberry's Grocery & Eatery ✪ ★ ⊂S
Staunton ▪ **(540) 885-4755**
7 S New St ▪ *Café* ▪ GF items marked on the menu include the mediterranean wrap, the grilled tempeh sandwich, the turkey reuben, the taj mahal salad, bagels, and scrambles. Owner Kathleen reports that diners should specify GF requests, and the kitchen will modify items to be GF. GF bread and wraps are available. ▪ *www.gocranberrys.com*

Dixie Bones BBQ $LD
Woodbridge ▪ **(703) 492-2205**
13440 Occoquan Rd ▪ *Barbeque* ▪ CEO Nelson reports that the restaurant is accustomed to serving GF diners, as they do it on a weekly basis. He notes that over half the menu is naturally GF or can be prepared GF. Managers are trained on the GF diet, so ask to speak with one upon arrival. ▪ *www.dixiebones.com*

Don's Woodfired Pizza, The   ★ $$LD
Sterling ▪ **(703) 444-4959**
21018 Southbank St ▪ *Pizza* ▪ GF pizza is available. ▪ *www.thedonspizza.com*

Duck Chang's Restaurant   ★ $LD
Annandale ▪ **(703) 941-9400**
4427 John Marr Dr ▪ *Chinese* ▪ Owner Peter reports that GF items include curry chicken, shrimp pepperada, and moo goo gai pan. GF soy sauce is available, so many other menu items can be modified to be GF. For dessert, they offer lychee nuts and taffy strawberries. ▪ *www.duckchangs.com*

Extreme Pizza   ★ $$LD
Henrico ▪ **(804) 360-3123**
11653 W Broad St ▪ *Pizza* ▪ GF pizza is available. ▪ *www.extremepizza.com*

Fellini's #9 $D
Charlottesville ▪ **(434) 979-4279**
200 West Market St ▪ *Italian* ▪ Owner Jaclyn reports that though less than half of the menu is naturally GF, the chef is trained on the GF diet and will prepare a short GF menu with advanced notice. She recommends calling the day before dining in, and if desired, requesting the flourless almond tart for dessert. ▪ *www.fellinis9.com*

Firebirds Wood Fired Grill   ✪ $$$LD
Fredericksburg ▪ **(540) 548-5100**
1 Towne Centre Blvd ▪ *American* ▪ GF menu includes a variety of salads and a selection of entrées. Examples include sirloin, filet mignon, ribs, and lobster tail. All locations report that servers are trained to alert the chef when a customer orders from the GF menu. ▪ *www.firebirdsrockymountaingrill.com*

Fireworks Pizza   ★ $LD
Leesburg ▪ **(703) 779-8400**
201 Harrison St SE ▪ *Pizza* ▪ GF pizza is available. Restaurant reports that GF pizza is available with any topping except meatballs, which are not GF. Many of the soups are also GF. Confirm timeliness of this information before dining in. ▪ *www.fireworkspizza.com*

First Watch - The Daytime Café   📖
Fairfax ▪ **(703) 978-3421**
9600 Main St

Fresh and Organic Café and Bakery
                                                   ★ ⊂S
Ashburn ▪ **(703) 723-1221**
44031 Ashburn Village Shopping Plaza #115 ▪ *Bakery & Café* ▪ GF flax seed bread, waffles, and baked goods are available. Manager Kevin notes that GF cheesecake and donuts are sometimes available on weekends or with advanced notice. ▪ *www.fresh-n-organic.com*

Frostings   ★ ⊂S
Glen Allen ▪ **(804) 360-2712**
11331 W Broad St ▪ *Bakery* ▪ Non-dedicated bakery offering GF chocolate and vanilla cupcakes every day. There is usually one more flavor available as the "weekly special." Possible special flavors include carrot cake, hummingbird cake, and coconut. Advanced notice of 48 hours is needed for

special orders of a dozen or more. ▪ *www.frostingsva.com*

Gabriel Archer Tavern, The　$LD
Williamsburg ▪ *(757) 229-0999*
5800 Wessex Hundred ▪ *American* ▪ Restaurant reports that GF diners are welcome. Alert a server upon arrival, and be specific about dietary needs. Limited GF offerings include salads, along with a meat and cheese platter.

Greene Turtle Sports Bar & Grill, The　✪ ¢LD
Fredericksburg ▪ *(540) 785-4832*
1 Towne Centre Blvd
Leesburg ▪ *(703) 777-5511*
603 Potomac Station Dr NE ▪ *American* ▪ GF menu includes spinach, artichoke, and jalapeno dip, buffalo chicken wings, roasted chicken, terrapin steak, apple walnut salad, french fries, crab soup, and more. ▪ *www.greeneturtle.com*

Jackson's　✪ $$LD
Reston ▪ *(703) 437-0800*
11927 Democracy Dr ▪ *American* ▪ The "low-gluten" menu includes the hickory grilled fish of the day, Hong Kong style sea bass, filet mignon, steak frites, a variety of salads, and more. For dessert, there's a warm flourless chocolate waffle. The menu is "low-gluten" rather than GF because items are prepared in the same kitchen as non-GF items.

Java Java　★ ¢S
Charlottesville ▪ *(434) 245-0020*
421 E Main St ▪ *Coffee Shop* ▪ GF muffins and biscotti are available. The restaurant recommends calling early in the day to reserve muffins, as they only make a few per day.

Kasha's Kitchen　★ ¢LD
Falls Church ▪ *(703) 533-8484*
1053 W Broad St ▪ *Vegetarian* ▪ GF bread is available. Manager Elise reports that many soups are also GF, and all sandwiches can be made with GF bread. ▪ *www.localdc.com/kennedys/*

Kona Grill　📖
Glen Allen ▪ *(804) 364-5660*
11221 W Broad St

La Sandia　$$LD
McLean ▪ *(703) 893-2222*
7852L Tysons Corner Ctr ▪ *Mexican* ▪ Manager Min reports that many things on the menu are naturally GF. He notes that the staff is "trained and very knowledgeable" about the GF diet. GF diners may order from the regular menu and alert the server that the dish must be GF. The server will discuss necessary changes with the kitchen and keep diners informed of these modifications. ▪ *www.modernmexican.com*

Lebanese Taverna　✪ ¢LD
McLean ▪ *(703) 847-5244*
1840 International Dr ▪ *Middle Eastern* ▪ GF menu includes lentil soup, lamb shanks, shwarma, chicken and rice, jumbo shrimp, and more. Any dish that normally includes bread can be made GF by substituting rice crackers and vegetables. ▪ *www.lebanesetaverna.com*

Legal Sea Foods　📖
McLean ▪ *(703) 827-8900*
2001 International Dr

Lone Star Steakhouse & Saloon　📖
Chesapeake ▪ *(757) 424-6917*
1570 Crossways Blvd
Colonial Heights ▪ *(804) 520-1009*
2001 Southpark Blvd
Danville ▪ *(434) 791-4428*
255 Lowes Dr
Fredericksburg ▪ *(540) 374-1565*
2051 Plank Rd
Hampton ▪ *(757) 262-0013*
1940 Power Plant Pkwy
Norfolk ▪ *(757) 466-0124*
450 N Military Hwy

Maggiano's Little Italy　★ $$$LD
McLean ▪ *(703) 356-9000*
2001 International Dr ▪ *Italian* ▪ GF pasta is available. Call individual locations to inquire about additional GF options. ▪ *www.maggianos.com*

Magnolia at the Mill   ★ $LD
Purcellville ▪ (540) 338-9800
198 N 21st St ▪ American Regional ▪ GF
pizza is available. Restaurant reports that
many items on the menu can also be
modified to be GF. Alert a server. Servers
are well-trained on the GF diet and know
which dishes can be prepared GF. ▪ www.
magnoliasmill.com

Mamma Lucia   ★ $$LD
Reston ▪ (703) 689-4894
1428 Northpoint Village Ctr ▪ Italian ▪ GF
pizza and pasta are available. The Elkridge,
Bethesda, and Shady Grove Rd locations
also offer GF beer. ▪ www.mammaluciares-
taurants.com

Manhattan Pizza   ★ $LD
Leesburg ▪ (703) 669-4020
647 Potomac Station Dr NE ▪ Pizza ▪ GF
pizza is available. At the time of publica-
tion, this was the only location with GF
pizza, but Ashburn location was expecting
to implement it in the near future. ▪ www.
manhattanpizza.com

Melting Pot, The   📖
Charlottesville ▪ (434) 244-3463
501 E Water St
Fredericksburg ▪ (540) 785-9690
1618 Carl D Silver Pkwy
Newport News ▪ (757) 369-9500
12233 Jefferson Ave
Reston ▪ (703) 264-0900
11400 Commerce Park Dr

Mike's American $$LD
Springfield ▪ (703) 644-7100
6210 Backlick Rd ▪ American ▪ The "low-
gluten" menu includes a variety of salads,
prime rib, filet mignon, and the fresh fish
of the day. For dessert, there is a warm
flourless chocolate waffle. The menu is
"low-gluten" instead of GF because items
are prepared in the same kitchen as non-
GF items. ▪ www.greatamericanrestaurants.
com

**Natalia's Elegant Creations Pastry
Shop and Café**   ✪★ ¢S

Falls Church ▪ (703) 241-8040
230 W Broad St ▪ Bakery & Café ▪
Non-dedicated bakery offering several GF
desserts and cookies. GF pies, cakes, and
muffins are available. For lunch, they offer
different GF options every day, including
soups. GF cakes are listed online and can
be ordered in advance. ▪ www.nataliasele-
gantcreations.com

Not Your Average Joe's   ✪ $$LD
Leesburg ▪ (571) 333-5637
19307 Promenade Dr ▪ American ▪ GF
menu includes rosemary-skewered fresh
scallops, fresh salmon filet, cobb salad,
NY strip, grilled chicken breast, and but-
terscotch pudding for dessert. ▪ www.
notyouraveragejoes.com

Original Pancake House, The   ★ ¢BL
Falls Church ▪ (703) 891-0148
370 W Broad St ▪ Breakfast ▪ GF pan-
cakes are available. Select locations may
serve other GF items. Call a specific loca-
tion to inquire. ▪ www.originalpancake-
house.com

Outback Steakhouse   📖
Bristol ▪ (276) 466-0100
3168 Linden Dr
Charlottesville ▪ (434) 975-4329
355 Albemarle Sq
Chesapeake ▪ (757) 465-1047
4312 Portsmouth Blvd
Christiansburg ▪ (540) 382-9596
295 Peppers Ferry Rd NE
Clifton ▪ (703) 818-0804
5702 Union Mill Rd
Colonial Heights ▪ (804) 520-4329
165 Southpark Cir
Danville ▪ (434) 792-0781
111 Enterprise Dr
Fairfax ▪ (703) 352-5000
10060 Fairfax Blvd
Fairfax ▪ (703) 978-6283
9579 Braddock Rd
Fredericksburg ▪ (540) 786-2343
2941 Plank Rd
Hampton ▪ (757) 838-3570
1700 W Mercury Blvd

Harrisonburg ▪ *(540) 438-0190*
261 University Blvd
Herndon ▪ *(703) 318-0999*
150 Elden St
Lynchburg ▪ *(434) 847-3646*
3121 Albert Lankford Dr
Mechanicsville ▪ *(804) 746-5277*
7420 Bell Creek Rd
Midlothian ▪ *(804) 739-9880*
6821 Chital Dr
Newport News ▪ *(757) 249-3637*
12258 Jefferson Ave
Norfolk ▪ *(757) 622-9101*
333 Waterside Dr
Roanoke ▪ *(540) 776-3238*
4380 Franklin Rd SW
Springfield ▪ *(703) 912-7531*
6651 Backlick Rd
Stafford ▪ *(540) 288-2614*
308 Worth Ave
Sterling ▪ *(703) 406-3377*
46300 Potomac Run Plz
Vienna ▪ *(703) 242-0460*
315 Maple Ave E
Warrenton ▪ *(540) 349-0457*
6419 Lee Hwy
Waynesboro ▪ *(540) 941-0087*
28 Windigrove Dr
Williamsburg ▪ *(757) 229-8648*
3026 Richmond Rd
Winchester ▪ *(540) 868-4156*
124 Kernstown Commons Blvd
Woodbridge ▪ *(703) 490-5336*
14580 Potomac Mills Rd

P.F. Chang's China Bistro   📖
Fairfax ▪ *(703) 266-2414*
4250 Fairfax Corner Ave
Mc Lean ▪ *(703) 734-8996*
1716M International Drive

Pei Wei Asian Diner   📖
Dulles ▪ *(703) 421-5590*
22000 Dulles Retail Plz Ste 190
Fairfax ▪ *(703) 803-4466*
4461 Market Commons Dr
Gainesville ▪ *(703) 753-3880*
5035 Wellington Rd
Herndon ▪ *(703) 251-0090*

2338 Woodland Crossing Dr Ste A
Leesburg ▪ *(703) 443-2411*
528A E Market St

Pizza Fusion   ★ $$LD
Glen Allen ▪ *(804) 381-4027*
11331 W Broad St ▪ *Pizza* ▪ GF pizza and brownies are available. ▪ *www.pizzafusion.com*

Pizza NY Margherita   ★ $LD
Gainesville ▪ *(703) 753-0744*
5115 Wellington Rd ▪ *Pizza* ▪ GF pizza crust is available. ▪ *www.pizzanymargherita.com*

Renatos $$$LD
Fredericksburg ▪ *(540) 371-8228*
422 William St ▪ *Italian* ▪ Manager Teresa reports that GF diners are frequent. Everything is made to order, which lowers the risk of cross-contamination. Alert a server upon arrival. If given advanced notice, Theresa can maybe GF pasta. ▪ *www.ristoranterenato.com*

Revolutionary Soup   ¢LD
Charlottesville ▪ *(434) 296-7687*
108 2nd St SW ▪ *Deli* ▪ Manager Alfonso reports that GF soups such as tomato basil and lamb curry are always available. Ask a server for the current GF soup options. ▪ *www.revolutionarysoup.com*

Silverado $$LD
Annandale ▪ *(703) 354-4560*
7052 Columbia Pike ▪ *American* ▪ The "low-gluten" menu includes a variety of salads, as well as smoked BBQ pulled pork, baby back ribs, hickory smoked black angus rib eye, and more. For dessert, there is a warm flourless chocolate waffle. The menu is "low-gluten" instead of GF because items are prepared in the same kitchen as non-GF items. ▪ *www.greatamericanrestaurants.com*

Southern Inn   ★ $$LD
Lexington ▪ *(540) 463-3612*
37 S Main St ▪ *American* ▪ Bookkeeper Mandy reports that they serve GF diners "pretty regularly," and that all servers are

trained to accommodate "dietary modifications." Menu items that can be prepared GF include spinach and artichoke dip, rigatoni bolognaise, and blackened chicken penne. GF pasta is not listed on the menu, but it is available. ▪ *www.southerninn.com*

SweetWater Tavern $$LD
Centreville ▪ *(703) 449-1100*
14250 Sweetwater Ln
Falls Church ▪ *(703) 645-8100*
3066 Gate House Plz
Sterling ▪ *(571) 434-6500*
45980 Waterview Plz ▪ *American* ▪ The "low-gluten" menu includes black angus prime rib (dinner only), wood-grilled filet mignon, hickory grilled pork chops, roasted chicken and more. For dessert, there is a warm flourless chocolate waffle. The menu is "low-gluten" instead of GF because items are prepared in the same kitchen as non-GF items. ▪ *www.greatamericanrestaurants. com*

Teddy's Pizza & Subs ★ $LD
Middleburg ▪ *(540) 687-8880*
9 East Federal St ▪ *Pizza* ▪ GF pizza is available.

Tony's NY Pizza ★ $$LD
Fairfax ▪ *(703) 502-0808*
13087 Fair Lakes Shopping Ctr ▪ *Pizza* ▪ GF pizza and pasta are available. Restaurant notes that GF diners are "common." GF spaghetti and cheese ravioli are available. Alert the counter attendant, who will discuss GF options in detail. ▪ *www. tonysnypizza.com*

Tortilla Factory Restaurant, The ✪ ¢LD
Herndon ▪ *(703) 471-1156*
648 Elden St ▪ *Mexican* ▪ GF menu includes carne asada, tacos de jefe, soups, salads, nachos, and more. Restaurant sells individual meals and bulk items to go. ▪ *www.thetortillafactory.com*

Trellis, The $$$LD
Williamsburg ▪ *(757) 229-8610*
403 Duke of Gloucester St ▪ *American* ▪ Restaurant reports that a number of menu items are naturally GF or can be modified to be GF, including steak and meat dishes. Alert a server upon arrival. ▪ *www.thetrellis.com*

Triple Oak Bakery 100% $$$$S
Sperryville ▪ *(540) 987-9122*
11692 Lee Hwy ▪ *Bakery* ▪ Dedicated GF bakery offering cakes, cupcakes, lemon curd tarts, cream puffs, apple turnovers, and more. Pumpkin, apple, and sweet potato pies are available. Cakes are sold by the slice or whole. Owner Brooke recommends calling beforehand because she sometimes steps out to deliver orders. ▪ *www.tripleoakbakery.com*

Uno Chicago Grill 📖
Chester ▪ *(804) 751-0400*
12211 Jefferson Davis Hwy
Falls Church ▪ *(703) 645-9590*
3058 Gate House Plz
Gainesville ▪ *(703) 754-1155*
7390 Atlas Walk Way
Kingstowne ▪ *(703) 822-0957*
5935 Kingstowne Towne Ctr
Manassas ▪ *(703) 365-0056*
10701 Bulloch Dr
Midlothian ▪ *(804) 763-4900*
13933 Hull Street Rd
Norfolk ▪ *(757) 466-0923*
5900 E Virginia Beach Blvd
Prince George ▪ *(804) 490-0060*
2070 Waterside Rd
Reston ▪ *(703) 742-8667*
11948 Market St
Sandston ▪ *(804) 328-0050*
5990 Audubon Dr
Tabb ▪ *(757) 886-9050*
5007 Victory Blvd
Williamsburg ▪ *(757) 220-5454*
205 Bypass Rd
Woodbridge ▪ *(703) 490-4883*
2680 Prince William Pkwy

Vespucci ★ $$$LD
Fairfax ▪ *(703) 272-8113*
10579 Fairfax Blvd ▪ *Italian* ▪ GF pasta is available. Chef Raymond reports that they are "absolutely" able to serve GF custom-

ers. He adds that all servers are "very well educated" about the GF diet, and that Chef Anna is an expert on it. ▪ *www.vespuccires-taurant.com*

Wildfire ✪★ $$$**LD**
McLean ▪ *(703) 442-9110*
1714 International Drive ▪ *Steakhouse* ▪ Extensive GF menu includes chicken and portobello mushroom skewers, sandwiches on GF buns, scallops, Long Island duck, filet mignon, and more. Flourless chocolate cake and GF beer is also available. ▪ *www.wildfirerestaurant.com*

Z Pizza ★ $**LD**
Falls Church ▪ *(703) 536-6969*
1051 W Broad St
Haymarket ▪ *(703) 753-7492*
5471 Merchants View Sq
Herndon ▪ *(703) 481-6580*
2320 Woodland Crossing Dr Ste C
Lorton ▪ *(703) 372-1538*
9451 Lorton Market St
Manassas ▪ *(703) 580-8100*
12817 Galveston Ct
Springfield ▪ *(703) 313-8181*
6699B Frontier Dr
Williamsburg ▪ *(757) 645-3303*
4902 Courthouse St ▪ *Pizza* ▪ GF pizza is available. ▪ *www.zpizza.com*

WASHINGTON

SEATTLE

94 Stewart $$$$**LD**
Seattle ▪ *(206) 441-5505*
94 Stewart St ▪ *Modern American* ▪ Manager Ben reports that most of the menu is naturally GF or can be modified to be GF. He notes that accommodating GF diners is "very doable," and that the kitchen frequently accommodates dietary requests. ▪ *www.94stewart.com*

Andaluca Restaurant ✪ $$$**BLD**
Seattle ▪ *(206) 382-6999*
407 Olive Way ▪ *Spanish Tapas* ▪ Extensive GF menu includes breakfast, lunch, and dinner selections. Examples are spinach frittata, a ratatouille omelet, crab tower salad, and seafood risotto. For dessert, they offer warm liquid chocolate cake and truffles. ▪ *www.andaluca.com*

Anthony's Bell Street Diner ✪ $$**LD**
Seattle ▪ *(206) 448-6688*
2201 Alaskan Way ▪ *Modern American* ▪ GF menu includes a seafood chop salad, sirloin steak, blackened rock fish, citrus salmon salad, garlic prawns, mussels, and edamame. Manager Michelle recommends alerting the server even if ordering from the GF menu.

Bambuza ✪★ ¢**LD**
Seattle ▪ *(206) 219-5555*
820 Pike St ▪ *Vietnamese* ▪ GF items marked on the menu include veggie salad rolls, cabbage chicken salad, pho, rice noodle stir fry, rice with broccoli. GF rice noodles are available. ▪ *www.bambuza.com*

Blue C Sushi ✪★ ¢**LD**
Seattle ▪ *(206) 467-4022*
1510 7th Ave
Seattle ▪ *(206) 633-3411*
3411 Fremont Ave N
Seattle ▪ *(206) 525-4601*
4601 26th Ave NE ▪ *Sushi* ▪ GF menu lists items on the sushi bar that are naturally GF, like the avocado roll and the snow crab California roll. GF tamari sauce is available. ▪ *www.bluecsushi.com*

Blue Dog Kitchen ★ ¢**BL**
Seattle ▪ *(206) 632-5132*
5247 University Way NE ▪ *Café* ▪ GF buttermilk, banana chocolate chip, and blueberry pancakes are available for breakfast only. These pancakes are labeled WF on the menu, but the restaurant confirms that they are GF. ▪ *www.bluedogkitchen.com*

Buca di Beppo   📖
Seattle ▪ *(206) 244-2288*
701 9th Ave N

Buckley's on Queen Anne   ★ *$$*LD
Seattle ▪ *(206) 691-0232*
232 1st Ave W ▪ *American* ▪ GF beer is
available. ▪ *www.buckleysseattle.com*

Café Flora   ✪★ *$$*BLD
Seattle ▪ *(206) 325-9100*
2901 E Madison St ▪ *World Cuisine, Veg-etarian* ▪ GF items marked on the menu
include Moroccan crepes, Oaxaca tacos,
and artichoke spinach pizza. Manager Al-berto reports that GF diners are welcome,
and he recommends alerting a server upon
arrival. GF pizza and desserts are available.
▪ *www.cafeflora.com*

Capital Grille, The   📖
Seattle ▪ *(206) 382-0900*
1301 4th Ave

Chaco Canyon Organic Café   ★ *$*BLD
Seattle ▪ *(206) 522-6966*
4757 12th Ave NE ▪ *Organic* ▪ GF bread,
beer, and soy sauce are available, as are
GF baked goods. Examples of GF entrées
include cilantro pesto pizza, the thai peanut
bowl, and the nacho plate. For dessert, they
offer a GF chocolate fudge brownie and a
raspberry tart, among other things. ▪ *www.chacocanyoncafe.com*

Chandler's Crab House   *$$$$*LD
Seattle ▪ *(206) 223-2722*
901 Fairview Ave N ▪ *Seafood* ▪ Manager
Ira reports that diners with special diets
come in "very frequently." He notes that
almost everything on the menu can be
modified to be GF. Confirm timeliness of
this information before dining in. Reserva-tions noting GF are recommended. ▪ *www.schwartzbros.com*

Cinnamon Works   ★ ¢S
Seattle ▪ *(206) 583-0085*
1536 Pike Pl ▪ *Bakery* ▪ Non-dedicated
bakery offering a limited variety of GF
items including banana bread, apple sauce

bread, cookies, scones, muffins, and gra-nola. Bakery advises that they make items
in the morning only, so sometimes they sell
out.

Daniel's Broiler   *$$$$*LD
Seattle ▪ *(206) 621-8262*
809 Fairview Pl N ▪ *Steakhouse* ▪ Manag-er Eric reports that steaks are naturally GF,
as are most menu items. Confirm timeli-ness of this information before dining in.
The kitchen takes dietary requests "very
seriously." Servers are trained to indicate
GF items. Eric notes that dishes can be
modified to be GF, as all food is made fresh
to order. Reservations noting GF are highly
recommended. ▪ *www.schwartzbros.com*

Flying Apron   100% ¢BL
Seattle ▪ *(206) 442-1115*
3510 Fremont Ave N ▪ *Bakery* ▪ Dedicated
GF bakery offering cookies, pies, cakes, and
more. GF calzones, pot pies, and bread are
also available. The lunch menu includes
soups, salads, pizzas, flat breads, and more.
▪ *www.flyingapron.net*

Flying Fish   *$$$*LD
Seattle ▪ *(206) 728-8595*
2234 1st Ave ▪ *Seafood* ▪ Manager Amy
reports that they can accommodate GF
diners "really easily," and they do it "all the
time." She recommends making a reserva-tion noting GF, but adds that this is not
necessary. All servers are very knowledge-able about the GF diet. ▪ *www.flyingfishse-attle.com*

Garlic Jim's   ★ *$$*LD
Seattle ▪ *(206) 524-5467*
2400 NE 65th St
Seattle ▪ *(206) 937-5467*
4520 California Ave SW ▪ *Pizza* ▪ GF pizza
is available in the large size only. GF menu
also includes salads and hot wings. All
locations report that GF cheesecake is also
available. ▪ *www.garlicjims.com*

Hotwire Online Coffeehouse   ★ ¢S
Seattle ▪ *(206) 935-1510*
4410 California Ave SW ▪ *Coffee Shop* ▪

GF baked goods are available on Wednesdays and Thursdays. The coffee shop reports that GF selections vary each week, but standard fare includes cookies, muffins, cupcakes, and bars. ▪ *www.hotwirecoffee.com*

Kalia Indian Cuisine $LD
Seattle ▪ (206) 782-7890
8518 Greenwood Ave N ▪ Indian ▪ Owner Kalia reports that GF diners are welcome and notes that everything on the menu is GF. Alert the server upon arrival. ▪ *www.kaliacuisine.com*

Lombardi's   ✪★ $LD
Seattle ▪ (206) 783-0055
2200 NW Market St ▪ Italian ▪ GF menu offers small plates and salads, as well as meat and seafood entrées. Examples include caprese toscano, seafood caesar salad, chicken parmigiano, and a Tuscan rack of lamb. For dessert, they offer panna cotta and chocolate mousse. ▪ *www.lombardisitalian.com*

Macrina Bakery   ★ ¢LD
Seattle ▪ (206) 623-0919
1943 1st Ave S
Seattle ▪ (206) 283-5900
615 W Mcgraw St ▪ Bakery & Café ▪ Non-dedicated GF bakery offering just one GF treat: a flourless chocolate ganache cupcake. Manager Luke reports that they may develop more GF products soon. ▪ *www.macrinabakery.com*

Melting Pot, The   📖
Seattle ▪ (206) 378-1208
14 Mercer St

Old Spaghetti Factory, The   📖
Seattle ▪ (206) 441-7724
2801 Elliott Ave

Outback Steakhouse   📖
Seattle ▪ (206) 367-7780
13231 Aurora Ave N
Seattle ▪ (206) 262-0326
701 Westlake Ave N

P.F. Chang's China Bistro   📖
Seattle ▪ (206) 393-0070
400 Pine St Ste 136

Pizza Pi   ★ $D
Seattle ▪ (206) 343-1415
5500 University Way NE ▪ Vegan Pizza ▪ GF pizza is available in the 9-inch size. All toppings except for the "fake meat" are GF. For dessert, they offer an ice cream sundae or the cinnamon stix made with GF pizza dough. ▪ *www.pizza-pi.net*

Portage Bay Café   ★ $BL
Seattle ▪ (206) 547-8230
4130 Roosevelt Way NE ▪ American ▪ GF pancakes are available for breakfast only. ▪ *www.portagebaycafe.com*

Romio's Pizza & Pasta   ✪★ $$LD
Seattle ▪ (206) 782-9005
8523 Greenwood Ave N ▪ Pizza ▪ Extensive GF menu includes GF paninis, soups, and salads. GF pizza and pasta are available. ▪ *www.romiospizza.com*

Sunlight Café   ★ $BLD
Seattle ▪ (206) 522-9060
6403 Roosevelt Way NE ▪ Vegetarian ▪ Server Melissa reports that "most of the menu" is GF, and nearly all items can be made GF. Examples are enchiladas, falafel with a corn tortilla, and nachos. She notes that they have GF desserts "occasionally." GF tamari sauce is available. ▪ *www.sunlightcafe.blogspot.com*

Ten Mercer   ✪ $$D
Seattle ▪ (206) 691-3723
10 Mercer St ▪ Modern American ▪ GF menu includes appetizers and salads, as well as seafood and meat entrées. GF dessert options include vanilla bean custard and the flourless chocolate torte. Owner Brian suggests noting GF when making a reservation. ▪ *www.tenmercer.com*

Txori   ¢LD
Seattle ▪ (206) 204-9771
2207 2nd Ave ▪ Tapas ▪ Manager Joe reports that most of the menu is GF. Alert

the server, who will ensure that the dish is prepared properly. Joe reports all servers are knowledgeable about GF preparation. ▪ *www.txoribar.com*

Wheatless in Seattle   100% ¢B
Seattle ▪ *(206) 782-5735*
10003 Greenwood Ave N ▪ *Bakery & Café* ▪ Bakery and café offering GF sweets and savories. GF items include quiche, paninis, and frittatas, as well as cheesecake, peanut butter cookies, strudel, and cupcakes. Not all items are available every day. ▪ *www. wheatlessinseattle.com*

Wild Ginger Thai Restaurant $$LD
Seattle ▪ *(206) 623-4450*
1401 3rd Ave ▪ *Thai* ▪ Manager Brad reports that "a variety" of menu items are naturally GF. He notes that most seafood, meat, and vegetable dishes can be modified to be GF. Confirm timeliness of this information before dining in. Brad adds that they serve GF diners "every day," and that GF tamari sauce is available. ▪ *www. wildginger.net*

Zao Noodle Bar   ★ ¢LD
Seattle ▪ *(206) 529-8278*
2630 NE University Village St ▪ *Asian Noodles* ▪ Manager Robert reports that they have a computer system that identifies GF items. Rice noodles are available. ▪ *www.zaonoodle.com*

'Zaw Artisan Bake at Home Pizza ★ $D
Seattle ▪ *(206) 325-5528*
1424 E Pine St
Seattle ▪ *(206) 787-1198*
1635 Queen Anne Ave N
Seattle ▪ *(206) 623-0299*
434 Yale Ave N
Seattle ▪ *(206) 297-1334*
5458 Leary Ave NW ▪ *Pizza* ▪ GF pizza is available in the large size. Co-founder Greg cautions that they prepare GF crusts each day before opening, and they often sell out. Place orders as soon as possible after opening. ▪ *www.zaw.com*

WASHINGTON
ALL OTHER CITIES

Avellino   ★ ¢S
Bellingham ▪ *(360) 715-1005*
1329 Railroad Ave ▪ *Coffee Shop* ▪ GF baked goods like muffins, scones, and cookies are available. Barista Tracy reports that the GF options "change daily" and that they usually run out before close.

Avenue Bread & Deli   ★ ¢BL
Bellingham ▪ *(360) 715-3354*
1135 11Th St
Bellingham ▪ *(360) 715-3354*
1313 Railroad Ave
Bellingham ▪ *(360) 715-3354*
2301 James St ▪ *Bakery & Café* ▪ GF bread, called "Almost Bread," is available for sandwiches, and GF croutons, called "Almost Croutons," are available for salads. GF muffins, cookies, and brownies are also available. General Manager Danny recommends that GF customers "explain the level of sensitivity," as their bakeries handle large amounts of wheat. ▪ *www.avenuebread.com*

Bellagios Pizza   ✪★ $$LD
East Vancouver ▪ *(360) 567-1007*
322 SE 192nd Ave ▪ *Pizza* ▪ GF menu includes a variety of pizzas, salads, and appetizers. There is a GF "build your own pizza" option, and GF pizza dough is available for "take-&-bake." GF pizza is available in the 10-inch size only. ▪ *www.bellagiospizza.com*

Billy's Bar & Grill $$BD
Aberdeen ▪ *(360) 533-7144*
322 East Heron And G St ▪ *American* ▪ Manager Gary reports that GF diners "usually" have a plain grilled chicken breast or steak with a salad. He notes that "some" servers are aware of the GF diet, but all of the servers will communicate with the kitchen when alerted by a GF diner.

Bin on the Lake $$$D
Kirkland ▪ *(425) 803-5595*

1270 Carillon Pt ▪ American ▪ Restaurant notes that servers are trained on the GF diet, and they know which menu items are or can be modified to be GF. GF items on the menu include salads, seafood dishes, and steak. Confirm timeliness of this information before dining in. Reservations noting GF are recommended. ▪ *www.thewoodmark.com*

Bison Creek Pizza & Pub ★ ¢LD
Burien ▪ *(206) 244-8825*
630 SW 153rd St ▪ *Pizza* ▪ GF pizza is available in the 8-inch, 12-inch, and 14-inch sizes. GF crust can be prepared with any toppings except for the chicken, which is not GF. Confirm timeliness of this information before dining in. GF croutons are available for salads. GF beer is also available. ▪ *www.bisoncreekpizza.com*

Black Pearl ★ $LD
Bellingham ▪ *(360) 756-5003*
1255 Barkley Blvd ▪ *Vietnamese* ▪ GF soy sauce is available. Owner Layla reports that there is "tons of gluten-free stuff" on the menu, and that they serve GF diners "all the time." She recommends alerting a server, as all servers know what menu items are or can be modified to be GF. She cites the soups, vermicelli bowls, curries, and peanut dressing as a few items that are GF. Confirm timeliness of this information before dining in.

Blackbird Bakery ★ ¢S
Bainbridge Island ▪ *(206) 780-1322*
210 Winslow Way E ▪ *Bakery* ▪ Non-dedicated bakery offering GF rolls and a truffle torte, along with an assortment of cakes and desserts. Breads and pie shells are available by special order only. Cakes must be ordered 48 hours in advance.

Blue C Sushi ✪★ ¢LD
Bellevue ▪ *(425) 454-8288*
503 Bellevue Sq
Lynnwood ▪ *(425) 329-3596*
3000 184th St SW
Tukwila ▪ *(206) 277-8744*

468 Southcenter Mall ▪ *Sushi* ▪ GF menu lists items on the sushi bar that are naturally GF, like the avocado roll and the snow crab California roll. GF tamari sauce is available. ▪ *www.bluecsushi.com*

Bonefish Grill 📖
Bothell ▪ *(425) 485-0305*
22616 Bothell Everett Hwy
Richland ▪ *(509) 628-9296*
133 Gage Blvd

Breadline Café $BLD
Omak ▪ *(509) 826-5836*
102 South Ash Ave. ▪ *Café* ▪ Manager Janet reports that the restaurant has served GF diners before. She notes that while there are not many options for GF diners, there is an extensive list of salads, most of which are or can be modified to be GF. Confirm timeliness of this information before dining in. Janet also notes that it is possible to cook meat separately in order to make it GF. Alert a server, who will note the gluten allergy on the ticket that goes to the kitchen. ▪ *www.breadlinecafe.com*

Bridges Restaurant $$LD
Aberdeen ▪ *(360) 532-6563*
112 N G St ▪ *Steakhouse* ▪ Manager Jennifer reports that they serve GF diners "often." She recommends making reservations noting GF, since some of the "young servers" may not be fully educated on the GF diet. She further notes that all salmon, halibut, and steak dishes can be prepared GF upon request.

Buca di Beppo 📖
Lynnwood ▪ *(425) 744-7272*
4301 Alderwood Mall Blvd

Cafe at the La Conner Fruit & Produce Market, The ★ ¢BLD
La Conner ▪ *(360) 466-3018*
116 1st St ▪ *Italian* ▪ GF bread and cookies are available. Restaurant reports that they have GF spaghetti on Wednesday nights. Call at least a half day ahead for GF preparation.

Canyons Restaurant   ✪ $$LD
Bothell ▪ *(425) 485-3288*
22010 17th Ave SE
Monroe ▪ *(360) 805-5453*
14919 N Kelsey St
Mountlake Terrace ▪ *(425) 744-1525*
6003 244th St SW
Redmond ▪ *(425) 556-1390*
15740 Redmond Way ▪ *American* ▪ GF
menu includes Cajun blackened tuna, BBQ
chicken, and the southwest chicken fiesta
salad. Alert a server, who will notify the
kitchen. Managers are happy to accommo-
date special GF requests, even if they are
not on the GF menu. ▪ *www.canyonsrestau-
rant.com*

Carino's Italian   📖
Burlington ▪ *(360) 757-4535*
150 Cascade Mall Dr

Charlie's Safari   ★ $LD
Lacey ▪ *(360) 292-1600*
5400 Martin Way E ▪ *American* ▪ Man-
ager Melissa reports that they have recently
started to offer GF snack items such as
muffins and brownies. The only other GF
options are hot dogs and hamburgers with-
out buns, but Melissa notes that the chef
will be happy to accommodate GF requests
if at all possible. ▪ *www.charliessafari.com*

Coho Café $LD
Issaquah ▪ *(425) 391-4040*
6130 E Lake Sammamish Pkwy SE ▪ *Amer-
ican Regional* ▪ The restaurant reports that
several items are naturally GF. They also
note that the kitchen references a list of GF
items, and a special note is attached to GF
orders to prevent cross-contamination. ▪
www.cohocafe.com

Colophon Café   ★ ¢BLD
Bellingham ▪ *(360) 647-0092*
1208 11th St ▪ *American* ▪ At least two GF
soups are available every day, along with at
least one GF quiche with a potato crust. GF
cookies are available in at least one unique
flavor every day, and there is a GF version
of the peanut butter pie. They sponsor the

Bellingham Gluten Intolerant Group. ▪
www.colophoncafe.com

Country Cousin $BLD
Centralia ▪ *(360) 736-2200*
1054 Harrison Ave ▪ *American Regional* ▪
Sous-Chef Greg reports that they are happy
to modify any dish that a GF diner "has
a hankering for." Alert a server, who will
approach Greg or another chef for sugges-
tions about how to adapt menu items to be
GF.

Earls $LD
Bellevue ▪ *(425) 452-3275*
700 Bellevue Way NE ▪ *Global* ▪ Chef
Dell reports that all floor leaders are edu-
cated on the "gluten-aware" menu items,
which include chicken tacos, a variety of
steaks, and the cedar plank salmon, among
other things. Confirm timeliness of this
information before dining in. He recom-
mends calling ahead so that he can better
prepare, but he notes that prior notice is
not necessary. ▪ *www.earls.ca*

Extreme Pizza   ★ $$LD
Issaquah ▪ *(425) 837-1700*
660 Front Street North @ Gilman ▪ *Pizza*
▪ GF pizza is available. ▪ *www.extremepiz-
za.com*

Fairhaven Pizza   ★ $$LD
Bellingham ▪ *(360) 756-7561*
1217 Harris Ave ▪ *Pizza* ▪ GF pizza is avail-
able. ▪ *www.fairhavenpizza.com*

Flat Iron Grill $$$LD
Issaquah ▪ *(425) 657-0373*
317 NW Gilman Blvd Ste 28 ▪ *Modern
American* ▪ Owner Sean reports that they
serve GF diners "a lot." He notes that they
developed the menu with the GF diet in
mind, so many items are naturally GF.
Alert a server upon arrival. All servers are
trained on the GF diet and will be able
to assist in choosing a GF meal. ▪ *www.
theflatirongrill.com*

Foley's Pizza   ✪★ $LD
Bremerton ▪ *(360) 373-7222*

724 Lebo Blvd ▪ Pizza ▪ GF menu includes a variety of pizzas, including garlic chicken pizza and Hawaiian pizza. Owner Mona notes that GF pasta, cakes, and brownies are available by special order only. ▪ *www.foleyspizza.net*

Frankie's Pizza & Pasta   ★ $LD
Redmond ▪ (425) 883-8407
16630 Redmond Way ▪ Pizza ▪ GF pizza is available. "Low-Carb/Gluten-Free" menu includes a chicken italian sausage bake, chicken parmesan, shrimp sauté with gorgonzola cream sauce, chicken breasts with roasted garlic and artichoke sauce, along with other items. Not all items on this menu are entirely GF, so check with the server before ordering.

Friesenburgers   ✪★ ¢BLD
Tacoma ▪ (253) 203-6753
308 E 26th St ▪ American ▪ GF menu includes burgers, cheeseburgers, bison burgers, and salmon burgers. GF hamburger and hotdog buns are available. Sometimes, they also have GF desserts like carrot cake and brownies. Co-owner Michael reports that they have a dedicated fryer for GF french fries, and the entire staff is educated on the GF diet. ▪ *www.friesenburgers.com*

Garlic Jim's   ★ $$LD
Bellevue ▪ (425) 455-5467
1105 Bellevue Way NE
Bellevue ▪ (425) 643-8586
3080 148th Ave SE
Bothell ▪ (425) 483-5555
18404 120th Ave NE
Edmonds ▪ (425) 771-5467
9796 Edmonds Way
Federal Way ▪ (253) 838-7744
34024 Hoyt Rd SW
Issaquah ▪ (425) 427-5467
4520 Klahanie Dr SE
Kent ▪ (253) 639-0880
13121 SE Kent Kangley Rd
Kirkland ▪ (425) 822-8881
8431 122nd Ave NE
Lacey ▪ (360) 456-8100
5730 Ruddell Rd SE

Maple Valley ▪ (425) 433-2525
23330 Maple Valley Black Diamond Rd SE
Marysville ▪ (360) 651-5467
1246 State Ave
Mill Creek ▪ (425) 379-8900
3922 148th St SE
Monroe ▪ (360) 794-1100
14957 N Kelsey St
Mukilteo ▪ (425) 493-8646
10924 Mukilteo Spdwy
Redmond ▪ (425) 861-9000
11523 Avondale Rd NE
Renton ▪ (425) 228-5467
4004 NE 4th St
Snoqualmie ▪ (425) 888-2488
7328 Better Way SE
Tacoma ▪ (253) 286-5467
3602 6th Ave
Vancouver ▪ (360) 573-8400
13317 NE 12Th Ave ▪ Pizza ▪ GF pizza is available at all locations, and some locations have GF cheesecake for dessert. Certain locations are open for dinner only, so call ahead to confirm that they are open. ▪ *www.garlicjims.com*

Giggles Gluten-Free Custom Bakery
100% ¢S
Pasco ▪ (509) 521-3572
350 Tracie Rd ▪ Bakery ▪ Dedicated GF bakery offering bread, hamburger buns, muffins, cookies, pies, cakes, brownies, and more. In addition to fresh baked goods, they have GF frozen foods available to order. ▪ *www.glutenfreebakery.biz*

Greener Bean, The   ★ ¢S
Fircrest ▪ (253) 564-7336
1039 Regents Blvd ▪ Coffee & Café ▪ GF muffins are available. ▪ *www.greenerbeancoffee.com*

Gustav's Pub & Grill   ✪ $LD
Vancouver ▪ (360) 883-0222
1705 SE 164th Ave ▪ German ▪ GF menu includes mushroom schnitzel, salmon filet, rotisserie turkey, and sausage trio. Restaurant reports that GF diners come in "all the time." ▪ *www.gustavs.net*

Haley's Corner Bakery   100% ¢S
Kent ▪ (253) 852-4486
10216 SE 256th St ▪ *Bakery* ▪ Dedicated GF bakery offering a large menu with varieties of pizzas, breads, and baked goods. Baked goods include cakes, cheesecakes, coffee cakes, pies, cookies, muffins, scones, and more. ▪ *www.haleyscorner.com*

i.talia pizzeria   ¢LD
Olympia ▪ (360) 754-3393
2505 4th Ave W ▪ *Pizza* ▪ Manager Brian reports that the restaurant does serve GF diners, and he recommends alerting a server upon arrival or asking for him. While he notes that they do not serve GF pizza or pasta, he reports that most salads can be made GF. He also keeps corn tortillas in the back of the restaurant, and he can use them to "fake" a pizza. Confirm timeliness of this information before dining in.

Indulge Cupcakes   ★ ¢S
Sumner ▪ (253) 426-5260
1913 Main St ▪ *Bakery* ▪ GF cupcakes are available on Wednesdays or by special order. Available flavors include Granny's chocolate cupcakes and carrot cake cupcakes. ▪ *www.indulgecupcakes.com*

Jekyl and Hyde Deli & Ale House ★ ¢BL
Bellingham ▪ (360) 715-9100
709 W Orchard Dr ▪ *Deli* ▪ GF pizza is available, and GF bread is available for sandwiches. Any toppings can be put on the GF pizza crust, and sandwiches can be made to order with any available fillings. For dessert, there is GF bread pudding and cookies. GF beer is also available. ▪ *www.jhdeli.com*

LaFiamma Wood Fire Pizza   ★ $$LD
Bellingham ▪ (360) 647-0060
200 E Chestnut St ▪ *Pizza* ▪ GF pizza is available. Manager Suzanne notes that some salads and soups are GF. ▪ *www.lafiamma.com*

Lombardi's   ✪★ $LD
Everett ▪ (425) 252-1886
1620 W Marine View Dr

Issaquah ▪ (425) 391-9097
695 NW Gilman Blvd ▪ *Italian* ▪ GF menu offers small plates and salads, as well as meat and seafood entrées. Examples include caprese toscano, seafood caesar salad, chicken parmigiano, and a Tuscan rack of lamb. For dessert, they offer panna cotta and chocolate mousse. ▪ *www.lombardisitalian.com*

Maggiano's Little Italy   ★ $$$LD
Bellevue ▪ (425) 519-6476
10455 NE 8th St ▪ *Italian* ▪ GF pasta is available. Call individual locations to inquire about additional GF options. ▪ *www.maggianos.com*

McGrath's Fish House   ✪ $LD
Federal Way ▪ (253) 839-5000
1911 S 320th St
Vancouver ▪ (360) 514-9555
12501 SE 2nd Circle ▪ *Seafood* ▪ GF menu features a large selection of seafood entrees and appetizers, as well as salads and steaks. ▪ *www.mcgrathsfishhouse.com*

Melting Pot, The   📖
Bellevue ▪ (425) 646-2744
302 108th Ave NE
Spokane ▪ (509) 926-8000
707 W Main Ave
Tacoma ▪ (253) 535-3939
2121 Pacific Ave

Mercato Ristorante $$LD
Olympia ▪ (360) 528-3663
111 Market St. NW ▪ *Italian* ▪ The restaurant reports that it hosts GF diners "all the time." Items that can be modified to be GF include salads, chicken and mashed potatoes, asparagus, salmon, and prawns caprese. Confirm timeliness of this information before dining in. Alert a server, who will discuss GF options with the kitchen.

Mike's Four Star BBQ   ¢LD
Port Gamble ▪ (360) 297-4227
4719 NE State Hwy 104 ▪ *Barbeque* ▪ Owner Mike reports that nearly everything is GF, and they have a dedicated GF fryer. All of the seasonings and most of

the sauces are GF, as they are made from scratch. Mike recommends alerting the cashier upon ordering, and the cashier will know exactly what is and what is not GF, as all staff members are thoroughly trained. ■ *www.mikesfourstarbbq.com*

Mon Ami Crepes & Coffee ★ ¢S
Vancouver ■ *(360) 750-5693*
1906 Main St ■ *Crêpes* ■ GF crepes are available. Owner Jen recommends calling ahead to note GF.

Mora Ice Creamery ★ ¢S
Bainbridge Island ■ *(206) 855-8822*
139 Madrone Ln N ■ *Ice Cream* ■ GF ice cream cones are available. Restaurant reports that they are always well-stocked. ■ *www.moraicecream.com*

Mustard Seed Asian Café ★ $LD
Spokane ■ *(509) 483-1500*
4750 N Division St ■ *Asian* ■ Server Christina reports that the entire staff is "really educated" about the GF diet, and they will be able to discuss GF options. Examples of GF dishes include spicy caramel ginger chicken and almost any dish with the pork and pepper sauce. Confirm timeliness of this information before dining in. GF soy sauce is available. ■ *www.mustardseedweb. com*

Old Spaghetti Factory, The 📖
Lynnwood ■ *(425) 672-7006*
2509 196th St SW
Spokane ■ *(509) 624-8916*
152 S Monroe St
Tacoma ■ *(253) 383-2214*
1735 Jefferson Ave
Tukwila ■ *(206) 664-6800*
17100 Southcenter Pkwy Ste 160

Organic Comfort Food Café ✪★ $L
Puyallup ■ *(253) 770-6147*
210 W Pioneer ■ *Organic* ■ GF items marked on the menu include sandwiches, soups, mac and cheese, and more. GF bread and pasta are available. GF desserts include chocolate chip cookies, quinoa

chocolate cake, and bread pudding. ■ *www. comfortfoodcafe.org*

Outback Steakhouse 📖
Bellevue ■ *(425) 746-4647*
15100 SE 38th St Ste 500
Bothell ■ *(425) 486-7340*
22606 Bothell Everett Hwy
Bremerton ■ *(360) 479-4676*
5769 State Highway 303 NE
Burlington ■ *(360) 707-9942*
478 Andis Rd
Everett ■ *(425) 513-2181*
10121 Evergreen Way Ste 15
Federal Way ■ *(253) 839-1340*
2210 S 320th St Ste A6
Kennewick ■ *(509) 735-9304*
6819 W Canal Dr
Kirkland ■ *(425) 803-6880*
12120 NE 85th St
Olympia ■ *(360) 352-4692*
2615 Capitol Mall Dr SW
Puyallup ■ *(253) 864-7725*
12920 Meridian Street South
Spokane ■ *(509) 484-6956*
5628 N Division St Ste B-6
Spokane Valley ■ *(509) 892-6700*
14746 E Indiana Ave
Tacoma ■ *(253) 473-3669*
3111 S 38th St
Tukwila ■ *(206) 575-9705*
16510 Southcenter Pkwy
Union Gap ■ *(509) 469-4886*
2412 Rudkin Rd
Vancouver ■ *(360) 883-0005*
8700 NE Vancouver Mall Dr Ste 121

P.F. Chang's China Bistro 📖
Bellevue ■ *(425) 637-3582*
525 Bellevue Sq
Kennewick ■ *(509) 735-3270*
8108 W Gage Blvd
Lynnwood ■ *(425) 921-2100*
3000 184th St SW Ste 912

Pastazza ★ $$LD
Bellingham ■ *(360) 714-1168*
2945 Newmarket Pl ■ *Pasta* ■ GF pasta and pizza are available. Restaurant reports that all pasta sauces are GF. Alert a server, who

will report GF requests to the kitchen. ▪ *www.pastazza.com*

Pizza Works   ★ $$ LD
Bothell ▪ *(425) 821-1300*
14130 Juanita Dr NE ▪ *Pizza* ▪ GF pizza, spaghetti, meatballs, and desserts are available. GF items are made to order, so calling in advance is a recommended time saver. ▪ *www.pizza-works.net*

Ramblin Jacks $$ LD
Olympia ▪ *(360) 754-8909*
520 4th Ave E ▪ *American* ▪ Manager Shannon reports that GF diners come in "very frequently." She notes that several menu items are naturally GF or can be modified to be GF, including salads, turkey breast, smoked salmon, steaks, and grilled prawns. Confirm timeliness of this information before dining in. ▪ *www.ramblinrestaurants.com*

Rhapsody in Bloom Florist & Café Latte, A   ★ ¢S
Tacoma ▪ *(253) 761-7673*
3709 6th Ave ▪ *Bakery* ▪ Assorted GF cookies, cakes, muffins, and brownies are available. Located within the Rhapsody in Bloom Florist shop. Local musicians play weekly, according to a schedule on the website. ▪ *www.arhapsodyinbloomflorist.com*

Sages Restaurant   ✪★ $$ LD
Redmond ▪ *(425) 881-5004*
15916 NE 83rd St ▪ *Italian* ▪ There are separate GF menus for lunch and dinner. GF dinner menu includes manila clams, wild salmon picatta, and chicken gorgonzola, among other things. For dessert, they offer GF chocolate decadence. GF beer is available. ▪ *www.sagesrestaurant.com*

Savory Moment   ★ ¢S
Redmond ▪ *(425) 867-1516*
18005 NE 68th St ▪ *Take-&-Bake* ▪ They offer a huge number of GF "take-&-bake" options, including apple chicken sausage cassoulet, teriyaki chicken, pizza, macaroni and cheese, and many more. GF pasta,

bread, bagels, quiche, muffins, cookies, and more are available. ▪ *www.savorymoment.com*

Seastar Restaurant & Raw Bar ★ $$$$ LD
Bellevue ▪ *(425) 456-0010*
205 108th Ave NE ▪ *Seafood* ▪ GF soy sauce is available. Front-desk manager Joel notes that all servers are "very well-versed" on GF dining. He also notes that all dishes are made to order, so most menu items can be modified to be GF. Alert a server, who will indicate GF options. Reservations noting GF are recommended. ▪ *www.seastarrestaurant.com*

Spazzo Italian Grill & Wine Bar $$$ LD
Redmond ▪ *(425) 881-4400*
16499 NE 74th St ▪ *Italian* ▪ Chef Kris reports that they have one GF risotto dish, as well as a variety of "protein dishes" which are GF. Confirm timeliness of this information before dining in. Alert a server, who will speak to the chefs and managers. ▪ *www.schwartzbros.com*

Swan Café & Deli   ★ $ BLD
Bellingham ▪ *(360) 734-8158*
1220 N Forest St
Bellingham ▪ *(360) 734-8158*
315 Westerly Rd ▪ *Deli* ▪ Both locations offer GF breads, parfaits, cakes by the slice, and rolls. Baker Kristen notes that the selection can vary each day. She also notes that special orders can be accommodated with advanced notice of 72 hours or more. ▪ *www.communityfood.coop/deli*

Sweet Cakes   ★ ¢S
Kirkland ▪ *(425) 821-6565*
128 Park Ln ▪ *Bakery* ▪ GF cupcakes and bars are available. The bakery reports that GF cakes can be made if they are given notice 24 hours in advance. They also note that the entire staff is "well-versed" in GF baking. ▪ *www.sweetcakeskirkland.com*

Thai Bistro   ★ $ LD
Federal Way ▪ *(253) 874-8800*
34817 Enchanted Park Way South
Mill Creek ▪ *(425) 787-9707*

1018 164th St SE
Shoreline ▪ *(206) 533-6200*
18336 Aurora Ave N ▪ *Thai* ▪ GF soy sauce
and rice noodles are available. ▪ *www.*
thaibistro.us

Trumpeter Public House   ✪★ $$LD
Mount Vernon ▪ *(360) 588-4515*
416 Myrtle St ▪ *Modern American* ▪ GF
items marked on the menu include a
cheesesteak sandwich and ancho crusted
scallops, among many other things. Owner
Karen reports that all menu items are
naturally GF or can be modified to be GF.
She notes that dishes with bread and pasta
have GF substitutes, and GF sandwich buns
are available. Restaurant has dedicated GF
fryers. ▪ *www.trumpeterpublichouse.com*

Twigs Bistro & Martini Bar   ✪ $$$LD
Spokane ▪ *(509) 465-8794*
401 E Farwell Rd
Spokane ▪ *(509) 443-8000*
4320 S Regal St
Spokane ▪ *(509) 232-3376*
808 W Main Ave ▪ *Modern American* ▪ GF
menu includes steak penne, crab macaroni
and cheese, pesto margharita chicken,
burgers on GF buns, ahi sashimi, and
toasted pecan ceasar salad. GF menu was
created because a friend of one of the location's chefs is GF. ▪ *www.twigsbistro.com*

Typhoon!   ✪ $LD
Redmond ▪ *(425) 558-7666*
8936 161st Ave NE ▪ *Thai* ▪ There are
separate GF menus for lunch and dinner, and both are extensive. They include
starters, soups, salads, noodle dishes, rice
dishes, main courses, and more. Examples
of main courses are pineapple curry, cashew chicken, and Buddha's feast. ▪ *www.*
typhoonrestaurants.com

Wild Ginger Thai Restaurant   ★ $$L
Bellevue ▪ *(425) 495-8889*
11020 NE 6th St ▪ *Thai* ▪ Manager Brad
reports that "a variety" of menu items are
naturally GF. He notes that most seafood,
meat, and vegetable dishes can be modi-

fied to be GF. Confirm timeliness of this
information before dining in. Additionally,
he says that they serve GF diners "every
day," and that WF tamari sauce is available.
Reservations noting GF are recommended.
▪ *www.wildginger.net*

Wild Sage American Bistro   ✪★ $LD
Spokane ▪ *(509) 456-7575*
916 W 2nd Ave ▪ *Bistro* ▪ GF menu
includes soup and salad combinations, en-
trées such as pork marsala, seafood, steaks,
pastas, and desserts like coconut cream
layer cake and chocolate silk pie. The menu
is seasonal and subject to change. ▪ *www.*
wildsagebistro.com

Winger's Grill and Bar   ✪ ¢LD
Spokane ▪ *(509) 893-8057*
14742 E Indiana Ave
Tacoma ▪ *(253) 471-9464*
5221 Tacoma Mall Blvd ▪ *American* ▪ GF
menu includes double basted ribs, glazed
salmon, quesadillas with corn tortillas, and
a variety of salads. ▪ *www.wingers.info*

Woody's on the Water   ✪★ $$LD
Tacoma ▪ *(253) 272-1433*
1715 Dock Street East ▪ *Seafood & Steak-*
house ▪ GF menu includes appetizers, salads, and entrées such as a Moroccan spiced
breast of chicken, chicken and goat cheese
pizza, and Alaskan halibut. GF desserts
include brownies and chocolate raspberry
decadence cake. GF beer is also available. ▪
www.woodystacoma.com

Zao Noodle Bar $LD
Kent ▪ *(253) 373-0414*
504 Ramsay Way ▪ *Asian Noodles* ▪
GF noodles are available. The restaurant
reports that other dishes, such as several
chicken dishes, thai shrimp salad, and
eggplant curry, can be modified to be GF.
They also note that they frequently accommodate special dietary requests. ▪ *www.*
zaonoodle.com

Z'Tejas Southwestern Grill   ✪★ $LD
Bellevue ▪ *(425) 467-5911*
535 Bellevue Sq ▪ *Southwest* ▪ One-

page GF menu includes wild mushroom enchiladas and grilled salmon, along with smoked chicken and black bean salad. Frozen margaritas and GF beer are also available. ▪ *www.ztejas.com*

WEST VIRGINIA

Bakery, The   ¢S
Lewisburg ▪ (304) 645-1106
102 N Court St ▪ *Bakery & Café* ▪ Owner Lisa reports that although none of the baked goods are GF, they are happy to serve salads to GF diners. GF options include chicken salad, tuna salad, and more. Confirm timeliness of this information before dining in. The servers are aware of the GF diet, but Lisa emphasizes the importance of "letting them know." ▪ *www.thebakeryllcwv.com*

Chop House, The   ✪ $$$$D
Charleston ▪ (304) 344-3954
1003 Charlestown Center ▪ *Steakhouse* ▪ GF items marked on the menu include filets, salads, a swordfish steak, and Atlantic salmon. ▪ *www.thechophouserestaurant.com*

Eat 'n Park   📖
Bridgeport ▪ (304) 842-7668
100 Tolley Dr
Morgantown ▪ (304) 598-0020
353 Patterson Dr
Triadelphia ▪ (304) 547-9500
80 Fort Henry Rd
Weirton ▪ (304) 723-5179
226 Three Springs Dr

First Watch - The Daytime Café   📖
Charleston ▪ (304) 343-3447
164 Summers St

Hometown Market LLC   ★ ¢S
Buckhannon ▪ (304) 472-0686

39 College Ave ▪ *Sandwich & Soups* ▪ GF soups and rotating dessert items such as orange cornmeal cookies and pound cake are available at the deli. Store hosts GF samplings, where customers can try the GF bread or cake mixes sold in the grocery section of the store.

Later Alligator   ¢BL
Wheeling ▪ (304) 233-1606
2145 Market St ▪ *Modern American* ▪ Manager Amanda reports that although the restaurant does not offer any GF specialty items, many of the salads, such as the spinach salad with berries and walnuts, can be modified to be GF. Confirm timeliness of this information before dining in. She suggests that GF diners bring their own bread for sandwiches, and she notes that if enough demand arises for GF bread, they would be open to carrying it. Ask for Amanda or another manager upon arrival, and he or she will confer with the kitchen staff. ▪ *www.lateralligator.net*

Lone Star Steakhouse & Saloon   📖
Beckley ▪ (304) 255-7827
4288 Robert C Byrd Dr
Charleston ▪ (304) 926-8459
6515 Maccorkle Ave SE

Mountain People's Co-op   ★ ¢S
Morgantown ▪ (304) 291-6131
1400 University Ave ▪ *Bakery* ▪ GF baked goods, including brownies and cookies, are available. ▪ *www.mountaincoop.com*

Outback Steakhouse   📖
Barboursville ▪ (304) 733-1355
3417 US Route 60 E
Beckley ▪ (304) 255-5100
111 Hylton Ln
Bridgeport ▪ (304) 842-8915
3000 Meadowbrook Mall
Charleston ▪ (304) 345-0440
1062 Charleston Town Ctr
Martinsburg ▪ (304) 262-2406
790 Foxcroft Ave
Morgantown ▪ (304) 296-2896
510 Venture Dr

Parkersburg ▪ *(304) 422-3781*
1005 Grand Central Mall
Princeton ▪ *(304) 487-1971*
311 Greasy Ridge Rd

Panorama at the Peak $$$**LD**
Berkeley Springs ▪ *(304) 258-0050*
3299 Cacapon Road ▪ *Healthy American*
▪ Chef Scott reports that GF diners will
"absolutely" have "many options." He notes
that the chicken marsala, pot roast, and
the shepherd's pie, among others, can be
prepared GF. Alert a server, who will notify
the managers and Chef Scott. Scott will
approach the table to make suggestions.
For dessert, they have chocolate truffles. ▪
www.panoramaatthepeak.com

River City Ale Works $**LD**
Wheeling ▪ *(304) 233-4555*
1400 Main St ▪ *American* ▪ Manager Jason
reports that GF diners are accommodated
"all the time." The kitchen can modify most
things to be GF upon request. Possible GF
options include chicken breast, shrimp, sal-
ads, and several sides. Confirm timeliness
of this information before dining in. Upon
arrival, alert a server, who will go over GF
options in detail. ▪ *www.rivercitybanquets.*
com

Tidewater Grill   ✪ $$$**LD**
Charleston ▪ *(304) 345-2620*
1060 Charleston Town Ctr ▪ *Seafood* ▪
GF menu includes coconut crusted fried
shrimp, barbequed salmon, chicken artichoke pasta, and chargrilled chicken salad
julienne. GF pasta is available. Restaurant
recommends alerting the server upon arrival. ▪ *www.tidewatergrillrestaurant.com*

Uno Chicago Grill   📖
Huntington ▪ *(304) 697-8667*
279 9th St

WISCONSIN

MADISON

Biaggi's Ristorante Italiano   📖
Madison ▪ *(608) 664-9288*
601 Junction Rd

Bluephies Restaurant and Vodkato-
rium   ✪ $**LD**
Madison ▪ *(608) 231-3663*
2701 Monroe St ▪ *American* ▪ Items that
can be made GF are marked on the regular
menu. These limited GF options include
the chili burger, portobello sandwich, salmon BLT, and seared tuna. For dessert, they
offer flourless chocolate cake, chocolate
truffles, and more. ▪ *www.foodfightinc.com*

Bunky's Café   ✪★ $**LD**
Madison ▪ *(608) 204-7004*
2425 Atwood Ave ▪ *Italian & Mediter-*
ranean ▪ Italian and Mediterranean café
offering extensive GF options. GF bread,
pasta, and beer are available. GF pizza is
available for dinner only. For dessert, they
offer GF chocolate mousse pie, chocolate
or caramel toffee cheesecake, and lemon
mousse with ginger crust, among other
things. The café was established in honor of
a family legacy, which is reflected in both
the cuisine and the décor. They periodi-

BUNKY'S
◄ CAFE ►
ITALIAN▪MEDITERRANEAN
LOCAL INGREDIENTS • GLUTEN-FREE
Catering Available
Visit
our
NEW LOCATION!
OPEN: Tuesday-Thursday 11-2, 5-9
Friday 11-2, 5-10 • Saturday 11-10
Sunday 5-9 • Closed Monday
►2425 Atwood Avenue, Madison
608-204-7004 • www.bunkyscafe.net

cally host performers, including a Middle Eastern dance artist on the first and third Friday of every month. ▪ *www.bunkyscafe. net*

Cabana Room $LD
Madison ▪ (608) 257-3300
240 W Gilman St ▪ Global ▪ Chef Mark reports that the restaurant serves GF diners "every day." Upon arrival, alert the server or ask for Mark. Servers are trained to confer with the kitchen regarding what can be modified to be GF. Dishes that can be prepared to be GF include nachos, beef skewers, pork tacos, arroz con pollo, and vegetable curry. Confirm timeliness of this information before dining in. ▪ *www. thecabanaroom.com*

Chautara $$LD
Madison ▪ (608) 251-3626
334 State St ▪ Nepalese ▪ The restaurant reports that GF diners are easily accommodated. They recommend asking a server about GF options, as the staff is well-versed in GF dining.

Coopers Tavern, The   ★ $LD
Madison ▪ (608) 256-1600
20 W Mifflin St ▪ Pub Food ▪ Two kinds of GF beer are available. Owner Peter reports that they serve GF diners "five or six times a day." Alert a server, who will speak with the kitchen about modifying food to be GF. ▪ *www.thecooperstavern.com*

Eldorado Grill   ✪★ $$LD
Madison ▪ (608) 280-9378
744 Williamson St ▪ Southwest ▪ GF items marked on the regular menu include enchiladas, chalupas, fajitas, tacos, and quesadillas, among other things. GF beer and soy sauce are available. ▪ *www.eldoradogrill-madison.com*

Fresco Rooftop Restaurant & Lounge
                                         $$$D
Madison ▪ (608) 663-7374
227 State St ▪ American ▪ Manager Caitlin reports that they serve GF diners "all the time." She notes that they have a "scratch

kitchen" and make everything fresh, so they know every ingredient. In addition, the majority of menu items are or can be modified to be GF. She suggests alerting the server, who will notify the executive chef so that he will sanitize the cooking area before making GF food. ▪ *www.frescomadison.com*

Great Dane, The   ✪ $$LD
Madison ▪ (608) 284-0000
123 E Doty St ▪ American ▪ GF menu includes cheese and artichoke dip, nachos, and a variety of salads as starters. As entrées, it offers a cheeseburger and garlic shrimp, among other things. The Billiards Lounge provides five pool tables and a shuffleboard table for casual and serious gamers. ▪ *www.greatdanepub.com*

Johnny Delmonico's Steakhouse $$$LD
Madison ▪ (608) 257-8325
130 S Pinckney St ▪ Steakhouse ▪ Manager Craig reports that most menu items are naturally GF or can be modified to be GF. GF options include steaks, halibut, scallops, jumbo prawns, and mussels. Confirm timeliness of this information before dining in. Reservations noting GF are recommended. Alert a server upon arrival. ▪ *www.johnny-delmonicos.com*

Lee's Garden   ★ $LD
Madison ▪ (608) 829-1168
7475 Mineral Point Rd ▪ Chinese ▪ GF soy sauce is available, and the white sauce is also GF. Restaurant recommends alerting the server and specifying that the dish must be prepared with GF soy sauce.

L'Etoile Restaurant $$$$D
Madison ▪ (608) 251-0500
25 N Pinckney St ▪ Modern American ▪ Manager Talish reports that many items are naturally GF. He recommends making reservations noting GF, and explains that they will "coordinate with the kitchen" to make sure the meal is completely GF. He notes that they accommodate "dietary needs fairly regularly," so all servers are able to help. ▪ *www.letoile-restaurant.com*

Macha Teahouse   ¢L
Madison ▪ (608) 442-0500
1934 Monroe St ▪ *Teahouse* ▪ Owner Anthony reports that although the restaurant does not specially prepare GF food, some of the menu items, including the rice bowls with shiitake mushrooms and bok choy, are naturally GF. Confirm timeliness of this information before dining in. ▪ *www.machateahouse.com*

Melting Pot, The
Madison ▪ (608) 833-5676
6816 Odana Rd

Monty's Blue Plate Diner   ¢BLD
Madison ▪ (608) 244-8505
2089 Atwood Ave ▪ *American* ▪ Manager Alyssa reports that the restaurant is "very accommodating" of GF diners. She recommends alerting the server upon arrival, as most servers are knowledgeable about the contents of the food. She or Manager Joey is always available for consultation with GF diners. ▪ *www.montysblueplatediner.com*

Nitty Gritty, The   ✪★ ¢LD
Madison ▪ (608) 251-2521
223 N Frances St ▪ *American* ▪ GF menu includes spinach dip, nachos, and various burgers with no buns. There is a dedicated GF fryer that will be used upon request. GF beer is available. ▪ *www.nittygrittybirthdaybar.com*

Ocean Grill   ✪ $$$LD
Madison ▪ (608) 285-2582
117 Martin Luther King Jr Blvd ▪ *Seafood* ▪ GF menu lists naturally GF items on the regular menu and includes fresh oysters, prosciutto-wrapped scallops, seafood enchiladas with salsa verde, cedar plank salmon, peppercorn tuna, potato-crusted seabass, and more. ▪ *www.oceangrillmadison.com*

Otto's Restaurant & Bar $$$D
Madison ▪ (608) 274-4044
6405 Mineral Point Rd ▪ *Mediterranean* ▪ Restaurant reports that GF diners are welcome and that "most menu items" are naturally GF. Restaurant notes that it is important to alert the server upon arrival. ▪ *www.madison.com/otto*

Outback Steakhouse
Madison ▪ (608) 829-0505
279 Junction Rd
Madison ▪ (608) 241-0851
4520 E Towne Blvd

Restaurant Magnus   ✪ $$$D
Madison ▪ (608) 258-8787
120 E Wilson St ▪ *Modern American* ▪ Manager Prentiss reports that most of the menu is GF. GF items marked on the menu include salmon with fennel, venison carpaccio, steak with pate, lamb chops, and wild boar tenderloin. Reservations noting GF are recommended. ▪ *www.restaurant-magnus.com*

Samba Brazilian Grill $$$$D
Madison ▪ (608) 257-1111
240 W Gilman St ▪ *Brazilian Steakhouse* ▪ Manager Jennifer reports that they accommodate GF diners "every day." She notes that most of the menu is naturally GF, and any staff member can indicate which items are GF and which must be modified. There is also a listing of non-GF items, which is available upon request. ▪ *www.sambabrazil-iangrill.com*

Silly Yak Bakery and Bread Barn, The
★ ¢S
Madison ▪ (608) 833-5965
7866 Mineral Point Rd ▪ *Bakery* ▪ Non-dedicated bakery that has a very wide selection of GF baked goods, including a variety of breads, cinnamon rolls, brownies, cookies, and cakes. Most GF items are baked on Tuesdays and Saturdays. All GF items are baked in a dedicated kitchen. ▪ *www.sillyyakbakery.com*

Tex Tubb's Taco Palace $LD
Madison ▪ (608) 242-1800
2009 Atwood Ave ▪ *Tex-Mex* ▪ Manager Diana reports that they serve GF diners. She recommends asking for her upon arrival, or asking the server to speak with the

kitchen staff about the best GF options. She also notes that the enchiladas, cobb salad, and tacos with unfried corn tortillas are some meals that can be made GF. Confirm timeliness of this information before dining in. ▪ *www.textubbstacos.com*

Uno Chicago Grill   📖
Madison ▪ *(608) 244-3266*
3010 Crossroads Dr
Madison ▪ *(608) 833-7200*
7601 Mineral Point Rd

WISCONSIN
ALL OTHER CITIES

Beans & Barley Deli, Market, Café
                                    ✪★ ¢**BLD**
Milwaukee ▪ *(414) 278-7878*
1901 E North Ave ▪ *Café* ▪ Co-owner Pat reports that naturally GF items are now marked on the menu, but many unmarked items can be modified to be GF. GF bread, pasta, soy sauce, and beer are available. For dessert, GF cakes and cookies are available. ▪ *www.beansandbarley.com*

Bonefish Grill   📖
Brookfield ▪ *(262) 797-0166*
18355 W Bluemound Rd

Buca di Beppo   📖
Milwaukee ▪ *(414) 224-8672*
1233 N Van Buren St

Bucatini Trattoria & Pizzeria   ★ $**LD**
Middleton ▪ *(608) 824-0004*
1611 Deming Way ▪ *Italian* ▪ GF pasta is available for substitution into any pasta dish on the menu. Consult with the server when choosing a GF sauce. ▪ *www.bucatinitrattoria.com*

Café 4   ★ $**LD**
Mineral Point ▪ *(608) 987-2030*
20 Commerce St ▪ *Italian* ▪ GF quinoa

pasta is available with advanced notice. Restaurant recommends noting GF in reservations so they can be sure to have separate cooking utensils ready upon arrival. ▪ *www.fourcafe.com*

Café Calamari   ★ $$**D**
Williams Bay ▪ *(262) 245-9665*
10 E Geneva St ▪ *Italian* ▪ GF pasta and pizza are available. GF pasta can be substituted into any pasta dish, and the GF pizza crust can be prepared with any toppings. GF beer is also available. ▪ *www.cafecalamari.com*

Café Tarragon   ✪★ ¢**L**
Milwaukee ▪ *(414) 294-4300*
2352 S Kinnickinnic Ave ▪ *Organic & Raw* ▪ GF pasta and bread are available. All items on the menu are GF. ▪ *www.futuregreen.net*

Capital Grille, The   📖
Milwaukee ▪ *(414) 223-0600*
310 W Wisconsin Ave

Carrabba's Italian Grill   📖
Brookfield ▪ *(262) 797-2548*
18365 W Bluemound Rd
Greenfield ▪ *(414) 282-4158*
4765 S 76th St

Charcoal Grill   ✪ $$**LD**
Appleton ▪ *(920) 731-9600*
N140 Eisenhower Dr
Burlington ▪ *(262) 767-0000*
580 Milwaukee Ave
Grafton ▪ *(262) 375-1700*
1200 N Port Washington Rd
Kenosha ▪ *(262) 942-9896*
5745 75th St
Manitowoc ▪ *(920) 682-1000*
4101 Harbor Town Ln
New Berlin ▪ *(262) 432-3000*
15375 W Greenfield Ave
Plover ▪ *(715) 295-0200*
190 Crossroads Dr
Racine ▪ *(262) 639-2050*
3839 Douglas Ave
Racine ▪ *(262) 884-9400*
8300 Washington Ave ▪ *Barbeque* ▪ A

laminated list of GF items on the menu, with ordering instructions, is available. It includes chiles, spinach dip with tortilla chips, nachos, salads, and sandwiches without buns. Alert a server upon arrival. ▪ *www.charcoalgrill.com*

Cheese Factory Restaurant, The
✪ $**BLD**

Wisconsin Dells ▪ *(608) 253-6065*
521 Wisconsin Dells Pkwy S ▪ *Vegetarian*
▪ GF items marked on the vegan menu include the tofu "chicken" salad, thai bananas, hummus without the pita bread, and Malaysian coconut noodles, among other things. ▪ *www.cookingvegetarian.com*

Claddagh Irish Pub
$**LD**
Middleton ▪ *(608) 833-5070*
1611 Aspen Cmns ▪ *Irish* ▪ Manager Laura reports that GF diners can be accommodated. She notes that the restaurant has an internal list of items that can be modified to be GF. She recommends alerting the server, who will bring that list out and discuss it. Sandwiches without bread, Jameson steak, steak salad, baked cod, and corned beef and cabbage are examples of items that can be made GF. Confirm timeliness of this information before dining in. ▪ *www.claddaghirishpubs.com*

Crawdaddy's Restaurant
✪ $$**LD**
West Allis ▪ *(414) 778-2228*
6414 W Greenfield Ave ▪ *Cajun & Creole*
▪ GF menu includes appetizers, soups, salads, fish and seafood entrées, as well as meat dishes. Examples are the blackened catfish and the BBQ ribs. Manager Tyler cautions that many of the GF menu items are modified from regular menu items, so it is important to specify GF when ordering. ▪ *www.crawdaddysrestaurant.com*

Fifth Ave Restaurant & Lounge ✪★
¢**LD**
Antigo ▪ *(715) 623-2893*
714 5th Ave ▪ *American* ▪ GF pizza is available. Limited GF menu items include burger without buns, any sandwich without bread, and the taco salad.

Fireside Theater, The
$$$$**D**
Fort Atkinson ▪ *(800) 477-9505*
1131 Janesville Ave ▪ *American* ▪ Manager Jean notes that GF diners often eat at the restaurant, and the staff is "well-aware" of GF options. Baked chicken or baked fish is generally available for GF diners, and the chefs are accustomed to modifying dishes to be GF. Confirm timeliness of this information before dining in. ▪ *www.firesidetheatre.com*

Fontana Grill
$$$$**D**
Fontana ▪ *(262) 275-1433*
269 Fontana Blvd ▪ *Seafood & Steakhouse* ▪ Executive Chef Steven reports that the restaurant is "very sensitive" to GF diners. He recommends asking for Sous-chef Josh upon arrival, as he can discuss GF dining options with customers. Located in the Abbey Resort. ▪ *www.theabbeyresort.com*

Fork in the Roads Café
★ ¢**S**
Milwaukee ▪ *(414) 961-2597*
100 E Capitol Dr
Milwaukee ▪ *(414) 755-3202*
2826 S Kinnickinnic Ave ▪ *Café* ▪ GF pasta, chocolate cherry and chocolate chip cookies, cakes, and bars are available. The Capitol Drive location bakes their own tapioca popovers as well. Cafe is located in the Outpost Natural Foods Market. ▪ *www.outpostnaturalfoods.coop*

Fresh and Natural Foods
★ ¢**BLD**
Hudson ▪ *(715) 377-9913*
1701 Ward Ave ▪ *Deli* ▪ Deli is located in the Fresh and Natural Foods grocery store. GF sandwiches, pasta, and pizza are available. GF pastries and baked goods are also available. Many GF items are available on a "build your own" and on a "Grab N Go" basis. ▪ *www.freshandnaturalfoods.com*

GingeRootz Asian Grille
✪★ $**LD**
Appleton ▪ *(920) 738-9688*
2920 N Ballard Rd ▪ *Asian* ▪ GF menu offers appetizers, salads, and entrées such as chicken mixed vegetable and Hawaiian

style sweet and sour chicken. It also includes the customize-a-bowl option, which provides choices between noodles or rice, GF soy sauce or classic white sauce, and vegetables or meat. ▪ *www.gingerootz.com*

Ground Round   📖
Janesville ▪ *(608) 314-8540*
2753 Milton Ave
Neenah ▪ *(920) 725-1010*
1010 Cameron Way
Tomah ▪ *(608) 372-4000*
201 Helen Walton Dr Ste 1

Hackberry's Bistro   ★ $$**BLD**
La Crosse ▪ *(608) 784-5798*
315 5th Ave S ▪ *Organic American* ▪ GF bread, macaroons, and specialty cakes are available. GF pancakes and toast are available for breakfast and lunch. GF options are significantly more limited at dinner time. ▪ *www.pfc.coop*

Hubbard Avenue Diner, The   ✪ ¢**BLD**
Middleton ▪ *(608) 831-6800*
7445 Hubbard Ave ▪ *American* ▪ Extensive GF menu includes burgers without buns, fresh salmon salad, spicy szechuan salad, and thai chicken stir fry. Breakfast menu includes frittatas, egg scrambles, and omelets. Restaurant notes that some GF items are prepared on the same griddle as non-GF products. They recommend speaking with a server about whether or not a specific dish can be made separately. ▪ *www.hubbardavenuediner.com*

Imperial Garden West   ★ $**LD**
Middleton ▪ *(608) 238-6445*
2039 Allen Blvd ▪ *Chinese* ▪ GF soy sauce is available. Restaurant notes that many dishes can be made GF. Alert a server, who will notify the kitchen. ▪ *www.imperialgarden.com*

Johnny's Italian Steakhouse   ✪ $$$**LD**
Middleton ▪ *(608) 831-3705*
8390 Market St ▪ *Steakhouse* ▪ Extensive GF menu includes steak, salmon, and lobster salads, along with cedar plank and Atlantic salmon, pork chops, steaks, veal

parmesan, chicken piccata, and more. ▪ *www.johnnysitaliansteakhouse.com*

Lakefront Brewery   ★ ¢**D**
Milwaukee ▪ *(414) 372-8800*
1872 N Commerce St ▪ *Modern American* ▪ Lakefront Brewery has a restaurant that is open on Friday evenings only. The brewery's own GF beer, New Grist, is available. ▪ *www.lakefrontbrewery.com*

Libby Montana Restaurant, Bar, & Volleydome   ✪★ $**LD**
Mequon ▪ *(262) 242-2232*
5616 W Donges Bay Rd ▪ *American* ▪ GF items marked on the menu include chicken nachos, goat cheese and artichoke pizza, as well as some salads and meat entrées. GF pizza is available in the 10-inch size. GF beer is also available. For dessert, they offer flourless chocolate soufflé. ▪ *www.libbymontana.com*

Lone Star Steakhouse & Saloon   📖
Racine ▪ *(262) 554-4511*
5880 Durand Ave

Market Street Diner & Bakery   ✪ ¢**BLD**
Sun Prairie ▪ *(608) 825-3377*
110 Market St ▪ *American* ▪ GF menu includes warm roasted chicken and spinach salad, burgers without buns, meatloaf, and Santa Fe chicken. Egg scrambles and omelets are available for breakfast. Restaurant notes that they always clean the grill before preparing GF items. ▪ *www.marketstreetdiner.com*

Maxie's Southern Comfort $$**D**
Milwaukee ▪ *(414) 292-3969*
6732 W Fairview Ave ▪ *American Regional* ▪ Verteran Bartender Sam reports that all servers have been "forced to train and taste from the menu," so they are very knowledgeable about the ingredients of menu items. If there are any questions, the server will go "straight to the chef." Sam notes that there are several naturally GF options, including jambalaya and cajun seared ahi tuna. Confirm timeliness of this information before dining in. ▪ *www.maxies.com*

Melting Pot, The   📖
Appleton ▪ *(920) 739-3533*
2295 W College Ave
Brookfield ▪ *(262) 782-6358*
19850 W Bluemound Rd

Mitchell's Fish Market   ✪ $$$LD
Brookfield ▪ *(262) 789-2426*
275 N Moorland Rd ▪ *Seafood* ▪ Extensive GF menu includes pan-roasted wild blue mussels, blackened salmon spinach salad, grilled shrimp and scallop skewers, Shanghai seafood sampler, lobster tail, filet mignon, and live Maine lobster. Mini crème brulee is available for dessert. ▪ *www.mitchellsfishmarket.com*

Molly's Gluten Free Bakery   100% ¢S
Pewaukee ▪ *(262) 369-1404*
N47 W28270 Lynndale Rd ▪ *Bakery* ▪ Dedicated GF bakery carrying cakes, pie crusts, muffins, bread, bagels, mock rye bread, rolls, cookies and brownies. Everything is made fresh to order. The restaurant reports that bread needs to be ordered two days in advance. ▪ *www.mollysglutenfreebakery.com*

Monical's Pizza Restaurant   ★ $$LD
Arbor Vitae ▪ *(715) 358-9959*
360 US Highway 51 N ▪ *Pizza* ▪ GF pizza is available. ▪ *www.monicalspizza.com*

Nitty Gritty, The   ★ ¢LD
Middleton ▪ *(608) 833-6489*
1021 N Gammon Rd ▪ *American* ▪ GF beer is available. Restaurant has an internal list of dishes that can be prepared GF, including nachos and barbeque chicken salad. The downtown location has a WF fryer. Confirm timeliness of this information before dining in. ▪ *www.nittygrittybirthdayplace.com*

Nook Café   ¢BL
Kenosha ▪ *(262) 657-6665*
5703 6th Ave ▪ *Café* ▪ Manager Oliver notes that the restaurant is "not a GF facility." He reports that not all staff are educated on GF dining, but that there is "usually someone around who is aware."

He recommends calling in advance. ▪ *www.thenookcafe.com*

Original Pancake House, The   ★ ¢BL
Brookfield ▪ *(262) 797-0800*
16460 W Bluemound Rd ▪ *Breakfast* ▪ GF pancakes are available. ▪ *www.originalpancakehouse.com*

Outback Steakhouse   📖
Brookfield ▪ *(262) 796-9580*
1260 S Moorland Rd
Grand Chute ▪ *(920) 730-4329*
4287 W College Ave
Greenfield ▪ *(414) 817-1800*
7401 W Barnard Ave
Onalaska ▪ *(608) 781-4329*
311 Hampton Ct

Outdoorsman Restaurant, The
              ✪ ★ $$$BLD
Boulder Junction ▪ *(715) 385-2826*
10383 Main St ▪ *American Regional* ▪ GF menu includes sundried tomato shrimp, rib-eye steak, and orange ginger-glazed cornish game hen. GF beer is available. Staff is educated on the GF diet, as one of the chefs is GF. ▪ *www.outdoorsmanrestaurant.com*

Outpost Natural Foods Bakery   ★ ¢S
Milwaukee ▪ *(414) 961-2597*
100 E Capitol Dr
Milwaukee ▪ *(414) 755-3202*
2826 S Kinnickinnic Ave
Wauwatosa ▪ *(414) 778-2012*
7000 W State St ▪ *Bakery* ▪ All locations report that although the deli and bakery menus "switch all the time," there are always GF baked goods. GF cookies, muffins, cakes, and more are available. GF "take-&-bake" pizza is also available. Located in the Outpost Natural Foods market. ▪ *www.outpostnaturalfoods.coop*

River Room, The   ✪ $$BLD
Green Bay ▪ *(920) 437-5900*
200 Main St ▪ *American* ▪ GF menu contains regular menu items that can be modified to be GF. It includes breakfast, lunch, and dinner options.

Roots Restaurant & Cellar $$$$D
Milwaukee ▪ (414) 374-8480
1818 N Hubbard St ▪ Modern American ▪
Manager Blake reports that GF diners are
"easily" accommodated. He suggests talking to a server, who will alert the kitchen
and discuss possible GF options. Reservations noting GF are recommended. ▪ www.
rootsmilwaukee.com

Saz's State House $$LD
Milwaukee ▪ (414) 453-2410
5539 W State St ▪ American ▪ Server Ash-
ton reports that all BBQ sauces are GF. She
adds that a number of items, including the
ribs and any of the sandwiches without a
bun, can be prepared GF. Confirm timeliness of this information before dining in. ▪
www.sazs.com

Slow Pokes Local Food   ★ ¢LD
Grafton ▪ (262) 375-5522
1229 12Th Ave ▪ Take-&-Bake ▪ Cashier
Pamela reports that the store carries GF
"take-&-bake" pizzas and take out sandwiches with GF bread. GF muffins, cookies,
and granola are also available. ▪ www.
slowpokeslocalfood.com

Smokey's Bar-B-Que House   ✪★ $BLD
Lake Geneva ▪ (262) 249-3411
7020 Grand Geneva Way ▪ Global ▪
Extensive GF menu includes, among other
things, french toast for breakfast, white
chicken chili for lunch, and a variety of
BBQ sandwiches. GF hamburger and
hotdog buns are available, as are GF pizza
crusts and GF bread. Located in the Timber Ridge Lodge. ▪ www.timberridgeresort.
com

Stack'd   ★ $LD
Milwaukee ▪ (414) 273-7800
170 S 1st St ▪ American ▪ GF buns are
available for burgers. ▪ www.stackedbar.com

Sustenance Artisan Breads   ★ ¢S
Superior ▪ (715) 392-7004
1323 North Broadway ▪ Bakery ▪ GF
breads, pastries, and sometimes cookies are
available. Owner Dale reports that he only

bakes GF items on Tuesdays, Wednesdays,
and Saturdays. ▪ www.sustenanceartisan-
breads.com

Taste of Africa Restaurant $LD
Port Washington ▪ (262) 268-1007
117 E Main St ▪ African ▪ Dedicated GF
restaurant serves chicken, pork, beef, catfish, tilapia, shrimp, rice dishes, a variety of
sauces, and more. A selection of GF beer is
available. ▪ www.tasteofafrica2go.com

Tess Restaurant   ✪★ $$D
Milwaukee ▪ (414) 964-8377
2499 N Bartlett Ave ▪ Modern American ▪
GF items are marked clearly on the menu.
GF bread is always available, and GF pasta
is usually available. All desserts, including a
flourless chocolate cake and two flavors of
crème brûlée, are GF.

Uno Chicago Grill   📖
Appleton ▪ (920) 731-2111
W 3254 Van Roy Rd
Elm Grove ▪ (262) 821-1755
15280 W Bluemound Rd
Lake Delton ▪ (608) 253-2111
1000 South Wisconsin Dells Pwy
Menomonee Falls ▪ (262) 255-1440
W 180 N 9455 Premier Land

Urban Frog, The   ★ ¢BL
Green Bay ▪ (920) 490-1170
163 N Broadway ▪ Deli ▪ GF bread, pizza,
pasta, and hamburger buns are available.
GF wraps are available for sandwiches.
Many homemade soups, salads, and juices
are naturally GF. Owner Terry notes that
GF diners should alert the staff, who will
ensure a GF meal. ▪ www.urbanfrogdeli.com

Wright Place on 6th, The $$$D
Wausau ▪ (715) 848-2345
901 6th St ▪ Seafood & Steakhouse ▪
Chef Travis reports that they have a "fair
amount" of regular GF diners. He recommends reservations noting GF, and he will
come to the table to discuss GF options. ▪
www.wrightplaceon6th.com

WYOMING

Blue Lion, The $$$D
Jackson Hole ▪ *(307) 733-3912*
160 N Millward St ▪ *Global* ▪ Owner Ned
reports that they accommodate GF diners
"about once a month." He recommends
alerting a server, who can ensure that almost any meal is prepared GF. Steaks, seafood, and some appetizers can be prepared
GF. ▪ *www.bluelionrestaurant.com*

Bosco's Italian Restaurant ✪★ $$LD
Casper ▪ *(307) 265-9658*
847 E A St ▪ *Italian* ▪ GF pasta is available.
Other GF menu items include chicken
parmigiana, shrimp scampi, shrimp diablo,
veal piccata and more.

Bubba's Bar-B-Que $LD
Cody ▪ *(307) 587-7427*
512 Yellowstone Ave ▪ *Barbeque* ▪ Manager Darren reports that nearly the entire
menu is GF. The meats, such as the pork
special, the chicken, and the baby back
ribs, all come with a naturally GF rib sauce.
Confirm timeliness of this information
before dining in.

Chophouse Restaurant $$$LD
Gillette ▪ *(307) 682-6805*
113 S Gillette Ave ▪ *Steakhouse* ▪ General
Manger Lance reports that they serve GF
diners on a weekly basis. He adds that GF
diners should ask to speak with a manager
or a chef, as they are trained on the GF
diet. He further notes that all steaks and
all seafood options can be prepared GF
upon request. Confirm timeliness of this
information before dining in. ▪ *www.gil-
lettechophouse.com*

Graham's Gluten-Free Foods 100% ¢S
Riverton ▪ *(307) 857-6155*
414 E Main St ▪ *Take-&-Bake* ▪ Owner
Sheila reports that although she had to
close the store's GF deli, they are still selling

GF "take-&-bake" pizza. Many other GF
"take-&-bake" meals are also available. ▪
www.grahamsglutenfree.com

Jeffrey's Bistro $LD
Laramie ▪ *(307) 742-7046*
123 E Ivinson St ▪ *Fusion* ▪ Cook Paul
reports that all staff members are "pretty
educated" about the GF diet. Several items,
including stir fry, giant salads, and the
Bombay spinach with grilled chicken, can
easily be prepared GF. Confirm timeliness of this information before dining in. ▪
www.jeffreysbistro.com

La Cocina ✪ ¢LD
Casper ▪ *(307) 266-1414*
1040 N Center St ▪ *Mexican* ▪ GF menu
includes fajitas, quesadillas, tacos, and burritos. ▪ *www.lacocinacasper.com*

Los Agaves ¢LD
Sheridan ▪ *(307) 674-0900*
922 Coffeen Ave ▪ *Mexican* ▪ There is a
"GF guide" that explains what menu items
are GF and what modifications must be
made to make items GF. Manager Mabel
reports that "most of the menu," including enchiladas and tacos, can be made GF.
Alert a server, who will be knowledgeable
about GF and able help choose a GF meal.

Million Dollar Cowboy Steakhouse, The $$$D
Jackson Hole ▪ *(307) 733-4790*
25 N Cache Dr ▪ *Steakhouse* ▪ Chef Kevin
notes that most of the menu is naturally
GF. He also notes that GF diners are
welcome and that accommodating them is
"not a big deal at all." Reservations noting
GF are recommended. ▪ *www.cowboysteak-
house.net*

Nikai Sushi ★ $D
Jackson ▪ *(307) 734-6490*
225 North Cache ▪ *Sushi* ▪ GF teriyaki
sauce and GF soy sauce are available.
Manager Kieran reports that they serve "a
fair amount" of GF diners, and that "most"
of the servers are educated on the GF diet.
Alert a server, and if he or she cannot iden-

tify GF menu items, he or she will check
with a chef. ▪ *www.nikaisushi.com*

Outback Steakhouse   📖
Cheyenne ▪ **(307) 638-8171**
1626 Fleischli Business Pkwy
Evansville ▪ **(307) 235-0391**
229 Miracle Rd

Pearl St. Meat & Fish Company ★ ¢**BLD**
Jackson ▪ **(307) 733-1300**
260 W Pearl St ▪ **Deli** ▪ GF bread, pasta,
cookies, and cake are available. GF avail-
abilities change daily, but there are always
fruit, vegetable, meat, and soup options.
Examples include chili, ribs, smoothies,
and flourless chocolate cake. ▪ *www.pearlst-
meatandfish.com*

Rendezvous Bistro $$**D**
Jackson ▪ **(307) 739-1100**
380 S. Hwy. 89 / Broadway ▪ **Bistro** ▪
Business Manager Jessica reports that they
are happy to serve GF diners, and that
all staff members are informed about the
GF diet. She advises making reservations
noting GF, alerting the server upon arrival,
and using the word "allergy." Though the
menu changes frequently, a staff member
will be able to indicate GF items. ▪ *www.
rendezvousbistro.net*

Winger's Grill and Bar   ✪ ¢**LD**
Rock Springs ▪ **(307) 382-8002**
1675 Sunset Dr ▪ **American** ▪ GF menu
includes double basted ribs, glazed salmon,
quesadillas with corn tortillas, and a variety
of salads. ▪ *www.wingers.info*

Section 3: Gluten-Free Lists & Menus

User's Guide

In this section, you will find gluten-free lists and menus from more than 100 chain restaurants across the United States. (Some of these restaurants were also included in Section 2, either because they have extensive gluten-free options or because they are small, regional chains.)

While some chains are listed for their extensive gluten-free selections, others are listed simply because of their ubiquity. We know you can't always choose a restaurant with a great gluten-free menu. Sometimes, you just have to settle for your child's favorite, but not so Celiac friendly, fast food restaurant.

Gluten-Free Menu vs. Gluten-Free List

In general, a gluten-free menu will be available at the actual restaurant, while a gluten-free list is only available from the restaurant's corporate headquarters. Chains that report having gluten-free menus are flagged with an icon of a star inside a circle.

The gluten-free menus and lists for these chain restaurants were obtained from the restaurants' corporate headquarters.

Notes on Format and Editorial Process

Although we have reformatted some of the menus and lists for clarity and convenience, we have done our best to convey the same information that appears in the original lists. For example, if a company provides a list of all its items and highlights those that are gluten-free, we've included only the highlighted, gluten-free items.

We have also provided contact information for the restaurants' corporate headquarters, so you can stay informed about changes to their lists and contact them for access to the full, unabridged lists.

In this section, the notes attributed to restaurants are paraphrased comments from the restaurants' corporate headquarters and should be read in addition to (not in lieu of) the list that accompanies them.

Note: Some restaurants noted as gluten-free items that contain distilled vinegar. Distilled vinegar is considered by prominent dieticians and Celiac organizations to be gluten-free, so items that contain distilled vinegar are included in these lists as any other gluten-free item.

Do Not Order Directly From These Lists

Unfortunately, there's no such thing as worry-free gluten-free dining. By its nature, ordering a gluten-free meal will almost always take more time and effort than ordering a "regular" one. Our guide is meant to help you save time by honing in on the restaurants or dishes that are most likely to be suitable for a gluten-free diet. We aim to prevent you from spending hours chasing dead ends, to provide you more time to engage with the restaurant staff and make sure you have updated information.

To that end, we have provided these gluten-free lists and menus as a starting point for your research. We have not independently confirmed that each item on these lists is gluten-free, nor have we confirmed the ability of each chain restaurant location to prepare gluten-free foods. In addition, some of these gluten-free lists may have changed since the printing of this book.

It's also important to remember that compiling a gluten-free list or menu and transcribing dozens of gluten-free lists and menus involves a large amount of labor. It's entirely possible that, despite best efforts and substantial precautions, human errors were made – either in the process of developing or in that of transcribing these gluten-free lists and menus.

For these reasons, it's not a good idea to order directly from the lists or menus in this book without first independently confirming their contents with both the corporate headquarters and the specific restaurant location.

Finally, please use common sense when reviewing these lists and other information we've compiled from restaurants. For example, if a restaurant or list tells you that the hamburger is gluten-free, assume that only the patty is gluten-free. That is, unless you've independently confirmed that they have gluten-free hamburger buns. In general, if something seems unusual or not quite right, use your own good judgment and double-check the information.

Also, keep in mind that the creators of these lists may or may not be familiar with all the nuances of the gluten-free diet. For example, if you see french fries on the gluten-free list, don't assume they have a dedicated fryer without confirmation from the restaurant.

Not All Restaurants are Created Equal

We do not endorse or recommend any of the restaurants listed in this book. Just because a restaurant has a gluten-free list or menu doesn't mean you should eat there. Certain types of restaurants (e.g., buffets, sandwich or burrito shops) naturally present higher risk factors than others, and management responsiveness can vary or be otherwise hard to predict.

Before you eat at any restaurant, you should independently assess the likelihood for cross-contamination, expected responsiveness of the service, and other factors that may impact your ability to get a gluten-free meal. (Please see the Section 2 User's Guide for more details.)

Reasonable people will differ in the amount they want to risk in pursuit of restaurant dining. This Guide is designed to help you make intelligent, informed choices, but those choices are ultimately your own to make.

Always Get the Most Recent Information

We obtained these gluten-free lists in the spring of 2010. Each list indicates the date it was received in a field labeled "Confirmed." Please note, however, that the restaurant industry is dynamic: Menus, suppliers, supplier ingredients, management, etc. are always changing.

We've provided websites and, when possible, phone numbers for the corporate head-quarters of listed restaurants. Please use this information to get up-to-date lists!

A Note About Ingredient Lists

Many restaurants release complete ingredient lists that enumerate the contents of every dish on their menu. We have not provided these resources here, but you may find them useful in evaluating the safety of a restaurant's offerings. For ingredient information, please contact a restaurant's corporate headquarters directly.

Always Individually Verify Information

Even if you've received the most up-to-date gluten-free information from the restaurant's corporate office, don't stop there.

It's important to realize the limitations inherent in a gluten-free list from a large chain restaurant. There is no way for any restaurant, especially a large chain, to guarantee a gluten-free meal. For starters, large chains may use different suppliers in different regions, meaning that the same ingredient may have a different composition in the Midwest than it does on the East Coast, for example. A supplier can also change the composition of ingredients. Moreover, a restaurant may change suppliers at any time. And some restaurant locations may not follow corporate procedures or recipes as closely as others; this is especially true of smaller franchise operations without far-reaching quality assurance departments.

In addition, the staff of certain restaurants may not be specifically trained about Celiac disease or versed in the appropriate food handling techniques necessary to prepare a gluten-free meal. For example, some large fast food chains have gluten-free lists, but their average employees aren't trained to understand the gluten-free diet or to avoid cross-contamination. Until a particular restaurant has established a good track record, always assume that this will be the case. Use a gluten-free list or menu as a starting point only. It's up to you to order the correct food and ask for it to be prepared in a manner that will avoid cross-contamination (be specific – ask for clean gloves, clean utensils, etc.).

In addition, preparation techniques for certain dishes may vary by region or even by restaurant location. Menu items and their ingredients can change over time. And, no matter how careful the restaurant staff is, there's always a chance of cross-contamination, because there are almost always gluten-containing items in a restaurant's kitchen.

Don't Expect Any Guarantees

As we discussed, no restaurant can guarantee a gluten-free meal. And no restaurant will ac-cept any liability for damages that result from your use of their gluten-free lists or menus. It's unfortunate, but today's reality is that you're on your own out there. Therefore, please always be alert and use your own good judgment in choosing where and what to eat. Be careful, cautious and deliberate. Ask questions, collect up-to-date information, use common sense and make intelligent, informed decisions.

DINING OUT CHECKLIST

Before you visit a restaurant listed in this Guide, review this Summary Checklist and the User's Guides in Sections 2 and 3.

Before you Leave the House

☑ Research the restaurant. Is it a buffet, sandwich shop, or other type of cuisine that increases the risk of cross-contamination? If so, will you feel safe eating there?

☑ If dining at a chain restaurant, call the corporate office to request the most recent gluten-free menu or list. (See Section 3 for contact information.)

☑ Regardless of the type of restaurant, call the location you plan to visit in advance. Does the restaurant still have a gluten-free menu? (If not, can they accommodate you tonight?)

☑ Also, confirm that gluten-free specialty items are in stock. (E.g., if you're going for the gluten-free pasta, do they have it tonight?)

When You Get There

☑ Introduce yourself to the maitre d', and mention your dietary needs.

☑ Ask for the gluten-free menu, if applicable.

☑ Never make any assumptions. Present your dining card, even if they have a gluten-free menu. Ask a few questions. Confirm that they understand the diet, even if they have a gluten-free menu.

Also, review and use the tips and strategies on safe restaurant dining presented in the previous sections of this book.

And remember, there is no way any restaurant (or restaurant guide) can guarantee a gluten-free meal. Always independently verify information and be vigilant when eating out. A bit of caution goes a long way in getting a delicious, safe gluten-free meal.

Applebee's Neighborhood Grill & Bar $LD

(888) 592-7753
American
Confirmed: 4/2/2010

Triumph Notes: Wheat-free menu options can be found online, but there is no gluten-free list available.

Arby's ¢BLD

(800) 487-2729
American
Confirmed: 4/5/2010

Breakfast
Breakfast Bacon
Breakfast Syrup
Egg, Scrambled Mix
Egg, Scrambled Patty
Sausage Patty

Salads
Chopped Farmhouse Chicken-Roast
Chopped Italian Salad
Chopped Side Salad
Chopped Turkey Club

Salad Dressings
Balsamic Vinaigrette
Buttermilk Ranch
Dijon Honey Mustard

Meats
Corned Beef
Genoa Salami
Pecan Chicken Salad-Roast
Pepper Bacon
Pepperoni
Roast Beef
Roast Chicken
Roast Ham
Roast Turkey

Sides
Applesauce

Condiments
Banana Peppers
Bleu Cheese Spread
Chargrill Seasoning
Cheddar Cheese Sauce
Cheddar, Processed Slice
Cheddar, Sharp Natural Slice
Cheddar, Shredded
Chicken Club Sauce
Dijon Honey Mustard Sandwich Sauce
Dill Pickles
Garlic Buttered Onions
Gyro Sauce
Gyro Seasoning
Ketchup
Mayonnaise
Parmesan Peppercorn Ranch Sauce
Pepper & Onion Mix
Red Ranch Sauce
Red Wine Vinaigrette Sauce
Sauerkraut
Smoky Q Sauce
Spicy Brown Honey Mustard Sauce
Swiss Cheese, Big Eye Natural
Swiss Cheese, Slice Processed
Tartar Sauce
Thousand Island Spread
Yellow Mustard

Dipping Sauces
Arby's Sauce
Bronco Berry Sauce
Buffalo Dipping Sauce
Honey Dijon Mustard Sauce
Horsey Sauce
Marinara Sauce
Ranch Dipping Sauce
Spicy Three Pepper Sauce
Tangy Barbeque Sauce
Tangy Southwest Sauce

Desserts
Chocolate Swirl Shake
Jamocha Swirl Shake
Vanilla Shake

Beverages
1% Low Fat Chocolate Milk
2% Reduced Fat Milk

CapriSun
Coffee
Diet Blackberry Iced FruiTea
Diet Peach Iced FruiTea
Mandarin Peach Iced FruiTea
Orange Juice
Passion Fruit Iced FruiTea
SoBe Energy
Sweet Tea
Tropicana Fruit Punch
Tropicana Light Lemonade

Arby's Notes: Gluten-free items such as the Potato Cakes and Homestyle Fries may share a fryer with a variety of gluten-containing items, so cross-contamination may occur. Arby's and their regional vendors may vary menu items without prior notice, due to recipe changes, preparation techniques, or the season. Check the website for the most recent and accurate information. Arby's is not responsible for the use of this list, and menu items vary by location.

Triumph Notes: This list was marked November 2009. Contact Arby's directly for the latest list.

Au Bon Pain   ¢**BLD**
(800) 825-5227
Café
Confirmed: 4/1/2010

Soups
Black Bean
Curried Rice & Lentil
French Moroccan Tomato Lentil
Garden Vegetable
Old Fashioned Tomato Rice
Portuguese Kale
Potato Cheese
Southwest Tortilla
Vegetarian Chili
Vegetarian Lentil

Baja Fresh Mexican Grill   ¢**LD**
(562) 391-2400
Mexican
Confirmed: 4/1/2010

"Bare Style" Burritos (All)
Baja Ensalada (Carnitas, Chicken, Grilled Shrimp or Mahi Mahi, Grilled Vegetables, Rice & Both Varieties of Beans, Steak)
Baja Tacos —*request corn tortillas*
Dressings (All)
Salsas (All)

Baja Fresh Mexican Grill Notes:
Information is based on standard formulations as reported by manufacturers. There is no dedicated gluten-free fryer. Ingredient variations may occur because of recipe revisions, product assembly, ingredient substitutions, or suppliers. Baja Fresh is not responsible for an individual's reaction to any food product, and encourages diners to consult a medical professional with questions about safe dining.

Triumph Notes: This list was marked January 15, 2009. Baja Fresh confirmed that their "wheat-gluten-free" menu was free of wheat, rye, barley, and oats.

Baskin-Robbins   ¢**S**
(800) 859-5339
Ice Cream
Confirmed: 5/4/2010

Triumph Notes: No gluten-free list is available, but a chart specifying items containing wheat only is available online. Contact Baskin-Robbins directly for a copy of their wheat-free list.

BD's Mongolian Grill $$**LD**
Asian Stir-Fry
Confirmed: 4/5/2010

Sauces
Chili Garlic
Lemon
Mongo Marinara
Mustard
Spicy Buffalo
Sweet & Sour

BD's Mongolian Grill Notes: Kitchens are not gluten-free. The list provided is based on information from BD's suppliers. Variations may occur due to sampling, manufacturing, regional ingredient differences, the season, preparation, and ingredient substitutions. Cross-contamination may occur on the buffet. Products listed are produced in a facility that handles allergens. Check the website for updated information.

Triumph Notes: This list was marked "Modified 4/10."

Bertucci's　　✪ $LD
(800) 290-0280
Italian
Confirmed: 4/7/2010

Appetizers
Antipasto Misto
Mussels Caruso —*no grilled crostini*
Shrimp Scampi Appetizer —*no grilled crostini*

Soups
Sausage Soup

Salads
Caesar Salad —*no garlic croutons*
Grilled Chicken Chopped Salad
Insalata
Salad Giardino with Grilled Chicken
Salad Vivaldi con Pollo & Bello
Tomato & Mozzarella Caprese Salad
Venetian Spinach Salad with Grilled Chicken

Entrées
Balsamic Chicken

Eggplant Parma with String Beans
Filet Mignon with Chianti Sauce
Grilled Salmon Fillet
Grilled Steak & Chicken Combo
Pollo Sanremo with Half Insalata
Salmon Florentine

Side Dishes
Broccoli Romana
Fresh Asparagus
Red Skin Mashed Potatoes
Roasted Tuscan Vegetables
Spinach & Artichokes
String Beans

Desserts
Bomba
Chocolate Budino

Bertucci's Notes: Upon arrival, alert a manager to your dietary needs. Bertucci's assembled this menu with help from the Gluten Intolerance Group. Neither organization is responsible for its use. Individual restaurant managers and staff members are not trained on all aspects of Celiac Disease, and cannot provide advice on this issue. All questions should be directed to the corporate office. Individuals should consider this menu as it pertains to their own dietary needs.

Triumph Notes: This list was marked 11/09.

Biaggi's Ristorante Italiano　✪★ $LD
(309) 664-2148
Italian
Confirmed: 5/4/2010

Appetizers
Carpaccio —*no flatbread grissini*
Mussels in Tomato-Garlic Broth —*no grilled baguette crouton*
Tomato Mozzarella Caprese

Salads
Caesar Salad —*no croutons*

Chopped Chicken Salad —*no gorgonzola cheese*
House Salad
Messina Salad
Seared Salmon Salad
Spinach Salad —*no gorgonzola cheese*
Venetian Chicken Salad —*no gorgonzola cheese*

Entrées
Chicken Piemontese
Filet Mignon
Grilled Chicken Parmesan
Grilled Chicken Pietro
Grilled Pork Chops —*no parmesan-gorgonzola butter*
N.Y. Strip
Salmon & Shrimp Milanese
Seared Sea Bass

Pasta —*request gluten-free pasta*
Capellini Di Mare
Farfalle Alfredo
Linguini And Clams
Rigatoni Alla Toscana
Spaghetti Marinara

Pizza —*request gluten-free dough*
Chicken Piccante
Margherita Pizza
Mediterranean Pizza
Pepperoni Pizza
Sausage Pizza

Gluten-Free Sauces
Alfredo
Bolognese
Espresso Sauce
Italian Salsa
Mac & Cheese Sauce
Marsala
Pesto
Roasted Red Pepper Cream
Rum Caramel
Scallion Cream
Sun-Dried Tomato Cream
Tomato Sauce

Biaggi's Ristorante Italiano Notes: Note gluten-free when making reservations, and inform the server that your meal must be free of wheat, rye, barley, and oats. Biaggi's is not responsible for the use of this menu, or resulting damages or liability. Guests should review this information as it pertains to their individual needs.

Triumph Notes: This menu was marked 10.09.

Black Angus Steakhouse $$$ LD
(800) 382-3852
Steakhouse
Confirmed: 4/5/2010

Entrées
Steaks —*no seasoning*

Sides
Vegetables —*no seasoning*

Black Angus Steakhouse Notes: Upon arrival, alert the server to your dietary needs, and ask the server to notify the chefs and the managers. It is best to call ahead so the restaurant can prepare.

Black-eyed Pea   ¢ LD
(877) 584-3237
Southern
Confirmed: 4/7/2010

Salads
Classic Caesar Salad —*no dressing*
Signature House Salad —*request grilled chicken instead of fried, request red wine vinegar and oil dressing.*

From the Grill
Charbroiled Chopped Steak —*no seasoned rice, no gravy*
Grilled Chicken Breasts —*no seasoned rice*
Ranch Style Pork Chops
Top Sirloin Steak —*no onion rings*

Home Style Favorites

Roasted Turkey Breast Dinner —*no cornbread dressing, no turkey gravy*
Slow-Roasted Half Chicken

Seafood

Baked Cod —*no seasoned rice*
Grilled Atlantic Salmon —*no seasoned rice*
Grilled Cajun Catfish —*no seasoned rice*

Vegetable Garden

Baked Potato
Black-eyed Peas
Spinach
Steamed Broccoli
Sweet Kernel Corn
Tender Green Beans

Triumph Notes: This list was marked 4/8/2010.

Bob Evans Farms　　　　　ⒸBLD

(800) 939-2338
American
Confirmed: 4/14/2010

Bob Evans Farms Notes: Bob Evans does not publish a gluten-free list because ingredient and menu items may change.

Triumph Notes: Contact Bob Evans Farms directly for ingredient information.

Boloco　　　　　　　　　ⒸBLD

Mexican
Confirmed: 4/12/2010

Salads

Greek Salad

Breakfast —*request that it be served in a bowl*

Bacon and Egg
Egg and Cheese
Huevos Chorizo
Huevos Rancheros
Truck Stop

Burritos (Chicken, Steak, Tofu) —*request that it be served in a bowl*

The Buffalo
The Cajun
The Classic Burrito
The Summer Burrito

Smoothies

Berry Blitz
Cape Codder
Cracy
Jimmy Carter
Mango Passion
Milk Shake
Strawbana
Triathlete
Whey Out

Triumph Notes: This list is entitled the "Allergy Recommendations" list. The restaurant reports that they are "on the verge" of introducing a gluten-free dessert and a gluten-free tortilla.

Bonefish Grill　　　　　　✪$$LD

(866) 880-2226
Seafood
Confirmed: 4/9/2010

Starters & Sharing

Mussels Josephine
Saucy Shrimp

Grilled Fish*

Ahi Tuna
Atlantic Salmon
Chilean Sea Bass
Cold Water Lobster Tails
Gulf Grouper
Longfin Tilapia
Sea Scallops & Shrimp
Snake River Rainbow Trout

Grilled Specialties*

Filet Mignon
Lily's Chicken
Sirloin Steak

Greens
Bonefish Caesar —*no croutons*
Bonefish House
Chilled Asparagus
Florida Cobb Salad
Grilled Salmon and Asparagus Salad

Vegetables & Sides
French Green Beans
Garlic Whipped Potatoes
Herbed Jasmine Rice
Steamed Broccoli
Steamed Vegetable Medley

Signature Sauces
Chimichurri —*no Aji Panca rub*
Lemon Butter
Mango Salsa

Desserts
Crème Brulee
Macadamia Nut Brownie

Martinis & Cocktails
Black Cherry Guava Mojito
Bonefish Martini
Chocolate Martini
Classic Vodka Martini
Cosmopolitan
Espresso Martini
Hpnotiq Breeze Martini
Lemon Drop Martini
Lemongrass Martini
Ocean Trust Mango Martini
Perfect Patron Margarita
Pomegranate Martini
Raspberry Martini
Sour Apple Martini

Wines
Wines (All)

Bonefish Grill Notes: *With the exception of the zucchini and tomatoes, the seasonal vegetable garnish with entrees is gluten-free. Upon arrival, alert the server to your dietary needs. A registered dietitian at the Gluten Intolerance Group assembled this information, and it has not been verified by Bonefish Grill. Neither organization is responsible for its use or resulting damages or liability. Individuals should consider this menu as it pertains to their dietary needs.

Triumph Notes: This menu was marked 10/2008.

Boston Market   ¢ LD
(800) 365-7000
American
Confirmed: 4/5/2010

Salads —no dressing
Market Chopped Salad with Chicken
Market Chopped Salad

Entrées
Roasted Turkey Breast
Rotisserie Chicken

Sides
Butternut Squash (Regional)
Cinnamon Apples
Creamed Spinach
Fresh Fruit Salad
Fresh Steamed Vegetables
Garlic Dill New Potatoes
Green Beans
Mashed Potatoes
Sweet Corn

Sauces
Poultry Gravy

Boston Market Notes: Cross-contamination may occur. This list is based on information from manufacturers, and may change, so check back for the most recent and accurate information.

Bubba Gump Shrimp Co.   ✪ $$ LD
(949) 366-6260
Seafood
Confirmed: 4/20/2010

Appetizers
Old Fashioned Deviled Eggs
Traditional Shrimp Cocktail

Salads
Pear & Berry Salad
Tossed Chicken Cobb

Forrest's Favorites
Accidental Fish & Shrimp
Fresh Amberjack with Lobster Butter Sauce
Fresh Cajun Catfish
Fresh Tilapia with Mango Pineapple Salsa
Salmon & Veggie Skillet
Shrimp & Veggie Skewers

Sides
Shrimp skewer
Steamed Broccoli

Kids
Kid's Grilled Chicken

Desserts
Jenny's Mini's

Bubba Gump Shrimp Co. Notes:
Kitchens are not gluten-free, so cross-contamination may occur. Bubba Gump does not guarantee that any food items are gluten-free, as human error is possible and changes may occur with formulations, ingredients, brands, or suppliers. Menu ingredients have been confirmed gluten-free by the Gluten Detectives. Neither they nor Bubba Gump are liable for the food served.

Triumph Notes:
The gluten-free menu varies by location. This menu is provided for illustrative purposes only. This menu was marked 12/09.

Buca di Beppo   ✪ $LD
(612) 225-3400
Italian
Confirmed: 4/5/2010

Insalate
Apple Gorgonzola Salad
Chopped Antipasto Salad
Mixed Green Salad
Mozzarella Caprese

Entrées —*request that dishes not be dusted with flour*
Chicken Cacciatore
Chicken Limone
Chicken Marsala
Salmon Limone
Saltimbocca

Sides
Garlic Mashed Potatoes
Green Beans —*request that the dish be prepared separately*
Italian Broccoli Romano —*request that the dish be prepared separately*
Sausage & Peppers

Buca di Beppo Notes:
Kitchens are not gluten-free, so cross-contamination may occur. Buca di Beppo does not guarantee that any food is gluten-free. Alert a manager to your dietary needs before ordering.

Triumph Notes:
This menu was marked 2010.

Buffalo Wild Wings   ¢LD
American
Confirmed: 4/3/2010

Sides
Celery
Coleslaw

Dressings & Sauces
BBQ Ranch Dressing
Bleu Cheese Dressing
Caesar Dressing
Marinara Sauce
Queso Cheese Sauce
Ranch Dressing
Salsa
SW Ranch Dressing

Sauces
Blazin Wing Sauce
Caribbean Jerk Wing Sauce
Honey BBQ Wing Sauce
Honey Mustard Dipping Sauce

Hot BBQ Wing Sauce
Hot Wing Sauce
Mango Habanero Wing Sauce
Medium Wing Sauce
Mild Wing Sauce
Parmesan Garlic Wing Sauce
Spicy Garlic Wing Sauce
SW Chipotle
Sweet BBQ Wing Sauce
Wild Wing Sauce

Desserts
Ice Cream with Chocolate Sauce

Tenders
Naked Tenders with Seasoning

Wild Child(ren)
Kid's Ice Cream with Chocolate Sauce
Kid's Meal Naked Tenders

Buffalo Wild Wings Notes: Cross-contamination may occur, and Buffalo Wild Wings recommends that customers review preparation processes to ensure that food will meet their dietary needs. There are no dedicated gluten-free fryers. Allergen information is received from manufacturers.

Triumph Notes: Ingredient information was provided with the gluten-free list; contact the restaurant directly for the ingredient list.

Bugaboo Creek Steak House ✪ $$
LD

(800) 616-4664
Steakhouse
Confirmed: 4/2/2010

The Creek's Salads *—no croutons, request that salads are prepared in a separate bowl*
Alpine Chicken Salad
Bleu Mountain Steak Salad *—no onion strings, request un-marinated steak only*
Chicken Caesar Salad

Salad Dressings
Balsamic Vinaigrette
Blue Cheese Dressing
Caesar
Lite Olive Oil Vinaigrette
Parmesan Peppercorn
Thousand Island

Bugaboo Steaks
Black Magic Steak
Kain's Cast Iron Skillet Steak
Kansas City Bone-in NY Strip Steak
Lodge Center Cut Filet
Mountain Man Strip
Prime Rib *—no au jus sauce*
Timber Creek T-Bone Steak

Fish from the Grill
Daily Fresh Fish Fillet *—no rice*
Grilled Rainbow Trout

Mountain Outfitters' Specials
Campfire Cheesesteak *—no bun, no french fries*
Moosebreath Burger *—no bun, no french fries*
Roasted Half Chicken
Smoked Baby Back Ribs *—no french fries*

Sides
Baked Beans
Charlie's Smashed Potatoes
Fresh Steamed Vegetables
Grilled Onions
Mountain Loaded Baked Potato *—real bacon only*
Sautéed Mushrooms

Beverages
Glacier Freeze Smoothies
Moose Juices (All)
Rocky Mountain Mudslide

Bugaboo Creek Steak House Notes:
Kitchens are not gluten-free, so request that your meal is prepared in clean containers and on clean surfaces. Bugaboo Creek assembled this GF menu with help from the Gluten Intolerance Group.

Triumph Notes: This menu was marked updated April 15, 2009.

Burger King   ¢BLD
(305) 378-3535
American
Confirmed: 4/22/2010

Meats, Eggs, and Sides
Bacon Slice
Burger Shots Patty
Egg Omelet
Ham Slice
Hamburger Patty
Steakhouse XT Patty
Tendergrill Chicken Breast Filet
Whopper JR. Patty
Whopper Patty

Condiments
Breakfast Syrup
Grape Jam
Honey
Ketchup
Mayonnaise
Mustard
Sliced Pickles
Strawberry Jam

Sauces
A1 Thick and Hearty Steaksauce
BBQ Dipping Sauce
Buffalo Dipping Sauce
Caramel Sauce
Chocolate Fudge Sauce
French Fry Sauce
Honey Mustard Dipping Sauce
KEN'S (Honey Mustard, Light Italian, Ranch)
Marinara Sauce
Ranch Dipping Sauce
Smoky Cheese Sauce
Stacker Sauce
Sweet and Sour Dipping Sauce
Sweet Baby Ray's Hot 'n Spicy BBQ Sauce
Tartar Sauce
Vanilla Icing
Zesty Onion Ring Sauce

Desserts
Shakes (Chocolate, Strawberry, Vanilla)
Soft Serve in a Cup

Beverages
BK JOE Coffees

Cheeses
Processed American Cheese
Processed Cheddar (Sharp)
Processed Pepper Jack Cheese
Processed Swiss Cheese
Three Cheese Blend

Produce
BK Fresh Apple Fries
Carrots
Lettuce
Salad Mix
Slice Onions
Sliced Tomato

Burger King Notes: Fried items that are gluten-free may be fried in oil shared with gluten-containing items. Variations in gluten content may occur due to preparation, handling, suppliers, and formulations. People with "severe gluten intolerance" should not use this list. This information is based on ingredient profiles supplied by vendors. Burger King may change or update this list without prior notice, so take steps to obtain the most recent information before ordering a meal. No individual related to the Burger King Corporation is liable for any individual's reaction to food. Seek advice from a health care professional with specific questions about the gluten-free diet.

Triumph Notes: This list was marked January 2010.

California Pizza Kitchen $LD
Pizza
Confirmed: 4/2/2010

Dijon Balsamic Vinaigrette

Field Greens Salad with Gorgonzola —*no croutons*
Grilled Vegetable Salad —*no croutons*
House Salad —*no croutons*
Steamed Vegetables

California Pizza Kitchen Notes: Kitchens are not gluten-free. Cross-contamination may occur. Consult the server with specific questions.

Cantina Laredo   ✪ $$ LD
(800) 275-1337
Mexican
Confirmed: 4/5/2010

Aperitivos, Sopas y Ensaladas
Ceviche
Chicken Fajita Salad
Chili Con Queso
Chips and Red Salsa
Top Shelf Guacamole
Tortilla Soup

Entrées
Brisket Tacos
Camaron Poblano Asada
Camarones
Fajitas (Beef, Chicken) —*request corn tortillas*
Soft Tacos (Beef, Chicken) —*request corn tortillas*
Tacos Cascabel

Sides
Black Beans
Pinto Beans
Rice

Desserts
Flan

Cantina Laredo Notes: The kitchen also prepares gluten-containing items. Cantina Laredo assumes no responsibility for the use of this list, titled "Menu Options for Gluten Sensitive Guests." Consider this information in light of your individual needs.

Triumph Notes: This list was marked 8.09.

Capital Grille, The $$$$ LD
Steakhouse
Confirmed: 4/7/2010

Appetizers
Cold Shellfish Platter —*no mignonette sauce*
Oysters on the Half Shell —*no mignonette sauce*
Shrimp Cocktail
Wagyu Capaccio

Salad —*no cheese, request oil and lemon on the side instead of dressing*
Caesar Salad —*no croutons*
Garden Salad
Spinach Salad
Wedge Salad

Entrées
Fresh Lobster
Fresh Seared Salmon Fillet —*no citrus glaze*
Fresh Swordfish with Lemon Shallot Relish
Lamb Chops —*no cherry mostarda*
Roasted Chicken —*request with salt and pepper only*
Sesame Seared Tuna —*no ginger vinegar, no white soy*
Steak (All) —*no sauce*
Veal Chop —*no sauce*

Sides
Au Gratin Potatoes
Fresh Asparagus with Hollandaise
Roasted Crimini, Portabella, Shiitakes, and Oyster Mushrooms
Sam's Mashed Potatoes

Desserts
Crème Brulee
Flourless Chocolate Espresso Cake
Fresh Berries with Vanilla Ice Cream Sorbet

Capital Grille Notes: Upon arrival, alert a chef or manager to your dietary needs. Kitchens are not gluten-free, but all of these items are prepared with gluten-free recipes, as well as new tongs and pans. A gluten-free experience cannot be guaranteed.

Captain D's Seafood Kitchen   ¢LD
(615) 391-5461
Seafood
Confirmed: 4/5/2010

Baked Potato
Broccoli
Catfish
Cocktail Sauce
Corn on the Cob
Dressing (Blue Cheese, Honey Mustard, Ranch, Thousand Island)
Green Beans
Mayonnaise
Premium Shrimp
Roasted Red Potatoes
Seasoned Rice
Seasoned Tilapia
Shrimp Scampi
Shrimp Skewers
Side Salad
Sliced Cheese
Sweet Chili Sauce
Tartar Sauce
Wild Alaskan Salmon Salad
Wild Alaskan Salmon

Captain D's Seafood Kitchen Notes:
The kitchens are not gluten-free, so cross-contamination may occur. Menu items and ingredients may vary at franchised locations.

Carino's Italian   ✪$LD
(512) 263-0800
Italian
Confirmed: 4/5/2010

Caesar Salad —*no croutons*
Chicken Marsala —*no flour on chicken, request sautéed green beans, garlic sautéed spinach, or potatoes instead of pasta*
Chicken Scaloppini —*no flour on chicken, request sautéed green beans, garlic sautéed spinach, or potatoes instead of pasta*
Grilled Citrus Balsamic Salmon —*request sautéed green beans, garlic sautéed spinach, or potatoes instead of pasta*
House Salad —*no croutons, request house chianti vinaigrette, creamy gorgonzola, ranch, roasted garlic ranch, signature caesar, or sun-dried tomato balsamic vinaigrette*
Italian Chili
Italian Pot Roast —*request potatoes*
Italian Wedge
Jalapeno Garlic Tilapia —*no flour on tilapia, request sautéed green beans, garlic sautéed spinach, or potatoes instead of pasta*
Kid's Grilled Chicken —*request sautéed green beans or potatoes instead of pasta*
Lemon Rosemary Chicken —*request garlic sautéed spinach, potatoes, green beans, or vegetables instead of pasta*
Roasted Garlic Potato Soup —*no croutons*
Shrimp Scampi with Garlic Toast —*no garlic toast*
Vanilla Ice Cream

Carino's Italian Notes: Alert the server to your dietary needs, and specify the modifications necessary to make a gluten-free meal. Ask to speak with a manager if any concerns arise. Carino's designed this menu with help from the Gluten Intolerance Group. Neither organization is responsible for its use or information therein. Menu options may vary by location.

Carl's Jr.   ¢BLD
(877) 799-7827
American
Confirmed: 4/7/2010

Triumph Notes: Carl's Jr. did not provide a gluten-free list; however, ingredient information is available by contacting them directly.

Carrabba's Italian Grill   ✪★ $LD
(813) 288-8286
Italian
Confirmed: 4/24/2010

Antipasti
Cozze in Bianco
Shrimp Scampi —*no garlic toast*

Zuppe & Insalate —*for all salads, request no croutons and a fresh mixing bowl*
House Salads (House, Italian, Caesar, Mediterranean)
Insalata Carrabba Caesar —*request that the chicken/shrimp be made without grill baste*
Insalata Fiorucci
Insalata Johnny Rocco —*request that the seafood be made without grill baste*
Insalate Carrabba —*request that the chicken be made without grill baste*
Mama Mandola's Sicilian Chicken Soup — *no pasta*

Wood-Burning Grill* —*no grill baste; if ordering soup, request no pasta; if ordering salad, request no croutons and a fresh mixing bowl*
Chicken Bryan
Chicken Gratella
Chicken Marsala
Filet Fiorentina
Grilled Salmon (Gluten-Free Fish Sauces: Bellimbusto, Citriolini, Denisco, Ferre, Lemon Butter, Livornese, Mostarda, Nino, Nocciola, Positano, Roasted Tomato, Salsa di Pepperoni, Salsa Verde, Sundried Tomato Pesto, Tomato Basil, Tri-Bell Pepper)
Pollo Rosa Maria
Sirloin Marsala

Dolci
John Cole

Beverages
Wines (All)

Birra
Redbridge

Specialty Drinks
Carrabba-Rita
Carrabba's Chocolate Martini
Citrotini
Cosmopolitan
Pomegranate Martini

Carrabba's Italian Grill Notes: * The grill is not dedicated gluten-free. Carrabba's has assembled this menu with help from the Gluten Intolerance Group. Neither organization is responsible for its use or consequential damages. Carrabba's has not independently verified the information provided by GIG. Staff is not trained on all aspects of Celiac Disease or the gluten-free diet. Please direct questions and requests to GIG or Carrabba's corporate office. Customers should consider this information as it pertains to their own dietary needs.

Champps Americana $LD
(800) 229-2118
American
Confirmed: 4/12/2010

Champps Burger —*no bun, no cheese, request one of the following sides: steamed vegetables, fresh fruit, broccoli, grilled veggies, jasmine rice*
Chicken Salad —*no bread*
Cobb Salad —*no blue cheese, no cheddar cheese, request Greek dressing*
Fajitas —*no tort set, no cheddar cheese*
Garden Salad —*no croutons, no cheese*
Greek Chicken Salad —*no feta cheese*
Grilled Proteins (Chicken, Sirloin Steak, Un-Marinated Salmon) —*request one of the following sides: steamed vegetables, fresh fruit, broccoli, grilled veggies, jasmine rice*

Sauces and Dressing
Corn and Black Bean Salsa
Greek Dressing

Marinara Sauce
Pico de Gallo
White Queso

Kid's Menu
Grilled Chicken Tenders —*request one
of the following sides: fruit, steamed
vegetables (not steamed in pasta water)*
Hamburger or Cheeseburger —*no bun,
request one of the following sides: fruit,
steamed vegetables (not steamed in pasta
water)*

Champps Americana Notes: Kitchens are
not gluten-free, so cross-contamination
may occur. Upon arrival, alert a manager to
your dietary needs.

Triumph Notes: This list was marked April
2010.

Charley's Grilled Subs   ¢LD
(800) 437-8325
Sandwich Shop
Confirmed: 4/5/2010

Triumph Notes: Charley's does not have a
gluten-free list, but they do have an allergy
list that includes wheat. Contact Charley's
directly for the list.

Charlie Brown's Steakhouse   ✪$$$
LD
(800) 616-4664
Steakhouse
Confirmed: 5/4/2010

Appetizers
Grilled Shrimp —*no bread, no sauce, no
frizzled onions*

Soups
French Onion Soup —*no bread*

Salads
Caesar Salad —*no croutons*
Chicken Caesar —*no croutons*

Steakhouse Wedge Salad —*no toppings, no
frizzled onions*

Entrees
Chopped Steak —*no toppings, no frizzled
onions*
Filet Mignon —*no toppings, no frizzled
onions*
NY Strip —*no toppings, no frizzled onions*
Porterhouse —*no toppings, no frizzled
onions*
Prime Rib —*no toppings, no frizzled onions*
Top Sirloin —*no toppings, no frizzled onions*
BBQ Ribs
Flounder —*request simply broiled*
Rack of Lamb —*no crust, no garlic aioli*
Roast Chicken —*no sauce*
Salmon —*no sauce, request un-marinated*
Tilapia —*no lemon butter sauce*
Twin Tails

Sandwiches
Burgers (All) —*no bread*
Chicken Salad —*no bread*
Hibachi Chicken Sandwich —*no bread*

Sides
Baked Potato
Coleslaw
Fresh Steamed Asparagus
Fresh Steamed Broccoli
Garlic Mashed Potatoes
Roasted Vegetable Medley
Sauteed Onions
Seasoned Rice
Sherried Button Mushrooms
Sweet Potato Mashed

Sauces & Condiments
Au Jus
Barbecue Sauce
Buffalo Wing Sauce
Cocktail Sauce
Guacamole
Honey Mustard Sauce
Ketchup
Marinara Sauce
Mayonnaise
Melted Butter

Mustard
Orange Horseradish Sauce
Salad Dressings (All EXCEPT Asian or
    Ranch)
Salsa
Sour Cream Horseradish Sauce
Sour Cream
Steak Sauce, A-1
Tomato Basil Bruschetta

Desserts
Ice Cream
Sugar Free Marble Cheesecake

Charlie Brown's Steakhouse Notes:
*Fried items, any sauces, side dishes,
starches or condiments not on this list
should be assumed to contain gluten. This
list has been assembled by an independent
registered dietician and is meant as a guide
only. Charlie Brown's is not responsible for
content provided by said dietician.

Cheddar's Casual Café   ¢LD
American
Confirmed: 4/8/2010

Entrées
Burgers (All EXCEPT Smokehouse
    Burger) —*no bun*
Grilled Catfish
Grilled Salmon
Lemon Pepper Chicken
Ribs —*no sauce*
Steak —*no onion straws*
Tilapia

Sides
Sides (All EXCEPT Broccoli Casserole)

Cheddar's Casual Café Notes:
Kitchens are not gluten-free and cross-
contamination may occur.

Cheeseburger in Paradise   ✪$LD
(813) 282-1225
American
Confirmed: 4/7/2010

Appetizers
Mini-Cheeseburgers —*no buns*

Soups & Salads
Calypso Chicken Salad
Costa Rican Steak Salad —*no wontons*
Son of a Sailor Salad —*no wontons*

Salad Dressings
Balsamic Vinaigrette, Buffalo Blue Cheese,
    Citrus Vinaigrette, Coconut Curry,
    Honey Mustard, Spicy Ranch

Burgers
Bacon Cheddar Burger —*no bun*
Baja Burger —*no bun*
BBQ Cheddar Burger —*no bun, no fried
    onion strings*
Cheeseburger in Paradise Burger —*no bun*
Mini-Cheeseburgers —*no bun*
Mushroom Swiss Burger —*no bun*
Veggie Burger —*no bun*

Island Specialties
BBQ Ribs
Parrot Beach Salmon —*no island rice, no
    teriyaki broccoli, no sauce, request that it
    be grilled or blackened*
St. Barts Citrus Chicken —*no island rice, no
    teriyaki broccoli*

Sandwiches
Bayside BBQ Chicken Sandwich —*no bun,
    no sweet potato chips*
Caribbean Chicken Sandwich —*no bun, no
    sweet potato chips*
Mahi Mahi Sandwich —*no bread, no sweet
    potato chips*

Sides
Coleslaw
French Fried Potatoes
Vegetable of the Day —*no roasted garlic
    butter*

Kids' Menu
Grilled Chicken Breast
Lil' Pirates Treat —*no Oreo cookie crumbles*
Mini-Cheeseburgers —*no bun*

Sensuous Treat
Copa Banana —*no nilla wafers*

Non-Alcoholic Beverages
Blackberry Sangria
Blueberry Mojito
Bottled Water
Cheeseburger in Paradise Cocktail
Flavored Iced Tea (Blueberry, Mango,
    Peach, Pomegranate, Raspberry)
Freshly Brewed Coffee
Freshly Brewed Iced Tea
Island Lemonade
Island Paradise
Jamaican Root Beer Float
Mouth-Watering Milkshakes
Red Bull
Silver Sunset
Strawberry Lemonade
Surfside Sodas
Tranquil Breeze

Cheeseburger in Paradise Notes: This
information was prepared by a registered
dietician with the Gluten Intolerance
Group (GIG) and has not been verified
by Cheeseburger in Paradise. Neither
organization is responsible for its use
or resulting damages. The management
teams and service staff are not trained on
the intricacies of Celiac Disease or gluten
intolerance and all questions should be
directed to GIG or the Cheeseburger
in Paradise corporate office. Consider
this information as it pertains to your
individual needs.

Chick-fil-A   ¢BLD
(404) 765-8000
American
Confirmed: 4/8/2010

Breakfast
American Cheese
Bacon
Egg
Hashbrowns —*only if cooked in a gluten-
    free fryer*

Sausage

Entrées
Chick-fil-A Chargrilled Chicken & Fruit
    Salad
Chick-fil-A Chargrilled Chicken Filet —*no
    bun*
Chick-fil-A Chargrilled Chicken Garden
    Salad
Tortilla Strips

Side Items
Carrot & Raisin Salad
Chick-fil-A Waffle Potato Fries —*only if
    cooked in a gluten-free fryer*
Cole Slaw
Fruit Cup
Side Salad

Condiments
Jelly (Apple, Grape, Mixed Fruit)
Ketchup
Light Mayonnaise
Mayonnaise
Mustard

Dipping Sauces and Dressings
Barbecue Sauce
Blue Cheese Dressing
Buttermilk Ranch Dressing
Buttermilk Ranch Sauce
Caesar Dressing
Chick-fil-A Buffalo Sauce
Chick-fil-A Sauce
Fat Free Dijon Honey Mustard Dressing
Honey Mustard Sauce
Honey Roasted BBQ Sauce
Light Italian Dressing
Polynesian Sauce
Reduced Fat Berry Balsamic Vinaigrette
    Dressing
Spicy Dressing
Thousand Island Dressing

Desserts
Blueberry Topping
Chocolate Syrup
Ice Dream Cup

Beverages
All

Chick-fil-A Notes: Customers should read ingredient lists with their physicians (available by contacting them directly). This information was assembled using information from suppliers.

Triumph Notes: This list was marked May 2008.

Chili's $LD

(800) 983-4637
Mexican
Confirmed: 4/6/2010

Soups
Chicken & Green Chile
Loaded Baked Potato
Sweet Corn

A Fresh Take On Salads —*no dressing, no croutons, no tortilla strips*
BBQ Smoked Chicken Salad
Caribbean Salad (Chicken Option Only) — *request honey lime dressing*
Chicken Caesar Salad
House Salad

Salad Dressings
Citrus Balsamic Vinaigrette
Honey Lime
Honey Mustard

Big Mouth Burgers —*no bun, no french fries, no O strings*
Bacon Burger
Ground Peppercorn Burger —*no bleu cheese dressing*
Mushroom-Swiss Burger
Oldtimer Burger

Flame-Grilled Greatness —*no condiments, no sides*
Classic Sirloin —*no garlic toast*
Flame Grilled Ribeye —*no garlic toast*
GG Salmon with Rice & Veggies
GG Sirloin with Veggies

Grilled Salmon with Garlic & Herbs with Rice & Veggies
Margarita Chicken with Rice & Black Beans —*no tortilla strips*
Monterey Chicken with Mashed Potatoes —*no gravy, no veggies*

New Tacos Wrapped in Flavor
Seasoned Ground Beef (Corn Tortillas Only) —*no cilantro sour cream*

Pepper Pals —*no sides, no bun*
Grilled Chicken Platter
Grilled Chicken Sandwich
Little Mouth Cheeseburger

Slow Smoke In-House Ribs
Original —*no sides*

Sides
Black Beans
Corn on the Cob
Fresh Vegetables
Loaded Mashed Potatoes
Mandarin Oranges
Mashed Potatoes —*no gravy*
Rice

Sauces & Extras
Avocado Slices
Bacon
Guacamole
Mixed Cheese
Original BBQ Sauce
Pico de Gallo
Salsa
Sauteed Mushrooms

Stupendously Sweet Endings
Chocolate Shake

Beverages
Electric Blue Blast
Rockin' Tropical Punch
Strawberry Lemonade
Tea (Blackberry, Mango)
Wine (Red, White)

Chili's Notes: This list is based on information provided by suppliers. A gluten-free meal cannot be guaranteed, as kitchens are not gluten-free and cross-contamination may occur. In addition, recipes, vendors, and preparation may change, among other things. Alert a manager to your dietary needs before ordering. Menus vary slightly by location.

Triumph Notes: This menu was marked valid 2/23/2010 - 4/11/2010. Contact Chili's for the latest list.

Chipotle Mexican Grill   ¢LD
Mexican
Confirmed: 4/16/2010

Chipotle Mexican Grill Notes: Servers handle wheat tortillas, lettuce, and cheese with gloved hands rather than with serving utensils. This means that there is a greater risk of cross-contamination with the aforementioned items than with other items on the menu. Ask the server to change gloves before preparing gluten-free food items.

Triumph Notes: No gluten-free list was provided by Chipotle.

Chuck E. Cheese's $LD
(888) 778-7193
American
Confirmed: 4/6/2010

Triumph Notes: Chuck E. Cheese's does not maintain a gluten-free list. However, ingredient information is available by contacting them directly.

CiCi's Pizza   ¢LD
(972) 745-4200
Pizza
Confirmed: 4/6/2010

Cheese

Ham
Pepperoni
Pizza Sauce
Sausage
Vegetables

CiCi's Pizza Notes: Gluten-free customers can request "crustless pizza."

Claim Jumper   ✪$$LD
(949) 756-9001
American
Confirmed: 4/22/2010

Salads
Chicken Caesar Salad —*no bread, no croutons*
Citrus Chicken Salad —*no bread, no bleu cheese crumbles*

Entrées
Giant Stuffed Baker
Roasted Tri-Tip —*no bread, no herb gravy*
Rotisserie Chicken —*no bread*
Shrimp Skewers —*no basmati rice*

Aged Steaks & Lobster —*no bread*
Certified USDA Prime Top Sirloin
Filet Mignon & Lobster Tail
Filet Mignon
Lobster Tail Dinner
New York Steak
Porterhouse Steak
Prime Rib
Ribeye Steak

Claim Jumper Notes: Upon arrival, alert the server to your dietary needs. The items on this list must be modified to be gluten-free. Kitchens are not gluten-free, so cross-contamination may occur.

Triumph Notes: This menu was marked 2009.08.19

Coco's Restaurant & Bakery   ¢BLD
(877) 225-4160
American
Confirmed: 4/6/2010

Breakfast Entrées
Mushroom & Tomato Egg White Scramble
Tomato Basil Egg White Omelette
Turkey Sausage and Eggs

Breakfast Sides
Breakfast Meats (Bacon, Sausage Links,
  Turkey Sausage)
Breakfast Potatoes
Eggs
Fresh Seasonal Fruit
Hash Browns

Entrées
Angus Top Sirloin with Wild Mushrooms
Angus Top Sirloin
Bistro Salmon with Fresh Tomato Salsa
Chicken Bruschetta and Fresh Spinach
Cobb Salad —*no croutons*
Greek Feta Salad
Southwest Angus Sirloin
Southwest Chicken Salad
Sun-dried Tomato Chicken
Taste of Season Salad

Sides
Baked Potato
Dinner Vegetables
Green Garden Salad —*no croutons*
Mashed Potatoes

Coco's Restaurant & Bakery Notes:
Kitchens are not gluten-free and frying
oil is shared, so cross-contamination may
occur. Coco's does not guarantee that any
food is gluten-free.

Coffee Bean & Tea Leaf, The ¢S
(800) 832-5323
Coffee Shop
Confirmed: 4/13/2010

Beverages
Coffees (All)
Teas (All)

Powders
Chocolate
Hazelnut

No Sugar Added Chocolate
No Sugar Added Vanilla
Powders (All Others)
Vanilla

Coffee Bean & Tea Leaf Notes: Cross-
contamination may occur during drink
preparation. Request that preparation
equipment be cleaned prior to preparing
your order.

Cold Stone Creamery ¢S
(866) 452-4252
Ice Cream
Confirmed: 5/4/2010

Fruit
Apple Pie Filling
Bananas
Black Cherries
Blackberries
Blueberries
Cherry Pie Filling
Maraschino Cherries
Peach Pie Filling
Pineapple Chunks
Raisins
Raspberries
Strawberries

Grab and Go Ice Cream
Peanut Butter Cup Perfection

Ice Cream
Amaretto Ice Cream
Banana Ice Cream
Black Cherry Ice Cream
Butter Pecan Ice Cream
Candy Cane Ice Cream
Cheesecake Ice Cream
Chocolate Dipped Strawberry Ice Cream
Chocolate Ice Cream
Chocolate Peanut Butter Ice Cream
Cinnamon Ice Cream
Coconut Ice Cream
Coffee Ice Cream
Cotton Candy Ice Cream
Dark Chocolate Ice Cream
Dark Chocolate Peppermint Ice Cream

Egg Nog Ice Cream
French Toast Ice Cream
French Vanilla Ice Cream
Ghirardelli Chocolate Ice Cream
Irish Cream Ice Cream
Macadamia Nut Ice Cream
Mango Ice Cream
Marshmallow Ice Cream
Mint Ice Cream
Mocha Ice Cream
Orange Dreamsicle Ice Cream
Peanut Butter Ice Cream
Pecan Praline Ice Cream
Pistachio Ice Cream
Pumpkin Ice Cream
Raspberry Ice Cream
Sinless Sans Fat Sweet Cream
Strawberry Cheesecake Ice Cream
Strawberry Ice Cream
Sweet Cream Ice Cream
Vanilla Bean Ice Cream
White Chocolate Ice Cream

Mix-Ins
Almond Joy Candy
Butterfinger Candy Bar
Chocolate Chips
Chocolate Shavings
Coconut
Gumballs
Gummi Bears
Heath Candy Bar
M & Ms Candy
Marshmallows
Peanut Butter
Peanut M & Ms
Reese's Peanut Butter Cup
Reese's Pieces
Snickers Candy
Toasted Coconut
White Chocolate Chips
York Peppermint Patties

Nuts
Cashews
Macadamia Nuts
Peanuts
Pecan Pralines

Pecans
Pistachio Nuts
Roasted Almonds
Sliced Almonds
Walnuts

Smoothie Products
Lemon Ice
Lifestyle Smoothie Mix
Mango
Orange Juice
Supplement- Antioxidant/Immune
Supplement- Anti-Stress
Supplement- Energy
Supplement- Protein

Sorbet and Yogurt
Lemon Sorbet
Raspberry Sorbet
Strawberry Mango Banana Sorbet
Tart and Tangy Yogurt (Berry, Plain)
Watermelon Sorbet

Toppings
Butterscotch Fat Free
Caramel Fat Free
Caramel
Chocolate Sprinkles
Cinnamon
Fudge Fat Free
Fudge
Honey
Marshmallow Crème
Rainbow Sprinkles
Redi Wip Original
Whipped Topping

Cold Stone Creamery Notes: This
information is based on standard
product formulations. Trace amounts of
gluten may be present in products due
to manufacturing facilities, preparation
differences, substitutions, the season, and
suppliers.

Triumph Notes: This list was marked
01/04/10.

Così   ¢**BLD**
Sandwich & Soups
Confirmed: 4/2/2010

Breakfast
Cosi Break Bar
Fruit Salad
Omelet
Strawberry Parfait

Soups
Tomato Basil Aurora

Salads
Bombay Chicken Salad
Caesar Salad —*no croutons*
Chicken Caesar Salad —*no croutons*
Cobb Salad
Greek Salad
Mixed Green Salad
Our Lighter Side Bombay Chicken Salad
Our Lighter Side Cobb Salad
Our Lighter Side Signature Salad
Salad Bruschetta
Signature Salad
Wild Alaskan Salmon Salad

Desserts
Ice Cream Scoop (Double or Triple)
Ice Cream Sundae (Medium or Large)
Whipped Cream

Frozen Beverages
Arctic Latte
Arctic Mocha
Chocolate Covered Strawberry
Mixed Berry
Pineapple Mango
Strawberry Banana

Hot Beverages
Americano
Café Au Lait
Cappuccino
Chai Tea Latte
Coffee
Espresso con Panna
Espresso Macchiato
Espresso
Hot Chocolate
Hot Cider
Hot Tea
Latte
Mocha
Steamer

Iced Beverages
Iced Chai Tea Latte
Iced Coffee
Iced Latte
Iced Mocha

Miscellaneous Beverages
Orange Juice
Syrups (Caramel, Grenadine, Hazelnut,
    Mint, Oregeat (Almond), Raspberry,
    Sugar Free Vanilla, Vanilla)
Wine

Cracker Barrel Old Country Store $**BLD**
(800) 333-9566
American
Confirmed: 4/20/2010

Salads —*no croutons*
All EXCEPT fried chicken tender salad and
    chunky (homemade) chicken salad

Grill Items
Bacon
City Ham
Country Ham
Eggs
Grilled Catfish
Grilled Chicken Tenders
Grilled Pork Chops
Grilled Trout
Hamburger Steak
Pork Sausage
Ribeye Steak
Sirloin Steak
Turkey Sausage

Side Items
Baked Potato
Carrots
Cole Slaw

Corn
Fried Apples
Green Beans
Mashed Potatoes
Pinto Beans
Turnip Greens

**Cracker Barrel Old Country Store
Notes:** Many gluten containing items,
are prepared in the kitchen, so cross-
contamination may occur. Upon arrival,
alert a manager to your dietary needs,
so the manager can ensure that every
possible precaution is taken to avoid cross-
contamination.

Triumph Notes: Their gluten-free list does
not contain wheat, rye, or barley. There is,
however, no mention of oats.

Culver's ButterBurgers & Frozen Custard ¢LD
(608) 643-7980
American
Confirmed: 4/5/2010

Soups
Baja Chicken Enchilada
Mushroom Medley
Potato Au Gratin

Garden Fresh Salads
Chicken Cashew with Flame Roasted
   Chicken
Strawberry Fields Salad

Salad Dressing
Bleu Cheese Fancy Chunky
Caesar Dressing
French Reduced Calorie
French
Ranch Buttermilk Gourmet
Ranch Reduced Calorie

Sides
Cole Slaw
Green Beans

Condiments
BBQ Sauce
Honey Mustard
Horseradish Sauce
Mayonnaise
Shrimp Cocktail Sauce
Sweet & Sour Dipping Sauce
Tartar Sauce

Cones and Frozen Custard
Chocolate Dish
Chocolate Frozen Custard (Pint, Quart)
No Sugar Added Caramel Fudge Swirl
Vanilla Dish
Vanilla Frozen Custard (Pint, Quart)

Malts, Shakes, Floats
Culver's Root Beer Float
Vanilla Shake

Toppings
Almond
Cashew
Chocolate Flake
Culver's Hot Fudge
M&Ms Minis
Peanut Butter
Pecan Halves
Reese's Peanut Butter Cups
Snickers Candy Bar Pieces
Spanish Peanuts

Drinks
Chocolate Milk Low Fat
Culver's Root Beer
Milk (2%)
Mocha N'iced Coffee
Tropicana Fruit Punch
Tropicana Pink Lemonade
Vanilla N'iced Coffee

Concrete Mixers
Pumpkin Pecan Concrete Mixer
Vanilla Concrete Mixer

Seasonal Items
Pumpkin Spice Shake

Special Treats
Cooler
Lemon Ice Smoothie
Lemon Ice

Culver's ButterBurgers & Frozen Custard Notes: Restaurants are often busy and cross-contamination may occur. It is important to be aware of the ingredients for all menu items. Upon arrival, alert a manager to your dietary needs and ask to see ingredient listings. Variations may occur due to changes in preparation, ingredients, recipes, and the season. Direct questions about food sensitivities to a medical professional. No Culver's employee or franchisee assumes responsibility for food sensitivity.

Triumph Notes: Ingredient information is available by contacting Culver's directly.

Dairy Queen   ¢LD
(952) 830-0200
American
Confirmed: 4/6/2010

Arctic Rush Slush
Soft Serve (Chocolate, Vanilla)

Beverages
Moolattes (Caramel, Mocha, Vanilla) —*no whipped topping*

Blizzards
Banana Split Blizzard
Butterfinger Blizzard
Hawaiian Blizzard
Heath Blizzard
M&M Blizzard
Reese's Peanut Butter Cup Blizzard
Strawberry Blizzard
Tropical Blizzard

Novelty Items
Buster Bar —*must be in a sealed plastic wrap*
Dilly Bar —*must be in a sealed plastic wrap*
DQ Fudge Bar

DQ Vanilla Orange Bar
Starkiss Bar

Toppings
Butterscotch
Chocolate
Hot Fudge
Marshmallow
Strawberry

Dairy Queen Notes: Many Blizzard candies and toppings contain gluten. Alert a server upon arrival, and request that the staff clean the Blizzard machine before blending your Blizzard to reduce the risk of cross-contamination. Even if such precautions are taken, cross-contamination may still occur with Blizzards or other items. Some locations use non-standard soft serve mix. Neither is covered by this list.

Triumph Notes: Listed items are only those reported to be gluten-free by Dairy Queen's corporate office. There is a full allergen chart available on the Dairy Queen website that lists products containing the wheat allergen.

Dave & Buster's $$LD
(888) 300-1515
American
Confirmed: 4/20/2010

Soups
Beef Broth
Chicken Broth

Salad —*no dressing, no tortilla strips*
Grilled Steak Salad —*no frazzled onions*
Honey Mustard Spinach Salad
House Salad
Sweet Apple Pecan Salad (Chicken, Shrimp)

Salad Dressings
Oil & Vinegar

Buster's Burgers —*no fries, no bun*
Bar Burger
Buster's Cheeseburger
Dave's Double Cheeseburgers
Monterey Burger

Chicken & Seafood —*request sides from GF list only*
Baked or Grilled Salmon
Lacy's Chicken
Plain Grilled Chicken

Grilled Steaks —*no frazzled onions, request sides from GF list only*
Chargrilled NY Strip
Chargrilled Sirloin Steak
NY Strip
Sirloin Steak

Sides
Edamame
Mixed Vegetable Medley
Sauteed Green Beans

Sauces & Extras
Guacamole
Pico de Gallo
Salsa
Sour Cream

Kids
Grilled Chicken
Kid's Burger —*no fries, no bun*

Dave & Buster's Notes: Dave & Buster's does not guarantee that any food items are gluten-free. Cooking equipment and preparation areas are not gluten-free, so cross-contamination may occur. Gluten-free items may share fryer oil with items containing gluten, so avoid all fried foods and garnishes. This list was made with help from a Food Safety Manager and Nutritionist.

Del Frisco's Double Eagle Steak House $$$$ **LD**
(316) 264-8899
Steakhouse
Confirmed: 4/5/2010

Appetizers
Marinated Shrimp —*no sauce, no marinade*
Oysters on the Half Shell —*no sauce*
Shrimp Cocktail —*no sauce*
Shrimp Remoulade —*no sauce*
Stone Crab Claws —*no sauce*

Salads
All —*no dressing, request vinegar as dressing*

Seafood
Australian Lobster Tail
Chef's Seafood Selection —*no sauce, request that it be cooked without oil*
Halibut —*no sauce, request that it be cooked without oil*
Salmon —*no sauce, request that it be cooked without oil*

Steaks & Chops
All EXCEPT Osso Buco —*no sauces, no starch*

Sides
Asparagus —*no sauce*
Fresh Vegetables —*no oil, request that they be steamed*

Desserts
Fresh Berries —*no sauce*

Del Frisco's Double Eagle Steak House Notes: These items must be ordered with the specified modifications.

Del Taco   ¢ **LD**
(800) 852-7204
Tex-Mex
Confirmed: 4/2/2010

Cheddar Cheese
Corn Tortillas
Del Scorcho Sauce

Fries
Green Sauce
Hamburger Patties
Hamburger Spread
Mild Sauce
Nacho Cheese Sauce
Regular Yellow Taco Shells

Denny's $ BLD
(800) 733-6697
American
Confirmed: 5/4/2010

Entrée/Salads
2 Egg & More Breakfast w/ Hash Browns —
  no bread
Bacon Cheddar Burger Patty with
  Grapes —*no bun*
Bacon
Beef Patty
Eggs/Omelets
Grilled Tilapia —*no rice pilaf*
Side Garden Salad —*no croutons, no
  dressing*
Sliced/Shaved Ham
Steak
Ultimate Omelette with Hash Browns —*no
  bread*

Sides/Sauces
Applesauce
Baby Carrots (Raw)
Black-eyed Peas
Celery Sticks
Corn
Cottage Cheese (check label)
Fresh Fruit
Fried Corn Tortilla (Used in Nachos)*
Green Beans
Hashed Browns
High Div'n Veggies —*no breadsticks, no dip*
Jump-shot Jello
Lemon Butter Sauce
Mashed Potatoes/Cheese
Olives
Pico de Gallo
Pinto Beans
Red Grapes

Regular French Fries*
Salsa
Sliced Cucumbers
Tartar Sauce
Tomato Slices
Vanilla Yogurt

Beverages
Coffee
Flavored Coffees
Fusion Favorites
Grapefruit Juice
Hot Chocolate
Lemonade
Milk (All EXCEPT Buttermilk)
Orange Juice
Raspberry Tea
Tea & Tea Chillers
Tomato Juice

Miscellaneous
American Processed Cheese
Banana
Butter
Cheddar Cheese
Cherry Flavoring
Cream Cheese
Honey
Jelly (Grape, Mixed Fruit, Strawberry)
Lemon Wedges
Lime Wedges
Maraschino Cherries
Margarine (Liquid, Whipped)
Pancake/Waffle Syrup
Red Wine Vinegar
Reduced Cal. French Dressing
Strawberries
Swiss Processed Cheese

Denny's Notes: * Verify that dedicated
gluten-free fryers are used for french fries
and corn tortillas before ordering. Upon
arrival, alert the server to your dietary
needs and ask the server to provide labels
for you to inspect. Also ask the server/
manager about cross-contamination and
request a dedicated fryer, clean grill, etc.
as necessary. This list covers menu items
that do not have gluten in their ingredient

list based on information provided by product vendors. Ingredients, regional menu offerings, and vendors are subject to change without prior notice. Product labels are available for inspection on-site if needed.

Triumph Notes: This list was marked October 2009.

Donatos $LD
(614) 416-7700
Pizza
Confirmed: 4/5/2010

Appetizers
BBQ Chicken Wings
Chicken Wings (Hot, Mild)

Salad —*no croutons, no dressing*
Caesar Side
Chicken Harvest Entrée
Italian Chef Entrée
Italian Side
Tuscan Chicken Entrée

Salad Dressings
1000 Island
Apple Cider Vinaigrette
Blue Cheese
Buttermilk Ranch
Creamy Caesar
Fat-free Ranch
Honey Dijon Mustard
Honey French
House Italian
Lite Italian
Sundried Tomato Caesar

Basic Pizza Ingredients
Pepperoni
Shredded Provolone Cheese
Sweet Pizza Sauce
Thin Pizza Sauce
Traditional Pizza Sauce

No Dough Pizza
Chicken Spinach Mozzarella
Classic Trio

Founder's Favorite
Fresh Mozzarella Trio
Hawaiian
Margherita
Mariachi Beef
Mariachi Chicken
Pepperoni Zinger
Pepperoni
Serious Cheese
Serious Meat
Vegy
Works

Donatos Notes: "No Dough" pizzas are prepared on a bed of soy crisps. Variations in ingredients may occur due to season, supplier, and region.

Triumph Notes: Ingredient list is available by contacting them directly. Donatos reports that they are testing a gluten-free pizza to sell in the future.

Eat 'n Park   ✪★ ¢BLD
(412) 461-2000
American
Confirmed: 4/6/2010

A La Carte Breakfast Items
Bacon
Canadian Bacon
Fresh Fruit Cup
Ham
Home Fries
Maple Syrup
Sausage
Strawberries (in Season)

Breakfast —*request a "Celiac-friendly" bun*
Cheese Omelette —*no toast*
Eat'n Smart Smile —*no toast*
Eggs Benedict —*no english muffin*
Eggs Breakfast —*no toast*
Ham and Cheese Omelette —*no toast*
Meat Lover's Omelette —*no toast*
Original Breakfast Smile —*no toast*
Super Omelette Smile —*no toast*
T-Bone Steak and Eggs Smile —*no toast*

Veggie Omelette —*no toast*
Western Omelette —*no toast*

Dinner —*request a "Celiac-friendly" bun*
Baked Cod —*no bread crumbs, no dinner rolls*
Beef Liver and Onions —*no dinner rolls*
Chargrilled Chicken —*no dinner rolls*
Chargrilled Sockeye Salmon —*no dinner rolls*
Chicken Stir-Fry —*no garden rice*
Eat'n Smart Cod Floridian —*no seasoning, no dinner rolls*
Ground Sirloin Steak —*no onion rings*
T-Bone Steak

Salads
Chicken Fajita Salad —*no tortilla bowl*
Grilled Chicken Portobella Salad —*no croutons*
Grilled Chicken Salad —*no french fries*

Salad Dressings
Salad Dressings (All)

Burgers —*request a "Celiac-friendly" bun*
Black Angus American Grill Burger —*no Texas toast*
Black Angus BBQ Bacon and Cheddar Burger —*no bun*
Black Angus Superburger —*no bun*
Classic Black Angus Burger —*no Kaiser roll*

Celiac-Friendly Sides
Apple Sauce
Baked Potato
Cottage Cheese
Fresh Broccoli
Fresh Fruit Cup
Garden Salad —*no croutons*
Homemade Chili
Mashed Potatoes —*no gravy*
Seasonal Vegetables

Eat 'n Park Notes: A "Celiac-friendly" bun can be substituted for any regular bread or bun. Alert the server to your dietary needs in order to help prevent cross-contamination. All fried items are prepared

in shared oil. Kitchens are not gluten-free, so cross-contamination may occur.

Triumph Notes: This menu is called the "Celiac Friendly" menu.

Einstein Bros. Bagels   ★ ¢ BLD
(800) 224-3563
Sandwich Shop
Confirmed: 4/20/2010

Triumph Notes: Einstein Bros. is currently testing gluten-free bagels in their Denver market, and reports that gluten-free bagels will soon be available nationwide. Contact Einstein Bros. for more information or for updates.

Famous Dave's Legendary Pit Bar-B-Que   ¢ LD
(952) 294-1300
Barbeque
Confirmed: 4/7/2010

Triumph Notes: A "Food Ingredient Information" packet is available by contacting Famous Dave's directly. It lists common allergens, including wheat. It does not list gluten as an allergen.

Fazoli's $ LD
Italian-American
Confirmed: 4/5/2010

Triumph Notes: No gluten-free list is available, but the restaurant provides an ingredients list. Contact Fazoli's directly for this list.

Firehouse Subs   ¢ LD
(877) 309-7332
Sandwich Shop
Confirmed: 4/1/2010

Chili, Soups, & Salads
Chief's Salad with Ham

Chief's Salad with Sliced Chicken
Chief's Salad with Turkey
Chili

Meats/Proteins
Bacon
Brisket
Chicken Breast (Sliced)
Corned Beef
Ham
Pastrami
Pepperoni
Roast Beef
Salami
Steak
Tuna Salad
Turkey

Side Items
Au Jus Onions and Peppers
Marinara Sauce
Mushrooms
Pickles

Dressings/Condiments/Toppings
Balsamic Dressing
Banana Peppers
Black Olives
Captain Sorensen Sauce
Cheese (All Varieties)
Fat Free Ranch Dressing
Fresh Lettuce, Tomato, Onions
Honey Mustard
Italian Dressing
Jalapeno Peppers
Mayo
Mustard (Brown, Yellow)
Ranch Dressing
Raspberry Vinaigrette
Thousand Island Dressing

Triumph Notes: This list was marked 3/16/2010.

First Watch The Daytime Café ✪¢
BL
(941) 907-9800
Healthy American
Confirmed: 4/1/2010

Egg-Cetera
Avocado Skillet —*no english muffin*
Breakfast Scramble —*no croissant, no hollandaise sauce*
Bubba's Benny —*no biscuits, no sausage gravy, no english muffin*
Burrito Vera Cruz —*no flour tortilla, no vera cruz sauce*
Caps Mushroom —*no english muffin*
Chickichanga —*no flour tortilla, no vera cruz sauce*
Eggs Benedict Florentine —*no english muffin, no hollandaise sauce*
Eggs Benedict Ham —*no english muffin, no hollandaise sauce*
Eggs Benedict Turkey —*no english muffin, no hollandaise sauce*
Ham Skillet —*no english muffin*
Joaquin Yahoo —*no english muffin*
Onion Skillet —*no english muffin*
Sonoran Fritatta —*no english muffin*
Veggie Skillet —*no english muffin*

Eggs and Omelettes
Acapulco Express —*no english muffin*
Bacado —*no english muffin*
Far West —*no english muffin*
Greek Fetish —*no english muffin*
Ham/Bacon/Sausage/and Cheese Omelettes —*no english muffin*
Killer Cajun —*no english muffin, no santa fe dressing*
Mushroom Omelette —*no english muffin*
The Works —*no english muffin*
Traditional —*no english muffin*
Veggie Omelette —*no english muffin*

Health Department
Fruit Bowl
Healthy Turkey Omelette —*no english muffin*
Lean Machine —*no muffin*
Power Wrap —*no tortilla wrap*
Siesta Key Cocktail —*no granola, no muffin*
Tri-Athlete —*no muffin*

Sandwiches —*no bread products, request to "build your own" with bread brought from home*
Al B. Core
BCB Burger
Beefeater
BLTE
Chicken Salad Melt
Grill Turkey —*no ranch dressing*
Monterey Club
Not Guilty Your Honor
Rueben
San Diego Chicken
Turkey Burger —*no dressing*

Wraps —*no tortilla*
Black and Blue —*no horseradish sauce*
Going Cold Turkey —*no ranch dressing*
Green Hamlet Wrap —*no honey dijon dressing*
Heard of Buffalo Chicken —*no ranch dressing*

Salad Bowl —*salad dressings vary by location, use with caution*
Cobb Salad —*no pita*
Fruity Chicken Salad —*no pita*
Pecan Dijon Salad —*no pita, no honey dijon dressing*
Santa Fe Salad —*no dressing, no croutons, no pita*

Salad Dressing*
Greek
House Dressing (Poppyseed Vinaigrette)
Oil and Vinegar (Cider, Rice, Wine)
Sweet and Sour

Side List / Extras —*no bread products*
Bacon
Fruit Cup
Ham
Potatoes
Salad Marinade
Salsa
Sausage
Turkey Patty
Turkey Sausage

Kids Menu
Bacon and Egg —*no toast*
Hot Dog —*no bun, no croissant*

First Watch The Daytime Café Notes:
*A "gluten-free guide" is available at the host stand. *Pre-made salad dressings may contain trace amounts of gluten, so exercise caution in choosing these products. If bringing gluten-free bread to the restaurant, do not send it to the kitchen in order to prevent cross-contamination. Product substitutions and changes may occur, so take care in selecting menu items to order. A registered dietician assembled this list, and it has not been verified by First Watch. First Watch is not responsible for its use and disclaims any resulting damages. Consider this information as it pertains to your individual needs.

Flat Top Grill $$D
(312) 284-6500
Asian Stir-Fry
Confirmed: 4/1/2010

Garlic Water
Ginger Water
Lemongrass Water
Meats —*request un-marinated (ask server for assistance)*
Nonfat Spicy Lime Basil
Rice Wine Vinegar
Sesame Oil
Vegetables (All)

Flat Top Grill Notes: Take your bowl to the grill station with a WHITE stick in it, so that the cooks prepare your food separately and prevent cross-contamination.

Triumph Notes: This list was marked Updated 12/21/09.

Fleming's Prime Steakhouse & Wine Bar $$$D

(949) 222-2223
Steakhouse
Confirmed: 4/1/2010

Appetizers
Chilled Seafood Tower
Lobster Bisque Soup
Lump Crab Louis Wraps
Seared Ahi Tuna —*request caper creole mustard sauce*
Shrimp Cocktail
Tenderloin Carpaccio —*no croutons*
Wicked Cajun Barbecue Shrimp —*no croutons*

Salads —*no croutons, no red onion balsamic vinaigrette*
Classic Caesar
Fleming's Salad
Fresh Mozzarella & Sweet Tomato
The Wedge

Chops & Meat
Double Breast of Chicken
Double Thick Pork Rib Chop
Nagle Veal Chop
New Zealand Lamb Chops
Prime Rib —*no au jus*

Seafood
Alaskan King Crab Legs
North Atlantic Lobster Tail
Salmon Nicoise Salad —*no crostini*
Seared Scallops —*no puff pastry*
Tuna Mignon

Steaks
Lite Filet Mignon with Fleming's Potatoes
Main Filet Mignon
Peppercorn Steak
Petite Filet Mignon
Porcini Rubbed Filet Mignon
Prime Bone-In Ribeye
Prime New York Strip
Prime Ribeye

Sides
Baked Potato (All Toppings)
Fleming's Potatoes
Grilled Asparagus
Mashed Potatoes (All Flavors)
Roasted Baby Carrots
Sautéed French Green Beans
Sautéed Mushrooms
Sautéed Spinach
Sautéed Sweet Corn

Sauces
"F17" Steak Sauce
Champagne Mint
Horseradish Cream
Horseradish Mustard
Jalapeno Pepper Sauce
Lemon Butter
Lobster Sauce
Madeira
Peppercorn
Porcini Mushroom Sauce
Smoked Jalapeno Aioli

Desserts
Crème Brulee
Mixed Berries with Whipped Cream and/ or Vanilla Ice Cream
Vanilla Ice Cream with Fudge Sauce

Fleming's Prime Steakhouse & Wine Bar Notes: Kitchens are not gluten-free. Upon arrival, alert the server to your dietary needs. This information is meant as an information resource only and is not a substitute for medical or dietetic advice. Fleming's is not responsible for individual reactions to food.

Fox and Hound Pub & Grille $LD

(800) 229-2118
American
Confirmed: 4/21/2010

Triumph Notes: No gluten-free list was provided. Restaurant recommends working with a manager on location to get a gluten-free meal.

Fuddruckers   ⊄LD

(512) 891-1300
American
Confirmed: 4/8/2010

Appetizers

Tricked Out Nachos —*no chili, no beef, no chicken*

Salads —*no croutons, no garlic toast, request only grilled chicken*

Market Toss Salad
Napa Valley Salad

Salad Dressings

Balsamic Vinaigrette
Blue Cheese
Buttermilk Ranch
Caesar
Fat Free Ranch
French
Olive Oil Light Vinaigrette
Ranch
Spicy Ranch
Thousand Island

Entrées

Chopped Steak

Sandwiches —*no bun*

Buffalo Burger
Dogzilla
Original Burger
Original Grilled Chicken Sandwich
   (Grilled Chicken Only)
Ostrich Burger
Ribeye Steak Sandwich
Slider Burger
The Works Burger
Three Cheese Burger

Side Items

BBQ Baked Beans
Fruit Cup
Grilled Mushrooms
Sweet Potato Fries
Wedge Cut Fries

Desserts

Hot Fudge and Caramel Ice Cream Sundae
Ice Cream (Chocolate, Vanilla, Strawberry)

Beverages

Milkshakes (All) —*no malt*

Kids' Menu Items —*no bun on sandwiches*

BBQ Baked Beans
Burger —*no bun*
Chocolate Shake —*no malt*
Fruit
Hot Dog —*no bun*
Sliced Apples
Strawberry Shake —*no malt*
Vanilla Shake —*no malt*
Wedge Cut Fries

Produce Bar Items

Banana Peppers
Diced Onions
Iceberg Lettuce
Jalapeno Slices
Lettuce Leaves
Onions
Pickle Slices
Pico de Gallo
Sweet Pickle Relish
Tomato Slices

Fuddruckers Notes: Ingredients of all foods on this list have been confirmed as gluten-free. However, human error, cross-contamination, and misinformation from suppliers may occur. Therefore, Fuddruckers does not guarantee that any of these items are gluten-free, and it is not responsible for the use or contents of this list and disclaims any liability.

Garbanzo's   ⊄LD

Mediterranean
Confirmed: 4/1/2010

Babaganoush
Chicken Schwarma
Cilantro Sauce
Falafel
Garbanzo Signature Teas

Green Chili Sauce
Grilled Eggplant
Hard-Boiled Egg
Hummus
Mediterranean Garlic Sauce
Mediterranean Lentil Soup
Moroccan Bean Soup (Bowl, Cup)
Olive Oil
Pickled Eggplants
Pickles
Red Cabbage
Red Chili Sauce
Rice
Romain Lettuce (Chopped)
Steak Schwarma
Tahini Sauce
Vegetable Salad

Garbanzo's Notes: Garbanzo's cannot guarantee that cross-contamination will not occur, but they do have a protocol in place to ensure a safe dining experience. Notify a manager upon arrival, and they will take the necessary precautions.

Triumph Notes: This list was marked March 9, 2010. An ingredient list is available by contacting them directly.

Golden Corral $LD
Buffet
Confirmed: 4/5/2010

Breakfast
Apple Juice
Bacon
Breakfast Links
Breakfast Sausage Patties
Corned Beef Hash
Liquid Eggs
Orange Guava Juice
Orange Juice
Scrambled Eggs
Shredded Hash Browns
Split Smoked Sausage
Whole Eggs

Proteins
BBQ Chicken (Leg Quarter)

BBQ Pork Ribs
BBQ Pork
Brisket (Ham)
Brisket (Pitt)
Carved Turkey
Flame Broiled Glazed Pork Ribs
Grilled Pork Chops
Ham Strips, Cold
Pork Loin Roast
Pulled Chicken (Salad Bar)
Rotisserie Chicken (Breast, Wing)
Salmon, Whole Carved
Sausage (Cajun, Italian Roped)
Sirloin
Turkey Strips, Cold

Vegetables/Side Dishes
Baked Potato
Baked Sweet Potato (NOT Sweet Potato Casserole)
Broccoli Salad
Broccoli
Cauliflower
Creamed Corn
Creamed Spinach
Key West Blend
Mashed Potatoes
Sugar Snap Peas
White Rice (NOT Rice Pilaf)

Desserts
Candy Corn
Chocolate Icing
Gummie Bears
Jelly Beans
Orange Slices
Sherbets (Orange)
Soft Serve (Chocolate, Vanilla)
Sugar Free Jello
Sugar Free Pudding
Whipped OnTop

Miscellaneous
BBQ Sauce
Caesar Dressing
Cajun Mayo
Cole Slaw
Dijon Honey Mustard
Fat Free French Dressing

Fat Free Ranch Dressing
French Dressing
Mayonnaise
Oil & Vinegar
Ranch Dressing
Solid Margarine

Promotions
Applewood Grill: Spinach Applewood
  Bacon Salad
Great American Seafood Tour: Grilled
  Lemon Pepper Tilapia, Salmon
  Lemonata, Tilapia Florentine
Oceans of Shrimp: Baked Fish with Shrimp
  and Lemon Herb Sauce, Shrimp Scampi

Golden Corral Notes: Kitchens are not
gluten-free, so cross-contamination may
occur. Cross-contamination may also
occur in the buffet line, as customers serve
themselves.

Ground Round $ⅬⅮ
(207) 865-4433
American
Confirmed: 4/22/2010

Baby Back Ribs —*no bread*
Boneless Chicken Dinner
Broiled Scallops —*no garlic butter*
Bruchetta Chicken (Grilled)
Chicken Caesar Salad —*no bread, request
  dressing on the side, request that the salad
  not be mixed*
Chopped Beef Steak —*no gravy*
Fajitas (Beef, Chicken) —*no sizzle sauce, no
  flour shells*
Grilled Chicken and Spinach Salad —*no
  bread*
Grilled Chicken Club Salad —*no bread,
  request dressing on the side, request that
  the salad not be mixed*
Ground Rounder or Specialty Burger
  (Any) —*no bun, no flour tortillas, no rye
  bread, no onion tanglers, no tortilla soup,
  no tortilla strips, no onion rings, no Texas
  toothpicks*
Margarita Grilled Chicken

Orange Grilled Salmon —*no orange glaze*
Original Chicken Wings (Buffalo [mild,
  medium, hot], Honey BBQ)
Ribs and Chicken —*no bread*

Salad Dressings
Balsamic Vinaigrette
Blue Cheese
Caesar
Honey Mustard
Italian
Ranch
Thousand Island

Side Items
Baked Potato
Black Beans
Broccoli
Caesar Salad —*no croutons*
Cole Slaw
House Salad —*no croutons*
Redskin Mashed Potato —*no gravy*
Vegetable of the Day

Beverages
Flavored Lemonades
Iced Tea
Lemonade

Ground Round Notes: This list is based
on suppliers' ingredient information. Upon
arrival, alert a manager to your dietary
needs. Ground Round does not guarantee
that any food is gluten-free. Variations in
local menus, ingredients, suppliers, recipes,
and preparation techniques may occur. In
addition, kitchens are not gluten-free, so
cross-contamination may occur.

Triumph Notes: GF menu is available in
some locations, but not all, as locations are
franchised. Contact the location directly to
confirm they carry the GF menu.

Hard Rock Café   ★ $ⅬⅮ
(407) 445-7625
American
Confirmed: 4/21/2010

BBQ Chicken
BBQ Ribs
Burger —*no bun*
Cobb Salad
Haystack Salad —*no tortilla straws*
Honey Citrus Salad
Hot Fudge Sundae
Ice Cream
Milk Shakes
Salmon
Skins
Strip and Sirloin —*no gravy*
Wings

Hard Rock Café Notes: Hard Rock does not guarantee that any food is gluten-free, as products may be made on shared equipment or in shared plants. Kitchens are not gluten-free. Contact the location you plan to visit in advance, and speak to the General Manager about how the staff can accommodate you.

HuHot Mongolian Grill $LD
(888) 751-3461
Asian Stir-Fry
Confirmed: 4/20/2010

Appetizer Sauces
Sweet and Sour Dipping Sauce

Sauces
Black Thai Peanut
Kung Pao…Yow!
Not So Sweet and Sour
Yellow Belly Curry

Noodles
Pad Thai Noodles

HuHot Mongolian Grill Notes: Grills are communal, so cross-contamination may occur. Ask the cook to clean an area of the grill for gluten-free meal preparation. Cooks can use separate spatulas, but HuHot still does not guarantee that cross-contamination will not occur.

IHOP   ¢BLD
(818) 240-6055
Breakfast
Confirmed: 4/6/2010

6 oz. Grilled Chicken Breast
Bacon
Broccoli —*no seasoning*
Fresh Fruit Bowl
Liquid Eggs
Mashed Potatoes —*no seasoning*
Salad —*no dressing, no croutons*
Shelled Eggs
Tilapia —*no seasoning*

IHOP Notes: Kitchens are not gluten-free, so cross-contamination may occur.

In-N-Out Burger   ¢LD
(800) 786-1000
American
Confirmed: 4/5/2010

Triumph Notes: There is no gluten-free list available. The restaurant reports that there is only one item which contains gluten, and that is the bun. Order any burger "protein-style" to have the sandwich wrapped in lettuce and eliminate the bun.

Islands Fine Burgers & Drinks   ¢LD
(760) 268-1800
Mexican
Confirmed: 4/5/2010

Cabo Loco Tacos —*request corn tortillas, no ranchero beans*
Grilled Chicken Tacos —*request onion, peppers, and corn tortillas, no ranchero beans*
Grilled Veggie Tacos —*request corn tortillas*
Kaanapali Kobb Salad —*no focaccia bread*

Islands Fine Burgers & Drinks Notes: Kitchens are not gluten-free and fry oil is shared, so cross-contamination may occur. These items were determined to be gluten free based on statements provided by ingredient vendors, which are subject to change. Menu items cannot be guaranteed to be gluten-free due to changes in suppliers, preparation, vendors, region, and season. This list is updated periodically, so obtain the most recent version before ordering.

Triumph Notes: This list was marked April 2009.

Jamba Juice   ¢S
(866) 473-7848
Juice & Smoothies
Confirmed: 5/6/2010

All Fruit Smoothies
Mega Mango
Peach Perfection
Pomegranate Paradise
Strawberry Whirl

Boosts
3G Charger
Antioxidant Power
Calcium
Flax & Fiber
Immunity
Matcha Green Tea
Soy Protein
Whey Protein

Classic Smoothies
Aloha Pineapple
Banana Berry
Caribbean Passion
Citrus Squeeze
Mango-A-Go-Go
Orange-A-Peel
Peach Pleasure
Pomegranate Pick-Me-Up
Razzmatazz
Strawberries Wild
Strawberry Surf Rider

Creamy Treats Smoothies
Chocolate Moo'd
Matcha Green Tea Blast
Orange Dream Machine

Peanut Butter Moo'd

Fruit Tea Infusions
Passion Fruit Tea
Pomegranate Fruit Tea
Prickly Pear Fruit Tea

Jamba Light Smoothies
Berry Fulfilling
Mango Mantra
Strawberry Nirvana

Juices
Carrot
Orange

Pre-Boosted Smoothies
Acai Super Antioxidant
Coldbuster
Protein Berry Workout (Soy, Whey)

Shots
Matcha Green Tea with OJ
Matcha Green Tea with Soymilk

Jason's Deli   ¢LD
(800) 444-3354
Deli
Confirmed: 4/6/2010

Soups
Red Beans and Rice with Sausage
Tomato Basil Soup
Tortilla Soup

Fresh Vegetables & Fruit
Broccoli Florets
Cauliflower Florets
Cherry Tomatoes
Organic Baby Carrots
Organic Field Greens
Organic Red Apple Slices
Organic Spinach
Purple Onion Rings
Red Bell Pepper Rings
Salad Bar Lettuce
Sliced Cucumbers
Sliced Mushrooms
Sprouts

Yellow Bell Pepper Rings

Homemade Recipes
American Potato Salad
Honeymustard Coleslaw
Mixed Fruit and Yogurt

Other Items (Salad Bar)
Artichokes
Bacon Bits
Cranberry Walnut Mix
Eggs
Italian Peppers
Jalapeno Peppers
Kalamata Olives
Red Pepper Hummus
Stuffed Green Olives

Protein Add Ons (Salad Bar)
Homemade Chicken Salad
Homemade Tuna Salad
Marinated Chicken Breast
Premium Ham
Roasted Turkey Breast
Smoked Turkey Breast

Salad Bar
Cheeses (Asiago, Cottage Cheese, Feta,
   Shredded Cheddar)

Salads & Fruit
Big Chef Salad —*no dressing*
Creamy Fruit Dip
Fresh Fruit Cup or Plate —*no fruit dip*
Homemade Salsa
Marinated Chicken Breast Salad —*no
   dressing*
Nutty Mixed-Up Salad (With or Without
   Chicken) —*no dressing*
Steamed Veggies
Twisted Turkey Salad (With or Without
   Dressing)

Dressings
1000 Island (Russian)
Blue Cheese
Caesar Dressing
Extra Virgin Olive Oil
Leo's Italian Dressing

Low Fat Honey Mustard
Organic Balsamic Vinegar (Bottle)
Organic Raspberry Vinaigrette
Ranch

Chips and Pickles
Baked Lays Chips
Blue Corn Tortilla Chips
Individual Potato Chips (To Go Chips)
Pickle (Dill Spears)
Ripple Chips (House Chips)

Potatoes
Plain Jane Potato
Pollo Mexicano Potato
Texas Style Spud - Beef

Side Items
American Potato Salad
Blue Corn Tortilla Chips
Homemade Guacamole
Homemade Salsa
Honeymustard Coleslaw
Roasted Red Pepper Hummus

Desserts
Chocolate Topping (For Ice Cream)
Ice Cream (Chocolate, Vanilla)

Build Your Own Cheeses
Finlandia Swiss
Jalapeno Pepper Jack
Mild Cheddar (Slices)
Provolone
Shredded Cheddar
Sliced American

Build Your Own Items
Build Your Own Spreads: Yellow Deli
   Mustard, Organic Stoneground Mustard,
   Mayonnaise, Smoked Pepper Cilantro
   Aioli, Leos Italian Dressing, Extra Virgin
   Olive Oil, Roasted Red Pepper Hummus,
   Homemade Guacamole

Build Your Own Meats
Homemade Chicken Salad w/ Almonds
Homemade Tuna Salad
Hot Corned Beef

Hot New York Style Pastrami
Premium Ham
Roast Beef
Roasted Turkey Breast
Smoked Turkey Breast

Build Your Own Toppings
Greek Peppers
Homemade Pico de Gallo
Leafy Lettuce
Organic Field Greens
Organic Spinach
Oven Roasted Tomatoes
Purple Onion Rings
Shredded Iceburg Lettuce
Sliced Avocado
Tomato Slice

Junior Meals
Kid's Baked Potato
Little Dippers - Apple Slices & Celery with
    Peanut Butter
Little Dippers - Blue Corn Chips with Salsa
Little Dippers - Broc & Carrots with Ranch

**Seasonal/Limited Time Offers/Special
    Boards**
Bacon Strips
Bronx Baker
Egg Salad - Build Your Own "Meat"
Pepperoni
Sauerkraut

Jason's Deli Notes: Kitchens are not
gluten-free, so cross-contamination may
occur. The availability and ingredient
profiles of these options are subject to
change at any time and according to
location for a variety of reasons including
variations in recipes, preparation, season,
and suppliers. Check back frequently for
updated and accurate information.

Triumph Notes: Restaurant reports that
there will be a GF menu beginning in the
Spring of 2010. There may also be gluten-
free bread available.

Jimmy John's Gourmet
Sandwiches   ¢LD
(217) 356-9900
Sandwich Shop
Confirmed: 4/12/2010

Bacon
Capicola
Ham
Mayo
Salami
Turkey

Johnny Rockets   ¢LD
(888) 856-4669
American
Confirmed: 5/4/2010

Triumph Notes: Johnny Rockets does not
provide a gluten-free list. Full ingredient
statements are available on the website,
with all ingredients that contain the wheat
allergen notated.

KFC   ¢LD
(800) 225-5532
Fried Chicken
Confirmed: 4/2/2010

Salads and More
Caesar Side Salad —*no dressing, no croutons*
Heinz Buttermilk Ranch Dressing
Hidden Valley The Original Ranch Fat Free
    Dressing
House Side Salad —*no dressing*
Marzetti Light Italian Dressing

Sides
Corn on the Cob
Green Beans
Potato Salad
Sweet Kernel Corn
Three Bean Salad

Sandwich Fixings
Monterey Jack Cheese Slices
Pepper Jack Cheese Slices

Pre-Shredded Lettuce
Tomato Slices

Sauces & Condiments
Colonel's Buttery Spread
Creamy Ranch Dipping Sauce Cup
Fiery Buffalo Wing Sauce
HBBQ Dipping Sauce Cup
Honey BBQ Wing Sauce
Honey Mustard Dipping Sauce Cup
Honey Sauce Packet
Pepper Mayonnaise
Spicy Mayonnaise
Sweet and Sour Dipping Sauce Cup
Tartar Sauce

Other
Jalapeno Peppers
Sargento Light String Cheese

KFC Notes: The availability and ingredient profiles of listed items may vary by location or change without prior notice due to supplier variations, recipe changes, and ingredient substitutions.

Triumph Notes: This list was marked April 2010.

Kona Grill   ✪ $$$ LD
(480) 922-8100
Modern American
Confirmed: 4/1/2010

Appetizers
Chicken & Shrimp Romaine Wraps —*no black bean garlic sauce, no ponzu*
Chicken Satay —*no hoisin dipping sauce*
Edamame

Dressings
Balsamic Vinaigrette
Honey Dijon
Oil & White Wine Vinegar

Entrées
Kona Filet
Kona Strip
Pan-Seared Ahi

Pork Tenderloin —*no almond crust, no onion strings, no red-pepper shiitake sauce*
Sweet-Chili Glazed Chicken —*no sweet chili glaze*
Sweet-Chili Glazed Salmon —*no sweet-chili glaze, request substitute for fried rice*

Salads and Sandwiches
Big Kahuna Cheeseburger —*no kaiser roll, request substitute for french fries*
Chef Salad —*request grilled chicken instead of macadamia nut chicken*
House Salad —*no croutons, request substitute for onion-soy vinaigrette*
Jerk Chicken —*no kaiser roll, no chipotle mayo, request substitute for french fries*
Roasted Asparagus Salad —*no goat cheese crostini*

Sides
Baby Bok Choy
Grilled Asparagus
Sauteed Spinach
Steamed Wok Vegetables
Sweet Rice
White Cheddar Mashed Potatoes
White Rice

Desserts
Ice Cream Scoop
Mochi, Ice Cream —*no wonton cup*
Passion Fruit Crème Brulee

Triumph Notes: This list was marked 111609.

Legal Sea Foods   ✪★ $$$ LD
(617) 530-9000
Seafood
Confirmed: 4/5/2010

Lunch
Classic Caesar Salad —*request gluten-free croutons, request gluten-free caesar dressing*
Crabmeat Salad —*no roll*
Crispy Sea Scallops —*in chick pea flour*
Crispy Shrimp —*in chick pea flour*

Grilled Atlantic Salmon
Grilled Chicken —*no roll*
Grilled Sea Scallops
Grilled Shrimp
Lobster Salad —*no bun*
Niman Ranch Burger —*no roll*
Shrimp and Garlic —*no pasta*

Appetizers
Crispy Montauk Calamari —*in chick pea flour*
Hot Lump Crab Dip with Seafood Chips
Jumbo Shrimp Cocktail —*no cocktail sauce, request lemon only*
Mussels
Pan Seared Raw Tuna "Sashimi" —*no sesame vinaigrette, no seaweed salad*
Steamers

Seafood Bar —*no cocktail sauce*
Raw Cherrystone Clams
Raw Littleneck Clams
Raw Oysters

Chowders & Salads
Classic Caesar Salad —*request gluten-free croutons, request gluten-free caesar dressing*
House Salad
Lite Clam Chowder —*no crackers*

Completely Legal
Baked Boston Scrod —*request gluten-free crumbs*
Baked Grey Sole —*request gluten-free crumbs*
Cioppino —*no bread*
Everything Tuna
Filet Mignon
Shrimp and Garlic —*no pasta*
Surf & Turf
Wood Grilled Assortment
Wood Grilled Swordfish

Legal Lobsters
Baked Stuffed Lobsters —*request gluten-free crumbs*
New England Lobster Bake —*no crackers*
Steamed Lobsters

Simply Legal —*if ordering crispy fried, request that it be fried in chickpea flour*
Atlantic Salmon
Rainbow Trout
Sea Scallops
Shrimp
Swordfish
Tuna

Sides
Baked Potato
Brown Rice
Jasmine Rice
Seasonal Vegetables
Steamed Broccoli
Steamed Snap Peas

Children's Menu
Cheeseburger —*no bun*
Fresh Cod Fish Sticks —*in chick pea flour*
Half Steamed Lobster
Hamburger —*no bun*

Desserts
Belgian Chocolate Mousse Parfait
Seasonal Fruit
Sorbet

Legal Sea Foods Notes: For safety's sake, substitutions are not allowed. Alert a manager upon arrival, and he or she will consult with you and follow your order through to its completion. All seafood and meat will be baked with gluten-free crumbs, fried in chick pea flour, pan-seared, steamed, or wood-grilled. Cookware and plates will be washed and dried before cooking and presentation. If you have any concerns about any item on the gluten-free menu, please consult a physician.

Triumph Notes: This list was marked 1209, and may vary slightly by location. The menu provided is for illustrative purposes only.

Lone Star Steakhouse & Saloon ✪

$$ LD

(800) 234-0888
Steakhouse
Confirmed: 4/5/2010

Big Lunch Salads —no croutons, request oil and vinegar instead of dressing

Big Garden Salad or Caesar Salad with Grilled Chicken —*request chicken without seasoning*
Signature Chicken & Wedge Salad —*request chicken without seasoning*
Signature Steak & Wedge Salad —*no bleu cheese crumbles, request steak medallions without seasoning*
Steakhouse Salad —*no bleu cheese crumbles, no crispy onion strings, request steak medallions without seasoning*

Lone Star Lunch Specialties

10 oz. Chopped Steak —*no seasoning, no rich mushroom gravy, no lemon butter*
6 oz. Lunch Sirloin —*no seasoning, no lemon butter*
6 oz. Mesquite-Grilled Chicken —*no seasoning, no sauce, no lemon butter*
7 oz. Delmonico —*no seasoning, no lemon butter*
8 oz. Garlic Lover's Medallions —*no seasoning, no garlic butter, no Texas rice*
Mesquite-Grilled Pork Chop —*no seasoning, no sauce, no lemon butter*
Mesquite-Grilled Shrimp —*no seasoning, no dressing, no lemon butter, no Texas rice*
Sweet Bourbon Salmon —*no sweet bourbon marinade, no seasonings*

Soup, Salad, or Baked Potato Combo (Pick One Salad and One Potato)

Classic Dinner Salad —*no croutons, request oil & vinegar dressing*
Oven-Baked Potato —*no sour cream*
Side Caesar Salad —*no croutons, request oil & vinegar dressing*
Signature Lettuce Wedge —*no bleu cheese crumbles, request oil & vinegar dressing*

Sweet Potato —*no cinnamon-sugar*

Big Salads —no croutons, no tortilla strips, request oil & vinegar instead of dressing

Big Garden Salad —*if adding grilled chicken breast, request chicken without seasoning*
Caesar Salad —*if adding grilled chicken breast, request chicken without seasoning*
Signature Chicken & Wedge Salad —*no bleu cheese crumbles, request chicken without seasoning*
Signature Steak & Wedge Salad —*no bleu cheese crumbles, request steak medallions without seasoning*
Steakhouse Salad —*no bleu cheese crumbles, no crispy onion strings, request steak medallions without seasoning*

A Cut Above Mesquite-Grilled Steaks

20 oz. Porterhouse —*no seasoning, no lemon butter*
6 oz. Bacon-Wrapped Sirloin —*no seasoning, no lemon butter*
Chopped Steak —*no seasoning, no rich mushroom gravy, no lemon butter*
Delmonico —*no seasoning, no lemon butter*
Five-Star Filet Mignon —*no seasoning, no lemon butter*
Garlic Lover's Medallions —*no seasoning, no garlic butter, no Texas rice*
New York Strip —*no seasoning, no lemon butter*
Peppercorn Ribeye —*no brandy cream sauce*
San Antonio Sirloin —*no seasoning, no lemon butter*
Texas Ribeye —*no seasoning, no lemon butter*

Pure Texas Specialties

Mesquite-Grilled Chicken —*no seasoning, no sauce, no lemon butter*
Mesquite-Grilled Pork Chops —*no seasoning, no sauce, no lemon butter*
Mesquite-Grilled Shrimp Dinner —*no seasoning, no dressing, no lemon butter, no Texas Rice*

Seafood Combo —*no sweet bourbon marinade, no dressing, no lemon butter, no seasoning*

Sweet Bourbon Salmon —*no marinade, no seasonings*

Steak Combos

5 Grilled Shrimp —*no dressing, no seasoning, no lemon butter*

6 oz. USDA Choice Center-Cut Sirloin —*no seasoning, no lemon butter*

BBQ Chicken Breast —*no sauce, no seasoning, no lemon butter*

Garlic Lover's Medallions & Shrimp —*no roasted garlic butter, no lemon butter, request steak medallions and grilled shrimp without seasoning*

Sweet Bourbon Salmon —*no marinade, no seasonings*

Texas Trio —*request steak medallions and chicken with no seasoning, no sauce, and no lemon butter, request grilled and unseasoned shrimp instead of breaded shrimp*

Great Add-Ons

5 Grilled Shrimp —*no dressing, no seasoning, no lemon butter*

Classic Dinner Salad —*no croutons, request oil & vinegar instead of dressing*

Side Caesar Salad —*no croutons, request oil & vinegar instead of dressing*

Signature Lettuce Wedge —*no bleu cheese crumbles, request oil & vinegar instead of dressing*

Great Sides of Texas

Baked Potato —*no sour cream*

Classic Dinner Salad —*no croutons, request oil & vinegar instead of dressing*

Jumbo Baked Sweet Potato —*no cinnamon-sugar*

Side Caesar Salad —*no croutons, request oil & vinegar instead of dressing*

Signature Lettuce Wedge —*no bleu cheese crumbles, request oil & vinegar instead of dressing*

Steamed Broccoli —*no seasonings*

Lone Star Steakhouse & Saloon Notes: Cross-contamination may occur. Lone Star does not guarantee that any food items are gluten-free.

Triumph Notes: This menu was marked 3/10.

LongHorn Steakhouse $$ **LD**

(407) 245-4835
Steakhouse
Confirmed: 4/6/2010

Salads —*no croutons, request that salad be tossed in separate bowl*

7-Pepper Salad
Caesar Side Salad
Chicken Caesar Salad
Grilled Salmon Salad —*no salmon marinade*
Mixed Green Side Salad
Sonoma Chicken Salad

Salad Dressings

Balsamic Vinaigrette
Bleu Cheese
Caesar
Chipotle Ranch
Fat-free Ranch
Honey Mustard
House
Oil and Vinegar
Ranch
Thousand Island

Burgers/Sandwiches

Bacon Cheese Burger —*no bun, no french fries*
Cheese Burger —*no bun, no french fries*
Honey Mustard Chicken Sandwich —*no bun, no french fries*
Shaved Prime Rib Sandwich —*no bun, no horseradish sauce, no french fries*

Chicken

Rocky Top Chicken —*no BBQ sauce*
Sierra Chicken

Legendary Steaks

Chop Steak —*no mushroom bordelaise sauce, no crisp onion straws, no french fries*
Fire-Grilled T-Bone
Flo's Filet
LongHorn Porterhouse
NY Strip
Peppered Bacon Wrapped Filet
Prime Rib —*no classic au jus, no french onion au jus, no roasted garlic cream sauce, no horseradish sauce*
Renegade Top Sirloin
Ribeye

Ribs, Chops, Etc.

Babyback Ribs —*no BBQ sauce, no french fries*
Cowboy Pork Chop —*no spiced apples, no french fries*

Seafood—*for all salmon, request no salmon marinade*

Flo's Filet and Lobster Tail
Flo's Filet and Salmon
LongHorn Salmon
Redrock Grilled Shrimp

Sides

Asparagus Spears
Baked Potato
Grilled Onions
Jalapeno Coleslaw
Mashed Potatoes
Sauteed Mushrooms
Seasonal Vegetables
Sliced Tomatoes
Sweet Potato

Kids Meals

Kid's BBQ Ribs —*no BBQ sauce, no french fries*
Kid's Cheese Burger —*no bun, no french fries*
Kid's Grilled Chicken Salad —*no croutons*
Kid's Grilled Chicken
Kid's Hot Dog —*no bun, no french fries*
Kid's Sirloin Steak —*no french fries*

Desserts

Fresh Fruit
Hot Fudge Sundae

LongHorn Steakhouse Notes: To prevent cross-contamination, request that all items be prepared in separate containers and on newly cleaned surfaces. Kitchens are not gluten-free. Ingredients, recipes, and preparation may vary, possibly affecting the stated contents of food items. There is no guarantee that food will be entirely gluten-free. Gluten-free diners should not rely on this information alone, and are responsible for their own dietary needs. LongHorn is not responsible for the use of this information and disclaims any liability. Consult a healthcare provider with concerns about consuming these items.

Luby's   ¢LD

(800) 886-4600
American Regional
Confirmed: 4/19/2010

Baked Chicken
Fresh Leafy Salad (Any), Mixed Field Greens with Oil and Vinegar
Fruit Salad
Steamed Fish Fillet
Turkey or Roast Beef —*no gravy*
Vegetables, Fresh Steamed or Sauteed (Any)

Luby's Notes: Upon arrival, alert a manager to your dietary needs. Kitchens are not gluten-free, so cross-contamination may occur.

Max & Erma's $LD

(866) 629-3762
American
Confirmed: 4/5/2010

6-1/2 oz. Sandwich Chicken Breast —*request that it be chargrilled with nothing on it*
Baked Potato

Laredo Steak —*no cactus butter*
Plain Hamburger —*no bun, no toppings*
Plain Salads —*request oil and vinegar dressing, confirm toppings are gluten-free*

Max & Erma's Notes: Kitchens are not gluten-free, so Max & Erma's does not guarantee that any food is gluten-free. This is a preliminary list. Inquire with the server for more information.

McAlister's Deli ¢LD
(888) 855-3354
Deli
Confirmed: 4/24/2010

Soup & Chili
Southwestern Roasted Corn Soup

Dressings and Extras
Bacon Bits
Bacon
Cheese (All)
Lite Sour Cream
Salad Dressings (All)

Sandwiches —no bread
Chicken Salad
Corned Beef
Roast Beef
Smoked Deli Turkey
Tuna Salad

Sides
Fajita Chicken Strips (NOT grilled chicken breast)
Fruit Salad
Mashed Potatoes —*no gravy*
Potato Salad
Steamed Broccoli and Carrots

Spuds
Plain Baked Potato with or without Land-O-Lakes Butter

McAlister's Deli Notes: This list was prepared with information provided by vendors. McAlister's Deli may vary vendors or ingredients without prior notice, and

they are not responsible for the accuracy or timeliness of this information. Contact the corporate office for updated gluten-free lists.

McDonald's ¢BLD
(800) 244-6227
American
Confirmed: 4/8/2010

Triumph Notes: McDonald's no longer maintains a gluten-free list. Ingredient information is updated periodically, and is available on the website.

Melting Pot, The ✪$$LD
(800) 783-0867
Fondue
Confirmed: 4/23/2010

Salads
Caesar Salad —*no croutons*
California Salad
Spinach Mushroom Salad
The Melting Pot House Salad —*no croutons*

Cheese Fondue —no bread, no chips, request a GF cheese dipper bowl, request that it be made with cornstarch
Cheddar Cheese Fondue —*request that it be made with Redbridge beer*
Fiesta Cheese Fondue —*request that it be made with Redbridge beer*
Spinach Artichoke Cheese Fondue
Traditional Swiss Cheese Fondue
Wisconsin Trio Cheese Fondue

Individual Entrée Selections
Breast of Chicken
Cedar Plank Salmon
Filet Mignon
Land & Sea
Pacific Rim —*request substitutions for teriyaki-marinated sirloin and potstickers*
Seafood Trio
Signature Selection —*request a substitution for teriyaki-marinated sirloin*

The French Quarter
The Vegetarian —*no batters, request substitutions for tofu, ravioli, and pasta*

Sides
Cold Water Lobster Tail

Entrée Cooking Styles
Bourguignonne —*no batters*
Coq au Vin
Court Bouillon
Mojo Style

Entrée Sauces
Curry
Ginger Plum
Gorgonzola Port
Green Goddess

Chocolate Fondue —*request GF dessert plate (strawberries, bananas, plain marshmallows, and pineapple)*
Bananas Foster
Chocolate S'mores —*no crushed graham crackers*
Cookies 'n Cream Marshmallow Dream —*no crushed Oreo cookies*
Disaronno Meltdown
Flaming Turtle
Pure Chocolate
Special Event
The Original
Yin & Yang

Beverages
Wines (All)

Specialty Drinks
Blackberry Sage Lemonade
Exotic Mojito
Love Martini
Mango Margarita
Meltini
Sangria
Yin & Yang

Melting Pot Notes: The Melting Pot has assembled this menu with help from the Gluten Intolerance Group. Neither organization is responsible for the use of this information, which The Melting Pot has not independently verified. Customers should consider this information as it pertains to their own dietary needs.

Triumph Notes: This list was marked updated 3/2010.

Miller's Ale House Restaurants $LD
(561) 743-2299
Seafood & Steakhouse
Confirmed: 4/1/2010

Salads —*no salad dressing, no croutons*
Caesar Salad (Grilled Chicken, Grouper, Mahi Mahi, Shrimp, Wild Alaskan Salmon)
Chef Salad —*no ham*
Summer Salad
Tossed Salad
Zinger Salad —*request grilled chicken*

Burgers —*no bun, request baked potato or steamed vegetables as sides*
Ale House Mini Burgers
Basic Burger
British Burger —*no swiss cheese*

Great Steaks —*no seasoning, request baked potato and steamed vegetables as sides*
12 oz. Choice Ribeye
12 oz. New York Strip
20 oz. Porterhouse
8 oz. Filet Mignon

House Specialties
Bahamian Dolphin
Grilled Pork Medallions —*request baked potato and steamed vegetables as sides*

Seafood —*no coleslaw, request baked potato or steamed vegetables as sides*
Catch of the Day
Grouper
Mahi Mahi
Wild Alaskan Salmon

Fresh Raw Bar *—no cocktail sauce*
Clams on the Half Shell
Raw Oysters
Steamed Clams
Steamed Oysters

Moe's Southwest Grill   ¢LD
(404) 705-4409
Southwest
Confirmed: 4/2/2010

Soups
Baja Chicken Enchilada Soup

Proteins
Fish
Ground Beef
Pork
Tofu

Beans
Black Beans
Pinto Beans

Dress It Up
Black Olives
Cheese
Chipotle Ranch
Cucumbers
Guacamole
Hard Rock Sauce
Jalapenos
Lettuce
Pico de Gallo
Queso (Cheese Sauce)
Rice
Rock 'n Roll Sauce
Salsa (El Guapo, Kaiser)
Sour Cream
Southwest Vinaigrette
Tomatillo Salsa
Veggies

Moe's Southwest Grill Notes: Corn chips
and corn tortillas are fried in the same
fryer as items containing gluten. This
information is based on standard recipe
formulations, as reported by suppliers.
Variations may occur due to changes in
supplier, ingredients or products, product
assembly, season, recipe revisions, or
ingredient substitutions. This may affect
the stated contents of food. Moe's is not
responsible for the use of this list or for any
reactions that arise from its use.

Triumph Notes: This list was marked
effective as of 2/25/2008.

Morton's The Steakhouse $$$$LD
(866) 667-8667
Steakhouse
Confirmed: 4/5/2010

Morton's The Steakhouse Notes: No
gluten-free list is available. However, upon
arrival, alert the server to your dietary
needs, or call ahead to speak with the
General Manager. They can arrange a meal
with the chef, as many menu items are
gluten-free with modifications.

Ninety Nine Restaurant   ✪★ $LD
(781) 933-8999
American
Confirmed: 4/2/2010

Fresh From the Garden
Caesar Salad *—no rustic bread*
Chicken Caesar *—no croutons, no rustic
bread*
Garden Salad *—no croutons*

Salad Dressings
Bleu Cheese, Buttermilk Ranch, Honey
Mustard, Northern Italian

Guest Inspired Chef Created
Broiled Sirloin Tips
Combo Creations (Fresh Cedar Plank
Salmon, Kickin' Shrimp Skewer, Top
Sirloin Steak) *—no honey butter biscuit*
Fresh Cedar Plank Salmon
NY Strip Sirloin
Prime Rib *—no au jus*
Smothered Tips
Top Sirloin Steak

Two Hands Required —*request gluten-free roll*

All Star Steakburger
Bacon & Cheese Steakburger
Mushroom & Cheese Steakburger

Classic Sides

Baked Potato
French Fries
Garlic Red Skin Mashed Potatoes
Load a Mashed or Baked Potato with
　Cheese, Bacon, & Chives
Seasonal Vegetables

Kid's Menu

Junior Steakburger with Cheese —*request a gluten-free roll*
Junior Top Sirloin Steak

Irresistible Endings

Hot Fudge Sundae

Ninety Nine Restaurant Notes: Upon arrival, alert a server to your dietary needs. This menu is not medical advice, and Ninety Nine is not responsible for its use or resulting reactions. There is no guarantee that foods from this menu are gluten-free.

Triumph Notes: This list was marked 4/10.

Noodles & Company　　　　ζ LD

(720) 214-1900
Pasta
Confirmed: 4/2/2010

Asian

Pad Thai

Proteins

Braised Beef
Sauteed Beef
Sauteed Shrimp

Extras

Cucumber Tomato Salad
Tossed Green Salad with Fat Free Asian
Tossed Green Salad

Noodles & Company Notes: Kitchens are not gluten-free and pasta is a central component of the menu, so cross-contamination may occur. Noodles & Company does not guarantee that any of these items are gluten-free. This guide is updated periodically, so check back for updated and accurate information.

Triumph Notes: This list was marked 1.20.10.

O'Charley's　　　　$ LD

(615) 256-8500
American
Confirmed: 4/6/2010

Asparagus
Baby Back BBQ Ribs
Baked Potato (Loaded), A La Carte
Baked Potato (Plain)
Bleu Cheese Steak Topping
Broccoli
Cajun Shrimp and Grits
California Chicken Salad —*no dressing*
California Shrimp Salad —*no dressing*
Cedar Planked Salmon
Cedar Planked Tilapia
Cheese Blend for Baked Potato
Dressings (Balsamic, Bleu Cheese,
　Cranberry Orange Vinaigrette, Honey
　Mustard, Honey Mustard Light, Ranch,
　Southwestern Ranch)
Eggs & Bacon
Eggs & Sausage
Eggs
Filet Mignon
Grilled Atlantic Salmon with Chipotle-
　BBQ Sauce
Grilled Atlantic Salmon
Grilled Chicken Breast (Pick 2/3 Lunch)
Jr. Grilled Chicken
Jr. Grilled Steak
Julienned Veggie Mix
Louisiana Sirloin
Margarine for Baked Potato
Mushrooms, Sauteed
Onions, Sauteed

Pick 2, Pick 3 Butcher's Cut Pemium USDA
  Sirloin
Ribeye
Salmon Chipotle
Salmon Dinner
Sausage Pattie
Smashed Potatoes, A La Carte
Soup, Overloaded Potato
Sour Cream for Baked Potato
Top Sirloin, Grilled
Your Favorite Rib-eye Steak

Old Spaghetti Factory, The ✪★ $LD

(503) 225-0433
Pasta
Confirmed: 4/1/2010

Salads
House Salad —*no croutons, request creamy
  pesto dressing or balsamic vinaigrette*

Baked Chicken —*request gluten-free
pasta*
With Marinara Sauce
With Mizithra Cheese & Browned Butter
  Sauce
With Sautéed Mushroom Sauce

Gluten Free Corn Rotelli (Add a Sicilian
Style Italian Sausage or Chicken
Breast) —*request gluten-free pasta*
With Marinara Sauce
With Mizithra Cheese & Browned Butter
  Sauce
With Sautéed Mushroom Sauce

Desserts
Ice Cream (Spumoni, Vanilla)

Beverages
Coffee
Iced Tea
Italian Cream Soda (Blackberry, Cherry,
  Orange, Raspberry, Strawberry)
Milk
Strawberry Lemonade
Tea

Old Spaghetti Factory Notes: Upon
arrival, alert the server to your dietary
needs and indicate modifications when
ordering. Kitchens are not gluten-free, so
cross-contamination may occur.

Olive Garden ✪★ $$LD

(800) 331-2729
Italian
Confirmed: 4/7/2010

Salads
Caesar Salad —*no croutons*
Garden Salad —*no croutons*

Entrées
Children's Grilled Chicken
Herb-Grilled Salmon
Mixed Grill —*no demi-glaze*
Mixed Grill with Chicken only —*no demi-
  glaze*
Pennine Rigate with Marinara —*request
  gluten-free pasta*
Steak Toscano

Olive Garden Notes: Variations in recipes
and preparation may occur. Therefore,
Olive Garden does not recommend relying
solely on this menu to ensure a meal will
be gluten-free. Olive Garden is not liable
for the use of this menu. Any medical
reactions related to items on this menu
should be directed to a physician. Contact
the corporate office for more information.

Triumph Notes: Call ahead to ensure
gluten-free pasta is available at the location
you'll be dining in.

On the Border Mexican Grill &
Cantina ¢LD

(800) 983-4637
Mexican
Confirmed: 4/6/2010

Appetizers
Guacamole & Guacamole Live —*no tortilla
  chips, no garnish*

Soups & Salads —, no tortilla strips, request salad dressings on the GF list only

Citrus Chipotle Chicken Salad
House Salad
Sizzling Fajita Salad (Chicken or Steak) —
no sour cream, no onions

Salad Dressings

Chipotle Honey Mustard
Fat Free Mango Citrus Vinaigrette
Smoked Jalapeno Vinaigrette

Fajita Grill —no condiments, no onions, no flour tortillas

Fajitas (Grilled Vegetable with Portabella
Mushrooms (Not Classic Veggies),
Mesquite-Grilled Chicken, Mesquite-
Grilled Steak, Pork Carnitas)
Sauces (Chipotle Honey, Tequila Lime
Chile)
Veggies (El Diablo)

Fresh Grill

Chicken Salsa Fresca
Tomatillo Chicken

OTB Taco Stand —request sides from the GF list only

Street-Style (Mini): Chicken, Steak

Sides

Black Bean & Corn Salsa
Black Beans
Cilantro Lime Rice
Corn Tortilla
Guacamole
House Vegetables
Mexican Rice
Mixed Cheese
Pico
Refried Beans —no blue corn chips

Sauces

Salsa
Tomato Salsa Fresca

Kids —request sides from GF list only

Kids Grilled Chicken Entrée

Kids House Salad —no dressing
Kids Mixed Vegetables
Strawberry Sundae

Beverages

Borderita Grande
Cuervo Paradise Rita
House Margarita
Iced Tea
Mango Passion Fruit Swirl Margarita
Milagro Agave Rita
Mojito
Perfect Patron
Sangria Swirl Margarita
Sangria
Shaken Margarita
Strawberry Lemonade
Wine (Red & White)

On the Border Mexican Grill & Cantina

Notes: Consult the manager before
ordering to check the information provided
is up to date and applicable to that location.
Kitchens are not gluten-free and fryer oil
is shared, so cross-contamination may
occur. On the Border does not guarantee
that any food is gluten-free. The gluten-free
list is based on food suppliers' ingredient
information; however, variations may
occur due to substitutions, recipe revisions,
preparation techniques, or the season. This
may affect the stated contents of food.

Triumph Notes: This list is valid until April
30, 2010, and was provided for illustrative
purposes. An updated list is available by
contacting On the Border directly for an
updated version.

Outback Steakhouse   ⊘ $$ LD
(813) 282-1225
Steakhouse
Confirmed: 4/28/2010

Aussie-Tizers to Share

Grilled Shrimp on the Barbie
Seared Ahi Tuna —no dressing

Salads —*request that salad be mixed in a separate bowl, request any dressing EXCEPT for Mustard Vinaigrette or Blue Cheese*

Chicken or Shrimp Caesar Salad —*no croutons*

Filet Wedge Salad

Queensland Salad —*no croutons*

Burgers & Sandwiches —*no bread, request veggies without seasoning or baked potato instead of fries*

Bacon Cheese Burger

Grilled Chicken & Swiss Sandwich

The Bloomin' Burger —*no Bloomin' Onion petals*

The Outback Burger

Outback Favorites

Alice Springs Chicken —*request veggies without seasoning or baked potato instead of fries*

Baby Back Ribs —*request veggies without seasoning or baked potato instead of fries*

Filet with Wild Mushrooms —*request veggies without seasoning, no wild mushroom sauce*

Grilled Chicken on the Barbie —*request veggies without seasoning or baked potato*

New Zealand Rack of Lamb —*request veggies without seasoning or baked potato, no cabernet sauce*

Sweet Glazed Pork Tenderloin —*request green beans without seasoning, veggies without seasoning, or baked potato, no crunchy crumb topping*

Perfect Combinations

Filet & Shrimp Scampi —*no garlic toast, no au jus*

Ribs & Alice Springs Chicken —*request veggies without seasoning or baked potato instead of fries*

Signature Steaks

New York Strip

Outback Special

Prime Rib —*no au jus*

Ribeye

The Melbourne

Victoria's Filet —*no blue cheese, no horseradish crumb crust*

Straight from the Sea —*request veggies without seasoning or baked potato*

Alaskan King Crab

Lobster Tails

Norwegian Salmon

Add On Mates

1/2 lb. Alaskan King Crab

Grilled Scallops —*no lemon pepper butter sauce*

Grilled Shrimp

Lobster Tail

Shrimp Scampi —*no garlic toast*

Freshly Made Sides

Dressed Baked Potato

Fresh Seasonal Veggies —*no seasonings*

Garlic Mashed Potatoes

Sweet Potato

Signature Side Salads —*no croutons, request that salad be mixed in separate bowl, request any dressing EXCEPT for Mustard Vinaigrette or Blue Cheese*

Caesar Salad

Classic Blue Cheese Wedge Salad —*no blue cheese dressing*

House Salad

Joey Menu (Kids Under 10) —*request veggies without seasoning or baked potato instead of fries*

Boomerang Cheese Burger —*no bread*

Grilled Chicken on the Barbie

Joey Sirloin

Junior Ribs

Spotted Dog Sundae —*no Oreo cookie crumbles*

Desserts

Chocolate Thunder from Down Under

Beverages

Acqua Panna

Red Bull
Royal Cup Coffee
San Pellegrino

After-Dinner Drinks
Disaronno Amaretto on the Rocks
Grand Marnier Straight Up
Kalua and Coffee

Outback Specialty Cocktails
Captain's Mai Tai
Down Under Sauza Gold Coast 'Rita
New South Wales Sangria
Sangria 'Rita
Sauza Gold Coast 'Rita
The Wallaby Darned
Top Shelf Patron Margarita

Outback Steakhouse Notes: Items may vary by location. If bringing your own GF bread, do not send it to the kitchen. This menu was produced in cooperation with the Gluten Intolerance Group (GIG), and Outback Steakhouse has not verified the information provided. Neither Outback nor GIG is responsible for its use. Consider this information as it pertains to your dietary needs.

Triumph Notes: This menu was marked 4/2010. Because menus may vary by location, this one is for illustrative purposes only.

P.F. Chang's China Bistro   ⊘★$LD
(866) 732-4264
Asian Fusion
Confirmed: 4/8/2010

Egg Drop Soup
Gluten Free Beef & Broccoli Lunch Bowl
Gluten Free Beef & Broccoli
Gluten Free Beef a la Sichuan
Gluten Free Buddha's Feast Lunch Bowl
Gluten Free Buddha's Feast
Gluten Free Cantonese Shrimp or Scallops
Gluten Free Chang's Chicken Lettuce Wraps
Gluten Free Chang's Lemon Scallops

Gluten Free Chang's Spicy Chicken
Gluten Free Dali Chicken
Gluten Free Fried Rice
Gluten Free Garlic Snap Peas
Gluten Free Ginger Chicken with Broccoli
Gluten Free Hong Kong Beef with Snow Peas
Gluten Free Mongolian Beef
Gluten Free Moo Goo Gai Pan Lunch Bowl
Gluten Free Moo Goo Gai Pan
Gluten Free Pepper Steak Lunch Bowl
Gluten Free Pepper Steak
Gluten Free Philip's Better Lemon Chicken
Gluten Free Salmon Steamed with Ginger
Gluten Free Shanghai Cucumbers
Gluten Free Shrimp with Lobster Sauce Lunch Bowl
Gluten Free Shrimp with Lobster Sauce
Gluten Free Singapore Street Noodles
Gluten Free Spinach with Garlic

P.F. Chang's China Bistro Notes: Upon arrival, alert a manager or chef to your dietary needs.

Panera Bread   ¢BLD
Café
Confirmed: 4/6/2010

Soups
Creamy Tomato —*no croutons*
Cuban Black Bean and Lentil
Low Fat Vegetarian Black Bean
Low-Fat Chicken Tortilla Soup
Low-Fat Vegetarian Southwest Tomato & Roasted Corn
Summer Corn Chowder
Turkey Chickpea Chili
Vegetarian Butternut Squash
Vegetarian Roasted Red Pepper & Lentil

Salads
Asian Sesame Chicken Salad —*no won ton noodles*
BBQ Chopped Chicken Salad
Caesar Salad —*no croutons*
California Mission Chicken Salad
Classic Café Salad

Greek Salad
Grilled Chicken Caesar Salad —*no croutons*
Mediterranean Salmon Salad
Salmon Caesar Salad —*no croutons*
Strawberry Poppyseed Salad with Chicken
Strawberry Poppyseed Salad

Salad Dressings
Asian Sesame Vinaigrette
Balsamic Vinaigrette
BBQ Ranch
Caesar
Greek
Poppyseed
Raspberry Vinaigrette
Roasted Garlic & Meyer's Lemon
    Vinaigrette
White Balsamic Vinaigrette

Sides
Panera Bread Potato Chips

Beverages
Coffee
Frozen Beverages (All)
Hot Chocolate
Juice (Apple, Orange)
Lattes (All)
Lemonade
Milk
Pumpkin Spice Latte
Soda (Bottled, Fountain)
Strawberry Smoothie
Tea (Chai, Regular)

Panera Bread Notes: Kitchens are not gluten-free, so cross-contamination may occur. Menu items are subject to change by location. Ingredient listings are available on the website. Recipes may change. To receive the most current information, contact your nearest Panera location and speak with a manager.

Pasta House Co., The   ✪ ★ $LD
(314) 535-6644
Pasta
Confirmed: 4/21/2010

Salads
The Pasta House Co. Special Salad

Entrée —*request gluten-free pasta*
Chicken Breast
Chicken Parmigiano
Mostaccioli
Pasta con Broccoli
Penne Alfredo
Penne Pomodoro
Penne with Red Clams
Sicilian Pesce

Desserts
French Vanilla Ice Cream
Spumoni Ice Cream

Pasta House Co. Notes: Upon arrival, alert the server to your dietary needs. The restaurant recommends calling ahead so that gluten-free pasta can be prepared in a timely manner. Cross-contamination may occur, and a gluten-free meal cannot be guaranteed.

Pei Wei Asian Diner   ✪ ¢LD
(480) 888-3000
Asian
Confirmed: 4/7/2010

Asian Chopped Chicken Salad —*no lime vinaigrette dressing, no wonton strips*
Pei Wei Spicy (Chicken, Shrimp)
Pei Wei Spicy Salad (Chicken, Shrimp)
Pei Wei Sweet & Sour (Non-Battered Chicken, Shrimp)
Vietnamese Chicken Salad Rolls —*no thai peanut sauce*

Pei Wei Asian Diner Notes: Kitchens are not gluten-free.

Pizza Hut   ¢LD
(800) 948-8488
Pizza
Confirmed: 4/14/2010

Triumph Notes: No gluten-free list is available. Contact Pizza Hut for more information.

Potbelly Sandwich Works ¢LD
(312) 951-0600
Sandwich Shop
Confirmed: 4/7/2010

Soups
Garden Vegetable

Side Salads
Coleslaw
Potato Salad

Salad Dressings
1000 Island
Buttermilk Ranch
Non-Fat Vinaigrette
Potbelly Vinaigrette

Shakes, Malts, & Smoothies —no cookies on straw
Banana
Boysenberry
Chocolate
Coffee
Dreamsickle
Mocha
Pineapple-Coconut
Strawberry
Vanilla

Cheese
American
Provolone
Swiss

Meats and Other Sandwich "Main Stuff"
Bacon
Egg (Breakfast Sandwiches Only)
Italian Meat - Capicolla
Italian Meat - Mortadello
Italian Meat - Pepperoni
Italian Meat - Salami
Jelly
Marinara
Mushrooms

Peanut Butter
Roast Beef
Sausage (Breakfast Sandwiches Only)
Smoked Ham
Turkey Breast

Salad Stuff
Artichoke Hearts
Blue Cheese
Cherry Tomatoes
Chick Peas
Cucumbers
Hard Boiled Egg
Roasted Red Peppers
Romaine, Iceberg, Radicchio, Carrot and Radish Blend

Sandwich Toppings
Hot Peppers (In Oil)
Iceberg Lettuce
Mayo
Mustard
Oil
Onions
Pickles
Tomatoes

Potbelly Sandwich Works Notes: Order salads without croutons. Upon arrival, alert a manager to your dietary needs so that he or she can take the precautions necessary in order to make gluten-free food. Because wheat bread is a central component of the menu, cross-contamination may occur. This list is based on information provided by suppliers. There is no guarantee that any food items are allergen-free. Food suppliers may vary ingredients, possibly affecting the stated contents of food. Check frequently for updated versions of this list.

Triumph Notes: This list was marked 1/28/2010.

Pret a Manger $BL
(646) 728-0505
Sandwich & Soups
Confirmed: 4/23/2010

Soups
Chicken & Mushroom
Chorizo & Butter Bean
Lentil & Bacon
Malaysian Chicken
Miso Soup
Moroccan Chicken
Mushroom Risotto
Pret Classic Tomato
Sag Aloo
Spinach & Nutmeg
Winter Vegetable

Salads —*no dressing*
Chef's Italian Chicken Salad
Chicken Caesar Salad (Airports Only)
Edamame Beans
French Dressing (Small or Large)
No Bread Wild Crayfish & Avocado
Tapas Salad
Tuna Nicoise Salad
Wild Crayfish & Salmon Salad (Airports Only)

Crisps & Snacks
Crisps - Croxton Manor Cheddar & Red Onion
Crisps - Maldon Sea Salt
Crisps - Parsnip, Beetroot, & Carrot
Crisps - Sea Salt & Organic Cider Vinegar
Crisps - Sweet Potato & Chipotle Chili
Dried Mango
Topcorn (Chocolate Crackle, Salted, Cheddar & Onion, Sweet & Salt)
Yoghurt Nuts

Pret Pots, Puddings & Fruit
Chocolate Moose
Kids Fruit Pot
Mango & Lime
Pret Caramel
Pret Fruit Salad
Seedless Grapes
Superfruit Salad
Tropical Fruit Sticks
Very Berry Pret Pot

Cold Drinks
Apple Juice

Carrot Juice
Mango & Orange Smoothie
Milk (Kids)
Orange Juice (Large)
Orange Juice
Pure Pret (Apple, Ginger Beer, Grape & Elderflower, Orange, Yoga Bunny)
Pure Pret Still (Elderflower Youth, Hippie, Lemon Aid, Pomegranate Power)
Strawberry Smoothie
Vanilla Bean & Honey Yoghurt Drink
Vitamin Volcano

Hot Drinks
12oz Cappuccino (With or Without Chocolate)
12oz Hot Chocolate
12oz Latte
12oz Mocha

Triumph Notes: This list was marked Monday 15 March to Sunday 9 May 2010. Contact Prêt a Manger for the most recent information.

Qdoba Mexican Grill   ¢ BLD
(888) 497-3622
Mexican
Confirmed: 3/23/2010

Triumph Notes: Qdoba does not have a traditional gluten-free list. Instead, they have a chart with wheat-containing items. Contact Qdoba for this list.

Red Lobster $$ LD
(800) 562-7837
Seafood
Confirmed: 4/6/2010

Appetizers
Chilled Jumbo Shrimp Cocktail —*no cocktail sauce*

Entrées
"Today's Fresh Fish" —*no seasonings, request that it be broiled*

Chicken —*no marinades, no sauces, no seasonings, request that it be broiled*
Live Main Lobster —*request that it be steamed and served with melted butter*
North Pacific King Crab Legs —*request that they be steamed and served with melted butter*
Shrimp —*no sauces, no seasonings, request that it be broiled*
Snow Crab Legs —*request that they be steamed and served with melted butter*
Steak —*no marinades, no sauces, no seasonings, request that it be broiled*

Sides
Steamed Asparagus —*no seasonings*
Steamed Broccoli —*no seasonings*

Children's Entrées
Broiled Fish —*no seasonings, request that it be broiled*
Chicken —*no marinades, no sauces, no seasonings, request that it be broiled*
Snow Crab Legs —*request that they be steamed and served with melted butter*

Red Lobster Notes: Alert a manager to your dietary needs. Confirm that chicken and steak items have not been pre-marinated. Red Lobster does not guarantee that any food is gluten-free. Kitchens are not gluten-free, so cross-contamination may occur. Ingredients may vary and recipes may change. Red lobster is not responsible for the use of this list and does not assume any liability for its use.

Red Robin Gourmet Burgers   ¢LD
(877) 733-6543
American
Confirmed: 4/6/2010

Salads —*dressings not included; pick from GF dressing list only*
Apple Harvest Chicken Salad —*no dijon vinaigrette, no candied walnuts, no bleu cheese crumbles, no other cheese*
Cobb Salad —*no bleu cheese crumbles, no black olives, no garlic bread*

Crispy Chicken Tender Salad —*no garlic bread, request grilled chicken breast instead of fried chicken tenders*
Dinner Salad —*no tortilla strips*
Mighty Caesar Salad —*request grilled chicken or salmon instead of blackened chicken, no croutons*
Side Caesar Salad —*no croutons, no garlic bread*

Salad Dressings —*verify with manager; ingredients vary by location*
Balsamic Vinaigrette
Blue Cheese
Creamy Caesar
Honey-Mustard Poppyseed

Entrées
Ensenada Chicken Platter —*no baja ranch dressing, no ancho marinade on chicken breasts, no tortilla strips, no tortilla cups*

Chicken Burgers —*request "protein-style" with lettuce instead of a bun, request sides from the GF list only*
California Chicken Burger

Classic Gourmet Burgers —*no Red Robin seasoning on beef patty, request "protein-style" with lettuce instead of a bun, request sides from the GF list only*
Guacamole Burger
Monster Burger
Royal Red Robin Burger
RR Bacon Cheeseburger
RR Gourmet Cheeseburger

Insanely Delicious Burgers request *"protein-style" with lettuce instead of a bun, request sides from the GF list only*
Bruschetta Chicken Burger —*request plain salsa instead of tomato-bruschetta salsa*

Other Favorite Burgers —*request sides from the gluten-free list only*

Grilled Salmon Burger —*no Country Dijon sauce, request "protein-style" with lettuce instead of a bun*

Grilled Turkey Burger —*no chipotle mayo, request "protein-style" with lettuce instead of a bun*

Lettuce Wrap Your Burger —*no Red Robin seasoning on beef patty*

Sides (Adults & Kids)

Celery Sticks
Dinner Salad —*no tortilla strips*
Guacamole
Mandarin Oranges
Melon Wedges
Salsa
Steamed Veggies
White Rice

Kid's Menu (Kids can also customize items on the adult menu) —*request sides from the GF list only*

Chick-on-a-Stick —*no teriyaki sauce, no ranch dressing*

Rad Burger with Beef Patty —*request "protein-style" with lettuce instead of a bun, no Red Robin seasoning on beef patty*

Rad Burger with Turkey Patty —*request "protein-style" with lettuce instead of a bun*

Red Robin Gourmet Burgers Notes: Ask a manager before ordering salad dressings, as ingredients may vary by location. Bleu cheese crumbles should not be used in any gluten-free dish. Kitchens are not gluten-free, so cross-contamination may occur. The broiler and fryer may not be gluten free, so inquire. This list is based on statements provided by suppliers. Ingredients may vary due to substitutions, alterations, or other reasons, so always check that you have the most recent information.

Triumph Notes: This list was marked valid through 5/1/10. It is provided for illustrative purposes only. This list expires monthly, so contact Red Robin for an updated version.

Rí Rá Irish Pub $LD
Irish
Confirmed: 4/15/2010

Lunch Entrées

Emigrant's Corned Beef & Cabbage —*no parsley sauce*

Lemon Broiled Haddock —*no crumb topping*

Dinner Entrées

Broiled Haddock —*no crumb topping*
Emigrant's Corned Beef & Cabbage —*no parsley sauce*
Gaelic Steak —*no Gaelic steak sauce*
Steak & Chips

Starters

Baked Spinach Dip —*request tortilla strips instead of baguette*

Hand Cut Chips
Pub Wings
Steamed Mussels —*no crostini*

Salads

Chop Chop
Pub Salad —*no croutons on the caesar*
Ri Ra Salad
The Bistro

Burgers —*no bun, no bread*

Black & Bleu
Paddy Melt
Pub Burger
The Ri Ra —*no onion rings*

Sandwiches —*no bread*

Bistro Chicken —*no bun*
Hummus Wrap —*no pita wrap, request as plate*

Rí Rá Irish Pub Notes: Do not order directly from this list. Upon arrival, alert the server to your dietary needs. This will trigger allergy protocols within the restaurant, from the floor to the kitchen. Kitchens are not gluten-free, so cross-contamination may occur.

Romano's Macaroni Grill $LD
(800) 983-4637
Pasta
Confirmed: 4/6/2010

Fresh Antipasti
Mediterranean Olives —*no peasant bread*
Mozzarella alla Caprese

Insalata —*no croutons*
Caesar Salad
Chicken Caesar
Fresh Greens Salad —*no dressing*
Parmesan-Crusted Chicken —*request grilled chicken breast*
Scallops & Spinach Salad
Warm Spinach Salad —*no goat cheese*

Salad Dressings
Balsamic Vinaigrette
Caesar
Mediterranean Vinaigrette
Peppercorn Ranch

Handcrafted Pasta
Sausage Salentino —*no pasta*
Shrimp Portofino —*no panko breadcrumbs, no pasta*

Mediterranean Grill
Aged Beef Tenderloin Spiedini —*no vegetables*
Calabrese Steak —*no sides*
Center-Cut Filet —*no sides*
Center-Cut Lamb Spiedini —*no vegetables*
Grilled Chicken Spiedini —*no vegetables*
Grilled Halibut —*no risotto*
Italian Sausage Spiedini —*no vegetables*
Jumbo Shrimp Spiedini —*no vegetables*

Sides
Grilled Asparagus
Spinach & Garlic

Kid's
Fresh Greens Salad
Grilled Chicken & Broccoli —*no pasta*

Desserts
Italian Sorbetto —*no biscotti*

Beverages
Italian & Italian Cream Sodas (Blackberry, Mango, Pomegranate, Sicilian Orange)
Tea (Blackberry Mint, Mango, Peach, Raspberry)
Wine (Red, White)

Romano's Macaroni Grill Notes: Upon arrival, alert a manager to verify the accuracy of this information. Neither the kitchen nor the frying oil are gluten-free, so cross-contamination may occur. Product information is provided by food manufacturers. Macaroni Grill is unable to guarantee that any food is gluten-free. Ingredients may vary due to recipe revisions, preparation techniques, or the season.

Triumph Notes: This menu expires on a monthly basis and is provided for illustrative purposes only. The menu was marked valid through 3/28/10. Contact Macaroni Grill for an updated version.

Rubio's Fresh Mexican Grill   ¢LD
(760) 929-8226
Mexican
Confirmed: 4/7/2010

Rubio's Fresh Mexican Grill Notes: Fried items are prepared in shared oil. Cross-contamination may occur.

Triumph Notes: Rubio's has a list of items that do contain gluten available on their website.

Ruby Tuesday $LD
American
Confirmed: 4/7/2010

Brunch —*no biscuits, no cookies*
Berry Good Yogurt Parfait —*no granola*
Mini Benedicts - Steak —*no bun, no seasoned potatoes*
Spinach & Mushroom Omelet —*no seasoned potatoes*
Steak & Eggs —*no crepe*
Western Omelet —*no seasoned potatoes*

Kids' Brunch —*no biscuits, no cookies*
Eggscellent Combo —*no bacon, no seasoned potatoes*

Create Your Own: Endless Fresh Garden Bar
Dressings: Balsamic Vinaigrette, French, Honey Mustard, Italian
Garden Bar Salads: Cucumber Salad
Toppings: Beets, Cottage Cheese, Cranraisins, Diced Eggs, Diced Ham, Diced Red Peppers, Edamame, Feta Cheese Crumbles, Garbanzo Beans, Green Peas, Shredded Cheddar Cheese, Shredded Parmesan Cheese, Sliced Black Olives

Salad Sensations
Asian Salmon Spinach Salad —*no wonton strips, no sesame-peanut dressing*
Avocado Shrimp Salad —*no wonton strips, no avocado ranch dressing*
Southwestern Beef Salad —*no tortilla chips, no southwestern ranch dressing*

Fork-Tender Ribs
Memphis Dry Rub Ribs (Half Rack or Full Rack) —*no mashed potatoes, no sour cream on the baked potato*

Handcrafted Burgers —*no bun, no pickle, no french fries, no Ruby's mayonnaise*
Alpine Swiss Burger
Bison Bacon Cheeseburger —*no bacon*
Boston Blue Burger —*no Boston barbecue sauce, no onion straws*
Classic Cheeseburger
Ruby's Classic Burger
Three Cheese Burger

Handcrafted Steaks —*no onion straws, no mashed potatoes, no sour cream on the baked potato*
Cowboy Sirloin (9 oz.) —*no Boston barbecue sauce*
Peppercorn Mushroom Sirloin (9 oz.) —*no parmesan cream sauce*
Petite Sirloin (7 oz.)
Rib Eye (12 oz.)
Steak & Lobster Tail
Top Sirloin (9 oz.)

Premium Sandwiches
The Ultimate Chicken —*no bun, no Ruby's mayonnaise, no bacon, no french fries*

Premium Seafood
Asian Glazed Salmon —*no sesame-peanut sauce, no brown-rice pilaf*
New Orleans Seafood —*no parmesan cream sauce, no brown-rice pilaf*
Steak & Lobster Tail —*no mashed potatoes, no sour cream on the baked potato*

Prime Burgers —*no bun, no french fries, no Ruby's mayonnaise*
Triple Prime Burger
Triple Prime Cheddar Burger
Triple Prime Havarti Burger

Specialties
Barbecue Grilled Chicken —*no barbecue sauce, no succotash, no mashed potatoes*
Chicken Bella —*no parmesan cream sauce, no mashed potatoes*
Chicken Fresco —*no lemon-butter sauce, no mashed potatoes*

Signature Sides
Baked Potato —*no sour cream*
Fresh Steamed Broccoli
Sauteed Baby Portabella Mushrooms
Sugar Snap Peas

Kids' Menu
Beef Mini Burgers —*no bun, no french fries*
Chop Steak —*no mashed potatoes*
Grilled Chicken

Desserts

Berry Good Yogurt Parfait —*no granola*

Ruby Tuesday Notes: Cross-contamination may occur. Fried items may be prepared in shared oil. Information has been provided by Ruby Tuesday's suppliers, and they cannot guarantee with absolute certainty that an item does not contain gluten. Ingredients may vary due to substitutions, regional availability, or variations in preparation.

Triumph Notes: This list was marked 04/01/10. Visit the Ruby Tuesday website often for the most recent gluten-free list.

Ruth's Chris Steak House $$$$D

(407) 333-7440
Steakhouse
Confirmed: 4/8/2010

Appetizers and Soups

Barbequed Shrimp —*no toast point*
Crabtini
Seared Ahi-Tuna
Shrimp Cocktail & Shrimp Remoulade

Salads —*request that salads be mixed in a separate bowl*

Caesar Salad —*no garlic croutons*
Lettuce Wedge
Ruth's Chop Salad —*no garlic croutons, no crispy onions*
Sliced Tomato and Onion
Steakhouse Salad —*no garlic croutons*
Vine Ripe Tomato and Buffalo Mozzarella

Salad Dressings

Balsamic Vinaigrette
Creamy Lemon Basil
Ranch
Remoulade
Thousand Island
Vinaigrette & White Vinaigrette

Seafood

Ahi-Tuna Stack
Barbequed Shrimp Entrée

Signature Steaks and Chops

Dinner Menu Steaks and Chops (All)

Specialty Entrees

Stuffed Chicken Breast

Entrée Complements

6 Large Shrimp

Potatoes

Baked
French Fries
Garlic Mashed
Lyonnaise
Shoestring

Vegetables

Broiled Tomatoes
Fresh Asparagus with Hollandaise Sauce
Fresh Broccoli
Sautéed Baby Spinach
Sautéed Mushrooms

Desserts

Chocolate Sin Cake
Fresh Berries and Cream
Ice Cream
Sorbet

Ruth's Classics Fall/Winter Menu

Braised Short Ribs
Caesar Salad —*no garlic croutons*
Filet & Shrimp
Filet
Green Beans with Roasted Garlic
Harvest Salad —*no crispy onions*
Lamb Chops
Mashed Potatoes
Ribeye
Sautéed Mushrooms
Steakhouse Salad —*no garlic croutons*
Stuffed Chicken Breast

Ruth's Chris Steak House Notes: Alert the manager or chef of dietary needs, as many of these items must be modified to be gluten-free. Kitchens are not gluten-free, so cross-contamination may occur. Ruth's Chris is not responsible for the use of this list, and cannot guarantee that any food item is in fact gluten-free.

Triumph Notes: This list is marked 11/5/09. List is for illustrative purposes only, and may not reflect current seasonal offerings.

San Francisco Soup Company ¢BLD
Sandwich & Soups
Confirmed: 4/7/2010

Signature Soups
Chilled Gazpacho
Mexican Chicken Tortilla
Organic Smoky Split Pea
Organic Tomato Bisque
Turkey Chili

Special Soups
BBQ Pork & Black Eyed Pea Soup
Black Bean Chili
Broccoli Cheddar
Caribbean Sweet Potato
Chicken Pozole
Chicken Provencal
Chicken Shitake Bok Choy
Chicken Tikka Masala Soup
Chicken with Wild Rice & Mushrooms
Chili Verde with Pork
Chilled Avocado & Cucumber
Chilled Thai Cucumber Honeydew
Cioppino Seafood Stew
Corned Beef & Cabbage
Cream of Asparagus with Chevre
Creole Vegetable
Curried Butternut Squash
French Onion Soup
Grilled Chicken & Artichoke with Sun-Dried Tomatoes
Grilled Chicken & Roast Corn Chowder
Hearty Beef Vegetable
Indian Lentil
Indian Mulligatawny
Kick A*S*S* Chili
Lobster Bisque
Manhattan Clam Chowder
Market Vegetable Soup

Mediterranean Lentil Stew with Spinach
Mexican Beef & Bean Chili
Moroccan Vegetable Stew
Organic Savory Lentil with Chicken Andouille Sausage
Organic Savory Lentil
Pizza Soup with Pepperoni & Sausage
Portabello Mushroom Chili
Potato Leek
Roasted Chicken with Summer Squash & Lime
Roasted Pumpkin Soup
Roasted Tomato Eggplant
Shrimp Bisque
Split Pea with Ham
Thai Red Curry Chicken
Tomato Basil
Vegetarian Thai Red Curry
Vegetarian Tortilla
West African Peanut with Chicken
Zucchini & Blue Cheese

Entrée Salad
Classic Cobb
Sensational Spinach

Side Salad
Fruit Salad
Mixed Greens
Spinach & Mushroom

Dressing
Balsamic Vinaigrette
Champagne Vinaigrette
Creamy Chipotle
Italian Vinaigrette
Low Fat Ranch
Low Fat Vinaigrette
Ranch
Raspberry Lime
Thousand Island

Triumph Notes: This list was marked March 2010.

Sbarro   ¢LD
(800) 456-4837
Italian
Confirmed: 4/5/2010

Salads
Green Salad

Schlotzsky's   ¢LD
(800) 846-2867
Deli
Confirmed: 4/7/2010

Au Jus
Corned Beef
Dijon Horseradish
Guacamole
Ham
Mayonnaise Light
Mushrooms
Non Dairy Creamer
Pastrami
Pickles
Potato Salad
Roast Beef
Sauerkraut
Turkey
Yeast

Soup
Broccoli Cheese Soup
Hearty Veg. Beef Soup

Dressing
Balsamic
Blue Cheese
Buttermilk Ranch
Caesar Packets
Caesar
French
Garlic
Greek
Honey Dijon
Light Italian
Light Ranch Packets
Raspberry
Salsa
Spicy Fat Free Ranch
Thousand Island

Shane's Rib Shack   ✪$LD
Barbeque
Confirmed: 4/2/2010

Salads *—no onion crisps, no garlic toast*
Beef Brisket
Grilled Chicken
The Shack (BBQ Chicken, Pork)

Plates *—no bread*
BBQ Chicken
Beef Brisket
Full Rack Ribs
Grilled Chicken Tenders
Half Chicken
Half Rack Ribs
Pork
Whole Chicken

Sides
Baked Beans
Cole Slaw
Collard Greens
Corn on the Cob
Green Beans
Side Salad

BBQ Sauce
Shane's Original BBQ Sauce

Shane's Rib Shack Notes: The gluten-free menu is based on product information provided by Shane's approved food manufacturers. Ingredients may vary, and substitutions may occur due to differences in regional suppliers, recipe changes, and the season. Shane's has not investigated potential sources of cross-contamination, and is not responsible for individual reactions to any food product. Alert a restaurant manager prior to placing an order to ensure the accuracy of this information.

Sheetz   ¢LD
(800) 487-5444
American
Confirmed: 4/8/2010

Salads *—no croutons, no bacon bits, no parmesan cheese*
Chef
Chicken Caesar

Garden
Grilled Chicken
Sliced Steak
Taco

Sandwiches —no bread products
Bacon
Deli Dog
Gourmet Burger
Grilled Chicken Breast Strips
Grilled Chicken Breast
Ham
Hot Dog Chili
Hot Dog
Jr. Burger
Pork BBQ
Turkey

Fried Items
French Fries
French Fry Platters

Shoney's   ¢ BLD
(615) 231-2333
American
Confirmed: 4/13/2010

Triumph Notes: An "Allergen Information" packet is available upon request. It lists common allergens, including wheat, but does not list gluten as an allergen. Contact Shoney's for this packet.

Sizzler $$ LD
(310) 846-8750
American
Confirmed: 4/7/2010

Triumph Notes: No gluten-free list is available. Sizzler does provide a chart indicating items that contain the wheat allergen. Contact Sizzler for this chart.

Smokey Bones Bar & Fire Grill $$ LD
Steakhouse
Confirmed: 4/7/2010

Fire Starters
Fire Stix
Smoked Wings

Salads and Soups
Charbroiled Chicken Caesar Salad —no croutons
Cobb Salad
Country Potato Soup (Cup or Bowl)
Nutty Grilled Chicken Salad
Side Caesar Salad —no croutons
Side Green Salad —no croutons

Chicken and Seafood —no bread
BBQ 1/2 Chicken
BBQ 1/4 Chicken
Bones Blackened Grouper
Fish and Chips
Flamed Seared Salmon Teriyaki
Grouper Grilled

Fire Grilled Steaks —no bread
10 oz Top Sirloin —not chipotle marinated
12 oz NY Strip Steak
7 oz Filet Steak
7 oz Top Sirloin —not chipotle marinated
Toppings (All EXCEPT Mushroom Sauce)

Smoked BBQ —no bread
Baby Back Ribs with Original, Brown Sugar, or Memphis Spice (All Sizes)
Sliced Smoked Turkey Breast
Smoked Beef Brisket
Smoked St. Louis Style Ribs with Original, Brown Sugar, or Memphis Spice (All Sizes)

Sides
Apples
Baked Potato
Broccoli
Coleslaw
Loaded Baked Potato
Loaded Mashed Potatoes
Mashed Potatoes —no gravy

Smokey Bones Bar & Fire Grill Notes: All items should be requested with the listed sides only and without bread. Because ingredients are subject to change and all items are hand-crafted, Smokey Bones does not guarantee that any food items are gluten-free. An independent registered dietician has reviewed these items.

Sonic　　　　　　　　　ⓒBLD
(866) 657-6642
American
Confirmed: 4/1/2010

Salad Dressings
Fat-Free Italian
Honey Mustard Dressing
Ranch Dressing
Reduced Calorie Ranch
Thousand Island Dressing

Grill Items
Bacon
Breakfast Sausage
Egg
Hamburger Patty
Hot Dog
Steak

Cheese
Shredded Cheddar Cheese
Shredded Colby Jack Cheese
Sliced American Cheese

Fried Items
French Fries*
Tots*

Sandwich Toppings & Dipping Sauces
Caramel Dipping Sauce
French Fry Sauce
Grape Jelly
Hickory BBQ Sauce
Honey Mustard Sauce
Ketchup
Maple Flavored Syrup
Marinara Sauce
Mayonnaise
Mustard Package
Mustard
Picante Sauce
Ranch Dressing Package

Relish Sweet
Strawberry Jam
Sweet and Sour Sauce
Taco Sauce
Tartar Sauce

Shakes, Drinks, & Toppings
1% Chocolate Milk
1% Milk
Blackberry Tea
Butterfinger
Butterscotch
Caramel Topping
Chocolate Fudge Topping
Coffee Creamer
Hazelnut
Hot Chocolate Cocoa Mix
Lemon Juice
M&Ms
Maraschino Cherries
Neutral Slush Base
Nut Topping
Peach Tea
Peanut Butter Topping
Pineapple Topping
Raspberry Tea
Reese's
Smoothie Powder
Soft Serve (Vanilla)
Strawberry Topping
Syrups (Blue Coconut, Bubble Gum, Cherry, Chocolate, Cream Pie, Grape, Green Apple, Low-Cal Diet Cherry, Orange, Watermelon)
Whipped Dessert Topping

Other
Apple Slices
Fritos Corn Chips
Green Chili Peppers
Roasted Corn and Black Bean
Sliced Dill Pickles
Sliced Jalapenos

Oil & Shortening
Bun Oil
Fryer Shortening

Sonic Notes: Kitchens are not gluten-free, and cross-contamination may occur, both with food items and blended or mixed drinks. Fried items, like french fries and tots, are not always prepared in dedicated fryers. Check the Sonic website for changes to this list.

Starbucks   ¢S
(800) 235-2883
Coffee Shop
Confirmed: 4/8/2010

Triumph Notes: Starbucks does not provide a gluten-free list, but it does report that bottled drinks and pre-packaged items are gluten-free as long as their labels describe them as such.

Steak 'n Shake   ¢LD
(877) 785-6745
American
Confirmed: 4/5/2010

Triumph Notes: Though no gluten-free list is available, there is a list of items that contain the wheat allergen. Contact Steak 'n Shake for a copy of this list.

Sullivan's Steakhouse $$$$LD
www.sullivansteakhouse.com
Steakhouse
Confirmed: 5/4/2010

Appetizer
Alaskan King Crab Legs
Chilled Seafood Sampler
Escargot —*no baguette*
French Onion Soup —*no croutons*
Fresh Oysters
Jumbo Lump Crabmeat
Oysters Rockerfeller
Seared Ahi Tuna
Shrimp Cocktail
Smoked Salmon —*no crustoni*
Steak Tartar —*no toast points*

Steamed Mussels —*no bread*
Stone Crab Claws
Tequila Lime Shrimp
Vegetable Gazpacho

Seafood
All Seafood

Steaks & Chops
All EXCEPT Sliced Steak with Lobster
    Newburg

Sides
Asparagus
Baked Potatoes
Broccoli Hollandaise
Creamed Corn
Green Beans
Hash Browns
Horseradish Mashed Potatoes
Sauteed Spinach
Skillet Steak Mushroom Caps

Sauces & Toppings
Bearnaise
Blue Cheese Crumbles
Carmelized Onions
Gorgonzola Garlic Butter
Green Peppercorn
Oscar Style
Sauteed Mushrooms

Dessert
Crème Brulee
Fresh Berries —*no Cookie Tuile*
Ice Cream & Sorbet

Taco Bell   ¢BLD
(800) 822-6235
Tex-Mex
Confirmed: 4/24/2010

Specialties
Tostada

Nachos and Sides
Mexican Rice
Pintos 'n Cheese

Condiments

Border Sauce (Fire, Hot, Mild)
Creamy Jalapeno Sauce
Fiesta Salsa
Guacamole
Pepper Jack Sauce
Pizza Sauce
Red Sauce
Reduced Fat Sour Cream
Salsa
Spicy Avocado Ranch Dressing

Beverages

Cherry Limeade Sparkler (16 oz., 20 oz.)
Classic Limeade Sparkler (16 oz., 20 oz.)

Taco Bell Notes: This list is based on standard product formulations. Ingredients and food products may vary due to ingredient substitutions, recipe revisions, or product preparation. Menu items may vary by location.

Triumph Notes: This list was marked current as of June 8, 2008.

Taco Cabana   ¢BLD

(800) 357-9924
Tex-Mex
Confirmed: 4/7/2010

Bacon
Barbacoa
Beef Fajita Meat
Beef Taco Filling (Chalupas, Crispy Tacos, Nachos)
Black Beans
Borracho Beans
Cheese, Shredded
Chicken Fajita Meat
Chicken Flameante (Rotisserie Chicken)
Chicken Flautas
Chorizo
Corn Tortillas (Can Be Substituted for Flour Tortillas in Fajitas, Plates, Tacos)
Eggs (Includes Scrambled Eggs and Whole Eggs)
Guacamole
Queso (Hot Cheese Topping)

Refried Beans
Rice
Salsas (Includes All Items Available on Salsa Bar)
Sour Cream
Stewed Chicken Taco Meat (Chalupas, Crispy Tacos, Nachos)
Tortilla Soup

Taco Cabana Notes: Corn tortilla chips and crispy taco shells are gluten-free, but they share a fryer with flour tortillas. This information was assembled using information from ingredient suppliers and is for Taco Cabana owned stores only; franchise locations may differ. Do not use this list as medical information.

Triumph Notes: This list was marked 01/01/10.

Taco John's   ¢BLD

(800) 854-0819
Tex-Mex
Confirmed: 4/15/2010

Sides

Refried Beans (With or Without Cheese)

Condiments

Bacon Ranch Dressing
Creamy Italian Dressing
Guacamole
Hot Sauce
House Dressing
Mild Sauce
Nacho Cheese Sauce
Pico de Gallo
Ranch Dressing
Roasted Green Chile Chipotle Sauce
Salsa
Sour Cream
Super Hot Sauce

Taco John's Notes: Kitchens are not gluten-free, so there is no guarantee cross-contamination will not occur. Taco John's uses shared frying oil, so otherwise gluten-free products, such as the Potato Oles, are fried in the same oil as gluten-containing products. Menu items co-branded with Steak Escape or Good Times Burgers & Custard may be cross-contaminated by items from the other brand. Taco John's disclaims responsibility for reactions caused by their food.

Triumph Notes: This list includes items marked as free of the "wheat" allergen on the Taco John's website. Corporate reports that the allergen listed as "wheat" on the website includes all gluten. There is no barley or rye in any of the menu items, and although the hamburgers contain only oats, they are listed online as containing wheat allergens. This list was marked Apr-2010.

TacoTime ¢LD
(480) 362-4800
Tex-Mex
Confirmed: 4/7/2010

Cheddar Fries
Cheese (Cheddar, Pepperjack)
Chicken
Green Sauce
Guacamole
Ketchup
Lettuce
Onions
Original Hot Sauce
Refritos (Cooked Pinto Beans)
Rice
Salsa Fresca
Salsa Verde
Shredded Beef
Sour Cream
Taco Meat
Tomatoes

TacoTime Notes: Mexi-Fries, Stuffed Fries, Taco Shells, and Taco Chips are fried in the same oil as gluten-containing products like flour tortillas. Cross-contamination may occur. TacoTime does not guarantee that any food is gluten-free. This list is subject to change at any time.

Triumph Notes: This list applies to all TacoTime locations in the United States, with the exception of restaurants in western Washington State (including Seattle).

TCBY ¢S
(800) 348-6311
Ice Cream
Confirmed: 4/7/2010

Hand Scooped Yogurt
All EXCEPT Chunky Chocolate Cookie Dough, Cookies & Cream, Peanut Butter Delight, Vanilla Fudge Brownie (No Sugar Added)

Toppings
All EXCEPT Butterfinger, Heath Candy Pieces, Reese's Pieces, Reese's Peanut Butter Cups, Snickers, Chocolate Cookies, Cookie Dough, Crumbled Brownies, Graham Crackers, Oreos, Waffle Cone Chips

TCBY Notes: TCBY cannot guarantee that food items are gluten-free. All products served on a cone contain gluten. Please note that regional vendors may vary ingredients and products, possibly affecting the stated contents of food.

Ted's Montana Grill $$LD
(404) 522-4123
Steakhouse
Confirmed: 4/7/2010

Starters
Grilled Shrimp —no bread

Salads —no croutons
Caesar Side Salad
Chopped Salad
Grilled Caesar Salad (Beef, Bison, Chicken, Salmon, Shrimp)
Grilled Salad (Beef, Bison, Chicken, Salmon, Shrimp)
House Salad
Vine-Ripened Tomato and Onion Salad

Wedge

Salad Dressings
Blue Cheese
Caesar
Creamy Vinaigrette
Honey Mustard
Thousand Island

Burgers and Chicken Sandwiches —no bun
America's Cup
Bleu Creek
C.O.B.
Cheese
George's Cadillac
Green & Hot
Kitchen Sink
Naked
New Mexico
Philly
S.O.B.
Skinny Dip
Spikebox
Swiss & Mushroom
Ultimate Skinny Dip
Vermejo

Entrees —no yeast roll, order with gluten-free sides only
Beer Can Chicken —*no chicken jus*
Bison Kansas City Strip Steak
Bison or Beef Delmonico
Bison or Beef Tenderloin Filet
Brick Chicken
Cedar Plank Salmon
Prime Rib —*no au jus*
Roast Turkey —*no dressing, no gravy*

Sides
Asparagus
Baked Potato
Broccoli
Cole Slaw
Cottage Cheese
French Fries
Mashed Potatoes
Sweet Potato
Vine-Ripened Tomatos

Kids' Menu —*order with gluten-free sides only*
Bar None Sliders —*no roll*
Cedar Plank Salmon

Desserts
Haagen-Dazs Ice Cream
Root Beer or Coke Float
Shakes

Ted's Montana Grill Notes: Kitchens are not gluten-free, but Ted's makes every effort to meet gluten-free needs. The listed menu items are gluten-free or can be with suggested changes. Alert a manager before ordering.

Texas Land & Cattle Steakhouse
✪ $$ LD
(316) 264-8899
Steakhouse
Confirmed: 4/7/2010

Lunch-Salad or Baked Potato Combo
House Salad —*no dressing, no croutons*
Oven Baked Potato —*no sour cream*
Side Caesar Salad —*no dressing, no croutons*
Signature Lettuce Wedge —*no bleu cheese crumbles, no dressing, no crouton toast*
Sweet Potato —*no cinnamon*

TXLC Lunch Favorites
6 oz. Lunch USDA Choice Sirloin —*no seasoning*
6 oz. Mesquite-Grilled Chicken —*no seasoning, no butter*
6 oz. Salmon Fillet —*no seasoning, no butter, request that salmon be un-marinated and un-smoked*
Classic Chopped Steak —*no rich mushroom gravy, no seasoning*

Signature Salads —*no dressing, no croutons, no tortilla strips, no cheese, no bacon, request vinegar and oil*
Chicken Caesar Salad —*no seasoning, no sauce, no marinade on chicken, no dressing*

Classic Cobb Salad —*no seasoning, no sauces on chicken, no dressing*
Mesquite-Grilled Salmon Caesar Salad —*no seasoning, no sauce, no marinade on salmon, no dressing*
Signature Steak & Wedge Salad —*no bleu cheese crumbles, no dressing, no seasoning on steak medallions*
Steakhouse Salad —*no bleu cheese crumbles, no dressing, no tortilla strips, no seasoning on steak medallions*

Great Steaks of Texas
Bacon-Wrapped Sirloin
Classic Chopped Steak —*no seasoning, no rich mushroom gravy*
Filet Mignon —*no seasoning*
New York Strip —*no seasoning*
Peppercorn Ribeye —*no brandy cream sauce*
Texas Bone-In Ribeye —*no seasoning, no onion strings*
Texas Ribeye —*no seasoning*
Texas-Sized Porterhouse —*no seasoning*
TXLC Sirloin —*no seasoning*

Other Great Tastes of Texas
Mesquite-Grilled Chicken —*no seasoning, no butter*
Mesquite-Grilled Shrimp —*no seasoning, no butter*
Pan-Seared Tilapia —*no seasoning, no butter, no lemon butter sauce*
Salmon Fillet —*no seasoning, no butter, request that salmon be un-marinated and un-smoked*

Texas Combinations
Garlic Steak & Shrimp —*no seasonings on sirloin, request grilled and un-marinated shrimp*
Grilled Chicken & Shrimp —*no seasoning, no butter, no marinade on chicken, request grilled and un-marinated shrimp*
New! TXLC Trio —*no seasoning on sirloin, request grilled and un-marinated shrimp instead of breaded shrimp, request no seasoning or sauce on chicken*

Add-Ons
4 Mesquite-Grilled Shrimp —*no marinade, no seasonings*
House Salad —*no dressing, no croutons*
Side Caesar or Spicy Caesar Salad —*no dressing, no croutons*
Signature Lettuce Wedge —*no bleu cheese crumbles, no dressing, no crouton toast*

Side Items
Baked Potato —*no sour cream*
Baked Sweet Potato —*no cinnamon*
House Salad —*no dressing, no croutons*
Side Caesar or Spicy Caesar Salad —*no dressing, no croutons*
Signature Lettuce Wedge —*no bleu cheese crumbles, no dressing, no crouton toast*
Steamed Broccoli —*no butter, no seasonings*

Texas Land & Cattle Steakhouse Notes:
Kitchens are not gluten-free, so cross-contamination may occur. There is no guarantee that food items are 100% gluten-free. If bringing your own gluten-free bread, which is not allowed in all locations, do not send it to the kitchen.

Triumph Notes: This list was marked 3/10.

Tokyo Joe's ★ ¢ⅅ
Japanese
Confirmed: 4/2/2010

Soups
Miso

Sauces/Dressings
Curry Sauce
Gluten Free Teriyaki
Honey Mango Dressing
Lemongrass Basil Dressing
Nikko Dressing
Wheat Free Soy Sauce (Stocked Behind Counter)

Protein
Chicken
Mahi Mahi
Pork

Salmon
Shrimp
Steak

Rice/Noodles
Rice (Brown, White)
Rice Noodles

Sushi
Joe's Roll
Nigiri (All EXCEPT eel)
Veggie Roll
Wasabi Paste
Yo Roll

Tokyo Joe's Notes: Kitchens are not gluten-free, so cross-contamination may occur. Tokyo Joe's may vary ingredients without prior notice. Consult the website for the most recent information.

Tony Roma's $$$LD
Steakhouse
Confirmed: 4/7/2010

Entrées
Grilled Chicken
Grilled Fish
Ribs
Steaks

Sauces
Barbeque Sauces (All)

Tony Roma's Notes: Shared oil is used for all fried foods and thus cross-contamination is expected with any fried menu item, such as french fries and tortilla chips.

UFood Grill   ¢LD
(617) 787-6000
American
Confirmed: 4/23/2010

Fired-up Burgers
All Meat Burgers —*no bun*

U Bowls
Southwestern Chicken

Wraps —*no tortilla*
Buffalo Bleu Chicken
Hamburger

Chili
Hearty Three-Bean Chili

Specialty Salads
Crispy Chicken Chopped Cobb —*request grilled chicken instead of crispy chicken*
Greek Salad
UFood Bistro Salad

Sides
Fresh Steamed Broccoli
Seasoned Black Beans
Side Salad
Steamed Veggie Medley
Sweet Potato Mash
Whole-Grain Brown Rice

Triumph Notes: This list was marked Feb_2010.

Uno Chicago Grill   ✪★ $LD
(866) 600-8667
American Regional
Confirmed: 4/1/2010

Great Greens —*no croutons, no breadstick*
Caesar Salad
Chicken Caesar Salad
Chopped Mediterranean —*no tortilla*
Classic Cobb Salad
House Salad

Salad Dressings
Balsamic Vinaigrette
Bleu Cheese
Caesar
Classic Vinaigrette
FatFree Vinaigrette
Honey Mustard
Low Fat Pomegranate Vinaigrette
Ranch

Burgers —*no bun*
Kid's Cheeseburger
The Uno Burger

Chicken
Baked Stuffed Chicken
Grilled Chicken Breast
Herb-Rubbed Breast of Chicken

Pizza —*request gluten-free crust*
Cheese Pizza
Pepperoni Pizza
Veggie Pizza

Smoke, Sizzle, & Splash
Cajun Blackened Mahi-Mahi
Chop House Classic
Grilled Shrimp and Sirloin
Lemon Basil Salmon
New York Strip Steak
Top Sirloin Steak

Sides
Red Bliss Mashed Potato
Skinless Baked
Steamed Broccoli
Steamed or Roasted Seasonal Vegetables
Whole Grain Brown Rice

Desserts
Bananas Foster
Ice Cream Sundae (Vanilla Ice Cream with
    Chocolate Sauce)

Beer
Redbridge

Drinks
Fresh Lemonade
Freshly-Brewed Lipton Iced Tea
Harney & Sons Premium Teas

Freezers
Chocolate Monkey
Raspberry Lime Ricky
Strawberry Smoothie
Tropical Fruit Freezer
Wildberry Mango Smoothie

Uno Chicago Grill Notes: UNO makes every effort to identify all gluten-containing items they purchase or prepare in the kitchen, but they are not responsible for any individual's reaction to any food, or for the use of this menu. This menu is for educational purposes only, and should not be considered medical advice. Uno disclaims responsibility for the use of this information.

Triumph Notes: The locations in downtown Chicago do not carry the GF pizza.

Wendy's   ¢ⓛⒹ
(614) 764-3100
American
Confirmed: 4/2/2010

Salads
Caesar Side Salad —*no croutons*
Side Salad
Southwest Taco Salad (Reduced Fat Sour
    Cream and Seasoned Tortilla Strips are
    GF)

Dressings
Ancho Chipotle Ranch Dressing
Classic Ranch Dressing
Fat Free French Dressing
Honey Dijon Dressing
Italian Vinaigrette Dressing
Light Classic Ranch Dressing
Supreme Caesar Dressing
Thousand Island Dressing

Meats
Grilled Chicken Breast
Hamburger Patty

Sides
Chili (Cheddar Cheese, Shredded, and Hot
    Chili Seasoning Packet are GF)

Baked Potatoes
Bacon & Cheese
Broccoli & Cheese
Chili & Cheese

Plain
Sour Cream & Chives

Condiments
American Cheese
Applewood Smoked Bacon
Bacon Jr.
Buttery Best Spread
Cheddar Cheese Sauce
Dill Pickles
Honey Mustard Sauce
Ketchup
Mustard
Natural Swiss Cheese
Ranch Sauce
Tartar Sauce

Beverages
Coffee
Hot Tea
Iced Tea
Sweet Tea

Frosty
Chocolate Frosty
Chocolate Fudge Frosty Shake
Coffee Toffee Twisted Frosty
Frosty-cino
M&Ms Twisted Frosty
Strawberry Frosty Shake
Vanilla Bean Frosty Shake
Vanilla Frosty

Wendy's Notes: There is no dedicated gluten-free fryer, so french fries may be cross-contaminated. Wendy's and their regional vendors may vary ingredients or products without prior notice, due to recipe revisions, product assembly, or the season. Menu items may vary by location. Wendy's is not responsible for an individual's reaction to any food products provided by their restaurants. Check website for frequent updates to the menu.

Triumph Notes: This list was marked April, 2010.

Wienerschnitzel   ¢ LD
(877) 709-3647
Sandwich Shop
Confirmed: 4/22/2010

Triumph Notes: There is no gluten-free list available, but the restaurant does provide a chart indicating items that contain the wheat allergen. Contact Wienerschnitzel for this chart.

Wingstop   ¢ LD
(972) 686-6500
Pub Food
Confirmed: 4/8/2010

Entrées
Wings (All EXCEPT Boneless Wing Strips)

Sides
All

Sauces
All

Wingstop Notes: There is a possibility that wings may be fried in shortening used for breaded wing strips that contain gluten, so cross-contamination may occur.

Yard House   ✪ $$$ LD
(800) 336-5336
Modern American
Confirmed: 4/7/2010

Appetizers & Starter Salads
Baby Leaf Spinach —*no portabella mushroom, no croutons, no candied walnuts*
Caesar Salad —*no croutons*
Chilled Edamame
Chopped Salad —*no bloody mary vinaigrette*
Grilled Artichoke —*no house fried potato chips*
Iceberg Wedge —*no bleu cheese dressing, no bleu cheese crumbles*

Lobster, Crab, & Artichoke Dip —*no pita, no tortilla chips, no panko*
Mixed Field Greens —*no croutons*
Spicy House Salad —*no wontons, no spicy peanut vinaigrette*
Spicy Tuna Roll —*no wasabi soy sauce, no fried ginger chips*
Spinach Cheese Dip —*no flat bread*
Summer Salad —*no candied walnuts*

Salad Dressings
Balsamic Vinaigrette
Caesar Dressing
Oil & Vinegar
Spiced Balsamic Vinaigrette

Entrée Salads
Ahi Crunchy Salad —*no wontons, no soy vinaigrette*
BBQ Chicken Salad —*no fried onions, no tortilla strips, no chipotle ranch dressing*
Grilled Hearts of Romaine —*no candied walnuts, no gorgonzola champagne vinaigrette*
New York Steak Salad —*no potato chips, no pickled egg, no gorgonzola dressing*
Seared Ahi Caesar —*no croutons*

Grilled Burgers —*no bread, no french fries, no chips*
Avocado & Swiss
BBQ Bacon & Cheddar
Classic Cheese
Pepper Jack —*no roasted green chilis*

Sandwiches —*no bread, no french fries, no chips*
Cuban Roast Pork Dip —*no bbq au jus*
Grilled Chicken & Avocado
Grilled Pastrami
Roasted Turkey Club
Seared Ahi Steak
Spicy Chicken Breast

Seafood —*request a sauce from the list provided*
Ginger Crusted Norwegian Salmon —*no panko, no peanut vinaigrette, no fried carrot strings*

Grilled Jumbo Shrimp —*no indonesian rice*
Pan Seared Ahi —*no chinese black bean sauce, no fried basil leaves*
Shrimp Rice Bowl —*no rice bowl sauce*

Steaks —*request a sauce from the list provided*
Grilled Rib Eye —*no marinade*
New York Steak —*no fries*
Pepper Crusted Filet —*no brandy cream sauce*
Top Sirloin —*no portabella, no marinade*

Sauces
Bearnaise
Buffalo
Cocktail
House Steak
Orange
Passion Fruit/Lemon Beurre Blanc
Porcini Mushroom
Spicy Peanut
Spicy Tomato
Sweet Chili
Tartar
Thai Basil Pesto

Desserts
Ice Cream (Caramel, Mango Sorbet, Vanilla)

Beer & Ciders
Ciders (Apple, Pear, Raspberry)
Redbridge Beer

Yard House Notes: Upon arrival, alert the server to your dietary needs. Consult with the server about the preparation methods of specific dishes. Kitchens are not gluten-free. Menu items were reviewed by Healthy Dining.

Triumph Notes: This list was marked 03.2010.

Zaxby's   ¢ⅬⅮ
(866) 892-9297
American
Confirmed: 4/27/2010

Triumph Notes: Zaxby's reports that the only item on their menu that does not contain gluten is their chicken wings. Ingredient statements for dressings and sauces are available. Contact Zaxby's for more information.

Zoe's Kitchen   ₵ⅬⅮ
(205) 414-9920
American
Confirmed: 4/8/2010

Salads
Chicken or Tuna Salad Sampler —*no pita bread, no pasta salad*
Greek Salad —*no pita bread*

Sandwiches —*no bread*
Chicken Salad
Egg Salad
Gruben
Ham and Swiss
Homemade Pimento Cheese
Lean Turkey Pita
Mediterranean Tuna
Tuna Salad
Turkey Sandwich

Sides
Fresh Fruit
Marinated Slaw
Potato Salad

Kid's Sandwiches —*no bread*
Chicken Salad Sandwich

Ham and Cheese
Turkey and Cheese

Zoe's Kitchen Notes: Upon arrival, alert a manager to your dietary needs. Kitchens are not gluten-free, and though the kitchen staff is trained on the risks of cross-contamination, it still may occur.

Zoup!   ₵ⅬⅮ
Soup
Confirmed: 4/7/2010

Soups
Fire Roasted Tomato Bisque
Frontier 7 Bean
Ginger Butternut Squash
Organic Carrot and Corriander
Potato Cheddar
Pumpkin Pie Bisque
Tomato Basil
Tomato Spinach and Brown Rice
Zesty 3 Pepper with Chicken

Salad Dressings
Caesar Dressing
Ranch Dressing

Snacks
Veggie Chips

Zoup! Notes: Menu items are constantly changing and rotating, so not all gluten-free items will be available all the time. Visit the website to sign up for daily menu emails.

Symbols Summary

Gluten-free menu is available on site. See the Section 2 User's Guide for more information about what constitutes a gluten-free menu.

Gluten-free specialty items, such as bread, beer, pasta, etc., are available. Always call ahead to confirm the availability of gluten-free specialty items. Restaurants may sell out and deliveries can arrive late.

100%   **This is a 100% gluten-free establishment.** No gluten on site.

This is a chain restaurant, and you can find its gluten-free menu or list in Section 3. More on this in the Section 3 User's Guide.

No Icon. None of the above apply. See the restaurant's description for information about its gluten-free accommodations.

B = Breakfast	**L** = Lunch	**D** = Dinner	**S** = Snack
¢ = under $10	**$** = $10 to $15	**$$** = $15 to $20	**$$$** = $21 to $29 **$$$$** = $30+